THE COMPANION TO JURI LOTMAN

THE COMPANION TO JURI LOTMAN

A SEMIOTIC THEORY OF CULTURE

Edited by
Marek Tamm and Peeter Torop

BLOOMSBURY ACADEMIC
LONDON • NEW YORK • OXFORD • NEW DELHI • SYDNEY

BLOOMSBURY ACADEMIC
Bloomsbury Publishing Plc
50 Bedford Square, London, WC1B 3DP, UK
1385 Broadway, New York, NY 10018, USA
29 Earlsfort Terrace, Dublin 2, Ireland

BLOOMSBURY, BLOOMSBURY ACADEMIC and the Diana logo are trademarks
of Bloomsbury Publishing Plc

First published in Great Britain 2022

A catalogue record for this book is available from the British Library.

Library of Congress Cataloging-in-Publication Data
Names: Tamm, Marek, editor. | Torop, Peeter, editor.
Title: The companion to Juri Lotman : a semiotic theory of culture /
edited by Marek Tamm and Peeter Torop.
Description: London ; New York : Bloomsbury Academic, 2022. |
Includes bibliographical references and index.
Identifiers: LCCN 2021031100 (print) | LCCN 2021031101 (ebook) | ISBN 9781350181618 (hardback) |
ISBN 9781350268197 (paperback) | ISBN 9781350181625 (pdf) | ISBN 9781350181632 (ebook)
Subjects: LCSH: Lotman, IŪ. M. (IŪriĭ Mikhaĭlovich), 1922–1993. | Semioticians–Russia
(Federation)–Biography. | Culture–Semiotic models. | Language and culture.
Classification: LCC P85.L68 C66 2022 (print) | LCC P85.L68 (ebook) | DDC 302.2092–dc23
LC record available at https://lccn.loc.gov/2021031100
LC ebook record available at https://lccn.loc.gov/2021031101

ISBN: PB: 978-1-3502-6819-7
HB: 978-1-3501-8161-8
ePDF: 978-1-3501-8162-5
eBook: 978-1-3501-8163-2

Typeset by Deanta Global Publishing Services, Chennai, India
Printed and bound in Great Britain

To find out more about our authors and books visit www.bloomsbury.com and sign up
for our newsletters.

CONTENTS

Contents

FIGURES

ACKNOWLEDGEMENTS

We remain deeply grateful to the contributors of this volume. All of them have invested time, energy and intellectual insights into making this volume possible in a very short time period.

Rhodri Mogford and Laura Reeves at Bloomsbury have been very supportive of the project throughout. Thanks are also due to the language editor of the volume, Daniel Allen.

We want to thank the Juri Lotman Semiotics Repository in Tallinn University for permission to use the photos and some of the archival materials in the volume.

Additionally, we acknowledge the financial support of the Tallinn University Rector's Fund for covering the costs of language editing. The publication costs were generously subsidized by the School of Humanities of Tallinn University and the Department of Semiotics of the University of Tartu (national professorship in semiotics of culture).

All translations, unless otherwise noted, are made by the respective authors of the chapters. A modified Library of Congress system was used in transliterating Russian names, titles and terms.

Marek Tamm and Peeter Torop
Tallinn and Tartu, 28 February 2021

CONTRIBUTORS

Edna Andrews is Professor of Linguistics and Cultural Anthropology, Nancy and Jeffrey Marcus Distinguished Professor, and Chair of the Linguistics Program at Duke University. She is a member of the Duke Institute of Brain Sciences and Center for Cognitive Neuroscience. Her books include *Markedness Theory* (Duke University Press, 1990), *Semantics of Suffixation* (Lincom Europa, 1996), *Conversations with Lotman: Cultural Semiotics in Language, Literature and Cognition* (University of Toronto Press, 2003) and *Neuroscience and Multilingualism* (Cambridge University Press, 2014).

Nutsa Batiashvili is Professor of Anthropology and Dean of the Graduate School at the Free University of Tbilisi. She holds a PhD in Anthropology from Washington University in St Louis, United States. She was a postdoctoral fellow at the University of Oxford. Her book *The Bivocal Nation: Memory and Identity on the Edge of Empire* (Palgrave Macmillan, 2018) is about a divided nation and polarized notions of nationhood. Recent projects include 'Anthropology of Anxiety' (funded by the Wenner-Gren Foundation) and 'Political and Cognitive Ecology of Heritage Objects in Upper Svaneti' (funded by the Templeton Foundation).

Taras Boyko is a researcher in semiotics and former lecturer at the University of Tartu. His research interests lie in semiotics of history, theory and philosophy of history, late medieval and early modern travel writing, and the Tartu-Moscow School of Semiotics. His main publications include 'Tartu-Moscow School of Semiotics and History' (*Historein*, 14, 2014), 'Describing the Past: Tartu-Moscow School Ideas on History, Historiography, and the Historian's Craft' (*Sign Systems Studies*, 43, 2015) and 'Reading Uspenskij: Soviet "Semiotics of History" in the West' (*Sign Systems Studies*, 45, 2017).

Caryl Emerson is A. Watson Armour III University Professor Emeritus of Slavic Languages and Literatures at Princeton University. Her work has focused on the Russian classics (Pushkin, Tolstoy, Dostoevsky), Mikhail Bakhtin and Russian music, opera and theatre. Recent projects include the modernist Sigizmund Krzhizhanovsky (1887–1950), the allegorical-historical novelist Vladimir Sharov (1952–2018) and the co-editing, with George Pattison and Randall A. Poole, of *The Oxford Handbook of Russian Religious Thought* (Oxford University Press, 2020).

Laura Gherlone is an adjunct professor of Russian Literature at the Centre for Comparative Literature of the Catholic University of Argentina, Buenos Aires. During the 2016–19 period she was a postdoctoral fellow in semiotics at the Centre for Language Research of the National University of Córdoba. Previously, she was a temporary research fellow in Italy. Her research deals with Juri Lotman's interdisciplinary thought – with a focus on his late theoretical production – in relation to the spatial turn, cultural affect theory and Latin American reflection on decoloniality.

Remo Gramigna is a postdoctoral researcher at the University of Turin, where he teaches semiotics. His academic research to date has mainly focused on the history of semiotics and semiotics of culture. He obtained his PhD in Semiotics and Culture Studies in Estonia, worked as a research fellow at the University of Tartu and lectured at the Department of Semiotics. His recent publications include *Augustine and the Study of Signs, Signification, and Lying* (De Gruyter, 2020). He has published in such journals as the *Journal for Communication Studies, Lexia, Sign Systems Studies* and *Versus*. He was among the editors of *Sign Systems Studies*.

John Hartley, AM, is an independent scholar, formerly a professor at Cardiff University, Queensland University of Technology and Curtin University. His research interests are in media, cultural, communication and journalism studies, creative industries and cultural science. Recent books include *Cultural Science* (with Jason Potts, 2014); *How We Use Stories and Why That Matters* (2020); *On the Digital Semiosphere* (with Indrek Ibrus and Maarja Ojamaa, 2021), published by Bloomsbury; and *Advanced Introduction to Creative Industries* (2021), published by Edward Elgar. He was the founding editor of the *International Journal of Cultural Studies* (Sage) and *Cultural Science Journal* (Open Access).

Indrek Ibrus is Professor of Media Innovation at Tallinn University's Baltic Film, Media and Arts School (BFM). His research interests include media innovation and evolution, datafication of culture, the evolving concept of public value in the context of Web 3.0 developments and the broader evolution of modern creative industries. He has published on mobile media, media innovation/evolution, media policy, metadata, transmedia and crossmedia production. He is a co-editor of *Crossmedia Innovations* (with Carlos A. Scolari, Peter Lang, 2012), editor of *Emergence of Cross-Innovation Systems* (Emerald, 2019) and co-author of *On the Digital Semiosphere* (with John Hartley and Maarja Ojamaa, Bloomsbury, 2021). He is also a co-editor of the journals *Baltic Screen Media Review* and *Cultural Science Journal*.

Tinatin Inauri is an undergraduate student at the School of Governance and Social Sciences at the Free University of Tbilisi, and is a writer and researcher for the news media broadcast 'Mtavari'. Her research interests include memory studies, nationalism and political cognition.

Ilya Kalinin is a professor at the Department of Liberal Arts and Sciences in Saint Petersburg State University. His research focuses on Russian Literature, early Soviet intellectual and cultural history, and on the historical and cultural politics of contemporary Russia. He is an author of 200 articles and an editor of five volumes on these topics. His book *History as Art of Articulation: Russian Formalists and Revolution* is forthcoming in Russian (Novoe literaturnoe obozrenie).

Eva Kimminich is Professor of Semiotics of Culture and Roman Literature at the Institute of Roman Languages in the University of Potsdam. She is the editor of the academic publication series 'Welt – Körper – Sprache. Perspektiven kultureller Wahrnehmungs- und Darstellungsformen' (Peter Lang), and has established the first German MA programme of Applied Cultural Studies and Cultural Semiotics. Her primary research fields are semiotics of sub-, popular and protest cultures, conspiracy theories and metaphors as cognitive concepts. For ten years she has been a committee member of the German Society of Semiotics.

Katalin Kroó is Professor at Eötvös Loránd University (Budapest), where she directs MA programmes in semiotics and a doctoral programme in comparative Russian literary studies. Her research areas are nineteenth-century Russian literature, literary theory and semiotics. Her latest work contextualizes the interpretation of Lermontov's novel poetics within a search for the disciplinary identification of literary semiotics (*Korunk hőse, korunk irodalomszemiotikája?* L'Harmattan, 2020). Her edited books include *Text within Text—Culture within Culture: Russian Literature (19th Century) in Contexts of Cultural Dynamics* (with Peeter Torop, L'Harmattan 2013) and *The Book Phenomenon in Cultural Space* (Eötvös Loránd University, 2019).

Kalevi Kull is Professor of Biosemiotics at the University of Tartu. He has worked as a field biologist and experimental ecologist, studied species coexistence mechanisms in rich communities, conducted research in mathematical and theoretical biology, biosemiotics, general semiotics, ecosemiotics and history of ideas, and written on the topic of ecological principles of living. He is the editor-in-chief of *Sign Systems Studies*, co-editor of *Semiotics, Communication and Cognition* (De Gruyter), *Biosemiotics* (Springer), and *Tartu Semiotics Library*, and the president of the International Society for Biosemiotic Studies.

Tatyana Kuzovkina is a senior researcher at the Juri Lotman Semiotics Repository in Tallinn University. She holds a PhD in Russian Literature from the University of Tartu (2007). Her research has focused on Lotman's life and work. In 1990–3, she was Lotman's personal assistant, and since 1997 has been cataloguing Lotman's archive. She has edited fourteen articles and five books by Lotman, has prepared for publication his self-portraits and correspondence and has authored research papers on his biography and legacy. Since 2009, she has been one of the main organizers of the Annual Lotman Days at Tallinn University and member of the editorial board of *Bibliotheca Lotmaniana* (Tallinn University Press).

Renate Lachmann is Professor Emerita of Slavic Literatures and Comparative Literature at Constance University, member of the Heidelberger Akademie der Wissenschaften and of the Academia Europaea. She is a member of the former scholarly group Poetik und Hermeneutik, and is former visiting professor at Irvine, Chicago, Prague et al. Her main research fields are rhetoric, literary theory, memory, fantastic literature and literature of the extreme/extraordinary. Her main books include *Gedächtnis und Literatur* (Suhrkamp, 1990), *Die Zerstörung der schönen Rede* (Fink, 1994), *Erzählte Phantastik* (Suhrkamp, 2002) and *Lager und Literatur. Zeugnisse des Gulag* (Konstanz University Press, 2019).

Jan Levchenko is Professor of Cultural Studies in the National Research University 'Higher School of Economics', Moscow. He holds a PhD in semiotics from the University of Tartu (2003). His books and edited volumes include *The Conceptual Glossary of Tartu-Moscow Semiotic School* (with Silvi Salupere, Tartu University Press, 1999, in Russian), *The Younger Formalists: A Russian Prose* (2007, in Russian), *Work and Service: In Memory of Rashit Yangirov* (2011, in Russian), *The Other Science: Russian Formalists in Search on Biography* (2012, in Russian) and *Era of Estrangement: Russian Formalism and the Humanities of the 20th c.* (with Igor Pilschchikov, 2018, in Russian).

Mihhail Lotman is Professor of Semiotics at the University of Tartu and Professor Emeritus of Semiotics and Literary Theory at Tallinn University. His research interests lie in the areas of general semiotics and semiotics of culture, as well as general poetics, rhetoric and Russian literature. His particular interests are associated with the study of versification: general, comparative, Russian and Estonian. He is the co-editor of *Studia Metrica and Poetica* and *Sign Systems Studies*.

Mari-Liis Madisson is a researcher of semiotics at the University of Tartu. Her scholarly interests lie primarily in cultural semiotics, media semiotics and political semiotics. Since 2014 she has taught multiple courses on online culture and critical media literacy. She is the author of *The Semiotic Construction of Identities in Hypermedia Environments: The Analysis of Online Communication of the Estonian Extreme Right* (Tartu University Press, 2016) and *Strategic Conspiracy Narratives: A Semiotic Approach* (with Andreas Ventsel, Routledge, 2020).

Andrey Makarychev is Professor of Regional Political Studies at Johan Skytte Institute of Political Science, University of Tartu. In recent years he has co-authored (all with Alexandra Yatsyk) three monographs: *Celebrating Borderlands in a Wider Europe: Nations and Identities in Ukraine, Georgia and Estonia* (Nomos, 2016), *Lotman's Cultural Semiotics and the Political* (Rowman and Littlefield, 2017)a and *Critical Biopolitics of the Post-Soviet: from Populations to Nations* (Lexington Books, 2020). He has co-edited a number of volumes, including *Vocabularies of International Relations after the Crisis in Ukraine* (Routledge, 2017) and *Borders in the Baltic Sea Region: Suturing the Ruptures* (Palgrave Macmillan, 2017).

Timo Maran is Professor of Ecosemiotics and Environmental Humanities at the University of Tartu. His research interests are semiotic processes in ecosystems and ecocultures, Estonian nature writing, zoosemiotics and species conservation, and semiotics of biological mimicry. He is the author of *Mimicry and Meaning: Structure and Semiotics of Biological Mimicry* (Springer, 2017) and *Ecosemiotics: The Study of Signs in Changing Ecologies* (Cambridge University Press, 2000). Timo Maran is also a writer, and has published five poetry collections.

Daniele Monticelli is Professor of Semiotics and Translation Studies at Tallinn University. His research is characterized by a wide and interdisciplinary range of interests which include theoretical and literary semiotics, philosophy of language, translation history and contemporary critical theory. He has researched the theoretical legacy of Juri Lotman, focusing particularly on Lotman's later works on the semiosphere and history and looking for points of contact with post-structuralism and critical theory. He has presented the results of his research in over eighty academic publications and been the initiator and editor of several collective volumes.

Winfried Nöth is Professor in Linguistics and Semiotics, Director of the Interdisciplinary Centre for Cultural Studies of the University of Kassel until 2009 and former visiting professor at Wisconsin and Humboldt Universities, and has been a professor in Cognitive Semiotics at Catholic University São Paulo (PUC) since 2010. He is author of *Handbook of Semiotics* (Indiana University Press, 1990) and co-author of *Semiotic Theory of Learning* (Routledge, 2018). He has edited *Origins of Semiosis* (De Gruyter, 1994), *The Crisis of Representation* (De Gruyter, 2003) and *Self-Reference in the Media* (De Gruyter, 2007), and published about 400 papers on general semiotics, cognitive semiotics, visual semiotics and Charles S. Peirce.

Maarja Ojamaa is a researcher at the Institute of Philosophy and Semiotics, University of Tartu. Her main research interests lie in semiotics of culture, adaptation and transmedia studies. She also co-leads with Peeter Torop the Transmedia Research Group, which creates open access online education platforms in cultural subjects for school students. Her recent publications include *On the Digital Semiosphere: Culture, Media and Science for the Anthropocene* (with John Hartley and Indrek Ibrus, Bloomsbury, 2021).

Katre Pärn is a lecturer at the Institute of Philosophy and Semiotics, University of Tartu, president of the Estonian Semiotics Association, and a member of the editorial board of the journal *Hortus Semioticus*. Her main fields of study are general semiotics and semiotics of culture, and her main research interests include semiotic modelling, semiotic functioning and relations between art and the media.

Igor Pilshchikov is Professor of Russian Literature at the University of California, Los Angeles, and Research Professor at Tallinn University, founding academic editor of the *Fundamental Digital Library of Russian Literature & Folklore* and the *Russian Virtual Library*, co-editor of *Studia Metrica et Poetica* (University of Tartu Press) and *Pushkin Review* (Slavica Publishers). He has published extensively in several areas, such as

Russian poetry in comparative perspective, the history of East/Central European literary theory, cultural semiotics, poetics, verse theory and digital humanities. Recent publications include articles and edited volumes on Russian formalism, the Prague School and the Tartu-Moscow School of Semiotics.

Nikolay Poselyagin is Associate Professor at the School of Philological Studies in the National Research University 'Higher School of Economics', Moscow. His research fields are semiotics, literary theory, critical thinking, cinema narratology and ideology, Russian and international politics. He has published works on the Tartu-Moscow School of Semiotics, Russian and Hollywood cinema, Russian literature, Russian and Soviet intellectual history and modern political ideologies.

Anti Randviir is Associate Professor at the Department of Semiotics in the University of Tartu. His main research areas are sociosemiotics, the semiotics of space and the Tartu-Moscow School of Semiotics. He has published *Mapping the World: Towards a Sociosemiotic Approach to Culture* (Tartu University Press, 2004), co-edited a special issue of *Semiotica* on 'Sociosemiotics' (with Paul Cobley, 2009) and authored many articles in various journals, including *Sign Systems Studies* and *Semiotica*.

Pietro Restaneo is a postdoctoral research fellow at the Institute for the European Intellectual Lexicon and History of Ideas (ILIESI), National Research Council (CNR) in Rome, Italy. He holds a PhD from La Sapienza University of Rome in theoretical linguistics and philosophy of language. He has published many articles about the history of linguistic ideas, about Antonio Gramsci's conception of language and about Juri Lotman's theory of power.

Merit Rickberg is the head of the Juri Lotman Semiotics Repository in Tallinn University and a doctoral student in semiotics and culture studies in the University of Tartu. Her main research interests are cultural universals in Juri Lotman's semiotics, semiotic theory of learning and semiotics of conflict. She is one of the founders of the *Education on Screen* project, which develops new education practices based on the framework of semiotics of culture.

Silvi Salupere is a lecturer of semiotics at the University of Tartu (Estonia), editor of *Sign Systems Studies*, *Tartu Semiotics Library* and *Acta Semiotica Estica*, and a translator. She has published articles on the history of the Tartu-Moscow School, Juri Lotman, cultural-semiotics and translation studies, and co-edited *Theoretical Schools and Circles in the Twentieth-Century Humanities* (with Marina Grishakova, Routledge, 2015) and *Beginnings of the Semiotics of Culture* (with Peeter Torop and Kalevi Kull, Tartu University Press, 2013).

Wolf Schmid is Professor Emeritus of Slavic Literatures at the Universität Hamburg. His publications include *Der ästhetische Inhalt* (The Peter de Ridder Press, 1977), *Puškins*

Prosa in poetischer Lektüre (Fink, 1991), *Ornamentales Erzählen in der russischen Moderne* (Peter Lang, 1992), *Proza kak poezija. Pushkin – Dostoevskij – Chekhov – avangard* (Inapress, 1994), *Narratology* (De Gruyter, 2010), *Narrative Motivierung. Von der romanischen Renaissance bis zur russischen Post-moderne* (De Gruyter, 2020), *Mental Events: Changes of Mind in European Narratives from the Middle Ages to Postrealism* (2021) and *Figurally Colored Narration* (forthcoming).

Andreas Schönle is Professor of Russian and Head of the School of Modern Languages at the University of Bristol as well as a Fellow of the British Academy. He is the author of four monographs and four edited volumes. His more recent monographs include *Architecture of Oblivion: Ruins and Historical Consciousness in Modern Russia* (Northern Illinois University Press, 2011) and *On the Periphery of Europe, 1762–1825: The Self-Invention of the Russian Elite* (with Andrei Zorin, Northern Illinois University Press, 2018).

Aleksei Semenenko is Associate Professor in Russian at the Department of Language Studies at Umeå University. He holds a PhD in Russian Literature from Stockholm University. He is the author of *Russian Translations of* Hamlet *and Literary Canon Formation* (Stockholm University, 2007) and *The Texture of Culture: An Introduction to Yuri Lotman's Semiotic Theory* (Palgrave Macmillan, 2012), and the editor of *Aksenov and the Environs* (with Lars Kleberg; Södertörns högskola, 2012). He has published works on translation, literature, censorship and semiotics, and is currently working on a project on neo-Soviet myths in Russia.

Elin Sütiste is Associate Professor at the Department of Semiotics in the University of Tartu. She works in the sphere of cultural semiotics, focusing mainly on semiotics of translation and history of translation. She has published articles on Estonian history of translation, on the notion of translation in the works of Roman Jakobson and of the Tartu-Moscow School of Semiotics. She has co-edited a volume *(Re)considering Roman Jakobson* (with Remo Gramigna, Jonathan Griffin and Silvi Salupere, University of Tartu Press, 2021) and a special issue of *Sign Systems Studies* on 'Semiotics of Translation and Cultural Mediation' (with Terje Loogus and Maarja Saldre, University of Tartu Press, 2012).

Marek Tamm is Professor of Cultural History at the School of Humanities in Tallinn University. His primary research fields are cultural history of medieval Europe, theory and history of historiography, and cultural memory studies. He has recently published *A Cultural History of Memory in the Early Modern Age* (co-edited with Alessandro Arcangeli, Bloomsbury 2020), *Juri Lotman – Culture, Memory and History: Essays in Cultural Semiotics* (Palgrave Macmillan 2019), *Rethinking Historical Time: New Approaches to Presentism* (co-edited with Laurent Olivier, Bloomsbury 2019), *Debating New Approaches to History* (co-edited with Peter Burke, Bloomsbury 2018) and *Afterlife of Events: Perspectives on Mnemohistory* (Palgrave Macmillan 2015).

Peeter Torop is Professor of Semiotics of Culture at the Institute of Philosophy and Semiotics in the University of Tartu. He is the co-editor of the journal *Sign Systems Studies*. His primary research fields are semiotics of translation and methodology of translation studies, transmedia studies, the Tartu-Moscow School of Semiotics, theory of culture, history of Russian literature and Dostoevsky studies. As a former student of Lotman, he has a long experience of interpreting his work. He has co-edited (with Indrek Ibrus) a special issue of the *International Journal of Cultural Studies* (2015), titled 'The Uses of Juri Lotman'. In 2009, he published in Russian an anthology of Lotman's writings, *Chemu uchatsia ljudi. Stat'i i zametki* (Tsentr Knigi).

Mikhail Trunin is a researcher at the School of Humanities at Tallinn University. His academic profile largely centres around research in the field of history of Russian literature and twentieth-century academic thought (mainly the Tartu-Moscow School of Semiotics in a cross-cultural context). He has edited two books: a correspondence between Juri Lotman and Boris Uspenskij (with Olga Kelbert and Boris Uspenskij, Tallinn University Press, 2016) and a collection of Lotman's lesser-known or neglected papers on structural methods in literary studies from 1965 to 1970 (with Igor Pilshchikov and Nikolay Poselyagin, Tallinn University Press, 2018).

Ekaterina Velmezova is Professor of Slavistics and of the History and Epistemology of Language Sciences in Eastern and Central Europe and Vice Dean of Research and PhD Studies at the Faculty of Arts of the University of Lausanne. Her work has focused on Czech and Russian ethnolinguistics, on the history of linguistics as reflected in the history of literature, on the history of structuralism, Russian semantics and semiotics. She is editor-in-chief of *Epistemologica et historiographica linguistica Lausannensia*, co-editor of *Slavica Helvetica* (Peter Lang) and associate editor of *Historiographia Linguistica* (Benjamins).

Andreas Ventsel is Associate Professor of Semiotics at the University of Tartu and a lecturer in Pallas University of Applied Sciences in Tartu. His research is interdisciplinary and includes semiotics, discourse theory, visual communication, rhetoric and political analysis. He has presented the results of the research on these topics in around 100 academic articles. He is the author of the books *Strategic Conspiracy Narratives: A Semiotic Approach* (with Mari-Liis Madisson, Routledge, 2020) and *Introducing Relational Political Analysis: Political Semiotics as a Theory and Method* (with Peeter Selg, Palgrave Macmillan, 2020).

James V. Wertsch is the David R. Francis Distinguished Professor at Washington University in St Louis and holds appointments in the Department of Anthropology and the Global Studies Program. His research has built on the ideas of Russian psychologists and semioticians, and his publications include *Vygotsky and the Social Formation of Mind* (Harvard University Press, 1985) and *Voices of the Mind* (Harvard University Press,

1991). More recently, he has employed the same conceptual framework to examine issues of national narratives and memory (*How Nations Remember: A Narrative Approach*, Oxford University Press, 2021).

Alexandra Yatsyk is a scholar in Russian and European cultural studies, and a former researcher at the University of Tartu. Her areas of expertise cover post-Soviet and East European identity-making, Russian influence in Europe, sport and cultural mega-events, biopolitics and art. She is the author of numerous articles and books, including the recently co-authored (with Andrey Makarychev) *Critical Biopolitics of the Post-Soviet: From Population to Nation* (Lexington, 2019), *Lotman's Cultural Semiotics and the Political* (Rowman & Littlefield, 2017) and *Celebrating Borderlands in a Wider Europe: Nations and Identities in Ukraine, Estonia and Georgia* (Nomos, 2016).

Sergey Zenkin is Research Professor of the Russian State University for the Humanities (RGGU, Moscow) and Professor of the Higher School of Economics (Saint Petersburg) and of the Free University (Moscow). He studies and teaches literary theory, history of ideas and French literature. His most recent books are *Cinq lectures de Roland Barthes* (Classiques Garnier, 2017), *La Forme et l'énergie: L'esthétique du formalisme russe* (Université de Clermont-Ferrand, 2018) and *Theory of Literature* (Novoe literaturnoe obozrenie, 2017, in Russian).

Suren Zolyan is a leading researcher at the Institute of Philosophy of the National Academy of Sciences of Armenia, and visiting professor at Immanuel Kant Baltic Federal University. In 1975–6, he was on an internship with Juri Lotman. He is the author of more than 200 publications on linguistics, semantics and semiotics, including 11 monographs. Some of his main works include *The Semantics and Structure of the Poetic Text* (1991 and 2014, in Russian), *The Language of the Political Conflict: The Logical-semantic Analysis* (2000, in Russian), *Explorations on the Semantic Poetics of Acmeism* (with Mihhail Lotman, 2012, in Russian) and *Juri Lotman: On Meaning, Text, History. Themes and Variation* (2020, in Russian).

INTRODUCTION
Marek Tamm and Peeter Torop

Juri Lotman[1] (1922–93), co-founder of the well-known Tartu-Moscow School of Semiotics, was one of the most original and prolific cultural and literary theorists and historians of the second half of the twentieth century. During his long academic career at the University of Tarty, he was active in a wide array of disciplines, from aesthetics to literary history, cultural history to semiotics, film studies to urban studies, poetics to robotics. He proposed new, original interpretations of a staggering range of cultural and other phenomena, from Russian literature to Dante Alighieri, daily life to duelling, puppet theatre to cinema, card playing to visual arts, architecture to animation, artificial intelligence to the human brain. His insights have been especially influential in conceptualizing the meaning-making practices in culture and society and have inspired the work of such diverse scholars as Jan and Aleida Assmann, Umberto Eco, Carlo Ginzburg, Stephen Greenblatt, Wolfgang Iser, Fredric Jameson, Julia Kristeva, Lev Manovich, Franco Moretti, Paul Ricoeur, Thomas Sebeok and Tzvetan Todorov.

Lotman left an immense intellectual inheritance. His bibliography contains more than 1,000 items, including some twenty monographs, and, in addition, twenty-five volumes of the *Trudy po znakovym sistemam* (Sign Systems Studies), the first semiotic journal in the world, which Lotman established and edited. Lotman's posthumously published selected works (1994–2003) fill nine vast volumes, or more than 6,000 pages, taken together. A significant portion of this oeuvre has been translated into about thirty languages. Lotman's first article in English was published on 16 October 1973 in the *Times Literary Supplement*, followed next year by six new translations. The first book renditions came out in the mid-1970s (*Analysis of the Poetic Text*, 1976; *Semiotics of Cinema*, 1976; *The Structure of the Artistic Text*, 1977), accompanied by some anthologies of Lotman's and his colleagues' writings (*Semiotics and Structuralism: Readings from the Soviet Union*, ed. H. Baran, 1976; *Soviet Semiotics: An Anthology*, ed. D. P. Lucid, 1977). In 1990, Lotman published a monograph titled *Universe of the Mind: A Semiotic Theory of Culture*, commissioned by the publishing house I.B. Tauris. Over the last decade, a new wave of English book translations has emerged: *Culture and Explosion* (2009), *The Unpredictable Workings of Culture* (2013), *Non-Memoirs* (2014), *Culture, Memory and History: Essays in Cultural Semiotics* (2019) and *Culture and Communication: Signs in Flux* (2020). According to the most recent bibliographic harvest, as of the end of 2020, 148 of Lotman's writings are available in English (see Gramigna in this volume).

Lotman's international reception remains unequal and diverse. Beyond the former USSR, his work has found particularly important resonance in some European countries, such as Germany (Aspisova 1998), Italy (De Michiel 1995) and Poland (Żyłko 2012; Faryno 2020), but even more so in Latin America (Cáceres 2003; Volkova Américo 2019) and in China (Chang, Han and Wu 2014; Zhang and Yan 2014). His welcome in the English-speaking world has been more complicated and ambiguous (Baran 1998; Blaim 1998; Winner 2002). Lotman elaborated most of his theories on the basis of Russian literary and cultural history, not widely known among Western scholars outside of Slavistics. William Mills Todd (2006: 347) has written pointedly: 'Nor did it help that Lotman had conducted his principal "field work" in a milieu, time, and place – the educated gentry of late-eighteenth- and early-nineteenth-century Russia – far removed from the presentist concerns of English and American cultural studies or from the Shakespearean Renaissance of American cultural poetics.' Lotman was neither able to (due to Soviet isolation and censorship) nor particularly interested in engaging in a serious discussion with contemporary theoretical trends, so he was absent from most of the intellectual debates that animated Western academia from the 1960s to 1980s. Todd, again, comments on this with the wisdom of hindsight: 'One can only imagine how much performance studies would have gained from witnessing Lotman's treatment of theatricality in dialogue with Erving Goffman's *Presentation of Self in Everyday Life*, or the cultural anthropology of the Tartu-Moscow school playing off the work of Western anthropologists such as Victor Turner, Clifford Geertz, Mary Douglas, or James Clifford' (2006: 347). When Geertz was asked in 2003 about the similarities between his and Lotman's ideas, his response illustrated the lack of serious interest: 'I have been told before that my ideas and those of Juri Lotman and the Tartu school are similar, but I had not read his work prior to producing my own and still do not know his well' (Gross and Tamm 2003: 329, see also Zorin 2001).

The study of Lotman's work in the English-speaking world started rather early, first in the form of introductions to various reprints and translations in the early and mid-1970s, then in critical engagements with some aspects of his work. In 1974, Ann Shukman dedicated her Oxford dissertation to Lotman's work, published three years later under the title of *Literature and Semiotics: A Study of the Writings of Yu. M. Lotman*. As of 2020, there are more than 200 research papers, books and dissertations in English discussing Lotman's ideas. Of special value are Edna Andrews's *Conversations with Lotman: The Implications of Cultural Semiotics in Language, Literature and Cognition* (2003), Peet Lepik's *Universals in the Context of Juri Lotman's Semiotics* (2008), Aleksei Semenenko's *The Texture of Culture: An Introduction to Yuri Lotman's Semiotic Theory* (2012) and Andrey Makarychev and Alexandra Yatsyk's *Lotman's Cultural Semiotics and the Political* (2017). In addition, there are a dozen special issues and anthologies in English dedicated to Lotman, most notably *Lotman and Cultural Studies: Encounters and Extensions*, prepared by Andreas Schönle (2006a).

This *Companion to Juri Lotman* represents a new step in Lotman studies. This is the very first attempt to provide a collective, systematic and interdisciplinary approach to Lotman's intellectual legacy, bringing together forty-three scholars from thirteen countries. Prepared with Lotman's centenary in mind (February 2022), this *Companion* is designed as a guide to the 'Lotmanian semiosphere', providing information about the context of his work, about the key concepts of his thinking and about the bearing of his work and its future potential in various academic disciplines. The *Companion* concludes with the first comprehensive bibliography of Lotman in English. The aim of this introduction is to provide some key elements for the understanding of Lotman's life and work, while briefly presenting the outline and content of the *Companion*.

Lotman in context

Lotman's thinking is grounded in the notion of context. Since his very first scholarly writings, context has been both an important conceptual tool and one of the main research objects (see Chapter 26). Applied to his own life and works, it is not easy to define or depict all the contexts that are relevant to understanding Lotman's thinking. In many respects, Lotman lived in and moved between very different contexts (see Chapter 1). Born and raised in Russian (Soviet) cultural milieu, his life was spent in Tartu, Estonia, a small university town at the periphery of the Soviet empire. This choice was a mere coincidence, but with major consequences, as Lotman liked to emphasize. In his *Non-Memoires*, he describes memorably his arrival in Tartu, in 1950, at the age of twenty-eight: 'Dressed in a slightly taken-in-black suit of my father's, which was my only "holyday" suit, I went to Tartu, and stayed there for the rest of my life' (Lotman [1995] 2014: 65). Tartu is a multicultural and multilingual town with a long and complex history, 'a meeting place' of peoples, religions and academic traditions, as Michel Espagne accurately writes (2010: 161). In an essay, published in Estonian in 1987 and titled 'Tartu as a Cultural Sign', Lotman explains his relationships with Tartu:

> Tartu is for me a 'town of culture' and this understanding forms the background to everything I see in this town. [. . .] According to my understanding, culture is not a passive storage, a simple bookcase, let it contain the dearest books to me (of course, books are the most important things in life!), but a generator, a machine that constantly reproduces itself, thus competing with life itself. Thus, Tartu is also a place where culture is constantly regenerated. It is the intellectual centre of the [Estonian] nation. And at the heart of this centre is the university, with its perpetually changing and therefore always of the same age student body. [. . .] And if Tartu is for me a sign that symbolizes culture, then the university is the symbol of this symbol. [. . .] It seems to me that even the air in Tartu must be imbued with culture, and that is why I find it very painful every time I encounter something that contradicts the nature of Tartu as a town of culture. (Lotman 1987: 51–2)

A few years before, Lotman had explained in an interview with Estonian daily *Noorte Hääl* (Voice of Youth) in the same atmospheric language the importance of Tartu for his life and thinking: 'I would not like to live in any other town. I would like to visit many other towns, but live only in Tartu. It seems to me that here the very air helps to work and think' (Lotman [1982] 2003: 81). It is not impossible to connect many of Lotman's key ideas to his everyday experience of Tartu. For instance, his deep belief in the importance of periphery and border zones in the dynamics of culture and generation of new ideas, argued eloquently in his programmatic essay 'On the Semiosphere' ([1984] 2005). It has also been claimed that 'Lotman turned Tartu's bilingual [Estonian–Russian] predicament into an epistemology and a worldview' (Beecher 2014: ix), considering that for Lotman, 'a minimally functional structure requires the presence of at least two languages and their incapacity, each independently of the other, to embrace the world external to each of them' (Lotman [1992] 2009: 2).

Lotman was able to transform Tartu, and, more specifically, the Department of Russian Literature at the University of Tartu, into a major 'intellectual magnet attracting people from all around the country: from Moscow and Leningrad, Armenia and Ukraine, the Baltic republics and Russian provincial cities, ranking from undergraduate students to renowned scholars' (Gasparov 1994: 735). The position of Tartu at the margins of the USSR allowed more academic freedom and made it possible for Lotman to invite to Tartu all of the most brilliant semiotically minded Soviet scholars, mainly from Moscow, and also to offer them publishing opportunities. This network of scholars, which included Vyacheslav Ivanov, Alexander Piatigorsky, Isaak Revzin, Vladimir Toporov, Boris Uspenskij and many more, developed gradually into what is now known as the Tartu-Moscow Semiotic School (see Chapter 6). The specificity of the Tartu-Moscow school was that its members had different cultural and linguistic affiliations and came from different, if overlapping, academic communities. 'Thus, we can only approach TMS as a translinguistic, transnational, transinstitutional, transdisciplinary association' which 'spanned all manner of borders, identities and domains: "Estonian", "Russian", "Soviet", "Orientalist", "Slavist", "linguist", "philosopher", "historian", "critic", and so on' (Pilshchikov and Trunin 2016: 384; see also Chapter 7). Lotman very much valued this heterogeneous and personal network, which formed the main context of his academic life, next to his cherished Department of Russian Literature (Kiseleva 2003). He admits this, for instance, in May 1968 in a letter to the Polish literary scholar Maria-Renata Mayenowa: 'for me, personal contacts form an absolutely necessary part of academic network' (quoted in Pilshchikov and Trunin 2016: 372fn3). A clear testimony of the importance of personal network is Lotman's epistolary archive, which includes some 2,500 different correspondents, most of whom lived far from Tartu.

However, we have to take into account yet another important context. Lotman spent almost all of his scholarly life in a totalitarian society, under the Soviet surveillance system and censorship. He was not free to write and publish on every subject he found important; rather, there was a permanent game of cat and mouse with the regime to keep pursuing his academic path. Many of Lotman's initiatives were aborted on various occasions, his publications were closely surveyed, censored and sometimes banned. He was neither allowed to invite non-Soviet scholars to Tartu (with a very few exceptions) nor allowed to travel to Western countries. In 1970, his apartment was searched and some of his manuscripts confiscated, and he was put under the close surveillance of KGB, not to speak about the daily fight for human and financial resources at the university.

In the situation of restricted freedom, it was particularly important for Lotman to root himself in the historical context, to recreate links with the forgotten or prohibited Russian academic tradition. One of the main strategies for this was the actualization of the heritage of early twentieth-century Russian humanities (Torop 2019; see also

Chapters 3, 4 and 5). The semiotic journal *Trudy po znakovym sistemam*, founded by Lotman in 1964, testifies to the various types of this strategy of actualization. The first type was evaluative actualization in the form of dedicating a series of volumes to predecessors: to Juri Tynianov (vol. 4, 1969), to Vladimir Propp (vol. 5, 1972), to Mikhail Bakhtin (vol. 6, 1973) and to Petr Bogatyrev (vol. 7, 1975). The second type is represented by reprint and archive publications of forgotten or unknown works, for example, by Pavel Florensky (vol. 3, 1967), Boris Jarkho (vol. 4, 1969), Boris Eikhenbaum, Florensky, Afanasy Selischev, Boris Tomashevsky (vol. 5, 1971), Olga Freidenberg, Sergei Bernstein (vol. 6, 1973) and Jan Mukařovský (vol. 7, 1975). As another form of actualization, we can mention the strategy of making allusions (when we can see accentuations, examples of retaking earlier excluded authors, or in some critical context the positive mentioning of certain exceptions, or making summaries). For example, in the first volume of *Trudy po znakovym sistemam* (1964) Lotman had to criticize the insufficiency of Russian formalism mostly for political reasons, but at the same time this created for him the opportunity to place Tynianov in the position of a positive exception, saying that there is not enough evidence to state that the works of Tynianov show the features of formalism (Lotman 1964: 10).

These forms of actualization demonstrate that one of Lotman's essential aims was to mediate the forgotten heritage of earlier generations. An active member of the Tartu-Moscow school, Dmitri Segal has called this attitude a 'semiotic historicism' that helped the new generation of scholars reconstruct their previously deprived sense of history: 'Thanks to semiotics we learned of another sense and understanding of history – a state of *existence* in history' (Segal [1993] 1998: 102). Ilya Kalinin (2009: 28) has fittingly summarized the situation: 'Soviet Semiotics is a typical case in which a scientific project that emerged and developed within the context of a severe ideological control over the production of historical knowledge not only solved its immediate scholarly problems, but also acted as a means of intellectual resistance to the official historical myths, as a form of their direct or latent demystification.' However, in the situation of censorship many contacts between Lotman and his predecessors are no longer immediately visible and have to be made explicit by contemporary interpreters (see Torop 2017; 2019).

Next to predecessors and teachers (we have to keep in mind the crucial role of Lotman's university instructors, especially Mark Azadovsky, Grigory Gukovsky, Nikolai Mordovchenko, Vladimir Propp, Boris Tomashevsky and Viktor Zhirmunsky), Lotman was very much aware of the new scholarly developments since the 1950s and their importance for his work: 'Structural-semiotic literary criticism takes into consideration the experience of all preceding literary scholarship. It has, however, its own specific character. It arose in the environment of that scientific revolution that has marked the middle of the twentieth century and is organically connected with the ideas and methodology of structural linguistics, semiotics, information theory and cybernetics' (Lotman [1972] 1976: 16). In this sense, another major scholarly context of Lotman's work is structuralism (in combination with cybernetics), the new epistemological platform he embraced in the early 1960s (for an excellent annotated collection of his structuralist works, see Lotman 2018) and never really abandoned, regardless of the new turns of his later work.

Lotman in concepts

Lotman's life work was to conceptualize the universe of the human mind in semiotic terms. He acknowledges that the semiotician has the habit of transforming the surrounding world so as to show up the semiotic structures: 'Everything that King Midas touched with his golden hand turned to gold. In the same way, everything which the semiotic researcher turns his/her attention to becomes semioticized in his hands' (Lotman 1990: 5). In this work of semiotization, Lotman was truly systematic and comprehensive. However, he never aimed to build a formalized metalanguage or to develop his own conceptual system. Lotman's semiotics has its own method, but almost no terminology. The conceptual analysis of Lotman's work is notoriously difficult, because, as Boris Gasparov has felicitously put it, 'in his theoretical claims, as well as in his concrete interpretations and findings, he was always delightfully inconsistent' (Gasparov 1994: 731). Lotman's work does not represent a unified doctrine, but a certain way of thinking based on seeing structure and systemicity in various meaning-making processes. Lotman's theories often emerged from empirical observation, and can be considered ad hoc theories. Aleksei Semenenko contends to the point: 'What distinguishes Lotman from many other theoreticians is that he never developed any theory for the sake of theory and even his most theory-laden works were as a rule based on actual historical material, ranging from medieval to modern literature' (Semenenko 2012: 7).

It is of major importance for Lotman's cultural semiotics to describe the same phenomenon once as a part, once as a whole, once as a sign, once as a sign system; once bounded and structured, once as an amorphous maze of boundaries. The accuracy of the study of cultural phenomena depends on how accurately the point of view of the cultural analyst is presented. In Lotman's approach, the most universal feature of human cultures is the need for self-description. Every culture has its own specific means for doing this – its languages of description. The descriptive languages facilitate cultural communication, perpetuate cultural experience, and model cultural memory. The more descriptive languages a culture has, the richer is that culture. Consequently, every culture is describable as a hierarchy of object languages and descriptive languages, where the initial object language is a so-called home language that is surrounded by semiotic systems related to everyday rituals and bodily techniques.

As a result of descriptive processes, one can talk about cultural self-models. Cultural self-description can be viewed as a process proceeding in three directions. Culture's self-model is the result of the first direction, the goal of which is maximum similarity to the actually existing culture. Secondly, cultural self-models may emerge that differ from ordinary cultural practice and may even have been designed to change that practice. Third, there are self-models that exist as an ideal cultural self-consciousness, separately from culture and not oriented towards it. By this formulation, Lotman does not exclude conflict between culture and its self-models. But the creation of self-models reflects the creativity of culture. In the 1980s, Lotman described creativity and unpredictability, calling on the work of Ilya Prigogine. In the article 'Culture as a Subject and Its Own Object', Lotman maintains: 'The fundamental problem in the semiotics of culture is the problem of meaning-making. We will define meaning-making as the capacity of a culture as a whole or of individual parts to produce new, non-trivial texts. We will define new texts as those that arise as a result of irreversible (as Prigogine used the term) processes, that is, texts that are to a certain extent unpredictable' ([1989] 2019: 85).

Lotman's conceptual development can be captured by the following sequence: language–text–culture–semiosphere. On the one hand, this represents the evolution of Lotman's conceptual thinking – moving from the particular to the general, as Ilya Kliger (2010: 263) has written: 'One might conceive of Lotman's intellectual trajectory, then, as moving outward from the particular to the general in a quest for a broader and broader conceptualization of all human activity, rooted in the fundamental belief that unless we can theorize the whole, no part can be properly understood.' But on the other hand, these conceptual elements can be considered part of an isomorphic series in which all elements are mutually connected and interdependent. According to this approach, the core principle of Lotman's conceptual thinking is the principle of *cultural isomorphism* 'which postulates that all semiotic entities from individual consciousness to the totality of human culture are based on similar heterogeneous mechanisms of meaning-generation' (Semenenko 2016: 494).

Lotman's theory of cultural semiotics started in the 1960s from the realization that in a semiotical sense culture is a multilanguage or polyglot system, where, in parallel to natural languages, there exist secondary modelling systems (mythology, ideology, ethics, etc.), which are based on natural languages, or which employ natural languages for their description or explanation (music, ballet) or language analogization (language of theatre, language of movies) (see Chapters 8 and 12). The next step was to introduce the notion of text as the principal concept of cultural semiotics (Chapter 9). On the one hand, text is the manifestation of language, using it in a certain manner. On the other hand, text is itself a mechanism that creates languages. From the methodological point of view, the concept of text was important for the definition of the object of research, since it denoted both natural textual objects (a book, picture, symphony) and textualizable objects (culture as text, everyday behaviour or biography, an era, an event). Text and textualization symbolize the definition of the object of study; the definition or framework allows in its turn the structuralization of the object either into structural levels or units, and also the construction of a coherent whole or system of those levels and units. The development of the principles of immanent analysis in various cultural domains was one of Lotman's fields of activity in the early 1970s (see Torop 2015).

For Lotman, text was the basic element of culture as well as culture itself. The prominence of text proves that Lotman's model of analysis is spatial in nature, since text refers to the boundedness of the object of analysis and its division into smaller bounded wholes (see Chapters 13 and 14). At the same time, Lotman immediately emphasized that the textual character of culture does not mean that culture is inherently static:

'Culture can be presented as an aggregate of texts; however, from the point of view of the researcher, it is more exact to consider culture as a mechanism creating an aggregate of texts and texts as the realization of culture' (Lotman and Uspensky [1971] 1978: 218) Thus, culture constitutes a kind of giant mechanism of text generation that constantly translates non-cultural messages into cultural texts (see Chapter 10).

In the late 1970s, Lotman created a typology distinguishing between cultural statics and dynamics. The basis for the typology is the distinction of the static and dynamic aspects of cultural languages. From the static aspect cultural languages divide into the discrete and the continual (iconic-spatial), and for Lotman this forms a semiotic primordial dualism. In discrete languages, sign comes first and meanings are created through the meanings of signs. In continual languages, text comes first and meaning emerges through holistic text that integrates even the most heterogeneous elements (see Chapter 16). These are the two languages between which it is difficult to create translatability.

The dynamic aspect of culture becomes increasingly important for Lotman, particularly in his later work, culminating in his views concerning the importance of unpredictable mechanisms and explosive situations in the development of culture (see Chapter 21). In dynamism, the simultaneity of the two processes in culture is important. On the one hand, in different fields of culture, specialization of cultural languages takes place as a result of autocommunication and identity searches (Chapter 11). On the other hand, on the level of culture as a whole there emerges integration of cultural languages as a possibility of self-communication and self-understanding. Yet the dynamism of integration is revealed in the simultaneity of the two processes. On the one hand, self-descriptions and alongside them also meta-descriptions or descriptions from the position of culture as a whole are created in different parts of culture. This is integration through autonomies. On the other hand, cultural languages diffuse and become creolized due to the communication between different parts of culture. Creolization is a feature of dynamism and an intermediary stage to reaching a new autonomy or pure (self)description.

Increasing interest in cultural dynamics let Lotman introduce in the early 1980s the concept of semiosphere (see Chapter 22). Although the attributes of semiosphere resemble those of text (definability, structurality, coherence), it is an important shift from the point of view of culture's analysability. Human culture constitutes the global semiosphere, but that global system consists of intertwined semiospheres of different times (the diachrony of semiosphere) and different levels (the synchrony of semiosphere). Each semiosphere can be analysed as a single whole, yet we need to bear in mind that each analysed whole in culture is a part of a greater whole, which is an important methodological principle. At the same time, every whole consists of parts, which are legitimate wholes on their own, which in turn consist of parts, and so on. It is an infinite dialogue of wholes and parts and the dynamics of the whole dimension. This means, as Kalevi Kull has happily recapitulated, that 'neither a sign, an organism, a text, or a culture can exist alone, singly – it always requires another sign, other organisms, texts, cultures, in order to exist, to live' (Kull 2005: 178). To put it differently, semiosphere is a concept that allows Lotman to reach a holistic analysis of dynamic processes in culture. A conceptual achievement which has not lost its importance and relevance in contemporary humanities.

Lotman in dialogue

Lotman was a profoundly dialogic thinker, like his important source of inspiration, Mikhail Bakhtin (see Chapter 5). 'No cognitive structure can be unistructural and monolingual', Lotman asserts ([1978] 2019: 36). One of his main ideas is that thought, like meaning, can arise only as a result of relations between two or more different entities. In human life, everything begins with the need for dialogue: 'the need for dialogue, *the dialogic situation*, precedes both real dialogue and even the existence of a language in which to conduct it' (Lotman 1990: 143–4). Cultural dynamics is based on the principle of dialogism, and all cultures are in constant dialogue with both their contemporaries and their past; dialogue is the fundamental characteristic of semiosphere. Therefore, it is very important to pay attention to the dialogic potential of Lotman's work, to map his prospective contribution to the development of new interdisciplinary conversations.

Mihhail Lotman (2007: 141) has mentioned that his father used to divide scholars into 'openers' and 'closers', similarly to Isaiah Berlin who divided writers and thinkers into two categories: hedgehogs, who 'relate everything to a single central vision, one system, less or more coherent', and foxes, 'who pursue many ends, often unrelated and even contradictory' (Berlin [1953] 1993: 3). The 'openers', according to Lotman, create novel ideas and approaches, open new avenues, but often do not take advantage of all the opportunities that they have made possible. Whereas the 'closers' construct systematic metalanguages and comprehensive descriptions. Lotman himself was clearly an 'opener', a paradigmatic academic 'fox', always after something new, and this is the main reason why his oeuvre is open to very different readings and uses. One could even say that, at the present, we don't have a single Juri Lotman, with a clear scholarly profile, but rather a great number of Lotmans, interpreted and shaped in very different ways in different disciplines. Lotman in Russian studies is not the same as Lotman in biosemiotics, Lotman in narratology is not the same as Lotman in cultural theory. Lotman's written legacy forms a giant *opera aperta*, 'an open work' (Eco 1962), permitting an infinite number of interpretations. This dialogic potential represents probably the most valuable feature of Lotman's intellectual inheritance and is very much the main raison d'être of this *Companion*.

True enough, we have to make a distinction between the actual and potential uses of Lotman in contemporary scholarship.[2] There are research fields where Lotman is very present and his work actively engaged with in various discussions. In semiotics he is considered one of the founding fathers of the discipline, one of the main representatives of the Saussurian tradition in semiotics (Chapter 2), creator of the field of cultural semiotics. In Russian literary studies, Lotman has inspired a great amount of research and is a towering figure in the study of late eighteenth-century and early nineteenth-century Russian literature and culture. Lotman has also offered some unexpected impulses or parallel ideas to French post-structuralism (Monticelli 2012; Landolt 2012, and Chapters 23 and 24) and American New Historicism (Schönle 2001; 2006b, and Chapter 27). He is currently being discovered in memory and media studies (Tamm 2015; 2019; Ibrus and Ojamaa 2020, and Chapters 17, 28, 32 and 33), and is discussed among historians and historical theorists (Boyko 2015; Tamm 2017; Monticelli 2020, and Chapters 18 and 25). Interesting attempts have been made to bring together Lotman and the (British) tradition of cultural studies (Schönle 2006a; Ibrus and Torop 2015a, and Chapters 30 and 31). He has been used in recent years to build a new platform for political semiotics and the semiotics of power (e.g. Makarychev and Yatsyk 2017; Selg and Ventsel 2020, and Chapters 20 and 29). The great potential of Lotman for life sciences has also been demonstrated, especially in the fields of biosemiotics and ecosemiotics (Kull 1999; 2015; Maran 2020, and Chapter 34). And last but not least, Lotman's early interest in the functioning of the human brain and artificial intelligence has made him a valuable partner in contemporary cognitive neuroscience (Andrews 2003; 2012, and Chapter 35). However, the last part of the *Companion* shows that most of Lotman's dialogic potential is still largely unexplored, and we hope very much to contribute with this collective effort to changing this situation.

We can see, for instance, that Lotman is an excellent guide in our new 'digital condition' (Stalder 2018), in making sense of the digital transmedia culture, as first studies have already demonstrated (Ibrus and Torop 2015b; Hartley, Ibrus and Ojamaa 2021). Lotman's conception of 'cultural polyglotism' (Lotman 1992) has gained new relevance in the contemporary technological context, which favours the travelling of texts between different cultural languages or media. We can 'read' a literary text in theatre or film language, such as a photo novel, comic or animation, or consume a book trailer or fanfiction, and so on. The transmedia approach to cultural texts enables us to analyse the quality of 'reading' in culture and the functioning of culture as education. The operation of culture as education was an important idea for Lotman. If film adaptations, for example, should have a greater prestige in a culture than literature, he considers the learning of written cultural heritage through audiovisual media a valuable compensation for in-depth knowledge of texts, which he described as 'stereoscopy':

> The normal condition for human activity, however, is one of insufficient information. No matter how far we extend our information networks, the demand for information will expand, outstripping the pace of our information gathering. As a result, no matter how quickly knowledge increases, ignorance will only increase. And, as cognitive activity becomes more efficient, it will become more complicated, not simpler. Under these conditions, insufficient information is compensated for stereoscopically, that is, by producing a completely different projection of reality – a translation into a completely other language. (Lotman [1978] 2019: 46)

Lotman believed in the capacity of semiotics to establish its identity in dialogue with other disciplines. On this belief he built the semiotic empathy both for the objects of research and for other disciplines. This empathy is an attitude that makes Lotman's legacy continually relevant, and his connections with the new orientations in contemporary academic disciplines exist implicitly even when they are not always explicitly comprehended.

Notes

1. Lotman's forename is often transliterated from the Russian, Юрий Лотман, as Yuri, Yury, Jurii or Jurij Lotman, but in this volume we adopt the spelling of Juri Lotman, because Lotman himself favoured this spelling when using Roman script.

2. As mentioned earlier, Lotman's reception has been global, even if geographically unequal (see also Chapter 7); in the following we focus deliberately on English-language scholarship, while knowing that the dialogic potential of Lotman has been used differently in different linguistic and cultural areas.

References

Andrews, E. 2003. *Conversations with Lotman: Cultural Semiotics in Language, Literature, and Cognition*, Toronto: Toronto University Press.

Andrews, E. 2012. 'Lotman and the Cognitive Sciences: The Role of Autocommunication in the Language of Memory', in S. Frank, C. Ruhe and A. Schmitz (eds), *Explosion und Peripherie. Perspektiven auf die Kultursemiotik Jurij Lotmans*, 175–92, Bielefeld: transkript.

Aspisova, O. S. 1998. 'Vospriatie moskovsko-tartuskoi semioticheskoi shkoly v Germanii', in S. Nekliudov (ed.), *Moskovsko-tartuskaia semioticheskaia shkola. Istoriia, vospominaniia, razmyshleniia*, 276–93, Moscow: Iazyki russkoi kul'tury.

Baran, H. 1998. 'Retzeptsii moskovsko-tartuskoi semioticheskoi shkoly v SSHA i Velikobritanii', in S. Nekliudov (ed.), *Moskovsko-tartuskaia semioticheskaia shkola. Istoriia, vospominaniia, razmyshleniia*, 246–75, Moscow: Iazyki russkoi kul'tury.

Beecher, D. I. 2014. *Ivory Tower of Babel: Tartu University and the Languages of Two Empires, a Nation-State, and the Soviet Union*, PhD Dissertation, University of California, Berkeley, Available online: https://escholarship.org/uc/item/9h90g470 (accessed 5 February 2021).

Berlin, I. [1953] 1993. *The Hedgehog and the Fox: An Essay on Tolstoy's View on History*, Chicago: Ivan R. Dee, Inc.

Blaim, A. 1998. 'Lotman in the West: An Ambiguous Complaint', in J. Andrew and R. Reid (eds), *Neo-Formalist Papers: Contributions to the Silver Jubilee Conference to Mark 25 Years of the Neo-Formalist Circle*, 329–37, Amsterdam: Rodopi.

Boyko, T. 2015. 'Describing the Past: Tartu-Moscow School Ideas on History, Historiography, and the Historian's Craft', *Sign Systems Studies* 43 (2/3): 269–80.

Cáceres, M. 2003. 'Lotman en español: Diffusion y recepción crítica', *Entretextos: Revista Electrónica Semestral de Estudios Semióticos de la Cultura* 2: 89–109.

Chang, H., Han, L. and Wu, S. C. 2014. 'The Reception of Tartu Semiotics in China: A Preliminary Survey and a Few Case Studies', *Chinese Semiotic Studies* 10 (1): 133–63.

De Michiel, M. 1995. 'O vospriiatii rabot Iu. M. Lotmana v Italii', in E. V. Permiakov (ed.), *Lotmanovskii sbornik*, vol. 1, 294–306, Moscow: IC-Garant.

Eco, U. 1962. *Opera aperta*, Milan: Bompiani.

Espagne, M. 2010. 'De Lotman à Parrot: pour une histoire régressive de Tartu-Dorpat', *Revue germanique internationale* 11: 161–74.

Faryno, J. 2020. 'Semiotyka Tartusko-Moskiewska w Polsce (1960–2000): (Materiały do bibliografii)', *Studia Litteraria Polono-Slavica* 5: 493–511.

Gasparov, B. 1994. 'In memoriam: Iurii Mikhailovich Lotman (1922–1993)', *The Slavic and East European Journal* 38 (4): 731–9.

Gross, T. and Tamm, M. 2003. 'Kultuur, tekst ja tähendus: Intervjuu Clifford Geertziga' [Culture, Text and Meaning: Interview with Clifford Geertz], in C. Geertz, *Omakandi tarkus: Esseid tõlgendavast antropoloogiast [Local Knowledge: Essays in Interpretative Anthropology]*, trans. T. Pakk-Allmann, 324–31, Tallinn: Varrak.

Hartley, J., Ibrus I. and Ojamaa, M. 2021. *On the Digital Semiosphere: Culture, Media and Science for the Anthropocene*, New York: Bloomsbury Academic.

Ibrus, I. and Ojamaa, M. 2020. 'The Creativity of Digital (Audiovisual) Archives: A Dialogue Between Media Archaeology and Cultural Semiotics', *Theory, Culture & Society* 37 (3): 49–70.

Ibrus, I. and Torop, P. (eds) 2015a. Special Issue: 'Uses of Juri Lotman', *International Journal of Cultural Studies* 18 (1): 151p.

Ibrus, I. and Torop, P. 2015b. 'Remembering and Reinventing Juri Lotman for the Digital Age', *International Journal of Cultural Studies* 18 (1): 3–9.

Kalinin, I. 2009. 'Tartusko-moskovskaia semioticheskaia shkola: semioticheskaia Model' kul'tury / kul'turnaia model' semiotiki', *Novoe literaturnoe obozrenie* 98: 27–56.

Kiseleva, L. N. 2003. 'Iu. M. Lotman – zaveduiushchii kafedroi russkoi Literatury', in A. D. Dulichenko (ed.), *200 let russko-slavianskoi filologii v Tartu*, 336–49, Tartu: Isdatel'stvo Tartuskogo Universiteta.

Kliger, I. 2010. 'World Literature Beyond Hegemony in Yuri M. Lotman's Cultural Semiotics', *Comparative Critical Studies* 7 (2–3): 257–74.

Kull, K. 1999. 'Towards Biosemiotics with Juri Lotman', *Semiotica* 127 (1/4): 115–31.

Kull, K. 2005. 'Semiosphere and a Dual Ecology: Paradoxes of Communication', *Sign Systems Studies* 33 (1): 175–89.

Kull, K. 2015. 'A Semiotic Theory of Life: Lotman's Principles of the Universe of the Mind', *Green Letters: Studies in Ecocriticism* 19 (3): 255–66.

Landolt, E. 2012. 'Histoire d'un dialogue impossible: J. Kristeva, J. Lotman et la sémiotique', *Langage et société* 141: 121–40.

Lepik, P. 2008. *Universals in the Context of Juri Lotman's Semiotics*, Tartu: University of Tartu Press.

Lotman, Ju. M. 1964. *Lektsii po struktural'noi poetike. Vyp. 1. Vvedenie, teoriia stikha*, Tartu: Izdatel'stvo Tartuskogo universiteta (*Trudy po znakovym sistemam*, 1).

Lotman, Yu. M. [1972] 1976. *Analysis of the Poetic Text*, trans. D. B. Johnson, Ann Arbor: Ardis.

Lotman, Ju. M. [1978] 2019. 'The Phenomenon of Culture', in J. Lotman, *Culture, Memory and History: Essays in Cultural Semiotics*, trans. B. J. Baer, ed. M. Tamm, 33–48, Cham: Palgrave Macmillan.

Lotman, Ju. M. [1982] 2003. 'Zhit' tol'ko v Tartu', in Ju. M. Lotman, *Vospitanye dushi*, 79–83, Saint Petersburg: Iskusstvo–SBK.

Lotman, Ju. M. [1984] 2005. 'On the Semiosphere', trans. W. Clark, *Sign Systems Studies* 33 (1): 205–29.

Lotman, J. 1987. 'Tartu kui kultuurimärk' [Tartu as Cultural Sign], in T. Matšulevits (ed.), *Meie Tartu [Our Tartu]*, 51–2, Tallinn: Perioodika.

Lotman, J. [1989] 2019. 'Culture as a Subject and Its Own Object', in J. Lotman, *Culture, Memory and History: Essays in Cultural Semiotics*, trans. B. J. Baer, ed. M. Tamm, 83–93, Cham: Palgrave Macmillan.

Lotman, Yu. M. 1990. *Universe of the Mind. A Semiotic Theory of Culture*, trans. A. Shukman, Bloomington, IN: Indiana University Press.

Lotman, Ju. M. 1992. 'Tekst i poliglotizm kul'tury', in Ju. M. Lotman, *Izbrannye stat'i v trekh tomakh*, vol. 1, 142–7, Tallinn: Aleksandra.

Lotman, J. [1992] 2009. *Culture and Explosion*, trans. W. Clark, ed. M. Grishakova, Berlin and New York: Mouton de Gruyter.

Lotman, Yu. M. [1995] 2014. *Non-Memoirs*, trans. C. L. Brickman, ed. E. Bershtein, Champaign, IL: Dalkey Archive Press.

Lotman, Ju. M. 2018. *O strukturalizme. Raboty 1965–1970 godov*, ed. I. A. Pilshchikov, with N. V. Poselyagin and M. V. Trunin, Tallinn: TLU Press.

Lotman, Yu. M. and Uspensky, B. A. [1971] 1978. 'On the Semiotic Mechanism of Culture', trans. G. Mihaychuk, *New Literary History* 9 (2): 211–32.

Lotman, M. 2007. 'Hirm ja segadus. Irratsionaalse semioosi poole' [Fear and Confusion: Toward the Semiosis of the Irrational], in J. Lotman, *Hirm ja segadus: Esseid kultuurisemiootikast [Fear and Confusion: Essays in Cultural Semiotics]*, trans. K. Pruul, ed. M. Lotman, 141–58, Tallinn: Varrak.

Makarychev, A. and Yatsyk, A. 2017. *Lotman's Cultural Semiotics and the Political*, Lanham: Rowman & Littlefield International.

Maran, T. 2020. *Ecosemiotics: The Study of Signs in Changing Ecologies*, Cambridge: Cambridge University Press.

Monticelli, D. 2012. 'Challenging Identity: Lotman's "Translation of the Untranslatable" and Derrida's *Différance*', *Sign Systems Studies* 40 (3/4): 319–39.

Monticelli, D. 2020. 'Thinking the New After the Fall of the Berlin Wall: Juri Lotman's Dialogism of History', *Rethinking History* 24 (2): 184–208.

Pilshchikov, I. and Trunin, M. 2016. 'The Tartu-Moscow School of Semiotics: A Transnational Perspective', *Sign Systems Studies* 44 (3): 368–401.

Schönle, A. 2001. 'Social Power and Individual Agency: The Self in Greenblatt and Lotman', *Slavic and East European Journal* 45 (1): 61–79.

Schönle, A. (ed.) 2006a. *Lotman and Cultural Studies: Encounters and Extensions*, Madison: The University of Wisconsin Press.

Schönle, A. 2006b. 'The Self, its Bubbles, and Illusions: Cultivating Autonomy in Greenblatt and Lotman', in A. Schönle (ed.), *Lotman and Cultural Studies: Encounters and Extensions*, 183–207, Madison: The University of Wisconsin Press.

Segal, D. M. [1993] 1998. '"Et in Arcadia Ego" vernulsia: nasledie moskovsko-tartuskoi shkoly semiotiki segodnia', in S. Nekliudov (ed.), *Moskovsko-tartuskaia semioticheskaia shkola. Istoriia, vospominaniia, razmyshleniia*, 99–112, Moscow: Iazyki russkoi kul'tury.

Selg, P. and Ventsel, A. 2020. *Introducing Relational Political Analysis: Political Semiotics as a Theory and Method*, Cham: Palgrave Macmillan.

Semenenko, A. 2012. *The Texture of Culture: An Introduction to Yuri Lotman's Semiotic Theory*, New York: Palgrave Macmillan.

Semenenko, A. 2016. '*Homo polyglottus*: Semiosphere as a Model of Human Cognition', *Sign Systems Studies* 44 (4): 494–510.

Shukman, A. 1977. *Literature and Semiotics: A Study of the Writings of Yu. M. Lotman*, Amsterdam, New York and Oxford: Elsevier North Holland.

Stalder, F. 2018. *The Digital Condition*, Cambridge: Polity Press.

Tamm, M. 2015. 'Semiotic Theory of Cultural Memory: In the Company of Juri Lotman', in S. Kattago (ed.), *The Ashgate Research Companion to Memory Studies*, 127–41, Farnham: Ashgate.

Tamm, M. 2017. 'Introduction: Semiotics and History Revisited', *Sign Systems Studies* 45 (3/4): 211–29.

Tamm, M. 2019. 'Introduction: Juri Lotman's Semiotic Theory of History and Cultural Memory', in J. Lotman, *Culture, Memory and History: Essays in Cultural Semiotics*, trans. B. J. Baer, ed. M. Tamm, 1–26, Cham: Palgrave Macmillan.

Todd, W. M., III 2006. 'Afterword: Lotman without Tears', in A. Schönle (ed.), *Lotman and Cultural Studies: Encounters and Extensions*, 345–52, Madison: The University of Wisconsin Press.

Torop, P. 2015. 'Cultural Semiotics', in F. Sharifian (ed.), *The Routledge Handbook of Language and Culture*, 170–80, London and New York: Routledge.

Torop, P. 2017. 'Semiotics of Cultural History', *Sign Systems Studies* 45 (3/4): 317–34.

Torop, P. 2019. 'Russian Theory and Semiotics of Culture: History and Perspectives', *Bakhtiniana: Revista de Estudos do Discurso* 14 (4): 19–39.

Volkova Américo, E. 2019. 'The Language of the Tartu-Moscow Semiotic School and the Translations of Yuri Lotman's Works in Brazil', *Bakhtiniana: Revista de Estudos do Discurso* 14 (4): 40–60.

Winner, T. G. 2002. 'How Did the Ideas of Juri Lotman Reach the West?', *Sign Systems Studies* 30 (2): 419–27.

Zhang, J. and Yan, Z. 2014. 'Former Soviet Cultural Semiotics in China: Reception and Transformation', *Chinese Semiotic Studies* 10 (1): 541–7.

Zorin, A. 2001. 'Ideology, Semiotics, and Clifford Geertz: Some Russian Reflections', *History and Theory* 40 (1): 57–73.

Żyłko, B. 2012. 'Lotman v Pol'she', *Novaia Pol'sha* 4: 67–73.

CHAPTER 1
LOTMAN'S LIFE AND WORK
Tatyana Kuzovkina

Juri Lotman was born in Petrograd (now Saint Petersburg) on 28 February 1922 into a family of Russian intelligentsia of Jewish descent. His parents, who came from Odessa, were the first generation to live in Saint Petersburg. His father was a lawyer who specialized in copyright matters. His mother was a dentist. They tried their best to give their children a well-rounded education by enrolling them in one of the best schools in the city, Petrischule. The children took music lessons at home as well as regularly visiting museums and the theatre. As a family, you could often find them reading out loud, drawing and publishing handwritten magazines. His older sister, Inna, became a composer, musicologist and teacher. His middle sister, Lidia, was a famous literary scholar who specialized in literature of the nineteenth century. His youngest sister, Victoria, became a cardiologist. In 1939 he graduated with a gold medal (first-class honours) and was admitted to the Faculty of Philology at Leningrad State University without having to take an entrance exam. In his first year he was drawn to the area of folklore. He attended the lectures of Mark Azadovsky and presented at a seminar of Vladimir Propp. Apart from this, he studied at one of Grigory Gukovsky's seminars on eighteenth-century Russian literature (1995a; 1995b[1]).

In October 1940, while Lotman was in his second year of university, he was called to serve in the military. During the Second World War he served as a signal operator in the artillery regiment. He was awarded three military orders and four medals. In 1986, in a letter to his close friend and colleague Boris Egorov, Lotman retrospectively penned his life motto: 'I have always considered circumstances unworthy of being blamed. Circumstances can break or destroy a great person, but they cannot become the defining factor of his life' (1997a: 348). During the war, he actively engaged in self-education: he studied French, read textbooks, articles and monographs on philosophy, the history of literature and Russian history and was interested in the era of Ivan Grozny. In letters to his sister, Lidia, in 1943, he had already begun to write statements about the need to look at culture as a whole, distinguishing between synchronic and diachronic levels. Judging by the letters, these perspectives were probably formed through the influence of Oswald Spengler's book *The Decline of the West*, upon which he happened to stumble (Kuzovkina 2020; Kuzovkina et al. 2021). After the war, Lotman completed another year and a half of mandatory service in the Soviet zone of occupied Germany. He worked as an artist in the regimental theatre. During his trips to Berlin, he would attend exhibitions and performances. Throughout his life he exercised his talent as a sketch artist, making random sketches during meetings and giving his cartoon drawings to friends (Kuzovkina and Daniel 2016).

Having returned to Leningrad in December 1946, Lotman resumed his studies at the university. He attended the lectures of Boris Tomashevsky, Boris Eikhenbaum, Arkady Dolinin and Viktor Zhirmunsky. During a seminar of Nikolay Mordovchenko he learned about literature, journalism, the movement of freemasonry in Russia during the eighteenth century and analysed Pushkin's *Eugene Onegin*. In the archives of the freemason Maksim Nevzorov, Lotman discovered the original Russian pamphlet entitled *Short Instructions for Russian Knights* by Matvey Dmitriev-Mamonov. The publication of this document was Lotman's very first scholarly article (1949), which became a significant piece in the study of the movement of social thought in Russia. Two articles that he had gathered to be published in a volume dedicated to the eighteenth century were given to Gukovsky but disappeared after his arrest. One of them referred to the French sources of Karamzin's articles in *The European Herald* (1995a: 34). The second appeared to be a correspondence with commentary between freemasons Aleksey Kutuzov and Ivan Turgenev (published in 1963). In addition to this, Lotman decided on the topic of his dissertation, which was actually written while he was still an undergraduate student (1995a: 40).

Lotman's final years at the university coincided with the Stalinist anti-Semitic campaign. From March to April 1949, during party meetings at Leningrad State University, the 'cosmopolitans' were exposed. Lotman's professors (Azadovsky, Zhirmunsky, Gukovsky, Eikhenbaum) were accused of 'servility to the West'. At a meeting at the Institute of Russian Literature (Pushkin House), a question was raised about Lotman's sister, Lidia, a student of Eikhenbaum who was 'infected with the ideology of cosmopolitanism and formalism' (Druzhinin 2012: 297–8). Lotman graduated from university with flying colours in 1950, but as a Jew he was not accepted into graduate school and was unable to find a job in Leningrad. He somehow heard that there was a need for lecturers at the Teachers Institute in Tartu and called the director, who decided to hire him regardless of his personal identity as a Jew. In Estonia, antisemitism was not as strong as it was in Moscow or Leningrad as the government's efforts were primarily aimed at combating 'bourgeois nationalism'. In the spring of 1949, there were mass deportations of the locals and 'purges' of the intelligentsia. Lotman later wrote that 'not knowing the language and circumstances' prevented him from seeing the tragedy of the situation in which he found himself (1995a: 40). Once he became a 'Russifier', Lotman behaved like an intellectual whose actions contributed to the establishment of a cultural dialogue. He studied Russian-Estonian literature and cultural connections (1958a; 1987a; Lotman and Isakov 1961), and wrote a literary textbook for Estonian schools (Lotman and Neverdinova 1982), a methodological guide for teachers (Lotman and Neverdinova 1984) and a textbook on Russian literature in Estonian (1982). Lotman worked for five years at the Teachers' Institute (1950–5), becoming a lecturer and the head of the department of Russian Language and Literature in 1952.

Simultaneously, starting in September 1950, he gave lectures on the history of Russian literature, criticism and journalism of the eighteenth and nineteenth centuries at the University of Tartu. In June 1954, he officially accepted a full-time position as associate professor in the Department of Russian Literature. During his time working at the university, in addition to teaching courses on the history of literature, Lotman gave lectures on linguistics, semiotics, analysis of literary texts, methods of teaching literature in schools and many specialized courses on the works of Karamzin, Pushkin, Lermontov, Baratynsky, Gogol, Tyutchev, the poetics of everyday behaviour, the history of the salons in Europe and Russia, film theory, the theory of prose and structural poetics. 'Until the mid 1980s, he taught at least ten hours a week, while in the 1960–70s [. . .] he taught 12–14 hours a week.' A total of eighty-four theses were defended with the guidance of Lotman (Kiseleva 1996: 7).

In 1951, Lotman was married to Zara Mints (1927–90), who was a graduate of Leningrad State University and a student of the leading specialist of the Silver Age, Dmitry Maksimov. After going to Tartu, she also initially worked at the Teachers' Institute; then in 1956, she became a senior lecturer in the Department of Russian Literature at the University of Tartu (from 1964 she worked as a lecturer and from 1979 a professor). Zara Mints headed the Silver Age study of Russian Literature in the department, was editor of the department's publications and assisted Lotman in preparing his works for publication.

In 1952, Lotman successfully defended his candidate's dissertation entitled *Alexander Radishchev in the Struggle with the Social and Political Views and the Bourgeois Aesthetics of Nikolay Karamzin*. Beginning in 1955, he started to cooperate with a newly formed group by studying the eighteenth century in the Pushkin House. Strict historicism, the study of literature as part of the movement of social thought, 'a thorough analysis of the breadth and depth of that era's cultural life' (1973a: 206, 210) is how Lotman characterized the method of his teacher, Nikolay Mordovchenko, whom Lotman followed. The end of the 1950s and beginning of the 1960s saw, in addition to the works of Karamzin and Radishchev, the advent of articles on subjects such as Russian–German literary ties (1959), the semiotics of everyday behaviour (1958b), the problems of cultural interpretation and the reception of the ideas of the Russian Enlightenment (1958c; 1967a).

From 1954 to 1960, the first steps towards the creation of a world-famous philological centre were made under the leadership of Lotman and Egorov, who was head of the department at that time. In many ways, the rector of the University of Tartu, physicist Fyodor Klement, made a large contribution to this initiative. At the Fourth International Congress of Slavists (Moscow 1958), *Studies on Russian and Slavic Philology* in the series *Acta Universitatis Tartuensis* were presented, with Lotman opening with a monograph on Andrei Kaysarov, a professor of Russian language and literature at the University of Tartu in the nineteenth century (1958). In 1959, Lotman received his first international invitation to the Schiller conference in the German Democratic Republic, although the trip did not take place due to the 'late submission of documents' (the official version). In 1961, at the University of Leningrad, Lotman successfully defended his doctoral dissertation, entitled *Paths of Development of Russian Literature in the Pre-Decemberist Period*. The subject was the development of literature in the pre-Pushkin period and the revised, traditional assessments of literary associations of that time, considering the overall historical and cultural background and clarifying their stylistic and ideological positions.

Figure 1.1 Juri Lotman in 1950s. © Juri Lotman Semiotics Repository, Tallinn University.

In the second half of the 1950s, Lotman carefully followed new methodological research initiatives in the humanities. He and his colleagues discussed Norbert Wiener's book *Cybernetics and Society* (Egorov 1999: 91–2) and different points of view on structural linguistics in the journal *Voprosy iazykoznaniia*. In 1960, Egorov moved to Leningrad, and Lotman became the professor and chair of the Department of Russian Literature (1963a).

Lotman's academic work cannot be divided into historical-literary and semiotic periods as his empirical and theoretical research go hand in hand, contributing to one another. With both of these academic streams, his research method continued to develop in a spiralling motion: at each new turn, he would gather new material, go into greater depth and complement that which had been discussed earlier. In September 1960, Lotman started to teach a course called 'Lectures on Aesthetics'.[2] The ideas for the course (e.g. comparing the writer as thinker to the writer as artist, or the need for a new scientific language) formed the basis of his first monograph on structural poetics.

In lectures he stated that a work of art is structural and that it has a purpose and a design. Its primary artistic structures (style and manner of writing) and its secondary artistic structures (subject, plot, composition, direct notes from the author) interact with each other in a complex way. In 1962, his first article was published on the problem of similarities between art and life. While relying on the definition of 'opposition' given in Nikolai Trubetzkoy's *Fundamentals of Phonology*, Lotman focused on the stages of aesthetic perception in particular, contrasting 'depicted ones with non-depicted ones' and concluding that 'differences in perception are relative, not objective' (1962a: 97). His second article discussed the difference between linguistic and literary concepts of structure. Lotman described both the text and underlying reality as a complex 'multi-level structure' (1963b: 48): 'both the system of the material world that surrounds a person, and their conscience, class and generation at each separate moment of their existence are not, in fact, amorphous but are instead linked through a rigid relational system within structures [. . .] these structures [. . .] are broad and difficult to see' (1963b: 52). This position was, in fact, a rudimentary form of the concept that he later developed under the name semiosphere. A year later, that article was translated into French (1964a).

In December 1962, a symposium on the structural study of sign systems was held in Moscow, after which the actions of Moscow's structuralists were harshly criticized by the ruling Communist Party and traditionalist scholars. The fate of the new academic stream was called into question. In the spring of 1963, Lotman began to correspond with Vladimir Toporov, and in the summer he met Vyacheslav Ivanov, Isaac Revzin, Boris Uspenskij and Alexander Piatigorsky, asking them if they would work with him (see Chapter 6). In August 1964, the first semiotics summer school on secondary modelling systems was held at Kääriku Sports Centre at the University of Tartu. The second was held in 1966, the third in 1968, the fourth in 1970 and the fifth (called the All-Union Symposium of Secondary Modelling Systems) in the winter of 1974. According to the participants, Lotman was the central figure of these academic meetings. This was due to 'the charm that radiated from his personality', 'the delicate balance between being human and also a professional', 'behind all that, one could feel a sense of self-worth to a degree that balance the natural way about him' (Toporov 1993: 70).

In 1964, a new series began to appear within the framework of the *Acta Universitatis Tartuensis*, entitled *Trudy po znakovym sistemam* (Sign Systems Studies). During Lotman's life, twenty-five volumes were published in this series, which also became the main platform for the Tartu-Moscow school. The series opened with Lotman's first semiotic monograph, *Lectures on Structural Poetics* (1964b). This was built on the theory that in a literary text the natural language becomes a system that models a new integrality which is, seemingly, a secondary modelling system. Lotman posed the problem of studying the text 'at the point of intersection within the text and extra-textual connections', distinguishing between 'common linguistic meanings, textual meanings and the functions of texts in their cultural systems' (Torop 1992: 10). Reports and articles of this period were influenced by the motto 'the study of literature must be a science' (1967b).

Figure 1.2 Juri Lotman in 1964. © Juri Lotman Semiotics Repository, Tallinn University.

Between them the monographs entitled *The Structure of Artistic Text* (1970) and *Analysis of the Poetic Text: The Structure of a Poem* (1972) summarized the results of the ten-year research study into text through a new methodological perspective. Lotman's theory of text can be schematically presented as follows: art generates a special type of language and helps a person 'decipher and turn [a huge amount of information] into signs' (1970a: 9); a literary text has expressivity, delimitation and a hierarchy of levels, and is 'the relationship between textual and extratextual systems' (1970a: 167), of which the meanings are formed by internal recoding as well as external recoding; 'the more different the structures are from each other', the more meaningful the 'act of switching' is (1970a: 50); irregularities in art 'gain structural meaning' (1970a: 94) because art has the ability to transform 'noise into information' (1970a: 99); the text as a structure is dynamic and within it, there is a constant battle between automation and de-automation (1970a: 95). Pragmatics of the text is also touched upon in Lotman's theory: 'perceiving the same text repeatedly reveals the evolution of the perceiving consciousness' (1970a: 167; see also Chapter 9).

Lotman develops these ideas by considering the specifics of cinematography in the monograph *Semiotics of Cinema and the Problems of Cinematic Aesthetics* (1973b), where the informative content of the text is expressed by the 'internal unexpectedness of the structure' (1973b: 73). Cinematography develops through the struggle of two tendencies: 'to seamlessly merge with life' and 'to reveal its own cinematographic specificities' (1973b: 28). Lotman compared the film frame as the smallest unit of which films are made of, with the word as the smallest unit of which literary texts are made of. He introduced the concept of the rhythm of film narration and studied in detail the poetics of montage as 'juxtaposition of heterogenous elements of a language' (1973b: 72). The book ended by discussing the artist's moral responsibilities, something that was uncommon for the 1970s but which was very characteristic of the late Lotman. He also considered complex semiotic systems in other types of art such as luboks (Russian popular prints) (1976), puppet theatrics (1978) and paintings (1986; 1997b) (see also Chapter 16).

At the end of the 1960s, the first articles in cultural theory appeared, mainly written in collaboration with Boris Uspenskij. Lotman understood culture as 'a set of non-hereditary information that is accumulated, stored and passed on' (1967c: 30); 'against the background of no culture at all, culture appears to be a sign system' (Lotman and Uspenskij 1971: 145), 'a nonhereditary memory of the community' which is expressed through 'a certain system of prohibitions and instructions' (Lotman and Uspenskij 1971: 147). Culture is a self-descriptive mechanism, and Lotman introduced a classification based on how close each culture's self-description is to reality (Lotman and Uspenskij 1971: 170). Articles about the culture in the 1960s–1970s, with the addition of some newer ones, were published in two small collections of articles entitled *Studies on the Typology of Culture* (1970b; 1973c). Lotman's culturological reflection helped him to further comprehend Soviet ideology, which was characterized, for example, by the following statement: 'when fighting for information, different historical and social groups seek to monopolize it', a lie 'grows on the same basis as information but takes the opposing side when it comes to social functionality' (1970b: 6). One of the fundamental positions of Lotman's cultural semiotics is the necessary presence of several languages in order for a culture to properly grow and function (1974; see also Chapter 10). His theoretical propositions were supported by research on the poetics of everyday behaviour in Russia during the eighteenth and nineteenth centuries, the importance of theatre and painting when it comes to coding the cultural behaviour of a person, and the semiotics of urban space (see Chapter 25).

Along with the structural-semiotic research that was coming out at the beginning of the 1960s, studies on Pushkin also began to develop. The acquisition of structural-semiotic methodology led to new ways of reading a text. In an article about the evolution of character building in *Eugene Onegin*, Lotman showed how the 'image structure' (1960: 168) of the heroes changed along with the evolution of the author's world view. What Pushkin considered ideal is evident in articles about the Tolstoyan trend in Russian literature and the ideological structure of *The Captains Daughter*: rejecting the 'principle of political structures' (1962b: 32) and aspiring to 'rise above the "cruel age"' while remaining human and holding on to human dignity (1962c: 20). In the article about the literary structures of *Eugene Onegin* (1966) and in a later monograph (1975), Lotman considered the main structural principle of the novel to have many different points of view and the poetics of contradictions which leads to the fundamental openness, incompleteness and dynamism of a text. In those years, Lotman did not abandon his research in the pre-Pushkin period of literature and French-Russian cultural ties but contributed in *The Complete Collection of Karamzin's Poems* (Karamzin 1966) as well as *Poets of the 1790–1810s* (Lotman and Al'tshuller 1971). Lotman also published an article entitled 'Rousseau and Russian Culture of the Eighteenth–Early Nineteenth Centuries' in the Russian edition of Rousseau's *Treatises* (1969).

In 1966 and 1967, Lotman and Mints visited Czechoslovakia to attend academic conferences (in Brno and Prague). In 1967, the first translations of Lotman's structuralist works appeared in *Strumenti critici* and in *Information sur les Sciences Sociales*. In 1968, he was elected a member of the International Association for Semiotic Studies, and from 1968 to 1985 served as vice president even though he was unable to attend their meetings in person.

In 1965, the first 'frosts' began to appear in Soviet politics, officially replacing the 'thaw' era. That September, the literary critic Andrei Sinyavsky and the translator and poet Yuli Daniel were arrested and a show trial was arranged for them. In 1966, the position of the general secretary of the Central Committee of the Communist Party of the Soviet Union was restored and was occupied by Leonid Brezhnev; at the same time, a fifth department of the KGB was created to combat the 'ideological sabotage of the enemy'. In 1968, human rights appeals to the rest of the world community began to be heard. Students of Lotman and Mints, a poet and friend of the couple, Natalya Gorbanevskaya, and a few scholars involved in the summer schools participated in protest movements. Philologists in Tartu caught the attention of the KGB during that time, causing the publication of collections and works from student conferences to be banned in 1968. In addition to this, the next edition of *Studies of Russian and Slavic Philology* was banned.

Lotman followed the events of the Prague Spring, and was strongly affected by the invasion of Soviet troops in Czechoslovakia on 21 August 1968. As acknowledged by Lotman himself, these events were a turning point in his attitude towards the Soviet state. He sympathized with the protest demonstrations in which Gorbanevskaya participated, and, in the summer of 1969, he took her son to his summer home for a while. On 30 January 1970, in connection with Gorbanevskaya's arrest, the Lotmans were put under surveillance and investigated (Kuzovkina 2015). Surveillance began, letters were revised and the semiotics summer school in 1972 was banned. Over the course of the next sixteen years, Lotman was prohibited from travelling to the foreign countries. In 1977, he was forced to leave his position of head of the department, and in 1980 was transferred to the Department of Foreign Literature. Serial editions from the department continued to be published, though they were put under significant restriction. From the mid-1970s, the University of Tartu, in accordance with the decisions of the State

Figure 1.3 Juri Lotman in 1972. © Juri Lotman Semiotics Repository, Tallinn University.

Press Committee, banned the publication of monographs, reduced the size of the *Acta Universitatis Tartuensis* series and no longer allowed 'the publication of new materials based on archival sources' (Isakov 1991: 9).

Lotman's works became even more famous. In the 1970s, three of his monographs on structural poetics were translated into several European languages. In 1974, a collection of articles on semiotic culture and literature was published in German, and then in Japanese in 1979. In 1975, a collection of articles by Lotman and Uspenskij was published in Italian. In 1977, Lotman was elected Honorary Fellow of the Semiotic Society of America and Corresponding Fellow of the British Academy.

The scholar's fame also grew within the USSR, and he was presented with many new and unexpected proposals for collaboration. For example, from 1971 to 1975 Mikhail Ignatev, the head of the Department of Cybernetics and Technology at the Leningrad State Institute of Aviation Instrumentation, invited Lotman and Egorov to take part in the development of artificial intelligence for a team of robots that were supposed to be used on the Moon. The literary scholars' task was to study the laws of communication in a group by role-playing and looking at the relationships between leaders and regular workers. They formed small teams of graduate students and young employees from the universities of Tartu and Leningrad and worked in the area of 'algorithmizing the behaviour of complex robotic manipulation systems using structural methods' (Egorov 1999: 208; Egorov, Ignatiev and Lotman 1995).

The 1980s were the final years of Lotman's academic research. Among his works in the area of structural semiotics, the most significant is considered to be the 1984 article 'On the Semiosphere', in which he discusses the global laws of the way culture functions. This programmatic article elaborated on the thoughts of Vladimir Vernadsky about the noosphere. The semiosphere, according to Lotman, is primary when it comes into relation with its conforming elements; it precedes any communicative act, and is 'a single mechanism (if not, an organism)' (1984: 7; see also Chapter 22).

In the 1980s, a group of scientists from the Leningrad Laboratory of Neurophysiology and the Behavioural Pathology of the Institute of Evolutionary Physiology and Biochemistry from the USSR Academy of Sciences (Lev Balonov, Vadim Deglin, Tatyana Chernigovskaya), who were studying the functional asymmetry of the brain, began to collaborate. Lotman applied the results of this research to his theory of culture, studying 'the relation of similarity between the mechanism of individual consciousness and the semiotic mechanism of culture' (1983: 16–17).

Lotman's long-term work on Pushkin was published in two books entitled *The Novel 'Eugene Onegin' by A. S. Pushkin: Commentaries* (1980) and *Aleksandr Sergeevich Pushkin: A Biography* (1981). The first work is a line-by-line commentary on the novel that helps the reader understand the author's intention and explains the reality, hidden quotations, literary context, polemical references, reminiscences and games that go on between the author and the reader. It also contains, for the first time in Lotman's literary career, lengthy chapters on the everyday culture of the eighteenth- and nineteenth-century nobility. In his biography of Pushkin, Lotman first discusses 'an internal psychological unity due to the unity of the individual including their willpower, intellect and self-awareness' (1997a: 346). The overall topic of the book is the formation of a sense of personal dignity, honour and integrity in one's home and personal life as it unfolds against a detailed historical background. In the chapters where Lotman analyses Pushkin, there are traces of Lotman's own autobiographical details. Many readers who knew Lotman personally saw features of him in his description of Pushkin. Miroslav Drozda, the Czech scholar of Slavic Studies, said in a letter to Lotman, 'when reading about Pushkin, I constantly thought about you, about your brave, creative work and about the endless source of lifegiving things that exist around you to which you pay close attention' (quoted in Kuzovkina 1999: 37). Similar features are to be found in Lotman's book *Creating Karamzin* (1987b). The position of Karamzin, who considered 'a life devoted to literature' to be a public service (1987b: 15–16), could be said to be analogous to Lotman's position. The events of 1968 caused Lotman to make the painful decision to join the work of the dissidents rather than continuing in academics (Kiseleva 2003: 347).

At one of the semiotic seminars in Tartu in 1985, Lotman made a report on the role of external factors in literary evolution in which he distinguished between two separate kinds of process: repetitive (reversible) and irreversible (with a 'historical, that is, temporary nature') (see also Chapter 21). In the latter process, chance plays a huge role, which Lotman associated with self-awareness and the act of individual choice: 'culture cannot be separated from acts of consciousness and self-awareness. Self-esteem is an essential part of it, therefore, the role of conscious processes is greatly increased because of it' (1989: 45).

In the second half of the 1980s, Lotman worked on a number of final projects that united his work. He prepared a book called *Universe of the Mind: A Semiotic Theory of Culture* (1990a) for a London publishing house (published in Russian in 1996) and compiled a three-volume collection of selected works for a Tallinn publishing house (1992–3). The collapse of the Soviet Union coincided with the peak of Lotman's popularity. His books about Pushkin and Karamzin were published in mass circulations across the USSR (900,000 copies of the two editions of Pushkin's biography were printed). From 1986 to 1991, he recorded thirty-three episodes with the Estonian television broadcasting network for a TV lecture series under the general title 'Conversations about Russian Culture', which were soon afterwards broadcast in Moscow. A large audience watched his lectures about human relationships, culture, intelligence and Pushkin and his entourage in order to gain moral support in a difficult time of historical and ideological change. Lotman received a large number of letters from grateful readers and viewers (Kuzovkina 2019), and he, along with Dmitry Likhachev and Andrei Sakharov, became one of the intellectual leaders of 'perestroika'. A book based on his main lectures and earlier articles was later published posthumously (1994a).

Lotman's popularity also grew in other countries. Until 1986, he was banned from going to foreign countries (his first trip was to the University of Bergen in Norway). Between 1987 and 1990, he gave lectures at universities in Finland, Italy, Germany, France and Sweden. In 1987, Lotman was elected member of the Norwegian Academy, and in 1989 of the Royal Swedish Academy; in the early 1990s, he was given honorary doctorates by several European universities (L'Université Libre de Bruxelles in 1990, Univerzita Karlova v Praze in 1991, Keele University, UK, in 1992). He was also elected to the Estonian Academy of Sciences and to the Estonian Writer's Union.

In 1989, during a one-year stay in Munich as the recipient of the Alexander von Humboldt Foundation Prize, Lotman suffered a stroke which caused his reading and writing abilities to decline drastically. From that moment on, the way he worked changed. All new texts (from personal letters to academic monographs) were dictated to his wife and then to his secretaries (Vladislava Gekhtman, Jelena Pogosjan and

Figure 1.4 Juri Lotman at the end of 1980s. © Juri Lotman Semiotics Repository, Tallinn University.

Tatyana Kuzovkina). This way of working led to Lotman having access to only a narrow selection of sources as he was only able to get acquainted with new texts audibly, and had to rely heavily on his memory. After leaving hospital, he dictated new episodes of *Conversations about Russian Culture* (1994a) to Zara Mints. He also worked with Pogosjan on a large project, studying the everyday life of the nobility (only the first part of it, *High-Society Dinners*, was finished, including daily menu items with comments from family members of aristocrat Pavel Durnovo from the mid-nineteenth century (Lotman and Pogosjan 1996).

On 25 October 1990, as a result of complications from surgery, Zara Mints passed away. It was very difficult for Lotman to deal with his loneliness, although he did continue to work anyway. By April 1991, a new theoretical book discussing the ideas of explosion in culture and history was ready for publication. The book was called *Praising Culture: Essays* and was supposed to be published by the Leningrad branch of publishing house Soviet Writer. After submitting the manuscript, Lotman began to work on a new book entitled *Culture and Explosion*, which he referred to as his main book (1997a: 425). In the winter of 1991, the Leningrad publishing house ceased to exist, and the manuscript for *Praising Culture* was returned to the author. While continuing to work on *Culture and Explosion*, Lotman added to it with fragments from *Praising Culture*. In February 1922, the manuscript was submitted to the new Moscow publishing house Gnozis, which printed 10,000 copies. The book became an intellectual bestseller immediately.

At the beginning of 1993, Lotman signed contracts with two Italian publishing companies for the publication of his books. One of them was Feltrinelli, to whom he gave *Culture and Explosion*. The other was the Venetian publishing company Marsilio, for whom he decided to prepare a new book by revising chapters from *Praising Culture* that had not been included in *Culture and Explosion*. This is how his last monograph, *The Unpredictable Workings of Culture,* was composed. It was first published in Italian (1994b; in Russian 2010).

Lotman's work in this last period is comparable to one unified text, one of the themes of which could be referred to as the understanding of the infiniteness of the existence of human individuality. According to Lotman, a person is simultaneously both immersed in and part of semiotic space: 'the human individual is isomorphic when it comes to the culture of the universe, but is also a part of that same universe' (2010: 185). His ability to focus on the problem of the individual in history also arose from the way he understood his own life experiences. From December 1992 and for the following four months, he dictated *Non-Memoirs* (1995a), fragments of military memoirs, to Pogosjan. At the same time, he dictated to me the article entitled 'Double Portrait', which was comparative sketches of his university professors (1995b). Lotman's once academic writing style became essay-like as he began to turn away from the rigid terminology of the structuralist period. Autobiography and academic research merged and became its own method.

In the final period of his life, Lotman created a large number of journalistic and popular scientific texts and addressed current events (collected in Lotman 2003). Often in his later years, his speeches sounded like teaching notes, such as, for example, in the obituary of Andrei Sakharov 'the most important thing I see in Sakharov is not that he is a scientist, though that is also very significant, and not even his [. . .] heroic acts [. . .] but his rehabilitation of the conscience as the basic principle of life' (1990b: 3). All of Lotman's later works can be summed up as having a common thread: his conscious intention – in a critical period of history, and in the final period of his creative biography – to create texts, both being of equal importance. This intention was described by Vyacheslav Ivanov, calling *Unpredictable Workings of Culture* 'part of Lotman's last will' and saying that the author 'is able to rise above and to pass on to the future what is most important, something achieved at the price of personal physical mortality' (Ivanov [2010] 2013: 7).

Juri Lotman passed away in Tartu on 28 October 1993 after a long illness. He was buried next to his wife, Zara Mints, in Raadi cemetery.[3]

Notes

1. Hereinafter, only the year of each cited work by Lotman will be mentioned in brackets.
2. There are notes of thirteen lectures by Zara Mints in the Lotman archives at the University of Tartu. The archives of Juri Lotman and Zara Mints are divided between two locations: Tallinn University (where their personal libraries are also kept) and the Research Library at the University of Tartu.

3. This chapter was written with the support of the Estonian Research Council (PUT1366) and the Tallinn University School of Humanities. Translated from Russian by Abigail Dewar (University of Alberta, Canada).

References

Druzhinin, P. A. 2012. *Ideologiia i filologiia. Leningrad, 1940-e gody. Dokumental'noe issledovanie*, vol. 2, Moscow: Novoe literaturnoe obozrenie.

Egorov, B. F. 1999. *Zhizn' i tvorchestvo Iu. M. Lotmana*, Moscow: Novoe literaturnoe obozrenie.

Egorov, B. F., Ignatjev, M. B. and Lotman, Iu. M. 1995. 'Iskusstvennyi intellekt kak metamekhanizm kul'tury', *Russian Studies* 4: 277–87.

Isakov, S. G. 1991. 'Ob izdaniakh kafedry russkoi literatury', in G. M. Ponomarieva and S. G. Barsukov (eds), *Trudy po russkoi literature i semiotike kafedry russkoi literatury Tartuskogo universiteta, 1958-1990: Ukazateli soderzhaniia*, 5–11, Tartu: Kompu.

Ivanov, V. V. [2010] 2013. 'Preface to the Russian Edition', in Ju. M. Lotman, *The Unpredictable Workings of Culture*, trans. B. J. Baer, ed. I. Pilshchikov and S. Salupere, 7–16, Tallinn: Tallinn University Press.

Karamzin, N. M. 1966. *Polnoe sobranie stikhotvorenii*, ed. Ju. M. Lotman, Moscow and Leningrad: Sovetskii pisatel'.

Kiseleva, L. N. 1996. 'Akademicheskaia deiatel'nost' Iu. M. Lotmana v Tartuskom universitete', *Slavica Tergestina* 4: 9–19.

Kiseleva, L. N. 2003. 'Ju. M. Lotman – zaveduiushchii kafedroi russkoi literatury', in A. D. Dulichenko (ed.), *200 let russko-slavianskoi filologii v Tartu*, 336–49, Tartu: Isdatel'stvo Tartuskogo Universiteta.

Kuzovkina, T. D. 1999. 'Oshchushchenie svobody. Iu. M. Lotman o Pushkine. Otkliki chitatelei', *Vyshgorod* 1–2: 33–43.

Kuzovkina, T. D. 2015. 'Odin den' professor Iu. M. Lotmana', *Novyi mir* 3: 140–53.

Kuzovkina, T. D. 2019. '"Besedy o russkoi kul'ture" Iu. M. Lotmana: tekst i auditoria', in M. Lotman, T. Kuzovkina and E. Pilarczyk (eds), *Dinamicheskaia struktura teksta*, 121–34, Krakow: Jagiellonian University Press.

Kuzovkina, T. D. 2020. 'O knige Oswalda Spenglera v pis'makh s fronta: k istorii formirovania kul'turologicheskikh idei Iuria Lotmana', in R. Mnih and O. Blashkiv (eds), *Oswald Spengler i slaviane*, 189–212, Siedlce: Instytut Kultury Regionalnej i Badań Literackich im. Franciszka Karpińskiego.

Kuzovkina, T. D. and Daniel, S. M. (eds) 2016. *Juri Lotmani autoportreed. Avtoportrety Iu. M. Lotmana. Juri Lotman's Self-Portraits*, Tallinn: TLU Press.

Kuzovkina, T. D., Naiditch, L. E., Obraztsova, N. Iu. and Superfin, G. G. (eds) 2021. *Lotmany: Semeinaia perepiska 1940-1946*, Tallinn: TLU Press.

Lotman, Ju. M. 1949. '"Kratkie nastavlenia russkim rytsariam" M. A. Dmitrieva-Mamonova: Neizvestnyi pamyatnik agitatsionnoi publitsistiki rannego dekabrizma', *Vestnik Leningradskogo universiteta* 7: 133–47.

Lotman, Ju. M. 1958a. *Andrei Sergeevich Kaisarov i literaturno-obshchestvennaia bor'ba ego vremeni*, Tartu: Isdatel'stvo Tartuskogo universiteta.

Lotman, Ju. M. 1958b. 'A. N. Radishchev i russkaia voennaia mysl' v XVIII v.', *Trudy po filosofii* 67: 194–207.

Lotman, Ju. M. 1958c. 'Radishchev i Mabli', *XVIII vek* 3: 276–308.

Lotman, Ju. M. 1959. 'Neue Materialien über die Anfänge der Beschäftigung mit Schiller in der russischen Literatur', trans. R. Richter, *Wissenschaftliche Zeitschrift der Ernst Moritz Arndt-Universität Greifswald* 8 (5/6): 419–34.

Lotman, Ju. M. 1960. 'K evolyutsii postroenia kharakterov v romane "Evgenii Onegin"', in *Pushkin: Issledovania i materialy*, vol. 3, 131–73, Moscow and Leningrad: Izdatel'stvo Akademii nauk SSSR.

Lotman, Ju. M. 1962a. Problema skhodstva iskusstva i zhizni v svete struktural'nogo podkhoda', in G. V. Krasnov and V. V. Pugachov (eds), *Tezisy dokladov 1-i nauchnoi regional'noi sessii*, 92–102, Gor'kii: Volgo-Viatskii sovet po koordinatsii i planirovaniu nauchno-issledovatel'skikh rabot po gumanitarnym chiklam.

Lotman, Ju. M. 1962b. 'Istoki "tolstovskogo napravlenia" v russkoi literature 1830-kh godov', *Trudy po russkoi i slavianskoi filologii* 5: 3–77.

Lotman, Ju. M. 1962c. 'Ideinaia struktura "Kapitanskoi dochki"', in *Pushkinskii sbornik*, 3–20, Pskov: Izdatel'stvo Pskovskogo universiteta.

Lotman, Ju. M. 1963a. '"Sochuvstvennik" A. H. Radishcheva. A. M. Kutuzov i ego pis'ma k I. P. Turgenevu', *Trudy po russkoi i slavianskoi filologii* 6: 281–97.

Lotman, Ju. M. 1963b. 'O razgranichenii lingvisticheskogo i literaturovedcheskogo poniatia struktury', *Voprosy iazykoznania* 3: 44–52.

Lotman, Ju. M. 1964a. 'Sur la délimitation linguistique et littéraire de la notion de structure', *Linguistics*, 6: 59–72.

Lotman, Ju. M. 1964b. *Lektsii po struktural'noi poetike. Vyp. 1. Vvedenie, teoriia stikha*, Tartu: Izdatel'stvo Tartuskogo universiteta (*Trudy po znakovym sistemam*, 1).

Lotman, Ju. M. 1966. 'Khudozestvennaia struktura "Evgenia Onegina"', *Trudy po russkoi i slavianskoi filologii* 9: 5–32.

Lotman, Ju. M. 1967a. 'Russo i russkaia kul'tura XVIII – nachala XIX veka', in M. P. Alekseev (ed.), *Epokha Prosveshchenia: Iz istorii mezhdunarodnykh sviazei russkoi literatury*, 208–81, Leningrad: Nauka.

Lotman, Ju. M. 1967b. 'Literaturovedenie dolzhno byt' naukoi', *Voprosy literatury* 1: 90–100.

Lotman, Ju. M. 1967c. 'K probleme tipologii kul'tury', *Trudy po znakovym sistemam* 3: 30–8.

Lotman, Ju. M. 1969. 'Russo i russkaia kul'tura XVIII – nachala XIX veka', in Zh.-Zh. Russo, *Traktaty*, 554–604, Moscow: Nauka.

Lotman, Ju. M. 1970a. *Struktura khudozhestvennogo teksta*, Moscow: Isskustvo.

Lotman, Ju. M. 1970b. *Stat'i po tipologii kul'tury: Materialy k kursu teorii literatury, 1*, Tartu: Izdatel'stvo Tartuskogo universiteta.

Lotman, Ju. M. 1972. *Analiz poeticheskogo teksta. Struktura stikha*, Moscow: Isskustvo.

Lotman, Ju. M. 1973a. 'Nikolai Ivanovich Mordovchenko: Zametki o tvorcheskoi individual'nosti uchenogo', *Istoriograficheskii sbornik* 1 (4): 205–13.

Lotman, Ju. M. 1973b. *Semiotika kino i problemy kinoestetiki*, Tallinn: Eesti Raamat.

Lotman, Ju. M. 1973c. *Stat'i po tipologii kul'tury: Materialy k kursu teorii literatury, 2*, Tartu: Izdatel'stvo Tartuskogo universiteta.

Lotman, Ju. M. 1974. 'Dinamicheskie mekhanizmy semioticheskih sistem', *Materialy I Vsesoyuznogo (5) simpoziuma po vtorichnym modeliruyushchim sistemam*, 76–81, Tartu: Izdatel'stvo Tartuskogo universiteta.

Lotman, Ju. M. 1975. *Roman v stikhah Pushkina 'Evgenii Onegin': Speckurs: Vvodnye lektsii v izuchenie teksta*, Tartu: Izdatel'stvo Tartuskogo universiteta.

Lotman, Ju. M. 1976. 'Khudozhestvennaia priroda russkih narodnyh kartinok', in I. E. Danilova (ed.), *Narodanaia graviura i fol'klor v Rossii XVII–XIX vekov: K 150-letiiu so dnia rozhdenia D. A. Rovinskogo*, 247–67, Moscow: Sovetskii khudozhnik.

Lotman, Ju. M. 1978. 'Kukly v sisteme kultury', *Dekotativnoe iskusstvo v SSSR* 2: 36–7.

Lotman, Ju. M. 1980. *Roman A. S. Pushkina 'Evgenii Onegin': Kommentarii: Posobie dlia uchitelia*, Leningrad: Prosveshchenie.

Lotman, Ju. M. 1981. *Aleksandr Sergeevich Pushkin: Biografia pisatelia: Posobie dlia uchitelia*, Leningrad: Prosveshchenie.

Lotman, Ju. M. 1982. *Vene kirjandus: Õpik IX klass* [Russian Literature: Textbook for 9th Grade], Tallinn: Valgus.

Lotman, Ju. M. 1983. 'Assimetria i dialog', *Trudy po znakovym sistemam* 16: 15–30.

Lotman, Ju. M. 1984. 'O semiosfere', *Trudy po znakovym sistemam* 17: 5–23.

Lotman, Ju. M. 1986. 'Natiurmort v perspektive semiotiki', *Veshch' v iskusstve* 17: 6–14.

Lotman, Ju. M. 1987a. 'Väga ühiskondlik, väga vajalik raamat: Professor Juri Lotman Jaan Krossi "Keisrihullust"' [A Very Social, Very Necessary Book: Professor Juri Lotman on Jaan Kross' "The Czar's Madman"], *Sirp ja Vasar*, 6 February: 7, 9.

Lotman, Ju. M. 1987b. *Sotvorenie Karamzina*, Moscow: Kniga.

Lotman, Ju. M. 1989. 'O roli sluchainykh faktorov v literaturnoi evoliutsii', *Trudy po znakovym sistemam* 23: 39–48.

Lotman, Yu. M. 1990a. *Universe of the Mind: A Semiotic Theory of Culture*, trans. A. Shukman, London and New York: I.B. Tauris.

Lotman, Ju. M. 1990b. 'Reabilitatsia sovesti', interv'iu s D. Kuzovkinym, *Alma mater: studencheskaia gazeta* 2: 3.

Lotman, Ju. M. 1992–93. *Izbrannye stat'i v trekh tomakh*, Tallinn: Aleksandra.

Lotman, Ju. M. 1994a. *Besedy o russkoi kul'ture: Byt i traditsii russkogo dvorianstva (XVIII– nachalo XIX veka)*, Saint Petersburg: Iskusstvo–SPB.

Lotman, Yu. M. 1994b. *Cercare la strada: Modelli della cultura*, trans. N. Marcialis, Venice: Marsilio.

Lotman, Ju. M. 1995a. 'Ne-memuary', ed. E. V. Pogosjan, in E. V. Permiakov (ed.), *Lotmanovskii sbornik*, vol. 1, 5–53, Moscow: IC-Garant.

Lotman, Ju. M. 1995b. 'Dvoinoi portret', ed. T. D. Kuzovkina, in E. V. Permiakov (ed.), *Lotmanovskii sbornik*, vol. 1, 54–71, Moscow: IC-Garant.

Lotman, Ju. M. 1996. *Vnutri mysliashchikh mirov: Chelovek – tekst – semiosfera – istoria*, ed. T. D. Kuzovkina, Moscow: Iazyki russkoi kultury.

Lotman, Ju. M. 1997a. *Pisma 1940–1993*, ed. B. F. Egorov, Moscow: Shkola 'Iazyki russkoi kultury'.

Lotman, Ju. M. 1997b. 'Portret', *Vyshgorod* 1–2: 8–31.

Lotman, Ju. M. 2003. *Vospitanie dushi: Vospominania. Besedy. Interv'iu. V mire pushkinskoi poezii (stsenarii). Besedy o russkoi kul'ture. Televizionnye lektsii*, eds. L. N. Kiseleva, T. D. Kuzovkina and R. S. Vojtekhovich, Saint Petersburg: Iskusstvo–SPB.

Lotman, Ju. M. 2010. *Nepredskazuemye mekhanizmy kul'tury*, eds. T. D. Kuzovkina and O. I. Utgof, Tallinn: Tallinn University Press.

Lotman, Ju M. and Al'tshuller, M. G. (eds) 1971. *Poety 1790–1810-kh godov*, Leningrad: Sovetskii pisatel'.

Lotman, Ju M. and Isakov, S. G. 1961. 'P. A. Viazemskii i Estonia', *Trudy po russkoi i slavianskoi filologii* 4: 293–5.

Lotman, Ju. M. and Neverdinova, V. N. 1982. *Uchebnik-khrestomatia po literaturnomu chteniu dlia IX klassa*, Tallinn: Valgus.

Lotman, Ju. M. and Neverdinova, V. N. 1984. *Kniga dlia uchitelia: Metodicheskie materialy k uchebniku-khrestomatii dlia IX klassa*, Tallinn: Valgus.

Lotman, Ju. M. and Pogosjan, E. A. 1996. *Velikosvetskie obedy: Panorama stolichnoi zhizni*, Sankt-Peterburg: Pechatnyi dvor.

Lotman, Ju. M. and Uspenskij, B. A. 1971. 'O semioticheskom mekhanizme kul'tury', *Trudy po znakovym sistemam* 5: 144–66.

Toporov, V. N. 1993. 'Vmesto vospominania', *Novoe literaturnoe obozrenie* 3: 66–77.

Torop, P. 1992. 'Tartuskaia shola kak shkola', in E. V. Permiakov (ed.), *V chest' 70-letia professora Iu. M. Lotmana. To Honour of professor Yu. M. Lotman*, 5–19, Tartu: Eidos.

PART I
LOTMAN IN CONTEXT

CHAPTER 2
LOTMAN AND SAUSSURE
Ekaterina Velmezova

Without belittling the successes and significance of de Saussure's ideas, we have the right to talk about the questions with which the science was faced subsequently, because each fruitful scientific idea requires its further development, and in a certain sense also a critical attitude towards it at the next stage of its development.

– Juri Lotman ([1984] 2002: 148)

Modern semiotics is commonly considered to derive from two sources: the American philosopher Charles Sanders Peirce (1839–1914) and the Swiss linguist Ferdinand de Saussure (1857–1913). Mihhail Lotman (2002b) has aptly called the first an atomistic approach to semiotics and the second a holistic one. Within the first tradition, the researchers' attention is focused on the sign in isolation, that is, on the relationship of sign to meaning, to addressee, and so on, whereas in the case of the second tradition, the researchers concentrate their attention on a language or text, that is, a mechanism which uses a certain set of elementary signs for the communication of content (Lotman and Uspenskij 1984: ix). Juri Lotman considered himself clearly to belong to the holistic tradition of semiotics, founded by Saussure. This chapter will explore more closely what Lotman owes to Saussure and what traces of Saussure's ideas can be found in Lotman's writings. Because of the limited length of the chapter, we will focus primarily on analysing Lotman's most important explicit references to Saussure (studies of Lotman's archives in the light of this problem should be conducted in the future). Another question which we will only briefly touch upon is that of 'implicit' references, that is, of Lotman's works in which he refers to Saussure without mentioning his name. However, even an analysis of Lotman's explicit references to Saussure is helpful to understanding several aspects of Lotman's work, including how his views changed over time.

Although Lotman did not publish any work entirely devoted to Saussure – nor did he publish anything with a title containing the name – Saussure is mentioned both in the relatively early works of Lotman and in the works written shortly before his death. The periodization of Lotman's work is a separate issue (see Salupere 2017: 26–31), but, in any case, Lotman's early work differs from his later work both in subject matter and in methodology, and it is in those works, which were written in the 1960s, that the name of Saussure is mentioned most frequently.

However, the place of Saussure's ideas in Lotman's works is determined not only by the moment in which a given text was written but also by the subject matter of a text. In Lotman's academic heritage, several main thematic components can be (conditionally) distinguished: Lotman worked on the history of Russian culture and literature as well as on more general problems, such as those associated with the study of texts (understood in the broad sense of the word) and with semiotics. It is in these works, which address questions of semiotics, that Saussure's name generally appears.

Before continuing, however, it is important to clarify that we refer here, in speaking of Saussure, to the *Course in General Linguistics* published in 1916 under his name by Charles Bally and Albert Sechehaye. It is to this book that Lotman, calling Saussure the 'founder' of the 'Geneva linguistic school' (Lotman [1972] 2002: 301), makes reference when he mentions Saussure (during Lotman's lifetime, two editions of the *Course* were published in Russian – one in 1933 and one in 1977). Of course, Lotman knew that this book was not written by Saussure himself. As he notices, 'We should keep in mind that Saussure (the genius of this scholar does not need any confirmation) is presented to us only in the notes of his students. As to pupils, they always see their teacher somewhat idealized, as a result of which he loses not so little of his value' (Lotman [1984] 2002: 149). He further develops this point, adding that, 'a large part of the philological heritage of Ferdinand de Saussure are the notes of his lectures, made by his students', and claiming that 'Saussurean linguistics', which presents 'a scientific system as a whole', can therefore be opposed in a sense to 'the very notes of Saussure's lectures' (Lotman [1984] 2002: 149).

As a whole, the 1960s in the USSR were a favourable era for the reception of the *Course*'s ideas in connection with the (belated) arrival of structuralism, the main ideas of which continue to be traced back to this book today (Velmezova 2018). The equivalence between the *Course* and the ideas of structuralism was also articulated by Lotman, who studied the *Course* as early as during his first year of university (Egorov 2009: 28). In the late 1960s, Lotman considered 'the influence of the fundamental ideas of modern structural linguistics – the works of F. de Saussure [. . .] and R. Jakobson' to be one of the 'main scientific factors [. . .] under the influence of which [. . .] the modern structural-semiotic study of literature' developed (Lotman [1968] 2018: 174). Lotman's reception of Saussure at this time was so positive that the mere fact of another researcher recognizing Saussure's merits could become an important parameter for Lotman to single out this colleague in a positive light, even despite maintaining certain theoretical disagreements with him (see, e.g. Lotman on V. V. Kozhinov, Lotman [1967b] 2018: 66).

What was of particular interest to Lotman in the *Course*, and to which of the ideas presented in this book did he refer most often? In a sense, the interests of the early Lotman in regards to Saussure are reflected in what the researcher wrote about the 'structural-semiotic study of literature in Czechoslovakia' (Lotman [1968] 2018: 180)[1], commenting upon Saussure's 'requirements to clearly distinguish between synchronic and diachronic (historical) approaches to language and other sign systems and to discern, as particular objects of study, language (*langue*) as a system of abstract ideal norms and speech (*parole*) as concrete linguistic matter' (Lotman [1968] 2018: 180–1; see also [1970] 2018: 360–1). The main focus here is the dichotomies of the *Course* and one of its main ideas, which would later become one of the main ideas of linguistic structuralism in general: the question of the relationship between the elements of a whole as determining the values of those elements.

From elements to their relations

Indeed, one of the main ideas of linguistic structuralism is the definition of the value of an element not taken by itself, but rather through its relationship to other elements of a whole system or structure (here, 'Lotman did not strive for a clear delineation' between the two [Salupere 2017: 45]) to which it belongs. The corresponding interpretation of the *Course* was shared by Lotman. It is therefore quite natural that Lotman already refers to Saussure in his early monograph devoted to 'structural poetics' ([1964] 1994). The 'pathos' of this book is 'structuralist-Saussurean': 'Linguistic elements and, by analogy, elements of artistic structure are determined not by their substantial properties, but by their relations with each other which condition their correlation and opposition' (Pilshchikov, Poselyagin and Trunin 2018: 15). Indeed, Lotman relies on the thesis of the importance of relations between linguistic elements, thereby appealing to the very essence of structuralism: 'in order for the speaker to be understood, the listener needs [. . .] a code that would allow for language signals to be classified and their meaning set. It establishes the relationship between signs, defining the structure of the language' (Lotman [1964] 1994: 66).

And further: 'F. de Saussure wrote: "Language is not a substance, but a relation"' (Lotman [1964] 1994: 67). In this sense, the phrase 'language is a form and not a substance' from the *Course in General Linguistics* (Saussure [1916] 1959: 122) could be paraphrased, but one of the main ideas of the *Course* was correctly conveyed by Lotman; in fact, his structuralist works were largely based on it. Here is what, for example, Lotman wrote in 1967: 'Traditional literary studies list and classify individual observable facts, while the structuralist researcher is always interested in relationships' (Lotman [1967a] 2018: 102).

The aforementioned 'correlation and opposition', or 'similarities and differences', are also mentioned in connection with Saussure's name (although not exclusively) in Lotman's other article written in 1967, in connection with the category of opposition. Lotman writes that considered as 'an effective means of constructing models of various structures', the term 'opposition' was, in particular, 'put by F. de Saussure on the basis of his system ("mechanism of similarity and difference")' (Lotman [1967b] 2018: 78). Here Lotman quotes Saussure approximately: both in the original and in the Russian-only edition of the *Course* available at the time, it is a question not of 'similarities and differences', but of 'identities and differences'[2] (cf. 'differences and identities' in the English translation of 1959 (Saussure [1916] 1959: 108)). The same statement is repeated in the monograph *Analysis of the Poetic Text*, where Lotman claims that 'F. de Saussure said that the entire structure of language is reducible to the mechanism of similarities and differences' (Lotman [1972] 1976: 33).

Therefore, the influence of Saussure on Lotman as a structuralist is obvious. However, as early as 1963, Lotman writes that, in the analysis of a literary text, 'the linguist will inevitably face the inadequacy of purely linguistic methods' (Lotman 1963: 46). 'In an ordinary language act', he explains, 'we are dealing with only one structure – the structure of language' (Lotman 1963: 45); language, according to this understanding, therefore has an amorphous content that is formed and regulated by the context. In the artistic world, however, content is structural, as it models the world. Thus, the specificity of verbal art lies in the inseparable unity of the structure of content ('the model of the world') and the structure of expression (language). Lotman writes: 'Therefore, there is a significant difference between the linguistic and literary concepts of structure. Linguistic structure is a condition, a *means* of conveying information, literary structure is its purpose and *content*' (Lotman 1963: 52). Although Saussure is not explicitly quoted here, the orientation of Lotman's work is clearly structuralist. However, the limits of the application of the main ideas of the *Course* to the study of literary problems were already apparent for Lotman; over time, this conviction would only become stronger.

On the science of *semiology*

If in the USSR of the 1960s structuralism could be associated with semiotics, one typical example of such a connection for Lotman was made in the book of 1973 on the *Semiotics of Cinema and Problems of Cinema Aesthetics* (Lotman [1973] 1981: 31). Quoting the 1933 Russian edition of the *Course*, Lotman draws an analogy between natural language and the language of cinema mentioning Saussure and citing the *Course*. Interestingly enough, he didn't explicitly refer here to the idea of Saussure's that seems most important for understanding Lotman's book: the very idea of semiology as 'a science that studies the life of signs within society' (Saussure [1916] 1959: 16), the science that linguistics is a part of – but, obviously, not only linguistics, as is shown in Lotman's book about the semiotics of cinema.

In the article 'Semiotics', written later for the *Literary Encyclopaedic Dictionary*, it is Peirce and Saussure ('philologist and anthropologist') who are referred to as the forerunners of modern semiotics (Lotman 1987), and in the introduction to the book *Universe of the Mind* (1990), Lotman names several aspects which, in their totality, constituted the field of semiotics at the end of the twentieth century. The first of these is 'the domain of knowledge whose object is the sphere of semiotic communication' (a line linking back to Saussure, with the concepts of language and communication in the centre) (Lotman 1990: 4). Moreover, 'even after Jakobson criticized [Saussure's works] and contrasted them with the ideas of C. S. Peirce', the ideas of Saussure, Lotman believes, 'remain in force as the foundations of semiotics' (Lotman 1990: 5).

On the whole, Lotman's semiotics is a clear example of how a scholar did not have to make every reference to Saussure's ideas explicit in order to base his thinking on them (on the closeness of Lotman's *semiotics* to Saussurean *semiology*, see also Salupere 2017: 61 and 63).

Dichotomies of the *Course in General Linguistics*

In his early works, Lotman already paid a great deal of attention to the oppositions presented in the *Course*, and on which Saussure's theories were largely based.

Language and *speech*

First, it was the opposition between language (*langue*) and speech (*parole*) that was, at the time, generally considered to be 'one of the most fundamental propositions of modern linguistics' (Lotman [1972] 1976: 19). Lotman thought that this opposition, as applied to literary studies, was a 'fruitful simplification', requiring 'a clear delineation of the object of research, an answer to the question of whether a certain amount of observed facts is being studied, or the writers', readers', researchers' models that serve to decipher the meaning of these facts' (Lotman [1967a] 2018: 103).

In *The Structure of the Artistic Text*, Saussure is mentioned twice, both times in reference to this dichotomy. Writing about acts of communication, Lotman makes a distinction between 'two different aspects of the communication system: a stream of individual messages embodied in some material substance' and 'an abstract system of invariant relations' ('speech' (*parole*) and 'language' (*langue*)), correspondingly, and drawing a parallel 'with the distinction of 'message' and 'code' in information theory' (Lotman [1970] 1977: 13).

Subsequently, it becomes clear that the opposition of language and speech will be necessary for Lotman in order to introduce the very concept of *text*, which would become key for him in the late 1960s and early 1970s (Chernov 1997: 8; Lotman [1994/2010] 2013: 52; see also Chapter 9): 'In terms of the Saussurean antinomy of language and speech, the text always belongs to the province of speech. Correspondingly, a text always has non-systemic as well as systemic elements' (Lotman [1970] 1977: 51–2).

Lotman highlights the opposition between structure ('language') and text ('speech') in all three published versions of his article 'Structuralism in Literary Studies' (Lotman [1967–8] 2018: 232; [1971] 2018: 239; [1972] 2018: 245); in *The Structure of the Artistic Text*, Saussure's opposition 'language vs speech' is also correlated with the opposition of structure and non-structure. Lotman states that 'the specific nature of a poetic text lies [. . .] in the fact that non-structural elements, peculiar to speech but not to language, acquire a structural character' (Lotman [1970] 1977: 154).

Lotman also returns – again regarding such an important concept for structuralists as structure – to the dichotomy of 'language vs speech' in the monograph *Analysis of the Poetic Text*: 'In each communication system', one can isolate 'that aspect of its invariant structure, which, following Ferdinand de Saussure, we call *language*, and that aspect of its variant realizations in different texts, which, in the same scientific tradition, is termed *speech*. [. . .] In information theory, the opposition of code (language) and communication (speech) approximately correspond to it' (Lotman [1972] 1976: 19).[3]

The relationship of 'language (code)' and 'speech (communication)' (*soobshchenie*, or 'message' in the original; see Lotman 1972: 20) is recognized as 'parallel' to the relationship between 'system' and 'text' (Lotman 1972: 20), while the relation of 'text (message) to code' Lotman would later call 'one of the main problems of semiotics' (Lotman [1980] 2002: 420).

Finally, Lotman resorted to the opposition of 'language vs speech', arguing about the problems of studying the history of culture and, in particular, about the 'problem of the relationship between historical-cultural typology and factual historical-cultural material – a relationship that to a certain extent corresponds to Saussure's opposition of language (*langue*) and speech (*parole*). The factual material will always be richer and more complex, more contradictory than typological schemes' (Lotman [1967a] 2018: 115).

Later, in the early 1980s, at a new stage of his academic path, Lotman wrote about two tendencies which can be discerned in the recent ('over the past fifteen years') development of semiotics:

> One is aimed at clarifying the original concepts and defining the procedures of generation. The striving for accurate modelling leads to the creation of metasemiotics: the object of research is not text as such, but models of texts, models of models, etc. The second trend focuses on the semiotic functioning of the real text. If, from the first position, contradiction, structural inconsistency, the combination of differently arranged texts within a single text formation, and semantic uncertainty are random and 'non-working' features which are possible to remove at the meta-level of text modelling, from the second position, they are the subject of particular attention. Using Saussurean terminology, one could say that in the first case, the researcher is interested in speech as the materialization of the structural laws of language, and in the second, the centre of attention is precisely those semiotic aspects that diverge from the linguistic structure. The first tendency is realized in metasemiotics, while the second one naturally gives rise to the semiotics of culture. (Lotman [1981] 2002: 84)

As in many other cases, when Lotman wrote about the opposition between language and speech, he did so without making direct reference to the *Course* – this Saussurean terminology had, by then, already entered into Lotman's academic idiom.

Synchrony and diachrony

In the preface to the *Universe of the Mind*, written shortly before Lotman's death, Lotman returns to Saussure's two dichotomies: (1) the opposition between language and speech ('or code and text'); and (2) the opposition between synchrony and diachrony. Regarding the latter opposition, Lotman quotes a passage from the *Course*, speaking of the structural nature of synchrony and accidental, according to Saussure, diachronic changes.

Discussing these two oppositions (language vs speech and synchrony vs diachrony), Lotman says that 'these ideas cannot be rejected by modern semiotics. [...] But from this we can see how deep are the transformations that even the fundamental propositions and the whole cast of semiotics have undergone in the second half of the twentieth century' (Lotman 1990: 6).

In the first case, this is, in particular, a change of focus from language-*langue* ('*the true and unique object of linguistics*' (Saussure [1916] 1959: 232)) to speech/text.[4] Moreover, as

Lotman wrote, 'in the real functioning of culture, very often language does not precede the text, but the text [. . .] precedes the appearance of language and stimulates it' (Lotman 1992: 472). If this is indeed the case, what should be considered a 'primary modelling system' and what a 'secondary'?

In the second case, it is, among other things, a more complex (in comparison with what Saussure proposed) relationship between the accidental and 'systemic' elements for a culture developing in time (cf. the interest, in Lotman's last works, in 'explosions' and the unpredictability of events following 'explosions' as inevitable components of culture and history; see also Chapter 21). As Umberto Eco noted, 'Lotman has managed to fuse the structural method (which takes a synchronic approach [. . .]) with his vocation as historian, [. . .] interested in explaining how a culture is formed and how different culture systems, distant from one another in time, can be compared' (Eco 1990: xi).

On the other hand, Lotman associated the opposition between synchrony and diachrony with the concept of 'systemic – non-systemic': 'It was already F. de Saussure who wrote about the need, while studying a semiotic object, to abstract away from some its insignificant features, speaking about the importance, within the limits of description of one synchronic state of language, to distract from 'unimportant' diachronic changes' (Lotman [1974] 1992: 91).[5]

Signified and signifier

Signifier and signified as components of the binary linguistic sign are discussed (without mentioning the *Course*) in the relatively early works of Lotman. He writes the following in *Analysis of the Poetic Text*: 'The concept of the sign – *the meaningful element of a given language* – lies at the basis of all language. The sign possesses a binary essence: being invested with a certain material expression that constitutes its formal aspect, it also has within the limits of a given language a certain meaning that constitutes its content' (Lotman [1972] 1976: 17).

Lotman also discussed the question of the conventional nature of the connection between the two components of a linguistic sign; language, with its signs-symbols, is simultaneously opposed to verbal art with its iconic signs (Lotman [1967a] 2018: 110).[6] He will return to this topic much later, in *Universe of the Mind*, writing about the 'debate' between 'those two linguists of genius, Saussure and Jakobson' (Lotman 1990: 17): the latter 'attacked Saussure's central proposition, the principle of the arbitrariness of the connection between signifier and signified in the sign. [. . .] Indeed, the language of the artistic text acquires secondary features of iconism, which sheds light on the problem of the 'untranslatability' of poetic language' (Lotman 1990: 17–18, cf. also 222).

Of course, here 'symbols' are used according to Peirce's terminology: 'Saussure contrasted symbols to conventional signs and emphasized their iconic nature' (Lotman 1990: 102; see also 179 and 259–60; [1981] 1993: 350; [1987] 1992: 191). Another example of how Lotman did not always follow Saussure's 'sign' terminology – and sometimes without even specifying it – can be found in his *Lectures on Structural Poetics*, where he discusses the reflections on the sign as far back as the works of Soviet linguist and psychologist N. I. Zhinkin (Lotman [1964] 1994: 63): 'sign' here refers to what Saussure called 'signifier'.

Syntagmatic and associative relations

In his early works, Lotman first distinguished, among the 'main types of structural studies of art', the so-called syntagmatic descriptions (Lotman [1967–8] 2018: 233). He pointed out that 'the mechanism of text description implies the distinguishing of paradigmatic and syntagmatic axes. The first give a set of possible structural elements and types of their relations (system), the second reveal sequences (text)' (Lotman [1967–8] 2018: 233–4; see also [1972] 1976: 37). Or again – here it is already a question of the description of culture using a number of oppositions – Lotman wrote that 'the definition of culture as subordinate to the structural rules of a sign system allows us to look at it as to a language in the general semiotic meaning of this term', reflecting about 'the legitimacy of extending to the analysis of culture those categories whose fruitfulness has already been proven in general semiotics (for example, the categories of code and message, text and structure, language and speech, distinction of paradigmatic and syntagmatic principles of description, etc.)' (Lotman [1970] 2002: 148). Although Lotman does not mention here either Saussure or his *Course*, he may be implicitly referencing the opposition of syntagmatic and associative relations between language elements (Saussure [1916] 1959: 122ff).

Semiotic description and the 'world beyond its borders'

In the second half of the 1970s, one of the key concepts of philology – the concept of *text* – changed in Lotman's works, marking a departure from Saussure. Lotman's new understanding of *text* was 'much closer to Bakhtin semiotics and to Peirce semiotics than to Saussure semiotics' (Grzybek 1995: 250), if we bear in mind, in particular, semiotic doctrines based on the text and their 'gravitating', respectively, to the utterance (*vyskazyvanie*) or to language, to dynamics or to statics (see also Lotman [1984] 2002; Egorov 1999). However, while the works that Lotman wrote shortly before his death make fewer explicit references to Saussure, he still remains significant for Lotman at that time. Thus, in *Culture and Explosion*, the name of Saussure appears in the first pages. According to Lotman, one of the 'fundamental questions relating to the description of any semiotic system' is 'its relation to the extra-system, to the world which lies beyond its borders' (Lotman [1992] 2009: 1). Lotman draws a parallel with 'language creating its own world' (Lotman [1992] 2009: 1). Although this passage does not make reference to a specific fragment in the *Course*, it does take up, in particular, the Saussurean dichotomy of the signifier and the signified: in the latter case, it is not an object or part of the 'world existing outside of language' that is supposed, but a fragment of the 'conventional reality' created by the language. As we read in the *Course*, 'the linguistic sign unites not a thing and a name, but a concept and a sound image' (Saussure [1916] 1959: 66).

However, Lotman had thought about the 'extra-semiotic reality' in connection with the name of Saussure much earlier. In the early 1980s, in the preface to collection of articles *The Semiotics of Russian Culture*, Lotman and his co-author Boris Uspenskij spoke about 'a crucial difference between the understanding of non-semiotic reality in the Peircean and the Saussurean approaches': 'If in the former it exists as the object of logical models, then in the latter it acquires features of empirical reality. For this reason the first approach opens the way only to logical models, while the second affords the hope of reconstructing extratextual empirical reality by means of the text' (Lotman and Uspenskij 1984: x).

In the section of *Culture and Explosion* entitled 'In Place of Conclusions', Lotman returns (albeit without mentioning Saussure by name) to the key idea of structuralism going back to the *Course* – adding to it the opposition of synchrony and diachrony (statics and dynamics), to which the question of describing semiotic systems can be connected (see also Lotman [1974] 1992: 90ff):

> The idea that the starting point of any semiotic system is not the simple isolated sign (word), but rather the relation between at least two signs causes us to think in a different way about the fundamental bases of semiosis. The starting point occurs not in a single isolated model, but rather in semiotic space. This space is filled with a conglomeration of elements whose relations with each other may be encountered in a variety of ways [. . .]. These multilingual texts simultaneously include both possibilities, i.e. one and the same text may find itself in a state of non-intersection in relation to a given semantic range and in a state of identification with yet another. This variety in the possible connections between semantic elements creates a multi-dimensional point of view, which can only be fully understood in terms of the ratio of each element to the other and all elements to the whole. Furthermore [. . .] the system has a memory of its past states and an anticipation of potential 'future states'. Thus, semiotic space is simultaneously multi-dimensional in both the synchronic and diachronic sense. It benefits from fluid boundaries and the capacity to incorporate itself in explosive processes. (Lotman [1992] 2009: 172)

Thus, the ideas of the *Course* – for Lotman, the ideas of Saussure – are implicitly present in the conclusion to one of Lotman's last monographs.

Saussure . . . and the idea of the semiosphere

Discussing the insufficiency of Saussure's theories for describing culture in the early 1980s, Lotman singled out several statements in the 'scientific system' of 'Saussurean linguistics' that lead to paradoxes. One was the question of the necessity of the existence of different language-codes, which over time became more and more numerous: 'From the point of view of the classical doctrine of de Saussure, culture is an unimaginably wasteful mechanism' (Lotman [1984] 2002: 149). Another was the question of the 'secondary nature' of poetry, and so on: 'I will not enumerate other paradoxical situations in which we unwittingly find ourselves, strictly following the classical doctrine of de Saussure. Neither human culture nor the very existence of art falls within the framework of this conception. Such a universal fact [. . .] as the presence of at least two different communication systems in the semiotic mechanism of culture remains unexplained in particular' (Lotman [1984] 2002: 151).

The idea of the plurality of cultural codes and of the polyglotism of cultures, already present in Lotman's early works (Lotman [1970] 2002: 149), eventually leads him to the concept of the semiosphere, which is already a fundamental step forward compared to his early structuralist works. This is best seen in the article 'On the Semiosphere':

Contemporary semiotics is undergoing a review of some of its basic concepts. [. . .] at the heart of semiotics lie two scientific traditions. One of these goes back to Peirce-Morris and begins with an understanding of the sign as the first element of any semiotic system. The second is based on the theses of Saussure and the Prague school and has at its core the antinomy of language and speech (texts). However, despite the differences of these approaches, they share one important commonality: they are based on a simple, atomic element, and everything that follows is considered from the point of view of its similarity to this. Thus, in the first instance, the isolated sign is analysed, and all subsequent semiotic phenomena are considered as a succession of signs. The second point of view, in particular, is expressed by the urge to consider a single communicative act [. . .] as the prime element and model of any given semiotic act. As a result, the individual act of sign exchange has come to be regarded as a model of natural language, and models of natural languages – as universal semiotic models, whereas semiotics itself has sought to be understood as the extension of linguistic methods to objects not included in traditional linguistics. (Lotman [1984] 2005: 205–6)

But if, as Lotman writes, such an approach first justified itself as corresponding to the rule of scientific thinking 'to ascend from simple to complex', it is not free of danger 'that heuristic expediency [. . .] comes to be accepted as the ontological character of the object', while 'in reality, clear and functionally mono-semantic systems do not exist in isolation. [. . .] They function only by being immersed in a specific semiotic continuum, which is filled with multi-variant semiotic models situated at a range of hierarchical levels. Such a continuum we [. . .] will call the "semiosphere"' (Lotman [1984] 2005: 106).

It turns out, therefore, that Lotman was building his concept of the semiosphere – one of his main theoretical achievements, which would be key to many others – by arguing with Saussure while at the same time departing from his ideas.

Conclusions

Despite the fact that Lotman's concepts were in constant development, despite his shifting from a predominant interest in structural poetics to the problems of cultural theory, even despite his refusal to use rigid dichotomies, privileging rather the more complex structures, a number of constants were nevertheless invariably present in his research. One of these was the work of Saussure, and the ideas of the *Course in General Linguistics* that it stood for.

From a strictly textual perspective, the passages of the *Course* that were of interest to Lotman were by the 1960s already so well known that there was no need to refer to its specific pages, which explains the lack in Lotman's works – in most cases – of references to particular pages of the *Course* and, at times, his inexact citations. In general, certain terms from the *Course* obviously entered the academic idiom of Lotman: Saussure is considered among the origins of Lotman's metalanguage (Salupere 2017: 31).

From an epistemological point of view, Lotman realized the limits of the Saussurean approach in his early works when shifting the central focus of his research from 'primary' to 'secondary modelling systems'. It was in starting from Saussure – and arguing with him – that Lotman built the concept of semiosphere, which in many respects crowned his semiotic reflections. Therefore, in a sense, the work of the late Lotman supposes both a distinction between semiotics and structuralism and a certain return to structuralism and to Saussure, while realizing the impossibility of applying his concepts for semiotic studies beyond the 'primary modelling systems'.

Notes

1. On the absence of a clear division between 'structuralism' and 'semiotics' in the Tartu-Moscow school, see Segal 1974: 3–4; Salupere 2017: 13 and 58–69.

2. In the original: '*identités et différences*' (Saussure [1916] 1922: 151); in the Russian translation: 'tozhestva i razlitchiia' (Saussure [1916] 1933: 109).

3. See Pilshchikov 2018: 123. Lotman further expands the concept of language to include in it natural languages, artificial languages and 'secondary modelling systems' ('semiotic systems [. . .] all of which merge into a single complex semiotic whole – a culture' [Lotman [1972] 1976: 19]). Over time, however, Lotman would become more and more interested in the possibility of describing non-discrete languages (Lotman [1977] 2000: 566–7). On the correspondence of Lotman's definition of language to Saussure's *langage* rather than *langue*, and also on the *Course* as a possible source of Lotman's 'organistic' (*organisticheskii*) interpretation of 'language', see Salupere 2017: 52–3.

4. It is Lotman's 'textocentricity' that Mihhail Lotman considered as an important difference between the views of the Tartu-Moscow researchers and those of the 'schools of structuralism that existed by that time' (M. Lotman 1998: 676): 'there is no place for text in the Saussurean concept of linguistic activity.' On the contrary, for 'the semiotics of culture, it is the text that is the main wholeness [*tselostnost*']' (see M. Lotman 2002a: 14–16).

5. Lotman also touches upon the issue of isolating 'significant' and 'insignificant' elements in semiotic research in other texts (see, e.g. Lotman [1979] 1993: 312). In this sense, 'culture' could be opposed to 'non-culture' (Lotman and Uspenskij [1971] 1993: 326); cf. also the

remark that 'an object in the process of structural description is not only simplified, but also reorganized [*doorganizovyvaetsia*] [being endowed, by the researcher, with an organization that it initially might not have]' (Lotman [1974] 1992: 91).

6. Here Lotman speaks about *oboznachaiushchee* 'signifier' and *oboznachaemoe* 'signifed', while in the Russian-only edition of the *Course*, which existed at that time, we find *oznachaiushchee* and *oznachaemoe* (Saussure [1916] 1933: 77).

References

Chernov, I. A. 1997. 'Opyt vvedeniia v sistemu Iu. M. Lotmana', in Ju. M. Lotman, *O russkoi literature*, 5–13, Saint Petersburg: Iskusstvo–SPB.

Eco, U. 1990. 'Introduction', in Yu. M. Lotman, *Universe of the Mind: A Semiotic Theory of Culture*, trans. A. Shukman, vii–xiii, London and New York: I.B. Tauris.

Egorov, B. F. 1999. 'Bakhtin i Lotman', in B. F. Egorov (ed.), *Zhizn' i tvorchestvo Iu. M. Lotmana*, 243–58, Moscow: Novoe literaturnoe obozrenie.

Egorov, B. F. 2009. 'Iu. M. Lotman kak chelovek i iavlenie', in V. K. Kantor (ed.), *Iurii Mikhailovich Lotman*, 13–81, Moscow: ROSSPEN.

Grzybek, P. 1995. 'Bakhtinskaia semiotika i moskovsko-tartuskaia shkola', in E. V. Permiakov (ed.), *Lotmanovskii sbornik*, vol. 1, 240–59, Moscow: IC-Garant.

Lotman, Ju. M. 1963. 'O razgranichenii lingvisticheskogo i literaturovedcheskogo poniatiia struktury', *Voprosy iazykoznaniia* 3: 44–52.

Lotman, Ju. M. [1964] 1994. 'Lektsii po struktural'noi poetike', in A. D. Koshelev (ed.), *Iu. M. Lotman i tartusko-moskovskaia semioticheskaia shkola*, 17–245, Moscow: Gnozis.

Lotman, Ju. M. [1967a] 2018. 'Nekotorye itogi i problemy primeneniia tochnykh metodov v sovetskom literaturovedenii', in Ju. M. Lotman, *O strukturalizme. Raboty 1965–1970 godov*, ed. I. A. Pilshchikov, with N. V. Poselyagin and M. V. Trunin, 98–117, Tallinn: TLU Press.

Lotman, Ju. M. [1967b] 2018. 'O printsipakh strukturalizma v literaturovedenii ("Literaturovedenie dolzhno byt' naukoi")', in Ju. M. Lotman, *O strukturalizme. Raboty 1965–1970 godov*, ed. I. A. Pilshchikov, with N. V. Poselyagin and M. V. Trunin, 65–82, Tallinn: TLU Press.

Lotman, Ju. M. [1967–8] 2018. 'Strukturalizm v literaturovedenii (stat'ia dlia "Kratkoi literaturnoi entsiklopedii")' (variant 1), in Ju. M. Lotman, *O strukturalizme. Raboty 1965–1970 godov*, ed. I. A. Pilshchikov, with N. V. Poselyagin and M. V. Trunin, 232–38, Tallinn: TLU Press.

Lotman, Ju. M. [1968] 2018. 'Sovremennye perspektivy semioticheskogo izucheniia iskusstva', in Ju. M. Lotman, *O strukturalizme. Raboty 1965–1970 godov*, ed. I. A. Pilshchikov, with N. V. Poselyagin and M. V. Trunin, 167–86, Tallinn: TLU Press.

Lotman, Ju. M. [1970] 1977. *The Structure of the Artistic Text*, trans. R. Vroon, Ann Arbor: University of Michigan, Department of Slavic Languages and Literatures.

Lotman, Ju. M. [1970] 2002. 'Kul'tura i informatsiia', in Ju. M. Lotman, *Stat'i po semiotike iskusstva*, 143–53, Saint Petersburg: Gumanitarnoe agentstvo 'Akademicheskii proekt'.

Lotman, Ju. M. [1970] 2018. 'Ian Mukarzhovskii – teoretik iskusstva', in Ju. M. Lotman, *O strukturalizme. Raboty 1965–1970 godov*, ed. I. A. Pilshchikov, with N. V. Poselyagin and M. V. Trunin, 356–90, Tallinn: TLU Press.

Lotman, Ju. M. [1971] 2018. 'Strukturalizm v literaturovedenii (stat'ia dlia "Kratkoi literaturnoi entsiklopedii")' (variant 2), in Ju. M. Lotman, *O strukturalizme. Raboty 1965–1970 godov*, ed. I. A. Pilshchikov, with N. V. Poselyagin and M. V. Trunin, 238–44, Tallinn: TLU Press.

Lotman, Ju. M. 1972. *Analiz poeticheskogo teksta: Struktura stikha*, Leningrad: Prosveshchenie.

Lotman, Ju. M. [1972] 1976. *Analysis of the Poetic Text*, trans. D. B. Johnson, Ann Arbor: Ardis.

Lotman, Ju. M. [1972] 2002. 'Strukturalizm v literaturovedenii (stat'ia dlia "Kratkoi literaturnoi entsiklopedii")' (variant 3), in Ju. M. Lotman, *Stat'i po semiotike iskusstva*, 294–313, Saint Petersburg: Gumanitarnoe agentstvo 'Akademicheskii proekt'.

Lotman, Ju. M. [1972] 2018. 'Iskusstvoznanie i "tochnye metody" v sovremennykh zarubezhnykh issledovaniiakh', in Ju. M. Lotman, *O strukturalizme. Raboty 1965–1970 godov*, ed. I. A. Pilshchikov, with N. V. Poselyagin and M. V. Trunin, 244–51, Tallinn: TLU Press.

Lotman, Ju. M. [1973] 1981. *Semiotics of Cinema*, trans. M. E. Suino, Ann Arbor: University of Michigan.

Lotman, Ju. M. [1974] 1992. 'Dinamicheskaia model' semioticheskoi sistemy', in Ju. M. Lotman, *Izbrannye stat'i v trekh tomakh*, vol. 1, 90–101, Tallinn: Aleksandra.

Lotman, Ju. M. [1977] 2000. 'Kul'tura kak kollektivnyi intellekt i problemy iskusstvennogo razuma', in Ju. M. Lotman, *Semiosfera*, 557–67, Saint Petersburg: Iskusstvo–SPB.

Lotman, Ju. M. [1979] 1993. 'Teatral'nyi iazyk i zhivopis' (K probleme ikonicheskoi ritoriki)', in Ju. M. Lotman, *Izbrannye stat'i v trekh tomakh*, vol. 3, 308–15, Tallinn: Aleksandra.

Lotman, Ju. M. [1980] 2002. 'Semiotika stseny', in Ju. M. Lotman, *Stat'i po semiotike iskusstva*, 401–31, Saint Petersburg: Gumanitarnoe agentstvo 'Akademicheskii proekt'.

Lotman, Ju. M. [1981] 1993. '"Dogovor" i "vruchenie sebia" kak arkhetipicheskie modeli kul'tury', in Ju. M. Lotman, *Izbrannye stat'i v trekh tomakh*, vol. 3, 345–55, Tallinn: Aleksandra.

Lotman, Ju. M. [1981] 2002. 'Semiotika kul'tury i poniatie teksta', in Ju. M. Lotman, *Stat'i po semiotike iskusstva*, 84–90, Saint Petersburg: Gumanitarnoe agentstvo 'Akademicheskii proekt'.

Lotman, Ju. M. [1984] 2002. 'Nasledie Bakhtina i aktual'nye problemy semiotiki', in Ju. M. Lotman, *Istoriia i tipologiia russkoi kul'tury*, 147–56, Saint Petersburg: Iskusstvo–SPB.

Lotman, Ju. M. [1984] 2005: 'On the Semiosphere', trans. W. Clark, *Sign Systems Studies* 33 (1): 205–29.

Lotman, Ju. M. 1987. 'Semiotika', in V. M. Kozhevnikova and P. A. Nikolaeva (eds), *Literaturnyi entsiklopedicheskii slovar'*, 373–74, Moscow: Sovetskaia entsiklopediia.

Lotman, Ju. M. [1987] 1992. 'Simvol v sisteme kul'tury', in Ju. M. Lotman, *Izbrannye stat'i v trekh tomakh*, vol. 1, 191–9, Tallinn: Aleksandra.

Lotman, Yu. M. 1990. *Universe of the Mind: A Semiotic Theory of Culture*, trans. A. Shukman, London and New York: I.B. Tauris.

Lotman, Ju. M. 1992. 'Vmesto zakliucheniia. O roli sluchainykh faktorov v istorii kul'tury', in Ju. M. Lotman, *Izbrannye stat'i v trekh tomakh*, vol. 1, 472–9, Tallinn: Aleksandra.

Lotman, Ju. M. [1992] 2009. *Culture and Explosion*, trans. W. Clark, ed. M. Grishakova, Berlin and New York: Mouton de Gruyter.

Lotman, Ju. M. [1994/2010] 2013. *The Unpredictable Workings of Culture*, trans. B. J. Baer, ed. I. Pilshchikov and S. Salupere, Tallinn: TLU Press.

Lotman, Ju. M. and Uspenskij, B. A. 1971 [1993]. 'O semioticheskom mekhanizme kul'tury', in Ju. M. Lotman, *Izbrannye stat'i v trekh tomakh*, vol. 3, 326–44, Tallinn: Aleksandra.

Lotman, Ju. M. and Uspenskij, B. A. 1984. 'Authors' Introduction', in Ju. M. Lotman and B. A. Uspenskij, *The Semiotics of Russian Culture*, ed. A. Shukman, ix–xiv, Ann Arbor: Department of Slavic Languages and Literatures, University of Michigan.

Lotman, M. 1998. 'Posleslovie: Struktural'naia poetika i ee mesto v nasledii Iu. M. Lotmana', in Ju. M. Lotman, *Ob iskusstve*, 675–86, Saint Petersburg: Iskusstvo–SPB.

Lotman, M. 2002a: 'Semiotika kul'tury v tartusko-moskovskoi semioticheskoi shkole. Predvaritel'nye zamechaniia', in Ju. M. Lotman, *Istoriia i tipologiia russkoi kul'tury*, 5–20, Saint Petersburg: Iskusstvo–SPB.

Lotman, M. 2002b. 'Atomistic versus Holistic Semiotics', *Sign Systems Studies* 30 (2): 513–27.

Pilshchikov, I. 2018. 'Primechaniia [k stat'e Iu. M. Lotmana "Nekotorye itogi i problemy primeneniia tochnykh metodov v sovetskom literaturovedenii"]', in Ju. M. Lotman, *O strukturalizme. Raboty 1965-1970 godov*, ed. I. A. Pilshchikov, with N. V. Poselyagin and M. V. Trunin, 118–42, Tallinn: TLU Press.

Pilshchikov, I. A., Poselyagin, N. V. and Trunin, M. V. 2018. 'Problemy genezisa i evoliutsii tartusko-moskovskogo strukturalizma v rabotakh Iu.M. Lotmana 1960-kh i nachala 1970-kh godov', in Ju. M. Lotman, *O strukturalizme. Raboty 1965–1970 godov*, ed. I. A. Pilshchikov, with N. V. Poselyagin and M. V. Trunin, 7–62, Tallinn: TLU Press.

Salupere, S. 2017. *O metaiazyke Iuriia Lotmana: problemy, kontekst, istochniki*, Tartu: University of Tartu Press.

Saussure, F. de [1916] 1922. *Cours de linguistique générale*, Paris: Payot.

Saussure, F. de [1916] 1933. *Kurs obshchei lingvistiki*, trans. A. M. Sukhotin, Moscow: OGIZ – Sotsekgiz.

Saussure, F. de [1916] 1959. *Course in General Linguistics*, trans. W. Baskin, New York: Philosophical Library.

Saussure, F. de [1916] 1977. 'Kurs obshchei lingvistiki', trans. A. M. Sukhotin, rev. A. A. Kholodovich, in *Trudy po iazykoznaniiu*, 31–273, Moscow: Progress.

Segal, D. 1974. *Aspects of Structuralism in Soviet Philology*, Tel-Aviv: Papers on Poetics and Semiotics, 2. Available online: http://www.tau.ac.il/tarbut/pubtexts/segal/Segal-Aspects.pdf (accessed 7 December 2020).

Velmezova E. 2018. 'Le triomphe du structuralisme et le triomphe du "Cours de linguistique générale" en URSS dans les années 1950–1960', in M. W. Bruno, D. Chiricò, F. Cimatti, G. Cosenza, A. De Marco, E. Fadda, G. Lo Feudo, M. Mazzeo and C. Stancati (eds), *Linguistica e filosofia del linguaggio: Studi in onore di Daniele Gambarara*, 525–33, Milan: Mimesis.

CHAPTER 3
LOTMAN AND RUSSIAN FORMALISM
Mikhail Trunin

In his retrospective notes on the Tartu-Moscow School of Semiotics (hereafter TMS), Boris Uspenskij (2016: 699) indicated that the main path of research has always been 'from form to meaning'. This kind of thinking from Juri Lotman's close friend and long-term co-author more or less compels us to seek out Russian formalists among the precursors of the TMS. Nor are they difficult to find, since the very first steps of the TMS were characterized by reflection not only on its methods but also on its genesis. Close attention to the problem of genesis of the TMS was related to their need for self-legitimation in the field of scholarship, dictated largely by extra-scholarly circumstances.[1]

In this chapter, I will focus on two main topics; firstly, I will consider the basic points of interaction between Lotman's scholarship and that of his formalist predecessors, and then I will demonstrate the role Lotman assigned to Russian formalists in the genesis of the TMS.

The beginnings of a career in scholarship

For Lotman, Russian formalism was long synonymous with the Petrograd Society for the Study of Poetic Language (OPOIaZ). Until the early 1970s, members of the TMS knew very little about the other important centre of Russian formalism, the Moscow Linguistic Circle (MLC).

Lotman studied at Leningrad State University's Faculty of Philology and his instructors included prominent figures of the formalist school (Boris Eikhenbaum, Vladimir Propp, Boris Tomashevsky), as well as Grigory Gukovsky who is often considered among 'junior formalists' (*mladoformalisty*). It would be a stretch, however, to construct a direct scholarly genealogy from Petersburg formalism to Lotman. In fact, by the time Lotman graduated from the university in 1950, formalism had been doubly defeated, so to speak: firstly, when Viktor Shklovsky published his penitential newspaper article 'Pamiatnik nauchnoi oshibke' (Monument to a Scientific Error) in 1930 (see Erlich 1965: 118–39), and then when the Leningrad Faculty of Philology was demolished in 1949 as part of the so-called campaign against cosmopolitans. The main victims of this campaign were the professors Gukovsky, Mark Azadovsky, Eikhenbaum and Viktor Zhirmunsky: all four were fired, and Gukovsky was arrested soon after (he died of a heart attack in prison before the verdict was announced) (see Druzhinin 2012: 281–473).

Lotman's research advisor was Nikolai Mordovchenko (1904–51), who came from a younger generation of scholars than the formalists. Boris Egorov has characterized the student Lotman's choice as an unexpected one: 'he joined the special seminar of the outwardly unassuming, inconspicuous associate professor N. I. Mordovchenko' (Egorov 1999: 39). Lotman estimated Mordovchenko for his style of scholarship. In his works, Mordovchenko paid most attention to diligent fact-hunting, not to Marxist clichéd 'eloquence'. Thus, he was an antipode to the revolutionary Formalist theories, but also to orthodox Marxism, the only permitted 'theory' in the 1950s. Later, in his own research of the 1960s and 1970s, Lotman attempted to combine positivist fact-hunting with post-formalist (i.e. structuralist) conceptual framework.

At least thirteen years passed between Lotman's first scholarly publication (1949) and his first structuralist experiments. We might say it was during this period of time that Lotman, who began his academic career as a traditional literary historian, rediscovered the legacy both of his university instructors and of other Russian formalists. Lotman's voluminous doctoral thesis, *A. N. Radishchev v bor'be s obshchestvenno-politicheskimi vozzreniiami i dvorianskoi estetikoi Karamzina* (A. N. Radishchev in the Struggle with the Social and Political Views and the Bourgeois Aesthetics of Karamzin) (in two volumes, typewritten), contains not a single reference to works by representatives of the Russian formalist school. Lotman's first monograph, *Andrei Sergeevich Kaisarov i literaturno-obshchestvennaia bor'ba ego vremeni* (Andrei Sergeevich Kaisarov and the Literary-Social Struggle of His Time), published in Tartu in 1958 and dedicated to the memory of Mordovchenko, contains a single, lone reference to a particular historical-literary remark by Eikhenbaum.

As characterized by Mihhail Lotman, his father 'experienced an acute creative crisis' at the turn of the 1960s: 'the range of problems to which he had devoted his previous years of research had lost, if not his interest entirely, at least a significant part of its appeal. His initial dissatisfaction with himself, however, soon turned into an awareness of the crisis situation in Russian literary scholarship itself' (M. Lotman 1998: 675). One means of solving this crisis was to turn to the legacy of the Russian formalist school.

In search of a method

In the early 1960s, a circle of young linguists in Moscow that had come together around Vyacheslav Ivanov and Vladimir Toporov began developing a structuralist approach to the study not only of natural language but also of cultural phenomena, including verbal art. The Moscow circle preferred to call its method 'semiotic' (or 'structural-semiotic'), effectively using the concepts of 'semiotics' and 'structuralism' synonymously. In addition to Saussure, Jakobson and Lévi-Strauss, the Moscow scholars also relied on the work of OPOIaZ members, whose most important figure for them was Shklovsky. The published theses of the Symposium on the Structural Study of Sign Systems, held in Moscow in December 1962, lack any reference to the work of Tynianov or Eikhenbaum, while Shklovsky appears in the theses of Isaac Revzin, Alexander Zholkovsky and Yuri Shcheglov, as well as that of Boris Uspenskij.

As we know, Lotman was moving towards structuralism on a parallel course with the Moscow scholars until 1964. The structural approach attracted Lotman's interest for several reasons. Firstly, this approach offered a set of new tools for analysing literary texts that served as an alternative to those that the official Soviet literary studies could provide. Secondly, it conveyed an attitude towards a rigorously scientific, systematic and verifiable method. For Lotman, this was a means of solving the crisis: philology was transformed from a set of subjective interpretations and/or ideological dogmas into a serious science, one that was methodologically similar to the exact and natural sciences. The complex and multibranched terminology of the TMS also worked to ensure that this new approach acquired a rigorously scientific appearance. Herein lies yet another convergence between the Soviet structuralists and the Russian formalists, who had also actively developed a vocabulary of literary studies. For Lotman, who had turned to structuralism, this connection with formalist method was important, particularly the connection with OPOIaZ conceptual frameworks.

In order to demonstrate that the trajectory of his references to Russian formalist works was not, in fact, straight, let us consider two pairs of articles by Lotman that mark the transition away from his historical-literary studies and on to structuralist ones. Compare the article 'K evoliutsii postroeniia kharakterov v romane "Evgenii Onegin"' (On the Evolution of Character Construction in the Novel *Eugene Onegin*) (1960) with the article 'Khudozhestvennaia struktura "Evgeniia Onegina"' (The Artistic Structure of *Eugene Onegin*) (1966), and the article 'Ideinaia struktura "Kapitanskoi dochki"' (The Structure of Ideas in *The Captain's Daughter*) (1962) with the article 'O razgranichenii lingvisticheskogo i literaturovedcheskogo poniatiia struktury' (On Delimitation of Linguistic and Literary-historical Concepts of Structure) (1963). Both pairs can be interpreted as attempts to revise his own method. In his first major article on Pushkin's novel in verse, Lotman follows Gukovsky and Tomashevsky.[2] Its main idea is that the evolution of *Eugene Onegin*'s characters is motivated by the 'Zeitgeist'. The article references works by Tynianov and Eikhenbaum, but only their historical-literary works, not their conceptual-theoretical ones (Lotman 1960: 134, 143, 154). In the 1966 article, Lotman speaks explicitly of revising some of the provisions of his 1960 work. He now sees Pushkin's novel in verse as a model constructed according to certain rules, reflecting not so much the surrounding reality as creating (modelling) its own. Therefore, immanent analysis of the work as 'a system [. . .] of heterogeneous structures and elements' has now become fundamental (Lotman 1966: 31). By the second page of the article, Lotman is already explicitly listing scholars whose influence determined his new approach to Pushkin's novel:

The author believes that the knowledgeable reader will not miss the connection between the piece offered to his attention and some of the ideas set forth in the following works: Yu. Tynianov, *The Problem of Verse Language*, L[eningrad], 'Academia', 1924; M. Bakhtin, *Problems of Dostoevskii's Poetics*, second ed., M[oscow], S[ovetskii] P[isatel'], 1963; V. Shklovsky, '*Eugene Onegin* (Pushkin and Stern)', in *Essays on Pushkin's Poetics*, Berlin, 'Epokha', 1923; G. Vinokur, *Word and Verse in Eugene Onegin* ('Pushkin', collection of articles, M[oscow], G[osudarstvennoe] I[zdatel'stvo] Kh[udozhesvennoi] L[iteratury], 1941). The lecture on *Eugene Onegin* delivered by N. I. Mordovchenko in his course on the history of Russian literature at Leningrad State University's Faculty of Philology exerted a great influence on the course of the author's thought. Mordovchenko had intended to use the idea expressed here of a 'taxonomic structure' of characters as the basis for a book that unfortunately remained unwritten. (Lotman 1966: 6)

This statement is valuable primarily for the history of science, since it is more declarative than methodological in nature: in the actual text of his article, Lotman references Grigory Vinokur alone. A paradox is that in search for a solution to the methodological crisis Lotman combines such different scholars as late Tynianov, early Shklovsky, Bakhtin and late Vinokur.

'The Structure of Ideas in *The Captain's Daughter*' is his first article that uses the word 'structure' in its title, though even here it serves as a synonym for the word 'composition'. As an answer to a topical question for Soviet literary studies – how did Pushkin feel about the peasant revolt? – Lotman proposes we look not to the sphere of ideology, but to the very arrangement of Pushkin's text, which he analyses using traditional literary-historical methods in combination with analysis of the inner structure of the text (i.e. poetics). Lotman reconstructs Pushkin's 1830s world view not on the basis of direct judgements of the protagonists of *The Captain's Daughter*, but on the basis of how these judgements are combined into a whole, arranged by the author according to certain rules. In other words, as formulated in 1963: 'Any characterization of relations among the elements [. . .] of the whole, the entire sum of these relations, that is, its structure, affects the semantics of a text' (Lotman 1963: 51).

For Lotman, it was linguistics that had led to a breakthrough in the humanities in the 1950s. When approaching a literary text, however, 'the linguist will inevitably encounter the inadequacy of purely linguistic methods' (Lotman 1963: 46). He argues that the nature of the verbal sign in everyday communication fundamentally differs from that in a work of fiction: in the former case it is a linguistic structure as such, while in the latter it is a 'conceptual', 'extra-linguistic structure expressed through language' (Lotman 1963: 45, 49, 50). Lotman believes that, in everyday communication, 'the content of the information transmitted is amorphous; it does not possess its own internal structure. In an ordinary linguistic act, we are dealing with only one structure: the structure of the language itself' (Lotman 1963: 45). Lotman contrasts scientific and artistic language with spoken language (as languages that have a content structure versus a language with an amorphous content shaped and regulated by context). The specific nature of verbal art lies in the inseparable unity of its content structure (model of the world) and its expression structure (language). However, Lotman found it insufficient to base his own discussions of literature and culture on an exclusive reliance on linguistic tools. This is why he engaged seriously with the legacy of the Russian Formalist school with its analysis of the immanent structure of artistic texts. The book *Lektsii po struktural'noi poetike* (Lectures on Structural Poetics) should be treated as a milestone.

Peak interest[3]

Let us consider how Lotman's book draws on the work of Russian formalists to develop and deepen the reasoning that had already appeared in his 1963 article. For example, consider one paradoxical assertion: Lotman suggests that, 'while language allows for different ways of expressing the same content, there is no such possibility in art' (Lotman 1963: 52). We cannot say, however, that a work of art is so inimitable that different ways of expressing the same content are unacceptable within it: we need only recall the 'other editions and variants' section of academic editions of classical literature, the variability of folkloric text, and the role of improvisation in various forms of art (see Pilshchikov, Poseliagin and Trunin 2018: 9–12). While the 1963 article contains this line of thought in an attempt to criticize Hjelmslev's thesis that content is an 'amorphous continuum on which the formative action of languages has laid its borders' (Lotman 1963: 52), it appears in *Lectures on Structural Poetics* in the context of a dispute with Shklovsky:

> There is a profound difference between the linguistic and the literary-historical [*literaturovedcheskoe*] understanding of text. The language text allows for different expressions for the same content [. . .]. The text of a literary work is, in principle, individual. It is created for a given content and, due to the aforementioned specifics of the relation of content to expression in a literary text, it cannot be replaced by any equivalent expression without changing the plan of content. The connection between content and expression in a literary text is so strong that translation into another system of notation is, in essence, also not indifferent to content [. . .]. It is in a literary work that the word 'text' justifies its etymology (*textum* from *texto*: woven, interlaced). For it is the full wealth of oppositions of the plan of expression becoming differentiating features of the plan of content that gives the text both its extraordinary depth of meaning and an individuality irreducible to the mechanical sum of all the thoughts separately extracted from the plan of content.
>
> The definition of device follows from all the above. The device is above all meaningful [*soderzhatelen*]: it is a sign of content [*soderzhanie*]. But this is a special kind of meaningfulness: a work of art does not consist of devices the way a syntactic unit, according to certain rules, consists of lexical ones. Devices relate to the content not directly but indirectly, through the totality of the text. Furthermore, the device does not exist at all outside of its relation to the totality of the text. But nor is the text the highest level. It is mediated by numerous extra-textual relationships. (Lotman 1964: 159–60)

In this passage, Lotman is criticizing Shklovsky's concept of 'device' (*priyom*) and the mechanistic model of a literary work as a 'sum-total of devices' (Shklovsky 1921: 8). By the very first pages of his *Lektsii*, Lotman is already contrasting this 'mechanistic-inventorial' approach with Tynianov's functional approach, Gukovsky's historical-typological approach and Propp's protostructuralist approach: 'The main flaw of the so-called "formal method" is that it often led the scholars to the view of literature as a sum-total of devices, a mechanical conglomerate. A genuine study of a work of art is possible only if we approach the work as a single, multidimensional, functioning structure' (Lotman 1964: 13).

In his polemic with Shklovsky, Lotman delivered a hypothesis that made a highly favourable impression on readers of *Lektsii*, namely that an artistic work is not exhausted by its text. Through his book, and particularly in its final chapter, 'Textual and Extratextual Structures', Lotman repeatedly emphasizes the importance of 'separating relationships into intratextual and extratextual' (Lotman 1964: 155). Nor does this pertain only to the language of poetic texts: Lotman is already at the cusp of interpreting all cultural phenomena as fundamentally textual. In this respect, the literary text turns out to be comparable with the theatrical or visual text, with a set of generally known (for a given culture) facts, forms of behaviour (behavioural texts), and so forth. Lotman's conceptual framework suggests that extratextual relationships involve both the relationship of text to extratextual (extralinguistic) reality and the relationship of text to other texts that establish the horizon of readers' expectations. In constructing both the former and latter types of relationship, 'it is not only what is depicted, but also what is not depicted, that plays a major role' (Lotman 1964: 25). This thesis, stated at the beginning of the book, develops into a polemic with Shklovsky, who 'saw the purpose of the device "in having us perceive things [. . .] as artistic". However, the history of art knows of aesthetic systems and eras in the history of art when it was precisely the rejection of "artistry" that was perceived as the highest artistic achievement' (Lotman 1964: 160). The text cannot be understood without our knowing what is intentionally absent from it. Lotman gives this phenomenon a name: 'minus-device'. The term 'device' was obviously suggested by the formalists, and one source of Lotman's conceptual framework is Tynianov's argument about the effectiveness of the 'minus sign' (*otritsatel'nyi priznak*), as opposed to the 'polished device' (*sglazhennyi priyom*):

> In some historical periods, the 'bared' device becomes automatized like any other, which naturally gives rise to the need for a dialectically opposed 'polished' device. Under these conditions, a 'polished' device will be more dynamic than one that is bared, as it will shift, and thereby accentuate, the habituated relationship between the constructive principle and its material. The 'minus sign' in front of a 'polished' device comes into force in cases where the 'plus sign' of a bared device has been automatized. (Tynianov [1924] 2019: 157)

Here we arrive at the moment where Lotman distinguishes Tynianov's conceptual framework from that of other OPOIaZ members, defining it not as 'formalism' but as 'the attempt at transitioning to a representation of the functional nature of the artistic system' (Lotman 1964: 13). In other words, functionalism.

Tynianov's works turned out to harmonize with the structuralist-Saussurean spirit of *Lektsii*: 'Art is always functional, always a relationship' (Lotman 1964: 22). By analogy with linguistic elements, elements of an artistic structure are defined not by their substantial properties, but by their relations among one another and by their functions in an overall system. Mikhail Gasparov considered this thesis the main achievement of structuralist poetics: 'The most important and difficult thing in [Lotman's] theory of poetry is relativity. The poetics of structuralism is not a poetics of an artistic system's isolated elements, but of the relations among them' (Gasparov 1994: 12).

The opposition between the 'dynamic' Tynianov and the 'mechanistic' Shklovsky was the focal point around which Lotman built his understanding of Russian formalism in the late 1960s. We can see this clearly in an article written shortly after *Lektsii*, known by the title 'Literaturovedenie dolzhno byt' naukoi' (The Study of Literature Must be a Science). This title has often been interpreted as the motto of the TMS in the late 1960s, though it came not from Lotman but from the editorial board of the journal *Voprosy literatury*, where the article was published in early 1967. The author had another title in mind – 'O printsipakh strukturalizma v literaturovedenii' (On the Principles of Structuralism in Literary Studies) – and its first completed version was dated 1 August 1965 (Lotman 2018: 65–97). Since Lotman's article was published as a response to polemics about structuralism, roughly one-third of it is occupied by the polemics themselves. The other two-thirds, however, are devoted to presenting the basic principles of structuralism in literary studies.

Lotman's first argument already refers to the opposition described earlier: structuralism is not mechanistic, and 'one of structuralism's basic principles is its rejection of analysis based on a mechanical list of features: a work of art is not the sum of its features, but a functioning system, a structure' (Lotman 1967: 93–4; 2018: 71). His next argument states: 'Structuralism is not the enemy of historicism.' Studying any functioning system or structure presumes analysing it synchronically. However, the contrast between synchrony and diachrony is 'not fundamental, but heuristic in nature' (Lotman 1967: 94; 2018: 72). This issue had first been raised in an argument by Tynianov and Jakobson in their article 'Problems in the Study of Language and Literature', in which the co-authors announce their revision both of Saussure's 'synchronic conception' and of the early works of their own OPOIaZ colleagues (primarily Shklovsky): 'Pure synchronism is now revealed to be an illusion: each synchronic system has its own past and future as integral structural elements of the system' (Tynianov and Jakobson [1928] 2019: 280; see Pilshchikov and Trunin 2016: 375–7).

The year after the publication of these arguments, the section about the relationship between synchronic and diachronic approaches was included and expanded in section 1b of the *Theses* of the Prague Linguistic Circle (PLC; see Cercle Linguistique de Prague 1929), which was prepared by Jakobson. Also in 1929, in a newspaper article on the First International Congress of Slavists, Jakobson applied the term 'structuralism' borrowed from psychology to his new methodology for studying language and literature. The passage devoted to structuralism (Jakobson 1929: 11) was later quoted in English in a 'Retrospect' to the second volume of Jakobson's *Selected Writings*:

Were we to comprise the leading idea of present-day science in its most various manifestations, we could hardly find a more appropriate designation than structuralism. Any set of phenomena examined by contemporary science is treated not as a mechanical agglomeration but as a structural whole, and the basic task is to reveal the inner, whether static or developmental, laws of this system. (Jakobson 1971: 711)

As we can see, Jakobson and Tynianov already considered 'structure' (rather than form) the central concept of the humanities by the late 1920s. Though Lotman does not refer to these works in his *Lektsii* nor in his article published in *Voprosy literatury*, he saw in Tynianov and Jakobson the pioneers of the structural-functional approach to literature (see also Chapter 4).

Asserting the connection between structuralism and historicism is important not only from a methodological point of view but also from the point of view of the genesis of the TMS. One of Lotman's overarching thoughts in the late 1960s is to reclaim the tradition of the 1920s and to use it as a basis for creating new directions for scholarly research. Synchronic formalist methods dominated literary studies in the 1920s; they were supplanted by diachronic, historical-literary methods in the 1930s. For Lotman, the late 1960s were a time of synthesis. Later, whenever Lotman proposed different ways of describing the genesis of the TMS, he would invariably interpret the development of literary theory in terms of the Hegelian 'thesis–antithesis–synthesis' triad. The role of thesis was always played by OPOIaZ and the role of synthesis by the TMS, whereas the role of antithesis depended on which directions in scholarship Lotman and his associates considered most relevant at a particular time. They were the schools and scholars who focused on semantics without losing attention to form, such as the late Gukovsky's version of stadial literary evolution (as a neo-Hegelian antidote to official Marxism), successively, Marrist (predominantly, Olga Freidenberg's) paleontological semantics, the Prague School's (first and foremost, Mukařovský's) functionalist literary structuralism and semiotic aesthetics (with Tynianov as the main forerunner of Prague functionalism), and, eventually, Bakhtin's dialogism (see Pilshchikov, Poseliagin and Trunin 2018: 45–6).

Further development

In the late 1960s, Lotman became acquainted with the scholarly work of Jan Mukařovský, one of the founders of Czech structuralism, whose selected works he intended to publish in Russian (see Pilshchikov and Trunin 2018). In an introductory article to the then-failed publication of Mukařovský, Lotman wrote:

> Only the kind of critique of formalists that complimented analysis of the syntagmatic structure with a semantic one, that regarded the entirety of the artistic construction as a mutual tension between these two principles of organization, could be fruitful. Critique that simply tossed aside the very problem of syntagmatic analysis of a text's internal structure was a step backwards. (Lotman [1970] 1994: 13; 2018: 363)

The PLC develops OPOIaZ ideas to the point of denying some of its original, 'mechanistic' postulates. It was the Prague School, Lotman says, that 'managed to carry out constructive criticism of formalism, unwittingly confirming Y. N. Tynianov's proposition that there were no more dangerous critics in the field of culture than one's direct successors' (1994: 14; 2018: 365). Tynianov's appearance in these arguments is not by chance. As we saw earlier, Lotman singled out Tynianov among the formalists as the scholar with the greatest interest in the semantics of artistic form.[4]

Volume four of *Trudy po znakovym sistemam* was dedicated to the memory of Tynianov. In his introduction, Lotman summarized Tynianov's research hypostases and his role in the genesis of the TMS:

On the one hand, [Tynianov] was interested in overall questions of cultural evolution throughout his life. That said, the general trends [*zakonomernosti*] advanced were so abstract in nature that both artistic and ideological, philosophical, and political texts acted only as special cases of their realization [. . .]. The connection with the St. Petersburg school of studying Russian social thought [. . .] manifested in Tynianov's scholarly work as a persistent interest in history as a mobile and regular [*zakonomernyi*] process and in the problems of correlating an artistic order [*riad*] with the social, philosophical, and political orders external to it.

On the other hand, Tynianov was a researcher who clearly gravitated towards a linguistic method of analysis. He distinctly imagined that the internal organization of a text's structure can and should be the focus of completely independent research. [. . .] The combination of these two approaches defined the perspective that works of art are a system of functions rather than inventory of 'artistic devices'. This fruitful idea served as the basis for many subsequent structuralist works. The idea of 'functionalism', which is fully consistent with the general spirit of twentieth-century science, allows us to eliminate the antinomy between the dynamism of the object of study and the staticity of descriptive research. (Lotman 1969b: 5)

In addition to the characterization discussed earlier, another appears here that is both important and, at the same time, the most problematic: the dynamics (dynamism) of the object of study (Pilshchikov 2019a: 50; 2019b: 218–9). Lotman's article 'O nekotorykh printsipal'nykh trudnostiakh v strukturnom opisanii teksta' (On Some Principal Difficulties in the Structural Description of a Text), published in the same volume, begins with a well-known quotation from Tynianov's book *The Problem of Verse Language*: 'The form of a literary work should be understood as dynamic'. Lotman is apparently interpreting this Tynianov quote in the sense of historical variability as opposed to achronic staticity. Later, he says that 'in specific descriptions of texts [. . .] it is static modes that come to the fore', suggesting the following heuristic solution:

the dynamic structure would be built as a number of static models (a minimum of two) in a certain mobile relationship. From this it follows that static descriptions are not only something that, in themselves, are not faulty, but that on the contrary represent a necessary stage, without which functionally mobile constructions are also impossible. (Lotman 1969a: 478–9)

Lotman would later discuss the fact that dynamics can be described as a series of static states and diachrony as a set of successive synchronic snapshots in 'The Dynamic Model of a Semiotic System' (1974).

Side interest: Tynianov as historical novelist

Lotman's ideas described earlier about the genesis of the TMS and the role of Russian formalists in that genesis became canonical fairly quickly. This is, for example, precisely the same trajectory of scholarly thought Lotman outlined in his introduction to the book *Analysis of the Poetic Text* (Lotman 1972: 16–17). Fifteen years later, Boris Uspenskij would construct the genesis of the TMS the same way, explicitly naming OPOIaZ, the MLC and the PLC as its most significant precursors (Uspenskij 1987: 19–21).

Lotman's later research in the field of cultural typology and semiotics developed the ideas formulated in his structuralist works. Beginning in the mid-1970s, Lotman became increasingly interested in the culturological aspects of structural research and worked at developing an expansive theory of semiotics of culture. He began interpreting the philological term 'text' more and more broadly: from the setting down of a work of art (which need not be verbal), it became a particular action or phenomenon endowed with meaning, be it a text of literature, cinema, material culture or even everyday behaviour. It was this idea that synchronic analysis of text could be supplemented by diachronic analysis of its functioning in a changing historical context that allowed Lotman to compare artistic sign systems with non-artistic and pseudo-artistic ones, such as aestheticized or ideologically loaded behaviour. It is characteristic that, in this case, Lotman speaks not of 'semiotics' of behaviour but of 'poetics', perhaps in recollection of the Russian formalists (the idea itself goes back to Vinokur and Tomashevsky). It is also indicative that, in his series of articles devoted to everyday behaviour as an aesthetic phenomenon, references to general theoretical works of formalists were supplanted by references to formalist case studies (see Lotman 1975: 42–3), while references to the primary sources under analysis prevail in the next article from his cycle of behavioural studies, 'The Poetics of Everyday Behaviour in Eighteenth-Century Russian culture' (1977).

In his articles on behaviour, Lotman talks about the projection of fiction into reality. The opposite trend, the transformation of reality into fiction, is represented by the genre of historical novel. Here we find a place for another of Tynianov's hypostases, the historical novelist. Lotman did not leave behind any major works on the historical novel, but his thoughts about it have been found in a number of marginal texts from the 1980s. On 9 October 1982, in response to a request from the Estonian writer Jaan Kross to share his thoughts on the historical novel, Lotman wrote:

Tynianov made himself a novelist, I am convinced of this, because he literally suffered from the impossibility of understanding documents on the basis of these documents alone. For example, so little documentary data about Griboedov has come down to us that we are powerless to use it for unravelling the motives of his behaviour and the mystery of his personality. Tynianov creates a 'myth of Griboedov' through which he deciphers historical facts.

Tynianov spent his whole life thinking about Pushkin as a person, but the material crumbled in his hands. He invented a fictional story: his whole life, Pushkin was in love with [Ekaterina] Karamzina and bore this tragic, hidden love with him for all his years. Proving this idea was impossible, and so Tynianov, after trying to write an article on the subject that was completely unconvincing as scholarship, began writing a novel where he could explain Pushkin, freely creating a myth of Pushkin. That the novel turned out, it seems to me, unsuccessful is another matter [. . .]. But the principle of it is very clear. (Trunin 2013: 227)

Thus, Tynianov combined two hypostases in himself: the scholar-philologist and the historical novelist who claimed, 'Where the document ends is where I begin' (see Gasparov 1990). Here, though, was a problem for Lotman that he never fully solved. On the one hand, Lotman mostly praised Tynianov's courage in print (compare, however, the share of criticism in Lotman 1987: 13), as in the afterword to the Estonian translation of his novel *Pushkin*:

Tynianov took a step of enormous scientific courage and honesty: he objectified his scientific intuition and showed the reader Pushkin from two points of view: saying in his scholarly articles, 'Here he is, Pushkin; this is the way he is because that is how the documents I am analyzing depict him', and saying in his novel, 'This is the way he is because I am convinced that he was; I have studied him all my life, I have grown accustomed to him, and I can imagine him even in situations where no documents tell us anything. Furthermore, it is this belief of mine that will illuminate for you, explain and bind together the disparate documents that are mute without that belief'. (Lotman 1985: 461)[5]

Meanwhile, he was privately criticizing Tynianov for effectively the same thing: his bold treatment of historical facts that often approached taking direct liberties. In a letter to Boris Egorov dated 31 July 1984, he wrote, 'In a certain sense, Tynianov is like Bakhtin: his specific ideas are often false and his conceptual frameworks are biased [. . .]. But the overall orientation is extremely fruitful and fecund [. . .]. He was still a genius, although he was, I'd agree, unpleasant in many ways' (Lotman 1997: 331). Or in a 24 April 1986 letter to Boris Uspenskij: 'I'm currently studying Griboedov. What a man! And how shamelessly Tynianov lied about him in his novel and his scholarship' (Lotman and Uspenskij 2016: 591). Unfortunately, Lotman's studies of Griboedov did not translate into full-fledged publications, so we cannot know what exactly Tynianov's 'lies' included.

Something else is important here, however: Lotman had passed the peak of his interest in the legacy of Russian formalists around the turn of the 1960s–1970s.

Late Lotman

In the 1980s, Lotman coined the term 'semiosphere', a semiotic space in which all the texts of a particular culture are created and function. Since Lotman believed that the human being always dwells within culture and cannot go past its borders, semiotics would soon transform for Lotman into a universal science of human being. It is here that biological and natural science models prevailed over literary and textual models: firstly, Vladimir Vernadsky's theory of the noosphere, and then Ilya Prigogine's theory of explosion.

Similarly, in his books *Universe of the Mind* (1990) and *Culture and Explosion* (1992), Lotman refers to the works of Tynianov or Tomashevsky only in relation to particular issues. However, the genesis of Lotman's path as a scholar that we have described in this chapter did not escape the perceptive eye of Umberto Eco, who wrote the introduction to *Universe of the Mind* and placed the Tartu-Moscow school within a broader transnational context:

> During the Sixties, two disturbing words erupted into the calm waters of the European academic world: semiotics (or semiology) and structuralism. [. . .] Interest in structural studies of language had led (particularly through the influence of Roman Jakobson) to an interest in the works of the Prague School, and at the same time to the rediscovery of the Russian Formalists of the Twenties [. . .]. Alongside this growth of interest in Russian Formalism, during the early Sixties scholars in Italy and France were beginning to discover the semioticians at work during this period in Russia – principally in Moscow and Tartu [. . .]. However, at the centre of this new field of research, as both link and fulcrum (through the series *Trudy po znakovym sistemam* [. . .] produced in Tartu) stood the figure of Yuri Lotman. (Eco 1990: vii–viii)[6]

Notes

1. Lotman's academic career as a structuralist began with polemics in which his opponents allowed themselves such arguments as 'modern followers of OPOIaZ are reviving its worst aspects', which, in Soviet reality, resembled political accusations of 'formalism'. For a detailed description of these polemics, see Shukman 1977: 200–4; Seyffert 1985: 172–253; Pilshchikov, Poseliagin and Trunin 2018: 20–40.

2. In this article, Lotman relies on Tomashevsky as a textologist and scholar of Pushkin. Tomashevsky (the author of the formalist handbook *Theory of Literature (Poetics)*) distanced himself from formalism in the early 1930s. At the same time, Tomashevsky's seminal 'Literature and Biography' (1923) was, together with Tynianov's works, the main inspiration for Lotman's poetics of everyday behaviour.

3. This section is based on the works co-authored with Igor Pilshchikov; see Pilshchikov and Trunin 2016; Pilshchikov, Poseliagin and Trunin 2018.

4. A discussion of the concept of the 'dominant', which developed as a result of the productive interaction of Russian formalism and Czech structuralism, and which was subsequently adopted by Lotman and the TMS, is behind the scope of this chapter. For more on the dominant, see Pilshchikov 2016: 210–27; Pilshchikov, Poseliagin and Trunin 2018: 57–60; Pilshchikov 2019a: 52–9; 2019b: 219–20.

5. Published in Estonian, translated here from the Russian original, which is held at the Juri Lotman Semiotics Repository (Tallinn University).

6. This chapter was written with the support of the Estonian Research Council (PRG319). Translated from Russian by Brad Damaré. The author is grateful to Igor Pilshchikov for his help and critical comments.

References

Cercle Linguistique de Prague. 1929. 'Thèses', in *Mélanges linguistiques dédiés au Premier Congrès des philologues slaves, vol. 1 of Travaux du Cercle Linguistique de Prague*, 5–29, Prague: Jednota československých matematiků a fysiků.

Druzhinin, P. A. 2012. *Ideologiia i filologiia. Leningrad, 1940-e gody. Dokumental'noe issledovanie*, vol. 2, Moscow: Novoe literaturnoe obozrenie.

Eco, U. 1990. 'Introduction', in Yu. M. Lotman, *Universe of the Mind: A Semiotic Theory of Culture*, trans. A. Shukman, vii–xiii, London and New York: I. B. Tauris.

Egorov, B. F. 1999. *Zhizn' i tvorchestvo Ju. M. Lotmana*, Moscow: Novoe literaturnoe obozrenie.

Erlich, V. 1965. *Russian Formalism: History – Doctrine*, 2nd rev. edn, The Hague: Mouton.

Gasparov, M. L. 1990. 'Nauchnost' i khudozhestvennost' v tvorchestve Tynianova', in M. O. Tchudakova (ed.), *Tynianovskii sbornik 5: Chetvertye Tynianovskie chteniia*, 12–20, Riga: Zinātne.

Gasparov, M. L. 1994. 'Predislovie', in A. D. Koshelev (ed.), *Iu. M. Lotman i tartusko-moskovskaia semioticheskaia shkola*, 11–16, Moscow: Gnozis.

Jakobson, R. 1929, 'Romantické všeslovanství – nová slavistika', *Čin* (31 October): 10–12.

Jakobson, R. 1971. *Selected Writings, vol. 2: Word and Language*, The Hague and Paris: Mouton.

Lotman, Ju. M. 1960. 'K evoliutsii postroeniia kharakterov v romane "Evgenii Onegin"', in N. V. Izmailov (ed.), *Pushkin: Issledovaniia i materialy*, vol. 3, 131–73, Moscow and Leningrad: Izdatel'stvo Akademii nauk SSSR.

Lotman, Ju. M. 1962. 'Ideinaia struktura "Kapitanskoi dochki"', in M. Efimova (ed.), *Pushkinskii sbornik*, 3–20, Pskov: Pskovskii gosudarstvennyi pedagogicheskii institut.

Lotman, Ju. M. 1963. 'O razgranichenii lingvisticheskogo i literaturovedcheskogo poniatiia struktury', *Voprosy iazykoznaniia* 3: 44–52.

Lotman, Ju. M. 1964. *Lektsii po struktural'noi poetike. Vyp. 1: Vvedenie, teoriia stikha*, Tartu: Izdatel'stvo Tartuskogo universiteta (*Trudy po znakovym sistemam*, 1).

Lotman, Ju. M. 1966. 'Khudozhestvennaia struktura "Evgeniia Onegina"', *Trudy po russkoi i slavianskoi filologii* 9: 5–32.

Lotman, Ju. M. 1967. 'Literaturovedenie dolzhno byt' naukoi', *Voprosy literatury* 1: 90–100.

Lotman, Ju. M. 1969a. 'O nekotorykh printsipial'nykh trudnostiakh v strukturnom opisanii teksta', *Trudy po znakovym sistemam* 4: 478–82.

Lotman, Ju. M. 1969b. 'Ot redaktsii', *Trudy po znakovym sistemam* 4: 5–6.

Lotman, Ju. M. [1970] 1994. 'Yan Mukarzhovskii – teoretik iskusstva', in Ju. M. Lotman and O. M. Malevich (eds), Ya. Mukarzhovskii, *Issledovaniia po estetike i teorii iskusstva*, 8–32, Moscow: Iskusstvo.

Lotman, Ju. M. 1972. *Analiz poeticheskogo teksta: Struktura stikha*, Leningrad: Prosveshchenie.
Lotman, Ju. M. 1974. *Dinamicheskaia model' semioticheskoi sistemy*, Moscow: Institut russkogo iazyka AN SSSR.
Lotman, Ju. M. 1975. 'Dekabrist v povsednevnoi zhizni (Bytovoe povedenie kak istoriko-psikhologicheskaia kategoriia)', in V. G. Bazanov and V. E. Vatsuro (eds), *Literaturnoe nasledie dekabristov*, 25–74, Leningrad: Nauka.
Lotman, Ju. M. 1977. 'Poetika bytovogo povedeniia v russkoi kul'ture XVIII veka', *Trudy po znakovym sistemam* 8: 65–89.
Lotman, Ju. M. 1985. 'Tõnjanovi romaanist "Puškin"' [About Tynianov's Novel *Pushkin*], in J. Tõnjanov, *Puškin*, 456–62, Tallinn: Eesti Raamat.
Lotman, Ju. M. 1987. *Sotvorenie Karamzina*, Moscow: Kniga.
Lotman, Ju. M. 1997. *Pis'ma 1940–1993*, ed. B. F. Egorov, Moscow: Iazyki russkoi kul'tury.
Lotman, Ju. M. 2018. *O strukturalizme: Raboty 1965–1970 godov*, ed. I. A. Pilshchikov, with N. V. Poseliagin and M. V. Trunin, Tallinn: TLU Press.
Lotman, Ju. M. and Uspenskij, B. A. 2016. *Perepiska 1964–1993*, eds O. Ia. Kel'bert, M. V. Trunin and B. A. Uspenskij, Tallinn: TLU Press.
Lotman, M. 1998. 'Posleslovie: Struktural'naia poetika i ee mesto v nasledii Ju. M. Lotmana', in Ju. M. Lotman, *Ob iskusstve*, 675–86, Saint Petersburg: Iskusstvo–SPb.
Pilshchikov, I. A. 2016. 'Nepolnaia perevodimost' kak mekhanizm poznaniia i kommunikatsii', in V. V. Feshchenko (ed.), *Lingvistika i semiotika kul'turnykh transferov: Metody, printsipy, tekhnologii*, 203–33, Moscow: Kul'turnaia revoliutsiia.
Pilshchikov, I. 2019a. 'Dinamika teksta i dinamika literatury: formalizm – funktsionalizm – strukturalizm (istoriko-nauchnye tezisy)', in M. Lotman, T. Kuzovkina and E. Pilarczyk (eds), *Dinamicheskaia struktura teksta / The Dynamic Structure of Text*, 45–63, Kraków: Wydawnictwo Uniwersytetu Jagiellońskiego.
Pilshchikov, I. 2019b. 'The Prague School on a Global Scale: a Coup d'œil from the East', *Slovo a Slovesnost* 80 (3): 215–28.
Pilshchikov, I., Poseliagin, N. and Trunin, M. 2018. 'Problemy genezisa i evoliutsii tartusko-moskovskogo strukturalizma v rabotakh Ju. M. Lotmana 1960-kh i nachala 1970-kh godov', in Ju. M. Lotman, *O strukturalizme: Raboty 1965–1970 godov*, ed. I. A. Pilshchikov, with N. V. Poseliagin and M. V. Trunin, 7–62, Tallinn: TLU Press.
Pilshchikov, I. and Trunin, M. 2016. 'The Tartu-Moscow School of Semiotics: A Transnational Perspective', *Sign Systems Studies* 44 (3): 368–401.
Pilshchikov, I. and Trunin, M. 2018. 'Vokrug podgotovki i zapreta russkogo izdaniia rabot Yana Mukarzhovskogo pod redaktsiei Ju. M. Lotmana i O. M. Malevicha', in Ju. M. Lotman, *O strukturalizme: Raboty 1965–1970 godov*, ed. I. A. Pilshchikov, with N. V. Poseliagin and M. V. Trunin, 315–49, Tallinn: TLU Press.
Seyffert, P. 1985. *Soviet Literary Structuralism: Background. Debate. Issues*, Columbus, Ohio: Slavica.
Shklovsky, V. 1921. *Rozanov: Iz knigi 'Siuzhet kak iavlenie stilia'*, Petrograd: OPOIaZ.
Shukman, A. 1977. *Literature and Semiotics: A Study of the Writings of Yu. M. Lotman*, Amsterdam, New York and Oxford: North-Holland Publishing Company.
Trunin, M. V. 2013. 'Perepiska Ju. M. Lotmana s Jaanom Krossom ob istoricheskom romane', *Russkaia literatura* 3: 220–34.
Tynianov, Y. 2019. 'Literary Fact (1924)', in Y. Tynianov, *Permanent Evolution: Selected Essays on Literature, Theory and Film*, ed. and trans. A. Morse and P. Redko, 149–68, Boston: Academic Studies Press.

Tynianov, Y. and Jakobson, R. 2019. 'Problems of the Study of Literature and Language (1928)', in Y. Tynianov, *Permanent Evolution: Selected Essays on Literature, Theory and Film*, trans. and ed. A. Morse and P. Redko, 278–82, Boston: Academic Studies Press.

Uspenskij, B. A. 1987. 'K probleme genezisa tartusko-moskovskoi semioticheskoi shkoly', *Trudy po znakovym sistemam* 20: 18–29.

Uspenskij, B. A. 2016. 'O moskovsko-tartuskoi semioticheskoi shkole', in Ju. M. Lotman and B. A. Uspenskij, *Perepiska 1964–1993*, eds O. Ia. Kel'bert, M. V. Trunin and B. A. Uspenskij, 696–700, Tallinn: TLU Press.

CHAPTER 4
LOTMAN AND JAKOBSON
Igor Pilshchikov and Elin Sütiste

In autumn 1982 the Estonian journal *Keel ja Kirjandus* (Language and Literature) commissioned Juri Lotman to write an obituary of Roman Jakobson, who had died on 18 July 1982. Lotman admits in his article that at first he was incapable of fulfilling the request: 'in order to write an obituary, you need to get used to the idea that the person has died, to *feel* this idea' (Lotman [1983] 2003: 74). Only a few months later was he able to finish his necrology, when he had discovered for himself 'the main meaning, the "idea" of [Jakobson's] creative path'. This idea was that 'Roman Osipovich Jakobson was a romantic in science all his life'. One aspect of Jakobson's scientific 'romanticism' was his reinterpretation of 'structure' as a dynamic entity. In this respect, Lotman placed him among scholars such as Juri Tynianov (Jakobson's one-time co-author) and Jan Mukařovský (Jakobson's associate in the Prague Linguistic Circle), but also Mikhail Bakhtin (see Lotman 1969: 478; [1970] 1994: 11; 1978: 18–19; [1984] 2002: 148–9).

Another aspect emphasized by Lotman was Jakobson's interdisciplinary effort. The evolution of Jakobson's thought went through several stages (Pilshchikov 2022): formalist (1915–22), with a focus on linguistic poetics; functional-structuralist (1923–39), with a focus on Saussurean semiology reinterpreted as general aesthetics; neurolinguistic (1940–56), with a focus on phonology and the problems of aphasia; and structuralist-semiotic (1957–82), with a focus on semiotics as a universal science of communication via sign systems. The goals Jakobson pursued in his latest period were ambitious: finding a common approach to works of literature and non-verbal arts and, more broadly, to all cultural activities; the search for linguistic and mental universals; a synthesis of humanities and natural sciences; and studying language and culture as means of human communication.

In addition to dynamism and interdisciplinarity, Lotman highlighted yet another prominent feature of Jakobson's intellectual activities – his ability to connect people, propose new ideas, launch unexpected research programmes:

> I happened to read medical papers which assert that talent is a disease. Looking at the creative path of R. O. Jakobson, I would like to say that this is an infectious disease. Wherever the difficult fate of a mid-twentieth-century man took him, everywhere Jakobson attracted a group of scholars that soon grew into a scientific centre of global importance. (Lotman [1983] 2003: 75)

When still a student in Moscow, Jakobson was one of the founders of and active participants in both the Moscow Linguistic Circle (officially established in 1915) and OPOIaZ (semi-officially established in 1916). In 1920, Jakobson left Russia for Prague, where he participated in the founding of the Prague Linguistic Circle (in 1926) and was the first to use the term 'structuralism' to mark the new methods in the study of language and literature (Jakobson 1929b; 1929c). He became one of the leading proponents of Prague dynamic functionalism, which revised some Saussurean principles, such as the opposition of synchrony and diachrony (Tynianov and Jakobson [1928] 2019: 280; Havránek et al. 1929: 7–8; Jakobson 1929a). When in 1939 Hitler invaded Czechoslovakia, Jakobson (who was of Jewish origin) escaped to Scandinavia. There, he became associated with the Linguistic Circle of Copenhagen that Louis Hjelmslev had founded in 1931, following the example of the Prague Linguistic Circle, and then, when working in Sweden, turned to the study of language acquisition in children and aphasia from the point of view of linguistics (Jakobson [1941] 1968). In 1941, Jakobson managed to get to the United States, which became his homeland, although for many decades he made almost yearly visits to Europe, frequently visited the Soviet Union attending conferences in Russia, Estonia, and Georgia and at least sometimes pondered the possibility of returning to his original home city, Moscow.

In New York, along with several other linguists of the École Libre des Hautes Études (ELHE), where Jakobson also worked for some years, he became one of the founders of the Linguistic Circle of New York in 1943 (Toman 1995: 245–50, 298–9; Pilshchikov 2019: 40–1). Claude Lévi-Strauss, who attended Jakobson's lectures at ELHE (Lotman (1990: 225) called their meeting 'historic'), was excited by Jakobson's innovative approaches in linguistics and transferred this methodology to the study of social structures (see Chapter 7). It was also in the United States that Jakobson discovered for himself the American logician and semiotician Charles S. Peirce, whose works exerted a great influence on his understanding of the semiotic nature of language and communication. It was mainly thanks to Jakobson, who repeatedly evoked Peirce in his works that the latter became known in the field of linguistics and other humanities (Jakobson 1965a; 1977). Jakobson summed up his research evolution in the 'Retrospect' postscripts included in each volume of his multivolume *Selected Writings* as well as in the Jakobson–Pomorska *Dialogues* ([1980] 1983).

Lotman, who for the greater part of his life lived in the peripheral town of Tartu in (Soviet) Estonia, appears at first sight to have lived on a much smaller scale than Jakobson, who crossed continents, fled countries and created influential scholarly groups and associations, as it would seem, at the sweep of his hand. Nevertheless, like Jakobson, Lotman was a connecting figure for a large group of scholars who later became known as the Tartu-Moscow School of Semiotics (henceforward referred to as TMS; see also Chapter 6). Also like Jakobson, Lotman was a scholar of enormous erudition and scope, with his research interests ranging from the topic of card games in Russian literature to culture as a collective intellect, and much more.

There are a number of additional intersecting points in the lives of Lotman and Jakobson as well as a certain congeniality in their ways of thinking. One of the most important influences on both Jakobson and Lotman came from Russian formalism, although in somewhat different guises (see Chapter 3). While Jakobson himself was one of the leading Russian formalists, Lotman, who was twenty-six years younger, had several former members of the formalist associations, such as Boris Eikhenbaum, Boris Tomashevsky and Viktor Zhirmunsky, as his university professors. Both Lotman and Jakobson were influenced by Ferdinand de Saussure's legacy and to a certain extent overcame the constraints of Saussurean linguistics and semiology (see Chapter 2). While Lotman agreed with Jakobson's criticism of some of Saussure's ideas, such as the identification of synchronic relations as static (Lotman [1974] 1978: 19), he emphasized the continuing heuristic value of Saussure's opposition between diachrony and synchrony (Lotman 1967a: 94; 1987: 14; 1990: 5–6). By the end of the 1950s, both Jakobson and Lotman became interested in the developments of information theory and cybernetics and the possibilities these areas seemed to promise for the study of language and poetics. While both researchers were first and foremost philologists – scholars of language and literature – they were both convinced of the necessity of the semiotic study of other communication systems besides human language and verbal art. Jakobson repeatedly drew attention to the fact that 'all five senses carry semiotic functions in human society' (Jakobson [1968] 1971: 701) and that 'the study of communication must distinguish between homogeneous messages which use a single semiotic system and syncretic messages based on a combination or merger of different sign patterns' (Jakobson [1968] 1971: 705). Lotman conceived of the summer school of semiotics and the semiotic journal *Trudy po znakovym sistemam* as venues devoted primarily to 'extralinguistic' semiotic systems (see Lotman's letters to Vyacheslav Ivanov of 1964 in Lotman 1997: 647–8).

It may seem somewhat puzzling that two scholars of different generations, living on different continents and on different sides of the Iron Curtain, could have been so similar in their thinking and scholarly interests. The strangeness is even more pronounced considering that there are not even many traces of mail correspondence between Lotman and Jakobson: in Lotman's archives, kept at Tartu University Library and the Juri Lotman Semiotic Repository at Tallinn University, there are only a couple of postcards from Jakobson to Lotman and a few letters written to Lotman and his wife Zara Mints by Krystyna Pomorska, Jakobson's wife. The key to this puzzle seems to lie in the fact that the 'communication system' in use involved a whole network of means to overcome the communication barriers, including common elements in the scholars' background, their actual meetings, occasional letters, publications sent (with warm inscriptions on the off-prints) and avidly read, acquaintances who helped to get publications from one participant to another, greetings conveyed through mutual friends, and so forth.

Jakobson and Lotman: Elective affinities

Jakobson influenced Lotman's research in several fields. To begin with, he was a prominent scholar of Russia's most celebrated medieval epic, *Slovo o Polku Igoreve* (The Tale of Igor's Campaign). Lotman's analysis of the words 'honour' and 'glory' in the *Tale* (Lotman 1967b) is based on Jakobson's scholarly reconstruction of the text (Jakobson 1948a) and, in particular, on his conjecture about the correct reading of its concluding phrase:

'Glory to the princes, and [honour] to the retinue.'[1] In a later article devoted to this epic, Jakobson called Lotman's analysis an 'apt interpretation' (Jakobson [1973] 1985: 322). In the long-standing debate on the origin of the *Tale*, Lotman, like Jakobson, also supported the text's authenticity. Lotman fully accepted Jakobson's critique of the sceptic André Mazon, who considered the *Tale* an eighteenth-century literary hoax, and supplemented Jakobson's (1948b) linguistic counterarguments with culturological counterarguments, having demonstrated that the *Tale*'s aesthetic and ideology contradicts eighteenth-century taste (Lotman 1962). At the beginning of this century, Jakobson's argumentation was confirmed and supplemented by Andrei Zalizniak, an outstanding linguist and TMS member, who determinately proved the authenticity of the *Tale* (Zalizniak 2008).

Needless to say, Lotman – who was a superb scholar of Russia's greatest poet Alexander Pushkin – knew the work of Jakobson the Pushkinist. Jakobson's seminal article on the symbolism of statue in Pushkin was published in 1937 in Czech, but became widely known later, when it was translated into French (1973) and then into English (1975). The article aims to identify the 'invariable components or constants' of Pushkin's 'multiform symbolism', that is, the semantic 'invariants' characteristic of the poetics of one author or a particular group of his/her texts (Jakobson [1937] 1975: 1–2). Jakobson defined 'poetic mythology' as a system of these invariable constituents.

Lotman added a cultural dimension to Jakobson's description of 'the poet's individual mythology'. In 'The Symbol as Plot-Gene', he posed the problem of the relationship between individual and traditional symbolism:

> A poet's symbolic 'alphabet' is not just an individual matter: a poet may draw symbols from the arsenal of epoch, cultural trend or social circle. A symbol is bound to cultural memory [. . .] But it is the *system of relationships* which the poet establishes *between* the fundamental image-symbols which is the crucial thing. Symbols are always polysemic, and only when they form themselves into the crystal grid [*kristallicheskaia reshetka*] of mutual connections do they create that 'poetic world' which marks the individuality of each artist. (Lotman 1990: 86–7, original emphasis)[2]

In the mid-1950s, Jakobson was extensively engaged in theoretical problems of grammar. After his groundbreaking article on shifters (indexical elements of language) and verbal categories (Jakobson [1957] 1971; an article which was also frequently cited by Lotman), Jakobson raised the question of the significance of grammatical categories for poetics. Grammatical categories precondition the structure of any utterance, but in poetry they have an additional 'compositional function' (Jakobson and Pomorska [1980] 1983: 112). A milestone for post-war structuralism, the proceedings of the Warsaw congress *Poetics. Poetyka. Poetika* (1961), featured an article, the very title of which marked a new approach to the analysis of poetic texts: 'Grammar of Poetry and Poetry of Grammar' (Jakobson [1961] 1987). This article, first in this series examining the relationship of sound and grammar to poetic semantics, contains an analysis of two poems by Pushkin. The next work done in this vein was 'Charles Baudelaire's "Les Chats"' co-authored with

Lévi-Strauss ([1962] 1987). It was followed by grammatical analyses of several dozen poetic masterpieces in various languages 'selected from a great many poetic traditions of the last thirteen centuries' (Jakobson and Pomorska [1980] 1983: 113). These studies are collected in the third volume of Jakobson's *Selected Writings* (1981). For Lotman and other TMS participants, the very first, Pushkinian, article was of the utmost importance.

Jakobson provided a framework for the TMS's view of 'the artistic significance of grammatical forms in a poetic text, as well as to other examples in art where a text's formal elements are semanticized' (Lotman [1970] 1977: 17). 'Grammatical categories, as Roman Jakobson indicated, express relational meanings in poetry. It is these categories which [. . .] create a model of the poet's vision of the world, a structure of subject-object relations' (Lotman [1970] 1977: 164). Lotman pointed out that Jakobson's study was significant not only for the poetics of verbal texts but also for semiotics in general because 'the artistic function of grammatical categories is equivalent in certain respects to the play of geometric structure in spatial forms of art' (Lotman [1970] 1977: 158).

Another aspect of Jakobson's grammatical theories of the 1950s and 1960s was a functional similarity of pronouns and proper nouns. Lotman elaborated on these issues in a seminal work of cultural semiotics, 'Myth – Name – Culture', co-authored with Boris Uspenskij (Lotman and Uspenskij [1973] 1976).

Lotman ([1967] 2018: 235) considered Tynianov and Jakobson pioneers of the structural-functional approach to literature, whose work was continued by Jan Mukařovský and other representatives of the Prague School (Lotman [1968] 2018: 180–4; [1970] 1994; [1971] 2018: 240). The difference between structural elements is not material but functional. The function of any element of any structure, either linguistic or literary, is meaning-differentiation. It follows from this that the same material element 'acquires different meanings depending on which system of oppositions we include it in' (Lotman 1967a: 97). Following Jakobson, Lotman thought of these differences as of dichotomies (binary oppositions) rather than, for example, trichotomies (as in Peirce's semiotics). According to this view, any polynomial opposition can be reduced to a set of binary oppositions, and these oppositions are privative ('A vs –A' type) rather than equipollent ('A vs B' type).

Jakobson ([1973] 1990: 321) argued that 'binarism is essential; without it the structure of language would be lost': linguistic units, such as phonemes, are bound together by a system of binary oppositions (Jakobson [1976] 1990; see Chandler 2007: 90–3). Jakobson and Nikolai Trubetzkoy developed a method of analysis of binary oppositions for phonology, and then Jakobson extrapolated it to the analysis of various levels of the text, including the semantic level (Pomorska 1987: 5). In his manifesto of literary structuralism, 'Literary Studies Should Be a Science', Lotman calls binarism 'an effective means of constructing models of various structures' and compares Trubetzkoy's and Jakobson's approaches with such fundamentals of cognition as Hegel's 'Einheit der Gegensätze', Darwin's 'principle of antithesis' and Saussure's 'mécanisme linguistique des identités et des différences' (Lotman 1967a: 98).

In his early *Lectures on Structural Poetics* and the 1967 article, Lotman even attempted to introduce the concept of an 'archiseme' using the model of Trubetzkoy's 'archiphoneme'

(Lotman 1964: 102–3; 1967a: 98). Although in later versions of Lotmanian poetics this particular idea was given less prominence, in both the theoretical and practical sections of Lotman's *Analysis of the Poetic Text* ([1972] 1976) the Jakobsonian analysis of binary oppositions is consistently referred to and applied.

Jakobson's idea of 'frustrated (reader's) expectations' as the foundational principle of art (Jakobson 1960: 363, 366) was also inherited by Lotmanian poetics:

> Structural analysis assumes that the artistic device is not a material element of the text but a relationship. There exists a difference in principle between the absence of rhyme, on the one hand, in verse that does not yet imply the possibility of its existence (for example, ancient poetry, Russian bylina verse, etc.) or in verse having already rejected it so that the absence of rhyme enters into the readers' expectation, into the aesthetic norm of that kind of art (for example, contemporary *vers libre*), and, on the other hand, its absence in verse that incorporates rhyme into the characteristic features of the poetic text. In the first case, the absence of rhyme is not an artistically significant element; in the second, the absence of rhyme is the presence of non-rhyme, of minus-rhyme. In the epoch when the reader's consciousness, raised in the poetic school of Zhukovsky, Batiushkov, and the young Pushkin, identified Romantic poetics with the very concept of poetry, the artistic system of [Pushkin's] 'Anew, I visited . . .' ('Vnov' ia posetil . . .') produced an impression not of the absence of 'devices' but of their maximal saturation. But these were 'minus-devices', a system of consistent and conscious rejections felt by the reader. (Lotman [1972] 1976: 22–3; cf. an earlier version of the same passage in Lotman 1964: 51)

Another source of Lotman's concept of 'minus-device' was Tynianov's 'minus-sign' (literally, 'negative sign': *otritsatel'nyi priznak*) (Tynianov [1924] 2019: 157; see Chapter 3), Jakobson's concept of 'zero sign' (Jakobson [1939] 1971; see Tchougounnikov 2004) and the notion of a 'hole' as a functional entity in contemporary molecular physics (Lotman 1964: 59; see M. Lotman 1998: 683–4). Lotman's innovation is quite in the spirit of Tynianov and Jakobson themselves: 'minus-device' presupposes subtraction or negation, rather than plain absence; it is not a passive 'zero' but an active 'minus' (M. Lotman 1998: 684).

Lotman was not only a follower of Jakobson: he offered a revision of some of Jakobson's most important postulates. In his seminal 'Linguistics and Poetics', Jakobson identified six 'constitutive factors' of the act of communication: the addresser, the addressee, a code, a message, a context and a contact (Jakobson 1960: 353). Lotman adds emphasis to the difference of the grammar/code of the sender and the receiver of information. Jakobson himself (1961: 249–50) highlighted this difference; Boris Uspenskij (1967) soon recognized its fundamental significance for linguistics and semiotics, and other members of the TMS accepted this view. In *The Structure of the Artistic Text*, Lotman refers to Jakobson, who 'is correct in asserting that in the process of transmitting information, not one, but in fact two codes are employed, the one for encoding and the other for decoding the message' (Lotman [1970] 1977: 13, cf. 24; Lotman [1989] 2019: 84). In Lotman's 'Autocommunication: "I" and "Other" as Addressees', this difference is conceptualized as a precondition of self-communication (Lotman 1990: 20–2): although the sender and the receiver are the same person, they are not identical to each other and their languages are different. Therefore, autocommunication becomes a basic example of internal polyglotism of any semiotic system (M. Lotman 2002: 16–17; 2019: 258).

As the next step, Lotman offered a fundamental revision of Jakobson's schema of communication (see Pilshchikov 2016; 2021). First of all, unlike code, language has a history: 'language contains not only code, but also the history of code' (Lotman 1964: 48). Hence the intrinsic diachronicity of any synchronicity, of which Jakobson wrote, and the heterogeneity of language as opposed to the homogeneity of the code. Furthermore, in addition to the common 'macrohistory', language has an individual history – or rather, many individual histories: we all possess a unique version of a common language (our own idiolect). The act of communication thus becomes an act of translation from the speaker's idiolect to the listener's idiolect. As a result, the unity of communication factors envisioned by the theory is lost. Or, as Lotman put it:

> For [Jakobson], the essence of the communication process is that a certain message is transmitted from the sender to the receiver as a result of coding and decoding. The very basis of the act is that the receiver gets the same message [. . .] as the sender transmitted. A violation of adequacy acts as a defect in the functioning of the communication chain. (Lotman 1977: 7–8)

The idea that there exists content that precedes the message (and is thus independent of the message) is wrong:

> According to Ju. M. Lotman, the act of communication is by no means the transmission of a ready-made message: it is not only language that cannot exist before and outside text – the same holds about all the other components of Jakobson's scheme. Context is co-text (con-text), it cannot exist before text, and like every text is dependent on context, context is also dependent on text. The act of communication is an act of translation, an act of transformation: text transforms language and the addressee, it establishes contact between the addresser and the addressee, it even transforms the addresser. Moreover, text transforms itself and ceases to be identical to itself. (M. Lotman [1995] 2000: 27–8; cf. 2002: 16)

But if any communication is translation, a paradox arises: on the one hand, meaning is revealed or even formed only in the process of translation; on the other hand, any translation transforms the original meaning and generates a new one. Meaning turns out to be unequal to itself, incessantly transformed in the process of signification and resignification (semiosis).

Whereas Jakobson characterizes semiotic systems as having complete 'mutual translatability' (Jakobson 1959: 234) and 'interprets "untranslatability" as an obstacle to communication, which can be eliminated by certain procedures, Lotman sees in the phenomenon of untranslatability (or, more precisely, complicated translatability) a creative mechanism of culture' (Avtonomova 2009: 259). From the aforementioned follows the fundamental polyglotism of any act of communication (Avtonomova 2008: 551) and, eventually, polyglotism of culture.

Lotman and Jakobson: Encounters and crossings

It is difficult to say how many times Lotman and Jakobson met in person during Jakobson's seven visits to the USSR (in 1956, 1958, 1962, 1964, 1966, 1967 and 1979). He is not even mentioned in Lotman's letters written during and after the Fourth Congress of Slavists held in Moscow in 1958, where Jakobson played one of the leading roles. The best-documented instance of their meeting is that of the second summer school in Kääriku, a small place close to Tartu, held between 16 and 26 August 1966, in which also Jakobson and Pomorska participated. This episode is recorded in the memoirs of Vyacheslav Ivanov (1999), who travelled to Kääriku together with the Jakobsons.[3] Ivanov recalls that Jakobson and Pomorska were very eager to attend the summer school, although this was not an easy task to accomplish since due to the military airbase on the outskirts of Tartu, foreigners' entrance to the town was allowed only with special permission. Jakobson and Pomorska first applied for permission in Moscow, but were denied; they then reapplied in Leningrad and received permission. When they were already in Tallinn, the local KGB detained them for two days for the purpose of rechecking their documents. When Ivanov, Jakobson and Pomorska finally arrived at the summer school, it had already started, but Jakobson joined in with great vigour. Ivanov remarks that Jakobson offered his comments after almost every presentation. This is also confirmed by Boris Uspenskij:

> Speaking of our foreign colleagues, it is important to name R. O. Jakobson – he read and appreciated our works and was very interested in them (as for us, we all knew his publications and learned from them). When he came to Tartu [and Kääriku], he took the floor after every presentation and attended meetings from morning till night. (Trunin 2016)

The memoirists' observations are supported by one of the two extant postcards from Jakobson to Lotman. The card is sent from Warsaw and is dated 21 September 1966, that is, about a month after the summer school, and contains the names of (some of) the participants. The message on the card is laconic: 'Participated in the discussion after the presentations of Serebrianyi, Ivanov–Toporov, Lekomtsev, Lekomtseva (both presentations), Uspenskij, Toporov, Nekliudov, Karpinskaia, Paducheva, Ogibenin, Ivanov. In the discussion after my presentation participated Levin, Segal, Revzin, Lotman, Ivanov, and Lesskis' (Tartu University Library, F135, s.1698).

Ivanov recalls the special atmosphere of the summer school:

> An unusual session took place in the evening at the fireplace, when Roman [Jakobson] and Petr Grigorievich Bogatyrev reminisced of their early activities in the Moscow Linguistic Circle. During more than a half a century, Russian humanities had continued to develop in one direction, without interruption, despite all the turns of history. The fact of that evening itself held a miracle: knowledge kept coming through despite all the prohibitions. But neither of the two speakers displayed any pompous solemnity. [. . .] Discussions about art and science continued during walks in the woods, joint meals at the dormitory cafeteria and other activities. We sang 'Gaudeamus igitur . . . '. In Roman's apartment my birthday was celebrated during which Roman as a cheerful host treated everybody to sweets. (Ivanov 1999: 243–4)

The letter dated 26 November 1967 (i.e. more than a year after the summer school of 1966), addressed to Lotman and Mints and signed by Krystyna Pomorska, includes the latter's warm response to the summer school:

> In the letter, I'd like to convey as lively as possible my deep gratitude and appreciation to you both for all the care, hospitality and such an abundance of intelligent, invigorating air that empowered us both [= Pomorska and Jakobson] at your conference. We talk about it and recall it all the time. Besides wonderful and interesting scientific conversations, everything was excellent also because of the selection of people present along with the prevailing atmosphere of scientific discipline and friendliness, devoid of any pretentiousness, and strive to arrive at scientific truth. (Tartu University Library, F135, s. Bp1147; translation by Taras Boyko)

One of the most important differences between Lotman and Jakobson, related to their intellectual temperaments and research agendas, was recorded by Ivanov, who recalled their meeting in Kääriku:

> Along with me [i.e. Vyacheslav Ivanov], Jakobson proposed analyses of texts of certain genres as well as work on methods of description and recording of obtained results. Lotman insisted on broader and more general theoretical projects. Iurii Levin noted that [Lotman and Jakobson] represented two different approaches. [. . .] [Jakobson] was attracted to constructs bridged with natural sciences and mathematics. In this sense, he was in tune with our semioticians like [Iurii] Lekomtsev. (Ivanov 1999: 243; translation by Taras Boyko, modified)

While interest in precise and mathematical methods in application to the study of language and literature was not foreign to Lotman, and Jakobson, in his turn, did not shy away from making broad generalizations, the differences that Ivanov registers remind us of Lotman's own retrospective remarks ([1995] 2014: 77) on the relations between the different strands of the TMS: orientation towards complex models (Tartu scholars) versus simple models (Moscow scholars). Lotman explains that just as we cannot obtain a calf if we put together lots of veal cutlets, we cannot arrive at a holistic phenomenon of culture by summing up simple texts, and concludes: 'Complex systems require complex models' (Lotman [1990] 1991: 91).

Another notable difference between Lotman and Jakobson lies in their attitude to the 'founding fathers' of semiotics, Saussure and Peirce (see M. Lotman 2002: 11–12). Jakobson was more critical of certain Saussurean principles than Lotman, while Lotman, who was certainly familiar with the main ideas of Peirce, never became as active a proponent of the American semiotician as Jakobson. Lotman preferred Saussure's more holistic view which gave preference to the system, to the whole – to that 'semiotic space outside of which semiosis cannot exist' (Lotman [1984] 2005: 208). At the same time, Lotman accepted both Jakobson's critique of Saussure's principle of arbitrariness of the linguistic sign and Jakobson's concept of iconism (Lotman 1990: 17–18, 222), which was to a great extent an elaboration on, and reinterpretation of Peirce's classification of signs (Liszka 1981; Eco 1987; Gvoždiak 2017).

In the very first chapter of *Universe of the Mind*, Lotman refers to Jakobson's 'Quest for the Essence of Language' and points out that, in this article, 'Jakobson makes an exceedingly subtle analysis of the features of iconism inherent in the language of everyday usage, i.e. the presence of artistic potential in language as such' (Lotman 1990: 18). In chapters 3 and 4 of the same book, Lotman elaborates on the idea of iconism and also accepts and develops another fundamental idea of Jakobson: that of the dichotomy of metaphor (similarity) and metonymy (contiguity) in the organization of any cultural text. According to Jakobson, two linguistic axes – the metaphorical axis and the metonymical axis – are associated with the opposition of two types of artistic speech (poetry and prose), two types of artistic attitude (lyric and epic), two types of literary trend (metaphor predominates in romanticism and symbolism, whereas metonymy prevails in realism) and two types of speech disorder in aphasia (Jakobson 1935; [1941] 1968). In 'Linguistics and Poetics', Jakobson suggested describing the functioning of poetic language as a specific interaction of the metaphorical and metonymical axes (i.e. those of similarity and contiguity), which he identified with the two types of structural relationship underlying the operations of selection and combination performed in text construction: '*The poetic function projects the principle of equivalence from the axis of selection into the axis of combination.* Equivalence is promoted to the constitutive device of the sequence', and 'similarity is superimposed on contiguity' (Jakobson 1960: 358, 371, original emphasis). Thus, according to Jacobson, the poetic function builds sequences (syntagmatics, a combination *in praesentia*) on the principles of equivalents (paradigmatics, a selection and substitution in absentia) (Lotman 1990: 39).

In Lotman's article 'Literary Structuralism', which was commissioned by *Kratkaia literaturnaia entsiklopediia* (The Concise Literary Encyclopaedia) in the late 1960s but remained unpublished in Lotman's lifetime due to censorship (see Pilshchikov 2012; 2015;

Pilshchikov and Trunin 2018), he described this thesis as Jakobson's main contribution to text analysis:

> The procedure of text description involves distinguishing the paradigmatic and syntagmatic axes. The former defines a set of possible structural elements and types of their relations (a system), the latter produces sequences (a text). The dialectics of the relationship of these axes in the poetic text was revealed by R. Jakobson. (Lotman [1967] 2018: 233–4)

Lotman refers to this definition in *The Structure of the Artistic Text* (Lotman [1970] 1977: 78, 86) and uses it for interpreting grammatical meanings in poetry in *Analysis of the Poetic Text* (Lotman [1972] 1976: 72–3).

Since the projection of one axis onto another in the poetic text transforms syntagmatic relations into paradigmatic ones, Lotman puts an equation mark between Jakobson's formula and Tynianov's celebrated principle of 'the unity and density of the verse series' (Tynianov [1924] 1981: 57–63), according to which syntactic relations in a poetic line are perceived as semantic relations (Lotman [1970] 1977: 86). This insightful interpretation seems to remain unnoticed by the historians of ideas in the humanities.

Ivanov (1999: 248) writes that Lotman asked him several times to request Jakobson to co-sign the 'Theses on the Semiotic Study of Cultures' that were written together by Lotman, Ivanov, Toporov, Uspenskij and Piatigorsky ([1973] 2013). A precedent text and generic model for this important self-statement were the 1929 'Theses' of the Prague Linguistic Circle (see Chapter 7) and, possibly, the no-less-celebrated 1935 'Theses', in which the problems of dynamism of structure were discussed (Havránek et al. 1929; 1935). Jakobson co-authored both, and his participation in the 1973 Theses would have had not only practical but also symbolic significance. However, he never responded to the repeated requests in any way.

Overall, nevertheless, Lotman and Jakobson always remained supportive and respectful of each other. Jakobson's preface to Tzvetan Todorov's anthology of Russian Formalist writings in French translation ends with praise for 'the young researchers from Moscow, Leningrad and Tartu' (Jakobson 1965b: 13). In the 1973 'Postscriptum' to *Questions de poétique*, Jakobson named Lotman among the creators of the grammar of poetry who are equally apt in linguistic and literary analysis (Jakobson 1973: 487). He also contributed an article to the Festschrift dedicated to Lotman's sixtieth birthday, in which he famously called Lotman 'farsighted to the degree of clairvoyance' (Jakobson 1984: 65).

In his obituary for Roman Jakobson, Lotman wrote:

> Looking at the destiny of scholars who entered science at the same time as Jakobson, we can often notice how the youthful romanticism of scientific ideas became over the years replaced – either by free will or conditioned by situation – with scientific classicism, dry decent academicism, sometimes simply with tiredness [. . .]. Jakobson never got old, never tired, never became 'decent'; he was and

remained a rebel in science – a revolutionary who irritates, creates turmoil, does not settle for common, domesticated ideas but leads us into the storm of new, uncommon, stunning thoughts and hypotheses. (Lotman [1983] 2003: 75, compare Avtonomova 2015)

Jakobson did not live to see the last decade of Lotman's life nor witness the developments of his thinking. It can be assumed, however, that he would have been very interested in Lotman's ideas of unpredictability, of explosive and gradual changes in culture. Like Jakobson, Lotman remained mentally young and agile until the end of his life. Now it is up to those who come after to continue the dialogue with the rich legacy of both scholars.[4]

Notes

1. The only extant Old Russian text reads, literally: 'Glory to the princes and the retinue. Amen.'
2. Written in 1985.
3. Taras Boyko (2021) gives an account of Jakobson's and Pomorska's visit to Kääriku and compares Ivanov's memoirs with those by Boris Egorov, Alexander Zholkovsky and Mihhail Lotman.
4. This chapter was written with the support of the Estonian Research Council (PRG319).

References

Avtonomova, N. S. 2008. *Poznanie i perevod: Opyty filosofii iazyka*, Moscow: ROSSPEN.
Avtonomova, N. S. 2009. *Otkrytaia struktura: Iakobson – Bakhtin – Lotman – Gasparov*, Moscow: ROSSPEN.
Avtonomova, N. S. 2015. 'Lotman i Jakobson: mezhdu "urokom" i "ekzamenom"'. *Vestnik RGGU. Seriia: Literaturovedenie. Iazykoznanie. Kul'turologiia* 7: 11–27.
Boyko, T. 2021. 'Roman Jakobson and Estonia', in E. Sütiste, R. Gramigna, J. Griffin and S. Salupere (eds), *Re-considering Roman Jakobson*, 241–54, Tartu: Tartu University Press.
Chandler, D. 2007. *Semiotics: The Basics*, 2nd edn, London and New York: Routledge.
Eco, U. 1987. 'The Influence of Roman Jakobson on the Development of Semiotics', in M. Krampen, K. Oehler, R. Posner and T. A. Sebeok (eds), *Classics of Semiotics*, 109–28, New York: Plenum.
Gvoždiak, V. 2017. 'Jakobson and Peirce: Deep Misunderstanding, or Creative Innovation?', in M. Švantner and V. Gvoždiak (eds), *How to Make Our Signs Clear: C. S. Peirce and Semiotics*, 106–18, Leiden and Boston: Brill-Rodopi.
Havránek, B., Jakobson, R., Mathesius, V., Mukařovský, J., Trnka, B. et al. 1929. 'Thèses', in *Mélanges linguistiques dédiés au Premier Congrès des philologues slaves*, vol. 1 of *Travaux du Cercle Linguistique de Prague*, 5–29, Prague: Jednota československých matematiků a fysiků.
Havránek, B., Jakobson, R., Mathesius, V., Mukařovský, J. and Trnka, B. 1935. 'Úvodem', *Slovo a slovesnost* 1 (1): 1–7.
Ivanov, V. V. 1999. 'Buria nad Newfoundlandom: iz vosmpominanii o Romane Jakobsone', in H. Baran and S. Gindin (eds), *Roman Jakobson: Teksty, dokumenty, issledovania*, 219–53, Moscow: RGGU. [A slightly abriged version was published as 'O Romane Jakobsone (Glavy iz vosmpominanii)', *Zvezda* 7 (1999): 139–64.]

Jakobson, R. 1929a. *Remarques sur l'évolution phonologique du russe compare à celle des autres langues slaves, vol. 2 of Travaux du Cercle Linguistique de Prague*, Prague: Jednota československých matematiků a fysiků.

Jakobson, R. 1929b. 'Romantické všeslovanství – nová slavistika', *Čin* 1 (31 October): 10–12.

Jakobson, R. 1929c. 'Über die heutigen Voraussetzungen der russischen Slavistik', *Slavische Rundschau* 1 (8): 629–46.

Jakobson, R. 1935. 'Randbemerkungen zur Prosa des Dichters Pasternak', *Slavische Rundschau* 7 (6): 357–74.

Jakobson, R. 1937. 'Socha v symbolice Puškinově', *Slovo a slovesnost* 3 (1): 2–24.

Jakobson, R. [1937] 1973. 'La statue dans la symbolique de Pouchkine', trans. M. Derrida, in R. Jakobson, *Questions de poétique*, ed. T. Todorov, 152–89, Paris: Seuil.

Jakobson, R. [1937] 1975. 'The Statue in Puškin's Poetic Mythology', in R. Jakobson, *Puškin and His Sculptural Myth*, trans. and ed. J. Burbank, 1–44, The Hague and Paris: Mouton.

Jakobson [1939] 1971. 'Signe zéro', in R. Jakobson, *Selected Writings, vol. 2: Word and Language*, 211–19, The Hague and Paris: Mouton.

Jakobson, R. [1941] 1968. *Child Language, Aphasia and Phonological Universals*, trans. A. R. Keiler, The Hague and Paris: Mouton.

Jakobson, R. 1948a. 'Essai de reconstruction du *Slovo* dans sa langue originelle', in *La Geste du prince Igor', épopée russe du douzième siècle,* texte établi, traduit et commenté sous la direction d'H. Grégoire, de R. Jakobson et de M. Szeftel, 150–78, New York: Rausen Brothers.

Jakobson, R. 1948b. 'L'authenticité du *Slovo*', in *La Geste du prince Igor', épopée russe du douzième siècle,* texte établi, traduit et commenté sous la direction d'H. Grégoire, de R. Jakobson et de M. Szeftel, 235–360, 363–80, New York: Rausen Brothers.

Jakobson, R. 1957. 'Shifters, Verbal Categories, and the Russian Verb', in R. Jakobson, *Selected Writings, vol. 2: Word and Language*, 130–47, The Hague and Paris: Mouton.

Jakobson, R. 1959. 'On Linguistic Aspects of Translation', in R. A. Brower (ed.), *On Translation*, 232–9, Cambridge, MA: Harvard University Press.

Jakobson, R. 1960. 'Linguistics and Poetics', in T. A. Sebeok (ed.), *Style in Language*, 350–77, Cambridge, MA: MIT Press.

Jakobson, R. 1961. 'Linguistics and Communication Theory', in *Structure of Language and Its Mathematical Aspects*, vol. 12 of Proceedings of Symposia in Applied Mathematics, 245–52, Providence, RI: American Mathematical Society.

Jakobson, R. [1961] 1987. 'Grammar of Poetry and Poetry of Grammar', in R. Jakobson, *Language in Literature*, eds K. Pomorska and S. Rudy, 121–44, Cambridge, MA, and London: The Belknap Press of Harvard University Press.

Jakobson, R. 1965a. 'Quest for the Essence of Language', *Diogenes* 51: 21–37.

Jakobson, R. 1965b. 'Vers une science de l'art poétique', in *Théorie de la littérature: Textes des Formalistes russes*, ed. and trans. T. Todorov, 9–13, Paris: Seuil.

Jakobson, R. [1968] 1971. 'Language in Relation to Other Communication Systems', in R. Jakobson, *Selected Writings, vol. 2: Word and Language*, 697–708, The Hague and Paris: Mouton.

Jakobson, R. 1973. 'Postscriptum' in R. Jakobson, *Questions de poétique*, ed. T. Todorov, 485–504, Paris: Seuil.

Jakobson, R. [1973] 1985. 'When a Falcon Has Molted', in R. Jakobson, *Selected Writings, vol. 7: Contributions to Comparative Mythology. Studies in Linguistics and Philology, 1972–1982*, ed. S. Rudy, with a preface by L. R. Waugh, 321–31, Berlin, New York and Amsterdam: Mouton.

Jakobson, R. [1973] 1990. 'Some Questions of Meaning', in R. Jakobson, *On Language*, eds L. R. Waugh and M. Monville-Burston, 315–23, Cambridge, MA: Harvard University Press.

Jakobson, R. [1976] 1990. 'The Concept of Phoneme', in R. Jakobson, *On Language*, eds L. R. Waugh and M. Monville-Burston, 217–41, Cambridge, MA: Harvard University Press.

Jakobson, R. 1977. 'A Few Remarks on Peirce, Pathfinder in the Science of Language', *MLN* 92 (5): 1026–32.

Jakobson, R. 1981. *Selected Writings, vol. 3: Grammar of Poetry and Poetry of Grammar*, ed. with a preface, by S. Rudy, The Hague, Paris and New York: Mouton.

Jakobson, R. 1984. 'Iz kommentariia k stikham Maiakovskogo "Tovarishchu Nette – parokhodu i cheloveku"', in M. Halle, K. Pomorska, L. Matejka and B. Uspenskij (eds), *Semiosis: Semiotics and the History of Culture. In Honorem Georgii Lotman*, 65–9, Ann Arbor: Michigan Slavic Publications.

Jakobson, R. and Lévi-Strauss, C. [1962] 1987. 'Charles Baudelaire's "Les Chats"', in R. Jakobson, *Language in Literature*, eds K. Pomorska and S. Rudy, 180–97, Cambridge, MA, and London: The Belknap Press of Harvard University Press.

Jakobson, R. and Pomorska, K. [1980] 1983. *Dialogues*, trans. C. Hubert, with a foreword by M. Halle, Cambridge, MA: MIT Press.

Liszka, J. 1981. 'Peirce and Jakobson: Towards a Structuralist Reconstruction of Peirce', *Transactions of the Charles S. Peirce Society* 17 (1): 41–61.

Lotman, Ju. M. 1962. '"Slovo o polku Igoreve" i literaturnaia traditsiia XVIII – nachala XIX v.', in D. S. Likhachev (ed.), *'Slovo o polku Igoreve' – pamiatnik XII veka*, 330–405, Moscow and Leningrad: AN SSSR.

Lotman, Ju. M. 1964. *Lektsii po struktural'noi poetike. Vyp. 1. Vvedenie, teoriia stikha*, Tartu: Izdatel'stvo Tartuskogo universiteta (*Trudy po znakovym sistemam*, 1).

Lotman, Ju. M. 1967a. 'Literaturovedenie dolzhno byt' naukoi', *Voprosy literatury* 1: 90–100.

Lotman, Ju. M. 1967b. 'Ob oppozitsii "chest" – slava" v svetskikh tekstakh Kievskogo perioda', *Trudy po znakovym sistemam* 3: 100–12.

Lotman, Ju. M. [1967] 2018. 'Strukturalizm v literaturovedenii. 1', in Ju. M. Lotman, *O strukturalizme. Raboty 1965–1970 godov*, ed. I. A. Pilshchikov, with N. V. Poselyagin and M. V. Trunin, 232–8, Tallinn: TLU Press.

Lotman, Ju. M. [1968] 2018. 'Sovremennye perspektivy semioticheskogo izucheniia iskusstva', in Ju. M. Lotman, *O strukturalizme. Raboty 1965–1970 godov*, ed. I. A. Pilshchikov, with N. V. Poselyagin and M. V. Trunin, 167–206, Tallinn: TLU Press.

Lotman, Ju. M. 1969. 'O nekotorykh printsipial'nykh trudnostiakh v strukturnom opisanii teksta', *Trudy po znakovym sistemam* 4: 478–82.

Lotman, Ju. M. [1970] 1977. *The Structure of the Artistic Text*, trans. G. Lenhoff and R. Vroon, Ann Arbor: University of Michigan, Department of Slavic Languages and Literatures.

Lotman, Ju. M. [1970] 1994. 'Jan Mukařovský – teoretik iskusstva', in J. Mukařovský, *Issledovaniia po estetike i teorii iskusstva*, trans. V. A. Kamenskaia, ed. with a commentary by Ju. M. Lotman and O. M. Malevich, preface by Ju. M. Lotman, 8–32, Moscow: Iskusstvo.

Lotman, Ju. M. [1971] 2018. 'Strukturalizm v literaturovedenii. 2', in Ju. M. Lotman, *O strukturalizme. Raboty 1965–1970 godov*, ed. I. A. Pilshchikov, with N. V. Poselyagin and M. V. Trunin, 238–44, Tallinn: TLU Press.

Lotman, Ju. M. [1972] 1976. *Analysis of the Poetic Text*, ed. and trans. D. Barton Johnson, Ann Arbor: Ardis.

Lotman, Ju. M. [1974] 1978. 'Dinamicheskaia model' semioticheskoi sistemy', *Trudy po znakovym sistemam* 10: 18–33.

Lotman, Ju. M. 1977. *Kul'tura kak kollektivnyi intellekt i problemy iskusstvennogo razuma*, Moscow: AN SSSR. Nauchnyi sovet po kompleksnoi probleme 'Kibernetika'.

Lotman, Ju. M. 1978. 'Dinamicheskaia model' semioticheskoi sistemy', *Trudy po znakovym sistemam* 10: 18–33.

Lotman, Ju. M. [1983] 2003. 'Poslednii ekzamen, poslednii urok . . . (Neskol'ko slov o Romane Osipoviche Jakobsone)', in Ju. M. Lotman, *Vospitanie dushi*, 74–7, Saint Petersburg: Iskusstvo–SPB.

Lotman, Ju. M. [1984] 2002. 'Nasledie Bakhtina i aktual'nye problemy semiotiki', trans. from the German by T. Semenova, in Ju. M. Lotman, *Istoriia i tipologiia russkoi kul'tury*, 147–56, Saint Petersburg: Iskusstvo–SPB.

Lotman, Ju. M. [1984] 2005. 'On the Semiosphere', trans. W. Clark, *Sign Systems Studies* 33 (1): 205–29.

Lotman, Ju. M. 1987. 'O problemakh i itogakh semioticheskikh issledovanii', *Trudy po znakovym sistemam* 20: 12–16.

Lotman, Ju. M. [1989] 2019. 'Culture as a Subject and Its Own Object', in J. Lotman, *Culture, Memory and History: Essays in Cultural Semiotics*, trans. B. J. Baer, ed. M. Tamm, 83–93, Cham: Palgrave Macmillan.

Lotman, Ju. M. 1990. *Universe of the Mind: A Semiotic Theory of Culture*, trans. A. Shukman, London and New York: I.B. Tauris.

Lotman, Ju. M. [1990] 1991. 'Zametki o tartuskikh semioticheskikh izdaniakh', in *Trudy po russkoi literature i semiotike Tartuskogo univetsiteta 1958–1990. Ukazateli soderzhania*, 89–92, Tartu: Tartuskii universitet.

Lotman, Ju. M. [1995] 2014. *Non-Memoirs*, trans. C. L. Brickman, Elmwood Park, IL: Dalkey Archive Press.

Lotman, Ju. M. 1997. *Pis'ma 1940–1993*, ed. B. F. Egorov, Moscow: Shkola 'Iazyki russkoi kul'tury'.

Lotman, Ju. M., Ivanov, V. V., Pjatigorskij, A. M., Toporov, V. N. and Uspenskij, B. A. [1973] 2013. 'Theses on the Semiotic Study of Cultures (as Applied to Slavic Texts)', in S. Salupere, P. Torop and K. Kull (eds), *Beginnings of the Semiotics of Culture*, 53–77, Tartu: University of Tartu Press.

Lotman, Ju. M. and Uspenskij, B. A. [1973] 1976. 'Myth – Name – Culture', in H. Baran (ed.), *Semiotics and Structuralism: Readings from the Soviet Union*, trans. W. Mandel, H. Baran and A. J. Hollander, 3–32, White Plains, NY: International Arts and Sciences Press.

Lotman, M. 1998. 'Struktural'naia poetika i ee mesto v nasledii Iu. M. Lotmana', in Ju. M. Lotman, *Ob iskusstve*, 675–86, Saint Petersburg: Iskusstvo–SPB.

Lotman, M. [1995] 2000. 'A Few Notes on the Philosophical Background of the Tartu School of Semiotics', *S: European Journal for Semiotic Studies* 12 (1): 23–46.

Lotman, M. 2002. 'Semiotika kul'tury v tartusko-moskovskoi semioticheskoi shkole. Predvaritel'nye zamechaniia', in Ju. M. Lotman, *Istoriia i tipologiia russkoi kul'tury*, 5–20, Saint Petersburg: Iskusstvo–SPB.

Lotman, M. 2019. '(Re)constructing the Drafts of Past', in J. Lotman, *Culture, Memory and History: Essays in Cultural Semiotics*, trans. B. J. Baer, ed. M. Tamm, 245–65, Cham: Palgrave Macmillan.

Pilshchikov, I. A. 2012. 'Nevyshedshaia stat'ia Iu. M. Lotmana "Strukturalizm v literaturovedenii"', *Russkaia literatura* 4: 46–69.

Pilshchikov, I. A. 2015. 'La perception de la poétique structurale en URSS à la fin des années 1960 et au début des années 1970 (Les avis des critiques internes de la Petite encyclopédie littéraire sur l'article non publié de Youri Lotman "Le structuralisme dans les études littéraires")', trans. M. Regamey and E. Velmezova, *Slavica Occitania* 40: 121–46.

Pilshchikov, I. A. 2016. 'Nepolnaia perevodimost' kak mekhanizm poznaniia i kommunikatsii', in V. V. Feshchenko (ed.), *Lingvistika i semiotika kulturnykh transferov: metody, printsipy, tekhnologii*, 203–33, Moscow: Kul'turnaia revoliutsiia.

Pilshchikov, I. A. 2019. 'Prazhskaia shkola na "perekrestke kultur" (O mnogoiazychii v nauchnoi perepiske i izdaniakh Prazhskogo lingvisticheskogo kruzhka)', *Rhema* 3: 25–52.

Pilshchikov, I. A. 2021. 'El esquema comunicativo de Roman Jakobson entre lenguas y continentes: historia cruzada del modelo teórico', trans. A. Belousova and S. Páramo, *Revista de Estudios Sociales* 77: 2–20.

Pilshchikov, I. A. 2022. 'Jakobson, Roman Osipovich', in A. A. Kholikov and O. A. Kling (eds), *Russkie literaturovedy XX veka: Biobibliograficheskii slovar'*, vol. 2, Moscow and Saint Petersburg: Nestor-Istoriia (forthcoming).

Pilshchikov, I. A. and Trunin, M. V. 2018. 'Stat'ia Iu. M. Lotmana o strukturalizme dlia "Kratkoi literaturnoi entsiklopedii" (istoriia nesostoiavsheisia publikatsii)', in Ju. M. Lotman, *O strukturalizme. Raboty 1965–1970 godov*, ed. I. A. Pilshchikov, with N. V. Poselyagin, and M. V. Trunin, 209–31, Tallinn: TLU Press.

Pomorska, K. 1987. 'Introduction', in R. Jakobson, *Language in Literature*, eds K. Pomorska and S. Rudy, 1–11, Cambridge, MA, and London: The Belknap Press of Harvard University Press.

Tchougounnikov, S. 2004. 'La notion de "signe zéro" dans la pensée formaliste et structuraliste russe (le cas de Roman Jakobson et Iouri Lotman)', *Slovo* 30/31: 327–43.

Toman, J. 1995. *The Magic of a Common Language: Jakobson, Mathesius, Trubetzkoy, and the Prague Linguistic Circle*, Cambridge, MA: MIT Press.

Trunin, M. 2016. '"...takoe iavlenie prirody: utverzhdayet, chto Boga net, khotia sam kak angel": Boris Uspenskij i Mihhail Lotman o semiotike i sovetskom nauchnom byte', *Colta*, 6 April, Available online: http://www.colta.ru/articles/literature/10671 (accessed 15 February 2021).

Tynianov, Yu. [1924] 1981. *The Problem of Verse Language*, trans. and ed. M. Sosa and B. Harvey, Ann Arbor: Ardis.

Tynianov, Yu. and Jakobson, R. [1928] 2019. 'Problems of the Study of Literature and Language', in Yu. Tynianov, *Permanent Evolution: Selected Essays on Literature, Theory and Film*, trans. and ed. A. Morse and P. Redko, 278–82, Boston: Academic Studies Press.

Uspenskij, B. A. 1967. 'Problemy lingvisticheskoi tipologii v aspekte razlichenia "govoriashchego" (adresanta) i "slushaiushchego" (adresata)', in *To Honor Roman Jakobson: Essays on the Occasion of his Seventieth Birthday*, vol. 3, 2087–108, The Hague: Mouton.

Zalizniak, A. A. 2008. *'Slovo o polku Igoreve': vzgliad lingvista*, 3rd augmented edn, Moscow: Rukopisnye pamiatniki Drevnei Rusi.

CHAPTER 5
LOTMAN AND BAKHTIN
Caryl Emerson

In October 1983, Lotman presented a paper at an International Bakhtin Colloquium in Jena (then East Germany) on Bakhtin's legacy in relation to present-day semiotics (Lotman [1984] 2002). Bakhtin had died eight years earlier. His trademark concepts of dialogue, heteroglossia, chronotope and carnival had begun to boom in the West, reaping disciples as well as detractors. Neither Bakhtin nor Lotman was by temperament a polemicist. But several of Bakhtin's provocative private jottings sceptical of structuralism, semiotics and codes had been published posthumously in 1979, and Lotman must have been eager to set things straight. How he did so, where their perspectives differ, and whether at base these two world-class theorists are antagonistic, complementary or simply working in parallel universes, is the burden of the present chapter.

Those private jottings by Bakhtin from the 1960s to 1970s, lapidary and for that reason lamentably quotable, have long sat at the centre of the dialogic-semiotic divide. We begin with them. In one place Bakhtin objects to Lotman having called the 'multi-styled nature' of Pushkin's *Eugene Onegin* a 'recoding', in this case of romanticism into realism. Such a procedure, Bakhtin objects, can only lead to 'a falling away of that most important *dialogic* aspect', since 'a code presupposes content to be somehow ready-made and presupposes the realization of a choice among various *given* codes' (Bakhtin [1970] 1986: 135; 1979: 339; 2002: 394). Two further jottings continue the offensive. 'Semiotics deals primarily with the transmission of ready-made communication using a ready-made code. But in live speech, strictly speaking, communication is first created in the process of transmission, and there is, in essence, no code.' This pronouncement generates several memorable definitions: 'Context and code. A context is potentially unfinalized; a code must be finalized. A code is only a technical means of transmitting information; it does not have cognitive, creative significance. A code is a deliberately stopped, killed context' (Bakhtin [1970] 1986: 147; 1979: 352; 2002: 380, 431). Finally, near the end of some comments on methodology in the humanities, Bakhtin remarked: 'My attitude toward structuralism. I am against enclosure in a text. Mechanistic categories: "oppositions", a shift of codes [. . .]' (Bakhtin [1970] 1986: 169; 1979: 372; 2002: 434). The objection to 'recoding' in *Onegin* was a misreading of Lotman's intent (Reid 1990: 314–7). But Bakhtin's more general remarks against impersonal system and closed structures, jotted down late in life, resonate with the opening sentence of his maiden publication, a six-paragraph treatise, 'Art and Answerability', published in 1919: 'A whole is called "mechanical" when its constituent elements are united only in space and time by some external connection and are not imbued with the internal unity of meaning' (Bakhtin 1990: 1; 2003: 5).

If Lotman, preparing for his 1983 talk, had been fretting over these fragments of a rival worldview he wished to placate, his response was a tour-de-force.

Lotman began by assuring his Jena audience that Bakhtin, like so many strong minds of his era, had learned a great deal from Saussure, all the while aware that the great Swiss linguist's work was incomplete. Among the positive lessons Bakhtin learned were the dynamic nature of the linguistic sign and the dialogism of language; among the paradoxes remaining was the fact that real-life senders and receivers rarely encode and decode the same message. Except in elementary semiotic systems like road signs or traffic signals, equivalency never means identity. Art, like all higher-level human exchange, assumes that no information transfer is, or should be, duplicative. Communication is neither mimicry nor obedience. The minimum for any creative semiotic transfer is not some ready-made code but two differently equipped consciousnesses who desire to make contact (Lotman's example is the mother who talks, or babbles, with her infant: the two have utterly different languages yet understand each other perfectly). Bakhtin appreciated this. But his adjustments to strict Saussurean doctrine could not be grounded scientifically because he lived and worked in the 1920s and 1930s. Bakhtin was obliged to express himself in a 'somewhat impressionistic manner'. As a result, Bakhtinian concepts in circulation today have been used to justify a huge amount of 'empty eclectic chatter' (Lotman [1984] 2002: 152). But – Lotman informed the hall – we no longer have the right to employ dialogue as some slapdash metaphor. We can now define it objectively: dialogue is 'a mechanism for assimilating new information' (Lotman [1984] 2002: 154). All semiotic systems more complex than road signs are dialogic, dynamic and have a history. To 'have a history' means to change and to remember the changes. It was Bakhtin's genius to grasp this dynamic: that culture must simultaneously 'unify a semiotic situation' (to ensure information exchange) and 'de-unify it' (to guarantee the creation of new texts) (Lotman [1984] 2002: 156). By the end of his talk, semiotics seemed wholly reconciled with dialogics and with Bakhtin's fluid notion of the centripetal–centrifugal forces of language (Bakhtin [1934–35] 1981: 270–3).

How had these two critical schools ended up on the same side? After Lotman's death, his lifelong friend and Tartu colleague Boris Egorov suggested that Lotman had rather too easily assimilated Bakhtinian ideas at the Jena Colloquium. Downplaying the differences and ignoring the evolution of his own thought, Lotman had tactfully disarmed the delegates in advance, as if to say: 'Here you've been reproaching us for our "Saussurean" narrow-mindedness, but we're in complete solidarity with your opposition to Saussure!' (Egorov 1998: 86; 1999: 245–6).[1] Or as one Lotman scholar later remarked, apparently Bakhtin 'can be equally described as a total antagonist of semiotic theories and as one of the founding fathers of modern semiotics' (Semenenko 2012: 47).

Dialogue versus code, carnival body versus mortal poet

The backstory is complex. Mikhail Bakhtin (b. 1895) and Juri Lotman (b. 1922) belonged to very different generations: the first a pan-European of the Symbolist era raised on Kant and Schelling, and the second wholly formed by Soviet reality. Although Bakhtin endured chronic illness, arrest and internal exile, whereas Lotman survived only front-line service throughout the Second World War followed by surveillance and harassment, both adjusted to political pressure in ways that maximized their independence and creativity. In his final 'semiospheric' decade, Lotman experimented with asymmetry, randomness, nontranslatability, the productiveness of interrupted messages and explosive zones. In thus distancing himself from the hardwired structuralist typologies of the 1960s, he appeared to draw closer to a holistic Bakhtinian personalism centred on individual voice, body and unrepeatable context. But in fact, the mechanistic structuralism of that first post-Stalinist decade had been adopted quite consciously to benefit individual voices and bodies. Human experience had been co-opted by a mandatory 'Marxist-Leninist humanism' that had stuffed literary studies with its sentimentalisms and political taboos – and 'objectively' quantified language, incomprehensible to party watchdogs, was one way to break free of that suffocating template. The history of these two titanic thinkers contains several look-alike moments, analogous benefits achieved by dissimilar routes. Take only the cluster of concepts around explosion noted earlier. In one jotting from his working notebooks of the 1960s–1970s, published in Lotman's lifetime, Bakhtin faulted the humanities of his day for its 'trivially human attitude toward the future (desire, hope, fear)' – life lived in the narrow space of Small Time. 'There is no understanding of evaluative non-predetermination, unexpectedness, as it were "surprisingness", absolute innovation, miracle, and so forth' (Bakhtin [1970] 1986: 167; 1979: 370; 2002: 429). We sense here the energy of Lotman's unpredictable explosions. But Lotman grounded his new models in the chemistry and physics of Ilya Prigogine, whose ideas of non-equilibrium and bifurcation in self-organizing systems were profoundly inspirational for him in the mid-1980s (Grishakova 2009: 178–80). Although Bakhtin too was a keen student of contemporary advances in physics, his plea for receptivity to the absolutely new and miraculous emerged from a very different conceptual universe.

In his corrective to the Jena presentation, then, Boris Egorov had good reason to press the case for a fundamental divergence. Bakhtin, Egorov affirmed, was a 'free and creative Christian' in the style of the *fin-de-siècle* intelligentsia, and this 'religiosity' of his world view, curious about sinfulness, guilt, redemption and grace, marked him off from Lotman's 'atheism', a result of his 'family and social upbringing' (Egorov 1998: 87; 1999: 247). Furthermore, Bakhtin was consistently cool towards the Formalist School, foundational for most early semioticians. Bakhtin, a neo-Kantian and (in Egorov's assessment) a non-Hegelian, shared little metaphysical ground with Lotman, whose university teachers in Leningrad were permeated by Hegelian dialectics and Marxist method (Egorov 1998: 91; 1999: 252). Significantly, Bakhtin, who died in 1975, could not have known Lotman's great works of literary history from the 1980s, above all the biographies of Pushkin and Karamzin. Just how important these latter studies are for humanizing the concept of 'code' has been argued eloquently by David Bethea. In novelistic prose – Bakhtin's preferred domain – codes suggest unfreedom, formulaic or cartoon-like characters, the tedium of automatized plots. But in the realm of poetry (say, the Onegin stanza) or the lived lives of poets (say, Pushkin's fatal duel), the code, assimilated as inner discipline, is excruciatingly alive and fertile. Among Lotman's most profound insights, Bethea concludes, is that the creative poetic personality (and the creative text) uses 'code' as a precondition to be confronted, respected and *overcome*; it is not a 'ready-made plot' or a 'totalizing model to follow' (Bethea 1997: 8). A code, once consciously taken on, produces change, but this change is not predictable. It takes its time, and along the way the poet always has choices. One's code, in short, is part of one's responsible context – not opposed to it.

Yet Bakhtin's jottings on this topic suggest that he retained until the end a blunt, elementary notion of 'code', never refining it much beyond Morse code or a system of traffic signals. Most likely, Bakhtin was using the word 'code' not as a precise methodological tool but more as a cognitive outer limit. The polarized binaries for which Bakhtin is famous (dialogue/monologue, novel/epic, carnival life/official life, personality/thing) are usually intended in this way, not as absolutes but as directions that tempt the mind. They resemble 'parameters of possibility' rather than 'essences' (Denischenko 2017: 257). For Bakhtin, to think or act by code is to act passively, to seek equivalency and stasis. Lotman does not agree, and offers another model of human agency. A useful metric here is their respective investment in space and in time.

In 2019, Mihhail Lotman opened his Afterword to a collection of his father's essays with this summing-up of the history of the Tartu-Moscow Semiotic School. 'From the semiotics of text, it evolved into the semiotics of culture, and from that, into the semiotics of mental processes and the semiosphere', he wrote. 'In conjunction with that, the centre of attention shifted from the semiotics of space to the semiotics of time' (M. Lotman 2019: 245). Early Tartu scholarship favoured studying the text as an immanent or closed structure, a practice that protected it against those critics (mainstream Marxists are meant) who insisted that texts were the passive results of sociocultural conditioning. But as structural linguistics gave way in the 1970s to more interactive, biosemiotic models, the text was reconceived as a thinking and responsive structure (if not yet quite an organism). In his final period, Lotman devoted increasing attention to duration: how it is differently experienced by authors and readers and by chroniclers and historians, how temporal categories are embedded in natural languages and how we learn over time by talking to ourselves (M. Lotman 2019: 254–6).

Bakhtin's thought evolved as well. His earliest scenarios were also spatial, and almost as static as Lotman's early grids: an 'I' faces an 'other', each supplementing the other's vision with its unique 'horizon'. Only in 1929, with his study of Dostoevsky, did the dialogic word – coupled with the responsive ear – displace the visualizing eye. Paramount now became degrees of speaking and listening. In this dynamic, as Michael Holquist has shown, dialogism indeed owes a debt to Saussure. But where Saussure despairs of any satisfying scientific study of the utterance (*parole*) and retreats into the generalizable social space of the *langue*, Bakhtin picks up the challenge, making the 'speaking subject the site of meaning' (Holquist 1990: 42–7). Peter Grzybek goes further. In 'Bakhtinian semiotics', not only must code, context and utterance be 'interpersonal' at every point, but every given utterance is so fused with its individualized context that no 'linguistic or semiotic apparatus can be used to describe it' (Grzybek 1995: 241–2). Here too we must speak of limits. Authors desiring to grant maximum articulation to the largest discrete number of voices in their texts strive towards polyphony. Polyphonic writing is not just dialogue taken to extremes, however. Dialogue is linear, open-ended, freely developing and often uncoordinated. The spatial organization of polyphony is more harmonious and 'chordal'. It strives for the benevolent 'coexistence and interaction' of maximally diverse elements, non-coerced and freely expressed unto eternity (Bakhtin [1963] 1984: 28). This euphonious ideal lends polyphonic design the aura of utopian religiosity that Egorov sensed in Bakhtin (and that Bakhtin sensed in Dostoevsky). Lotman also found the concept of polyphony congenial, although he tilted it towards structure rather than a chorus of voices. Every text contains a 'polylogue of different systems', Lotman writes, and (citing Bakhtin's book on Dostoevsky as his inspiration) 'the poetic (artistic) text is in principle polyphonic' (Lotman [1972] 1996: 112).

In the 1930s, Bakhtin shifted ground again, into an area that would also become definitive for Lotman: philosophy of culture. In Bakhtin's thought, 'the notion of polyphony was gradually ousted by that of heteroglossia', Galin Tihanov writes. 'Whereas polyphony encapsulates a mixture of aesthetic but also moral overtones – listening to the other, not placing oneself above him or her – heteroglossia [. . .] promotes a more neutral view of language and the novel, one that makes no moral demands' (Tihanov 2019: 102). This apparent farewell to all lingering traces of an ethical Kantian framework culminates in Bakhtin's magnum opus from the mid-1930s, a treatise on grotesque matter, ambivalence and laughter as defences against our fear of death, packaged as a book on François Rabelais.

The carnival body became a global hit. Praised as freedom-bearing and condemned as anarchist and Stalinist, this surreal organism has been identified with the archaic and pagan as well as with Christian transubstantiation. Perhaps the carnival body, so resilient and free of pain, creates around itself its own semiosphere, which some scholars have begun to politicize as a site for accommodating historical trauma (Makarychev and Yaksyk 2017: 74–7). For the body in carnival is remarkable for the unimportance of its face, eyes and speaking mouth. It has few organs of individuation, scarcely any places of storage or accumulation and no memory. These bodies are important to Bakhtin largely as points of exchange and transit, as orifices. Elements pass through them. It is commonplace to note that carnival time lacks the patience to develop a network of dialogic words. Often overlooked is the fact that bodies in carnival are as asexual as they are amoral; they reproduce because they are somatically programmed to do so, like single-celled organisms, but they are not attracted to one another aesthetically or erotically (about this Bakhtin is explicit). The only appetite that matters – this is the famine-ridden Stalinist 1930s – is hunger for food. Otherwise Bakhtin's carnival bodies are as depersonalized and interchangeable as any mechanistic actants that populate Lotman's early semiotic texts.

Bakhtin's book on Rabelais appeared in 1965. Its rigid separation of carnival license from official seriousness, as well as its metaphysics of laughter, fascinated humanists and historians alike. With consummate tact, the Tartu semioticians also weighed in. As Natalya Avtonomova has observed, Lotman, while unfailingly respectful of Bakhtin, at the same time 'constantly attempts to translate Bakhtin's set of concerns directly into terminology close to him': polyphony becomes 'a play of subsystems'; dialogue, 'conflicting systems' or information transfer; carnival, 'the invasion of dynamic structures into a sacral world' (Avtomonova 2008: 132). She adds that regarding carnival, 'Lotman allowed himself to criticize directly only the epigones of Bakhtin'. One example will suffice. In 1976, the eminent medievalist Dmitry Likhachev, working with the folklorist Alexander Panchenko, undertook to investigate 'cultures of laughter' in Ancient Rus' (Likhachev 1976). Following Bakhtin, they had devised a strict dualistic model, in which a carnivalesque 'anti-culture' full of promiscuous minstrels and scandalous holy fools was as free and fearlessly subversive as the official culture (church and state) was unfree, pious and obedient. Two years after Bakhtin's death, the Soviet journal *Voprosy literatury* published an essay by Boris Uspenskij and Juri Lotman laying out their objections to the Likhachev thesis (Uspenskij and Lotman 1977). While praising its boldness and originality (the semiotic vocabulary and binary elegance of the model must have appealed to them), as historians they were sceptical. The codes were ill-suited to the context. The two-way laughter celebrated by Bakhtin in sixteenth-century France, which supposedly empowered commoners on the public square by allowing them to praise and blame in a single ambivalent gesture, could not be translated from the early French Renaissance into Russian medieval culture. Bakhtin's assumption that 'laughter elevates medieval man into a popular carnival utopia, snatching him out from under the power of social institutions' (Uspenskij and Lotman 1977: 153), is misleading as a cultural universal. Pre-modern Russia was organized into two zones, sanctity versus Satan; it contained no neutral or ambivalent secular sphere. Laughter was not 'outside the system' but an inversion of the system, not liberating but blasphemous and demonic. Although Orthodox writ allowed inner merriment expressed by a smile, 'Christ never laughed' (Uspenskij and Lotman 1977: 154), devils laugh. Liturgical parody arrived in seminaries late and under Polish influence. The Muscovite public square, from Ivan the Terrible to Peter the Great, was more often the site of torturing than of feasting. If the torturers laughed, it was not infectious or participatory; the spectators did not join in. Likewise, native Russian holy foolishness was not comic, democratic or progressive, as the Likhachev team optimistically claimed. It was specular and performative, intended to strike terror in onlookers, not mirth. In a cautionary footnote, Uspenskij and Lotman warn against any 'mechanical extension of Bakhtin's ideas into areas where their very application should be the subject of specialized research' (Uspenskij and Lotman 1977: 152n2).

Thus did the Tartu scholars, after their historical turn, issue an early warning against a faddishly globalized Bakhtin. Nevertheless, for all its fantasized status in history, the porous and anaesthetized carnival body, which never complains or registers an insult, remains a stunning metaphor for one constant of Bakhtin's world view: his conviction that the space of our inner intimate self is too unfinalized, too much in flux, ever to be known or owned. We are all carnival space to the extent that we are conduits. If Lotman will eventually devise an internal grid where 'autocommunication' is possible and valid, thereby generating a theory of creativity out of internally circulating elements (Lotman

1990: 20–35), Bakhtin avoids such subjectivizing exercises. My 'I' has no private realm of which 'I' can be aware. Only some outside other can stabilize me temporarily, 'sediment' me out into bounded form. The absence in Bakhtin of the ineffable, of any domain of radical mystery or any interior space that is in principle inaccessible to others, makes him a most unusual personalist as well as a highly unconventional Christian (even in Egorov's 'free and creative' sense). Tihanov refers to this world view as Bakhtin's 'wry and difficult – decentered – humanism' (Tihanov 2019: 102), noting that it places him outside classical identitarian versions of subjectivity. Lotman's humanism, for all its residual vocabulary of mechanism and semiotic device, might more comfortably house the recesses of individualized consciousness.

Bakhtin's time, Lotman's space (a balance sheet)

Both Bakhtin and Lotman moved from studying the singular structured text (or interpersonal scenario) to broader cultural inquiries with a historical dimension. For this purpose Bakhtin equipped himself with the *chronotope*, a time–space marker that Lotman credited with 'significantly advancing the study of a genre typology for the novel' (Lotman [1987] 1993: 91). Peeter Torop sees evidence of Bakhtin's chronotopic idea in Lotman's move from 'decoding' to 'communication and circulation' and then to 'a new understanding of holism' (Torop 2009: xxxiv–v). In this evolution from 'mathematical procedures to a biological, organismic approach', which has been compared to 'the shift from Newtonian to relativistic physics' (Mandelker 1994: 385), modelling systems are softened to semiospheres that contain no dead codes, no unresponsive or irresponsible non-holistic parts. Lotman's application of semiotic categories to the biography of individual poets is the capstone to this evolution.

Can we imagine Bakhtin in the role of biographer? Only with difficulty; he had no voice for it. The life stories he trusted are the ones fixed in novels. Real human lifespans are precious, but petty and fragile. Rather than reconstitute historical persons in their own Small Time, Bakhtin preferred to animate and even anthropomorphize historical forces (epicness, novelness, cultures of laughter, genre memory going back millennia and infinite Great Time). On a human scale, space interested Bakhtin if there was a boundary passing through it – the thresholds, doors and stairwells in Dostoevsky, with a person on either side – or alternatively, if this space could grow, digest or excrete something (a womb, a stomach, a bowel). The one spatial distinction Bakhtin took seriously was inside versus outside. In the spirit of his dialogic personalism, he recast this dynamic as 'I' versus 'other', entities that occupy fundamentally non-coincident spaces. But beyond this brute division, Bakhtin appears to have had limited theoretical interest in spatial categories. When he jotted down in the early 1970s that he was 'against enclosure in a text', his word for enclosure, *zamykanie*, comes from the Russian verb 'to lock up'. Spatial thinking, unless it served the developmental energies of time, was a prison. Carnival escapes this unfreedom by defining useful space not as a storeroom but as a conduit. But what about our ordinary answerable lives lived in non-carnival space?

Again Bakhtin's working notebooks provide clues. In the loose pages that precede his laconic comment on structuralism, he identifies two opposing limits towards which our thought and practice strive: 'reification' (*oveshchestvlenie*: better would be 'thing-ification') and 'personalization' (Bakhtin 1986: 168; 2002: 432). An isolated 'I', while possible in logical relations, is impossible with persons, who come into being only on a boundary with other persons and thus are always in flux. Implicit here is that a lone 'I' is tantamount to a thing, and *things*, being reified, exist in space. They can be shoved around, deadly and mutely, by a single unimplicated outside agent. *Persons*, in contrast, cannot be shoved around because they enable each other reciprocally. Although they face one another spatially as subjects, their function is to grow, resist, interact and answer back. So the question for every person is not 'who am I?' or even 'where am I?' but rather, how long do I have to become someone else, and how can you help me in this task?

It is tempting to speculate on Bakhtin's hopefulness about time (his belief that time generates value) and his fatality about space (his sense that it traps). One contributing factor might have been his own condition as an invalid – a chronic bone disease since childhood – and his final decades as an amputee. About the loss of his right leg in 1938 Bakhtin was cheerfully matter-of-fact; it saved his life, the pain was far less, 'I could walk very well with crutches' and could even run and climb (*Mikhail Bakhtin* [1973] 2019: 47). But there were many bedridden months, and moving was always a self-conscious task. If the impression we receive from Lotman's memoirs – or, as he preferred, non-memoirs – is of a vigorous young man in constant movement, hauling equipment along dangerous fronts during four years of total war, then the normal default state for Bakhtin, young and old, is an armchair.

This physical fact has stimulated fascinating work in unexpected places, including Bakhtin and the performing arts. The theatre scholar and actor trainer Dick McCaw, discussing the topic of Bakhtin's philosophy of the moving body, notes that for Bakhtin, a 'concrete embodied whole' is almost always envisioned as static and 'egocentric' (located at the centre of surrounding space) rather than as allocentric (only one of multiple objects in space) (McCaw 2018: 238). Bakhtin gives us concrete bodies, but we don't see them *moving*; they do not dart left or right, nor glance round at themselves to fill out their horizon. This fixity in space, McCaw suggests, limits Bakhtin's understanding of the nimbleness and agency of the actor. It also affects his readings of plays. In his ruminations on theatre and drama, Bakhtin, a classicist by training, was drawn to tragedy: Oedipus and then Shakespeare. King Lear and Macbeth are trapped inside the royal crown; refusing to partake in larger life cycles, they exhibit 'the logic of any self-asserting life, which is hostile to replacement and renewal' (Bakhtin [1944] 2014: 527). Power that tries to stop time becomes first criminal and then fatal. Consider in contrast Lotman's effervescent discussions of Shakespeare: two comedies where space, not time, is the generative dimension (Lotman 1990: 151–7). *The Comedy of Errors* and *As You Like It* are based on mythological plots organized cyclically, peopled by twins and doubles. The romantic couples in these comedies duplicate one another and can be stacked in a single space. When the cast is 'unwound', all confusions cease and happy endings ensue – not because they are predetermined (that is a temporal calculation) but because they have always occupied the same ground. Only Melancholy Jaques, with his litany of life's seven ages, remains outside this fertile plot-space, looking in.

If Lotman delights in space filled with potential relations unthreatened by the passage of time, then Bakhtin is far more dependent on time's beneficent energy. The future must be richer than the world now. In December 1943, a dark year, Bakhtin jotted down some thoughts on cognition and violence. Trying to know any image, he wrote, is 'an attempt to circumvent the object from the side of the future [. . .] to deprive it of an open-ended future, to present the object with all of its boundaries [. . .]. The object is all here and nowhere else; and if it is all here, in its entirety, then it is dead and can be devoured' (Bakhtin ([1943] 2017: 204–5). A cognized thing is no longer benevolently 'finalized' by an other, as it was in Bakhtin's early writings; now it is violated. Spatial thinking is tyrannical: it behaves like a bad code. Only the future holds out freedom.

If Bakhtin sat still and moved most comfortably through time, then Lotman was a highly appreciative student of space. This virtuosity was shared by the Tartu community and reflected in its pathbreaking work on the semiotics of the city and the subsequent 'Petersburg text'. (A telling detail: Bakhtin celebrates Rome and Constantinople in his essays on the history of the novel, but for him, cities are valuable not as structures with buildings and streets but as mixing chambers for multiple languages.) Space for Lotman is more than geography or Cartesian extension, however. It is also metaphysical, mathematical and topological. On this point, Lotman was very aware of how he differed from Bakhtin.

In 1983, Lotman wrote a revealing letter to one of his external PhD students, Larisa Lvovna Fialkova. Fialkova was writing a dissertation on Nikolai Gogol, and in Lotman's view she had used far too much Bakhtin in it. Succumbing to academic fashion, Fialkova had taken up 'ready-made templates', plugged them in, and distorted her subject. As Lotman explained:

> For Bakhtin, as a person of modernist culture, as for Einstein who was also a modernist, chronotopes exist: time as the fourth dimension. But for Gogol and medieval culture more broadly [. . .] it wasn't that way at all. Space was far more universal. Time began with the Fall and would end with the Trumpet of the Archangel. But authentic space is eternal (the space of Platonic ideas, not its shadow in the material world). Bakhtin proceeds from the idea of physics (the theory of relativity) and looks at space and time as phenomena of a single order'. But for the semiotic structuralist, 'space is that multitude of objects (points) between which there is a relationship of continuity. In this sense one can speak of semantic space, the space of coloration, ethical space, temporal space, and even the space of physical space. [. . .] Space is the universal language of all modelling.' (Lotman 1997: 719–20)

Lotman reiterates this argument in his essay on spatial semiotics from the same decade (Lotman [1986] 1998). For Bakhtin, he notes, 'artistic time is the fundamental structural element, and space behaves as a dependent variable in the genre continuum'

(Lotman [1986] 1998: 442). In thus privileging time, Lotman seems to suggest, Bakhtin's very idea of chronotope is too secular, too dependent on the real experience of realistically drawn characters moving from birth to death, to adequately explain the richness of the world's genres.

Meeting up at the end

In 2010, Nikolai Vasiliev (literature professor and native son of Saransk, Bakhtin's academic home from 1936 to 1970) published a commemorative piece with the title 'Tartu-Saransk: Two Poles of "Provincial" scholarship' (Vasiľev [2010] 2013). He noted the isolation of Bakhtin and Lotman and their exile from the Centre, which both protected and constrained them. Beginning in the 1960s, Lotman had regularly sent Bakhtin the major Tartu publications, personally inscribed (Vasiľev [2010] 2013: 369–70). In 1970, responding to a question from the liberal journal *Novy Mir*, Bakhtin included the 'young researchers headed by Yuri M. Lotman' as among 'the most highly gratifying phenomena of recent years' (Bakhtin [1970] 1986: 2). Lotman first met the Bakhtins in the summer of 1970, in an old people's home outside Moscow (Egorov 1999: 255–6). On September 29 of that year, he wrote to Boris Uspenskij, saying that Bakhtin was living in unacceptable conditions, we should invite him here, and 'if he agrees, he and his wife can rent a good room in Tartu' (Lotman 1997: 512–13). Bakhtin declined to move to Tartu. But he had been formally rehabilitated two years earlier, regained his right to reside legally in Russia's larger cities, and was able, in 1971, to relocate in Moscow.

In February 1973, Lotman visited Bakhtin, now widowed, in his Moscow quarters. Bakhtin was 'fettered to his armchair' and cared for by a housekeeper. During these months, Bakhtin was being interviewed by Viktor Duvakin, whose seventeen hours of taped conversation constitute the closest Bakhtin ever got to writing 'memoirs'. But Lotman also left a portrait. In 1987, a volume of Bakhtin's writings was published in Estonian translation, for which Lotman wrote the introduction. It contains this personal moment:

> I had the good fortune to know Mikhail Bakhtin towards the end of his life. It was a profoundly sad, chain-smoking, monosyllabic man that I saw sitting opposite me. In a room whose whole interior bespoke a solitary old age, a crutch leaning against the table brought to mind the fact that the master of the house had had a leg amputated and was forced to spend endless hours in an armchair, frozen in contemplation. Fate had robbed him of so much, but up to the end it could not take from him the greatest treasure – his ability to give himself fully, unreservedly over to contemplation. Bakhtin [. . .] was more than just a scholar, he was a thinker. Thinking was his main activity, it was the field that he cultivated all his life industriously as a ploughman, and it was the domicile where he, who had been homeless almost all his life, found shelter. Bakhtin was a fabulous interlocutor. And I mean interlocutor, not narrator. In conversation he would frequently stay silent and for long periods. But he had a talent

for sympathetic silence, creating thereby a benevolent and confidential atmosphere without which conversation is impossible. His ability to divine another person's thoughts was astounding. Occasionally it could even embarrass his interlocutor. Nowadays we are losing the art of conversation; we hurry to set out our own ideas and hardly ever listen to what is being said to us. Our conversations have become arbitrarily linked up monologues, resembling absurdist theatre. This is due to our outsized self-admiration and lack of interest in other persons. Mikhail Bakhtin, although seemingly lost in deep thought, was brimming with interest in the other person. He grasped others' ideas with such ease that one could think he had thought it all over himself long ago, knew it all, and was interested not in bare authorless thoughts but in the thinking interlocutor – in the person who created the thought and the thought that expressed the person. (Lotman 1987: 5–6)[2]

In 1992, Lotman, now also widowed and ailing, dictated his 'non-memoirs'. Its final paragraph resonates with Bakhtin's plea in 1919 that at the end of the day, or of the life, there would be 'unity of meaning'. 'A snake sheds its skin when it grows', Lotman noted in his non-memoirs (Lotman [1995] 2014: 79). 'This is a perfect symbolic expression of scholarly progress. [. . .] All that remains is to hope that the snake, having shed its skin, changed its colour, and increased its size, will still preserve the very unity of itself.'

Notes

1. Egorov appended a fuller version of this essay to his biography of Lotman published one year later. Its three additional pages discuss Lotman's personal relationship with Bakhtin since their first meeting in 1970 to Lotman's remarks at a commemorative evening for Bakhtin in April 1975.

2. Cited portion translated from the Estonian by Triinu Pakk. The original Russian text has been lost, so the translation into Estonian, by Malle Salupere, is the only extant version of the introduction.

References

Avtonomova, N. S. 2008. 'Bakhtin i Lotman: Na podstupakh k otkrytoi strukture . . ', *Kul'turologiia* 1: 123–42.

Bakhtin, M. M. [1934–35] 1981. 'Discourse in the Novel', in *The Dialogic Imagination: Four Essays by M. M. Bakhtin*, trans. C. Emerson and M. Holquist, ed. M. Holquist, 259–422, Austin: University of Texas Press.

Bakhtin, M. M. [1943] 2017. 'Ritorika, v meru svoei lzhivosti . . .' [bilingual text], ed. and trans. I. Denischenko and A. Spektor, *Slavic and East European Journal* 61 (2): 202–15.

Bakhtin, M. M. [1944] 2014. 'Bakhtin on Shakespeare: Excerpt from "Additions and Changes to Rabelais"', trans. S. Sandler, *PMLA* 129 (3): 522–37.

Bakhtin, M. [1963] 1984. *Problems of Dostoevsky's Poetics*, ed. and trans. C. Emerson, Minneapolis: University of Minnesota Press.

Bakhtin, M. M. [1970] 1986. 'Response to a Question from the *Novy Mir* Editorial Staff', in *Speech Genres and Other Late Essays*, trans. V. W. McGee, 1–7, Austin: University of Texas Press.

Bakhtin, M. M. 1979. *Estetika slovesnogo tvorchestva*, eds. S. S. Averintsev and S. G. Bocharov, Moscow: Iskusstvo.

Bakhtin, M. M. 1986. *Speech Genres and Other Late Essays*, trans. V. W. McGee, Austin: University of Texas Press.

Bakhtin, M. M. 1990. *Art and Answerability: Early Philosophical Essays by M. M. Bakhtin*, eds. M. Holquist and V. Liapunov, Austin: University of Texas Press.

Bakhtin, M. M. 2002. *Sobranie sochinenii*, vol. 6, eds. S. G. Bocharov and L. A. Gogotoshvili, Moscow: Russkie slovari. Iazyki slavianskoi kul'tury.

Bakhtin, M. M. 2003. *Sobranie sochinenii*, vol. 1, eds. S. G. Bocharov and N. I. Nikolaev, Moscow: Russkie slovari. Iazyki slavianskoi kul'tury.

Bethea, D. M. 1997. 'Bakhtinian Prosaics versus Lotmanian "Poetic Thinking": The Code and its Relation to Literary Biography', *Slavic and East European Journal* 41 (1): 1–15.

Denischenko, I. M. 2017. 'Beyond Reification: Mikhail Bakhtin's Critique of Violence in Cognition and Representation', *Slavic and East European Journal* 61 (2): 255–77.

Egorov, B. F. 1998. 'M. M. Bakhtin i Iu. M. Lotman', in N. A. Pan'kov (ed.), *Bakhtinskie chteniia III. Materialy mezhdunarodnoi nauchnoi konferentsii, Vitebski, 23–25 iiunia 1998 g.*, 83–96, Vitebsk: Izdatel'stvo Vitebskogo universiteta.

Egorov, B. F. 1999. *Zhizn' i tvorchestvo Iu. M. Lotmana*, Moscow: Novoe literaturnoe obozrenie.

Grishakova, M. 2009. 'Afterword. Around Culture and Explosion: J. Lotman and the Tartu-Moscow School in the 1980s–90s', in J. Lotman, *Culture and Explosion*, trans. W. Clark, ed. M. Grishakova, 175–87, Berlin and New York: Mouton de Gruyter.

Grzybek, P. 1995. 'Bakhtinskaia semiotika i moskovsko-tartuskaia shkola', E. V. Permiakov (ed.), *Lotmanovskii sbornik*, vol. 1, 240–59, Moscow: IC-Garant.

Holquist, M. 1990. *Dialogism. Bakhtin and his world*, London: Routledge.

Likachev, D. S. and Panchenko, A. M. 1976. '*Smekhovoi mir' Drevnei Rusi*, Leningrad: Nauka.

Lotman, Ju. M. [1972] 1996. 'Analiz poeticheskogo teksta', in Ju. M. Lotman, *O poetakh i poezii*, 17–252, Saint Petersburg: Iskusstvo–SPB.

Lotman, Ju. M. [1984] 2002. 'Nasledie Bakhtina i aktual'nye problemy semiotiki', trans. T. Semenova, in Ju. M. Lotman, *Istoriia i tipologiia russkoi kul'tury*, 147–56, Saint Petersburg: Iskusstvo–SPB.

Lotman, Ju. M. [1986] 1998. 'K probleme prostranstvennoi semiotike', in Ju. M. Lotman, *Ob iskusstve*, 442–4, Saint Petersburg: Iskusstvo–SPB.

Lotman, Ju. M. 1987. 'Kutse dialoogile' [Invitation to Dialogue], trans. M. Salupere, in M. Bahtin, *Valitud tööd* [Selected Works], ed. P. Torop, 5–14, Tallinn: Eesti Raamat.

Lotman, Ju. M. [1987] 1993. 'Siuzhetnoe prostranstvo russkogo romana XIX stoletiia', in Iu. M. Lotman, *Izbrannye stat'i*, vol. 3, 91–106, Tallinn: Aleksandra.

Lotman, Ju. M. 1990. 'The Semiosphere and the Problem of Plot', in Yu. M. Lotman, *Universe of the Mind: A Semiotic Theory of Culture*, trans. A. Shukman, 151–70. Bloomington: Indiana University Press.

Lotman, Ju. M. [1995] 2014. *Non-Memoirs*, ed. E. Bershtein, trans. C. L. Brickman, Champaign, IL: Dalkey Archive Press.

Lotman, Ju. M. 1997. *Pis'ma 1940–1993*, ed. B. F. Egorov, Moscow: Iazyki russkoi kul'tury.

Lotman, Ju. M. 2019. *Culture, Memory and History: Essays in Cultural Semiotics*, ed. M. Tamm, trans. B. J. Baer, Cham: Palgrave Macmillan.

Lotman, M. 2019. 'Afterword: (Re)constructing the Drafts of the Past', in J. Lotman, *Culture, Memory and History: Essays in Cultural Semiotics*, ed. M. Tamm, trans. B. J. Baer, 245–65, Cham: Palgrave Macmillan.

Makarychev, A. and Yatsyk, A. 2017. *Lotman's Cultural Semiotics and the Political*, Lanham: Rowman & Littlefield.

Mandelker, A. 1994. 'Semiotizing the Sphere: Organicist Theory in Lotman, Bakhtin, and Vernadsky', *PMLA* 109 (3): 385–96.

McCaw, D. 2018. 'Toward a Philosophy of the Moving Body', in S. N. Gratchev and H. Mancing (eds), *Mikhail Bakhtin's Heritage in Literature, Arts, and Psychology*, 237–54, Lancing: Lexington Books.

Mikhail Bakhtin. The Duvakin Interviews [1973] 2019. Eds. S. N. Gratchev and M. Marinova, trans. M. Marinova, Lewisville, PA: Bucknell University Press.

Reid, A. 1990. 'Who is Lotman and Why is Bakhtin Saying Those Nasty Things about Him?', *Discours social / Social Discourse* 3 (1/2): 311–24.

Semenenko, A. 2012. *The Texture of Culture: An Introduction to Yuri Lotman's Semiotic Theory*, New York: Palgrave Macmillan.

Tihanov, G. 2019. *The Birth and Death of Literary Theory: Regimes of Relevance in Russia and Beyond*, Stanford, CA: Stanford University Press.

Torop, P. 2009. 'Foreword: Lotmanian Explosion', in J. Lotman, *Culture and Explosion*, trans. W. Clark, ed. M. Grishakova, xxvii–xxxix, Berlin and New York: Mouton de Gruyter.

Uspenskij, B. A. and Lotman, Ju. M. 1977. 'Novye aspekty izucheniia kul'tury Drevnej Rusi', *Voprosy literatury* 3: 148–66.

Vasil'ev, N. L. [2010] 2013. 'Tartu-Saransk: dva poliusa "provintsial'noi" nauki', in N. L. Vasil'ev, *Mikhail Mikhailovich Bakhtin i fenomen 'Kruga Bakhtina'*, 355–70, Moscow: Kn. dom. 'Librokom'.

CHAPTER 6
LOTMAN AND THE TARTU-MOSCOW SCHOOL OF SEMIOTICS

Merit Rickberg and Silvi Salupere

In the 1960s two groups of humanities scholars in the USSR who shared a mutual interest in structural studies started an academic collaboration that later became known as the Tartu-Moscow School of Semiotics (TMS). The sources and analyses devoted to the TMS can broadly be divided into three categories: academic works published in the West during the period of the school (e.g. Eimermacher 1971; Meletinsky and Segal 1971; Rewar 1976; Lucid 1977; Shukman 1977; Portis-Winner and Winner 1976; Seyffert 1985; Rudy 1986; Chernov 1988); the reflections and memories of participants and students of the school from the late 1980s and early 1990s (e.g. Koshelev 1994; Permiakov 1995; Nekliudov 1988); and the post-factum academic research of the TMS since the 1990s (e.g. M. Lotman [1996] 2000; Waldstein 2008; Salupere 2012; Semenenko 2012; Salupere and Torop 2013; Torop 2014; Grishakova and Salupere 2015; Pilshchikov and Trunin 2016; Gherlone 2020; Avtonomova 2021).

One of the threads that runs through many of these works is a discussion of the applicability of the notion of 'school' for this group of scholars. The lack of shared methodology, the plurality of metalanguages, the all-encompassing scope of possible research objects and the ad hoc approach in building theoretical frameworks can easily raise doubts as to whether this collaboration was grounded in sufficient scientific unity to justify the title of school. However, the common ground becomes more evident when we take Juri Lotman's understanding of school as the point of departure for exploring this phenomenon. From Lotman's perspective, communication inside the TMS was best described as a 'chain of conversations' (Lotman [1990] 1998: 85). These conversations – whether they took the form of academic gatherings, collective publications or personal letters – offered participants the possibility to learn from each other, to challenge one another, to be inspired and to be united in common interests and at times divided in disputes. Hence, the differences between the participants served as catalysts for developing their individual creative work. From this point of view, the multiplicity that can seem problematic in the light of the canonical meaning of 'school' paradoxically appears to be the uniting factor in the case of the TMS.

Lotman had a central role in facilitating the conversations in the TMS. He was the initiator and organizer of the academic gatherings and the creator and main editor of the journal *Trudy po znakovym sistemam* (Sign Systems Studies) – both of which served as the main platforms of dialogue for the members of the school. In these activities, he managed to bring together some of the most notable Soviet scholars who were interested in the study of semiotics, among them Vyacheslav Ivanov, Alexander Piatigorsky,

Vladimir Toporov, Boris Uspenskij, Isaak Revzin, Juri Levin, Boris Gasparov and many others. It is relevant to point out that the name 'Tartu-Moscow' (or Moscow-Tartu), which in the very initial stage of the school corresponded to the geographical location of the scholars involved in the group, later had a merely conditional character, as the school included members from cities such as Leningrad, Yerevan, Riga, Vilnius and others.

The multifaceted nature of the TMS and the separate academic paths of its members make it difficult to fit the evolution of the ideas inside this school into one coherent story. Such attempts at narration often lead to equating the theoretical path taken by Lotman with the story of the TMS as a whole, and as such they fail to present the complexity of the communication between this group of scholars. This is why in this chapter our focus will be on the TMS as an academic and historical phenomenon instead. Adopting Lotman's perspective of 'school', we will give an overview of the historical context and the course of the various TMS conversations with the aim of explicating how the school functioned in its time, as well as clarifying the role it played for Lotman as a scholar.

The beginning of structural studies in Moscow

The emergence of the TMS falls into the time frame of Khrushchev's Thaw – a period of reform in the USSR from the mid-1950s to the mid-1960s characterized by political, economic and cultural liberalization. This reformation of the Soviet system brought about significant changes in the field of science as well. For the story of the TMS, the most relevant change was the re-evaluation of such research areas as cybernetics, structural linguistics and information theory, which later served as steppingstones in the development of Soviet semiotics. Before the 'thaw', at the beginning of the 1950s any research that dared to establish a dialogue with the aforementioned disciplines ran the risk of being labelled 'reactionary pseudoscience'.

However, such negative official evaluations were not enough to stop the increasing attention towards these new disciplines. In the field of humanities, this interest was driven mainly by the search for an 'exact language' of science. According to Slava Gerovitch: 'Cybernetics, with its promise of making scientific knowledge objective by translating it into the "exact" mathematical language of computer algorithms, naturally appealed to the young generation of Soviet linguists' (Gerovitch 2002: 228). Gerovitch points out that Soviet research in this field differed significantly from Western cybernetics: 'They viewed the works of Western cyberneticians as a point of departure, rather than as a theoretical canon' (Gerovitch 2002: 249). This creative approach, using conceptions of cybernetics as mainly a generator of individual ideas, was also inherent to Lotman's works (Salupere 2015: 65).

Against the backdrop of the 'thaw', it became possible for scholars to make some initial steps towards permitting cybernetics and structural linguistics. One such step was the formation of the Seminar on the Application of Mathematical Methods in Linguistics in 1956, which was initiated by renowned Soviet mathematician Andrey Kolmogorov and organized under the philological faculty of Moscow University by two young scholars, who some years later were both also involved in the formation of the TMS, linguist and a polymath Vyacheslav Ivanov, and a mathematician Vladimir Uspenskij. In the same year, Ivanov, together with Isaak Revzin, who was also later an active member of the TMS, took part in the founding of the Association for Machine Translation. In 1959, the Academy Council of Cybernetics was established, which led to the official 'rehabilitation' of cybernetics and structuralism finally in 1960 when the presidium of the Academy of Sciences issued a decree that ordered the establishment of divisions of structural and applied linguistics in several of its institutes (Gerovitch 2002: 241–2). This decree also included a resolution for the formation of the Institute of Semiotics in Moscow in the upcoming years. Reflecting on the effect of this decree, Vladimir Uspenskij has written that although this plan was not realized, the mere statement of such a plan had a significant moral and psychological effect on the development of semiotics in the Soviet Union (V. Uspenskij 1995). In the same year, the Division on Structural Typology of the Institute of Slavic and Balkan Studies at the Academy of Sciences in Moscow was opened, and in 1962 this division organized the first conference in the USSR devoted to semiotics (Shukman 1977: 186–9).

The conference, titled the Symposium on the Structural Study of Sign Systems, is where the story of the TMS usually begins. There are a couple of reasons for this. Firstly, there were in total twenty-eight participants at the symposium, seventeen of whom later became members of the TMS. Secondly, news of the symposium caught the attention of scholars in Tartu and eventually led to the establishment of contact between the two circles. The fact that news of such a small academic gathering reached the outskirts of the Soviet Union points to a peculiar characteristic of the Soviet information field: the role critical reviews played in disseminating information about either forbidden or ideologically questionable texts. Although semiotics was not forbidden, it was still considered suspect and so the conference proceedings, printed in rather small numbers, fell under harsh criticism. Reviews condemning the content of the proceedings in great detail, with long quotes from the original texts, were published in various journals with large circulations. One of the participants in the symposium, Boris Uspenskij, recalled with gratitude how 'these journals accidentally ended up advertising our research by spreading our programme and ideas to wider audiences' (B. Uspenskij 1987: 23).

The first steps in Tartu

The semiotic ideas discussed in the symposium resonated with the ideas of an active group of scholars working in the Department of Russian Literature at the State University of Tartu. Boris Egorov, Juri Lotman, Zara Mints and Igor Chernov gave a methodological seminar throughout the late 1950s and early 1960s dealing with the newest ideas of cybernetics, information theory and structural linguistics (M. Lotman [1996] 2000: 32). Methodological seminars were a compulsory part of academic life for university staff in the Soviet Union. However, such seminars were usually led by assigned members of the Communist Party, with the only method under discussion supposed to be Marxism.

According to Egorov (1994), the unusual situation of their seminar was to some extent caused by the fact that most of their collective had arrived in Estonia from Leningrad and were also members of the Communist Party. In the context of Estonia, such criteria immediately made them seem more trustworthy in the eyes of the officials. For that reason, they didn't need to be controlled as closely as their Estonian colleagues and were thus given the opportunity to lead their own seminars.

In addition to the methodological seminars, in the years 1958–63 Lotman was reading a course in structural poetics, which, later with the help of his wife and colleague Zara Mints, who was transcribing his lectures[1] (Egorov et al. 2012: 83), was turned into his first semiotic monograph *Lectures on Structural Poetics* (Lotman 1964). After finding out about the Symposium on the Structural Study of Sign Systems in 1962, the Tartu group decided to establish contact with the scholars in Moscow.

In that year, Lotman sent his student Igor Chernov to meet the Symposium participants. Chernov brought back to Tartu the infamous book of abstracts published for the event. Closer familiarization with these ideas encouraged Lotman to pursue direct collaboration with Moscow linguists, and in 1963 he went to the capital to propose co-operation in organizing a conference dedicated to structural studies. 'Lotman had the stroke of genius to invite the Moscow scholars to transfer their activities (informal semiotic gatherings and publications), which had turned out to be impossible in Moscow, to Tartu' (Grishakova and Salupere 2015: 176). The offer was accepted, and the planning of the first summer school of semiotics began.

Before the first summer school

The possibility of organizing a summer school in Tartu devoted to semiotics is predominantly explained by the milder political climate of this 'provincial' location compared to the central regions of the Soviet regime (Waldstein 2008: 35). Without downplaying the relevance of such geopolitical peculiarities, it seems important to stress that in the Soviet society a single actor at a high position often had a much greater influence over the course of events than the general rules governing the whole system. In the case of the summer school, this single actor was the rector of the University of Tartu (1951–70), Feodor Klement. Klement possessed a flair for genuine science and genuine scientists (V. Uspenskij 1995: 4) without paying much attention to whether they had backgrounds suitable to holding academic positions, and thus was entirely in support of Lotman. The fact that the fourth summer school that took place the same year that Klement retired, 1970, remained the last one, despite Lotman's enormous efforts to continue with these gatherings, confirms the importance of the role that he played for the TMS.

The first summer school was planned for the late summer of 1964. From the very beginning Lotman envisioned it not as an academic event in its traditional sense. His aim was to create conditions for scholars to truly live together for a determined period of time (Lotman [1990] 1998: 85), enabling free and uninhibited discussions outside of the event's 'official programme'. For Lotman it was important to keep the number of participants as low as possible for a couple of reasons. Firstly, in this way it would be possible to have a real discussion between scholars (Lotman 1997: 675–6). Secondly, carefully selecting the participants and keeping a strict limit was a necessary measure 'given a situation in which academic structures were infiltrated with KGB agents' (Grishakova and Salupere 2015: 177). Lotman shared his plan for the summer school in a letter to Vyacheslav Ivanov dated 31 January 1964:

> Before the symposium commences we should (and we must) plan preliminary topics and a range of questions to be discussed. (I don't want it to be loaded with 'planned' works, to avoid the mad dashing about of ordinary conferences, and instead to have time for conversations on a free range of topics even during walks. A place has been chosen for this purpose – not Tartu, but in a forest, by a lake. And most importantly, there should be no outsiders and we could talk according to the 'Hamburg score'[2]). There is already a preliminary name: 'Summer School of Semiotics (Extra-linguistic Sign Systems)'. (Lotman 1997: 646–7)

This preliminary name for the event was eventually discarded by the organizers as too risky and replaced with a safer and much less comprehensible title, Summer School of Secondary Modelling Systems. This name was proposed by Vladimir Uspenskij, who spent the summer of 1964 in Estonia in Elva, a town close to Tartu where Lotman's family were also summering. On one of their many walks Lotman shared his concern about the title of the event with Uspenskij. As Uspenskij recalls, by that time the word 'semiotics' had already fallen into disrepute (see V. Uspenskij 1995: 106). Inspired by the concept of 'modelling semiotic systems', which was introduced in the proceedings of the 1962 Moscow Symposium, Uspenskij proposed the idea of replacing the word 'semiotics' in the title with 'secondary modelling systems'. Uspenskij explained his choice:

> For me, this title had the following important values: (1) it sounded very scientific; (2) it was completely incomprehensible; (3) if really needed, it could have been explained: primary modelling systems that model reality are natural languages, and all the rest that build upon them are secondary. I did not hide from Lotman the mocking and hooliganish character of my suggestion, but to my surprise he became immediately attached to it. He explained that incomprehensibility is not a property of parody, as I mistakenly believed, but a characteristic of a sophisticated science. (V. Uspenskij 1995: 106–7)

Summer school of secondary modelling systems

The first summer school was held from 19 to 29 August 1964 at the university sports centre in Kääriku – a secluded and naturally beautiful place in southern Estonia. The gathering lived up to Lotman's expectations: there were around thirty participants, who embraced a simple country lifestyle and had plenty of time to engage in informal dialogue that fostered an interdisciplinary exchange of ideas. As remembered by Egorov: 'During the 50 years of my academic career, I have never seen anything comparable in terms of novelty, brilliance, productivity, candour and solidarity. Those 10 intense days provided so many ideas and were so stimulating that their effect lasted for several years afterwards' (Egorov 1994: 85). After 1964, the summer school gatherings were planned for every two years, with the next three, held in 1966, 1968 and 1970, following this time frame as well as the general organizational pattern (Salupere 2012). By the time of the second summer school, these events had become well known, and as the invitations were limited to a closed circle, participation was seen as an indication of a certain status (Salupere 2012: 307).

The summer school events managed to take in a couple of foreign guests as well.[3] Roman Jakobson from the United States, who was attending another conference in Moscow at the time, managed to join the semiotic gathering in 1966, which was quite extraordinary in the context of the Soviet regime as 'due to the presence of a Soviet garrison, Tartu was a "closed" town: to travel to Tartu, Western guests needed a special permission which was not easy to obtain' (Grishakova and Salupere 2015: 177). The fourth summer school was attended by another guest from the United States, the linguist and semiotician Thomas Sebeok, who gave a talk on types of sign. This gathering was centred around the topic of semiotics of culture, and laid the initial groundwork for the establishment of semiotics of culture as a separate scientific discipline three years later in the 'Theses on the Semiotic Study of Cultures' (Lotman et al. [1973] 2013), co-authored by Lotman, Ivanov, Piatigorsky, Toporov and B. Uspenskij. All the summer school meetings were accompanied by published proceedings (although the content of the proceedings did not always entirely match the actual presentations); the theses presented in these proceedings were often later also developed into articles published in the TMS journal *Trudy po znakovym sistemam* (see Salupere and Torop 2013: 21).

In 1970, new rector Arnold Koop was assigned to the University of Tartu, with whom Lotman did not manage to continue similar co-operation as he had had with Klement. There was an unsuccessful struggle to stage the next summer school. Eventually they managed to pull off a four-day event in February 1974 called the First All-Union Symposium on Semiotics of the Humanities, which took place in Tartu. Although much different from the summer gatherings in both organization and atmosphere, the event brought together the same circle of participants. With that the series of regular semiotic gatherings of the TMS came to an end. However, the network created through the summer school events remained in close contact through various academic events and gatherings. There was also an attempt to reanimate the TMS gathering in 1986, when a summer school took place in Kääriku, but it was an entirely different event (Salupere 2012: 309).

Despite the fact that the summer school tradition was short-lived, it managed to maintain the central position for the school's self-description. In the memories of the participants, the summer school gatherings were mainly connected with the notion of freedom through the liberating atmosphere, which, according to Mihhail Lotman, 'did not concern merely scholarly or academic liberty – against the background of the Soviet reality, the summer school meetings were perceived as safety valves in the stale atmosphere of Soviet non-liberty' (M. Lotman [1996] 2000: 30). For example, Toporov recalls that it was like 'being outside this world with its topical affairs, it was a feeling of emancipation, a sensation of the proximity of the space of liberty and the impending meeting with it, a euphoria of spirit' (Toporov 1994: 336). Boris Gasparov ([1989] 1994: 280–1) has described these regular trips to Tartu as a spiritual experience that gave the feeling of internal independence, of entering a mental space protected from a hostile environment. And Vladimir Uspenskij remembers that 'for some the feeling of being in a sanctuary was the most prevalent, for others, it was the cognizance of truth revealed in this sanctuary (even if it may have been imaginary). Both, nevertheless, have an emotionally enlightening impact' (V. Uspenskij 1995: 108).

Lotman had a central role in creating this specific ambience of freedom in the summer school gatherings (something that has been emphasized by many of the participants). As the oldest among them, he managed to create an exceptional, dialogic atmosphere in which everybody was equal, where everyone had the right to their own opinion, where people were passionate about science but where everything went smoothly, playfully and cheerfully. Boris Uspenskij has quoted Roman Jakobson's impression of the extraordinary organization of the school:

> I have never seen an arrangement like that. The participants at the conference probably had the impression that there was no arrangement at all – all presentations and speeches took place as if by themselves, discussions arose spontaneously. But behind it all there was the iron grip of the supervisor of the conference, Juri Lotman – a magnificent, incomparable organizer! (B. Uspenskij 1987: 24)

Uspenskij remarked that he had great pleasure in hearing this, since he knew for certain that, in fact, nothing was indeed organized – everything proceeded by its own accord. If there was an instance of organization, it was Lotman's personality rather than his iron grip (B. Uspenskij 1987: 24).[4]

In many ways, the experience of the summer school served as a model that set the standards for the overall academic communication in the TMS. For Juri Lotman, the dominant principle of this communication was a dialogue based on difference. In an essay titled 'Winter Notes on Summer Schools', Lotman writes:

> Diversity of interests, difference in mentality and age – their dissimilarity in everything – led to continuous and productive dialogue between the participants. [. . .] These meetings were so dense with fruitful contradictions that it is difficult to describe them as a single system. (Lotman [1990] 1998: 85)

Although these words were meant to describe the gathering in Kääriku, they illustrate well Lotman's perception of the TMS in general as well as reflecting his own theoretical understanding of non-trivial communication.[5]

Trudy po znakovym sistemam

The appreciation of difference and the understanding of its creative value in communication seems to be one of the reasons why attempts at unification at the theoretical or methodological level inside the school were not forced and why the individuality of each scholar was put above the theoretical coherence of the group (see Lotman [1990] 1998: 87). Recognition of the individual style and personal opinion of each member of the TMS was also a guiding principle for *Trudy po znakovym sistemam* (Torop 1995: 226). Especially telling in this regard is the editorial board's foreword to the second volume of *Trudy po znakovym sistemam*, which gathered a collection of papers, mainly presented at the first summer school in August 1964 and published in 1965:

> The range of questions that arise when dealing with topics of myth, folklore, ritual, literature and visual arts as modelling sign systems is so diverse and the number of unresolved issues so vast, that the participants of the summer school did not always succeed in reaching a consensus. The editors did not consider it useful to artificially unify different points of view. However, the general focus of the research, as the editors believe, gives the collection the necessary unity, at the same time, not taking away the opportunity of the participants to seek scientific truth in the direction which they personally find most fruitful. (Redkollegiia 1965: 6)

The first issue of the journal *Trudy po znakovym sistemam* was published in 1964 making it the first semiotic journal in the world, which also contributed significantly to the establishment of the TMS's international reputation (Grzybek 1998: 424). Alongside the summer school gatherings, the journal became the main platform for the academic activity of the TMS. Under the leadership of Lotman as the main editor, twenty-five issues were published between 1964 and 1992 with topics ranging from 'mythology, religion, folklore, medieval art, music, theatre, cinema and painting, to etiquette, card games and cartomancy, prophecies, divination, and nonsense poetry' (Grishakova and Salupere 2015: 179). As the main editor, Lotman was the one who connected this variety into a whole through forewords, notes and comments. He made links between the texts, reflected over polemical questions and through that established a dialogue between the various lines of thoughts presented in the journal.

At the same time, the journal served not only as means for dialogue between members of the TMS but also as a way to re-establish the disrupted communication with the past. According to Peeter Torop (2019: 23), the journal's efforts to reconstruct tradition and connect itself to the forgotten or repressed cultural-scientific achievements of the first decades of the twentieth century was a part of the professional attitude of TMS scholars. Hence, the decision to create a separate section in *Trudy po znakovym sistemam*[6] for archival publications and historical overviews of the structuralist movement in science (Issakov 1991: 8) was a particularly significant step in the Soviet context 'in view of the radical disruptions and discontinuities that country suffered during the first half of the twentieth century' (Rudy 1986: 559). In this section, readers of the journal were introduced to the works of such prominent thinkers as 'Czech structuralist and semiotician Jan

Mukařovsky, Russian philosophers Gustav Shpet and Pavel Florensky, and literary scholars Boris Eikhenbaum, Boris Tomashevsky, Olga Freidenberg, Boris Yarkho' (Grishakova and Salupere 2015: 174), and many others. In addition, through special issues devoted to single authors, the journal established direct links with the heritage of Juri Tynyanov, Vladimir Propp, Mikhail Bakhtin, Petr Bogatyrev and Dmitry Likhachov. Considering that any connections with the previously harshly condemned formalism were still deemed ideologically questionable and could have attracted trouble from above, Lotman added an editorial commentary for the Reviews and Publications section to explain its function: 'an inalienable part of any legitimate scientific movement is the realization of the relation of its research method to preceding scientific and cultural traditions' (Lotman 1967: 363).

Dialogues in the TMS

In one of his articles, Boris Uspenskij has framed the communication in the TMS as a dialogue between two cultural traditions (see B. Uspenskij 1987). It was the combination of two different directions of philological thought – one that originated in Leningrad and the other in Moscow. As Lotman, Mints and Egorov had all studied philology in Leningrad, their education background was linked to the strong tradition of literary studies in this city and the influence of the OPOIaZ movement (Society for the Study of Poetic Language). At the same time, the Moscow side of the school was tightly connected to the Moscow Linguistic Circle. Boris Uspenskij (1987: 19) has recalled that although at first this difference of cultural platforms between the Moscow linguists and literary scholars from Tartu was clearly evident, it turned out to be extremely rewarding as well, as both sides managed to mutually enrich their work and infected each other with their interests.

The academic communication between Moscow and Tartu was also rewarding in a purely pragmatic sense and benefitted both sides in various ways. As noted by Maxim Waldstein, 'Tartu and Estonia appeared to be Lotman's primary organizational and political resources. An opportunity to meet periodically in a distant place and to publish in a practically uncensored series was more than the Muscovites could wish for at that point' (Waldstein 2008: 36). Although the claim that *Trudy po znakovym sistemam* was practically uncensored is an overstatement, for many scholars publishing an article on semiotics in this journal was probably their only possibility of getting published at all (Chernov 1988: 16). At the same time, for Lotman and his Tartu colleagues, collaboration with Moscow was a chance to resolve some of the limitations imposed by the peripheral location of the University of Tartu. Thanks to their Moscow colleagues, scholars in Tartu were able to get information about books and journals that would not otherwise have reached the poorly supplied libraries of the Soviet periphery. In addition, the connections of the Moscow structuralists, both inside the USSR and to Western scholars, allowed Lotman to expand his academic network immensely.

When talking about the influence the members of the group had on each other's work, it is not always easy to track the links of this communication in a way that would enable us to reproduce the movement of ideas between scholars. Especially considering the importance of face-to-face communication between the participants of the school. In this aspect, it is also necessary to note that for Lotman the intellectual outcome of free academic discussions – whether in the form of university seminar or summer school – belongs equally to every participant, meaning that each one of them had the right to develop these ideas further in their own way without feeling that they were stealing something (see Pesti 2001). This is why the main direct indication of the mutual influences are the co-authored works of the members. For Lotman, the main collaborator was Boris Uspenskij, with whom he wrote many articles that appear central to his own semiotic theory, including 'On the Semiotic Mechanism of Culture' (1971), 'Myth – Name – Culture' (1973) and 'The Role of Dual Models in the Dynamics of Russian Culture' (1977). For Uspenskij, whose academic work before this collaboration had remained predominantly within the limits of linguistics, these were the first steps towards implementing a more holistic approach in cultural semiotics (Lepik 2008: 24).

Lotman published only one article with Piatigorsky, an analysis of the semiotic relationship between text and function (Lotman and Piatigorskij [1968] 1977). However, some authors indicate that Piatigorsky's influence on Lotman's understanding in regard to text–reader dynamics dates back to his much earlier writings (see Shukman 1977; Grishakova and Salupere 2015). Although Lotman did not co-author any papers with Vyacheslav Ivanov (apart from the *Theses*), it is evident that Ivanov's work regarding the functions of the left and right hemispheres of the brain in the basic codes of culture (Ivanov 1978) had a direct impact on Lotman's later writings, where he deals with similar ideas (see, e.g., Lotman 1981; 1983; 1984). In regard to Ivanov's influence on the other members of the group, it is necessary to mention his encyclopaedic knowledge of Western semiotic literature, which enabled the TMS to be up-to-date with the developments of this field in the wider world. The significance of Vladimir Toporov as a dialogue partner for Lotman might not appear as relevant at first glance, considering that their works do not seem to have much in common; however, from the last letter that Lotman sent to Toporov, on the 26 August 1993, we can read that it is exactly their opposing interests that Lotman cherishes as value in itself:

> I am forever grateful for meeting you – as a person and a scholar. [. . .] From the very beginning, you and I took very different paths at scientific crossroads, however it seems to me that this did not separate us, but – on the contrary – somehow brought us even closer together. (Lotman 1997: 690)

It is impossible for us here to list all the meaningful connections made over the course of the TMS's existence that affected Lotman as a scholar. However, there is one more member we need to mention here, Zara Mints. Despite the fact that they have only one officially co-written article published in *Trudy po znakovym sistemam* (Lotman and Mints 1981), Mints, as the first reader and critic of Lotman's works and the main copyeditor of all of his texts, can without doubt be considered one of Lotman's most important dialogue partners.

For the Tartu branch of the school, and for Lotman in particular, it was also essential to be able to develop scientific ideas in dialogue with students.[7] In his *Non-Memoirs*, Lotman reflects on the importance of lecturing for him:

> Working with students was an enormous pleasure. [. . .] Four to six hours of lectures a day did not tire me. On the contrary, the unexpected discovery that during the lectures I was able to come up with fundamentally new ideas, and that by the end of the class I could manage to develop interesting and unexpected concepts, was incredibly inspiring. (Lotman 1995: 40)

It is important to note here that Lotman's pedagogical activity was not explicitly connected with semiotics, and the wide range of courses he read over the years at the University of Tartu were devoted to Russian cultural and literary history (see Kiseleva 1996). However, for Lotman these two spheres – history and semiotics – were inherently inseparable. As a cultural historian, Lotman saw turning to semiotics as a necessary step to overcome the limits of traditional historical writing and approached it as an opportunity to create a new academic basis for historical research. According to him, this balance between empirical material and abstract modelling in scientific research was what defined the Tartu-Moscow group as a school: 'Here is the fundamental difference between our understanding of semiotics and Western semiotics, that remains fixated on the abstract models. For us, however, abstract models were a necessary discipline of the mind, which served as a new tool for studying the traditional material' (Lotman [1990] 1998: 86).

Notes

1. These transcripts that precede the 1962 Symposium and give evidence of the specific and independent development of the structuralist ideas in Tartu are preserved at Juri Lotman Semiotics Repository at Tallinn University and await publication.

2. Honestly and without deductions.

3. There are sources claiming that Julia Kristeva was also a guest at Kääriku in 1969 (see Waldstein 2008: 99; Landolt 2011: 135); however, this information appears to be incorrect.

4. Apart from Lotman's extraordinary personality as the main organizing principle of the gatherings, the summer school gatherings owe a great deal to Ann Malts, a colleague of Lotman at the University of Tartu, who was the main coordinator of these events and made sure that everything ran smoothly.

5. For Lotman, the value of dialogue is linked not to the intersecting parts of the informational spheres of communication partners, but to the transfer of information between non-intersecting parts. The more difficult and inadequate the translation of one non-intersecting part of the space into the language of the other, the more valuable, in informative and social terms, the fact of this paradoxical communication becomes (Lotman [1992] 2009: 5–6).

6. The Reviews and Publications section was present in issues 3–9. The reason why we cannot find it in later issues might be connected on the one hand with the fact that the sizes of the

volumes were drastically reduced after the tenth issue; on the other hand, it is the result of a prohibition on publishing archival materials in University publications (see Torop 1995: 225).

7. The majority of school members from Moscow worked at the institutions of the Academy of Sciences, which meant that they had no direct contact with students, which, as Waldstein (2008: 36) points out, is the main opportunity to reproduce as a school proper.

References

Avtonomova, N. 2021. 'Yuri Lotman and the Moscow-Tartu School of Semiotics: Contemporary Epistemic and Social Contexts', in M. F. Bykova, M. N. Forster and L. Steiner (eds), *The Palgrave Handbook of Russian Thought*, 737–53, Cham: Palgrave Macmillan.

Chernov, I. 1988. 'Historical Survey of Tartu-Moscow Semiotic School', in H. Broms and R. Kaufmann (eds), *Semiotics of Culture: Proceedings of the 25th Symposium of the Tartu-Moscow School of Semiotics, Imatra, Finland, 27th–29th July 1987*, 7–16, Helsinki: Arator.

Egorov, B. 1994. 'U istokov Tartuskoi shkoly: vospominaniia o 1950-kh godakh', *Novoe literaturnoe obozrenie* 8: 78–85.

Egorov, B., Kuzovkina, T. and Poseljagin, N. (eds) 2012. *Iu. M. Lotman, Z. G. Mints – B. F. Egorov. Perepiska 1954–1965 gg*, Tallinn: Tallinn University Press.

Eimermacher, K. (ed.) 1971. *Teksty sovetskogo literaturovedcheskogo strukturalizma*, Munich: Wilhelm Fink.

Gasparov, B. [1989] 1994. 'Tartuskaia shkola 1960-kh godov kak semioticheskii fenomen', in A. D. Koshelev (ed.), *Iu. M. Lotman i tartusko-moskovskaia semioticheskaia shkola*, 279–94, Moscow: Gnozis.

Gerovitch, S. 2002. *From Newspeak to Cyberspeak: A History of Soviet Cybernetics*, Cambridge, MA: The MIT Press.

Gherlone, L. 2020. 'In the Footsteps of the Semiotic School of Moscow-Tartu / Tartu-Moscow: Evaluations and Perspectives', *Semiotica* 235: 229–41.

Grishakova, M. and Salupere, S. 2015. 'A School in the Woods: Tartu-Moscow Semiotics', in M. Grishakova and S. Salupere (eds), *Theoretical Schools and Circles in the Twentieth-Century Humanities: Literary Theory, History, Philosophy*, 173–95, New York and London: Routledge.

Grzybek, P. 1998. 'Moscow-Tartu School', in P. Bouissac (ed.), *Encyclopedia of Semiotics*, 422–25, New York and Oxford: Oxford University Press.

Issakov, S. 1991. 'Ob izdaniiakh kafedry russkoi Literatury', in S. Issakov (ed.), *Trudy po russkoi literature i semiotike kafedry russkoi literatury Tartuskogo universiteta 1958–1990: ukazateli soderzhaniia*, 5–11, Tartu: Kafedra Russkoi Literatury Tartuskogo Universiteta.

Ivanov, V. 1978. *Chet i nechet. Asimmetriia mozga i znakovykh system*, Moscow: Sovetskoe radio.

Kiseleva, L. 1996. 'Akademicheskaia deiatel'nost' Iu. M. Lotmana v Tartuskom universitete', *Slavica Tergestina* 4: 9–19.

Koshelev, A. D. (ed.) 1994. *Iu. M. Lotman i tartusko-moskovskaia semioticheskaia shkola*, Moscow: Gnozis.

Landolt, E. 2011. 'Odin nevozmozhnyi dialog vokrug semiotiki: Iuliia Kristeva – Iurii Lotman', *Novoe literaturnoe obozrenie* 3: 135–50.

Lepik, P. 2008. *Universals in the Context of Juri Lotman's Semiotics*, Tartu: Tartu University Press.

Lotman, Ju. M. 1964. *Lektsii po struktural'noi poetike. Vyp. 1. Vvedenie, teoriia stikha*, Tartu: Izdatel'stvo Tartuskogo universiteta (*Trudy po znakovym sistemam*, 1).

Lotman, Ju. M. 1967. 'O zadachakh razdela obzorov i publikatsii', *Trudy po znakovym sistemam* 3: 364–5.

Lotman, Ju. M. 1981. 'Mozg – tekst – kul'tura – iskusstvennyi intellekt', *Semiotika i informatika* 1: 13–7.

Lotman, Ju. M. 1983. 'Asimmetriia i dialog', *Trudy po znakovym sistemam* 16: 15–30.

Lotman, Ju. M. 1984. 'O semiosfere', *Trudy po znakovym sistemam* 17: 5–23.

Lotman, Ju. M. [1990] 1998. 'Zimnie zametki o letnikh shkolakh', in S. Nekliudov (ed.), *Moskovsko-tartuskaia semioticheskaia shkola. Istoriia, vospominaniia, razmyshleniia*, 85–8. Moscow: Iazyki russkoi kul'tury.

Lotman, J. [1992] 2009. *Culture and Explosion*, trans. W. Clark, ed. M. Grishakova, Berlin: Mouton de Gruyter.

Lotman, Ju. M. 1995. 'Ne-memuary', in E. V. Permiakov (ed.), *Lotmanovskii sbornik*, vol. 1, 223–39, Moscow: IC-Garant.

Lotman, Ju. M. 1997. *Pis'ma 1940–1993*, ed. B. Egorov, Moscow: Shkola 'Iazyki russkoi kul'tury'.

Lotman, Ju. M. and Mints, Z. G. 1981. 'Literatura i mifologiia', *Trudy po znakovym sistemam* 13: 35–55.

Lotman, Ju. M. and Piatigorskij, A. [1968] 1977. 'Text and Function', in D. P. Lucid (ed. and trans.), *Soviet Semiotics: An Anthology*, 125–35, Baltimore, MD: Johns Hopkins University Press.

Lotman, Ju. M. and Uspenskij, B. A. 1971. 'O semioticheskom mekhanizme kul'tury', *Trudy po znakovym sistemam* 5: 144–66.

Lotman, Ju. M. and Uspenskij, B. A. 1973. 'Mif – imia – kul'tura', *Trudy po znakovym sistemam* 6: 282–303.

Lotman, Ju. M. and Uspenskij, B. A. 1977. 'Rol' dual'nykh modelei v dinamike russkoi kul'tury (do kontsa XVIII veka)', *Trudy po russkoi i slavianskoi filologii* 28: 3–36.

Lotman, J., Ivanov, V., Pjatigorskij, A., Toporov, V. and Uspenskij, B. [1973] 2013. 'Theses on the Semiotic Study of Cultures (as Applied to the Slavic Texts)', in S. Salupere, P. Torop and K. Kull (eds), *Beginnings of the Semiotics of Culture*, 53–77, Tartu: University of Tartu Press.

Lotman, M. [1996] 2000. 'A Few Notes on the Philosophical Background of the Tartu School of Semiotics', *S: European Journal for Semiotic Studies* 12 (1): 23–46.

Lucid, D. P. (ed.) 1977. *Soviet Semiotics: An Anthology*, Baltimore, MD: Johns Hopkins University Press.

Meletinsky, E. and Segal, D. 1971. 'Structuralism and Semiotics in the USSR', *Diogenes* 19 (73): 88–115.

Nekliudov, S. (ed.) 1988. *Moskovsko-tartuskaia semioticheskaia shkola. Istoriia, vospominaniia, razmyshleniia*, Moscow: Iazyki russkoi kul'tury.

Permiakov, E. V. (ed.) 1995. *Lotmanovskii sbornik*, vol. 1, Moscow: IC-Garant.

Pesti, M. 2001. 'Intervjuu: Peeter Torop väidab, et tööturg hakkab väärtustama semiootikuid' [Interview: Peter Torop Asserts that Job Market Will Valorize the Semioticians], *Eesti Päevaleht*, 29 March. Available online: https://epl.delfi.ee/artikkel/50873875/b-intervjuu-peet er-torop-vaidab-et-tooturg-hakkab-vaartustama-semiootikuid-b? (accessed 7 January 2021).

Pilshchikov, I. and Trunin, M. 2016. 'The Tartu-Moscow School of Semiotics: A Transnational Perspective', *Sign Systems Studies* 44 (3): 368–401.

Portis-Winner, I. and Winner, T. 1976. 'The Semiotics of Cultural Texts', *Semiotica* 18 (2): 101–56.

Redkollegiia 1965. 'Ot redaktsii', *Trudy po znakovym sistemam* 2: 5–8.

Rewar, W. 1976. 'Tartu Semiotics', *Bulletin of Literary Semiotics* 3: 1–16.

Rudy, S. 1986. 'Semiotics in U.S.S.R.', in T. A. Sebeok and J. Umiker-Sebeok (eds), *The Semiotic Sphere*, 555–82, New York and London: Plenum Press.

Salupere, S. 2012. 'Tartu Summer Schools of Semiotics at the Time of Juri Lotman', *Chinese Semiotic Studies* 6: 303–11.

Salupere, S. 2015. 'The Cybernetic Layer of Juri Lotman's Metalanguage', *Recherches sémiotiques/ Semiotic Inquiry* 35 (1): 63–84.

Salupere, S. and Torop, P. 2013. 'On the Beginnings of the Semiotics of Culture in the Light of the Theses of the Tartu-Moscow School', in S. Salupere, P. Torop and K. Kull (eds), *Beginnings of the Semiotics of Culture*, 15–37, Tartu: Tartu University Press.

Semenenko, A. 2012. *The Texture of Culture: An Introduction to Yuri Lotman's Semiotic Theory*, New York: Palgrave Macmillan.

Seyffert P. 1985. *Soviet Literary Structuralism: Background, Debate, Issues*, Columbus, OH: Slavica Publishers.

Shukman, A. 1977. *Literature and Semiotics: A Study of the Writings of Yu. M. Lotman*, New York and Oxford: North-Holland Publishing Company.

Toporov, V. 1994. 'Vmesto vospominaniia', in A. D. Koshelev (ed.), *Iu. M. Lotman i tartusko-moskovskaia semioticheskaia shkola*, 330–48, Moscow: Gnozis.

Torop, P. 1995. 'Tartuskaia shkola kak shkola', in E. V. Permiakov (ed.), *Lotmanovskii sbornik*, vol. 1, 223–39, Moscow: IC-Garant.

Torop, P. 2014. 'The Tartu-Moscow School of Semiotics and the Possibilities of Cultural Analysis', *Chinese Semiotic Studies* 10 (1): 109–17.

Torop, P. 2019. 'Russian Theory and Semiotics of Culture: History and Perspectives', *Bakhtiniana: Revista de Estudos do Discurso* 14 (4): 19–39.

Uspenskij, B. 1987. 'K probleme genezisa tartusko-moskovskoi semioticheskoi shkoly', *Trudy po znakovym sistemam* 20: 18–29.

Uspenskij, V. 1995. 'Progulki s Lotmanom i vtorichnoe modelirovanie', in E. V. Permiakov (ed.), *Lotmanovskii sbornik*, vol. 1, 99–127, Moscow: IC-Garant.

Waldstein, M. 2008. *The Soviet Empire of Signs: A History of the Tartu School of Semiotics*, Saarbrücken: VDM Verlag.

CHAPTER 7
LOTMAN IN TRANSNATIONAL CONTEXT
Igor Pilshchikov

The intellectual lineage of Juri Lotman's legacy can best be understood in a broader European and global context. The methodological impetus gained from Baudouinian and Saussurean linguistics and the conceptual transfer of the paragons of *fin-de-siècle* German formal art criticism to Russia created the formalist breakthrough of the 1910s. The theory of literature and poetic language developed by Russian formalists in the 1920s revolutionized twentieth-century humanities. The Russian Formalist School did not possess internal methodological unity and did not manage to create a new scientific paradigm (in Thomas Kuhn's sense of this word). From the Kuhnian standpoint, formalism, as Peter Steiner pointed out, 'can be termed an "interparadigmatic stage" in the evolution of Slavic literary scholarship' (Steiner 1984: 269). In 1926, Roman Jakobson, ex-president of the Moscow Linguistic Circle and a former member of OPOIaZ (the two foremost formalist associations in Russia), co-founded a new linguistic circle in Prague. An innovative scientific paradigm was established by the Prague Linguistic Circle in the mid-1930s when its leaders, including Jakobson and Jan Mukařovský, proposed a programme that integrated structural linguistic and semiotic methods for the study of Slavic languages, literatures and cultures. Hence, formalism and its successor, structuralism, started to spread across Europe and America (after Jakobson's emigration to the United States).

An encounter between Jakobson and Claude Lévi-Strauss in the New York-based École Libre des Hautes Études (ELHE) in 1942 resulted in Lévi-Strauss's transfer of structuralist methods to anthropology. In New York, Jakobson collaborated with the Czechoslovak government in exile and positioned himself, in his own words, as a representative of 'the Prague school of linguistics and literary history' (Toman 1995: 247). On the other hand, ELHE was a sui generis French 'university in exile' supported by the Rockefeller Foundation and Charles de Gaulle's *France Libre* (Rutkoff and Scott 1983). ELHE employed prominent scholars who left France and Belgium under threat of persecution – some of them, like Lévi-Strauss, due to their Jewish origin. Lévi-Strauss's subsequent return to France prompted the formation and development of French structuralism and semiotics. Jakobson was also a paternal figure for the Tartu-Moscow School of Semiotics (henceforward referred to as TMS), as is confirmed by interviews with the members of the School taken by Kalevi Kull and Ekaterina Velmezova (Velmezova and Kull 2011: 300–1; 2017: 413–5; Kull and Velmezova 2018: 186).

A distinctive feature of the TMS was the combination of structuralist and semiotic approaches to culture. This synthesis originates in Prague, from which it came to Tartu primarily via Jakobson (Pilshchikov and Trunin 2016: 377–8). Moreover, Jakobson and his lifelong friend Petr Bogatyrev not only were among the founders of the Moscow and Prague Linguistic Circles but also participated in the Kääriku/Tartu Summer School on Semiotics. The seventh volume of the University of Tartu periodical *Trudy po znakovym sistemam* was dedicated to the memory of Bogatyrev and included an obituary authored by Lotman. In it, he characterized Bogatyrev as 'the living history of semiotic research' and recalled 'a memorable evening by the fireplace' at the Second Semiotic School held in Kääriku in 1966, 'during which P. G. Bogatyrev and R. O. Jakobson shared their memories of the Moscow Linguistic Circle and the first steps of semiotic research in Moscow, Petrograd and Prague' (Lotman 1975: 5–6).

Contemporary cultural mobility studies emphasize the importance of academic mobility – either voluntary or involuntary – for the development of scientific theories. Emigration, exile or retreat function as 'a meeting place' where important transfers and encounters happen. Edward Said maintains that 'the point of theory [. . .] is to travel, always to move beyond its confinements, to emigrate, to remain in a sense in exile. [. . .] This movement suggests the possibility of actively different locales, sites, situations for theory, without facile universalism or over-general totalizing' (Said 2000: 451–2). Referring to Said's 'Travelling Theory', Galin Tihanov emphasizes 'the enormous importance of exile and emigration for the birth of modern literary theory in Eastern and Central Europe' (Tihanov 2019: 12). Tellingly, of the six representative biographies Tihanov mentions (the lives of Georg Lukács, Viktor Shklovsky, Roman Jakobson, Nikolai Trubetzkoy, Petr Bogatyrev and René Wellek), four belong to former members of the Prague Circle and four belong to scholars of Russian origin.

In a 1934 article titled 'About the Premises of the Prague Linguistic School', Jakobson described the Prague School as a 'symbiosis of Czech and Russian thought' (Jakobson 1934: 8). He did not mention German thought as its third constituent (obviously for political reasons), but vaguely indicated other Western influences. This definition is confirmed by the origins of the core members of the Prague Linguistic Circle, which included not only local Czechs and Germans but also Russian émigré scholars of both Russian and Jewish backgrounds (Toman 1995: 103–35; Pilshchikov 2019a). The Prague School was polygenetic because it elaborated on both the Russian formalist tradition and the Czech version of Herbartian aesthetics (Steiner 1982b).

Jakobson posited that the wide-ranging national and cultural origins of its members contributed to the symbiotic nature of the Prague School: 'The School's originality is manifested in the selection of new ideas and their connection into a systematic whole. Czechoslovakia lies at the crossroads of various cultures, and its distinctive character consists [. . .] in the creative merging of streams whose sources are at some distance from one another' (Jakobson 1934: 8). In another article of the Prague period, he made polygeneticism into a principle for a school of thought: '[O]nly bidirectional wholes create cultural movements distinguished by significant [literally: far-reaching] export values' (Jakobson 1938: 233). For Jakobson, structuralist theory developed for the advancement of Slavic Studies was 'a systematically organized creation [. . .] of cultural export', aimed for particular 'markets of cultural retail' (Jakobson 1929: 637; see Avtonomova and Gasparov 1997).

Interwar Prague was one of the places open for transcultural contact, 'the "free market of ideas"' (Steiner 1982b: 179) or – in terms of Stephen Greenblatt's 'Mobility Studies Manifesto' – 'a "contact zone" where cultural goods were exchanged' (Greenblatt 2009: 251), 'contact zone' being Mary Louise Pratt's concept that refers to 'social spaces where cultures meet, clash and grapple with each other, often in contexts of highly asymmetrical relations of power' (Pratt 1999: 34). Prague – a remnant of the collapsed Austrian-Hungarian Empire, a nexus for the construction of a new cultural and political Central European identity, and an asylum for émigrés from the collapsed Russian Empire – provided fertile ground for literary and cultural theory that 'developed at the intersection between national enthusiasms and a cultural cosmopolitanism that transcended local encapsulation and monoglossia' (Tihanov 2019: 11–2).

Lotman described the same phenomenon in an unpublished article of the early 1970s entitled 'Nekotorye problemy sravnitel'nogo izucheniia khudozhestvennykh tekstov' ('Issues in the Comparative Study of Artistic Texts'), in which he elaborated on the theory of 'cultural areals' formed under the influence of Jakobson's and Trubetzkoy's theory of *Sprachbünde*. Lotman wrote:

An aggregate of cultures with certain common codes forms a cultural areal. An intra-areal exchange is always more intensive. Of special interest for comparative studies, in this respect, are those geographic regions where cultures of different types have co-existed and found themselves in close spatial communication for a long time. Examples of such regions are Transcaucasia, the Baltic countries, the Mediterranean, and Central Europe. (Lotman 1971: 16)

Lotman's Estonia, home to the Tartu School, can likewise be characterized as a place open for intercultural contact, Pratt's and Greenblatt's 'contact zone'. The regime of transcultural displacement and forced academic mobility was also relevant for the birth of the TMS. First and foremost, Lotman himself moved to Estonia in 1950 because he was unable to find a job in his native Leningrad due to the Soviet 'anti-cosmopolitan' (i.e. anti-Semitic) campaign of 1949 and the anti-Semitic policy that followed. But the Moscow branch had a similar start. In 1959, Vyacheslav Ivanov, then an associate professor at Moscow State University, was expelled from his alma mater for the 'antipatriotic actions and behaviour' manifested in his defence of the 'anti-Soviet' poet and novelist Boris Pasternak and the 'renegade' and 'US citizen' Roman Jakobson (quoted in Vroon and Pilshchikov 2018: 165–6). Jakobson, whom Ivanov met in person for the first time in 1956 (when Jakobson came to Moscow for preparation of the Fourth Congress of Slavists), became a 'model' scholar for him. Ivanov accepted Jakobson's research programme of developing a single methodology for the multifarious study of languages, literatures, arts, folklore, myths and other constituents of traditional and modern cultures in the framework of structural and semiotic approaches (Krylov 2007; Pilshchikov and Vroon 2018). Ivanov accompanied Jakobson on his academic trips to the Soviet Union, including a visit to Tallinn, Tartu and Kääriku in 1966 (Ivanov 1995: 171–3; [1995] 2010; 1999).

In 1961, Ivanov was invited to join the newly founded Structural Typology Sector of the Institute of Slavic Studies in Moscow, and in 1963 he was appointed head of the Sector. His predecessor in this position was Vladimir Toporov, his college friend in the recent past and co-author in the nearest future. In 1962, Ivanov and Toporov organized the Moscow Symposium on the Structural Analysis of Sign Systems. This event is generally acknowledged to be the symbolic birthday of 'Soviet' semiotics (Baran 1976: xi; Seyffert 1985: 14, 164–71; Poselyagin 2011). The Symposium consistently sought to develop a unified semiotic approach to different disciplines within the humanities. For the ruling orthodox Marxists, the Symposium was so uninhibited and unusual in its methods that the academic establishment in Moscow reacted with unanticipated severity. Semiotic research was persecuted and largely suppressed, and the semioticians' regular meetings were moved, of necessity, to Estonia. As Ivanov testifies in his later memoir, in the early 1970s semiotics was 'semi-forbidden in Moscow [. . .] and only permitted as an import from Tartu' (Ivanov 1998: 10).

Lotman and Ivanov got to know each other in 1963 (Ivanov 1995: 173). In 1964, Lotman published his first major book of literary theory, *Lektsii po struktural'noi poetike* (Lectures on Structural Poetics), which was also the first issue of *Trudy po znakovym sistemam* (Lotman 1964). Ivanov joined the editorial board of *Trudy po znakovym sistemam*, and a semi-official association was formed that became known as the Tartu-Moscow or Moscow-Tartu School of Semiotics. The general consensus was that the Tartu branch was headed by Lotman, and the Moscow branch by Ivanov and Toporov. Therefore, Ivanov's expulsion from Moscow University became the first step towards the self-organization of what would become known as 'Soviet' structuralism and semiotics. The attribute 'Soviet' is used in scare quotes here because the TMS was never fully accepted by the official academic authorities in the USSR and remained a semi-formal (although not completely prohibited) movement in the humanities.

In the perspective of the 'Travelling Theory' concept, the School's forced move to Tartu is significant. Beginning in 1964, Ivanov, Toporov and several other linguists and semioticians from Moscow (including Boris Uspenskij, soon to become Lotman's collaborator and co-author) became regular participants in the Summer School of Semiotics. The meetings took place in Kääriku near Tartu in 1964, 1966, 1968 and 1970 (see Chapter 6). The next meeting was to be held in Yerevan, Armenia, in 1972, or Kääriku in 1973, but was suppressed, and in 1973 only a *Collection of Essays on Secondary Modelling Systems* was published. In winter 1974, the All-Union Symposium for the Study of Secondary Modelling Systems was held in Tartu. Each venue was followed by publications of *Synopses* or *Materials*, most of them edited by Lotman.

On the occasion of the fiftieth anniversary of the Moscow Linguistic Circle in 1965, Jakobson published an article with a long descriptive title: 'An Example of Migratory Terms and Institutional Models' (Jakobson [1965] 1971). Here he pointed out the fact that the Moscow Linguistic Circle served as an institutional model for both the Prague Linguistic Circle and another important centre of European structuralism, the Linguistic Circle of Copenhagen. Both circles were even intentionally named to recall their Moscow predecessor. An important feature of the Prague Linguistic Circle, however, was its combination of the features of two Russian formalist associations – the Society for the Study of Poetic Language (OPOIaZ), based in Petrograd/Leningrad, and the Moscow Linguistic Circle (MLC). The Prague Circle combined the MLC-type organizational structure with regular meetings with OPOIaZ-type self-promotion based on the Circle's periodical, *Travaux du Cercle Linguistique de Prague*, published from 1929 to 1939.

Ten years later, in 1975, Vyacheslav Ivanov published an article entitled 'Sign Systems of Academic Behaviour', in which he developed Jakobson's typology of semi-formal academic communities and traced the organizational structure of the TMS back to the Prague School and its kernel, the Prague Linguistic Circle, and even further back to the Moscow Linguistic Circle (Ivanov 1975). Ivanov classified the TMS in the same taxon as the Prague Circle:

> A necessary condition for the fruitfulness of periodic meetings of scientific groups, the members of which are usually separated in space (these meetings excepted), is a preliminary distribution of written synopses of keynote presentations. This is, in particular, exemplified by the experience of the summer school of semiotics periodically organized by Prof. Ju. M. Lotman in Tartu since 1964. [. . .] International recognition and sober critical assessment of the achievements of the Tartu School, as well as the Prague Linguistic Circle, were made possible only thanks to their publications. (Ivanov 1975: 4)

From this point of view, the role of Tartu periodicals, proceedings and collected essays is hard to overestimate – in relation to both the international standing of the TMS and its self-organization.

Lotman and Uspenskij considered the Moscow Linguistic Circle and OPOIaZ, as well as their traditions preserved in Moscow and Leningrad Universities, as the main predecessors of the TMS. In the paper 'The Problem of the Genesis of the Tartu-Moscow School of Semiotics', Uspenskij stated that the School 'unifies two traditions: the Moscow linguistic tradition with the Leningrad literary-historical [*literaturovedcheskaia*] tradition, which mutually enrich each other. This symbiosis has proven extraordinarily fruitful for both traditions' (Uspenskij 1987: 21). Uspenskij's paper was first delivered as a talk at the Institute of Language and Literature of the Academy of Sciences of the GDR in Berlin in 1981. The next year, in a paper entitled 'Universitet – nauka – kul'tura' ('University – Science – Culture'), which remained unpublished until recently, Lotman described the genesis of the TMS in a similar way, but added the University of Tartu with its 'Europeanness':

> The alumni of Moscow University and Leningrad University formed the Soviet school of semiotics as a synthesis of these two traditions in the humanities. To them, a third tradition was added: the University of Tartu. This was no accident: the University of Tartu had its own, well-established linguistic school, and, moreover, was always typified by a high spirit of academic tolerance and openness to European-wide cultural trends. (Lotman [1982] 2016: 684–5)

Linguistic and cultural polyglotism are indispensable fundamentals in Lotman's concept of the semiosphere (Lotman [1984] 2005). Moreover, 'no semiotic mechanism can function as an isolated system within a vacuum', as Lotman put it in 'Culture as a Subject and Its Own Object'. He emphasized that meaning-making 'assumes the introduction of texts from outside the system and their specific, unpredictable transformation between the time they enter and leave the system' (Lotman [1989] 2019: 86, 85). It should be noted in this context that the term 'Tartu School' itself came 'from the outside': it was first used by the Czech scholar Miroslav Drozda in an article published in a Yugoslav journal (Drozda 1969).

The TMS was an open, multicultural and interlingual phenomenon in terms both of its external relations and its internal social structure, which unified scholars of Estonian, Russian and Jewish origins (Pilshchikov and Trunin 2016). The TMS members not only had different cultural and linguistic affiliations; they also came from overlapping, but different academic communities. The school was not a single homogeneous institution, but a translinguistic, transnational, transinstitutional, transdisciplinary association, otherwise known as an 'invisible college' as Igor Chernov and Peeter Torop suggested (Chernov 1988: 8; Torop 1995: 233), using a term introduced by Diana Crane (Crane 1972; cf. Vihalemm and Müürsepp 2007: 174). This 'invisible college' spanned all manner of borders, identities and domains: 'Estonian', 'Russian', 'Soviet', 'émigré', 'Orientalist', 'Slavist', 'linguist', 'philosopher', 'historian', 'critic' and so on.

The question of the 'geographical territorialization' of Lotman's theory can also be approached from a different angle. It is not unusual today to describe French structuralism and post-structuralism as 'French Theory', although it has been argued that 'French Theory' is, ironically, 'a peculiarly American construct that can only be understood as the product of the blinkered enthusiasm of Anglo-Saxon academics for a range of thought they have not properly understood' (Baring 2011: 1). The early ancestors of the 'French Theory' – Russian formalism and the Bakhtin circle – as well as their continuation in the TMS have sometimes been called 'Russian theory' (Zenkin 2004; Zenkine 2006; Depretto 2010; Torop 2017, 2019) despite this theory's apparently German and partly Polish roots (Jakobson [1943] 1971; Romand and Tchougounnikov 2009; Dmitrieva, Zemskov and Espagne 2009; Dmitriev 2010; Espagne 2014). Similarly, the research programme developed by the Prague Linguistic Circle in the 1920s and 1930s, and its extension, the Prague School, earned the name 'Czech theory' (Gvoždiak 2016; Velmezova 2016), despite Jakobson's description of its symbiotic transnational nature. The unique combination of (post)-Lotmanian cultural-semiotics and (post)-Uexküllian biosemiotics developed in Tartu has been referred to as 'Estonian theory' (Tamm and Kull 2015; 2020), despite its mixed German-Russian origins (Torop 2000; Kull et al. 2011; Deely 2012; Kull and Peng 2013). It becomes clear from this brief overview that historians of ideas include Jakobson in both the 'Russian' and 'Czech' theories, and Lotman is likewise included in both the 'Russian' and 'Estonian' theories.

At first glance, postulating the existence of geographically, culturally and nationally specific theories seems to contradict the notion of the international and universal nature of human knowledge. However, these terms have gained a foothold in the history of the humanities for delineating 'a particular historico-geographical *crystallization*' of a wider methodology (Steiner 1982a: xi), a specific culturally and geographically located '*condensation* of theories within the heterogeneous network of cultural communication' accompanied by 'the evolution of certain local peculiarities which then lend support to the thinkers' pursuits and form a mental atmosphere, powerfully shaping the ideas and questions raised by those participating in it' (Tamm and Kull 2016: 76; my emphasis in both quotations). Therefore, terms such as 'Russian theory' or 'Estonian theory' should be understood as descriptions of open systems of ideas favoured in particular cultures and societies, rather than generated by those cultures and societies 'independently' from others. The same can be applied to definitions such as the 'Prague School' or the 'Tartu-Moscow School'. A 'school' can be considered an emergent property of certain persons interacting with each other (Sutrop 2015). This also involves places of interaction (countries and cities, universities, research institutes, private homes, etc.) and means of interaction (correspondence, conferences, collaboration, and so on). Although all interactions are embedded in a cultural and historical context, a school's borders cannot be clear-cut: as Margus Ott remarked (private communication), every 'school' extends to infinity (cf. Sooväli and Ott 2020). At the same time, this infinity is not homogeneous, and interactions between its heterogeneous parts ('crystallizations' or 'condensations') are important stages in the development of human knowledge. Therefore, different theories 'can easily have some parts in common, and many scholars may well belong to both, or several, at once' (Tamm and Kull 2016: 77; 2020: 30–1).

A transnational approach to the study of the typology and history of literary and cultural theories can help us to outline several cross-cultural transfers of theoretical concepts and research tools from linguistics to literary theory and structural anthropology and further to semiotics and cultural studies. The global 'transcultural trajectory' of this process (Tamm 2020: 143–4) can be schematically divided into the following five stages of ex-, de- and re-territorialization (Pilshchikov 2019b: 224): (1) the transfer and transfiguration of formalist ideas ('Russian theory') from Russia to Europe with the formation of Prague structuralism; (2) the export of Central European structuralist and semiotic concepts ('Czech theory') to the United States and then to France; (3) their re-importation to the USSR ('Soviet' literary structuralism and semiotics); (4) the subsequent post-structuralist reaction in France – exported soon to the United States as 'French Theory'; and (5) the post-Soviet elaboration of the legacy of structuralism and semiotics ('Estonian theory').

This outline is not only schematic but also incomplete. Firstly, each stage is, in effect, polygenetic, so it can be easily built into the indigenous histories of territorialized national traditions as well. Secondly, the scheme does not include quite a few important phenomena such as Danish glossematics, or Italian structuralism and semiotics, or Polish formalism, structuralism and semiotics. Thirdly, we should take into account the parallel development and mutual awareness of different schools.

This reciprocity explains bidirectional processes, such as the numerous translations of Lotman into Italian and the growing interest in the theoretical works of Umberto Eco in late Soviet and post-Soviet Russia. It also sheds new light on the simultaneity of such events as Lotman's postscript to the Russian edition of Eco's *The Name of the Rose* (Lotman 1989) and Eco's introduction to the Anglophone edition of Lotman's *Universe of the Mind* (Eco 1990), which played a crucial role in establishing the international reputation of Lotman's theories.

A telling example is a reciprocal interest of Lotman and Maria-Renata Mayenowa, the indisputable leader of Polish studies in poetics and semiotics. Mayenowa was a disciple of Manfred Kridl, founder of the Polish Formalist School. Polish formalists were highly indebted to Russian formalism and at the same time leaned upon their native Polish philosophical tradition (Pomorska 1968: 13; Karcz 2002; Mrugalski 2018). Later, Mayenowa organized and headed what now is known as the Department of Theoretical Poetics of the Institute of Literary Studies at the Polish Academy of Sciences in Warsaw. Mayenowa contributed a lot to our understanding of Lotman. She published a review of the first four volumes of *Trudy po znakovym sistemam* and Lotman's *The Structure of the Artistic Text* (1970) in the Amsterdam-based journal *Russian Literature* (Mayenowa 1972),[1] and contributed a paper, 'Lotman as a Historian of Literature', to a special issue of *Russian Literature* devoted to Lotman (Mayenowa 1977). Mayenowa and Lotman discussed various scientific and organizational questions in their vast correspondence, which is preserved in archives at Tartu, Tallinn and Warsaw. A planned annotated publication of these letters will hopefully enable us to demonstrate how Polish scholars, however specific their approach to culture may have been (see Mayenowa 1983; Łebkowska 2012; Kola and Ulicka 2015), contributed to the general development of semiotics and cultural theory.

Another evidence of Lotman's transnational horizon is his interest in similar, sometimes interrelated, developments of structural poetics and cultural semiotics in (the now former) Czechoslovakia and the (now former) Soviet Union. In the October 1968 issue of the most authoritative Estonian linguistic and literary journal *Keel ja Kirjandus* ('Language and Literature'), Lotman published an article in Estonian under the title 'Kunsti semiootilise uurimise tulemusi tänapäeval' ('Recent Achievements in the Semiotic Study of Art') (Lotman 1968). The article places Soviet semiotics in an international context – primarily Czechoslovak, Polish and French. However, an extensive section devoted to structuralist and semiotic research in Czechoslovakia was entirely excluded from the published text. It was most likely censored after the suppression of the 'Prague Spring' and the invasion of the Warsaw Pact troops in Czechoslovakia in August 1968. This section discussed the works of the Prague School and, in particular, the theoretical achievements of Mukařovský and his followers. Lotman was very impressed by a Festschrift prepared by Mukařovský's disciples on the occasion of his seventy-fifth birthday (Jankovič, Pešat and Vodička 1966), calling it 'the summa of contemporary Czech structural literary studies' (Lotman [1968] 2018: 183).[2]

In the late 1960s, together with his friend Oleg Malevich, a prominent Russian scholar of Czech culture, and Malevich's wife Viktoria Kamenskaia, a leading translator from Czech and Slovak, Lotman started working on a two-volume edition of Mukařovský's works on structural poetics and aesthetics. The manuscript, which opens with Lotman's introductory article 'Jan Mukařovský – teoretik iskusstva' ('Jan Mukařovský as Art Theorist') and concludes with meticulous annotations compiled by Lotman and Malevich, was submitted to the Moscow-based publishing house Iskusstvo in summer 1969. The mid-1960s was the most important stage in the history of the reception of the Prague School by the Tartu and Moscow structuralists. The Russian edition of Josef Vachek's *Dictionnaire de linguistique de l'École de Prague* appeared in 1964 (Vachek [1960] 1964), and a collection of Russian translations of the most important linguistic works of the Prague Linguistic Circle was published three years later (Kondrashov 1967). A book representing Mukařovský's works on literary theory and semiotic aesthetics was slated to be next in this series. However, it was banned – presumably as a reaction to the Prague events of 1968[3] – and the two volumes edited by Malevich and Lotman saw the light of day only after the collapse of the Soviet Union, as two separate books printed by different publishers (Mukařovský 1994; 1996).

Of special importance for the evolution of the TMS were 'Theses on the Semiotic Study of Cultures', a collective manifesto presented at the Seventh International Congress of Slavists held in Warsaw in 1973. A precedent text and generic model for this important self-statement were the collective 'Thèses du Cercle Linguistique de Prague', which had been presented at the First International Congress of Slavists in Prague in 1929. In the 1973 'Theses', Lotman and his co-authors described semiotic research as both self-cognition of Slavic culture(s) and a transnational effort:

> [Semiotic] investigation is not only an instrument for the study of culture but is also part of its object. Scientific texts, being metatexts of the culture, may at the same time be regarded as its texts. Therefore any significant scientific idea may be regarded both as an attempt to cognize culture and as a fact of its life [. . .]. From this point of view we might raise the question of modern structural-semiotic studies as phenomena of Slavic culture (the role of the Czech, Slovak, Polish, Russian, and other traditions). (Lotman et al. [1973] 2013: 77)

A single, homogeneous history of semiotics and cultural theory would be both an empirical and a theoretical dead-end: these systems are polygenetic in origin, and their development is multidirectional. Recent methodological advances in *histoire croisée* ('entangled history'), which describes intellectual evolution as a transcultural and multilateral process, encourage investigating the relationships between scholars of different cultural, national and ethnic backgrounds in terms of reciprocity and reversibility (Werner and Zimmermann 2006).

The research of these relations can clarify the heretofore underestimated role of the TMS as a synthesis between 'Western' and 'Eastern' intellectual traditions. From the 1960s to 1990s, the TMS served, despite the Iron Curtain, as an intermediary between Western and Eastern academic communities from France and Italy to Czechoslovakia and Poland, and from Russia to China and Japan. It comes as no surprise, then, that Lotman's archives in Tartu and Tallinn contain a great deal of documentation of the TMS's international connections. In particular, the archives contain Lotman's correspondence with Estonia's and Russia's leading intellectuals, as well as prominent structuralists and semioticians worldwide. Tallinn University Press has started publishing these materials in the *Bibliotheca Lotmaniana* book series. These publications will substantially enrich and complicate our present picture of how the TMS fits into the history of structuralism and semiotics writ large. This approach does not aspire to regularize the past, reconcile conflicts and produce a unified (hi)story. Rather, on the narrative level an 'histoire croisée' research project will result in an ensemble of mutually complementing histories of Lotmanian semiotics.

The schools of semiotics that emerged from Tartu over the last sixty years have had an outsized global impact, fundamentally affecting humanistic inquiry not just in Europe, but the world over. In the 1970s, many representatives of the TMS emigrated to Israel, Western Europe and North America. The evolution of the former members of the TMS, including Lotman's former mentees, who continued to work in new cultural and linguistic contexts, has not yet been written. A separate branch is now developing in independent Estonia and is known as 'New Tartu Semiotics' (Torop 2000).

Although the first English-language monograph on Lotman was published long ago (Shukman 1977) and 'Lotman's work has been gradually generating interest in English-language cultural studies for several years' now (Ibrus and Torop 2015: 5), in the English-speaking world he remains insufficiently known among literary and cultural theorists outside Slavistics (Blaim 1998; Winner 2002; Shukman 2005; Schönle and Shine 2006: 6; Todd 2006; Platt 2008: 321; Kull 2011a: 344–5). The reception of Lotmanian semiotics in Slavic countries, France, Italy and Germany has in general been more positive than the Anglo-American reaction, but also diverse. In terms of their political ideology, these European interpreters of Lotman were either left-wing or conservative thinkers. In terms of institutional classification, they were either academic scholars (e.g. in Poland, Italy and West Germany; see Żyłko 2012; Faryno 2020; De Michiel 1995; Eimermacher 1995) or members of avant-garde groups (for example, *Tel Quel* in France; see also Chapter 23).

In contrast, more recent Lotmanian studies that have emerged in Latin America[4] and China[5] are quite a departure from what we are accustomed to seeing. The question of why and how Lotman's semiotics is understood and applied in other cultural-linguistic contexts, especially non-Western ones, is very interesting but remains largely unanswered. This research is yet to be done.[6]

Notes

1. See also Lotman's important but not widely known reply: Lotman 1974.

2. The full text of the article was published only recently with our annotations (Lotman [1968] 2018). The title of the Russian original is, in fact, 'Sovremennye perspektivy semioticheskogo izucheniia iskusstva' ('Contemporary Perspectives on the Semiotic Study of Art').

3. See our detailed reconstruction of the history of this unrealized edition based on numerous archival documents (Pilshchikov and Trunin 2018).

4. See Arán and Barei 2006; Barei and Gómez Ponce 2018; Machado and Barei 2019.

5. See Kull 2011b; Chang, Han and Wu 2014; Peng and Jiang 2014; Kull and Magnus 2014.

6. This chapter was written with the support of the Estonian Research Council (PRG319). I am grateful to Ainsley Morse, who provided generous feedback as well as thorough and thoughtful copyediting.

References

Arán, P. O. and Barei, S. 2006. *Texto / memoria / cultura: El pensamiento de Iuri Lotman*, 2nd rev. edn, Córdoba: El Espejo Ediciones.

Avtonomova, N. S. and Gasparov, M. L. 1997. 'Jakobson, slavistika i evraziistvo: dve kon'iunktury, 1929–1953', *Novoe literaturnoe obozrenie* 23: 87–91.

Baran, H. 1976. 'Introduction', in H. Baran (ed.), *Semiotics and Structuralism: Readings from the Soviet Union*, vii–xxvi, White Plains, NY: International Arts and Sciences Press.

Barei, S. and Gómez Ponce, A. (eds) 2018. *Lecciones sobre la cultura y las formas de la vida. Encuentro Córdoba-Tartu*, Córdoba: Editorial del Centro de Estudios Avanzados.

Baring, E. 2011. *The Young Derrida and French Philosophy, 1945–1968*, Cambridge: Cambridge University Press.

Blaim, A. 1998. 'Lotman in the West: An Ambiguous Complaint', in J. Andrew and R. Reid (eds), *Neo-Formalist Papers: Contributions to the Silver Jubilee Conference to Mark 25 Years of the Neo-Formalist Circle*, 329–37, Amsterdam: Rodopi.

Chang, H., Han, L. and Wu, S. C. 2014. 'The Reception of Tartu Semiotics in China: A Preliminary Survey and a Few Case Studies', *Chinese Semiotic Studies* 10 (1): 133–63.

Chernov, I. A. 1988. 'Historical Survey of Tartu-Moscow Semiotic School', in H. Broms and R. Kaufmann (eds), *Semiotics of Culture: Proceedings of the 25th Symposium of the Tartu-Moscow School of Semiotics, Imatra, Finland 27th–29th July, 1987*, 7–16, Helsinki: Arator.

Crane, D. 1972. *Invisible Colleges: Diffusion of Knowledge in Scientific Communities*, Chicago and London: University of Chicago Press.

De Michiel, M. 1995. 'O vospriiatii rabot Iu. M. Lotmana v Italii', in E. V. Permiakov (ed.), *Lotmanovskii sbornik*, vol. 1, 294–306, Moscow: IC-Garant.

Deely, J. 2012. 'The Tartu Synthesis in Semiotics Today Viewed from America', *Chinese Semiotic Studies* 8: 214–26.

Depretto, C. 2010. '[Review of] Tynianovskii sbornik 13: XII–XIII–XIV Tynianovskie chteniia. Issledovaniia. Materialy. Moskva: Vodolei, 2009', *Revue des études slaves* 81 (4): 601–5.

Dmitriev, A. N. 2010. 'Obraztsovaia "russkaia teoriia", ili Zapadnoe nasledie formal'noi shkoly', in J. Axer and I. M. Savel'eva (eds), *Natsionalnaiia gumanitarnaia nauka v mirovom kontekste: opyt Rossii i Pol'shi*, 63–91, Moscow: The Higher School of Economics Publishing House.

Dmitrieva, E. E., Zemskov, V. B. and Espagne, M. (eds) 2009. *Evropeiskii kontekst russkogo formalizma: K probleme esteticheskikh peresechenii. Frantsiia, Germaniia, Italiia, Rossiia*, Moscow: IMLI.

Drozda, M. 1969. 'Tartuska škola', *Umjetnost riječi* 1/2: 87–106.

Eco, U. 1990. 'Introduction', in Yu. M. Lotman, *Universe of the Mind: A Semiotic Theory of Culture*, trans. A. Shukman, vii–xiii, London and New York: I. B. Tauris.

Eimermacher, K. 1995. *Wie grell, wie bunt, wie ungeordnet: Modelltheoretisches Nachdenken über die russische Kultur*, Bochum: Universitätsverlag Dr. N. Brockmeyer.

Espagne, M. 2014. *L'ambre et le fossile: Transferts germano-russes dans les sciences humaines*, Paris: Armand Colin.

Faryno, J. 2020. 'Semiotyka Tartusko-Moskiewska w Polsce (1960–2000): (Materiały do bibliografii)', *Studia Litteraria Polono-Slavica* 5: 493–511.

Greenblatt, S. 2009. 'A Mobility Studies Manifesto', in S. Greenblatt (ed.), *Cultural Mobility: A Manifesto*, 250–3, Cambridge: Cambridge University Press.

Gvoždiak, V. 2016. *Česká teorie: Tendence moderní české sémiotiky*, Olomouc: Univerzita Palackého v Olomouci.

Ibrus, I. and Torop, P. 2015. 'Remembering and Reinventing Juri Lotman for the Digital Age', *International Journal of Cultural Studies* 18 (1): 3–9.

Ivanov, V. V. 1975. 'Znakovye sistemy nauchnogo povedeniia', *Nauchno-tekhnicheskaia informatsiia. Seriia 2: Informatsionnye protsessy i sistemy* 9: 3–9.

Ivanov, V. V. 1995. 'Goluboi zver': Vospominaniia [Part 3]', *Zvezda* 3: 155–96.

Ivanov, V. V. [1995] 2010. 'Jakobson in My Life: An Excerpt from *The Blue Beast*', trans. M. H. Heim, in T. M. Nikolaeva (ed.), *Issledovaniia po lingvistike i semiotike: Sbornik statei k jubileiu Viach. Vs. Ivanova*, 605–10, Moscow: Iazyki slavianskikh kul'tur.

Ivanov, V. V. 1998. 'Predislovie', in V. V. Ivanov, *Izbrannye trudy po semiotike i istorii kul'tury, vol. 1: Znakovye sistemy. Kino. Poetika*, 9–12, Moscow: Iazyki russkoi kul'tury.

Ivanov, V. V. 1999. 'O Romane Iakobsone (Glavy is vosmpominanii)', *Zvezda* 7: 139–64.

Jankovič, M., Pešat, Z. and Vodička, F. (eds) 1966. *Struktura a smysl literárního díla: Janu Mukařovskému k 75. narozeninám*, Prague: Československý spisovatel.

Jakobson, R. 1929. 'Über die heutigen Voraussetzungen der russischen Slavistik', *Slavische Rundschau* 1 (8): 629–46.

Jakobson, R. 1934. 'O předpokladech pražské lingvistické školy', *Index* 1 (6): 6–9.

Jakobson, R. 1938. 'Význam ruské filologie pro bohemistiku', *Slovo a slovesnost* 4 (4): 222–39.

Jakobson, R. 1971 [1943]. 'Polish-Russian Cooperation in the Science of Language', in R. Jakobson, *Selected Writings, vol. 2: Word and Language*, 451–5, The Hague and Paris: Mouton.

Jakobson, R. [1965] 1971. 'An Example of Migratory Terms and Institutional Models (On the Fiftieth Anniversary of the Moscow Linguistic Circle)', in R. Jakobson, *Selected Writings, vol. 2: Word and Language*, 527–38, The Hague and Paris: Mouton.

Karcz, A. 2002. *The Polish Formalist School and Russian Formalism*, Rochester: University of Rochester Press, and Kraków: Jagellonian University Press.

Kola, A. A. and Ulicka, D. 2015. 'From Circles to the School (and Back Again): The Case of Polish Structuralism', in M. Grishakova and S. Salupere (eds), *Theoretical Schools and Circles in the 20th-Century Humanities: Literary Theory, History, Philosophy*, 63–83, New York and Abington: Routledge.

Kondrashov, N. A. (ed.) 1967. *Prazhskii lingvisticheskii kruzhok: Sbornik statei*, Moscow: Progress.

Krylov, S. A. 2007. 'Akademik Viacheslav Vsevolodovich Ivanov: Kratkii ocherk nauchnoi deiatel'nosti', in L. G. Nevskaja, E. V. Pchelov, T. N. Sveshnikova, and K. Herold (eds), *Viacheslav Vsevolodovich Ivanov, vol. 30 of Rossiiskaia Akademiia nauk. Materialy k biobibliografii uchenykh. Literatura i iazyk*, 8–37, Moscow: Nauka.

Kull, K. 2011a. 'Juri Lotman in English: Bibliography', *Sign Systems Studies* 39 (2/4): 343–56.

Kull, K. 2011b. 'Introducing Tartu Semiotics for Chinese Semiosphere', *Chinese Semiotic Studies* 5 (1): 229–32.

Kull, K. and Magnus, R. (eds) 2014. *Semiotics of Life: Approaches from Tartu / 生命符号学：塔尔图的进路*, trans. J. Peng and L. Tang, Chengdu: Sichuan University Press.

Kull, K. and Peng, J. 2013. 'On the "New Tartu School"', *Chinese Semiotic Studies* 9 (1): 284–91.

Kull, K., Salupere, S., Torop, P. and Lotman, M. 2011. 'The Institution of Semiotics in Estonia', *Sign Systems Studies* 39 (2/4): 314–42.

Kull, K., Velmezova, E. 2018, 'Semiootikast ja semiootika ajaloost Peet Lepikuga' [About Semiotics and History of Semiotics with Peet Lepik], *Acta Semiotica Estica* 15: 176–95.

Łebkowska, A. 2012. 'Polski wariant strukturalizmu a współczesny dyskurs literaturoznawczy', in D. Ulicka, and W. Bolecki (eds), *Strukturalizm w Europie środkowej i wschodniej: Wizje i rewizje*, vol. 92 of *Z Dziejów Form Artystycznych w Literaturze Polskiej*, 405–17, Warsaw: Instytut Badań Literackich Polskiej Akademii Nauk.

Lotman, Ju. M. 1964. *Lektsii po struktural'noi poetike. Vyp. 1. Vvedenie, teoriia stikha*, Tartu: Izdatel'stvo Tartuskogo universiteta (*Trudy po znakovym sistemam*, 1).

Lotman, Ju. M. 1968. 'Kunsti semiootilise uurimise tulemusi tänapäeval' [Recent Achievements in the Semiotic Study of Art], *Keel ja Kirjandus* 10: 577–85.

Lotman, Ju. M. [1968] 2018. 'Sovremennye perspektivy semioticheskogo izucheniia iskusstva', in Ju. M. Lotman, *O strukturalizme. Raboty 1965–1970 godov*, ed. I. A. Pilshchikov, with N. V. Poselyagin and M. V. Trunin, 167–206, Tallinn: TLU Press.

Lotman, Ju. M. 1971. 'Nekotorye problemy sravnitel'nogo izucheniia khudozhestvennykh tekstov', Unpublished typescript (24 pp.), Tallinn University, Juri Lotmani Semiootikavaramu (The Juri Lotman Semiotic Repository), fond 1.

Lotman, Ju. M. 1974. 'Neskol'ko zamechanii po povodu stat'i prof. Marii R. Mayenowoi "Poetika v rabotakh Tartuskogo universiteta"', *Russian Literature* 6 [3 (2)]: 83–9.

Lotman, Ju. M. 1975. 'Pamiati Petra Grigor'evicha Bogatyreva', *Trudy po znakovym sistemam* 7: 5–6.

Lotman, Ju. M. [1982] 2016. 'Universitet – nauka – kul'tura', in J. M. Lotman and B. A. Uspenskij, *Perepiska 1964–1993*, eds. O. Ia. Kel'bert, M. V. Trunin and B. A. Uspenskij, 679–88, Tallinn: TLU Press.

Lotman, Ju. M. [1984] 2005. 'On the Semiosphere', trans. W. Clark, *Sign Systems Studies* 33 (1): 205–29.

Lotman, Ju. M. 1989. 'Vykhod iz labirinta', in U. Eco, *Imia rozy*, trans. E. A. Kostiukovich, 468–81, Moscow: Knizhnaia palata.

Lotman, Ju. M. [1989] 2019. 'Culture as a Subject and Its Own Object', in J. Lotman, *Culture, Memory and History: Essays in Cultural Semiotics*, trans. B. J. Baer, ed. M. Tamm, 83–93, Cham: Palgrave Macmillan.

Lotman, Ju. M., Ivanov, V. V., Pjatigorskij, A. M., Toporov, V. N. and Uspenskij, B. A. [1973] 2013. 'Theses on the Semiotic Study of Cultures (as Applied to Slavic Texts)', in S. Salupere, P. Torop and K. Kull (eds), *Beginnings of the Semiotics of Culture*, 53–77, Tartu: University of Tartu Press.

Machado, I. and Barei, S. (eds) 2019. *Bakhtiniana: Revista de Estudos do Discurso 14 (4)*, a special issue devoted to Juri Lotman.

Mayenowa, M. R. 1972. 'Poetika v rabotakh Tartuskogo universiteta', *Russian Literature* 2 [1 (2)]: 152–65.

Mayenowa, M. R. 1977. 'Lotman as a Historian of Literature', *Russian Literature* 5 (1): 81–90.

Mayenowa, M. R. 1983, 'Structural Thought in Poland', *Russian Literature* 13 (3): 313–31.

Mrugalski, M. 2018. 'Le "formalisme" polonais et l'héritage du formalisme russe', trans. J. Conan and P. Roussin, *Communications* 103: 213–31.

Mukařovský, J. 1994. *Issledovaniia po estetike i teorii iskusstva*, trans. V. A. Kamenskaia, ed. with a commentary by Ju. M. Lotman and O. M. Malevich, preface by Ju. M. Lotman, Moscow: Iskusstvo.

Mukařovský, J. 1996. *Struktural'naia poetika*, trans. V. A. Kamenskaia, ed. with a commentary by Ju. M. Lotman, and O. M. Malevich, preface by Ju. M. Lotman, Moscow: Iazyki russkoi kul'tury.

Peng, J. and Jiang, S. 2014. 'Research on Tartu (and Moscow) Semiotics in China: A Review of Past Three Decades', Abstract of the paper presented at the 12th World Congress of the International Association for Semiotic Studies (IASS/AIS), 'New Semiotics Between Tradition and Innovation', panel 'Tartu School: Old and New', Sofia, 16 September 2014, Available online: http://semio2014.org/bg/tartu-school-old-and-new (accessed 27 January 2021).

Pilshchikov, I. A. 2019a. 'Prazhskaia shkola na "perekrestke kul'tur" (O mnogoiazychii v nauchnoi perepiske i izdaniiakh Prazhskogo lingvisticheskogo kruzhka)', *Rhema* 3: 25–52.

Pilshchikov, I. 2019b. 'The Prague School on a Global Scale: A Coup d'œil From the East', *Slovo a slovesnost* 80 (3): 215–28.

Pilshchikov, I. A. and Trunin, M. 2016. 'The Tartu-Moscow School of Semiotics: A Transnational Perspective', *Sign Systems Studies* 44 (3): 368–401.

Pilshchikov, I. A. and Trunin, M. V. 2018. 'Vokrug podgotovki i zapreta russkogo izdaniia rabot Jana Mukarzhovskogo pod redaktsiei Ju. M. Lotmana i O. M. Malevicha', in Ju. M. Lotman, *O strukturalizme. Raboty 1965–1970 godov*, eds. I. A. Pilshchikov, with N. V. Poselyagin and M. V. Trunin, 315–49, Tallinn: TLU Press.

Pilshchikov, I. A. and Vroon, R. 2018. 'Vyacheslav V. Ivanov (1929–2017) and His Studies in Prosody and Poetics', *Studia Metrica et Poetica* 5 (1): 106–39.

Platt, K. M. F. 2008. '[Review of] Schönle, A. (ed.), *Lotman and Cultural Studies: Encounters and Extensions*, Madison: University of Wisconsin Press, 2006', *The Russian Review* 67 (2): 321–22.

Pomorska, K. 1968. *Russian Formalist Theory and its Poetic Ambiance*, The Hague and Paris: Mouton.

Poselyagin, N. 2011. 'Rannii rossiiskii strukturalizm: "dolotmanovskii" period', *Novoe literaturnoe obozrenie* 109: 118–34.

Pratt, M. L. 1991. 'Arts of the Contact Zone', *Profession '91*: 33–40.

Romand, D. and Tchougounnikov, S. (eds) 2009. *Psychologie allemande et Sciences Humaines en Russie: anatomie d'un transfert culturel (1860–1930)*, Auxerre: Sciences Humaines.

Rutkoff, P. M. and Scott, W. B. 1983. 'The French in New York: Resistance and Structure', *Social Research* 50 (1): 185–214.

Said, E. W. 2000. 'Travelling Theory Reconsidered', in E. W. Said, *Reflections on Exile and Other Essays*, 436–52, Cambridge, MA: Harvard University Press.

Schönle, A. and Shine, J. 2006. 'Introduction', in A. Schönle (ed.), *Lotman and Cultural Studies: Encounters and Extensions*, 3–35, Madison: The University of Wisconsin Press.

Seyffert, P. 1985. *Soviet Literary Structuralism: Background. Debate. Issues*, Columbus, OH: Slavica.

Shukman, A. 1977. *Literature and Semiotics: A Study of the Writings of Yu. M. Lotman*, Amsterdam, New York and Oxford: Elsevier North Holland.

Shukman, A. 2005. '[Review of] Andrews, E., *Conversations with Lotman: Cultural Semiotics in Language, Literature, and Cognition*, Toronto, Buffalo and London: University of Toronto Press, 2003', *Slavic Review* 64 (3): 690–91.

Sooväli, J. and Ott, M. 2020. 'On Territorialisation of Theory', in A. Kannike, J. Pärn and M. Tasa (eds), *Interdisciplinary Approaches to Culture Theory*, 67–72, Tartu: University of Tartu Press.

Steiner, P. 1982a. 'To Enter the Circle: The Functionalist Structuralism of the Prague School', in P. Steiner (ed.), *The Prague School. Selected Writings, 1929–1946*, ix–xii, Austin: University of Texas Press.

Steiner, P. 1982b. 'The Roots of Structuralist Esthetics', in P. Steiner (ed.), *The Prague School. Selected Writings, 1929–1946*, 174–219, Austin: University of Texas Press.

Steiner, P. 1984. *Russian Formalism: A Metapoetics*, Ithaca, NY and London: Cornell University Press.

Sutrop, M. 2015. 'What is Estonian Philosophy?', *Studia Philosophica Estonica* 8 (2): 4–64.

Tamm, M. 2020. 'Introduction: Cultural History Goes Global', *Cultural History* 9 (2): 135–55.

Tamm, M. and Kull, K. 2015. 'Eesti teooria' [Estonian Theory], *Akadeemia* 4: 579–625.

Tamm, M. and Kull, K. 2016. 'Toward a Reterritorialization of Cultural Theory: Estonian Theory from Baer via Uexküll to Lotman', *History of the Human Sciences* 29 (1): 75–98.

Tamm, M. and Kull, K. 2020. 'Estonian theory', in A. Kannike, K. Pärn and M. Tasa (eds), *Interdisciplinary Approaches to Culture Theory*, 30–66, Tartu: University of Tartu Press.

Tihanov, G. 2019. *The Birth and Death of Literary Theory: Regimes of Relevance in Russia and Beyond*, Stanford, CA: Stanford University Press.

Todd, W. M., III 2006. 'Afterword: Lotman without Tears', in A. Schönle (ed.), *Lotman and Cultural Studies: Encounters and Extensions*, 345–52, Madison: The University of Wisconsin Press.

Toman, J. 1995. *The Magic of a Common Language: Jakobson, Mathesius, Trubetzkoy, and the Prague Linguistic Circle*, Cambridge, MA: MIT Press.

Torop, P. 1995. 'Tartuskaia shkola kak shkola', in E. V. Permiakov (ed.), *Lotmanovskii sbornik*, vol. 1, 223–39, Moscow: IC-Garant.

Torop, P. 2000. 'New Tartu Semiotics', *S: European Journal for Semiotic Studies* 12 (1): 5–22.

Torop, P. 2017. 'Semiotics of Cultural History', *Sign Systems Studies* 45 (3/4): 317–34.

Torop, P. 2019. 'Russian Theory and Semiotics of Culture: History and Perspectives', *Bakhtiniana: Revista de Estudos do Discurso* 14 (4): 19–39.

Uspenskij, B. 1987. 'K probleme genezisa tartusko-moskovskoi semioticheskoi shkoly', *Trudy po znakovym sistemam* 20: 18–29.

Vachek, J. [1960] 1964. *Lingvisticheskii slovar' Prazhskoi shkoly*, trans. from French, German, English and Czech by I. A. Mel'chuk and V. Z. Sannikov, ed. with an introduction by A. A. Reformatskii, Moscow: Progress.

Velmezova, E. 2016. '"Czech Theory", Czech Semiotics', *Sign Systems Studies* 44 (4): 630–33.

Velmezova, E. and Kull, K. 2011. 'Interview with Vyacheslav V. Ivanov about Semiotics, the Languages of the Brain and History of Ideas', *Sign Systems Studies* 39 (2/4): 290–313.

Velmezova, E. and Kull, K. 2017. 'Boris Uspenskij on History, Linguistics and Semiotics', *Sign Systems Studies* 45 (3/4): 404–48.

Vihalemm, R. and Müürsepp, P. 2007. 'Philosophy of Science in Estonia', *Journal for General Philosophy of Science / Zeitschrift für allgemeine Wissenschaftstheorie* 38 (1): 167–91.

Vroon, R. and Pilshchikov, I. 2018. 'Vyach. Vs. Ivanov kak issledovatel' russkoi i mirovoi literatury', *Novoe literaturnoe obozrenie* 153: 163–76.

Werner, M. and Zimmermann, B. 2006. 'Beyond Comparison: *Histoire croisée* and the Challenge of Reflexivity', *History and Theory* 45 (1): 30–50.

Winner, T. G. 2002. 'How Did the Ideas of Juri Lotman Reach the West?', *Sign Systems Studies* 30 (2): 419–27.

Zenkin, S. N. (ed.) 2004. *Russkaia teoriia. 1920–1930-e gody: Materialy 10-ch Lotmanovskikh chtenii. Moskva, dekabr' 2002 g.*, Moscow: RGGU.

Zenkine, S. 2006. 'Forme interne, forme externe. Les transformations d'une catégorie dans la théorie russe du XXe siècle', *Revue Germanique internationale* 3: 63–76.

Żyłko, B. 2012. 'Lotman v Pol'she', *Novaia Pol'sha* 4: 67–73.

PART II
LOTMAN IN CONCEPTS

CHAPTER 8
LANGUAGE
Suren Zolyan

Introduction

The scholarly heritage of Juri Lotman is, first of all, semiotics, cultural theory, history of literature, and literary criticism. However, in any matter he turned to, he always refers to languages of the domain under consideration – languages of the brain, culture, behaviour, science, etc. Therefore, regarding Lotman's view on language, some clarifications and reservations should be made. Lotman, having expertise in linguistic issues, nevertheless did not consider himself a linguist, although, among his friends and co-authors, there were outstanding linguists with whom he could conduct professional conversations on equal terms. Lotman did not pretend to do linguistic research. For him, linguistics was the standard of scholarship for the humanities:

> A literary scholar of a new type is a researcher who needs to combine a wide knowledge of independently obtained empirical material with the skills of deductive thinking developed by the exact sciences. He/she must be a linguist (since at present linguistics has 'pulled ahead' among the humanities and it is here methods of a generally scientific relevance are often developed), and possess skills of working with other modelling systems [. . .]. He/she must accustom to cooperate with mathematics, and ideally – to combine a literary scholar, a linguist and a mathematician in oneself. (Lotman 1967: 100)

In linguistics, he saw and found 'precise' ('objective') tools for describing other semiotic systems, which would help rid the humanities of its inherent 'subjectivism':

> Without taking into account the achievements of modern linguistics, the science of literature will not develop its own, urgently necessary methodology for the structural study of artistic phenomena, a methodology that would allow getting rid of ignoring the artistic nature of verbal art and from subjectivism in its interpretation. (Lotman 1963: 52)

I can cite an illustrative episode from 1976, when I was on an internship under Lotman's supervision at the University of Tartu. He recommended reading books on cultural theory as little as possible and instead studying original sources and authentic documents. As usual, Lotman backed up theoretical statements with salient comparisons. He compared my desire to study the theory of culture with someone going to a restaurant and instead of choosing delicious food starts eating the menu. A menu, of course, is needed to choose what to eat. Without it, the diner will have to try everything before understanding what he or she wants. 'Menu' is a method which general linguistics provides. As for 'food', these are the texts and facts of this or that particular culture; in this way, Lotman characterized the relationship between method and object in semiotics. As for theory and methodology, according to Lotman, there were few worthy books, in fact only about ten seminal books on linguistics. It is easy to see that Lotman himself did not follow this approach because, as is clear from his works, he read many more than just a dozen books. However, addressing language as a whole, and not citing peculiar linguistic facts, the circle to which he refers is, in fact, rather limited: these are Saussure and Jakobson, and to a lesser degree Trubetzkoy, Mukařovský, the Prague School, Hjelmslev and Benveniste.

In his works, primarily in research on the semiosphere and the 'self-expansion of meaning' in the process of communication, he outlined those issues that have become relevant for the linguistics of the next generation. Since the subject of this chapter is Lotman's conception of natural language, leaving aside its semiotic extensions and extrapolations associated with it, we shall consider only those directly related to linguistic problems. The term 'language' in Lotman's work is one of the most frequent, used in almost all of his publications, although with different meanings starting from the broadest interpretation, in which *language* is understood as any sign and even non-sign system (e.g. the language of nature), to the extremely narrow (e.g. language as a writer's particular style). For Lotman, these meanings were internally related, with the concept of natural language being central: a secondary modelling system's definition as a sign system, based on the primary modelling system, that is, natural language, presupposes it. At the same time, poetic language was also considered by Lotman a secondary modelling system, albeit the most closely related to language and using its system of signifiers. Moreover, Lotman considered an artistic/poetic text not as a complication of 'ordinary' texts, but, on the contrary, as a prototypical manifestation of linguistic activity when addressing processes of the active transmission of information. At the same time, unambiguously interpreted texts are to be considered special, or degenerate cases, or they are extreme cases of the 'passive' transmission of information.

> It is not a case that artistic texts are extreme expressions of some normal non-artistic texts, but, I think, non-artistic texts are a particular case of artistic ones [. . .]. The generative active meaning-producing function of a text message is expressed most fully in artistic texts, but it is inherent in all texts in general. Similarly, as the function of the passive transmission is [at some degree] also present in artistic texts, but it is extremely manifested, probably, in the street signalling. (Lotman 1981: 8)

Thus, two linguistics are possible: in the traditional model, language is considered a tool for the transmission of information and aims to preserve meaning; in the prototypical model, language is to be compared to a street signalling system that does not allow distortion or ambiguity. However, based on different axiomatics another kind of linguistics is also possible, in which the function of meaning production is to be considered cardinal; therefore, language is manifested as a system, oriented not so much towards transmission of ready information, but towards its transformation and the creation of new meanings.

Not being a professional linguist, Lotman did not undertake to develop such a linguistic theory but transferred this approach to semiotics as an extension peculiar to language in its artistic (poetic) function. He did not pay special attention to consider the notion of 'natural language', referring to prominent structuralists' works mentioned earlier. Lotman pointed out issues beyond the common linguistic description and, according to the concepts of the founding fathers of structuralism, beyond the border of the ordinary language. Therefore, in the dichotomy *language and speech*, he is interested in speech, or, more precisely, in implementation of speech in the text (Lotman did not use the term *discourse*). Rather than the systems and structures themselves, Lotman considered their manifestations and transformations in the process of communication. Because of this, Lotman's views of language are of particular interest to linguistics as he presents the perspective of its neo-structuralist version.

Word and context

Probably only one of Lotman's articles can be put under the heading of proper linguistics: 'On the Delimitation of the Linguistic and Literary Notions of Structure' (Lotman 1963), published in the leading Soviet linguistic journal *Voprosy jazykoznania* (Issues of Linguistics).[1] In this article, Lotman does not intervene in a discussion of linguistic problems per se, although his approach to describing meaning was in many ways ahead of the lexicological concepts of that time (see below). The very fact of its publication at a time when other central publishing venues in the USSR were practically closed to Lotman due to his structuralist stand was a breakthrough. It made possible subsequent publications and stimulated the development of structural linguistic poetics. Unfortunately, the article went unnoticed in linguistics, although it could have opened a new approach for the semantics of that time by addressing lexical meaning in a social context. Lotman's experience as a historian of literature and social thought influenced his interest in the sign's social aspects. For him, the social nature of language and all other sign systems functioning in society was apparent: 'The definition of language as a communicative system implies the character of its social function: language provides the exchange, storage, and accumulation of information in the collective that uses it' (Lotman 1973: 4).

Lotman formulates this general view in relation to lexical semantics. Starting with the obvious statement that a word acquires meaning only in context, Lotman takes the next step, unusual for linguists: he presumes that context could be insufficient. The historian's experience allows him to see what was then (and still is) insufficiently taken into account in linguistics: a word is not only a unit from a dictionary; it is also an element of some ideological system (worldview, literary trend, scientific discipline, etc.). The same linguistic expressions as 'natural state', 'man', 'citizen' receive different, sometimes opposite interpretations in political philosophy and journalism (see Lotman 1963: 45–6). Therefore, a linguistic analysis should be supplemented by the 'structural-ideological' method, as Lotman baptized it:

> In this case, experiments on the comparative categorization of formally identical, but semantically different (included in different systems) terms used by different publicists of the same era would provide very interesting data. Thus, the structural-ideological method will reveal an interesting difference in using the same terms by close publicists, for example, Chernyshevsky and Dobrolyubov. However, approaching such work, the linguist will inevitably face the inadequacy of purely linguistic methods. He will have to restore the ideological structure, the interdependence of its constituent concepts, before establishing the specifics of terms, i.e., signs that serve to convey them. (Lotman 1963: 46)

It is easy to see that the approach proposed by Lotman is currently actively used in linguistics, for example, on the one hand, in the analysis of concepts in cognitive linguistics and, on the other, in the methods of corpus linguistics, discourse analysis and critical discourse analysis. The article also contains hints of today's frame analysis, the description of a situation through ordered relationships between components. Lotman uses the term 'structural situation' to explain how a speaker can identify the appropriate meaning of a polysemantic word.

> The semantic content of the utterance 'My table is the second one' is determined by the situation which not expressed in words – it happens in a sanatorium. From all the numerous connections of the structural concept of 'sanatorium', only one feature is important in this case: the situation 'a sanatorium' excludes all situations 'not a sanatorium' and, therefore, cuts off all redundant meanings of the word table. (Lotman 1963: 51)[2]

In this article, Lotman presumes not only that the semantics of the language forms a certain structure but also that the 'amorphous material of content', as he names it following Hjelmslev's terminology, is endowed with some structure. This statement seems to him so bold that he makes some reservations:

> Both the system of the material world around a person, and the consciousness of a person, class, generation at each separate moment of their existence are not amorphous phenomena but connected by a strict system of relations into structures. Consequently, it is possible to speak about the amorphousness of the 'content material' of a language only with certain reservations. However, another thing should be taken into account: these structures are so vast and difficult to detect, their very structurness is so hidden from an observer, and may be revealed only as a result of research efforts, that in comparison with the evidently closed system of a language they appear as open and amorphous. (Lotman 1963: 52)

Leaving linguists to do their job of studying language, Lotman adopts their method. The proposed two-component scheme, in which linguistic structures appear as substance and precondition for expression of literary structures, was then generalized as the concept of secondary modelling systems, the main tool in the methodological box of the Tartu-Moscow school. This conception was firstly articulated as a distinction between linguistic and literary structures:

> In verbal art, the content structure is realized through a language's structure, forming a complex whole. Thus, there is a significant difference between the linguistic and literary concepts of structure. A linguistic structure is a condition, a means of transmitting information; a literary structure is its purpose and content. (Lotman 1963: 53)

However, Lotman does not depart at all from the linguistic aspects of the 'content plan'. This issue continues to be relevant to him, and not only a literary text but also the semantics of the language as a whole turns out to be a two-level entity. He distinguishes between two levels of its 'objectivity', that is, these are worlds inside and outside of language:

> The plane of content, as conceived by F. de Saussure, is a conventional reality. Language creates its own world. At the same time, the question arises as to the level of adaptability of a world created by language towards a world existing outside of language, i.e. beyond its borders [. . .]. In this way, initially, the existence of two levels of objectivity may be surmised: one relates to the world of languages (this is objective from its point of view) and one relates to the world outside the borders of language. One of the key problems is that of the translation of the world of the content of the system (its internal reality) to the reality that lies outside, beyond the borders of language. (Lotman [1992] 2009: 1–2)

Thus, it is assumed that there are two semantics, two '*levels of objectivity*', one of them is outside the language, and the other is the intralinguistic content plan that pretends to reflect the first. This can remind us of the classical distinction between 'sense' and 'meaning', *Sinn* and *Bedeutung*. However, Lotman draws a conclusion that is the opposite of the generally accepted one: instead of searching for an ideal language, due to which objects from these two domains can be brought into rigid correspondence, he concludes that such an operation is impossible if using only one language:

> Out of this, two specific issues arise: 1. The necessity that more than one language (a minimum of two) is required in order to reflect a given reality. 2. The inevitable fact that the space of reality cannot be represented by a single language but only by an aggregate of languages [. . .]. The idea of an optimal model, consisting of a single perfect universal language, is replaced by the image of a structure equipped with a minimum of two or, rather, by an open number of diverse languages, each of which is reciprocally dependent on the other, due to the incapacity of each to

express the world independently. These languages superimpose themselves on each other in such a way as to reflect one and the same thing in diverse ways, so that they appear to be situated on a 'single plane' and form its internal borders. Their mutual untranslatability (or limited translatability) represents a source of adjustment of the extra-lingual object to its reflection in the world of languages. (Lotman [1992] 2009: 2–3)

Rethinking Saussure: From structures to text

Saussure is one of the most frequently mentioned names by Lotman; at the same time, he is a constant subject of reflection on the methodology of linguistics and semiotics (see Chapter 2). This attitude is both respectful and polemical:

> To generalize about the attempt to develop principles for a theory of semiotics since the first premises were formulated by Ferdinand de Saussure is to come to the paradoxical conclusion that any reconsideration of basic principles has been certain confirmation of their stability, while any attempt to stabilize the methodology of semiotics has led inevitably to a reconsideration of these very principles. (Lotman [1974] 1977: 193)

In the brief chapter 'After Saussure' in his *Universe of the Mind* (1990: 4–6), Lotman summed up his attitude to Saussure's theory as the foundation of semiotics, highlighting the points that remain relevant and make further development possible. At the same time, in other chapters of his last books (1990; [1992] 2009; [1994/2010] 2013) he refers to points that require revision. This concerns, firstly, the very nature of a sign. On this point, referring to Roman Jakobson, Lotman speaks of the deterministic nature of the relationship between the signified and the signifier.[3] Secondly, he insists on introducing dynamism into the synchronous description of language as a system. As a historian of literature and culture, Lotman considers the diachronic (evolutionary) dimension to be so essential that he concludes by distinguishing the concepts of 'code' and 'language' on this basis, which he had previously used as interchangeable. A language is a code, endowed with a history and an inherent capacity for transformation:

> In fact, the substitution of the term 'language' by the term 'code' is not as harmless as it seems. The term 'code' carries with it the idea of an artificial, newly created structure, introduced by instantaneous agreement. A code does not imply history, that is, psychologically it orients us towards artificial language, which is also, in general, assumed to be an ideal model of language. 'Language', albeit unconsciously, awakes in us an image of the historical reach of existence. Language – is a code plus its history. (Lotman [1992] 2009: 4)

It seems to us that both of these aspects, as Lotman presents them, relate more to semiotics. The closest to linguistics is the reinterpretation of the fundamental 'language–

speech' dichotomy, or, in other terms, 'system–text'.⁴ In a still unpublished presentation, Lotman articulated the issue as follows:

> I don't want to in any way cast a shadow on the classic works of Ferdinand Saussure, on which we all stand. However, the time comes to reconsider essential things. In particular, the relationship between text and language. A text is presented in this classical scheme as a kind of materialization of a system. And what is significant in a text was thought of as being present in a language. Thus, a text was a kind of packaging, a kind of box that conveyed systemic meanings. (Lotman 1981: 6)

However, as we have noted, in 1963 it was pointed out that this approach was inadequate since between a system and texts intermediate levels and mechanisms with a certain autonomy function. In linguistics, the awareness of this situation led to the actualization of the concept of discourse (it was present in Saussure's notes, but was removed by Sechehaye and Bally; see Bouquet 2004: 210–14), as well as to the development of pragmatics. Lotman could have relied on Benveniste's idea to transcend Saussurian semiotics in two directions:

> This transcendence is achieved through two channels: in intralinguistic analysis, through the opening of a new dimension of meaning, that of discourse (which we call semantic), henceforth distinct from that which is connected to the sign (which we call semiotic); and in the translinguistic analysis of texts and other manifestations through the elaboration of a metasemantics founded on the semantics of enunciation. (Benveniste [1969] 1981: 23)

Needless to say, one can find many affinities between Lotman's and Benveniste's ideas (see Gramigna 2013). However, the solution proposed by Lotman is different: it is not an intra-systemic complication but a synthesis of heterogeneous semiotic principles and mechanisms crucial for the 'system–text' dichotomy. Thus, a literary text is the product of at least two different systems. For this reason, elements that seem to be non-systemic concerning one system at the same time appear as a manifestation of another.

At the beginning (Lotman 1963), this provision was formulated in relation only to the literary text, since it imitates reality and must create an 'illusion of non-systemic character'. Then this is formulated as a property of the text:

> Literature imitates reality; it creates a model of the extra-systemic out of its own inherently systemic material. In order to appear 'accidental', an element in a work of art must belong to at least two systems and must be located at their intersection. That aspect of the element which is systemic from the point of view of one system will appear 'accidental' when viewed from the vantage of the other [. . .]. The capacity of a textual element to enter into several contextual structures and to take on a different meaning in each context is one of the most profound properties of the artistic text. (Lotman [1970] 1977: 59–60)

Next, this provision was generalized so that any text can be recognized as the product of at least two systems. Thus, it must have a multidimensional and heterogeneous structure, with the mutual complementarity between discrete and continual generative mechanisms being crucial. The asymmetry of the left and right brain hemispheres was an effective exemplification of this conception (Lotman had previously referred to this dichotomy, although he described it as a difference between logical and mythological mechanisms of meaning formation). Lotman does not enter into polemics with Saussure regarding the adequacy of the 'language–speech' dichotomy; rather, he invited the great predecessor to divide the spheres of interest: Saussure is interested in language and system, and Lotman in speech and text.[5] With this in mind, it is clear that Lotman's departure from linguistics is more an issue of terminology than methodology. The linguistics of speech is understood by him as the semiotics of the text. Moreover, text was considered by Lotman not as a linguistic phenomenon, but as 'the mutual relationship among the system, its realization, and the addresser-addressee of the text' (Lotman and Piatigorsky [1968] 1978: 233). Therefore, the notion of the text becomes a dynamic entity; it is not an immanent object, but a complex relation (function in the mathematical sense) between four variables: language (sign system), a composition consisting of signs (i.e. a text in the narrow sense of the word), the addressee–addresser and a context (for more detail, see Zolyan 2016; 2020).

Text rather than structure turns out to be the initial object of consideration, entailing a change in the entire architecture of the linguistic system. According to Peeter Torop, 'from understanding a text as a manifestation of language, Lotman moved on to understanding that text generates its own language' (Torop 1995: 228; see also: M. Lotman 1995; 2019). In this area, he proposed several ideas that are different from the linguistic doctrine of structuralism and which have become, perhaps, the most promising characteristics of the Tartu-Moscow Semiotic School as well as Lotman's main contribution to the theory of language. Mihhail Lotman highlights the following:

The Tartu-Moscow school's specific feature is its emphasized textocentricity: its conceptual system is not focused on the language, the sign, the structure, the binary oppositions, or the grammar rules but on the text. Even descriptions of linguistic structure recede into the background since the Tartu-Moscow school undermined the very principle of automatic inference of text from language [. . .]. From the point of view of Lotman, language and text are fundamentally not reducible to each other, and in some properties, a text is larger than language: The text contains several elements that cannot be derived from the language: the marking of the beginning and the end, compositional principles, etc. Unlike a language, a text is endowed with meaning, and this meaning is inseparable from text structures; therefore, the text is subject not only to description, but also to interpretation, whereas a number of possible interpretations are in principle unlimited. Text is almost never a product of the implementation of only one language; in principle, any text is polylingual. (M. Lotman 1995: 214, 218).

It should be added that Lotman thought of the unlimited semiotic heterogeneity of the text as a dynamic equilibrium between different subtext-structures that created some integral unity: 'A text is a moment of balance between the tendency of its functional disintegration into two or several texts and complete unification as an internally homogeneous entity' (Lotman 1982: 4). This approach is applicable to a language: 'When we say: "some natural language", then it will be easy to demonstrate that this is a heterogeneous system, which is a mix of several systems; however, it is essential that at the same time this entity is aware of itself as one language, and that this complex system is aware of itself as one, and this ensures its internal circulation' (Lotman 1981: 5).

Thus, an extremely important property was introduced, that is, the presence of mechanisms ensuring an intra-systemic integrity, something that is sometimes not adequately taken into account when emphasizing the heterogeneity of some semiotic entities. Misunderstanding and insufficiently mastered deconstruction procedures or discourse analysis often lead to a situation in which the very concept of the text can be lost: text as a structural and semantic unity dissolves in an amorphous intertextual or contextual semiosis or breaks up into unrelated components. Therefore, it is crucial to identify internal interaction mechanisms between heterogeneous structures and sublanguages, but within an integral wholeness. 'The absent structure' (i.e. moveable and decentralized) is transformed by Lotman into an integrating one.

Conclusion

Although structuralism was not completely banned in the USSR, except in linguistics, it was the subject of harsh criticism, becoming political accusations of servility to 'bourgeois science'. According to the official 'methodology', the function of the humanities was to justify the Soviet party-state ideological dogmas. Accusations of being a structuralist constantly persecuted Lotman and caused the withdrawal from publication of many of his works (for more detail, see Pilshchikov et al. 2018). In such a situation, writing about some methodological issues that could not be solved within the framework of structuralism, or criticizing the fundamental stands of structuralism, could seem like a rejection of the scientific approaches and adoption of an officially permitted point of view. Moreover, in some of the theses of the politically ideologized French post-structuralism, Lotman saw motives close to those of the Soviet critics, and his attitude towards 'various Tel-Quels' was very ironic (see Salupere 2017: 19–22 and Chapter 23).[6] Soviet critics of structuralism did not offer anything new; rather, their goal was to prohibit such development, meaning that Lotman could indulge in no solidarity with them. At the same time, if we analyse the extensions proposed by Lotman, it becomes obvious that they were oriented not to negating but to developing the structural method, giving it a multidimensional and non-linear character. Another matter is that Lotman envisaged this development not in the framework of linguistics, but in semiotics and communication theory.

For all the conventionality of the demarcation of structuralism from post-structuralism, it is usual to associate its beginning with Jacques Derrida's famous presentation at the conference in Johns Hopkins University in 1966 (Derrida 1967). At this conference, designed to emphasize the role of Claude Lévi-Strauss, Derrida made several provisions in which the very concept of 'structure' and the absolute privileged 'centre' associated with it was subjected to deconstruction. Another signal of the 'change of milestones' can be considered the release of Umberto Eco's book *The Absent Structure* (1968) in which the concept of 'structure' also becomes the main object of criticism.

In the 1960s–1970s, Lotman put a lot of effort into describing structuralism and the structural method (see Lotman 2018). However, and this seems rather strange, Lotman did not make the notion of structure a subject of special consideration; instead, he gave some general characteristics[7] or referred to Benveniste's article (Lotman [1970] 1977: 210). Perhaps this concept seemed to him intuitively clear and did not need special consideration. There is no indication that the revision of the basic ideas of Saussurian structuralism, which started in the 1960s–1970s, in any way influenced Lotman's concept. Meanwhile, already retrospectively analysing Lotman's works, some researchers portray him as a dedicated post-structuralist (Zhivov 2009: 22; Smirnov 1996: 330). However, such a characterization, emphasizing the similarities, does not take into account the significant discrepancies between Lotman's conception and French post-structuralism. The similarities are relatively superficial due to the common domain of problems, but not the proposed solutions: 'This means that Lotman came to the fundamental questions, only superficially inherent of poststructuralism, and the answers to these questions were to be found in the searches of the next years' (Torop 1995: 231). In this case, since we are considering linguistic aspects, the attitude towards Saussure's heritage can be taken as the main point of divergence. It is more appropriate to see in Lotman's approaches a special version of structuralism, free from both classical dogmatism and the ideologized voluntarism of post-structuralists.

As it seems, the analysis of Lotman's linguistic views allows us to determine more correctly his place in the paradigms of modern humanitarian knowledge. There is no doubt that Lotman remained true to Saussurian structuralism's fundamental principles, and in this sense, of course, was a structuralist. But at the same time, he foresaw and, to a large extent, formulated the development that these principles can receive if they are given a dynamic character. We prefer to discuss the emergence of a certain formative context for neo-structuralism *avant la lettre* (this term was introduced in Zolyan and Lotman 2012; its development is given in Zolyan 2021). As it seems, recently the 'hero of our time' is not a phoneme, a favourite object of early structuralism, and not a sentence, a darling entity of generativism, but a text studied as a totality of its multidimensional heterogeneous semantic compositions, a plurality of languages of generation and interpretation, and flexible context-based communicative characteristics. Language units are defined according to their functions in text production, processing, and interpretations. The text acts both as a structure and as an operation (action); and heterogeneous textual and subtextual structures considered as a complex of non-linear functions in communication may become the main object and concept of this new theoretical framework. This approach is deduced from Lotman's works. This creates an opportunity for a new neo-structuralist or even neo-Saussurian version of linguistics.[8] It will continue the traditions of a systemic-structural approach to language, in which the formalism of such a description will be supplemented by constructivism, in its dynamic conjugation with the processes of communication and meaning production.

Notes

1. With some reservations, Lotman's article on Rousseau's concept of the origin of language (Lotman 1989) can also be mentioned, as well as a series of articles on the concept of text, although in these the linguistic approach is mainly a subject of polemical discussion.

2. In the USSR, vacationers in sanatoriums and rest homes had to sit at tables in a dining room assigned to them by the administration. In large sanatoriums, the reference to the table number was a kind of address.

3. As usual in his polemics with Saussure, Lotman refers to the authority of Jakobson: 'The language of Khlebnikov, the language of the Russian Futurists, was for Jakobson not an anomaly, but the most consistent realization of the structure of language, and one of the most important stimuli to his later phonological researches. From his experience of studying poetic language came his sensitivity to the aesthetic side of semiotic systems. This explains the intensity of his criticism of Saussure when he attacked Saussure's central proposition, the principle of the arbitrariness of the connection between signifier and signified in the sign. (See Roman Jakobson, *Quest for the Essence of Language*.)' (Lotman 1990: 17). See also Avtonomova 2015.

4. Lotman equated the notions of 'text' and 'speech', as opposed to the concepts of 'system' and 'language', thereby combining the dichotomies of Saussure and Hjelmslev: 'During the next stage, the centre of attention shifted to texts ("speech" in the terminology of Saussure) and, in particular, unique artistic texts, and to the tension between the iterative and the non-iterative' (Lotman [1994/2010] 2013: 32).

5. 'At the Second School, Roman Osipovich Jakobson said [. . .] that I am not interested in structures anymore, I am interested in texts. And in general, he said, it is interesting to revise Saussure in terms of texts' (Lotman 1981: 2).

6. Lotman avoided entering into a public discussion; however, he had expressed his attitude in his private letters. In particular, he wrote to Boris Uspenskij: 'During these days I looked through some of the discussions about structuralism in France – and there they say the same thing as Kozhinov and Palievsky' (Uspenskij 2016: 128).

7. Cf.: 'Any characteristic of the relations between the elements of this whole, the entire sum of these relations, that is, the structure, affects the semantics of the text' (Lotman 1963: 51). In his last work, he even, perhaps ironically, proclaimed himself non-prepared on this issue: 'The next essential step taken by the discipline was the formulation of a general theory of structures, a theory that linked all forms of organisation in the world – from physical to cultural phenomena. Although this is a problem that inevitably arises in any discipline, I do not consider myself prepared to resolve it' (Lotman [1994/2010] 2013: 35).

8. Let us remember that Lotman had no opportunity to be acquainted with Saussure's archival notes, which were published later. The theory of language that remained in the outline was

called by its publisher the semiotics of interpretation (Bouquet 2004: 205). The developments suggested by Lotman largely coincide with Saussure's reflections, which primarily relates to the relationship between language and speech (Saussure 2006).

References

Avtonomova, N. 2015 'Lotman i Jakobson: mezhdu "urokom" i "ekzamenom"', *Vestnik RGGU. Seriia 'Literaturovedeniie. Iazykoznaniie. Kul'turologiia'* 7: 11–27.

Benveniste, É. [1969] 1981. 'The Semiology of Language', trans. G. Ashby and A. Russo, *Semiotica*, supplement, 5–23.

Bouquet, S. 2004. 'Saussure's Unfinished Semantics', in C. Sanders (ed.), *The Cambridge Companion to Saussure*, 205–18, Cambridge: Cambridge University Press.

Derrida, J. 1967. 'La structure, le signe et le jeu dans le discours des sciences humaines', in J. Derrida, *L'écriture et la différence*, 409–28, Paris: Seuil.

Gramigna, R. 2013. 'Juri Lotman and Émile Benveniste', *Sign Systems Studies* 41 (2/3): 339–54.

Lotman, Ju. M. 1963. 'O razgranichenii lingvisticheskogo i literaturovedcheskogo poniatiia struktury', *Voprosy iazykoznaniia* 3: 44–52.

Lotman, Ju. M. 1967. 'Literaturovedeniie dolzhno byt' naukoi', *Voprosy literatury* 1: 90–100.

Lotman, Ju. M. [1970] 1977. *The Structure of the Artistic Text*, trans. R. Vroon, Ann Arbor, MI: University of Michigan, Department of Slavic Languages and Literatures.

Lotman, Ju. M. 1973. *Semiotika kino i problemy kinoestetiki*, Tallinn: Eesti Raamat.

Lotman, Ju. M. [1974] 1977. 'The Dynamic Model of a Semiotic System', *Semiotica* 21: 193–210.

Lotman, Ju. M. 1981. *Doklad 13 marta v Tartuskom universitete*. Juri Lotman Semiotics Repository, Tallinn University. F 1 (YU. Lotman). Typescript.

Lotman, Ju. M. 1982. 'Ot redaktsii', *Trudy po znakovym sistemam* 15: 3–9.

Lotman, Ju. M. 1989. 'Slovo i iazyk v kul'ture Prosveshcheniia', in *Vek Prosveshcheniia: Rossiia i Frantsiia: Le Siècle des Lumières: Russie: France (Materialy nauchnoi konferentsii (1987))*, 6–18, Moscow: Nauka.

Lotman, Ju. M. 1990. *Universe of the Mind: A Semiotic Theory of Culture*, trans. A. Shukman, London and New York: I.B. Tauris.

Lotman, Ju. M. [1992] 2009. *Culture and Explosion*, trans. W. Clark, ed. M. Grishakova, Berlin and New York: Mouton de Gruyter.

Lotman, Ju. M. [1994/2010] 2013. *The Unpredictable Workings of Culture*, trans. B. J. Baer, Tallinn: TLU Press.

Lotman, Ju. M. 2018. *O strukturalizme. Raboty 1965-1970 godov*, ed. I. A. Pilshchikov, with N. V. Poselyagin and M. V. Trunin. Tallinn: Izdatel'stvo TLU.

Lotman, Ju. M. and Piatigorsky, A. M. [1968] 1978. 'Text and Function', trans. A. Shukman, *New Literary History* 9 (2): 233–44.

Lotman, M. Ju. 1995. 'Za tekstom: Zametki o filosofskom fone tartuskoi semiotiki (Stat'ia pervaia)', in E. V. Permiakov (ed.), *Lotmanovskii sbornik*, vol. 1, 214–22, Moscow: IC-Garant.

Lotman, M. Ju. 2019. 'Tekst v kontekste Tartuskoi shkoly: problemy i perspektivy', *Slovo.ru: baltiiskii aktsent* 10 (4): 45–58.

Pilshchikov, I. A., Poselyagin, N. V. and Trunin, M. V. 2018. 'Problemy genezisa i evoliutsii tartusko-moskovskovskogo strukturalizma v rabotakh Iu. M. Lotmana 1960-kh i nachala 1970-kh godov', in Ju. M. Lotman, *O strukturalizme. Raboty 1965-1970 godov*, ed. I. A. Pilshchikov, with N. V. Poselyagin M. V. Trunin, 7–63, Tallinn: Izdatel'stvo TLU.

Salupere, S. 2017. *O metaiazyke Iuriia Lotmana: problemy, kontekst, istochniki*, Tartu: University of Tartu Press.

Saussure, F. de 2006 *Writings in General Linguistics*, eds. S. Bouquet and R. Engler, Oxford: Oxford University Press.

Smirnov, I. 1996. 'O vremeni v sebe: Shestidesiatyie gody — ot Afin do akhinei', in A. M. Piatigorsky, *Izbrannyie trudy*, 318–35, Moscow: Iazyki slavyanskikh kul'tur.

Torop, P. 1995. 'Tartuskaia shkola kak shkola', in E. V. Permiakov (ed.), *Lotmanovskii sbornik*, vol. 1, 223–39, Moscow: IC-Garant.

Uspenskij, B. A. (gen. ed.) 2016. *Ju. M. Lotman – B. A. Uspenskij. Perepiska 1964–1993*, Tallinn: Izdatel'stvo TLU.

Zhivov, V. 2009. 'Moskovsko-tartuskaia semiotika: ee dostizheniia i ee ogranicheniia', *Novoie literaturnoie obozreniie* 98: 11–26.

Zolyan, S. T., 2016. 'Iurii Lotman o tekste: idei, problemy, perspektivy', *Novoie literaturnoie obozreniie* 3 (139): 63–96.

Zolyan, S. 2020. *Iurii Lotman: O smysle, tekste, istorii. Temy i variatsii*, Moscow: Iazyki slavianskikh kul'tur.

Zolyan, S. 2021. 'Kak primirit' Lumana s Sossiurom: printsip vnutrisistemnoi differentsiatsii kak osnova neostrukturalistskogo podkhoda', *Voprosy iasyknozaniia* 1: 121–41.

Zolyan, S. and Lotman, M. 2012. *Issledovaniia v oblasti semanticheskoi poetiki akmeizma*, Tallinn: Izd-vo Tallinnskogo universiteta.

CHAPTER 9
TEXT
Aleksei Semenenko

The concept of text is central in Juri Lotman's theory and unites all other key concepts, such as culture, dialogue, language, (auto-)communication and semiosphere. If we were to formulate the main principle of Lotman's semiotics, we could call it the principle of *textuality of culture*, the assumption that culture is a complex text that in turn consists of a hierarchy of texts within the texts. The following sections of this chapter will thus discuss different levels of textual organization, from an individual text to larger entities.

Text vs sign

The very first thing that has to be mentioned is that in Lotman's terminology the definition of text is much broader than the concept of literary work: it is multimodal, polyglot and transcends the limits of literature, or any single sign system. Secondly, Lotman ([1984] 2005: 205) opposes the text to the sign and distinguishes between two scientific traditions: one that goes back to Peirce and Morris and prioritizes the sign as the basic element of semiotic systems, and the other, which he himself advocates, based on Saussure and the Prague School, which focuses on the text. If the former is concerned with models and 'models of models', the latter focuses on actual texts and their functioning in the semiosphere. The 'textual' approach emphasizes the non-systemic and irregular features, whereas the 'sign approach' removes or neutralizes these contradictions through building models (Lotman [1981] 2002: 158). The text thus becomes the main basic unit of semiosis, the product of communication and the main object of semiotic study, and in that sense it is opposed to the concept of sign. The only time Lotman equates the text with the sign is when he describes the artistic text as an integral sign, meaning that it is perceived holistically, in its entirety (Lotman [1970] 1977: 22; 1964: 140).

The primacy of text over such metaconstructions as language, code or sign was a 'trademark' trait of the Tartu-Moscow Semiotic School, a theoretical stance that was shared by the majority of its scholars, who maintained that the sign is not the primary element of semiosis but the product of analysis (M. Lotman 2002: 37; see also M. Lotman 2019; Chernov 1988: 13; Ivanov 1976: 3). Today, semioticians are used to juxtaposing the Saussurian (dual) and Peircian (triadic) models of sign, but for Lotman ([1970] 1977: 13) the focus was on another dichotomy, that of *la langue* (which he reinterpreted as 'an abstract system of invariant relations') and *parole* ('a stream of individual messages'). This comparison notwithstanding, Lotman was far from treating texts as a mere reflection of natural language.

Text and language

It seems logical to assume that one has to know some language in the first place in order to create texts in that language. Lotman argues that, paradoxically – paradoxes are frequent in his works because he uses them not as a rhetorical figure but as a methodological tool – language is not the main prerequisite of a dialogue, but it is the dialogic situation which 'precedes both real dialogue and even the existence of a language' (Lotman 1990: 143). In other words, it is the text that creates its own language(s) and context(s) (M. Lotman 2002: 34). Furthermore, 'the relationship of text and system in an artistic work is not the automatic realization of an abstract structure in concrete form, but is always a relationship of struggle, tension, and conflict' (Lotman [1972] 1976: 123–4), and it is not only the text that changes but the addressee as well (Lotman [1977] 1982).

As an example, Lotman (1990: 143–4) refers to the situation in which the need for dialogue between the mother and her newborn child creates unique texts and idiosyncratic languages. In this situation, the need to impart a message comes first, even before knowing any language. Even in a 'traditional' mode of communication, the intention to create a text *is* the necessary condition of any dialogue, and it is the text that determines which language(s) to use, not excluding the possibility of creating new ones. Thus, the conventional (at least in the 1960s–1970s) scheme of communication

$$\text{addressee} \rightarrow \text{Text}^1\left(\text{Lang}^1\right) \rightarrow \text{addresser}$$

transforms into

$$\text{Text}^1 \rightarrow \left[\sum \text{Lang}^{1,2,3,n}\right] \rightarrow \text{Text}^{2,3,4,n}$$

The particularity of Lotman's model is that it is not just a single code serving as a channel of communication but multiple overlapping codes that produce a (potentially endless) number of new texts. That is how the text both transmits messages and serves as a generator of new ones (Lotman 1990: 13). It is important to note that in this scheme, $\text{Text}^{2,3,n}$ should not be interpreted as a multiplicity of meanings that can be extracted from one text because in this view meaning is something external to the text.

Text as a meaning-generating mechanism

The *meaning-generating* function of the text is intrinsically linked with the text's *polyglotism*. This crucial idea is often reiterated in Lotman's works and appears as early as 1970: 'The text belongs to *two* (or several) languages *simultaneously*' (Lotman [1970] 1977: 298, here and henceforth original emphasis).[1] These languages may be overlapping, but they should not be identical because – here's another paradox – 'A text that is absolutely comprehensible is at the same time a text that is absolutely useless' (Lotman 1990: 80). Again, every act of communication presupposes *translation* between different codes and languages because generation of meaning between identical codes is simply impossible:

> If we assume an addresser and an addressee possessing identical codes and fully devoid of memory, then the understanding between them will be ideal, but the value of the transferred information will be minimal and the information itself – severely limited. Such a system cannot fulfil all the multivariate functions that are historically attributed to language. You could say that, ideally, an identical addresser and addressee would understand each other very well, but they would not be able to talk about anything. (Lotman [1992] 2009: 4)

In other words, both understanding and misunderstanding (or rather non-comprehension) are necessary conditions for communication because only difference can create meaning. This is the essential paradox of human cultures: every attempt to convey some information (informative function) inevitably creates possibilities for interpretation and the creation of new information (modelling function). But how are these functions manifested in the 'physical' properties of the text?

The structure of the artistic text

It is not a coincidence that Lotman's first monograph was titled *The Structure of the Artistic Text* (1970). In this book, Lotman returns to such long-debated questions as the text's structure and meaning, form versus content, text versus reality. First of all, Lotman emphasizes the idea that any text – and an artistic text even more so – is perceived holistically. Its elements (signs) are packed inside one another like Matryoshka dolls (Lotman [1970] 1977: 23), that is, they are connected not only syntagmatically but also *hierarchically*, on all levels. *'Beauty is information'*, states Lotman aphoristically, pointing out that the structure of the artistic text already bears some potential information (Lotman 1964: 100). Therefore, the structure of an artistic text is meaningful by itself, and if this structure is altered, the text will convey different ideas (Lotman [1970] 1977: 12).

This is a transparent reference to the writings of the Russian Formalists and especially Juri Tynianov, whose theoretical works Lotman particularly valued (see Chapter 3). Lotman ([1970] 1977: 51–3) distinguishes three main characteristics of the artistic text: structure (*strukturnost'*), expressedness (*vyrazhennost'*) and boundary (*otgranichennost'*).

Structure

The concept of structure is used by Lotman as a substitute for an imprecise notion of form which unavoidably triggers a long-standing discussion on the relationship between form and content in the text. Lotman has always stressed that the artistic text is a *complexly constructed meaning* (Lotman ([1970] 1977: 12; [1972] 1976: 35): 'Under the complex operations of meaning-generation language is inseparable from the content it expresses [. . .] the ideas of an artist *are a text*' (Lotman 1990: 15, 237). Indeed, if we consider content and form as separate entities, then the whole point of art turns out to be pointless: Why bother to write a poem or make a film if you can just summarize its main ideas? The content of the artistic text is thus inseparable from the artistic structure in which it is expressed: 'Consequently, an artistic idea is inconceivable outside a structure. The dualism of form and content must be replaced by the concept of "idea" as something realized in a corresponding structure and non-existent outside that structure' (Lotman [1970] 1977: 12).

The genesis of this methodological standpoint is traced back to the Russian Formalists and Tynianov ([1924] 1965: 27–8), who already in 1924 pointed out that the perception of content and form as separate categories is misleading, and a (literary) work should be analysed as an integral entity the elements of which are in a relative and dynamic relationship to one another. The same idea is encountered in the works of the Bakhtin circle: for example, Pavel Medvedev argued that the 'meaning of art is completely inseparable from all the details of its material body' and that the work of art is 'meaningful in its entirety' (Bakhtin and Medvedev [1928] 1991: 12).

Lotman, however, differentiates between different pragmatics of a text: for example, the scholarly text has a different creative potential and 'gravitates towards monosemy', whereas the artistic text gravitates towards ambiguity and a multitude of possible interpretations (Lotman [1972] 1976: 122). These are the two main, albeit opposing, forces of human culture – the desire to reduce the entropy and ambivalence in communication and the inherent *unpredictability* of textuality. The unpredictability (of the artistic text) presupposes an interpreter; the goal of the scientific text is to reduce the interpretive possibilities as much as possible. The scientific text 'looks at the world as something already made, constructed', whereas the artistic text creates a world of its own 'in which are embedded mechanisms of unpredictable self-development' (Lotman 1990: 236).

Expressedness

Structure is closely connected with the concept of expressedness, which describes the relationship of the system and the text and how the system manifests itself in the text. This concept is obviously close to Tynianov's 'literary function' which he defines as 'the interrelationship of a work with literary order' (Tynianov [1927] 1977: 74). The expressedness of the text allows us to define a text as belonging to any category, be it literature, genre or any other criterion. Keeping in mind that a work of art lies at the intersection of several deciphering codes, we inevitably compare any text to other similar texts that we deem to belong to the same system: for example, a poem is compared with other poems, genres, subgenres and styles, alongside the existing conventions regarding rhyme, metre, etc. It is important to note that this is not an absolute criterion, and different addressees will have different perception of a text due to different competence and knowledge of the system(s).

The system that is 'reflected' in a *literary* text is of course natural language, but Lotman ([1972] 1976: 17) argues that 'language in relation to literature functions as a material substance similar to paint in painting, stone in sculpture, and sound in music', in other words, literature, as a separate sign system, deforms and transforms the 'usual' relations in language, creating new meanings.[2] Furthermore, 'In a work of art *deviations* from the structural organization can be as meaningful as the realization of the latter' (Lotman ([1972] 1976: 120). In general, expressedness also refers to the material substance of the text, its 'physical envelope' – for example, the paper quality of a printed novel, a streamed video on a computer screen, the layout of a newspaper, a text message on the screen of a smartphone – all of which to various extents influence our perception of a given text.

Boundary

Last but not least, another mechanism of meaning generation is boundary, both of the semiotic space and the text itself: 'Because the semiotic space is transected by numerous boundaries, each message that moves across it must be many times translated and transformed, and the process of generating new information thereby snowballs' (Lotman 1990: 140). This feature of the text is seemingly too obvious: any text is delimited and has a boundary that distinguishes it from other texts, non-texts and extratextual reality. In narratives, for example, the beginning and the end of the text serve as its temporal boundary: the plot unfolds in time, and its elements are perceived consequently and not simultaneously as, for example, in a picture or sculpture (see Chapter 13). For the plot, the category of end is especially important; it is what makes a text meaningful: 'That which is without end is without sense' (Lotman [1992] 2009: 161). In visual arts, the concept of the frame is what delimits the boundaries of the text; whenever we enclose a piece of reality in a physical or metaphorical frame, it *becomes* the artistic text.[3] This innocuous feature exposes one of the core problems of human semiosis, the relationship between the continuity of life and the discrete nature of the text. Lotman ([1970] 1977: 75) describes it as the ability of art to transform 'noise', non-semiotic reality, into information, and the continuous flow of reality into discrete, *meaningful* and analysable entities.

In his several works, Lotman explains this phenomenon through the concept of montage, borrowed from film theory: 'One of the basic elements of the concept "shot" is the *boundary of the artistic space*. [. . .] reproducing a visual and movable image of life, cinematography subdivides it into segments' (Lotman [1973] 1976: 24). Lotman once more cites Tynianov, who argues that 'the visible world is presented on film not as it is but in its semiotic interdependence' (cited in Lotman [1972] 1976: 161). Thus, the text is not a mere 'reflection' of life, not its copy, but a model that recreates life by means of its own semiotic logic: 'Being spatially limited, a work of art is a model of an infinite universe' (Lotman [1970] 1977: 210).

Any text is always perceived in relation to *non-texts* and extratextual reality as such. Again, this relation is not absolute but relative: for example, for most people the fight between a snake and an eagle is just an episode of life, but a Greek oracle may interpret it as a message from the gods. The semiotization of reality – assignment of meaning to the continuity of life – and the desemiotization of texts – when the semiotic frame is ignored, and a text is considered to be a non-text – is something that we experience in our lives on a daily basis.

However, this is just one side of the text's relation to the extratextual reality. Already in the 1962 article 'The Problem of Similarity of Art and Life from the Structuralist Point of View', Lotman ([1962] 1998: 383) argues that the text is perceived in a dual way: in its relation to both what is being recreated (reality) and what is *not* being recreated (the multiplicity of possible texts). Lotman introduces the term 'minus-device'[4] (and, consequently, 'minus-context' and 'minus-trope'), or *the meaningful absence of structural elements*. Some elements are not formally present in the text and are located 'between' the shots of the film or the passages of the written text, but the reader/viewer would reconstruct them on their own: some are reconstructed almost automatically, and some require an interpretive effort on part of the addressee. This is especially characteristic of the marked structural elements; for example, in narratives, open endings that presuppose multiple interpretations serve as an explosive element with a strong meaning-generating potential (Lotman [1970] 2000: 430).

Lotman argues that the problem of meaningful absence is especially important for historical studies of distant epochs and/or cultures. For example, travellers in an 'exotic' land (which Russia was for many Europeans in various epochs) would tend to describe everything they experience in a foreign country as a norm, not being able to differentiate between the normal and the extraordinary in the daily life of the locals (Lotman [1976] 1993: 138–44). The same problem is valid for the study of cultures which left after themselves only a handful of artefacts/documents; a text from such a culture cannot be perceived on the background of the multitude of textual material with which it can be compared: 'And so, when historians pick up a text, they must distinguish between what constitutes an event from their point of view and what was an event worthy of remembering from the point of view of the author of the text and his or her contemporaries' (Lotman [1992] 2019: 190). This principle of the differential character of the text which can be perceived as meaningful only in relation to other texts goes back both to Saussure – 'in language there are only differences' (Saussure 1966: 120) – and to Peirce (1931–4: 5.289): 'At no one instant in my state of mind is there cognition or representation, but in relation of my states of mind at different instants there is.'

The invariant and typology of cultures

If any text is produced in its own specific culture, is it possible to reconstruct this culture, or some features of it, from one text? Contrariwise, is it possible to describe a given culture as a text? In a 1969 article, Lotman maintains that it is possible to 'obtain a textual construct which will be the invariant of all the texts belonging to the given cultural type', and this 'cultural text' will represent 'the most abstract model of reality from the position of a given culture' (Lotman [1969] 1975: 100–1). Culture can therefore be studied as an exceptionally complex text that consists of a hierarchy of 'texts within the texts' (Lotman [1992] 2009: 77). An example of this approach is evident in Lotman's ample commentary to Pushkin's *Eugene Onegin* (Lotman 1980), in which he reconstructs the main features of the culture of the Russian nobility of that time in order to position the text in its specific semiosphere.

The invariant is a pragmatic and functional concept because it facilitates our comprehension of texts and allows us to make assumptions about texts, structures and cultures we are not familiar with. In other words, it allows the recipient to inductively make connections between the microstructure (a single text) and the macrostructure (from a group of texts to culture). It is a known fact that all texts of an unfamiliar genre, an art form or a whole sign system might seem indistinguishable from one another, and individual peculiarities of a given text – especially idiosyncratic and irregular ones – will be ignored. Lotman explains this by the fact that in this case our attention is fixed on the *systemic* elements or the invariant system of relations (Lotman [1970] 1977: 54–5). For example, Russian eighteenth-century comedies, or Hollywood blockbusters, or late night TV shows all may be described as texts with a similar invariant structure that can serve as a model for recognition and creation of other texts.

An example of how a single text can influence a whole culture is discussed in Lotman's 1985 article on Vasili Trediakovsky's translation in 1730 of a novel by Paul Tallemant (le Jeune) *Le Voyage à l'île d'amour* (1663). In France, it was an average novel of the *salon* culture, but when transferred onto the Russian soil that lacked any of the contexts of the source culture, it acquired a very different meaning and became *the* novel, the literary standard and at the same time a textbook of romantic behaviour (Lotman [1985] 1992: 27). That is how a single text became a model not only in literature but also in everyday life.

On a higher level, it would be possible to classify and compare various cultures by analysing what kind of invariant text a culture constructs of itself, both in diachronic and in synchronic perspective. In other words, it would be possible to construct a cultural *typology*:

> Culture can be presented as an aggregate of texts; however, from the point of view of the researcher, it is more exact to consider culture as a mechanism creating an aggregate of texts and texts as the realization of culture. An essential feature for the typology of culture is its self-appraisal in this regard. While it is typical of some cultures to regard themselves as an aggregate of normative *texts* [. . .] others model themselves as a system of *rules* that determine the creation of texts. (Lotman and Uspensky [1971] 1978: 218)

In this paper, Lotman and Uspenskij contrast European Neo-Classicism (which they term a rules-oriented or content-oriented culture) with European Realism of the nineteenth century (defined as a text-oriented or expression-oriented culture) (Lotman and Uspensky [1971] 1978). They mention the concept of self-description or the metalevel of culture, that is, its 'ideal self-portrait' (Lotman [1977] 1979: 92) expressed in normative texts: grammars, chronicles, textbooks, critical works, etc. Because these texts tend to describe the norm and ignore cultural 'aberrations', in this self-description culture is presented as more organized, systemic and logical than it really is. The goal of the typological description of cultures is therefore to create 'a grammar of cultural languages' (Lotman [1966] 1977: 216) that can be used for comparative studies but also to reveal their normative discourses and ideologies.

Memory of the text

One of the oft-repeated thoughts in Lotman's works is that every text is also a vehicle of collective memory (see Chapter 17). The concept of memory is crucial for Lotman's approach because it is closely related to the thesis of cultural isomorphism of individual and collective consciousness, according to which culture is understood as the non-hereditary collective memory (Lotman and Uspensky [1971] 1978: 213). However, Lotman brings our attention to the fact that cultural (and human) 'memory is not an immobile store, but an apparatus for active and ever new modelling, although it is directed towards the past' (Lotman [1977] 1979: 95). In other words, it behaves as a human memory and therefore inherits its entropic features: it may forget, it may transform old memories and create new ones, up to the point of 'going out of its mind' (Lotman [1977] 1979: 85).

The mnemonic function of the text is manifested not in storing information inside itself but in its intertextual ability to link to other texts and other hierarchical structures on different levels (genres, themes, motifs, contexts, etc.). That is how the text creates its own 'meaning-space', its own semiosphere:

> The sum of the contexts in which a given text acquires interpretation and which are in a way incorporated in it may be termed the text's memory. This meaning-space created by the text around itself enters into relationship with the cultural memory (tradition) already formed in the consciousness of the audience. As a result the text acquires semiotic life. [. . .] Nowadays *Hamlet* is not just a play by Shakespeare, but it is also the memory of all its interpretations, and what is more, it is also the memory of all those historical events which occurred outside the text but with which Shakespeare's text can evoke associations. (Lotman 1990: 18–19)

From the point of view of information theory, producing endless interpretations should be considered counterproductive for any text because it seems to contradict its primary function, the transfer of information. In human semiosis, however, and especially in artistic texts, 'noise' and entropy on the contrary enrich the semiotic space of a text and facilitate its preservation in cultural memory.

Mythological texts

The text's memory is a key element of *mythological* texts, which constitute the core of any culture. Similar to Claude Lévi-Strauss, Roland Barthes and others, Lotman and his colleagues at the Tartu-Moscow School understand by myth a special type of texts that is not limited to folklore. In their terminology, myth is rather a means of preserving cultural identities, from individual consciousness to whole civilizations. On an individual level, myth 'organizes the world of the listener' rather than serves as a source of new information – 'Myth always says something about me' (Lotman 1990: 153), – and on the collective level, myths preserve world views, ideologies (the focus of Roland Barthes's *Mythologies*, [1957] 1972) and the model of the universe in general.

The main difference between mythological texts and non-mythological texts (which Lotman calls *plot-texts* at some point) is that the former are oriented towards *autocommunication*. In a 1973 article, Lotman juxtaposes two types of text that require opposite techniques of reading, a *note* and a *knot* on a handkerchief:

> Both are supposed to be read, but the character of 'reading' will be profoundly different. In the first case, the message is contained in the text and can be extracted from it. In the second case, the 'text' performs a mnemonic function and reminds the reader of something they already know. There is no message that can be extracted from this text. (Lotman [1973] 1998: 438)

The knot functions here not as a source of information but as a catalyst of memory, and in that sense is purely autocommunicative. This is the case of the 'I–I' communication – in contrast to the usual 'I–s/he' communication, – when information is transferred not in space but in time (Lotman 1990: 21–2). In this act of communication, it is not the text that is changed but the addresser's individual semiosphere, causing the addresser to perceive old information as new (see also Chapter 11).

In his several works, Lotman introduces the dichotomy of mythological texts versus *plot*-texts. Lotman argues that because myth is oriented towards maintaining a certain world view, mythological texts appear to be cyclical and *non-discrete*, that is, they are perceived as a whole and cannot be segmented (i.e. analysed). Plot-texts, on the other hand, are usually linear and may be subdivided into smaller elements. 'Plot is a "revolutionary element" in relation to the world picture' (Lotman [1970] 1977: 238), and in that sense is not limited to narratives, it is a category of textual structure that presupposes a different technique of reading. Plot-texts are *descriptive* in a broad sense of the word and polylinguistic; as a consequence, their comprehension is linked with *translation* and *interpretation*. Mythological texts tend to be monolingual, and their comprehension relies to a great extent on *recognition* and recollection; strictly speaking, in myth no new messages are possible, and every text is not learned but recognized (Lotman and Uspenskij [1973] 1977).

This is of course an abstraction, an ideal opposition of the two 'primordial' types of texts that correspond to the two types of consciousness (Lotman 1990: 153). Further, Lotman argues that modern artistic texts are a result of a mutual interference of these two types. In practice, there are very few purely 'plotless' texts, and practically any modern text can be perceived as mythological and, depending on the context, can be used as such by different communities in order to preserve certain identities and values.

Conclusion: Isomorphic textuality

This chapter reviewed the main features of Lotman's approach to textuality, which in a very condensed form can be summarized as follows: 'Lotman studies culture as a very complex polyglot text which is isofunctional and isomorphic to individual intellect' (Semenenko 2012: 86). This law of cultural isomorphism is reflected in the following key points that have been discussed in the chapter:

- Text is a meaning-generating mechanism;
- Text is polyglot, that is, it lies at the intersection of at least two languages;
- Text is the primary unit of (human) semiosis;
- Mythological texts are oriented towards recognition rather than description;
- Text is a vehicle of collective memory;
- Culture is a hierarchy of texts within the texts which functions both as a generator of texts and as a text itself.

Notes

1. Later on, Lotman extends this heterogeneity onto cognition: 'within one consciousness there are as it were two consciousnesses. The one operates as a discrete system of coding and forms texts which come together like linear chains of linked segments. In this system the basic bearer of meaning is the segment (= the sign), while the chain of segments (= the text) is secondary, its meaning being derived from the meaning of the signs. In the second system the text is primary, being the bearer of the basic meaning. This text is not discrete but continuous. Its meaning is organized neither in a linear nor in a temporal sequence, but is "washed over" the n-dimension semantic space of the given text (the canvas of a picture, the space of a stage, of a screen, a ritual, of social behaviour or of a dream). In texts of this type the text is the bearer of the meaning' (Lotman 1990: 36).

2. See also Lotman and Pjatigorskij ([1968] 1977). This idea can be traced back to Tynianov ([1924] 1965) who speaks of different meaning-altering devices and introduces the notion of 'the compactness of the verse series', which means that verse is able to change and transform syntactical and semantic relations of natural language.

3. The concept of the text frame was also developed by Lotman's close colleague Boris Uspenskij (1970: 181–214), who argues that any text creates a special world with its space and time, the world to which we are related as outside observers and the rules of which we have to accept in order to make sense out of our interaction with it.

4. The term 'device' (*priem*) is again borrowed from the Russian Formalists (Lotman 1964: 59; [1970] 1977: 103).

References

Bakhtin, M. and Medvedev, P. [1928] 1991. *The Formal Method in Literary Scholarship: A Critical Introduction to Sociological Poetics*, trans. A. J. Wehrle, Baltimore, MD: Johns Hopkins University Press.

Barthes, R. [1957] 1972. *Mythologies*, trans. A. Lavers, New York: Noonday Press.

Chernov, I. 1988. 'Historical Survey of Tartu-Moscow Semiotic School', in H. Broms and R. Kaufmann (eds), *Semiotics of Culture: Proceedings of the 25th Symposium of the Tartu-Moscow School of Semiotics, Imatra, Finland, 27th–29th July, 1987*, 7–16, Helsinki: Arator.

Ivanov, V. 1976. *Ocherki po istorii semiotiki v SSSR*, Moscow: Nauka.

Lotman, Ju. M. [1962] 1998. 'Problema skhodstva iskusstva i zhizni v svete stuktural'nogo podkhoda', in Ju. M. Lotman, *Ob iskusstve*, 378–86, Saint Petersburg: Iskusstvo–SPB.

Lotman, Ju. M. 1964. *Lektsii po struktural'noi poetike. Vyp. 1. Vvedenie, teoriia stikha*, Tartu: Izdatel'stvo Tartuskogo universiteta (*Trudy po znakovym sistemam*, 1).

Lotman, Ju. M. [1966] 1977. 'Problems in the Typology of Texts', in D. P. Lucid (ed. and trans.), *Soviet Semiotics: An Anthology*, 119–24, Baltimore, MD: Johns Hopkins University Press.

Lotman, Ju. M. [1969] 1975. 'On the Metalanguage of a Typological Description of Culture', *Semiotica* 14 (2): 97–123.

Lotman, Ju. M. [1970] 1977. *The Structure of the Artistic Text*, trans. R. Vroon, Ann Arbor: University of Michigan, Department of Slavic Languages and Literatures.

Lotman, Ju. M. [1970] 2000. 'Stat'i po tipologii kul'tury', in Ju. M. Loman, *Semiosfera*, 391–459, Saint Petersburg: Iskusstvo–SPB.

Lotman, Ju. M. [1972] 1976. *Analysis of the Poetic Text*, trans. D. B. Johnson, Ann Arbor: Ardis.

Lotman, Yu. M. [1973] 1976. *Semiotics of Cinema*, trans. M. E. Suino, Ann Arbor: University of Michigan.

Lotman, Ju. M. [1973] 1998. 'Kanonitcheskoe iskusstvo kak informatsionnyi paradoks', in Ju. M. Lotman, *Ob iskusstve*, 436–41, Saint Petersburg: Iskusstvo–SPB.

Lotman, Yu. M. [1977] 1979. 'Culture as Collective Intellect and the Problems of Artificial Intelligence', in L. M. O'Toole and A. Shukman (eds), *Dramatic Structure: Poetic and Cognitive Semantics*, 84–96, Oxford: Holdan Books.

Lotman, Yu. M. [1977] 1982. 'The Text and the Structure of Its Audience', *New Literary History* 14 (1): 81–7.

Lotman, Ju. M. 1980. *Roman A. S. Pushkina Evgenii Onegin, kommentarii: posobie dlia uchitelia*, Leningrad: Prosveshchenie.

Lotman, J. [1984] 2005. 'On the Semiosphere', trans. W. Clark, *Sign Systems Studies* 33 (1): 205–29.

Lotman, Ju. M. [1985] 1992. '"Ezda v ostrov liubvi" Trediakovskogo I funktsii perevodnoi literatury v russkoi kul'ture pervoi poloviny XVIII veka', in Ju. M. Loman, *Izbrannye stat'i*, vol. 2, 22–8, Tallinn: Aleksandra.

Lotman, Yu. M. 1990. *Universe of the Mind: A Semiotic Theory of Culture*, trans. A Shukman, London and New York: I.B. Tauris.

Lotman, J. [1992] 2009. *Culture and Explosion*, trans. W. Clark, ed. M. Grishakova, Berlin: Mouton de Gruyter.

Lotman, J. [1992] 2019. 'A Divine Pronouncement or a Game of Chance? The Law-Governed and the Accidental in the Historical Process', in J. Lotman, *Culture, Memory and History: Essays in Cultural Semiotics*, trans. B. J. Baer, ed. M. Tamm, 189–99, Cham: Palgrave Macmillan.

Lotman, Ju. M. 1993. 'Smert' kak problema siuzheta', in V. Polukhina, J. Andrew and R. Reid (eds), *Studies in Slavic Literature and Poetics. Vol. XX: Literary Tradition and Practice in Russian Culture: Papers from an International Conference on the Occasion of the Seventieth Birthday of Yu. M. Lotman*, 1–15, Amsterdam: Rodopi.

Lotman, Ju. M. and Pjatigorskij, A. M. [1968] 1977. 'Text and Function', in D. P. Lucid (ed. and trans.), *Soviet Semiotics: An Anthology*, 125–35, Baltimore, MD: Johns Hopkins University Press.

Lotman, Yu. M. and Uspensky, B. A. [1971] 1978. 'On the Semiotic Mechanism of Culture', trans. G. Mihaychuk, *New Literary History* 9 (2): 211–32.

Lotman, Yu. M. and Uspensky, B. A. [1973] 1977. 'Myth–Name–Culture', in D. P. Lucid (ed. and trans.), *Soviet Semiotics: An Anthology*, 233–52, Baltimore, MD: Johns Hopkins University Press.

Lotman, M. 2002. 'Umwelt and Semiosphere', *Sign Systems Studies* 30 (1): 33–40.

Lotman, M. 2019. 'Tekst v kontekste tartuskoi shkoly: problemy i perspektivy', in S. T. Zolyan, *Iurii Lotman: O smysle, tekste, istorii. Temy i variatsii*, 277–94, Moscow: IaSK.

Peirce, C. S. 1931–34. *Collected Papers*, vol. 5, eds. C. Hartshorne and P. Weiss, Cambridge, MA: Harvard University Press.

Saussure, F. de [1916] 1966. *Course in General Linguistics*, eds. C. Bally and A. Sechehaye with A. Riedlinger, New York: McGraw-Hill.

Semenenko, A. 2012. *The Texture of Culture: An Introduction to Yuri Lotman's Semiotic Theory*, New York: Palgrave Macmillan.

Tynianov, I. [1924] 1965. *Problemy stikhotvornogo iazyka: stat'i*, Moscow: Sovetskii pisatel'.

Tynianov, I. [1927] 1977. *Poetika. Istoriia literatury. Kino*, Moscow: Nauka.

Uspenskij, B. A. 1970. *Poetika kompozitsii*, Moscow: Iskusstvo.

CHAPTER 10
CULTURE
Mihhail Lotman

It is at the same time easy and difficult to write about the concept of culture in the work of Juri Lotman. It is easy because almost all of Lotman's writings in semiotics, but also in other fields, are in one way or another related to culture. Even the bibliography alone would encompass over 100 titles. But the difficulty relates to terminology. As noted by one benevolent critic of his first works of semiotics, Lotman is a stranger to terminological rigorism. To this, Lotman reacted with a smile: that was mildly put. He did not concern himself with a systematization of terminology and on many occasions used ad hoc terms according to specific needs. One must also keep in mind that Lotman often makes use of metaphors. Sometimes he refers to semiotic objects as mechanisms; on other occasions he discusses them as organisms. However, there are times where he uses both metaphors at once. In reading Lotman's texts, one ought to concentrate on his approach as a whole and on its dynamics and not get caught up in particular terms. One must further consider that the terminological apparatus of Lotman becomes more simplified over time and that he will start avoiding specific terms.

Formation of the concept of culture

During his high school years, Lotman was foremost interested in biology and entomology and undertook serious preparations for this field. Entomological parallels helped him to describe various cultural phenomena. Nevertheless, literature and history formed the focal point of his university studies. He constantly reflected on the phenomenon of art and one can discern from his early correspondence embryonic ideas about structural poetry. Already in his letters during military service one can encounter the approach to culture as a whole and as an integral organism (see Kuzovkina et al. 2021). In these letters, which were written years before reading Saussure, Lotman differentiates synchrony from diachrony, but also displays a clear preference for synchrony, since according to him, the 'organic' connection is more important than the genetic.

As concerns Lotman's approach to culture in his semiotic works, despite the fact that his views were subject to significant change, the nucleus remained the same. It is characterized by a holistic view of culture, both in its structural sense (the internal construct of culture) and in its functional sense (culture's relation to surrounding reality). Culture is a sovereign domain. Here, Lotman is opposed to several traditions of approach to culture at once. Above all, one must name Marxism, positivism, and German philosophy of culture.

Marxism was the official ideology of the Soviet Union. It was mandatory to quote Lenin, although in discussions the positivist approach of the nineteenth century was preferred, according to which culture is divided into two fields: material and non-material (in Soviet terminology, 'spiritual', from German phrase '*die Geistige Kultur*'), with only the latter being discussed as culture *stricto sensu*: culture without an adjective meant intellectual culture, arts etc., in the opposite sense it needed the adjective 'material'. Lotman was critical of both Soviet Marxist culturology and German philosophy of culture with its distinction between culture and civilization. First of all, because, for him, culture is an integral whole and – let us note in advance – the entire field of culture is an integral semiotic whole. Firstly, objects of the so-called material culture are also signs, and serve as message carriers; secondly, the boundary between the material and the spiritual in culture is always conditional, and it is never predetermined. One must also remember that the concept of material culture originates from archaeology and ethnology and that it originally came from research dealing with societies that were either temporally or spatially distant, that is, the cultures of 'them', not the cultures of 'us', and the messages of these were at least partially incomprehensible to scholars.

As to the epistemological basis of Lotman's semiotics of culture, it formed, in the first place, under the influence of Kant's philosophy: a semiotic structure must be approached foremost by deriving from its immanent properties (compare Kant's 'the thing-in-itself'). Only after that should the given structure be approached in interaction with other things (Kant's 'the thing-for-other-things'). Later, Leibniz's monadology was added as a more adequate methodological basis. Culture as a monad does not rule out other monads, although it does presume their existence. However, Lotman does not quite use the term 'monad' as Leibniz does. According to Lotman, culture itself is composed of different monads and all cultures together also form a monad. Here the particularity of Lotman's semiotic perspective becomes apparent, which is characterized, firstly, by the abandonment of causal explanations of cultural phenomena in favour of structuralist explanations that focus on isomorphism between cultures as semiotic phenomena, and, secondly, by giving up the relationship between a part and the whole: in semiotic systems, a part can contain the whole to which it itself belongs.

Lotman's concept of the semiotics of culture had already been broadly developed in his early work, although it improves and evolves significantly later on. One can often encounter the genesis of future concepts in his earlier writings. All of this presents me with difficult choices: whether to discuss the problems found in these works thematically or chronologically. It seems that neither of these solutions can be strictly adhered to and here I try to present a hybrid approach and to discuss the concept of culture both thematically and in chronological order.

Culture as a sign

In order to understand the foundations of Lotman's approach to culture, one must first outline his views on semiotics, which are far from trivial. This is rendered more complicated by the fact that Lotman has never once described this in a separate text (Semenenko 2012: 7); rather, it must be reconstructed in the similar manner which he himself uses to reconstruct the content of lost or even unwritten texts or the mindset of various authors.

When Lotman's approach to culture is discussed, usually the focus is on either his results in studies of Russian culture or on the various semiotic models of culture beginning from medieval socio-semiotic understandings and ending with the semiosphere. What are usually overlooked, however, are the principles of Lotman's semiotics, which are very different from the understandings that have been developed in other semiotic schools. Of those principles, the most important is that each semiotic object can be understood at the same time both as a sign and as text: for example, each text can function as a simple sign, each sign can be interpreted as text.

To say that each element of a text can be meaningful is to say that the concept of text in the given case is identical to the concept of sign (Lotman [1970] 1977: 22). At first, this is only applied to works of art and other works which belong to the secondary modelling systems, but in his later studies Lotman concludes that this can be applied to all types of text, because each text is potentially an artistic one. The text itself is a potential object, it becomes actualized not due to its immanent properties, but by fulfilling a particular cultural function: a text is something that functions as a text (Piatigorsky 1962; Lotman and Piatigorsky 1968). Firstly, the text can therefore exist as a text only in the context of culture, and any materially one and the same object or phenomenon can function in one culture as an element of its language, in another as a picture or commodity or then as a material object without general significance or meaning. Secondly, textuality is a universal cultural function. Just as there cannot be texts outside of culture, a culture that lacks texts cannot exist either.

The following analysis allows for an even more courageous conclusion: with a certain level of generalization, one can speak of the isomorphism of all semiotic systems.

> Meaning-making occurs at all structural levels of a culture. [. . .] Systems of this type – ranging from minimal semiotic entities to global ones [. . .] acquire structural isomorphism, despite their material differences. This makes possible the construction of a minimal model for such systems, on the one hand, while turning out to be extremely valuable for analyzing the process of meaning-making, on the other. (Lotman [1989] 2019: 85)

This means that sign, text and culture are, in a certain sense, isomorphic (cf. Semenenko 2016: 494). How do we understand this? It seems almost self-evident that a sign is an elementary semiotic element, a text is a complex of signs and a culture is a system of numerous texts, languages and artefacts. Lotman's approach to signs differs significantly from those of Peirce and Saussure. As with Saussure, it is pointless to talk about single signs outside of a sign system in his work, but unlike Saussure, each sign is a realization of several (at least two) sign systems. If we take the spelling of whichever word, then it is coded at once with the means of both natural language and typographical shapes. Neither graphics nor acoustics are components of natural language; they are autonomous from language. One cannot necessarily understand a language, but still enjoy calligraphy or typography or enjoy (or detest) the melody of a language. One must separately emphasize that language and its graphical manifestation (e.g.) are not merely two detached systems, but they are semiotic systems of a different type.

Here, one must make an important clarification. One of the key concepts of the Tartu-Moscow school is 'secondary modelling systems' (see Chapter 12). In its first version, this represented semiotic systems that are more complicated than natural language and contain natural language as its component. In such cases, natural language appears as a primary, but literature in the role of secondary, modelling system. One can deduce from this that natural language is the primary modelling system par excellence. Such understanding was expressed by Vladimir Uspenskij, who offered this term for a conference and publications. This approach became subject to justified criticism from scholars like Thomas A. Sebeok (1988) or Han-liang Chang (2003) because it is obvious that language itself is based on other sign systems. Deriving from Peirce, Sebeok and Marcel Danesi offered a different solution. They divide the modelling systems into three groups in accordance with the Peircian three types of sign relation: primary modelling systems are iconical, secondary indexical and tertiary symbolical (Sebeok and Danesi 2000: 10). This is indeed as in Peirce's approach, according to which firstness always comes first, secondness second and thirdness third. One must concur with Chang (2003) in that natural language is a complicated system which cannot be considered primary in the absolute meaning. However, Lotman's concept is something entirely different when compared to the first definitions by both Sebeok and Danesi, and V. Uspenskij.

The treatment of primary and secondary sign systems in the Tartu-Moscow school is purely relative: a primary sign system is primary only in respect of a given secondary system, and a secondary sign system is secondary only in respect of a given primary system. The fact that poetry is a secondary sign system in respect to natural language does not mean that natural language cannot be secondary to some other system. To focus on secondary modelling systems meant that at the centre of attention were complicated systems consisting of several subsystems. A similar conclusion was reached by Winfried Nöth (2006), who emphasized the relative nature of firstness and secondness.

If culture is a text, then what is its message; if culture is a sign, then what does it mean? The answer to the first question depends on the position of culture as a recipient/interpreter of a text. Lotman offers three main opportunities: culture from the perspective of itself, culture from the perspective of another culture and culture as understood by its researcher. For itself, culture is a universal text which consists of many texts and also contains information from the reality outside of culture; from other cultures come reflections and meta-descriptions of it, while both reflections from other cultures and self-presentations can be quite biased. As a text, culture is dynamic; with its message being in constant change, it incorporates new information from the external world and reconstructs its content. A significant aspect is how culture wants to appear to itself, what it tries to present to others and what to conceal. From the perspective of another culture, it is important to what extent it speaks the language of the culture of interest, to what degree one wants to delve into it and how benevolently or malevolently it is regarded (Semenenko 2012: 54–5).

In the case of meta-descriptions, the position of the interpreter is extremely important: do they belong to a given culture, how fluent are they in the language of that culture, what are their own metalanguage and scientific paradigms: Are they trying to make it explicit from the languages of the culture they are studying or are they deriving from universal typological criteria?

Just as every text, culture can be reduced to a sign. This sign usually appears as a designation, for example 'people' (in the language of Matsés), or 'people + a specifying epithet', 'people of the land' (the self-designation of Estonians until the nineteenth century), 'people of the straits' (the Tlingit), 'people of the river' (Matsés in the Quechua language), etc.; or, such designations as 'German culture' or the 'Russian Romantic age'. Each such designation carries in itself narratives which may be expanded into texts. It is important not only that the sign contains the information previously embedded in it but also that the sign itself has the potential to expand. 'A sign models its content' (Lotman [1970] 1977: 21). At first, this applied to texts and signs of art in Lotman's concept, but according to his later understandings, this applies to all signs and texts. Semiotic objects beginning from signs and concluding with the semiosphere have creative potential; they can not only transmit ready-made information but also generate new information. Lotman compares this to Heraclitus's self-increasing Logos (Lotman [1981] 1988: 56; [1992] 2004: 159).

No sign or text can exist in a vacuum; the prerequisite for the existence of each sign is other signs, the prerequisite for each text is other texts, and for each culture, other cultures (Lotman [1984] 2005). Behind the growth of the meaning of the sign are contacts with other signs and their appearance in various texts and cultural contexts. However, what and how a sign, text or culture incorporates something into itself is determined not only by context but also by the immanent properties of semiotic structures, their ability and readiness to acquire new information.

Even more, in communicating with the surrounding environment, the semiotic structure is the active participant; context is not primary in relation to the text, and it is not predetermined (M. Lotman 2000). Context is the context of *that* text which is formed as a result of active interactions. Lotman thus demonstrated that language is not always primary in relation to text(s), a language cannot exist without texts, just as texts cannot exist without language (Lotman 1990: 31–2). Similarly, the recipient of a text does not exist before the text, and a text has the ability to choose and form its own audience (Lotman [1977] 1982).

Here, there is an obvious parallel to Jakob von Uexküll's concept of Umwelt: unlike the environment, which is independent of an organism, the Umwelt is specific to a given organism and has largely designed it (M. Lotman 2002; Kull and Lotman 2012). The semiotic structure as an organism is a consistent metaphor for Lotman (Tamm 2019: 8), and he employs it even when describing the semiosphere, which he calls an 'organism made up of organisms' (Lotman [1989] 2019: 89).

The boundaries of culture

Culture, like all other semiotic structures, is limited both temporally and spatially, with Lotman having repeatedly emphasized that the spatial boundaries are the most important for culture, as for text, and that even the temporal dimension can be interpreted in spatial terms (e.g. Lotman 1997: 719–20). The metalanguage of culture operates in spatial terms because this approach corresponds to the nature of culture. Culture is a semiotic space that also accommodates physical space as part of itself (see Chapter 14). In discussing the boundaries of culture Lotman departs from the same logic he used to discuss the boundaries of text, which he referred to as a frame.

A boundary is an area of heightened semiosis, which at once belongs and does not belong to the structure being framed, with the boundaries of the boundary itself not being determined but rather being the result of text or culture and its exterior dialogue. As one example, Lotman cites painting. In classicist and realist art, the frame of the painting exists almost outside of the text itself (almost meaning that it must warrant independent attention neither for its artistic value nor for its robustness), whereas in baroque or modernist art, the frame can form an integral whole with the painting. In *The Structure of the Artistic Text*, Lotman cites as an example the way an undesired junction can form between the frame and the painting, which did not seem relevant at the moment of the framing, but which may induce a comedic effect for the modern observer (Lotman [1970] 1977: 209).

The boundary of culture is above all semiotic, but it often expresses itself with physical signs: even nomadic peoples, who do not have their own locus, have in some way delineated their territory. In such cases, the sign must be comprehensible to representatives of other cultures as well. Signs of this nature form something akin to a lingua franca. For example, hunter-gatherers in the Amazon mark their temporary territory with freshly broken wood. The same is also done by the so-called uncontacted peoples, whose language is understood by nobody. Nevertheless, they recognize the boundary signs of others and mark their own territory in a similar way. A broken tree as an object may be so insignificant that a European anthropologist would not even notice or interpret it. For them, a broken tree is merely an object and not a sign. However, this is noticed by local guides, who draw the attention of anthropologists to this border sign. Since a boundary is foremost a sign, it is intended for those with the ability to comprehend it. Therefore, as with text, the boundary of a culture is at once a sign of both the interior and the exterior of the culture. A border sign warns (other) people, but not animals, who possess entirely different devices for delimitation.

The interior and exterior space of culture

A mandatory property of culture is its delimitation and differentiation from the world exterior to culture. The exact nature of the world exterior to culture largely depends on the culture itself, on the text that it creates about itself. On the most general level, the cultural space is surrounded by non-culture, following Rousseau's lead; this is often named as nature (Lotman et al. [1973] 2013: 53–4). Rousseau inverts the model of the ruling culture by switching positive signs to negative ones and vice versa. Nevertheless, the principle of the model remains the same: culture and non-culture do not need each other.

If one were to treat culture not from an internal, but an external perspective, then non-culture becomes an unavoidable correlate of culture. Although on a declarative level, nature was primary to Rousseau and culture as a perversion of nature secondary, it is clear even in his case that nature is a construction that he poses as an opposition to culture by assigning to nature as positive all the properties that have been altered or are missing altogether in culture. Culture models not only itself but also non-culture, which is specific namely to a given culture. In such a case, the border becomes a membrane absorbing from non-culture the necessary information, which is translated by a culture into its own proper language and then assimilated or rejected (Lotman et al. [1973] 2013: 54). For example, official Soviet culture vigilantly observed the culture of the 'rotten West', in order to demean it. Lotman emphasized that during certain stages of culture, a need develops not only to isolate oneself from barbarians, who have been relegated almost to the status of nonhumans, but also to learn from them.

Enlighteners and the Romanticists were not the first admirers of the 'noble savage'. In ancient Greek culture, the Scythian philosopher Anacharsis allegedly tried to teach the Greeks the principles of a simple and noble life and reproached them for their ethnic restrictions. Although he is said to have been active in sixth century BC Athens, he became a kind of cult figure much later, during the Hellenistic period, when 'nature peoples' and 'barbarians' began to be idealized. Anacharsis can be considered the first noble savage in European culture. In his lectures, Lotman cited as an example another Anacharsis, Jean-Baptiste de Cloots, who changed his first name to Anacharsis. Cloots was a Prussian baron-turned French philosopher, an ardent republican, who journeyed to Paris in 1789 in order to herald the revolution in the name of mankind. He was received with jubilation, and he became a member of the Convent, but when the Convent adopted a law against foreigners in 1793, he was expelled, arrested and sentenced to death. Upon hearing of his sentence, Anacharsis Cloots said: 'It is extraordinary that a man fit to be burned in Rome, fit to be hanged in London, fit to be wheeled in Vienna would be guillotined in Paris.' As he was being escorted to his execution, the crowd accompanied him shouting: 'The Prussians to the guillotine!' Lotman cited Anacharsis Cloots as an example of how a cultural situation can change drastically in a very short time. Cloots, who was a Dutchman born in Germany and who was raised in the spirit of French culture, assumed the identity of the 'noble savage' Anacharsis in order to act in the name of not a nation but the whole of humanity, and was heralded as such; then, only a few years later, he was no longer just a human, but a German. The culture of Revolutionary France closed itself off from foreign influence.

Culture as a text

Each culture contains many texts, but even as a whole it can be approached as a message. This message ensures the identity of the carriers of this culture, secures their memory, customs and norms. Here, text is approached in the most general sense, not only as merely written, and not even merely as verbal. Some norms and taboos are never verbally fixated. These messages are encoded in other sign systems. What is more, no culture is homogenous from the perspective of the use of sign systems. Even in the most archaic or primitive societies, where no specific sign systems relating to social or professional stratification have been identified, there are always fundamental differences between the codes used by males and females. For example, information that mothers transmit to daughters, firstly, is concealed from men and, secondly, is usually non-verbal. The same applies to the objects belonging to men and women – apart from practical purposes, they were signs too, but the semiosis of objects belonging to men and that of women is different. Men's things have names, sometimes even proper names (this especially pertains to weapons), and they are given a name, they are boasted about and they can be offered as gifts; different narratives can apply to them. Objects and acts pertaining to women are much more clandestine, and it is not customary to talk about them or to gift them (women's objects are never part of rituals such as potlach, see Godelier 1998; about the specifics of the female world in Russian culture of the eighteenth and nineteenth centuries, see Lotman 1994: 46–135.)

For decades, Lotman worked in the field of cultural typology by constantly discovering new possibilities to typologize (however, a discussion of this would not fit well within the limits of this chapter). Let us mention only one of the first because it had significant consequences even outside the context of the Tartu-Moscow school.

A cultural text is inextricably linked to its structure, and Lotman ([1967] 1977) highlights four different cultural types from the perspective of semiotics in Russian culture starting from the Middle Ages up to the twentieth century: the semantic or symbolic, the syntactic, the asemantic and asyntactic and the semantic-syntactic. Since Lotman broadly uses parallels with other European cultures, his typology is not just limited to the different mechanisms of Russian culture.

In codes that represent a *semantic type* of culture, the syntactic is either reduced or missing altogether: each sign has a particular narrative related to it. This is particularly characteristic of Russian culture during the twelfth and thirteenth centuries. The model of this culture is characterized by the understanding that in the beginning was the Word. The world appears as a word, the act of creation represents the creation of the word and by the word. The world is divided into two: the one that has a meaning that can be expressed in words and the one that is meaningless and unimportant. The latter exists, but at the same time it does not: this was daily life. In his later works, Lotman emphasized that this was a women's world, we only know about women in Russian culture when they commit acts that have been encoded in the terms of the masculine world, for example when they are saints, meaning they give up everything relating to the corporeality or daily life of women, or the opposite is true, that is, they are criminals or avengers (Lotman 1994). The second characteristic of such a culture is the indivisibility of meaning. Illustrating this, Lotman cites the discussion of Czech theologist and writer Tomáš Štítný ze Štítného (1331–1401) over the Eucharist: each piece of the Sacramental bread is the entire body of the Lord, not a component of it. In a similar fashion, the face of the human is at once reflected in the mirror as a whole and in every individual fragment. What is disintegrated, is the signifier, not the signified. The text of such culture evolves not in the horizontal, but in the vertical dimension: wisdom is not based on finding new knowledge and texts, but on delving into old texts, which ideally form a singular text – Scripture. All new information is either integrated into this text or ignored. Anything 'new' that cannot be interpreted in the terms of the old appears unimportant and dangerous.

The *syntactic* culture type begins to replace the semantic one during the sixteenth and seventeenth centuries, and begins to prevail in Peter the Great's 'Regular State', or rather in the model which was the basis for this society. Peter detested the entire old order, but foremost its symbols. Practicality came to replace spiritual ideals, with it beginning to rule both in the stately and the ecclesiastical spheres. Instead of delving into the content of the text, one must orient oneself to common sense even in the religious sphere. However, the reduction of meaning did not mean its complete disappearance. In the horizontal dimension, meaning continued to grow, and the semantic connection between signs was replaced by the syntactic one. For example, the value of a human being was not determined by their holiness or – at least on a declarative level – their origins, but by their achievements: nobles had to serve, and the emperor himself learned handicrafts and began his military career demonstratively as a bombardier; the value of a human was determined by their social position, that is, their relationships with other people. Belonging to a larger whole became a cultural value, to be means to be a part of something. Unlike in semantic cultures, the parts in syntactic culture do not present a whole, their value lies in being a part. The whole cannot be symbolized through its parts, but through the sum of its fractions which have been syntactically arranged. While a semantic culture is oriented towards eternity, then for syntactic culture the direction of the axis of time is important; the adding up, then ordering of new elements is what ensures progress. The 'new' becomes positive and valuable, and the 'old' grows to have a negative connotation as a hurdle to progress. It is notable that the structure, which is on a declarative level, pointed against semioticity and hierarchies of meaning, leads to an even more rigid semiotization in Russia during the eighteenth century, although this semioticity is different when compared to the earlier version: the rigid bureaucratic system smooths over individual meanings and assigns them its own parts of meaning laying claim to the universal.

The *asemantic and asyntactic* type expressed itself as a cultural ideal in Continental Europe and in Russia as well during the Enlightenment. Its cultural codes are different from both medieval pansymbolism and the syntactic nature of bureaucratic absolutism. Unlike with medieval semiosis, the superior value is attributed to those things that cannot be used as signs in the minds of the enlighteners. While such semiotic phenomena as orders, uniforms, occupations, reputation and money are central to a syntagmatic structure, they are considered to be fake and worthless by the enlighteners, who value genuine, simple and essential objects that are not signs and which cannot be used as signs, according to them – for example, bread, water, love, life itself. According to Rousseau, all signs either lie or can be utilized for the purposes of lying. Unlike previous syntactic codes, the Enlightenment originates from the assumption that separately existing things own the greatest importance and also the greatest realness – they are not fractions, but their wholeness is not total; they are elementary, but they are elements of nothing.

The *semantic-syntactic* type of culture begins to dominate as an ideal during the Romanticist era. This is characterized by a drive to create a model of the world that would present it as at once meaningful and whole. Whereas Rousseau was undeniably the leading figure of the Enlightenment in the context of Russian culture, Hegel became the leader during the Romantic age. The era is characterized by explosive developments in historicism, evolution and dialectics. The world consists of real things and circumstances or facts, which express profound spiritual developments. This model provides a double meaning to objects and events. Using a syntactic projection, this ties them to the course of history, using a semantic one it opens their hidden meaning in material objects and in life itself. Unlike medieval culture, Romanticism is characterized by the urge to comprehend the meaning of evolution and history.

Although the described types constitute simplified models, they rarely appear in their pure form in cultural history. The wheels of different cultural mechanisms turn at different speeds. This ensures the internal diversity of a culture. Each text of a culture is heterogenous. One must even emphasize that there are always at least two types: the ruling and the subordinate. What is more, there is often a tendency in the ruling cultural type to preserve its opposite. Thus, by constantly fighting against their Classicist enemies, Russian Romanticists were at least subconsciously interested in its existence and as representatives of the latter, the Classicist worldview continued to exist as a phantom. On the other hand, the 'archaicists' (Juri Tynianov's term) pressured by Romanticists could become in many ways more modern and radical than Romanticists (Lotman 1986).

To sum up, let us emphasize again that a text created by culture is inextricably related to the type of culture. As with text, where idea and structure are inseparably linked (Lotman emphasized repeatedly that distinguishing between form and content is misleading and called for these terms to be abandoned), so is culture, approached as text, a meaningful structure.

Instead of a conclusion: Culture as a text and a metatext

The cultural typology outlined in the previous section is one of many found in Lotman's work. Cultures are differentiated based on whether they are open or closed, oriented towards tradition or innovation, towards syntagmatics or paradigmatics (Lotman 1968).

Cultures based on having an 'I–He' channel of communication are differentiated from those in which the autocommunication (i.e. the 'I–I' channel of communication) is dominant (Lotman [1970a] 1977); then there are cultures oriented towards an existing model, and those oriented towards grammar, that is, algorithm (these distinctions largely correspond to the distinction between semantic and syntactic structures, but with a different logic behind the classification); and there is a distinction made between cultures in which the creation of signs characteristic of the dominant hemisphere of the brain is prevalent and those where the semiosis is similar to what happens in the non-dominant hemisphere of the brain (Lotman [1981] 1992).

The results of typology depend on its purposes and the metalanguage used. Culture is at once a text and metatext of itself. It is one of the most complex topics in Lotman's semiotics of culture. On the one hand, he emphasizes several times that culture must be distinguished from its models and that one and the same culture or cultural situation can be presented in very different semiotic models. On the other hand, it is not always apparent in his writings if he is talking about Russian culture or its semiotic model. Things are rendered complicated by the fact that the culture and its models as well are both semiotic structures, and the metalanguage used to describe culture must be as adequate as possible for the language of the culture itself. Lotman was thus sure that the most adequate models of culture are spatial, the best method of analysis is founded on binary oppositions.

It is characteristic that both Lotman and his long-term co-author Boris Uspenskij saw here not a lack of an approach, but a strength. For example, when I discussed with Uspenskij the methodological basis of the Tartu-Moscow school after Lotman's death, I asked him, among other things, whether being binary is an immanent property of Russian culture or if it is merely a model, he replied instantaneously, 'It is both!' and explained that these are the very descriptions using that type of metalanguage that paint an accurate picture of Russian culture, since the metalanguage is adequate to its object (see Lotman and Uspenskij [1977] 1985).

Lotman calls the semiotic structure a monad; however, as explained earlier, unlike Leibniz's monad, the semiotic monad can contain an unlimited number of other monads, and, most importantly, it can contain itself. The monad can instil itself into itself, translate itself into its own terms, 'digest' itself in the semiotic sense (Lotman [1989] 2019). The system describes itself by employing its own language as metalanguage, with the result that two texts are equivalent, but not identical and the relationship between them can become inverted. The meta-description becomes part of the described system, and the object language becomes a metalanguage. Lotman emphasizes that the urge to describe oneself is an inseparable characteristic of culture. Culture makes use of different languages and forms to describe itself, with the description itself may not necessarily be the primary intention of the author. Culture describes itself in human and social sciences, but also in the arts, with the poetic (aesthetic) function of language being very close to metalanguage (M. Lotman 2011). It is also one of the reasons why Lotman pays so much attention to the role of art in culture.

References

Chang, H. 2003. 'Is Language a Primary Modeling System? On Juri Lotman's Concept of Semiosphere', *Sign Systems Studies* 31 (2): 1–15.

Godelier, M. 1998. *The Enigma of the Gift*, trans. N. Scott, Cambridge: Polity Press.

Kull, K. and Lotman, M. 2012. 'Semiotica Tartuensis: Jakob von Uexküll and Juri Lotman', *Chinese Semiotic Studies* 6 (1): 312–23.

Kuzovkina, T. D., Naiditch, L. E., Obraztsova, N. Iu. and Superfin, G. G. (eds) 2021. *Lotmany: Semeinaia perepiska 1940–1946*, Tallinn: TLU Press.

Lotman, Ju. M. [1967] 1977. 'Problems in the Typology of Culture', in D. P. Lucid (ed. and trans.), *Soviet Semiotics: An Anthology*, 213–21, Baltimore, MD: Johns Hopkins University Press.

Lotman, Ju. M. 1968. 'Semantika chisla i tip kul'tury', in Ju. M. Lotman (ed.), *III Letniaia shkola po vtorichnym modeliruiushchim sistemam. Tezisy*, 103–9, Tartu: Tartuskii Gosudarstvennyi Universitet.

Lotman, Ju. M. [1970] 1977. *The Structure of the Artistic Text*, trans. R. Vroon, Ann Arbor, MI: University of Michigan, Department of Slavic Languages and Literatures.

Lotman, Ju. M. [1970a] 1977. 'Two Models of Communication', in D. P. Lucid (ed. and trans.), *Soviet Semiotics: An Anthology*, 99–101, Baltimore, MD: Johns Hopkins University Press.

Lotman, Yu. [1977] 1982. 'The Text and the Structure of Its Audience', *New Literary History* 14 (1): 81–7.

Lotman, Ju. M. [1981] 1988. 'The Semiotics of Culture and the Concept of a Text', *Soviet Psychology* 26 (3): 52–8.

Lotman, Ju. M. [1981] 1992. 'Mozg – tekst – kul'tura – iskusstvennyi intell'ekt', in Ju. M. Lotman, *Izbrannye stat'i v trekh tomakh*, vol. 1, 25–33, Tallinn: Aleksandra.

Lotman, J. [1984] 2005. 'On the Semiosphere', trans. W. Clark, *Sign Systems Studies* 33 (1): 205–29.

Lotman, Ju. M. 1986. 'Arkhaisty-prosvetiteli', in M. O. Tchudakova (ed.), *Tynianovskii sbornik. Vtorye tynianovskie chtenia*, 192–207, Riga: Zininte.

Lotman, J. [1989] 2019. 'Culture as a Subject and Its Own Object', in J. Lotman, *Culture, Memory and History: Essays in Cultural Semiotics*, ed. M. Tamm, trans. B. J. Baer, 83–93, Cham: Palgrave Macmillan.

Lotman, Yu. M. 1990. *Universe of the Mind: A Semiotic Theory of Culture*, trans. A. Shukman, Bloomington: Indiana University Press.

Lotman, J. [1992] 2004. *Culture and Explosion*, trans. W. Clark, ed. M. Grishakova, Berlin and New York: Mouton de Gruyter.

Lotman, Ju. M. 1994. *Besedy o russkoi kul'ture: Byt i traditsii russkogo dvorianstva (XVIII–nachalo XIX veka)*, Saint Petersburg: Iskusstvo–SPB.

Lotman, Ju. M. 1997. *Pis'ma 1940–1993*, ed. B. F. Egorov, Moscow: Shkola 'Iazyki russkoi kultury'.

Lotman, Ju. M. and Piatigorsky, A. M. 1968. 'Tekst i funktsia', in Ju. M. Lotman (ed.), *III Letniaia shkola po vtorichnym modeliruiushchim sistemam. Tezisy*, 74–88, Tartu: Tartuskii Gosudarstvennyi Universitet.

Lotman, Ju. M. and Uspenskij, B. A. [1977] 1985. 'Binary Models in the Dynamics of Russian Culture (to the End of the Eighteenth Century)', in A. D. Nakhimovsky and A. S. Nakhimovsky (eds), *The Semiotics of Russian Cultural History*, 30–66, Ithaca, NY and London: Cornell University Press.

Lotman, Ju. M., Ivanov, V. V., Pjatigorskij, A. M., Toporov, V. N. and Uspenskij, B. A. [1973] 2013. 'Theses on the Semiotic Study of Cultures (as Applied to Slavic Texts)', in S. Salupere, P. Torop and K. Kull (eds), *Beginnings of the Semiotics of Culture*, 53–77, Tartu: University of Tartu Press.

Lotman, M. 2000. 'A Few Notes on the Philosophical Background of the Tartu School of Semiotics', *S: European Journal for Semiotic Studies* 12: 23–46.

Lotman, M. 2002. 'Umwelt and Semiosphere', *Sign Systems Studies* 30 (1): 33–40.

Lotman, M. 2011. 'Linguistics and Poetics Revisited', in M. Lotman and M.-K. Lotman (eds), *Frontiers in Comparative Prosody*, 15–53, Frankfurt am Main: Peter Lang.

Nöth, W. 2006. 'Yuri Lotman on Metaphors and Culture as Self-referential Semiospheres', *Semiotica* 161 (1/4): 249–63.

Piatigorsky, A. 1962. 'Nekotorye obshie zamechania otnositel'no rassmotrenia teksta kak raznovidnosti signala', in T. N. Moloshnaia (ed.), *Strukturno tiplogitcheskie issledovania*, Moscow: Izdatel'stvo Akademii Nauk SSSR.

Sebeok, T. A. 1988. 'In What Sense is Language a 'Primary Modelling System?', in H. Broms and R. Kaufmann (eds), *Semiotics of Culture. Proceedings of the 25th Symposium of the Tartu–Moscow School of Semiotics, Imatra, Finland, 27th–29th July, 1987*, 67–80, Helsinki: Arator.

Sebeok, T. A. and Danesi, M. 2000. *The Forms of Meaning: Modeling Systems Theory and Semiotic Analysis*, Berlin and New York: Mouton de Gruyter.

Semenenko, A. 2012. *The Texture of Culture: An Introduction to Yuri Lotman's Semiotic Theory*, New York: Palgrave Macmillan.

Semenenko, A. 2016. '*Homo polyglottus*: Semiosphere as a Model of Human Cognition', *Sign Systems Studies* 44 (4): 494–510.

Tamm, M. 2019. 'Introduction: Juri Lotman's Semiotic Theory of History and Cultural Memory', in J. Lotman, *Culture, Memory and History: Essays in Cultural Semiotics*, trans. B. J. Baer, ed. M. Tamm, 1–26, Cham: Palgrave MacMillan.

CHAPTER 11
COMMUNICATION
Winfried Nöth

The concept of communication and its status in Lotman's oeuvre

Communication is a key concept in Juri Lotman's writings, but only three of his essays and book chapters in English (see Gramigna, in this volume) carry the word 'communication' in their titles: his early papers 'Two Models of Communication' ([1970b] 1977) and 'Primary and Secondary Communication-Modelling Systems' ([1974] 1977) and his chapter on 'Autocommunication' in *Universe of the Mind* (1990). Nevertheless, the titles of many other of his papers can be read like chapters of a theory of communication. Among these are 'language' ([1970a] 121977: 7), 'code' ([1970a] 1977: 23), 'dialogue' (1983; 1985; 1990: 143), 'audience' (1983), 'author-to-audience' (1990: 63), 'rhetoric' (1990: 36), 'cultural interaction' ([1983] 2019: 67) and, of course, 'culture' ([1992] 2009; 2019) in its 'organic link with communication' (1990: 20).

Furthermore, many of the key terms of communication theory are also keywords of Lotman's theoretical vocabulary. *The Structure of the Artistic Text* ([1970a] 1977), for example, abounds with terms borrowed from communication and information theory. Its glossary of terms, contained in the Portuguese translation of 1978, for example, lists, in the alphabetical order of their English translation: addressee, addresser, code, codification, communication, dialogue, entropy, information, language, listener, message, receiver, receptor, redundancy, sender, sign, sign model, speaker, storage, transmission, transmit and transmitter.

Commentators on Lotman's work have dedicated more titles to Lotman's theory of communication than Lotman himself. Andrews (1999) wrote on Lotman's 'Communication Act and Semiosis', Kull (2005) on certain paradoxes of communication according to Lotman, Gretchko (2012) on Lotman's model of communicative asymmetry, Gherlone (2016) on otherness in the communication theory of Vygotsky, Bakhtin and Lotman, Laas (2016) on the concept of dialogue in Peirce, Lotman and Bakhtin, and Konstantinov (2017) on Lotman's model of communication in art. Communication as well as autocommunication are also among the keywords of monographs and their chapters dedicated to Lotman's semiotics of culture, for example, Reid's book on Lotman's and Bakhtin's theory of literary communication (1990), Semenenko's introduction to Lotman's semiotics of culture (2012), Lorusso's *Cultural Semiotics* (2015: 67–115) and Schönle's collective volume on *Lotman and Cultural Studies* (2006).

Lotman's concepts of communication and autocommunication are inseparable from others of his key concepts, in particular, language, dialogue, culture, translation and semiosphere. Often, these concepts are defined in terms of communication and vice versa. Lotman writes that communication is only possible within culture, but at the same time, he argues that outside the semiosphere of culture 'there can be neither communication nor language' (1990: 124). For him, art is one of the means of communication since it 'creates a bond between the sender and receiver' and serves as a 'method of storage and transmission of information' ([1970a] 121977: 7, 23).

Communication is structured in the form of semiotic systems defined, in turn, in terms of communication. The primary semiotic system, natural language, is an 'ordered system which serves as a means of communication and employs signs' ([1970a] 1977: 6) and 'the most powerful system of communication in the human collective' ([1970a] 1977: 9). Other semiotic systems are secondary but may even be more effective than communication in natural language. Art, for example, is a system of communication that 'can effect a revolution in methods of storage and transmission of information' ([1970a] 1977: 23). Literary communication is but a special instance of communication so that 'one should bear in mind that the "author–reader" scheme is derived from an analysis of the act of communication' ([1970a] 1977: 295fn5).

Roots in information theory and structuralism: Jakobson and Saussure

Lotman's theory of communication has two theoretical roots to which the author of *Universe of the Mind* (1990) acknowledges his indebtedness in the first two chapters of his book: Ferdinand de Saussure's model of the 'speech chain' of 1916 and Roman Jakobson's communication model of 1960, whose roots, in turn, are in cybernetics and information theory. From both authors, Lotman adopts the basic framework, but at the same time, he transforms the models of his sources into a model of his own.

In Lotman's paper on 'Two Models of Communication', the point of departure is the communication model that Roman Jakobson (1960) had proposed under the influence of Shannon and Weaver's information theory and Karl Bühler's functional linguistics (cf. Nöth 2013). Less interested in Jakobson's 'functions' (cf. M. Lotman 2019: 239), Lotman focuses on the basic elements of the classical model of information transfer from a sender to a receiver, as outlined by Shannon and Weaver ([1949] 1963):

> The general concepts of communication theory are elaborated on the basis of the scheme 'transmitter–message–receiver', which is supposed to cover all communication situations. [. . .] Given a code, a text is introduced that is encoded in the code's system, transmitted and decoded. Ideally, the text coincides at entrance and exit; in practice, a decrease in information occurs. In this scheme, the code constitutes the constant and the text is the variable. (Lotman [1970b] 1977: 99)

In *Culture and Explosion*, Lotman showed once more his indebtedness to Jakobson's model by declaring that this 'long-established communication model [. . .] perfected by R. O. Jakobson [. . .] has become the basis for all models of communication' ([1992] 2009: 4), but now, Lotman reduces this model to its very skeleton, when he cites it diagrammatically, as shown in Figure 11.1.

addresser   addressee
                        text

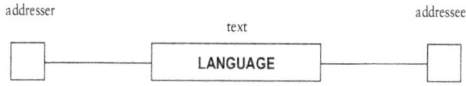

Figure 11.1 Jakobson's communication model presented diagrammatically by Lotman ([1992] 2009: 4).

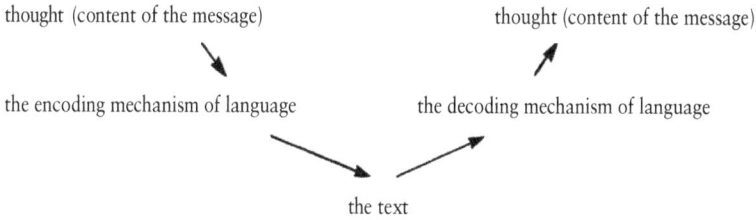

thought (content of the message)   thought (content of the message)

the encoding mechanism of language   the decoding mechanism of language

the text

Figure 11.2 Lotman's model of communication (Lotman 1990: 11).

Figure 11.3 Saussure's diagram of the speech chain (Saussure [1916] 1969: 11).

Saussure's influence is apparent in the model of communication presented on the first page of *Universe of the Mind* (1990: 11), where Lotman describes communication 'from the perspective of a receiver' (alias addressee), as shown in Figure 11.2.

The main difference between the linear Shannon/Weaver/Jakobson model 'addresser – message – addressee' and this new model consists in the element of mental processing, which it interprets as one of encoding the addresser's thought into the form of a text and of decoding the text in the addressee's mind in the reverse order. The message is thus traced back to the ideas that give rise to a text and forward to those created in the receiver's mind. This additional distinction is undoubtedly inspired by the diagram of the speech chain, in which Ferdinand de Saussure also distinguished between the phases of the association of a 'mental fact' (alias 'thought') with the phonetic expression into which it is then encoded in the addresser's mind and the reverse process in the addressee's mind (Saussure [1916] 1969: 11; see Figure 11.3). While Lotman adopts the rudiments of the theory of communication of his sources, his transformations of other elements of their communication models are programmatic and decisive. Firstly, Lotman rejects the idea of perfect symmetry between the addresser's message and the addressee's interpretation as represented in Saussure's mirror-symmetric diagram or Shannon/Weaver model, replacing it with a theory of asymmetry at the root of communication (cf. Gretchko 2012). Secondly, Lotman rewrites the information-theoretical code theory by introducing the idea of the duality of the codes underlying any message. Thirdly, he reinterprets the cognitive theory of encoding and decoding a message as one that implies processes of translation. Fourthly, he introduces, as a complement to the theory of communication between a sender and another receiver, the theory of autocommunication. And fifthly, he replaces and redefines the notion of the message in terms of a theory of texts. The sum total of these innovations, to be examined in detail in the following, constitutes the originality and distinctive features of Lotman's semiotic theory of communication. The topics are closely interlinked and overlap in several respects.

Code differences as the source of the fundamental asymmetry of communication

An early programmatic outline of the fundamental asymmetry of communication is the paper 'The Text and the Structure of its Audience' ([1977] 1982), in which Lotman identifies the differences between the codes of the addresser and the addressee of a message as well as differences between their cultural memories as sources of asymmetry in communication:

> It is obvious that when the codes of addresser and addressee do not coincide (and they coincide only as a theoretical assumption which is never realized in practical communication), then the text of the message is deformed in the process of decoding by the receiver. [. . .] Dialogic speech is distinguished not only by the common code of two juxtaposed utterances but also by the presence of a common memory shared by addresser and addressee. The absence of this factor makes a text undecipherable. ([1977] 1982: 81)

In 1990, Lotman takes up this argument of asymmetry again and extends it to its further consequences in communication. In contrast to the message transmitted by a machine, a text created by an addresser and the interpretation by its addressee are never identical. T_1, the addresser's 'text', differs creatively from T_2, the text as interpreted by the addressee. 'Instead of a symmetrical transformation, there is an asymmetrical one, instead of identity between the elements which compose T_1 and T_2, there is a conventional equivalence between them' (Lotman 1990: 13–14).

The symmetrical models of communication of information theory do not apply to cultural communication since they interpret differences between the message as encoded by a sender and decoded by a receiver as the result of undesirable *noise* or distortion, which the system tends to eliminate 'not only through the redundancy of its structure but also the systemic nature of its construction' ([1970a] 1977: 70). In cultural communication, in contrast, code differences and the resulting differences between T_1 and T_2 are not a disadvantage but an advantage in communication since they are the source of innovation and creativity. A text coded in absolutely the same way in which it is decoded is indeed 'absolutely comprehensible', but at the same time, it is 'absolutely useless' (Lotman 1990: 80). 'For a fairly complex message to be received with absolute identity, conditions are required which in naturally occurring situations are practically unobtainable: addressee and addresser have to have wholly identical codes, that is, to be in fact semiotically speaking a bifurcation of one and the same personality' (Lotman 1990: 12–3). Without code differences, communication would even be 'insipid' (Lotman [1992] 2009: 5). If we assume an addresser and an addressee processing identical codes and fully devoid of memory, then the understanding between them might be ideal. However, the value of the transferred information will be minimal. 'The ideal of information of this type is found in the transfer of commands', but in 'normal human communication', the 'non-identity' of speaker and hearer must be presupposed (Lotman [1992] 2009: 4–5).

Due to the non-identity of the minds of the addresser (A) and the one of the addressee (B) as well as to the differences in their cultural memory, the 'lingual spaces' of A and B are never congruent. Instead, these spaces merely overlap, as with the following two intersecting circles A and B (Lotman [1992] 2009: 5):

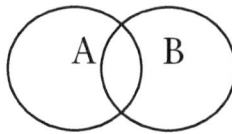

This difference between the semiotic spaces of A and B is the source of permanent tension and conflict between two opposing forces in cultural communication (Lotman [1992] 2009). On the one hand, there is a 'struggle to facilitate understanding', which results in the attempt to extend the area of intersection between A and B; on the other, there is 'the struggle to amplify the value of the communication', which results in an effort to amplify the semiotic spaces in which A and B do not intersect (Lotman [1992] 2009). We are therefore faced with the following paradox: communication is only possible within the semiotic domain of intersection between A and B, but it is only informative if transfers take place between the nonintersecting domains. Hence, 'we are interested in communication in the very sphere which complicates communication and, in actual fact, renders it impossible' (Lotman [1992] 2009: 5–6). This leads to the paradoxical insight that communication is not simply determined by the goal of mutual understanding. Instead, 'not only understanding but also misunderstanding is a necessary and useful condition in communication' (Lotman 1990: 80).

The fundamental asymmetry of communication is thus only a particular manifestation of the asymmetry within the more general semiotic sphere of culture, the *semiosphere*, outside of which there is no communication (Lotman 1990: 124–7). This asymmetry is the source of information and creativity, in a permanent process of translation between heterogeneous languages. Since immersion within the cultural semiosphere is a prerequisite of communication but communication is not possible without its semiotic space, we are again faced with a paradox: 'All participants in the communicative act must have some experience of communication, be familiar with semiosis before they can communicate. [. . .] The semiotic space necessary for the existence and functioning of languages [. . .] has prior existence and is in constant interaction with languages' (Lotman 1990: 123; cf. Nöth 2014b). Hence, the semiosphere must have been created by communication, but at the same time, communication presupposes it, so that communication is not the interaction of fully autonomous agents. The addresser and the addressee have the semiosphere as their co-agents in any act of communication.

As an alternative to symmetry, Lotman proposes enantiomorphy as an adequate model of communication, which is the property of an image that differs from its mirror image as do the gloves for the right and left hand. The two forms are invariant, but they do not coincide:

> The simplest and most widely disseminated form of combination of a structural identity and difference is enantiomorphism, mirror symmetry, through which both parts of the mirror are equal, but unequal through superposition, i.e. relating one to the other as right and left. Such a relationship creates the kind of correlative difference that distinguishes both identity – rendering dialogue useless – and non-correlative difference – rendering it impossible. If dialogic communication is the basis of meaning generation, then enantiomorphism divides the unity. [. . .] Mirror symmetry creates the necessary relations between structural diversity and structural similarity, which allow dialogic relationships to be built. On the one hand, the systems are not identical and give out diverse texts, and on the other, they are easily converted, ensuring mutual translatability. We may say that, in order for dialogue to take place, the participants must be distinct and yet simultaneously contain within their structure a semiotic image of counter-agent [. . .] Thus enantiomorphism represents the primary 'mechanism' of dialogue. (Lotman [1984] 2005: 220–1)

Cerebral asymmetry and the duality of codes underlying communication

The functional asymmetry of the two hemispheres of the human brain and its relevance to communication is Lotman's topic in his essay on 'Asymmetry and Dialogue' (1983). Although this essay has received much attention in the West, having become the subtitle of the books into which his writings on cultural semiotics were first translated into Italian (1985) and Spanish (1996), it has not yet been translated into English. Semenenko (2012: 141–2) gives a comprehensive English summary of its main ideas.

As early as 1979, Lotman had interpreted the asymmetry of the two cerebral hemispheres of the human brain as a model of the asymmetry of culture in general: 'The analogy between the asymmetry of culture and the asymmetric structure of the brain highlights the problem of the correlation of discrete and non-discrete languages and the problem of the mutual equivalence of the texts created in them' (1979: 94). The argument is indebted to Ivanov's neurosemiotic treatise of 1978, *Evens and Odds: Asymmetry of the Brain and Sign Systems*, which interprets the lateralization of brain function as the cause of the differences in the cognitive processing of analogue and discrete information. At the time, the left hemisphere was thought to control language and logic, while the right hemisphere was supposed to handle spatial information and visual comprehension. Lotman develops this neurocognitive theory into a model of the asymmetric structure of culture and communication as the 'exchange of texts' in general:

> A minimal thinking apparatus must include at least two differently constructed systems to exchange the information they each have worked out. Studies carried out on the specific functioning of the large hemispheres of the human brain have revealed a profound analogy between it and the organization of culture as a collective intellect. In both cases we find there are at least two essentially different ways of reflecting the world and working out new information and that in both cases there are complex mechanisms for exchanging texts between these systems. In both cases we observe a generally analogous structure: within one consciousness there are as it were two consciousnesses. [. . .] Both the individual and the collective consciousness, contain two types of text-generator: one is founded on discreteness, the other is continuous. (Lotman 1990: 36)

The duality of communication via two channels is thus a second duality besides the one due to the differences between the addresser's and the addressee's codes. It is a duality that leaves its traces within each message since 'to be defined as "text", a message should be at least dually coded' (Lotman [1981] 1988: 53). The sources of this duality, 'bilingualism' or even 'polyglotism' are many (Lotman [1989] 1997: 12), but among the most important of them is the simultaneity of analogue and discrete or the iconic and the symbolic codedness (Lotman's term: 'conventional', [1972] 1976: xi) of any meaningful message. The text exchanged in communication is polyglot since 'more than one language (a minimum of two) is required [. . . which] superimpose themselves on each other in such a way as to reflect one and the same thing in diverse ways' (Lotman [1992] 2009: 2).

In sum, the consequences of the duality of the minds of both addressers and addressees in communication are that

> each of them is simultaneously both participant in the dialogue (as part of the semiosphere) and the space of dialogue (the semiosphere as a whole), in each can be seen manifestations of 'rightism' and 'leftism' and, whether lying to the right or left, each also includes within itself, at the lowest level, structures belonging to both right and left. (Lotman [1984] 2005: 225)

Communication as translation

At its bottom, communication means *translation*, since any act of communication presupposes two or more semiotic systems between which information is exchanged and thereby translated. Since even 'the elementary act of thinking is translating', dialogical communication is even more so (Lotman 1990: 143). 'Asymmetry is to be seen first, in the difference between the semiotic structures (languages) which the participants in dialogue use; and second, in the alternating directions of the message-flow' (Lotman 1990), in which the participant's roles switch continuously from addresser to addressee.

Translation proper can serve as a model of what goes on in the encoding and decoding of a message:

> The very fact that one and the same poem can be translated by different translators in many ways testifies to the fact that in place of a precise correspondence to text T_1 in this case there is a certain space. Any one of the texts $t_1, t_2, t_3 \ldots t_n$ which fill this space may be a possible interpretation of the input text. Instead of a precise correspondence, there is one of the possible interpretations. (Lotman 1990: 14)

Translation in communication begins with the process of bridging the gap between the non-intersecting parts of the codes of A and B represented above as two intersecting circles: 'The more difficult and inadequate the translation of one non-intersecting part of the space into the language of the other, the more valuable [. . .] this paradoxical communication becomes. [. . .] The translation of the untranslatable may, in turn, become the carrier of information of the highest value' (Lotman [1992] 2009: 5–6). Lotman describes the bridging of the communicative gap between the addresser and the addressee as the paradox of 'bridging the unbridgeable' (cf. Kull 2005; Monticelli 2012).

Furthermore, translation is also a characteristic of intercultural communication. Although a cultural semiosphere is a system closed within the external boundaries that constitute and delimit its identity, it is still able to absorb influences from other semiospheres, from foreign or even alien cultures through translation. The boundary that seems to constitute a culture as a closed system thus

> both separates and unites. It is always the boundary of something and so belongs to both frontier cultures, to both contiguous semiospheres. The boundary is bilingual and polylingual. The boundary is a mechanism for translating texts of an alien semiotics into 'our' language, it is the place where what is 'external' is transformed into what is 'internal', it is a filtering membrane which so transforms foreign texts that they become part of the semiosphere's internal semiotics while still retaining their own characteristics. (Lotman 1990: 136–7)

As Kotov and Kull recapitulate, the boundary between two semiospheres, according to Lotman, 'is a bilingual translation filter that translates external texts and messages into the semiosphere's internal language and through which the semiosphere comes into contact with nonsemiotic or other semiotic spaces' (Kotov and Kull 2011: 182–3). Hence, the semiosphere is defined by its untranslatability, which threatens its identity, as well as by its translatability across its boundaries, which is a prerequisite of intercultural communication:

> Just as in mathematics the border represents a multiplicity of points, belonging simultaneously to both the internal and external space, the semiotic border is represented by the sum of bilingual translatable 'filters', passing through which the text is translated into another language (or languages), situated outside the given semiosphere. 'The isolated nature' of the semiosphere subsists in the fact that it cannot be contiguous to extra-semiotic texts or non-texts. In order that these may be realized, they must be translated into one of the languages of its internal space, in other words, the facts must be semioticized. In this way, the border points of the semiosphere may be likened to sensory receptors, which transfer external stimuli into the language of our nervous system, or a unit of translation, which adapts the external actor to a given semiotic sphere. (Lotman [1984] 2005: 205)

Translation is furthermore implied in the process of exchange between symbolic and iconic, discrete and non-discrete cognition and communication, although Lotman's premise is the fundamental untranslatability between these two modes of communication: 'When we are dealing with discrete and non-discrete texts, translation is in principle impossible. The equivalent to the discrete and precisely demarcated semantic unit of one text is, in the other, a kind of semantic blur with indistinct boundaries and gradual shadings into other meanings' (Lotman 1990: 37). However, this untranslatability is not a dilemma, but a source of cultural growth, for 'it is precisely in these situations that efforts to translate are most determined and the results most valuable. For the results are not precise translations, but approximate equivalences determined by the cultural-psychological and semiotic context common to both systems' (Lotman 1990).

To communicate means to translate; it presupposes 'some form of translation between signs, where there are at least two distinct sign systems involved. [...] There is no singular communication act, but at least a doublet at its inception', says Lotman in dialogue with Andrews (2003: 35). Hence, there is always some 'filtration of external communications and the translation thereof into its own language, as well as the transformation of external non-communication into communications, i.e., the semiotization of incoming materials and the transformation of the latter into information' (Lotman [1984] 2005: 210).

> If the same extralinguistic reality is represented in language, the new text appears to be a translation from a different language. The presence of diverse mental subjects that translate the same reality into the individual languages of each particular consciousness is transformed, after a new translation of all these texts into a language common to all of them, into a variety of texts that represent the same object in different ways and impart to culture as a whole its stereoscopic quality. (Lotman [1974] 1977: 96)

The text as an agent in communication

Lotman's substitution of the 'message' in the information-theoretical model of communication with the 'text' is as original as it is characteristic of his text semiotics. This conception of the text is not restricted to verbal messages. Lotman speaks of pictorial texts, verbal and non-verbal texts (1990: 55). As Lorusso (2015: 84) recapitulates, the text is 'the prime element – the base unit – of culture (see Lotman and Uspensky [1971] 1978) and anything that has a significant role in a culture can be regarded as a text, from an architectural structure to a toy, a painting, a fashion, or a doll'.

Whereas in information theory, the message is a target value to be kept error-free in its transfer from addresser to addressee, the text in Lotman's model is a participant in communication with a life of its own. T_1, the text as conceived by the addresser, translates itself into T_2, the text as interpreted by the addressee, and thus begins to act on its own:

> Insofar as the translated text and the response received from it must produce, from some other third point of view, the *unitary text*, and through this, each of them, from their own point of view, becomes not only a separate text but has the tendency to become a text in another language; the translated text must, anticipating a response, conserve within itself an element of transference into the other language. Otherwise, dialogue is not possible. (Lotman [1984] 2005: 218)

By substituting the notion of the message for the one of 'text', Lotman transforms the object of transmission, as conceived in information technology, into the one of a 'meaning-generating mechanism' (1990: 11–119). Neither is the text a mere product, or intellectual property, of an author nor is it the product of a reader's mind. It is an *agent* in communication who 'can create its own audience, meaning, and reader (Lotman [1977] 1982). The text modifies the receiver (Lotman [1974] 1977; [1977] 1982). The text not only stems from the context but also expands the context of the given text, changing it' (M. Lotman 2019: 239).

The text is not just a sign that reminds us of the author's ideas; it has a memory of its own. As M. Lotman points out,

> a culture creates, reproduces, and constantly reads its own texts (Semenenko 2012: 100–3). Here lies a certain parallel with human memory: a person's memory is not separate from the person, and the person remembers who they are by constantly consulting their memory, reproducing and modifying it. So, too, does a text. It changes over time, losing a part of its information while expanding it at the same time. (M. Lotman 2019: 249)

The agency of the text consists in its capacity to evoke 'external associations (quotes, reminiscences, allusions, hints, etc.), and to bring fragments of other texts into the text, often not as deliberate wilful of the author' (M. Lotman 2019: 248).

In J. Lotman's words, it is not the addresser who aims to influence the thoughts of the addressee but the very text that 'strives' to do so since 'a text and its readership are in a relationship of mutual activation: a text strives to make its readers conform to itself, to force on them its own system of codes, and the readers respond in the same way. The text as it were contains an image of its "own" ideal readership, and the readership one of its "own" text' (Lotman 1990: 63).

In this perspective, the audience is not really in dialogue with the author. Instead, the dialogue is between the audience and the very text. The agency of the text is triggered in a process that Lotman compares to the chemical process of autocatalysis. Moreover, Lotman describes the text as an agent with thoughts of its own, which make the text a 'thinking structure': 'The idea that "thinking" semiotic structures need an initial impulse from another thinking structure and that text-generating mechanisms need a text from outside to set them going reminds us on the one hand of so-called autocatalytic reactions' (1990: 3). As an agent in communication, the text as well as the other constituents of Lotman's model of communication

> no longer inhabit separate parts of the life of a society but, rather, they place themselves within a unitary fabric in which experiences, texts, models, gestures and code communicate with each other and, thus, work. Lotman is quite clear on this: one must reject the concept of an artistic work – or any text, for that matter – as something isolated, removed from context, and always identical to itself. This kind of text does not exist, but even if it did, it would be totally useless from the cultural-functional point of view. A text needs an exchange in order to exist; it thrives on exchanges, as we have already seen. The central role of texts played in cultural life is due to their 'nature', which corresponds to the living nature of culture (both chaotic and ordered at the same time). (Lorusso 2015: 86)

Lotman's theory of the text as a generator of meaning is quite in accord with Charles S. Peirce's theory of the agency of the sign, with which Lotman was apparently unfamiliar. What Peirce calls 'sign' is Lotman's 'text'. Peirce was perhaps still more radical in attributing life to signs (cf. Nöth 2014a), but Lotman undoubtedly also considered the text as an agent in semiosis and communication. While Peirce wrote, 'For every symbol is a living thing, in a very strict sense that is no mere figure of speech. The body of the symbol changes slowly, but its meaning inevitably grows, incorporates new elements and throws off old ones' (CP 2.222, 1901), Lotman's version of the 'life of the text' (Lorusso 2015: 83–8) is the following:

> For a text, like a grain of wheat which contains within itself the programme of its future development, is not something given once and for all and never changing. The inner and as yet unfinalized determinacy of its structure provides a reservoir of dynamism when influenced by contacts with new contexts. [. . .] One might expect a text as it lives through the centuries to become faded and

to lose the information contained in it. Yet texts that preserve their cultural activity reveal a capacity to accumulate information, i.e. a capacity for memory. (Lotman 1990: 18)

Autocommunication

In contrast to communication theorists who postulate that communication by definition takes place between a sender and a receiver, both of whom need to be two different individuals, Lotman (1990: 20–2) introduces the concept of *autocommunication*, defined as the transmission of a message from a present I to a future I, who reinterprets the same message in a new context. In contrast to communication that Lotman dubs 'I–HE' communication, autocommunication is communication within an 'I–I system', which implies the transformation of a text into a new message, 'restructuring the actual "I" itself' (1990: 22). Lotman's distinction between the 'I–I' and the 'I–HE' type of communication goes back to his paper of 1970, where he first discussed both modalities of communication as 'two models of communication', defined as 'internal' versus 'external' communication ([1970b] 1977).

Again there is a parallelism with Peirce of which Lotman was not aware. Peirce's theory of autocommunication is encapsulated in his dictum that 'thinking always proceeds in the form of a dialogue – a dialogue between different phases of the ego – so that, being dialogical, it is essentially composed of signs' (CP 6.6, 1906). Lotman, by contrast, introduces the code as a determinant. 'In the "I–I" system, the bearer of the information remains the same but the message is reformulated and acquires new meaning during the communication process. This is the result of introducing a supplementary, second, code; the original message is recoded into elements of its structure and thereby acquires features of a *new* message' (Lotman 1990: 22). Although 'code' is not a term of his vocabulary, Peirce would otherwise agree with Lotman. In autocommunication, texts transform the addressee in its self-dialogue, argues Lotman: 'The "I–I" system qualitatively transforms the information, and this leads to a restructuring of the actual "I" itself' (Lotman 1990: 22). Peirce could only agree with Lotman. He would argue that the self changes in autocommunication because 'the fact that every thought is a sign, taken in conjunction with the fact that life is a train of thought, proves that man is a sign' since 'my language is the sum total of myself; for the man is the thought' (CP 5.314, 1868).

References

Andrews, E. 1999. 'Lotman's Communication Act and Semiosis', *Semiotica* 126 (1–4): 1–16.

Andrews, E. 2003. *Conversations with Lotman: Cultural Semiotics in Language, Literature, and Cognition*, Toronto: University of Toronto Press.

Gherlone, L. 2016. 'Vygotsky, Bakhtin, Lotman: Towards a Theory of Communication in the Horizon of the Other', *Semiotica* 213 (1–4): 75–90.

Gretchko, V. 2012. 'Jurij Lotmans Modell der kommunikativen Asymmetrie: Entstehung und Implikationen', in S. K. Frank, C. Ruhe and A. Schmitz (eds), *Explosion und Peripherie: Jurij Lotmans Semiotik der kulturellen Dynamik revisited*, 79–96. Bielefeld: transcript.

Ivanov, V. V. [1978] 1983. *Gerade und Ungerade*, trans. W. Petri. Stuttgart Hirzel. [Russian original: Chet i nechet: Asimmetriia mozga i znakovykh system], Moscow: Sovetskoe Radio.

Jakobson, R. 1960. 'Linguistics and Poetics', in T. A. Sebeok (ed.), *Style in Language*, 350–77, Cambridge, MA: MIT Press.

Konstantinov, M. 2017. 'Model of Communication Act in Art: Ju. M. Lotman', *European Philosophical and Historical Discourse* 3 (1): 98–104.

Kotov, K. and Kull, K. 2011. 'Semiosphere Is the Relational Biosphere', in C. Emmeche and K. Kull (eds), *Towards a Semiotic Biology: Life is the Action of Signs*, 179–94, London: Imperial College Press.

Kull, K. 2005. 'Semiosphere and a Dual Ecology: Paradoxes of Communication', *Sign Systems Studies* 33 (1): 175–89.

Laas, O. 2016. 'Dialogue in Peirce, Lotman and Bakhtin: A Comparative Study', *Sign Systems Studies* 44 (4): 469–93.

Lorusso, A. M. 2015. *Cultural Semiotics: For a Cultural Perspective in Semiotics*, New York, NY: Palgrave MacMillan.

Lotman, J. [1970a] 1977. *The Structure of the Artistic Text*, trans. R. Vroon, Ann Arbor, MI: University of Michigan, Department of Slavic Languages and Literatures.

Lotman, Yu. M. [1970b] 1977. 'Two Models of Communication', in D. P. Lucid (ed. and trans.), *Soviet Semiotics: An Anthology*, 99–101, Baltimore, MD: Johns Hopkins University Press.

Lotman, Yu. M. [1972] 1976. *Analysis of the Poetic Text*, ed. and trans. D. B. Johnson, Ann Arbor, MI: Ardis.

Lotman, Yu. M. [1974] 1977. 'Primary and Secondary Communication-Modelling Systems', in D. P. Lucid (ed. and trans.), *Soviet Semiotics: An Anthology*, 95–8, Baltimore, MD: Johns Hopkins University Press.

Lotman, Yu. M. [1977] 1982. 'The Text and the Structure of its Audience', trans. A. Shukman, *New Literary History* 14 (1): 81–7.

Lotman, J. M. 1978. *A estrutura do texto artístico*, trans. M. do C. Vieira Raposo and A. Raposo. Lisboa: Estampa.

Lotman, Yu. M. 1979. 'Culture as Collective Intellect and the Problems of Artificial Intelligence', in L. M. O'Toole and A. Shukman (eds), *Dramatic Structure: Poetic and Cognitive Semantics*, 84–96, Oxford: Holdan.

Lotman, Yu. M. [1981] 1988. 'The Semiotics of Culture and the Concept of a Text', *Soviet Psychology* 26 (3): 52–8.

Lotman, Yu. M. 1983. 'Asimmetriia i dialog', *Trudy po znakovym sistemam* 16: 15–30. [Italian trans. in Lotman 1985: 91–110. Spanish in Lotman 1996: 26–40.]

Lotman, J. [1983] 2019. 'Toward a Theory of Cultural Interaction: The Semiotic Aspect', in J. Lotman, *Culture, Memory and History: Essays in Cultural Semiotics*, ed. M. Tamm, trans. B. J. Baer, 67–81, Cham: Palgrave Macmillan.

Lotman, Yu. M. [1984] 2005. 'On the Semiosphere', trans. W. Clark, *Sign Systems Studies* 33 (1): 205–29.

Lotman, J. M. 1985. *La semiosfera: L'assimetria e il dialogo nelle strutture pensanti*, ed. and trans. S. Salvestroni, Venice: Marsilio Editori.

Lotman, J. [1989] 1997. 'Culture as Subject and Object of Itself', *Trames* 1 (51/46): 7–16.

Lotman, Yu. M. 1990. *Universe of the Mind: A Semiotic Theory of Culture*, trans. A. Shukman, Bloomington, IN: Indiana University Press.

Lotman, J. [1992] 2009. *Culture and Explosion*, trans. W. Clark, ed. M. Grishakova, Berlin: de Gruyter Mouton.

Lotman, J. M. 1996. *La semiosfera I: Semiótica de la cultura y del texto*, trans. D. Navarro, Valencia: Frónesis Cátedra.

Lotman, J. 2019. *Culture, Memory and History: Essays in Cultural Semiotics*, trans. B. J. Baer, ed. M. Tamm. Cham: Palgrave Macmillan.

Lotman, M. 2019. 'Afterword: (Re)constructing the Drafts of Past', in J. Lotman, *Culture, Memory and History: Essays in Cultural Semiotics*, trans. B. J. Baer, ed. M. Tamm, 245–65, Cham: Palgrave Macmillan.

Lotman, Yu. M. and Uspensky, B. A. [1971] 1978 'On the Semiotic Mechanism of Culture', trans. G. Mihaychuk, *New Literary History* 9 (2): 211–32.

Monticelli, D. 2012. 'Challenging Identity: Lotman's "Translation of the Untranslatable" and Derrida's Différance', *Sign Systems Studies* 40 (3/4): 319–38.

Nöth, W. 2013. 'Human Communication from the Semiotic Perspective', in F. Ibekwe-SanJuan and T. M. Dousa (eds), *Theories of Information, Communication and Knowledge: A Multidisciplinary Approach*, 97–119, Heidelberg: Springer.

Nöth, W. 2014a. 'The Life of Symbols and Other Legisigns: More than a Mere Metaphor?', in V. Romanini and E. Fernández (eds), *Peirce and Biosemiotics: A Guess at the Riddle of Life*, 171–82, Heidelberg: Springer.

Nöth, W. 2014b. 'The Topography of Yuri Lotman's Semiosphere', *International Journal of Cultural Studies* 174: 1–17.

Peirce, C. S. 1931–58. *Collected Papers*, vols. 1–6, ed. C. Hartshorne and P. Weiss, vols. 7–8, ed. A. W. Burks, Cambridge, MA: Harvard University Press (quoted as CP).

Reid, A. 1990. *Literature as Communication and Cognition in Bakhtin and Lotman*, New York, NY: Garland.

Saussure, F. de [1916] 1969. *Course in General Linguistics*, trans. W. Baskin, New York: McGraw-Hill.

Schönle, A. (ed.) 2006. *Lotman and Cultural Studies: Encounters and Extensions*, Madison: The University of Wisconsin Press.

Semenenko, A. 2012. *The Texture of Culture: An Introduction to Yuri Lotman's Semiotic Theory*, New York: Palgrave Macmillan.

Shannon, C. E. and Weaver, W. [1949] 1963. *Mathematical Theory of Communication*, Urbana: University of Illinois Press.

CHAPTER 12
MODELLING
Katre Pärn

The problematics of models and modelling was central to Juri Lotman's thinking and to the cultural semiotics of the Tartu-Moscow school (TMS), especially in the 1960s and 1970s. This coincided with a rise in attention to models and modelling in various disciplines that was influenced particularly by the emergence of cybernetics at the end of 1940s, and among other things had turned models into objects of study for philosophy of science (Kortlandt 1972: 127). Within these discussions, modelling came to be conceived as a universal method of acquisition of scientific knowledge and, by extension, a universal means of cognition, an epistemological (or in Soviet terminology, gnoseological) tool. These notions were introduced into semiotics by scholars in Moscow and by Lotman in Tartu independently just before the 'official' birth of the school in 1964 (see Grzybek 1994; Grishakova and Salupere 2015). Thus, models and modelling were their shared interest and pivotal in providing a common theoretical ground for the TMS.

For Lotman and the TMS, the concepts 'model' and 'modelling' offered a means for viewing sign systems or semiotic systems more generally from the viewpoint of their functioning as means to organize cognition and knowledge about the world – as means of building world models and cognizing the world through those models. The concepts afforded a unitary basis for the study of an otherwise diverse collection of semiotic phenomena from sciences to arts, myths, games, fortune-telling, etc. However, they also allowed researchers to integrate semiotic systems with semiotic subjects beyond the problem of communication. Accordingly, semiotics was conceived as the study of modelling systems, modelling and world models, and the semiotics of culture as the study of secondary modelling systems, that is, higher-order modelling systems that constitute culture as a system of semiotic systems.

Although secondary literature habitually refers to the semiotic modelling theory of Lotman or the TMS, neither provided an explicit and cohesive presentation of a general theory of modelling. Rather, we find elements of such theory scattered around in their writings on a great variety of topics, offering the possibility of reconstructing it from different perspectives and with different emphases. The following overview is but one of the possibilities.

Background: Model, structure, system

'Model', 'modelling' and 'modelling system', as well as related terms like 'structure', 'system', 'relation', 'function', 'isomorphism', 'information', and so on, were elements of a metalanguage that formed part of a broader quest for a new methodology for humanities – the structural-semiotic method, as it became to be called. There were two main requirements for the new metalanguage/methodology. Firstly, it had to be applicable in all human sciences (Lotman 1964: 15), that is, it should provide a common ground for description of the diverse objects of study found within the humanities. Lotman notes that the then-current terminology of various humanistic disciplines was applicable in neighbouring fields only metaphorically, and does not, as a rule, form a coherent and rigorous conceptual system (Lotman 1964: 15). Secondly, the methodology should insert humanities into the cycle of 'general scientific knowledge' (Lotman 1964: 15). The ultimate aim was, thus, to go beyond the unification of humanities and to achieve metalinguistic and methodological convergence of humanities and natural sciences in line with 'the steady process of developing a single universal methodology for all sciences' (Lotman 1964: 11), an intellectual ambition that was widespread at the time.

With these aims in mind, Lotman and the TMS adopted a metalanguage that had already had considerable cross-disciplinary success, and could thereby act as a point of convergence of diverse disciplines and phenomena. Although the particular goal of developing a unified methodology for (human) sciences was later abandoned, it is nevertheless relevant background for understanding their metalanguage, 'modelling' included. Moreover, the generalizing mode of thinking associated with this goal, as well as many of the core ideas developed during this period, remained implicitly or explicitly central throughout Lotman's works.

While the structural method of TMS is habitually viewed in the context of structural linguistics or cybernetics and information theory, a significant inspiration for TMS thinking was also mathematical structuralism (particularly Nicolas Bourbaki), including their ideas on structure, model and isomorphism.[1] Mathematics, as Lotman notes, is not just a 'separate branch of science but [. . .] a method of scientific thinking' (Lotman 1964: 11), and the unification of sciences entailed 'mathematization' of the humanities. However, the mathematics that was seen as relevant to provide the scientific foundation for the humanities was not mathematics as a study of quantities but of relations, of structures. Still, it was less about literal application of mathematics and more about the abstract and generalizing mode of thinking in terms of structures as non-substantial systems of relations and their morphisms that was the source of inspiration for the structural-semiotic approach.[2] It allowed scholars to bridge seemingly disparate fields of studies and phenomena, which was crucial in view of the diversity of study objects for semiotics as well as the humanities more broadly.

Thus, Lotman begins with the most general and structural, that is, relational, notion of model, borrowed from Victor Shtoff, as 'a structure [i.e. system of relations] that is similar or considered as similar to another structure' (Lotman 1964: 16). The notion of structure allowed Lotman to integrate the issue of models and modelling with those of order and organization that were central in his concept of culture. Culture organizes/orders/structures the world around people, models and modelling systems as structural and structuring phenomena therefore play a key role in the mechanism of culture. While models are embodied in some material, they themselves are intangible systems of relations. That is, 'model' does not refer to a text but to an internal structure of a text. In the case of artworks, Lotman speaks also of the structure of ideas (or ideas realized in structures) as the 'model' embodied by a text created in a language. He exemplifies this by using the architectural plan of a building, an idea of the building that is not realized in brick walls but in the proportions of the building (Lotman [1970] 1977: 12).

As also follows from this definition, another key characteristic of a model is its similarity to the modelled object. However, the similarity is structural, an identity of structure, it is not perceptual or a similarity in elements. But for Lotman, similarity is always coupled with dissimilarity, as will be explained in the following text. Finally, models are also semiotic – created by means of languages (in the broad sense) in order to communicate, transmit information about some sphere of objects. The emphasis on communication brings into the picture the author (whose idea or thought is realized by a structure) and a receiver with their respective models of the world, as well as the problem of (mis)comprehension. (Common) language is an intermediary between the author and the receiver that should ideally ensure or at least aid in apprehending the model (Lotman [1970] 1977: 12–3). But this also means that models are not simply reflections of (the structure of) their object but must also 'obey the laws of semiotic systems' (Lotman 1964: 40).

As a result, 'modelling' can be conceived on two levels. Firstly, modelling is something that someone does when building models. Lotman calls it 'modelling activity' (Lotman [1967] 2011: 250). On this level, modelling is always pragmatic. Secondly, modelling is something that modelling systems do. Modelling systems have their own (mainly historical-conventional) internal structures, which imply certain world models and modelling capacities. Any act of modelling entails both of these levels. It should be added that in semiotics, model and modelling are at the same time object- and meta-concepts. On the object level, the model is a certain kind of phenomenon studied in semiotics, on the metalevel, 'model' is a theoretical concept; semiotics not only builds theoretical models but also models various phenomena as 'models'. The duality of metalanguage and its application on different levels of generality is quite characteristic in Lotman works (e.g. the concepts of text or semiosphere) (see Torop 2005).

Model, modelling and cognition

Another relevant background for Lotman's notion of model was philosophy of science (or theory of science, as he called it in Lotman 1964: 15), or general gnoseological discussions (e.g. Grzybek 1994: 290; Segre [1975] 1978: 528–9). The discussions not only provided a general view of models and modelling in science but also connected the problem of modelling with that of cognition and acquisition of knowledge. The functional perspective on models as means of cognition and of knowing reality was central to Lotman, as well as the question of cognitive/gnoseological merits and the specificity of art when viewed as modelling, and in comparison to other forms of modelling.

When Lotman defines, in his paper 'The Place of Art Among Other Modelling Systems', the model as 'an analogue of an object of cognition that substitutes it [productively] in the process of cognition' (Lotman [1967] 2011: 250, translation adjusted), he is summarizing the key characteristics assigned to models in then-current philosophical discussions: model is a reflection or reproduction of an object that functions as its replacement in research process or in cognition more generally, and the study of model yields new information about the object (i.e. Kortlandt 1972: 127–8).

Although the definition foregrounds similarity or analogy, Lotman also emphasized the cognitive import of the necessary difference between a model and its object. Thus, while models and modelling are a means of cognition or knowing through the reconstruction of objects, whereby the value or truthfulness of knowledge is (at times naively) assigned on the basis of similarity or analogy between the model and the object (Lotman 1964: 17), for Lotman, the crucial cognitive value of a model is in its difference from the object or world as perceived. By studying the model or cognizing an object through the model the difference allows us to find out something about the object that would be impossible or difficult otherwise, for example by direct observation. To be useful, a model should be more abstract than its object, a simplified reproduction, whereby only certain aspects of the object are reproduced (selected). Abstraction is one of the key cognitive functions of models. Moreover, the gradual rise in the level of abstraction allows us to move from observable similarity to apprehending internal, structural similarity (Lotman 1964: 29, 24–5). At the same time, that which has been selected will always imply that which has not. The latter is cognized in relation to the former as a 'minus' sign. Thereby, the model affords comparison between objects that have the selected features, as well as those that do not, or have some other feature (Lotman 1964: 25–6). Any change in the selection changes the cognitive configuration of the sphere of the objects.

Moreover, models are realized in some substance or material (sign system) that is different from that of the object itself. From this perspective, Lotman defines modelling as a 'creative process' characterized by '*the transformation of the dissimilar into the similar*' (Lotman 1964: 27, original emphasis). In this context, he makes an explicit distinction between the modelling (creation of similarity) and semiotic (being composed of signs) aspects of art. We deal with modelling function in the case of production of similarity, while the primary function of signs is communication, transmission of information. In the combination or co-presence of the functions we have communicative systems that perform modelling function and vice versa (Lotman [1971] 1977: 15). Accordingly, semiotic modelling systems are the kind of sign systems (means of communication) that can be used to describe or represent reality (or some part of it), as they have the 'rules of analogy' (Lotman [1967] 2011: 250) necessary for this.

Due to the use of a modelling system, the similarity between the model and its object is not natural or unconditional but conditional (or conventional, *uslovnyi*) (Lotman [1967] 2011: 250). This becomes most obvious in the case of models created by means of a symbolic modelling system that does not have 'natural' or perceptual similarity to the sphere of objects they represent. From that also follows Lotman's oft-repeated thesis (e.g. [1970] 1977; [1973] 1976) that in order to understand a work of art (or any model), one has to learn its language of modelling. And of course, this motivates the need for the semiotic study of these systems in the first place, since this assigns to modelling systems certain agency in cognitive and knowledge processes.

The recreation through difference and selection of relevant features is also related to Lotman's broader interests and ideas concerning the theoretical modelling of 'thinking devices' (human intellect, text, culture). Among the key characteristics of an intellectual object, in Lotman's view, are its capacity to create new information (through non-trivial translation) and freedom of behaviour (capacity to make choices among alternatives) (Lotman [1990] 1992: 30–1). While he does not discuss it explicitly in terms of models and modelling, it is evident that modelling (in his view artistic modelling in particular) bears consequence for the genesis of intellect, that is, it transforms (translates) its object productively while making choices along the way.[3]

In order to understand the agency or cognitive role of models and modelling systems, an important context is also Lev Vygotsky's theory of the role of signs and culture in the development of higher psychological functions, and in self-organization through internalization of signs. Accordingly, Lotman points to the role of sign systems in the (self-)organization of human intellect and behaviour, as well as in the organization of the surrounding world (e.g. Lotman [1970] 1977: 8; [1967] 2011: 268–9; Lotman and Uspensky [1971] 1978). Moreover, in his 'The Place of Art . . .' Lotman even differentiates between various types of modelling on the basis of which sphere they primarily organize: scientific models organize intellect while play-type models organize behaviour, and art as their combination organizes both (Lotman [1967] 2011: 268–9). This viewpoint on models as means for organizing or guiding thinking and behaviour can explain how models of something can become models for something – for thinking and behaving in a certain way.

One of the issues that backgrounded Vygotsky's ideas on self-organization by means of signs was his debate with Pavlonian view that behaviour is causally guided by external stimuli. Vygotsky, in turn, expounded on how humans, by means of the internalized signs and cultural systems, become capable of creating by themselves and for themselves the stimuli that guide their activity (Valsiner and Van der Veer 2000: 365). And Lotman's views on art bear witness to the possibility to change one's life via models that are at the same time similar to and different from the existing world, a combination of recreation of the world, subjective creativity and intent, and modelling systems (culture).

In one way or another, Lotman's interest in models went beyond the issues of modelling in the research process (e.g. Revzin [1962] 1966) or models as textualized structures of ideas and meanings, keys to decoding texts or situations. Models and modelling were seen as the fundamental elements and mechanisms of cognition and behaviour that are essential for the intelligent functioning of any semiotic subject from the individual to culture as a whole.

Model and modelling systems

The concept 'modelling systems', and particularly 'secondary modelling systems' is the hallmark of the TMS. The TMS semiotics of culture was the study of culture as a system of secondary modelling systems built upon (a) primary modelling system(s).

While natural language is taken as a prototypical modelling system, the concept itself is broader and applied with different degrees of generality. Modelling systems included individual languages of culture as well as more general cultural systems such as myth, folklore, religion, cartomancy, science, art and so on. This flexibility of the term is understandable when it is recognized as an abstract meta-concept that foregrounds the structural and relational nature of any semiotic system, while bracketing their material or substantial aspects. In a more technical sense, 'modelling system' designates an invariant structure (of ideas) that is observable within a certain set of texts. Whether particular modelling system is embodied by one specific substance or can be expressed in a variety of languages or modes, is secondary. In contemporary approaches, this can be seen connected to the issue of transmediality.

The conception of natural language as modelling system relates to Saussure's notion of language (*langue*) as a system of interdependent signs defined by their mutual relations, as well as to Sapir-Whorf's hypothesis that connected the structural aspect of language with that of world modelling. The distinction between primary and secondary modelling systems has received a great amount of scholarly attention (e.g. Sebeok 1988; Birnbaum 1990; Jules-Rosette 1993; Grzybek 1994; Chang 2003; Põhjala 2008; M. Lotman 2012; Semenenko 2012; Gramigna 2013). The distinction does not emerge from the interest in the application of linguistic models to the study of cultural phenomena, but primarily from the role assigned to natural language in human life and among other sign systems. This entails a claim to the primacy of natural language (relative to other languages) as means of modelling and communication in culture and in cognition. Lotman views natural language as 'one of the earliest [and] the most powerful system of communication in the human collective [that] by virtue of its very structure [. . .] exerts a powerful influence on human psyche and over many aspects of social life' (Lotman [1970] 1977: 9), and as the 'language of our consciousness' (Lotman [1970] 1977: 9; Lotman [1967] 2011: 250). According to this view, secondary modelling systems (the languages of culture) add additional means of modelling and communicating, as well as additional structures and models to the linguistic universe and consciousness. In this regard, the notion of secondary modelling systems has also been related to that of discourse (Greimas and Courtés 1982: 84).

The existence of secondary modelling systems also means that culture and human consciousness are not simply linguistic, determined by natural language or a linguistic world model. What is characteristic to culture as well as to cognition is polyglotism (e.g. Lotman 1992: 143), the co-presence of diverse modelling systems that provide a stereoscopic world view (Lotman [1990] 1992: 29), the possibility to model the world from different viewpoints. Accordingly, Lotman emphasizes the necessity of at least two languages for any kind of 'thinking device'. The plurality of modelling systems allows us to attain a certain degree of cognitive independence from any particular modelling system (and the world model implicit in it) and to create non-trivially new information. Later, he added 'the structural model of space' as another primary modelling system next to natural language (Lotman 1992: 142), which allowed him to arrive at a more complete theory that entails the core element – the presence of at least two languages – necessary to explain the emergence of culture.

However, more important than the classification or hierarchy of languages was the view that culture is not composed of static and fixed sets of modelling systems. New secondary structures emerge in culture constantly, and so culture becomes increasingly more diverse and complex. While initially the problem of modelling systems, their structure and function were foregrounded, soon texts became a more central problem of semiotics of culture, not only as the expressions of world models but also as a complex point of convergence of several semiotic structures and a mechanism that gives rise to new languages. Texts create their own languages, new idiosyncratic systems of modelling the world. This also leads to a more dynamic view of culture not as a hierarchy of mutually correlated sign system but as a generative and changing system.

Modelling, translation and creativity

According to Lotman's approach, modelling activity is translation. As he describes it in 'The Place of Art . . .': 'the content of art as a modelling system is the world of reality, translated to the language of our consciousness, translated in turn to the language of the given form of art' (Lotman [1967] 2011: 250). Impressions of the world are first formulated as a thought[4] and thereafter expressed in some secondary modelling system. Sometimes Lotman uses the concepts of coding and recoding to describe the process of (re)modelling whereby structures are transformed into new structures that preserve certain structural identity, allowing them to be taken as pragmatically or conditionally equivalent to their objects. Moreover, the plurality of modelling systems available in culture intensifies the need to translate information from one modelling system to another. At each stage we have a modelling system with its specific internal structure and modelling capacity, and the idea of modelling as creation of similarity in dissimilarity extends to the sphere of translation.[5] Modelling can be viewed not only as translation but also the other way around – every act of translation is also an act of modelling.

Lotman ([1990] 1992: 25–6) distinguishes between two types of communication and text in culture (see also Chapter 11). The first type aims to convey information without loss or change (which are considered flaws); therefore, meaning is based on the structure of language and translation is algorithmic and reversible. Ideal modelling systems for this kind of communication are artificial and formal languages. The second kind is oriented towards the transformation of information and the creation of new information through non-trivial shifts in meaning. The equivalence between the source and the new text is more flexible. The innovation can emerge from incidental changes or even mistakes, or from untranslatability (lack of equivalences) between the modelling systems of the original and the new text, which makes the result to an extent unpredictable and the translation irreversible. This kind of text always 'knows' more than the initial message, as Lotman notes ([1990] 1992: 27). In the first case, text is created from language and follows its rules; in the second case, text can create its own language ([1990] 1992: 27). Lotman views the second type of communication as characteristic of the arts.

While Lotman does not use this terminology, these could also be seen as two kinds of modelling and model. It also comes as no surprise that in discussions on modelling in science, analogies, metaphors, concepts borrowed from other fields and disciplinary languages – in Lotman's terms various non-trivial translation blocks ([1990] 1992: 27) – came to be regarded as an important source of creativity in science (e.g. Black 1962; Hesse 1966; Hoffman 1980; Arbib and Hesse 1986; Maase et al. 1995; Knudsen 2005). Or as Lotman himself notes while comparing artistic text with the kind of text that aims for singularity of meaning: 'An artistic text is constructed differently: each detail, but also the text as a whole is a part of different systems of relations; as a result, it has multiple different meanings concurrently. This is apparent in metaphor, but is a more general property' (Lotman [1967] 2011: 262, translation adjusted).

Conditionality, dual cognition and play-type modelling

Thus, model is a semiotic construct that can substitute (be taken as an equivalent of) its object due to similarity or analogy with it. Yet the similarity between a model and its object is conditional, created via the rules of analogy of a modelling system. It is similar or equivalent in terms of its modelling system. Therefore, the substitution itself is conditional – a model is not its object but can replace it under certain conditions. Accordingly, Lotman ([1967] 2011: 252) distinguishes modelling activity or the activity of using a model (i.e. plotting one's route with the help of a map) from practical behaviour (passing from one place to another via the route): the latter is used to achieve something in the real world, and the former is purely conditional and done in order to acquire knowledge about the world. In 'normal' circumstances no-one confuses the two forms of activity.

On the basis of the awareness of their conditionality, Lotman distinguishes between different types of modelling activity. Firstly, scientific-cognitive modelling is aware of its conditionality and its clear-cut separation from practical activity. But secondly, in the case of play-type modelling (playful behaviour), conditional and practical activity are realized simultaneously: an activity is practically realized while keeping in mind the conditionality of the situation ([1967] 2011: 254). The cognitive value of play is in learning to master such twofold behaviour ([1967] 2011: 254). Thirdly, he views the creation or use of artistic models as the combination of the former two types of modelling. Art is dual, like play: one has to relive (cognitively and emotionally) the modelled situation as if it was real while knowing that it is not (without acting upon this immediately) ([1967] 2011: 260). And similarly to scientific-cognitive modelling, it aims to capture the world in conditional language and provide means for knowing it ([1967] 2011: 265). Lotman considers this dual attitude in modelling semantically richer, as it allows us to assign meaning to models on both planes, or, more specifically, it affords the awareness that other meanings or interpretations are simultaneously possible ([1967] 2011: 264).

This does not conclude the differences he outlines between art, play and science; however, the idea of different attitudes towards conditionality of models is one of the more interesting and unexplored strains of thought in his discussion on modelling. After all, it's not just a change in models and modelling systems but also a change in attitude towards them that has brought about paradigm shifts in various cultural systems and in culture as a whole.

Self-modelling and autocommunication

In addition to the issue of the cultural and cognitive role of arts as modelling systems, another topic to receive notable attention was the role of self-modelling and self-models (or in alternative terminology self-knowledge and self-description) in culture (or by extension in any semiotic system) and in the genesis of culture more specifically. It is the core of cultural autocommunication.

Self-modelling is seen as a central and obligatory mechanism of (any) culture that ensures the homogeneity and individuality of a culture – 'every historically given culture generates some special model of culture peculiar to itself' (Lotman and Uspensky [1971] 1978: 211). Lotman notes that the 'individual' can emerge in two ways: through differentiation of some whole into autonomous elements or through integration of independent elements into a whole of a higher order (Lotman [1990] 1992: 32). While he regards the latter as more characteristic to culture, in view of self-bounding (culture's differentiation of itself from non-culture or alien culture, or the world or humanity in general) we can see both processes at work in cultural self-modelling.

Self-model emerges at a certain stage of development of culture when it becomes self-conscious (Lotman and Uspensky [1971] 1978: 227), foregrounds self-modelling texts and creates a conception of itself (Lotman [1971] 2010: 419). Its main function is the structural unification of culture by creating a 'unified, artificially schematized image' that provides unity and order, regulates culture as an information reservoir and curates cultural memory as well as culture's future prospects (Lotman and Uspensky [1971] 1978: 227). Cultural self-modelling, as with any other kind of modelling, is about creating similarity and order in difference and diversity. However, as a mechanism of self-regulation it became a central issue in his system-theoretically oriented conception of semiosphere (Lotman [1984] 2005; [1992] 2004).

The relationship between culture and its self-model can be quite complex. Lotman ([1971] 2010: 420) outlines three possible forms of self-modelling: (1) the self-model should be as similar to the actual cultural reality as possible; (2) the self-model differs from cultural reality and aims to change it, and concurrence between the two is perceived as an ideal state to be achieved; (3) the self-model is idealistic self-cognition that exists apart from everyday reality and is not meant to be achieved. This relates to the issue of cognitive/gnoseological value of difference in models, but we can also draw a parallel between the attitude towards self-models and the attitude towards conditionality of models, which Lotman discussed in the context of art, play and science.

Self-models are self-descriptions on a metalevel of culture (Lotman [1984] 2005: 212). While various metalanguages and models built in these languages partake in the cultural autocommunication, the self-model of culture is of a higher order of structural unity. The meta-descriptions of various parts of culture can become elements of the self-model of the culture. In this context, Lotman outlines another difference between natural and human sciences. While with science, metalanguages and created models must 'stand outside' of their objects, with sciences that study mind or cognition (i.e. semiotic and cultural sciences), this is achieved only in part, since the sciences as well as their metalanguages are 'inside' the object (Lotman [1990] 1992: 32). Thereby the knowledge produced in human sciences is always latently part of culture's self-knowledge, which creates – as an informational reserve – new possibilities for its self-modelling.

In place of conclusions

The problematics of modelling and models runs in various guises through Lotman's works. These were perhaps among the most general notions that pertained both to the object and metalevel of semiotic studies, providing thereby one of the most efficient means of unifying and extending semiotics across the diversity of objects and concerns. While the problematics of modelling was more explicit in his earlier writings, the outcomes of these discussions informed his later works. Yet there was a notable shift from the interest in invariant structures and their variations forming the core of the initial problematics of modelling, to viewing culture as a dynamic and self-organizing – self-modelling – system.

One could claim that Lotman applied throughout his life a method of thinking/ modelling that was isomorphic and stereoscopic. A method of discovering conceptual equivalence or analogy between ideas that seemed sometimes divergent, and at the same time acknowledging the value of their difference, retaining the plural metalanguage that allowed to move between the various ways of describing and modelling the object of study, and to 'observe' it from different theoretical angles.

Over the past few decades, there has been a growth in interest in models and modelling in semiotics as well as in other fields. Sebeok's and Danesi's effort to develop Lotman's and the TMS ideas further into a more cohesive and general semiotic theory of modelling systems that would bridge umwelt and culture, humans and other species (Sebeok and Danesi 2000; Danesi 2015) invigorated interest in modelling across different branches of semiotics, including biosemiotics, whereby attempts have been made to extend the notions beyond culture, human cognition and across species (e.g. Deely 2007; Kull 2010; Maran 2020; see Chapter 34). Space and spatiality have been foregrounded in approaches to modelling (e.g. Nöth 2006; Chien 2014; see Chapter 14) and there is a newfound interest in the topics of play and play-type modelling (Thibault 2016). The concepts of model, modelling systems and the spatiality of culture are promising in the studies of intermediality and transmediality (e.g. Saldre and Torop 2012; Ojamaa 2015; see Chapter 32), and so on. As concepts that are at the same time abstract and fundamental, yet central in cognition and culture, or in life generally, they still hold great potential both in being extended to new domains of enquiry as well as in bringing together diverse fields of studies.

Notes

1. The list of influences could be, of course, extended. Moreover, more than any single or specific source, Lotman's approach is characterized by bringing together ideas from very diverse sources.

2. The aim of modelling semiotics after mathematics is also evident, for example in Ivanov's remark that 'the fundamental role of semiotic methods for all the related humanities may with confidence be compared with the significance of mathematics for the natural sciences' (Ivanov [1962] 1978: 202). Of course, the role of (non-quantitative) mathematics in structural studies was already emphasized in the 1950s by Lévi-Strauss (e.g. in papers collected in his *Structural Anthropology*, [1958] 1963), who had co-operated with Bourbaki while developing his study on the structure of kinship.

3. We could also relate this to more broader discussions on the problem of choice and its semiotic function (e.g. Kull 2015).

4. We might today call it perhaps 'mental model'. However, it's important to note that in this view mental models also resort to some kind of modelling system – mind is not languageless.

5. Or vice versa, to recall Roman Jakobson's (1959: 233) idea of equivalence in difference.

References

Arbib, M. and Hesse, M. B. 1986. *The Construction of Reality*, Cambridge: Cambridge University Press.

Birnbaum, H. 1990. 'Semiotic Modeling Systems, Primary and Secondary', *Language Sciences* 1: 53–63.

Black, M. 1962. *Models and Metaphors*, Ithaca, NY and London: Cornell University Press.

Chang, H. 2003. 'Is Language a Primary Modeling System? On Juri Lotman's Concept of Semiosphere', *Sign Systems Studies* 31 (2): 1–15.

Chien, J.-P. 2014. 'Schemata as the Primary Modelling System of Culture: Prospects for the Study of Non-verbal Communication', *Sign Systems Studies* 42 (1): 31–41.

Danesi, M. 2015. 'Signs, Forms, and Models: Modeling Systems Theory and the Study of Semiosis', *Language and Semiotic Studies* 1 (1): 95–105.

Deely, J. 2007. 'The Primary Modelling System in Animals', in S. Petrilli (ed.), *Philosophy of Language as the Art of Listening: On Augusto Ponzio's Scientific Research*, 161–79, Bari: Edizione dal Sud.

Gramigna, R. 2013. 'The Place of Language Among Sign Systems: Juri Lotman and Émile Benveniste', *Sign Systems Studies* 41 (2/3): 339–54.

Greimas, A. J. and Courtés, J. 1982. *Semiotics and Language: An Analytical Dictionary*, trans. L. Crist, D. Patte, J. Lee, E. McMahon II, G. Phillips and M. Rengstorf, Bloomington: Indiana University Press.

Grishakova, M. and Salupere, S. 2015. 'A School in the Woods: Tartu-Moscow Semiotics', in M. Grishakova and S. Salupere (eds), *Theoretical Schools and Circles in the Twentieth-Century Humanities. Literary Theory, History, Philosophy*, 173–95, New York and London: Routledge.

Grzybek, P. 1994. 'The Concept of "Model" in Soviet Semiotics', *Russian Literature* 36: 285–300.

Ivanov, V. V. [1962] 1978. 'The Science of Semiotics', trans. D. Bradbury, *New Literary Criticism* 9 (2): 199–204.

Jakobson, R. 1959. 'On Linguistic Aspects of Translation', in R. A. Brower (ed.), *On Translation*, 232–39, Cambridge, MA: Harvard University Press.

Jules-Rosette, B. 1993. 'Semiotic Modelling Systems: The Contribution of Thomas A. Sebeok', *Semiotica* 96 (3/4): 269–83.

Hesse, M. 1966. *Models and Analogies in Science*, Indiana, IN: University of Notre Dame Press.

Hoffman, R. R. 1980. 'Metaphor in Science', in R. P. Honeck and R. R. Hoffman (eds), *Cognition and Figurative Language*, 393–423, Hillsdale, NJ: Lawrence Erlbaum Associates.

Kortlandt, F. H. H. 1972. *Modelling the Phoneme: New Trends in East European Phonemic Theory*, The Hague and Paris: Mouton.

Knudsen, S. 2005. 'Communicating Novel and Conventional Scientific Metaphors: A Study of the Development of the Metaphor of Genetic Code', *Public Understanding of Science* 14: 373–92.

Kull, K. 2010. 'Umwelt and Modelling', in P. Cobley (ed.), *The Routledge Companion to Semiotics*, 43–56, London: Routledge.

Kull, K. 2015. 'Evolution, Choice, and Scaffolding: Semiosis is Changing its Own Building', *Biosemiotics* 8: 223–34.

Lévi-Strauss, C. [1958] 1963. *Structural Anthropology*, trauss. C. Jacobson and B. Grundfest Schoepf, New York: Basic Books.

Lotman, Ju. M. 1964. *Lektsii po struktural'noi poetike. Vyp. 1. Vvedenie, teoriia stikha*, Tartu: Izdatel'stvo Tartuskogo universiteta (*Trudy po znakovym sistemam*, 1).

Lotman, J. [1967] 2011. 'The Place of Art Among Modelling Systems', trans. T. Pern, *Sign Systems Studies* 39 (2/4): 249–70.

Lotman, J. [1970] 1977. *Structure of an Artistic Text*, trans. R. Vroon, Ann Arbor: University of Michigan.

Lotman, Ju. M. [1971] 2010. 'Problema 'obucheniia kul'ture' kak tipologicheskaia kharakteristika', in Ju. M. Lotman, *Semiosfera*, 417–24, Saint Petersburg: Isskustvo–SPB.

Lotman, J. [1973] 1976. *Semiotics of the Cinema*, trans. M. E. Suino, Ann Arbor: University of Michigan Press.

Lotman, J. [1984] 2005. 'On Semiosphere', trans. Wilma Clark, *Sign Systems Studies* 33 (1): 205–29.

Lotman, Ju. M. [1990] 1992. 'Mozg – tekst – kul'tura – iskusstvennyi intellekt', in Ju. M. Lotman, *Izbrannye stat'i v trekh tomakh*, vol. 1, 25–33, Tallinn: Aleksandra.

Lotman, Ju. M. 1992. 'Tekst i poliglotizm kul'tury', in Ju. M. Lotman, *Izbrannye stat'i v trekh tomakh*, vol. 1, 142–7, Tallinn: Aleksandra.

Lotman, J. [1992] 2004. *Culture and Explosion*, trans. W. Clark, ed. M. Grishakova, Berlin and New York: Walter de Gryter.

Lotman, Yu. M. and Uspensky, B. A. [1971] 1978. 'On the Semiotic Mechanism of Culture', trans. G. Mihaychuk, *New Literary History* 9 (2): 211–32.

Lotman, M. 2012. 'Sekundaarne modelleeriv süsteem' [Secondary Modelling System], in M. Lotman, *Struktuur ja vabadus I. Semiootika vaatevinklist [Structure and Freedom I: From the Point of View of Semiotics]*, 102–24, Tallinn: TLÜ Kirjastus.

Maasen, S., Mendelsohn, E. and Weingart, P. (eds) 1995. *Biology as Society, Society as Biology: Metaphors*, Dordrecht: Kluwer Academic.

Maran, T. 2020. *Ecosemiotics: The Study of Signs in Changing Ecologies*, Cambridge, UK: Cambridge University Press.

Nöth, W. 2006. 'Yuri Lotman on Metaphors and Culture as Self-referential Semiospheres', *Semiotica* 161 (1/4): 249–63.

Ojamaa, M. 2015. *The Transmedial Aspect of Cultural Autocommunication*, Tartu: University of Tartu Press.

Põhjala, P. 2008. 'Loomulik keel kui primaarne modelleeriv süsteem. Ühe mõiste elulugu' [Natural Language as Primary Modelling System: Story of a Concept], *Acta Semiotica Estica* 5: 83–96.

Revzin, I. I. [1962] 1966. *Models of Language*, trans. N. F. C. Owen and A. S. C. Ross, revised by the author, London: Methuen & Co.

Saldre, M. and Torop, P. 2012. 'Transmedia Space', in I. Ibrus and C. A. Scolari (eds), *Crossmedia Innovations: Texts, Markets, Institutions*, 25–44, Frankfurt etc.: Peter Lang.

Sebeok, T. A. 1988. 'In What Sense is Language a 'Primary Modelling System?', in H. Broms and R. Kaufmann (eds), *Semiotics of Culture. Proceedings of the 25th Symposium of the Tartu-Moscow School of Semiotics*, Imatra, Finland, 27th–29th July, 1987, 67–80, Helsinki: Arator.

Sebeok, T. A. and Danesi, M. 2000. *The Forms of Meaning: Modeling Systems Theory and Semiotic Analysis*, Berlin and New York: Mouton de Gruyter.

Semenenko, A. 2012. *The Textuality of Culture: An Introduction to Yuri Lotman's Semiotic Theory*, New York: Palgrave Macmillan.

Segre, C. [1975] 1978. 'Culture and Modeling Systems', trans. J. Meddemmen, *Critical Inquiry* 4 (3): 525–37.

Thibault, M. 2016. 'Lotman and Play: For a Theory of Playfulness Based on Semiotics of Culture', *Sign Systems Studies* 44 (3): 295–325.

Torop, P. 2005. 'Semiosphere and/as Research Object of Semiotics of Culture', *Sign Systems Studies* 33 (1): 159–73.

Valsiner, J. and Van Der Veer, R. 2000. *The Social Mind: Construction of the Idea*, Cambridge: Cambridge University Press.

CHAPTER 13
NARRATION
Wolf Schmid

The event

Juri Lotman's approach to the structure of the poetic text, based on Roman Jakobson's categories of equivalence and co-opposition (*so-protivopostavlenie*) of elements, has lost some interest since its virulence in the 1970s. In contrast, the more recent narratological concept, which Lotman developed only in the 1970s,[1] is increasingly being taken up and expanded in international literary criticism[2] and has been applied in numerous analyses.[3] Central to Lotman's contribution to the theory of narrative are the categories of plot, event and figure.[4] Among the three categories, the key role is played by the event.

What is an event? Lotman's famous definition is: 'An event in a text is the shifting of a persona across the borders of a semantic field' (1970: 282; [1970] 1977: 350). This definition contains a number of assumptions.

1. Lotman thinks of the semantic relations of a text in categories of space.[5] The reason for this is that we tend to present the abstract spatially. Lotman uses topological terms as the basis for his definition, but he stresses the normative relevance of the definition by pointing out that normative values tend to be described by spatial images and oppositions. Thus, Lotman's spatial semantics should be understood as a metaphor for non-spatial, normative values. In the artistic text, the language of spatial relations with the terms *high–low, right–left, open–closed* and others also expresses non-spatial relations as *valuable–not valuable, good–bad, mortal–immortal* and so on (see also Chapter 14).

2. The most important topological feature of space is the border dividing the entire space of the narrative world into two mutually non-intersecting semantic fields, the internal structure of which is different. So in a fairy tale the space is divided into *home* and *forest*. In literature, the opposition of the two semantic fields is realized in many different ways, often in a metaphorical, non-topological manner: such as the opposition of *wealth* and *poverty, heaven* and *earth* or *earth* and *underworld*. Borders in a narrated world which do not divide semantic fields and thus are not associated with semantic values are without meaning for the event.

3. The main property of the border is its impermeability (*nepronitsaemost'*). Whereas most inhabitants of the semantic field A are neither willing nor able to cross the border and penetrate into the field B, some are both willing and able to do so. The latter are mobile or dynamic personae, the former immobile. Immobile figures cannot constitute a plot, because this always requires movement. The immobile figures, however, often serve as obstacles that stand in the way of crossing borders. In the picaresque novel, we observe a typical complication: characters who are mobile protagonists in certain episodes can become obstacles for other characters in other episodes, that is, they can

constitute the border, so that one and the same element of the text can assume different plot functions.

In his presentation of the concept of event, Lotman refers to a number of Russian predecessors who – according to him – had prepared the way to his theory: Boris Tomashevsky's concept of event in his *Theory of Literature* (1925), Aleksandr Veselovsky's (1940) concept of motif, Viktor Shklovsky's syntagmatic-functional analysis ([1925] 1990) and Vladimir Propp's ([1928] 1956) syntagmatic analysis of the fairy tale. The strongest influence was undoubtedly exerted by the latter's functional approach, although Lotman ([1987] 1997: 712) cautions against applying the Propp model to non-folkloric narrative genres. However, the reference to predecessors applies only in general. The specific idea of the event as a transgression of a border between semantic fields is not found in any of the 'forerunners' mentioned. But Lotman's overall approach to event may be inspired by Goethe's definition of the plot of the novella as an 'unprecedented incident' (*ereignete unerhörte Begebenheit*).[6]

The term *plot* (*siuzhet*) sometimes appears in Lotman (1970) as a synonym of *event*, although in most cases it designates a *chain of events*.[7] The crossing of the border usually does not happen as a single act, but in the form of a chain of events, a plot. In contrast to Shklovsky, who uses the term *siuzhet* to denote a formative *enérgeia* (Schmid 2018) that transforms the *fabula* (the narrative material), Lotman's *sjuzhet* is the – not quite explicitly defined – summary term for the unity of the depicted action in a work. Lotman's term in its English translation must by no means be identified with Edward Morgan Forster's (1927) *plot* in its opposition to *story*. Lotman's term *plot* is without a counter term.

In terms of the plot, Lotman distinguishes two types of text: the plotless text and the text with a plot. The former has a classificatory character and establishes a certain world order that does not change. Plotless texts include the telephone directory, the calendar and descriptions in which nothing happens. Plot texts represent incidents, events, changes of the world order. 'The plot text is a struggle between some order, classification or model of the world and its destruction' (Lotman [1973] 1976: 65). The plotless text is primary, the plot text is secondary. 'What the plotless text establishes as an impossibility is the very thing that constitutes the content of the plot. The plot is the 'revolutionary element' in relation to the world picture' (Lotman [1970] 1977: 238).

What makes Lotman's border model attractive for narratology?

Lotman's approach is attractive for narratology because it models the narrative event as a transgression of an established border in the multiple meanings this term can obtain depending on the respective narrative world.[8] At the border there are all kinds of barrier. This can be the adversaries in a fairy tale, the waves and winds hostile to Odysseus, the false friends in a picaresque novel or the false clues in a detective novel (Lotman [1970] 1977: 240–1). Examples of border crossing mentioned by Lotman: a living person descends into the realm of shadows, a commoner falls in love with an aristocrat and a pauper obtains wealth ([1973] 1976: 65–6).

Lotman underlines the *prohibitive* character of the border in different formulations. 'The movement of the plot, the *event*, is the crossing of that forbidden border which the plotless structure establishes' ([1970] 1977: 238). '[A]n event always involves the violation of some prohibition and is always a fact which takes place, though it need not have taken place' ([1970] 1977: 236). 'The structure of the world faces the hero as a system of prohibitions, a hierarchy of boundaries which it is forbidden to cross' ([1973] 1976: 65).

Some of the examples Lotman gives, however, suggest a broader definition of the term event. *Anagnórisis* ('recognition'), which Aristotle cites as an example of 'the reversal from ignorance to knowledge' (ἐξ ἀγνοίας ἐις γνῶσιν μεταβολή; *Poetics* 1452a), must also be seen as the crossing of a border. In the history of narrative literature, most reversals ultimately prove to be mental events (Schmid 2017, 2021).

In the history of the English novel, we observe a transition from social to mental transgressions. Compare Richardson's *Pamela* with Austen's *Emma*. The former consists mainly of a social advancement. Richardson has great difficulty in psychologically motivating his heroine as she succumbs to the brutal aristocratic wooer Squire B. In Austen's novels, on the other hand, the focus is on the process of an inner transformation that is not associated with social gain. *Pride and Prejudice*, which seems to contradict this assertion, is also about the fact that the bourgeois Elizabeth Bennet and the aristocratic Fitzwilliam Darcy only come together when they have both overcome the weaknesses of pride and prejudice, which they have in common. The mental event in *Emma* is the titular heroine's gradual insight into the cardinal errors she has made in judging her fellow human beings.

The mental event may even consist in the renunciation of an intended action, for example in overcoming an intention to murder, as is the case with Dmitri Karamazov, who has already raised the pestle against his father, but does not carry out the intended blow. Mental events are often *paradoxical* in the original meaning of the word, that is, they are παρὰ τὴν δοξάν, 'contrary to all expectation',[9] both against the expectation of the environment and against the expectation of the character concerned.

What an event is depends on the *context*. Lotman demonstrates context sensitivity using the example of a married couple arguing about abstract art. When the police are called and they establish that no beating has taken place, they refuse to put the case on record. For them nothing has happened. For a psychologist, however, or an art historian, the dispute can constitute an event (Lotman [1970] 1977: 234). The epoch-context is also decisive for whether an event has occurred or not. Lotman gives numerous examples of how certain events in Old Russian literature were evaluated differently from how they are interpreted in modern times. Every cultural context has its own ideas of norm and deviation and thus its own ideas of what an event is.[10]

Context sensitivity is related to *subject* dependence, which, though not explicitly elaborated by Lotman, results from his approach. Within the same context, changes can be judged differently from different positions. Such positions are the authors and readers of the works but also instances inherent in the works such as narrators, characters and fictional readers. And it can be controversial among the characters of a narrated world whether a certain action or change of situation is an event or not.

The border between two semantic fields can be more or less impermeable. As a consequence, events are *gradable*. 'The less probability that a given event will take place [. . .] the higher the rank of that event on the plot scale' (Lotman [1970] 1977: 236). Although this aspect has not been particularly elaborated by Lotman, his brief suggestions have subsequently led to an in-depth discussion of the gradability of *eventfulness*, the latter being a category that does not yet occur with Lotman but is suggested by his overall approach.[11]

Lotman mentions different versions of what follows the border crossing (Lotman [1970] 1977: 241). Once the agent has crossed the border, he enters another semantic field. When he adapts to the new field and its values, the movement is over, and the agent is transformed from a mobile into an immobile persona. But if the hero does not merge with the new semantic field the plot does not come to an end. The agent can return to the first semantic field affirming its values and norms or remain in motion and strive to another change.

The culture-specific 'plot space'

The acting character of a verbal or cinematic narrative need not necessarily be a human figure, as Lotman points out in the important essay on the plot space of the nineteenth-century Russian novel (Lotman [1987] 1997). In the novel as in the film, carriers of plot development can also be things, symbols or signs that have internal freedom and the capacity for active behaviour, for independent execution of actions. The socioculturally marked objects are not neutral, but remind us of preceding traditions and contain in themselves, in a folded state, a spectrum of possible plot developments and thus condition the richness of the novel genre, a realm of realized and unrealized possibilities, which Lotman calls the 'plot space' (*siuzhetnoe prostranstvo*). The plot space, with its possibilities and clichés, is specific to a culture. In the aforementioned essay, Lotman reconstructs the 'Russian plot' created by Pushkin and Gogol. In contrast to the Western European novel, which can be generally understood as a variation on the theme of 'Cinderella' with a clearly developed ending, the Russian novel, with its cyclical time, lack of a clear ending, and repetitive plot, is more oriented towards myth.

'Depth' as a concept of cinematic narration

The structure of cinematic narration can be used to highlight the mechanics of any artistic narration. Thus, for example, shots segmenting a film into sections function similarly to chapters, which have a beginning and an end and in this respect are homeomorphous to the whole text. In this connection, Lotman mentions a compositional device, which in cinematography is called 'depth' (Russian and French: *plan*, German: *Einstellung*). Depth is not simply the size of the depiction, but its relation to the frame. Close and long-range shots also exist in verbal narration when identical space or attention is devoted to phenomena of differing quantity. If segments of a text differ from each other in terms of the quantitative aspect of their content we speak of different 'depths', that is, the shots have a differing range (distance and proximity). The semantic yield of the diversity of shots of the same thing in various ways and different nuances is expressed by Lotman as follows: 'The comparison of individual "shot-segments" activates the multiplicity of elements of the content plane, lending them the significance of differential features and thereby suggesting the semantic content' (Lotman [1970] 1977: 264).

The viewpoint of the text

Questions of point of view play a lesser role in Russian literary studies as a whole than in Western criticism, where countless typologies compete with each other. Two theorists are an exception. In Mikhail Bakhtin's 'metalinguistic' works, especially from the 1920s (Bakhtin [1929] 1984; [1929] 2000; Vološinov [1929] 1973; [1929] 1993), the manifold relationships that the 'positions of meaning' (*smyslovye pozitsii*) of the instances of the text can establish are illuminated. Boris Uspenskij (1970; [1970] 1973) offers an important model of stratification in five levels for the complex phenomenon of viewpoints.[12] In explicit recourse to these two authors, Lotman investigates the problem of viewpoint, but does not raise the question of the narrator's or a character's point of view, rather the viewpoint of the whole artistic text.

The concept of 'artistic point of view' is defined 'as the relation of the system to its subject' (i.e. 'a consciousness capable of engendering a similar structure') (Lotman [1970] 1977: 265). The viewpoint of a text is more directly than other elements of the artistic structure related to the task of constructing a picture of the world, of expressing the position of the author, to the problems of truth. In a parkour through texts from various epochs, Lotman sketches the increasing differentiation of the point of view. In sacred texts, which in the Middle Ages occupied the highest place in the cultural system, we find an agreement of their viewpoint with the general orientation of the culture by virtue of the fact that the creator of the world was thought of as the creator of the 'inspired' texts. In the classicist poetry of the eighteenth century, all subject-object relations expressed in the text converged in one fixed focus that was extended beyond the limits of the author's person and coincided with the universal concept of truth. In Romantic narratives, the points of view are united in the author's personality. The diversity of viewpoints was achieved in Russian literature only in Alexander Pushkin's verse novel *Eugen Onegin*. Paradoxically, the necessary 'effect of simplifying was achieved by sharply increasing the degree of complexity of the text's structure' (Lotman [1970] 1977: 270). The author employs various styles with a fixed point of view and presents the same content from various stylistic positions. The sequence of semantic-stylistic breaks creates not a focused but a scattered point of view that is perceived as the illusion of reality itself. In this way, the artistic model reproduces the inexhaustibility of reality in every interpretation.

Lotman concludes his considerations on point of view with an outlook on the evolutionary role of the device: 'In its battle with opposing systems, the point of view not only damages, but also resurrects and activates these systems' (Lotman [1970] 1977: 279).

Additions to Lotman's event model

Based on Lotman's model, Michael Titzmann introduces two further categories. The first one is the category of the *meta-event*. 'A meta-event is present if a character crosses the border of two semantic spaces and through this event the represented world order is transformed in time itself [. . .] A meta-event is thus a revolutionary event: not only the state of the character but that of the world changes' (Titzmann 2003: 3081). The second extension of Lotman's model proposed by Titzmann is the concept of a *modalization* of semantic spaces (Titzmann 2003: 3082). Semantic spaces can be specified by a certain modality, such as reality versus desire or illusion.

An example of a transgression from a real into an imaginary space are those events in Chekhov's narrative worlds that take place only in the imagination. In the short story *In the Cart*, the young village schoolmistress on her way home from town has to stop her cart in front of a train barrier. As the train passes, she believes that in one of the first-class windows she recognizes her long-dead mother, of whom only a completely faded photograph remains. In the imagination triggered by the memory, she leads a life that is far removed from her joyless everyday life. And for the first time in the thirteen years of her existence as a teacher, she remembers with amazing clarity her mother, father, brother, the Moscow apartment, all the objects down to the last detail; she hears the piano playing, her father's voice and she is young and beautiful, just as she was then, sitting in the bright, warm room in the circle of her loved ones. Meanwhile, the handsome, but somewhat run-down, single neighbour of the manor, who has long occupied the imagination of the lonely heroine, has approached the railway barrier in his four-in-hand carriage. At the sight of him, the teacher feels a happiness never experienced before. And it seems to her as if her father and mother never died, as if she never became a teacher herself, as if everything had been a long, heavy, strange dream and as if she had now woken up. From the world of imagination, however, the harsh call of the coachman soon summons her back. The crossing of borders has led her into an imaginary space.

The origin of the plot

In a special article, the significance of which is widely underestimated, even among experts, Lotman (1973b; [1973] 1979) poses the question of the origin of the plot. This question is answered not in a historical but in a typological way. Lotman assumes the existence of two opposing text types, the archaic mythical and the more recent plot text. The former has no linear time and no plot in our understanding lacking the categories beginning and end. 'The text is thought of as a mechanism which constantly repeats itself, synchronized with the cyclical processes of nature' ([1973] 1979: 161). This text type does not tell of the new, the unheard-of, but rather depicts the continual flow of cyclical processes in nature.[13] Human life is regarded as a constantly recurring cycle. The world in this text type is topologically structured. This means that phenomena that for us are only similar are identified in this text type. 'Characters and objects mentioned at different levels of the cyclical mythological mechanism are different proper names for the same thing' ([1973] 1979: 162). Mythical texts played a classifying, stratifying and regulating role. In their orientation towards iso- and homomorphisms and by reducing the diversity and variety of the world to invariant images, mythological texts occupied the place of science. The problem is that the corresponding texts are not handed down to us in their original form, but only in retellings in the form of plot texts. So we have to reconstruct them from their narrativized shape.

Why does the plot text emerge? The mythological text needed as a counterpoint form a text organized in accordance with linear temporal motion, representing not laws but anomalies. Such were the tales about 'incidents', 'news', 'novellae'. Whereas statutory and normative texts of both a sacral and a scientific character developed from the mythological text, from the second text type historical texts, chronicles and annals emerged. There is an essential pragmatic difference between the primordially opposed text types: 'Myth always speaks about me. "News", an anecdote speaks about somebody else. The first organizes the hearer's world, the second adds interesting details to his knowledge of this world' ([1973] 1979: 163). Lotman's decisive move in his genealogy amounts to the following definition: 'The modern plot-text is the fruit of the interaction and reciprocal influence of these two typologically age-old types of text' ([1973] 1979).

The whole article about the origin of plot is dedicated to the individual steps of translating mythological texts into the language of discrete-linear systems. The first step of such a translation was the loss of isomorphism between levels of text. The characters were no longer perceived as different names for the same person. The most obvious result of the linear unfolding of cyclical texts was the appearance of doubles, which is illustrated by Lotman using the example of Shakespeare's *Comedy of Errors*. The appearance of different characters is the result of the same process: the semantic field as well as the figures and the boundaries and their transgressions are split up. Thus, Lotman comes to a surprising conclusion: 'the more noticeably the world of the characters is reduced to singularity (one hero, one obstacle), the nearer it is to the primordial mythological type of structural organization of the text' ([1973] 1979: 168).

The transition to eschatological narration entailed the linear development of plot: 'The action [. . .] was constructed as narration about the gradual enfeeblement of the world (the ageing of a god) after which came his death, dismemberment, torture, eating, burial [. . .], and resurrection, which portended the destruction of evil and its final eradication' ([1973] 1979: 169). The reciprocal influence of the two text types – one describing the normal course of events and the other telling of deviations, incidents – determined the development of the narrative genres. The texts of the first group, which define the order of the world, form the central cultural mechanism, the plot texts, which carry a world view in which chance reigns, form its periphery. The two types of text fight for the leading position in the hierarchy of the respective culture. Their conflict takes on a new meaning with the emergence of art: 'In an artistic text it turns out to be possible to realize that optimal correlation of the two groups in which the conflicting structures are disposed not hierarchically, that is to say on different levels, but dialogically on one level' ([1973] 1979: 175). Lotman illustrates this 'dialogic' narrative structure with the example of Dostoevsky's novels, especially *The Devils*, referring to Bakhtin's well-known dialogicity concept. The conclusion is: 'if dialogism is the penetration of the wide variety of life into the regulating sphere of theory, at the same time mythologism penetrates into the sphere of the excess' ([1973] 1979: 179).

In the unfolding of the mythological text, there are correlations of beginning and end on the one hand and birth versus death on the other, which no longer constitute the standard schema for modern man. One example is the conversion of Saul to Paul. The story begins with Saul's passionate persecution of the Christians. The Damascus experience describes the death and the (re-)birth of the hero. The narrative does not begin with the hero's birth and does not end with his death. Categories such as 'unity of action' and the 'logic of character' do not provide a basis for the uniting of Saul and Paul into one person.

In the later development of literature, this schema for the construction of character became the basis for plots of 'enlightenment' or a sudden change of nature, that is, a mental event, as, for example, in fairy tales with a fundamental transformation of the hero, or in stories about great sinners who become righteous men.[14] Here we are dealing with one character consisting of two opposite parts, whereby the transition from one to the other is seen as renewal.

Conclusion

Lotman's concepts of semantic space, border and transgression provide useful tools to help analyse plot, the heart of any narrative. His historical-typological derivations give a view of the archaic basic structures in our everyday and literary plots. Lotman concludes his essay on 'The Origin of Plot in the Light of Typology' by discussing the life-philosophical relevance of the plot:

> Plot represents a powerful means of making sense of life. Only as a result of the emergence of narrative forms of art did man learn to distinguish the plot aspect of reality, that is, to break down the non-discrete flow of events into discrete units, to connect them to certain meanings (that is to interpret them semantically) and to organize them into regulated chains (to interpret them syntagmatically). [. . .] By creating plot-texts, man learnt to distinguish plots in life and thus to make sense of life. ([1973] 1979: 182–3)

Notes

1. The following works by Lotman are especially relevant to his narratology: *The Structure of the Artistic Text* (1970) and 'The Origin of Plot in the Light of Typology' (1973). In the sense of a broad concept of narratology, Lotman's film-theoretical studies deserve attention: *Semiotics of Cinema* (1973), and especially the chapter 'Plot in Cinema' (Lotman [1973] 1976).

2. The narratological theory appears only in Lotman's second part of *The Structure of the Artistic Text* (1970: 255–342; [1970] 1977: 209–84). In *Lektsii po struktural'noi poetike* (1964), there is still no trace of narratological interest.

3. Cf. as a pioneering study the application of Lotman's narratological concept to the analysis of German short stories in Heuermann, Hühn and Röttger 1982: 115–96.

4. The most important treatises on Lotman's concept of narrativity are in chronological order: Heuermann, Hühn and Röttger 1982: 59–67; Renner 1983; Krah 1999; Titzmann 2003; Renner 2004; Hauschild 2009; Hühn [2009] 2014: 170–3; Gruber 2014: 68–84.

5. See the chapter 'The Problem of Artistic Space', which in *The Structure of the Artistic Text* precedes the chapter 'The Problem of Plot'. Renner (1983) explains the spatial concept that Lotman uses metaphorically in categories of set theory. Critical of Lotman's hermeneutical model and Renner's attempt at an inductive application: Meister 2003: 91–5. Lotman's plot and event categories are taken up and further developed in the sense of a formalization by Krah 1999, Titzmann 2003 and Renner 2004. An overview of these approaches is provided by Hühn [2009] 2014: 170–3.

6. Words spoken to Eckermann, 25 January 1827.

7. On the correlation of the Russian terms *siuzhet*, *tema* and *motif*, see Lotman 1970. Lotman also mentions here the possibility that individual words in a text can 'unfold into whole sujet constructions' (*razvertyvat'sia v siuzhetnye postroeniia*). We have this process in the procedure of unfolding microtexts, semantic figures, proverbs and idioms, a procedure we often find in the prose of Alexander Pushkin (cf. Schmid [1996] 2013: 86–7).

8. The term *transgression* corresponds to the Russian *prestuplenie*, which designates *crime*. In his novel *Crime and Punishment* (*Prestuplenie i nakazanie*), Dostoevsky activates the meaning of *prestuplenie* as *crossing a border*. The verbs *perestupit'* and *pereshagnut'* ('to transgress') occur several times in the meaning 'to exceed a prohibition limit'. Raskolnikov cannot forgive himself for not showing himself to be up to the task and has not shown himself to be an 'extraordinary man' in cold blood, indifferent to remorse. He understands that he did not cross the border: 'it wasn't a human being I killed, it was a principle! So I killed the principle, but I didn't cross the border [*perestupit'-to ne perestupil*]. I stayed on this side' (Dostoevsky 2007: 274). The amoral cynic Svidrigailov clearly understands Raskolnikov's motives: '[He] suffers still, from the thought that though he knew how to devise the theory he was unable to step over [*pereshagnut'*] without hesitation' (491).

9. Aristotle defines paradox as that which contradicts general expectation (*De arte rhetorica* 1412a 27).

10. The dependence of event and eventfulness on the historical, sociocultural and literary context in British fiction is demonstrated in Hühn 2010.

11. Cf. Schmid 2003: 23–29; 2010: 8–12 for a catalogue of two basic conditions of events (reality, resultativity) and five criteria for the measure of eventfulness (relevance, unpredictability, persistence, irreversibility, non-iterativity). Members of the Hamburg Interdisciplinary Center for Narratology have combined the concept of eventfulness with schema theory (especially Hühn 2008: 144–9). Eventfulness is constituted by deviation from a script, a

break with expectations like the paradox that violates the doxa (what is generally considered true, what is generally expected). In works by members of the Hamburg group, lyrical poetry has also been analysed under the aspect of the Lotmanian eventfulness: Hühn and Kiefer 2005; Schönert, Hühn and Stein 2007.

12. Details and criticism in Schmid 1971.

13. There is a tendency in Russian modern literature to realize structures of the archaic mythical text in the medium of the plot text. The result of this tendency is the so-called ornamental prose, which is more widespread in Russian culture than in any other. Ornamentalization here concerns not only the level of discourse, where it leads to sound repetition, rhythmization and similar poetic devices of equivalence, but also the level of the story, which is subjected to paradigmatization, that is, the formation of equivalent thematic units. A master of ornamentalism is Yevgeny Zamyatin, who in a series of stories (*The Dragon, The Cave, Mamaj*) realizes the mythical existence in the Soviet world. The most striking collision of mythical thinking and modern conception of the world he succeeds in the narrative *The Flood*. The heroine acts in harmony with the cycles of nature, the times of day and the seasons. When the water rises in the autumnal Neva, the blood rises in her; she is – as she perceives – connected to the river as if through underground veins (cf. Schmid 1998).

14. Lotman mentions Lev Tolstoy's novel *Resurrection* as an example based on this schema. Dostoevsky's novels *Crime and Punishment* and *The Brothers Karamazov* (Schmid 2017: 249–300) also stand in this tradition of the European novel of conversion and purification. One can say that the development of this schema culminates in the event-optimistic novels of the great Russian realists.

References

Bakhtin, M. [1929] 1984. *Problems of Dostoevsky's Poetics*, ed. and trans. C. Emerson, Minneapolis: University of Minnesota Press.

Bakhtin, M. [1929] 2000. 'Problemy tvorchestva Dostoevskogo', in M. M. Bakhtin, *Sobranie sochinenii*, vol. 2, 5–175, Moscow: Russkie slovari.

Dostoevsky, F. 2007. *Crime and Punishment*, trans. R. Pevear and L. Volokhonsky, London: Vintage.

Forster, E. M. 1927. *Aspects of the Novel*, London: Edward Arnold.

Gruber, C. 2014. *Ereignisse in aller Kürze. Narratologische Untersuchungen zur Ereignishaftigkeit in Kürzestprosa von Thomas Bernhard, Ror Wolf und Helmut Heißenbüttel*, Bielefeld: Transcript Verlag.

Hauschild, Ch. 2009. 'Jurij Lotmans semiotischer Ereignisbegriff. Versuch einer Neubewertung', in W. Schmid (ed.), *Slavische Erzähltheorie. Russische und tschechische Ansätze*, 141–86, Berlin and New York: De Gruyter.

Heuermann, H., Hühn, P. and Röttger, B. 1982. *Werkstruktur und Rezeptionsverhalten: Empirische Untersuchungen über den Zusammenhang von Text-, Leser- und Kontextmerkmalen*, Göttingen: Vandenhoeck & Ruprecht.

Hühn, P. and Kiefer, J. 2005. *The Narratological Analysis of Lyric Poetry: Studies in English Poetry from the 16th to the 20th Century*, Berlin and New York: De Gruyter.

Hühn, P. 2008. 'Functions and Forms of Eventfulness in Narrative Fiction', in J. Pier and J. Á. García Landa (eds), *Theorizing Narrativity*, 141–63. Berlin and New York: de Gruyter.

Hühn, P. [2009] 2014. 'Event and Eventfulness', in P. Hühn, J. C. Meister, J. Pier and W. Schmid (eds), *Handbook of Narratology*, 159–78, 2nd edn, fully revised and expanded, Berlin and Boston: de Gruyter. Available on-line (2013) in P. Hühn, J. Ch. Meister, J. Pier, and

W. Schmid (eds), *The Living Handbook of Narratology*, http://www.lhn.uni-hamburg.de/node/39.html (accessed 19 December 2020).

Hühn, P. 2010. *Eventfulness in British Fiction*, with contributions by M. Kempf, K. Kroll and J. K. Wulf, Berlin and New York: de Gruyter.

Krah, H. 1999. 'Räume, Grenzen, Grenzüberschreitungen. Einführende Überlegungen', *Kodikas/Code* 22 (1–2): 3–12.

Lotman, Ju. M. 1964. *Lektsii po struktural'noi poetike. Vyp. 1. Vvedenie, teoriia stikha*, Tartu: Izdatel'stvo Tartuskogo universiteta (*Trudy po znakovym sistemam*, 1).

Lotman, Ju. M. 1970. *Struktura khudozhestvennogo teksta*, Moscow: Iskusstvo.

Lotman, J. [1970] 1977. *The Structure of the Artistic Text*, trans. R. Vroon, Ann Arbor: University of Michigan, Department of Slavic Languages and Literatures.

Lotman, Ju. M. 1973a. *Semiotika kino i voprosy kinoestetiki*, Tallinn: Eesti Raamat.

Lotman, Ju. M. 1973b. 'Proiskhozhdenie siuzheta v tipologicheskom osveshchenii', in Ju. M. Lotman, *Stat'i po tipologii kul'tury*, vol. 2, 9–41, Tartu: Izdatel'stvo Tartuskogo universiteta.

Lotman, J. [1973] 1976. 'Plot in Cinema', in J. Lotman, *Semiotics of Cinema*, trans. M. E. Suino, 65–76, Ann Arbor: University of Michigan Press.

Lotman, Ju. M. [1973] 1979. 'The Origin of Plot in the Light of Typology', trans. J. Graffy, *Poetics Today* 1: 161–84.

Lotman, Ju. M. [1987] 1997. 'Sjuzhetnoe prostranstvo russkogo romana XIX stoletiia', in Ju. M. Lotman, *O russkoi literature*, 712–29, Saint Petersburg: Iskusstvo–SPP.

Meister, J. C. 2003. *Computing Action: A Narratological Approach*, Berlin and New York: de Gruyter.

Propp, V. [1928] 1956. *Morphology of the Folktale*, trans. L. Scott, Austin, TX: University of Texas Press.

Renner, K. N. 1983. *'Der Findling'. Eine Erzählung von Heinrich von Kleist und ein Film von George Moorse. Prinzipien einer adäquaten Wiedergabe narrativer Strukturen*, Munich: Fink.

Renner, K. N. 2004. 'Grenze und Ereignis. Weiterführende Überlegungen zum Ereigniskonzept von J. M. Lotman', in G. Frank and W. Lukas (eds), *Norm – Grenze – Abweichung. Kultursemiotische Studien zu Literatur, Medien und Wirtschaft. Michael Titzmann zum 60. Geburtstag*, 357–81, Passau: Stutz.

Schmid, W. 1971. 'Review of Uspenskij 1970', *Poetica: Zeitschrift für Sprach- und Literaturwissenschaft* 4: 124–34.

Schmid, W. [1996] 2013. *Proza Pushkina v poeticheskom prochtenii. "Povesti Belkina" i "Pikovaja dama"*. 2nd rev. edn, Saint Petersburg: Izd-vo S.-Peterb. un-ta.

Schmid, W. 1998. 'Ornamental'nyi tekst i mificheskoe myshlenie v rasskaze E. I. Zamiatina "Navodnenie"', in W. Schmid, *Proza kak poeziia. Pushkin – Dostoevskii – Chekhov – avangard*, 2nd rev. edn, 328–44, Saint Petersburg: Inapress.

Schmid, W. 2003. 'Narrativity and Eventfulness', in T. Kindt and H.-H. Müller (eds), *What Is Narratology? Questions and Answers Regarding the Status of a Theory*, 17–33, Berlin: de Gruyter.

Schmid, W. 2010. *Narratology: An Introduction*, Berlin and New York: de Gruyter.

Schmid, W. 2017. *Mentale Ereignisse. Bewusstseinsveränderungen in europäischen Erzählwerken vom Mittelalter bis zur Moderne*, Berlin and Boston: de Gruyter.

Schmid, W. 2018. 'Energeia, an Underestimated Facet of Šklovskij's Concept of Sujet', in C. Depretto, J. Pier and P. Roussin (eds), *Le formalisme russe cent ans après* (Communications, no. 103), 55–62. Paris: Seuil.

Schmid, W. 2021. *Mental Events: Changes of Mind in European Narratives from the Middle Ages to Postrealism*, Hamburg: Hamburg University Press.

Schönert, J., Hühn. P. and Stein, M. 2007. *Lyrik und Narratologie. Text-Analysen zu deutschsprachigen Gedichten vom 16. bis zum 20. Jahrhundert*, Berlin and New York: de Gruyter.

Shklovsky, V. [1925] 1990. *Theory of Prose*, trans. B. Sher, Normal, IL: Dalkey Archive Press.

Titzmann, M. 2003. 'Semiotische Aspekte der Literaturwissenschaft: Literatursemiotik', in R. Posner, K. Robering and T. A. Sebeok (eds), *Semiotik/Semiotics. Ein Handbuch zu den zeichentheoretischen Grundlagen von Natur und Kultur/A Handbook on the Sign-Theoretic Foundations of Nature and Culture*, vol. 3, 3028–103, Berlin: De Gruyter.

Tomaševskij, B. 1925. *Teoriia literatury. Poetika*. Leningrad: Gosizdat.

Uspenskij, B. A. 1970. *Poetika kompozitsii. Struktura khudozhestvennogo teksta i tipologiia kompozitsionnoi formy*, Moscow: Iskusstvo.

Uspensky, B. [1970] 1973. *A Poetics of Composition: The Structure of the Artistic Text and Typology of a Compositional Form*, trans. V. Zavarin and S. Wittig, Berkeley, Los Angeles and London: University of California Press.

Veselovskij, A. 1940. *Istoricheskaia poetika*, ed. V. M. Žirmunskij, Leningrad: Goslitizdat.

Vološinov, V. [1929] 1973. *Marxism and the Philosophy of Language*, trans. L. Matejka and I. R. Titunik, Cambridge, MA and London: Harvard University Press.

Vološinov, V. [1929] 1993. *Marksizm i filosofiia jazyka: Osnovnye problemy sociologicheskogo metoda v nauke o iazyke*, Moscow: Alkonost.

CHAPTER 14
SPACE
Anti Randviir

Space shares a common feature with many other fundamental and recurring concepts in Juri Lotman's work; it lacks a very clear-cut and univocal definition. Likewise it has to be admitted that his understanding and evolution of comprehending space has found little specific treatment (see Torop 2005; Randviir 2007; Remm 2010; Hess-Lüttich 2012; Lagopoulos and Boklund-Lagopoulou 2014). Characteristically for Lotman and cultural semiotics in general, the usage of 'space' often entails balancing between the object level and metalevel, and the notion of space obtain not only several metalinguistic meanings but also meanings that blend together the text of culture and metatexts that describe that culture. This has been acknowledged by Lotman himself: 'space often obtains a metaphorical character whereby metaphorism is included into the language of the scholarly description' (Lotman 1986: 4). Furthermore, it seems appropriate to infer that in that metaphorism there lies also a hint at space as a binding structure of physical and semiotic phenomena, or at least of the ontological and epistemic realms: 'In connection with that, the notion of space contains a contradiction: it is filled with both mathematical and everyday-life contents' (Lotman 1986: 4).

It appears that this twofold field of application of space as a category and further metaphorical understanding of it not only has enhanced the view on the physical and the mental dimensions as analysable via a common key notion of space and the relevant toolkit but also has facilitated a view to see the physical and the purely semiotic as immanently bound together. This led Lotman and the Tartu-Moscow school to the perplex of text, culture and space, or the textual, the cultural, and the spatial phenomena as intertwined; but perhaps even more interestingly, to such a confusion of these phenomena where they could even change positions and become turned into each other. One could raise a question about the status of space in text or in culture: Is that space real or is it a conglomeration of ideas, artefacts or other structures? Or, is it space that allows to articulate ideas and artefacts in texts and cultures; or vice versa, are articulated ideas and artefacts tools for expressing our spatial essence? In that sense – where is space? It must be stressed that these are not philosophical but methodological questions in the context of semiotics where relations between the physical and the semiotic environments are under inspection. We can find a reference to these very essential questions, as a clue to answers, in Lotman's hints at the status of space beginning from the textual level to even a much broader and fundamental phenomenon. He says: 'space in text is a modelling language by the help of which any meanings can be expressed as long as they obtain the character of structural relationships. Therefore, the spatial organisation is one of the universal means for building any cultural models' (Lotman 1986: 4). It seems that in principle we can even leave aside the issue of whether '*kul'turnykh modelei*' at the end of the citation rather refers to the object level and the building of 'cultural models' (such as artistic texts, e.g.), or to the metalevel and the creation of 'models of culture'. Reasons for that are even simpler than cases like the translational dilemmas of '*vtorichnye modeliruiushie sistemy*' or '*semiotika kul'tury*', because the building of cultural models on the object level and their description on the metalevel as models of culture are in (eternal and mainly retrospective) interdependence and movement. In this sense, 'the spatial organisation' and space itself are universal means and principle so-to-speak horizontally not only on the object level of the ontological building of culture but also on the vertical axis of description, going simultaneously for communication, autocommunication and metacommunication. Space, spatial language and the principle of spatial organization are a guarantee of the formation of the coherent meaningful sphere of culture. Apart from the concept of the semiosphere, this understanding is perhaps best exhibited in Lotman's proposal for a typology of cultures in which we can see the latter's proximity to the 'topology of cultures': the spatial arrangement of both the physical and the semiotic space are bound together (Lotman [1969] 1992). That 'topology' does not find explicit extended treatment in Lotman's works, but can be seen in the background of all of his studies of cultural texts laid out spatially, in space and forming cultural spaces.

Space: A(nother) primary modelling system

In accord with the general ideology of the Tartu-Moscow school, Lotman admits that culture is a set of 'superlinguistic semiotic systems – "secondary modelling structures"', but adds that 'culture is built on two primary languages', one of which is 'natural language used by man in everyday interaction' (Lotman [1969] 1992: 142). Culture is a phenomenon of polyglotism in the sense that 'its texts are always realized in the space of two semiotic systems as minimum' (Lotman [1969] 1992: 143), and it seems he is keeping in mind the so-to-speak traditional secondary modelling systems, mentioning their tying of words and singing, music, gestures. Besides the requirement of the existence of at least two semiotic systems for the creation of meaningful cultural phenomena, Lotman makes an important addition: 'the minimal working textual generator – is not an isolated text, but a text in context, a text in mutual interaction with other texts and the semiotic environment' (Lotman [1969] 1992: 147). The essence of that 'semiotic environment' poses a most interesting methodological issue for semiotics, and leads us to Lotman's second primary language, which appears to be 'the structural model of space'. Thereby he seems to assume that space, in this case, is a semiotic space as related to 'any activity of man as *Homo sapiens* as connected with classificatory models of space, its division into the "own" and the "alien" and translation of diverse social, religious, political, kinship and other associations into the language of spatial relationships' (Lotman [1969] 1992: 142).

It would seem natural that while the structural model of space is the second primary language on which culture is built, Lotman's logic of description of the build-up of culture ought to begin from the study of relations between the physical or ontological environment and the semiotic or cognized space. In order to speak about culture or semiosphere as a bounded semiotic reality, it would seem to be a natural prerequisite to first describe how physical entities are semiotized, translated into semiotic units. Yet Lotman's poetic vagueness surrounding the notion of space, leaves us oftentimes confused: Is he keeping in mind the physical space or the semiotic one? His hints at the metaphorical application of space suggest that the importance of the ontological reality is left behind for the sake of the semiotic or epistemic reality. Of course, from the semiotic viewpoint it might even be seen as justified, since semiotics, after all, studies meaningful phenomena, and therefore there might be no confrontations in taking both the physical and the semiotic space as belonging to the same, the already-semiotized reality – in the concept of cultural space, both have already merged into textual phenomena forming the discursive fabric of culture. Indeed, taking a look at relations between reality and semiotic reality in the age when the latter has been introduced at the level of virtual reality, and when this virtual reality is fused with the physical reality in the phenomenon of mixed reality, we can even see that regarding rigid differentiation between the ontological and the semiotic reality as unimportant was predictively justified for Lotman decades ahead of the mixtures mentioned.

Basic aspects of spatial modelling

Space *can* be selected as a viewpoint or principle of semiotic analysis, and issues connected with space and spatiality as a method *may* be taken as central for the semiotic metalevel. There *have* been attempts to introduce the idea of the 'spatial turn' into the row of other 'turns' in the humanities (cf. Döring and Thielmann 2009; for Lotman's case, Hess-Lüttich 2012). As from many other works treating the meaning of space and meanings in space, we can see from Lotman's contributions that from the semiotic viewpoint spatiality *must* be taken as a prerogative of semiosis. People live in space, place themselves and things in space, that is – we spatialize meaningful phenomena in the sense of arranging them into cognitive maps. In the formation of cognitive maps of both the physical and the semiotic environments, the structural and the processual issues come together. Taking into account Lotman's view on spatial modelling, we can maintain that the latter can be compared to what is called semiosis in other branches of semiotics. From here two important corollaries follow. Firstly, in the general aspect of modelling, it becomes natural that in his concept of space we can recognize at least three main issues: (a) there are things or structures that are spatial and these things often entail specific kinds of space, (b) there are processes by which diverse kinds of space are forged and (c) there are principles or features that are applied at the creation of spaces.

Spatial structures and specific kinds of space as spatial models of culture and cultural phenomena can be met in Lotman's works under notions like cultural space, textual space, space in text, text in space, artistic space, semiotic space, geographical space in literary texts and semiospherical space. As already mentioned, in the context of Lotman's logic of study, it is not much worth discussing whether these entities are treated metaphorically or not, since we are dealing with phenomena that already possess semiotic value. Processes of spatialization must be seen hand in hand with the concept of modelling (see Chapter 12); thus, attention is to be paid to communication, autocommunication and metacommunication, both on the level of the individual and culture. In the context of cultural semiotics, it is natural that these processes involve both the social dimension of interaction and the dynamism of texts in cultural tradition. These processes concern the creation and maintenance of meaningful spaces, and are to be seen as taking place both inside cultural spaces and between them. Among other important communication issues, we should keep in mind processes of mediation, translation, circulation of semiotic units and ideas. These interactions concern, for example, the creation of the homogenizing isomorphism that coheres cultural units, and the formation of boundaries as separating and connecting structures of semiotic systems. Spatial structures and process can be described by diverse characteristics and dimensions of space that appear in cultural semiotics and Lotman's works frequently in the shape of binary oppositions such as 'inside–outside', 'right–left', 'top–bottom', 'near–far', 'centre–periphery', 'own–alien' and so on. Since spatial modelling does not concern merely the physical space, but also such semiotic entities and topics that do not seem to relate to the physical ontology in the first place and are to be interpreted metaphorically, spatialization also means the creation of characteristics of so-to-speak conceptual fields and landscapes. Therefore, spatial modelling also entails such principles as 'static–dynamic', 'discrete–continuous', 'open–closed', 'homogeneous–heterogeneous', 'demarcated–unmarked' and so on.

The second major corollary arising from the equivalence of spatial modelling (as combined with natural language) and semiosis is that it is pivotal to understand that as in the culturally influenced process of modelling as the creation of meaningful spatial environment, the perceptual and the cognitive merge together, we must approach the indexical, the iconic and the symbolic relations of man with his environment as simultaneous and complex. This seems to explain Lotman's frequent negligence concerning differentiations of classes of sign in favour of treating them in a more general manner.

The functionality of 'space' and 'text'

The general principles of modelling and the semiosic cooperation of the primary modelling systems of natural language and space can be understood by recalling some of the basic aspects of the synoptic analysis of textual and spatial meaning-generating mechanisms. So, although the present volume covers some of these aspects (see Chapter 9), the notion of space requires that we contextualize them. Thinking in/about spheres was customary for Lotman, beginning from 'textual spaces' to individual's identity or, at the end, the semiosphere. The 'text', as a central notion of the Tartu-Moscow school, has a certain inner structure which is organized around or according to a certain dominant, that is, it is distinguished from the extratextual by a boundary (Lotman [1969] 1992: 392–8).

The qualities of text can be – and often have been – extrapolated to the level of culture, and thus one would rather keep in mind the notion of cultural space. Cultural spaces are also interpretable from an internal viewpoint that takes into account communicative cohesion entailing a certain autocommunicative whole. From such an internal viewpoint, a basic criterion for the definition of 'cultural space' is the existence of self-explanatory self-models (or 'automodels'). Such self-models have been explained and associated with textual terminology: 'A model of a given culture of itself which, as a rule, yields certain dominants in it on the basis of which there is built a unifying system that has to serve as a code for self-consciousness and self-identification of texts of the given culture' (Lotman 1971: 170).

An integrated cultural space, in turn, may be referred to as a textual conglomeration in which hermeneutic cultural movement where texts and metatexts exist in a dynamic cycle, where the cultural object-level and metalevel descriptions are interdependent, and where semiotic and physical aspects of space are joined in interaction. The afore-cited opinion of Lotman on the power of spatial organization as a modelling language for cultural texts (Lotman 1986: 4) further suggests that the development of metalanguage(s) in his works as in cultural semiotics in general has most frequently been extremely closely connected with objects in their so-to-speak innocent status on the research table, before an actual analysis begins. 'Texts' have often been replaced with 'textual spaces', and 'cultures' with 'cultural spaces', already on the so-to-speak 'object-level' (objects are defined with the preface *as* even prior to analysis). Space, in this respect, serves as a descriptor, and can be replaced by 'system', 'mechanism' (e.g. a 'system of culture' such as that of norms). This simplicity of replacing or loading objects of analysis with descriptive (or ideological, if you will) features prior to actual analysis has been admitted also by Lotman in his afore-cited view on the metaphoricity of space that is introduced into the language of investigative description where mathematical and behavioural contents meet. Apparently, this understanding made it easy for Lotman to talk about the aforementioned textual spaces often, whereas such textual spaces may extend to the field of describing behaviour, even lives of people, in textual terms. 'Behavioural texts' are, like any other cultural phenomena, built on natural language and belong, thus, to the realm of secondary modelling systems (see Lotman 1977: 66). Such phenomena are already described in entirely textual terms such as dominant (or constants of behaviour), genre, sujet, style, and so on (Lotman 1977: 66). The text is thus understood in broad terms and hints at phenomena created through secondary modelling systems based on natural language and spatial organization, bringing descriptive logic close to any other discipline (e.g. cultural and linguistic anthropology, ethnography, culture theory in general) that studies cultural or sociocultural phenomena in merely other terminology.

The interdependence of text and space comes to the fore extremely vividly today when modern technology itself forces us to see and talk about the hypertextual space of global communication. Now, communication, the nature of space and the structure of texts are intertwined, and we talk about intertextual spaces, intersemiotic and intersemiosic communication. On the one hand, it may seem as if textual spaces have, by the development of modern technology (the internet, hyperspace, cyberspace, virtual space, in fact also cosmic space) lost one of their originally inherent features, that of being bordered and structured thereby. On the other hand, these developments can also be seen in the light of those boundaries having been and being transformed from disjunctive into conjunctive.

Is there an end of space?

We can witness the aforementioned logical transformation, or presupposition of such a transformation, already in the concept of the semiosphere (Lotman 1984; see also Chapter 22). The semiosphere complicated the intertwined web containing 'text', 'space', 'culture', and so on, with the idea of linguistic interaction and internal translatability (Lotman 1984: 11–16). In a way, one may thus compare the semiosphere to 'linguistic spaces' in a wider sense, but also to 'translation spaces' also in a broader sense.

The inner organization of texts, spaces, textual spaces and spatial texts and their functioning as systems must be connected with their identity features, which are essentially connected with the notion of boundary. While, at first glance, boundary itself should not pose major methodological issues, we can eventually see that its very function and nature introduces contradictions to Lotman's semiotic logic. Being bordered is one of the most important features of the semiosphere (Lotman 1984: 7–11). This, however, raises several problematic and contradictory issues. Specifically, inasmuch as 'the notion of the semiosphere is connected with a certain semiotic uniformity and individuality' (Lotman 1984: 7), and 'both notions presuppose the semiosphere to be discriminated from the outer-semiotic or alien-semiotic space by a border' (Lotman 1984: 8), a question emerges: How does this border come into existence, or does it emerge at all, or is it somehow made up, fabricated? Lotman's claims inevitably lead to issues of the origin of that border in terms of its emergence either on the object level, or its generation on the metalevel. In other words, be the boundary at either at object level or at metalevel, it can only be outlined by contrasting an 'intrasemiotic' world with an 'outer-semiotic' world, and as far as the outer sphere is not semiotized, possibilities of differentiation are disregarded. Thus, the 'absolute border' simultaneously presumes and dismisses possibilities of describing a semiosphere, and makes the depiction of this border – as the semiosphere in toto – possible from a shifted (e.g. divine or extraterrestrial) viewpoint that would enable us to engage comparison of the internal and extra-semiospherical units. The original concept of the semiosphere is thus connected with understanding the semiotic reality of a community in totalitarian terms. It seems important to note that a totalitarian understanding of the semiosphere is, for Lotman, not an occasional affair. After two years of publishing the conception of the semiosphere, he maintains that the term refers to: 'the semiotic space of culture in which solely are possible semiotic processes' (Lotman 1984: 6). While, for Lotman here, 'the "closure" of the semiosphere lies in its inability to get involved with alien-semiotic texts or non-texts' (Lotman 1984: 8), then even the mechanism of autocommunication in the identity discourse shows that cohesive individual wholes result from cooperation between such semiotic realities (individuals, texts, cultures) that are dissimilar, 'alien' to each other at least to some extent (see the afore-cited Lotman 1992: 143, 147).

In case studies, from an internal viewpoint within a semiotic realm, the description of a meaningful world can be executed exactly against a background system which is often formed of the 'non-cultural' or 'non-textual'. In order to specify the identity discourse of a semiotic subject (individual, society, text, culture, semiosphere), that is, its (semiotic) boundaries, we must outline those borders somehow, and this can only be done by contrasting the outside of a semiotic reality with its interior. Here we are confronted with a paradoxical situation: in order to be able to talk about the semiotic subject and its individuality as a phenomenon based on contrast between the semiotized and non-semiotized world, and the dynamic border between them, we could conclude that this border is indefinable. More exactly, this boundary – and thus features resulting in the extent of the semiotic reality – cannot be circumscribed as persistent. This goes both for the semiotic metalevel, and all the more for the (hypothetically referred) semiotic reality on the object level: talking about the expanse of the meaningful world, we must – in order to describe its boundary – have semiotized elements of the (originally) 'meaningless world'. Evidently, thereby the latter elements are switched into the frame of the semiotic reality. With the intention of referring to the 'alien semiotic space' as a phenomenon outside the semiosphere, we must already have had it semiotized. Consequently, we should not equalize 'outside of semiotics' with 'alien semiotics', since the former cannot, in principle, be switched into (articulate) discourse. Therefore, when entities of a non-semiotized world are, through semiosis, incorporated into a textual output, they can be referred to as representing 'non-culture', of being 'alien-semiotic' or 'non-textual', rather than a sphere 'outside semiotic(s)'.

Because in connection with the creation of meaningfulness so many ambiguities appear at the definition of the semiotic subject and reality already due to the notion of the semiosphere, we probably should look for a more concrete phenomenon, or a category through which to delimit the semiotic subject. Proceeding from the aforementioned possibilities to distinguish between reality and the semiotic reality, we may face the verity that, by default, the topic ought to be concerned with the unreadable/incomprehensible/scarcely interpretable on the one hand and the readable/understandable/interpretable on the other. This involves the factor of viewpoint and deprives us of the overly categorical nature of Lotman's notion of the semiosphere. Since individuals can extend their horizons through learning, and cultures develop through innovation and discovery either through their inner potential or contacts with the 'other', the boundary of semiotic reality must be permeable, and semiospheres obtain the nature of open systems that *are* able to semiotize their outside: semiosis outside the semiosphere *must* be possible.

The application of a textual approach to cultural phenomena seems to imply that semiotic structures, or semiotic subjects, can but be set in such an environment which is demarcated from such 'different organisations' in the manner as 'culture' is opposed to its outside. The combination of textualist and spatial vocabulary does not entail as categorical oppositions as contained in Lotman's treatment of the semiosphere. We can meet evidence to this even in Lotman's own practical analysis of the so-called behavioural texts that are based on the dynamism between 'normal' and 'abnormal', 'normal' and 'artistic' spheres of behavioural modalities. Behavioural texts concern interaction between the cultural space both in the physical and in purely semiotic sense; for example: 'the Russia before Peter knew binary contrasting of the ritual and extra-ritual (non-ritual: *vneritual'noe*) space in the world and in the space of human settlement' (Lotman 1977: 77). That very contrasting of the ritual and the extra-ritual means that the latter had but to have been brought to consciousness, which is another proof that the semiosphere cannot do without its outside, and that the non-cultural, in this sense, has to be at least potentially meaningful (although presumably in a negative modality).

Spatialization and the 'real'

One must take Lotman's seemingly loose vocabulary very seriously, including the notion of space itself or other spatial structures and phenomena for which it almost impossible to find a univocal definition. The non-existence of such a singular meaning of/for space simply indicates that it has multiple meanings, areas and possibilities of application. Furthermore, when recalling a few available hints at the essence of space, it is mainly quickly tied with the other categories, becoming an adjective, feature or principle of other structures or arrangements (spatial structure, spatial organization, spatial expression, spatial and spatiotemporal characteristics, spatial metalanguage, spatial modelling, spatiotemporal continuum). Things, phenomena, events, individuals, meanings can be spatial, and in fact they always are, for we operate in both the physical and the semiotic reality with the help of cognitive maps. This means that space is turned into a *device* of semiotizing (let us remember Russian formalism and its discourse on art, estrangement and device), and although it is not possible to find a relevant longer treatment in Lotman's works, in the case of primary modelling, we are talking about spatialization as a process of creating the meaningful world.

In this manner, natural language and space as primary modelling systems go hand in hand: as with texts as cultural building blocks, we are talking about spaces, textualization and spatialization, which are probably to be viewed as complementary semiotic processes and procedures. 'Spatial texts', 'textual spaces' and the other metalinguistic combinations mentioned earlier therefore become quite natural, and as the textual and the spatial are intertwined, so the methodology and vocabulary that can be used to analyse either texts or spaces become applicable to both of these primary modelling systems. Furthermore, as texts (vocal, written, visual, even behavioural) can be traced back to natural language, natural language and space are fundamentally related: processes and products of language and space are intertwined and perhaps even integrated. Features of not only texts but also language and space are mutually explanatory. If space (or *spatiality*), like natural language, is a primary modelling system, then it is expected that it constitutes the elementary level of any cultural grammar on the one hand, and that all cultural and semiotic phenomena can be reduced to that elementary level on the other hand; there seems to be no logical alternative. Of course, we can see a third counterpart entering the scene, since notions like sujet, action, event, personage and so forth cannot but become dependent on text and space (see, e.g. Lotman 1988); thus, *time* not only complements the two, but can even be said to depend on them (cf. Lorusso 2019; Remm 2010). In the sense of cognitive mapping decisive for any semiotizing activity, the pretty-much-undefined category of space (added by 'spatialization' quite unused by Lotman) becomes a key that opens multiple functions, processes and phenomena of meaning-making. These can be approached through both the spatial and the textual analysis, since: 'The text of culture is a most abstract model of activity from the position of the given culture. Therefore it can be defined as a *picture of the world* of the given culture' (Lotman [1969] 1992: 389).

It seems that Lotman's treatments of space, and even more importantly the so-to-speak spatial issues have, as well as their historical theoretical value, an increasing importance for the study of contemporary and developing sociocultural issues. As mentioned, from the binding of the two primary modelling systems – natural language and space – there arose entanglement of the ontological and epistemic realities. Yet in spite of the confusion of the physical and the semiotic realities, text and space became operational concepts that are somewhat mutually explanatory. The semiotic essence of textual and spatial entities eventually does help to explain relationships between the semiosphere and its outside, both in aspects concerning the meaningful and the physical world, and also in those that have to do with relations between multiple dissimilar semiotic realities. As mentioned, it logically follows from Lotman's own discourse that semiospherical realities are, in fact, not such totalitarian spheres that could be seen as completely separate from their outside where any semiosis would be unimaginable. Rather, beyond the boundaries of cultural spaces there are alien semiotic, other semiotic realms loaded with negative or dangerous meanings, or with those that could be described as potentially semiotic. Thus, the outside of the semiosphere is a pool of novelty that can be imported into the 'own' as a source to overcome entropy.

Therefore, the semiotic processes that take place on borderlines obtain the highest importance as a key to the sustainability of cultural systems. The 'alien', the negative must be discovered and translated into the 'own' through intermediary positions characterized by the 'dangerous', the 'taboo' or other peripheral categories. In this way, the translation mechanisms and functions that are responsible for cultural dynamism on the axis of centre–periphery do not entail merely the liminal cultural areas and social entities, but also make possible exploration of/into the unknown. Translation of borderline and even further-off semiotic entities into the 'suitable' for the culture-core obviously does not concern only activities on an imaginable line between the 'own' and the 'alien'. Both cultural and social units are liminal in relation to the cultural mainstream, for example textual devices (genres, personages, topics) and social groups demarcated as deviant by their disobedience to sociocultural norms (subcultures, 'inconvenient' social groups). Since these units appear to be at least briefly stable in time, we can treat them as forming a third space in the topology of cultural spaces, as buffering translation zones between the 'own' and the 'alien'. That third space (not to be confused with the Third Space theory) inhabited by liminal cultural and social units is thus an area of translation and overlap of the semiosphere and its outside. Inasmuch as any cultural system, according to Lotman's view, is based on the primary modelling systems of natural language and space, that third space must be describable through textual and spatial features. Thus, their internal structure and borderline functioning can principally be subject not only to description but also to prediction of both the dynamism of the internal topology of a culture, involving interaction of textual units and norms of behaviour, and the interaction processes taking place in liminal sociocultural zones, like import of novel semiotic (as also physical) elements, exclusion of the 'unsuitable' and other borderline acts of semiotization.

Today it seems important that such liminal spaces and borderline semiosic processes are applicable not only to (historical) culture areas in the physical–artefactual–mentifactual sense but also to novel kinds of space such as virtual reality, mixed reality and augmented reality. Relations between the latter and the so-to-speak traditional cultural space simultaneously concern issues of communication because they can be seen as areas or results of communication, autocommunication and/or metacommunication (see also Chapter 11). What spaces are connected to what kind of reality can be solved by the logic of reference and deixis; therefore, the textual spatial modelling logic is again connected not only with the building of the semiosphere but also with the positioning of the self in cultural space, that is, with the identity discourse of the semiotic subject. In this sense, the topological structure and functioning of culture and the semiotic self are simultaneous, as are also the creation of the linguistic and spatial models of the semiosphere in both its structure and its expression that also involve, further on, secondary modelling systems. Modelling is a cognitive activity; hence, the analysis of culture can only centre on the (already) semiotized features of any social, cultural or physical phenomena. The mythological and the scientific, the traditional and the novel are a matter of decision made in the course of communication (in the public information space); it is also a matter of viewpoint whether to characterize as a so-to-speak ordinary daily interaction, autocommunication or metacommunication. Lotman's views on space are thus valid for very diverse cultural types and epochs, being also applicable to any possible future semiotic realities – as has already been shown by the age of several kinds of computerized reality that are striving towards artificial intelligence.

References

Döring, J. and Thielmann, T. (eds) 2009. *Spatial Turn: Das Raumparadigma in den Kultur- und Sozialwissenschaften*, Bielefeld: Transcript Verlag.

Hess-Lüttich, E. W. B. 2012. 'Spatial Turn: On the Concept of Space in Cultural Geography and Literary Theory, *Meta – Carto – Semiotics*', *Journal for Theoretical Cartography* 5: 27–37.

Lagopoulos, A. P. and Boklund-Lagopoulou, K. 2014. 'Semiotics, Culture and Space', *Sign Systems Studies* 42 (4): 435–86.

Lorusso, A. M. 2019. 'Between Times and Spaces: Polyglotism and Polychronism in Yuri Lotman', *Bakhtiniana: Revista de Estudos do Discurso* 14 (4): 83–98.

Lotman, Ju. M. [1969] 1992. 'O metaiazyke tipologicheskikh opisanii kul'tury', in Ju. M. Lotman, *Izbrannye stat'i v trekh tomakh*, vol. 1, 386–406, Tallinn: Aleksandra.

Lotman, Ju. M. 1971. 'Problema "obucheniia kulture" kak ego tipologicheskaia kharakteristika', *Trudy po znakovym sistemam* 5: 167–76.

Lotman, Ju. M. 1977. 'Poetika bytovogo povedeniia v russkoi kul'lture XVIII veka', *Trudy po znakovym sistemam* 8: 65–89.

Lotman, Ju. M. 1984. 'O semiosfere', *Trudy po znakovym sistemam* 17: 5–23.

Lotman, Ju. M. 1986. 'Ot redaktsii: K probleme prostranstvennoi semiotiki', *Trudy po znakovym sistemam* 19: 3–6.

Lotman, Ju. M. 1988. 'Siuzhetnoie prostranstvo russkogo romana XIX stoletii', in Ju. M. Lotman, *V shkole poeticheskogo slova: Pushkin. Lermontov. Gogol'*, 325–48, Moscow: Prosveshenie.

Lotman, Ju. M. 1992. 'Tekst i poliglotizm kul'tury', in Ju. M. Lotman, *Izbrannye stat'i v trekh tomakh*, vol. 1, 142–7, Tallinn: Aleksandra.

Randviir, A. 2007. 'On Spatiality in Tartu-Moscow Cultural Semiotics: The Semiotic Subject', *Sign Systems Studies* 35 (1/2): 137–59.

Remm, T. 2010. 'Spatial Metalanguage: The Ambiguous Position of Time in Concepts of Sociocultural, Social and Cultural Space', *Trames* 14 (4): 394–410.

Torop, P. 2005. 'Semiosphere and/as the Research Object of Semiotics of Culture', *Sign Systems Studies* 33 (1): 159–73.

CHAPTER 15
SYMBOL
Ilya Kalinin

General foundations of semiotics: Symbol and sign

The term 'symbol', derived from the ancient Greek verb 'συμβάλλω' ('to throw things together'), replicates in its meaning the polyvalence referenced in its inner form, projecting a collision of divergent implications within a single semantic field. The situation becomes more complex when we turn from the word's casual significance (according to which any sign that in addition to its narrow referent projects a more generalized meaning may be called a 'symbol') to its circulation in academic discourse (in which various traditions in the term's definition coexist, elevating its many distinct applications practically to the level of homonyms – which is quite possibly the proper stance to adopt, for instance, in comparison of the conceptions of symbol pertinent to the work of Charles Sanders Pierce and Pavel Florensky).

Juri Lotman begins his extended consideration of the nature and cultural mechanisms undergirding the function of this semiotic phenomenon – the article 'The Symbol in the Cultural System', published in a special issue of *Trudy po znakovym sistemam* on the symbol in 1987 – with a gesture towards the polyvalence of the word 'symbol' in relation to 'the semiotic sciences' (Lotman [1987] 1990a: 102). Lotman attributes the constitutive multiplicity of the term's meanings to the fundamental opposition of two traditions. The first of these is based on a rational and conventional understanding of the symbol's semiotic character, presupposing a conception of 'adequate translation of expression level into content level'. The second derives from a distinct position, according to which 'the content of a symbol irrationally glimmers through the expression level and the symbol as it were serves as a bridge between the rational world and a mystical one' (Lotman [1987] 1990a: 102).

Without great difficulty, one may discern the classical roots of these two traditions, in the former instance going back to the writings of Aristotle (chiefly his treatise *On Interpretation*) and in the latter to Plato's works (primarily to the dialogue *Cratylus*). In the most schematic account, one can trace the historical trajectory of the first tradition as a punctuated line extending from Aristotle to Cicero and Roman Stoicism, from there to Thomas Aquinas and medieval scholasticism, onwards to the *Port-Royal Grammar*, to the rhetorical conceptions of the French Enlightenment, and finally to the theories of Pierce and Saussure, foundational for opposed vectors of semiotic scholarship (Todorov [1977] 1984). An equally schematic account of the trajectory of the second tradition can trace it from Plato to Neoplatonism, onwards to Christian mysticism and Byzantine Hesychasm, thence to Renaissance conceptions of hermeticism and to European Romanticism, and finally to the language-philosophical speculations of

Russian Symbolism and Onomatodoxy (see Averintsev 2001: 155–61). The first tradition, founded on conceptions of the arbitrary, unmotivated and contingent nature of language, views the symbol as a deviation from the normatively conventional nature of language, approaching its inherent pretensions to a motivated or substantive relationship between the level of expression and that of content with suspicion, scepticism and irony. The second, considering language to be an instrument for insight into the true essence of being, affirms the isomorphism of the grammar of language and the 'grammar of the world',[1] perceives within the word/name an energetic impulse, linking in an unmediated manner – distinct of social convention – to its meaning, and conceives of the symbol as the highest form of linguistic expression (see, for instance, the definition of the symbol as the 'substantive identity of idea and object' in Losev [1930] 1993: 635).

However, beyond this rather obvious conceptual divergence, which one may articulate without great difficulty, lies an additional, terminological controversy, linked with perhaps the most authoritative semiotic classification of categories of sign, developed by Pierce in his works of the 1890s (see Peirce 1977). As is well known, Pierce proposed a tripartite typology based on the relationship between the sign and its object of reference. According to this schema, an 'icon' is based on a relationship of resemblance between the sign and the object to which it refers. An 'index' is based on a relationship of proximity in space or time between the sign and the object of reference. Finally, a 'symbol' arises on the basis of purely arbitrary connections – presupposing neither resemblance nor proximity – between sign and object.

Hence, Pierce's classification system applies the term 'symbol' to the category of signs that, in the tradition underlying his semiotics, most fully corresponds to the conventional nature of semiosis per se. Meanwhile, this same term found itself in the centre of the opposed tradition that conceives of 'symbol' as the embodiment of the organic and essential connection between sensible expression and supersensible content, between the limitations of form and the limitlessness of spirit, between the particular and the general, between the immanent and the transcendent. In consequence, the semantic field of the term 'symbol' became a space of tension between divergent interpretations, developed by the opposed traditions of thought concerning the nature of language and signs, based in turn on opposed philosophical platforms (derived from the Platonic philosophy of the One, on the one hand, and Aristotelian formal-rational philosophy, on the other). In effect, a peculiar conceptual conquest was staged: a term that had been consigned in the former tradition to the periphery, beyond the boundaries of its conception of the arbitrariness of the sign, was catapulted in the works of Pierce to the centre and rendered equivalent in its definition to the sign as such. Whereas previously *sign* and *symbol* were generally deployed to denote opposed entities (distinguished by qualities of arbitrariness and conditionality), at this point the symbol takes the position of fundamental category underpinning a quality of sign arbitrariness, and passes a quality of motivatedness (via resemblance or proximity) to the icon and the index.[2] Whereas previously it was primarily what we can call the 'mystical' philosophical tradition that was concerned with description of the 'symbol', seeking to discern beyond social convention a coveted horizon of convergence between the name and true knowledge of the world, Pierce's semiotic theory designated 'symbol' as the name of the conventional itself. This did little in support of clarity in the subsequent history of use of the term.

Symbol: Semantics

The specificity of Lotman's analytical work with the term 'symbol' lies in his efforts to mark out his own position in relation to the distinctions described earlier. It appears that the vector of Lotman's theoretical inclinations in relation to the phenomenon of the symbolic was conditioned by his central object of analysis (Russian culture), by the contextual underpinnings of his analytical apparatus,[3] and by his conceptual movement from description of the language of grammar to description of the multilingual rhetoric of the text (see M. Lotman 2002: 14–6; Kalinin 2003; 2009). In relation to each of these dimensions, interpretation of the symbol figures as a peculiar form of shifter,[4] bearing within itself its own symbolic dimension, that is, the characteristic conception of this semiotic phenomenon in Lotman's understanding of it, as well as an indexical dimension, directed in unmediated fashion to the object and method of research, as well as to the location in which the research was carried out. Ultimately, the symbol constituted both a cardinally important element of the language-object (myth, poetic language culture, i.e. everything that gravitates to meaning-creating mechanisms founded on the text's continuous nature, spatial iconicity, linguistic heterogeneity and semantic diffusion, in distinction from the discrete nature of language) and a no-less-important element of the metalanguage (a model of description for the very mechanisms of production and reproduction of culture, semioticization of experience, signifying dynamics of the text, principles of intersection of the synchronic and diachronic axes).[5]

Although he never offered explicit critique of Pierce's classification of signs and regularly employed the terms 'icon' and 'index', as defined in that context, Lotman relied on a fundamentally distinct understanding of 'symbol', at times resorting to caveats such as, 'we are not referring to the special meaning attributed to this term in the classification of Charles Peirce' (Lotman and Uspenskij [1973] 1977: 250), or clearly articulating that he, in his conception of the meaning of the term 'symbol', did not follow Pierce, who opposed it to the icon as a conventional type of sign.[6] As an alternative touchstone, Lotman referred to a no-less-authoritative predecessor, the founding figure of the distinct (structural) version of semiotics. Twice in articles devoted to the problem of the symbol (Lotman [1987] 1990a: 102; 1990c: 260), he turns to one and the same citation from Saussure's *Cours de linguistique générale*: 'One characteristic of the symbol is that it is never wholly arbitrary; it is not empty, for there is the rudiment of a natural bond between the signifier and the signified. The symbol of justice, a pair of scales, could not be replaced by just any other symbol, such as a chariot' (Saussure [1916] 1959: 68). It is precisely this rudimentary, naturalized connection between the signifier and signified, extending to culture's archaic strata, that becomes an object of the scholar's special attention; it is precisely here that Lotman discovers a semiotic resource that ensures the dynamic equilibrium of culture and the balance between persistence and the capability to change and adapt. It is symptomatic that, in his efforts to move away from Pierce's conception of symbol, Lotman refers to de Saussure, who, although he laid the cornerstone for a distinct model for semiotic description, nevertheless belongs to the same larger rational, positivistic tradition as does Pierce. Although Saussure, in distinction from Pierce, defines the 'symbol' in terms of 'a natural bond between the signifier and the signified', his assessment of this connection as *rudimentary* reflects his relegation of the symbol to the place of marginal phenomenon in the field of linguistic signification (see Culler 1976: 19–28; Todorov [1977] 1984: 255–70). Curiously enough, following the definition of 'symbol' cited by Lotman, Saussure proceeds to offer a qualification: 'The word symbol has been used to designate the linguistic sign, or more specifically, what is here called the signifier. Principle I in particular weighs against the use of this term' (Saussure [1916] 1959: 68). Lotman, however, chose not to reproduce this qualification.

In essence, Lotman, like Pierce, turns to 'symbol' as the quintessence of semiosis as such, yet in so doing defines this term in precisely the opposite manner to the American philosopher. Whereas for Pierce the symbol is the sign par excellence, in that it presents a case of pure conventionality (although it also possesses a certain degree of indexicality – 'proximity in a certain sphere of meanings'[7]), for Lotman and his colleagues the symbol in its semiotic nature synthesizes the features of index and icon, with emphasis on the factor of motivated conditionality (Barsukov et al. 1987: 86).

'A symbol, then, is a kind of condenser of all the principles of sign-ness and at the same time goes beyond sign-ness. It is a mediator between different spheres of semiosis, and also between semiotic and non-semiotic reality. In equal measure it is a mediator between the synchrony of the text and the culture's memory. Its role is that of a semiotic condenser' (Lotman [1987] 1990a: 111). In point of fact, this summary statement affirms the absolute semiotic functionality of the symbol, which unites all semiotic principles and breaks through to extra-semiotic reality, and which possesses characteristics of systematicity and historicity, realizing its invariable essence by means of its modulating variability (Lotman [1987] 1990a: 104). Although Lotman's thesis deploys the terminological apparatus of the rationalistic tradition of thought about the sign, with his fairly strained citation of de Saussure, its implicit claims may be translated with little difficulty into those of the Romantic philosophy of language (cf. De Man [1969] 1989: 187–228; 1984: 1–19; 1988) and those of its heirs in the philosophical and poetic thought of Russian symbolism (see Stolovich 2005: 341–63), who saw in the symbol the unity of phenomenon and noumenon, focus of the organic link between language and nature, synthesis of bodily and spiritual, dialectic of being and becoming, and embodiment of the universal in the particular.

There is a great deal of commonality between, on the one hand, Lotman's conception of the symbol as the locus of intersection of two languages caught 'in a situation of mutual untranslatability' (Lotman [1992] 1997: 417), along with the theory of the semiosphere that he in many ways based on this conception, and, on the other hand, the intellectual context of Russian thought of the late nineteenth century and first decades of the twentieth. These commonalities are apparent on several distinct levels, proceeding all the way from particular areas of enquiry to basic foundations. Hence, Lotman conceptualized the relationship between symbol and myth, among other things, by means of the procedure of predication, that is, the transformation of the symbol into the 'subject' of a mythological text and its subsequent acquisition of verbal linkages (Lotman and Uspenskij [1973] 1977: 241; Lotman [1987] 1990b). These relationships are described in similar fashion by the Symbolist poet Vyacheslav Ivanov, who considered myth to be a symbol that has acquired a 'verbal predicate' and has in this manner become the protagonist of a mythological drama (Ivanov 1916: 62).

The interest in space and its semiotic organization, characteristic of the Tartu-Moscow school as a whole and for Lotman in particular (see Chapter 14), blossomed in the late works of the latter into a sui generis 'spatial turn', discovering in space a symbolic resource for conceptual metaphorics, making it possible to address: (1) a 'spatial iconicity' counterpoised against the discrete linearity of conventional verbal signs; (2) the 'secondary iconization of the text' that arises in poetry (and in innovative cultural phenomena in general), constructing over and above the arbitrary chain of discrete signs a more complex level of organization, granting a non-linear – that is to say, spatial – structure of meaning (Lotman 1990d: 55), diffuse and polyvalent 'unity and density of the poetic series' (Tynianov 1924: 40); and (3) the semiosphere itself, likewise conceived as a *space* of intersection and mutual translation of various forms of language and methods of signification (see Chapter 22). There is little doubt that one may interpret the conceptual neologism 'semiosphere' with reference to the works of Vladimir Vernadsky and to his concepts of the bio- and noosphere (see Mandelker 1994: 385–96; Tamm 2019: 8), substantiating the organicist imagery of Lotman's discourse. It is no less relevant, however, to observe the spatial metaphorics that underlie the conception of the semiosphere, the theoretical pretext for which is to be found in the conception of space and spatiality ('all culture may be interpreted as activity for the organization of space') developed by Vernadsky's contemporary Florensky (Florenskij 1993: 55), whose works are also of widely recognized significance for Lotman (see, for instance, M. Lotman 1995: 219–20; Grigorieva 2006: 32–5).[8]

The revolutionary definition of the semiosphere as a space within which semiotic mechanisms operate that cannot be reduced completely to the structural conventionality of language and the discrete network of signs, reflecting in mirror image the persistent system of meanings (see, in particular, Lotman 1990; [1992] 2009), is founded on Lotman's characteristic interpretation of the symbol. Precisely this interpretation of the symbol as a phenomenon, the semiotic nature of which does not correlate with the normative conventionality of the sign, makes it possible to construct an alternative chain of semiotic phenomena, in distinction from the linear structure of language, a chain of phenomena of various levels that share a common nature: myth; poetic text; rupture in signification; the unpredictable mechanisms of culture; productive untranslatability from one language to another; the multilingual character of the semiosphere.

In all of these cases, what is at stake is affirmation of culture's irreducibility to the systematic, conventional and discrete character of language and sign and to the gradual nature of historical progress and the predictable direction of cultural processes that are undergirded by this conception of language. The semiotic pole of this structural monologism (one code; one language; one culture) is the symbol and the Neoplatonic tradition of its interpretation, founded not on the analytic segmentation of mutually equivalent series of signifiers and signifieds, but rather on the idea of their mutual inextricability, which rules out 'the possibility of expression being alienated from content' (Lotman 1990c: 255). The 'Empire of Signs', described by Roland Barthes ([1970] 1982), found itself set in opposition to the 'Czardom of the Symbol', the latter being comparable to Vladimir Solovyov's poetic world, which relied on the 'Platonic-romantic "dual reality"' (*dvoemirie*) and ideas about the totally symbolic, sign nature of all mundane life' (Mints [1979] 1999: 337).[9] In this manner, a conceptual antidote to structuralist theory was found in the theory – mystical in its intellectual genealogy – of the symbol, as it had been inherited most proximately in Symbolism and Russian religious philosophy, the living representative of which was Aleksei Losev, who by the 1970s had managed to translate the language of *Athonite* Onomatodoxy into that of the Marxist-Leninist theory of reflection (Losev [1973] 1991; 1976), although in the 1920s his works had still exhibited direct traces of the recent intellectual context (Losev [1927] 1993) or had concealed this context within historical studies of Classical ancient symbolism (Losev [1930] 1993).[10]

Nevertheless, the conceptual convergence of Lotman's semiotic theory and the 'mystical protosemiotics' of Russian Symbolism and Eastern Orthodox Onomatodoxy remains beyond the bounds of his works, glimmering behind his proposed interpretation of the symbol in the same manner as, beyond a symbolic form of expression as described in that same theory, there glimmers 'a higher and absolute non-semiotic reality'. The affirmation that the symbol 'serves as a bridge between the rational world and a mystical one' (Lotman [1987] 1990a: 102) could be presented in relation to sources on which Lotman's theory of the symbol was based, yet might be read as an (probably involuntary) auto-metadescription (a characteristic conceptual gesture for the style of thought of the Tartu-Moscow school).

Nevertheless, the search for intellectual convergences between these theories of the symbol cannot diminish the actual divergences between them, which extend far beyond matters of style and axiological register, despite Elena Grigoreva's claims that: 'The difference between Florensky's mystical semiotics and Lotman's positivistic semiotics is found at the evaluative, rather than the constructive level. Whereas Florensky makes extensive use of words such as "higher", "seeming", and "real", Lotman carefully avoids such expressions' (Grigorieva 2006: 34). In actuality, the difference between Lotman's semiotics and Symbolist theories of the symbol dating to the Silver Age lies at a considerably more foundational epistemological level. The Russian Symbolists and their heirs viewed the symbol as presenting an opportunity to grasp the truth of existence, conceiving it as an identity of idea and thing: 'In the *symbol* the very fact of the "internal" identifies with the fact of the "external" – *here, there is a material, real identity linking "idea" and the "thing", and not simply a linkage of meaning*' (Losev [1930] 1991: 49, my emphasis). Lotman saw the symbol as an opportunity for accurate interpretation of culture. This distinction is fully apparent if one compares Losev's definition of the symbol with the one offered in a work that appeared in its first version in *Trudy po znakovym sistemam* (Mamardashvili and Piatigorsky 1971). Subsequently, this work, authored by Merab Mamardashvili and Alexander Piatigorsky, appeared in a separate edition (Jerusalem, 1984) under the title *Metaphysical Considerations on Consciousness, the Symbol, and Language*: 'Every symbol includes and image, but cannot be reduced to it, for it presupposes the presence of a certain meaning, inextricably linked to the image, *but not identical with it*. The image and meaning are the two elements of the symbol, and are inconceivable without one another. For this reason, symbols exist as symbols (and not as things) only within interpretations' (Mamardashvili and Piatigorsky 1997: 135; my emphasis). Whereas in the first case we are dealing with the ontological identity of thing and idea, in the second we have an example of the semiotic distinction between meaning and image, bound together by complex relations of unity and non-identity, the reality of which relates not to being, but to the interpreting consciousness. Lotman's interpretation of the symbol was structurally isomorphic to its characteristic comprehension in myth and in those aspects of culture that actualized a mythic consciousness in one form or another. Diverging from this conception of the symbol in its epistemological function, it made it possible to realize the description of that which was incompatible with the cultural logic of classical rationalism.

Symbol: Syntax

Beyond interpretation of the semantic structure of the symbol, a non-trivial matter for contemporary scholarship, Lotman's work also poses the question of its role in the process of the syntagmatic unfolding of the plot. Of central importance in this regard is his article 'The Symbol as Plot-Gene' (Lotman [1987] 1990b). Leaving aside for the moment the biological implications of the metaphor of 'plot-gene', which was printed without quotation marks in the subsequent Russian edition (1996), let us turn to the conceptual armature of this text.

As in the case examined earlier, Lotman's interpretation of the symbol and its syntagmatic function stands in opposition to the conception of linearity. Whereas in the former instance its role as a 'semiotic condenser' was opposed to the linearity of the process of signification as it unspools through a chain of signs, the meaning of which is firmly fixed in the linguistic system, in the case of the 'gene-condenser' of the plot, the symbol motivates one or another plot twist, depending on which of its meanings acquires contextual actualization. Here, the symbol's polyvalence finds a new and additional foundation, one that is effected not via the semantic hierarchy rising from its concrete connotations to more and more generalized and universal meanings, but rather via the network of paradigmatic linkages, rendering pointless all debate concerning one or another comprehension of the symbolic meaning of this or that image of an artistic text, *taken in isolation* (Lotman [1987] 1990b: 83).

As raw material for his analysis, Lotman takes a number of works by Pushkin, studying their symbolic gene structure independently of their literary generic categorization (lyric, epic, drama). 'Pushkin's thought-paradigm is formed not by words but by model-images; these model-images have a syncretic verbal-visual existence and their contradictory nature means that it is possible to make different readings, as well as complementary ones (complementary, in Niels Bohr's sense, that is, readings that are equally adequate as interpretations and at the same time mutually exclusive of each other)' (Lotman [1987] 1990b: 83). Hence, the characteristic means of signification for the symbol undermines both Pierce's model and de Saussure's. In some sense, the model of semiosis proposed by Lotman is closer to de Saussure's, in that it depends on the principle of systematicity; yet, here the systematic has a completely different nature. Relationships within the 'thought-paradigm' that establishes one or another meaning for the symbol are rooted not in language, but rather arise on the level of the text. Reference to Niels Bohr's principle of complementarity terminates the principle of systematicity in its classical formation, shaped in terms of a finite number of elements and a finite number of relationships between them – in terms of dictionary and grammar, to use linguistic terminology. Further, in the case at hand, we see a qualitative leap from dictionary and grammar of language to 'model-images' and the rhetoric of the text, which might be compared with the leap from classical to quantum mechanics. The 'syncretic verbal-visual existence' and 'contradictory nature' of these model-images may be compared with the particle-wave nature of quantum objects. To be precise, the symbol, in Lotman's interpretation, itself takes the form of such a quantum object, that can be grasped as both particle and wave, verbal-discrete and visual-continual, linear and non-linear, conventional and motivated, allowing it to serve as condenser of 'readings that are equally adequate [. . .] and at the same time mutually exclusive of each other' (Lotman [1987] 1990b: 83). As stated earlier, the symbol appears here as a conceptual fulcrum, as an exemplary modelling object that makes it possible to outline the semiotic parameters that will subsequently be extended to more and more complex and manifold phenomena such as archaic myth, the individual mythology of the poet, mythological structures that run throughout the fabric of culture.

In analysis of Pushkin's idiosyncratic mythology, Lotman articulates a tripartite paradigm, the extreme points of which are three distinct factors, as follows: (1) the elemental-catastrophic, impersonal principle; (2) the principle of the world of civilisation; (3) the personal, human principle that is capable of entering into relationships with the first two (Lotman [1987] 1990b: 83). Displacing the binary oppositional scheme that is characteristic of structuralism with this tripartite paradigm, the corners of which are additionally defined via two distinct evaluative scales (elemental/orderly and personal/impersonal), Lotman discovers a dynamic and mobile combinatoric space of semantic manoeuvre.

In his subsequent account, Lotman demonstrates how given symbolic images in various Pushkin texts may take on this or that meaning, at times building on one another, at times contradicting one another, depending on which relationships are actualized at a given moment and on the conceptual and figural planes against which they appear. And so, the symbolic meanings of the figure of Peter the Great in *The Bronze Horseman* in opposition to the flood, on the one hand, and in opposition to Evgeny, on the other, are well nigh incompatible with one another, realizing as they do different pairs of differential features (civilization vs the elements, in the former instance, and the impersonal vs the personal, in the latter). Consequently, the figure of Peter becomes emblematic of the principle of rationality at one moment and of the irrational at another.

Furthermore, symbolic images may be projected into various conceptual fields. To continue with *The Bronze Horseman*, Lotman identifies several such fields, to which he relates the basic symbolic images of the poem (the elements, the monument, Evgeny):

> One such projection is a mythological one: water (or fire) – chiselled stone – a human being. When, however, the second member is historically interpreted as culture, *ratio*, authority, city or laws of history, then the first member will be transformed into the concept 'nature', 'unconscious element', 'rebellion', 'steppe', 'elemental opposition to the laws of history'. But this can also be interpreted as the opposition of 'wild freedom' to 'dead captivity'. The relationships of the first and second members of the paradigm to the third can be just as complex. (Lotman [1987] 1990b: 85)

Each turn of the interpretational screw, shifting analysis from one conceptual level to the next, leads to a successive resemantization of the entire chain of symbols. In addition, the conceptual antitheses and echoes between individual symbolic particles cannot be confined to the domain of a single text. The symbolic 'wave' creates a dynamic conceptual paradigm, connecting disparate texts, and so expanding even further its semantic range, rendering ever more complex and problematic the linear model of meaning's development.

In this manner, analysis of the syntactic valence of the symbol, laying bare its open structure, makes it possible to step from comprehension of the text as a realization of language's systemic potential (Saussure) to a model of the text as 'a meaning-generating mechanism'.[11]

Symbol: Pragmatics

The metaphor of the 'gene', that arose in the chapter dedicated to the role of the symbol in relation to plot (i.e. that 'the subsequent development of a plot is merely the unfolding of a symbol's hidden possibilities' (Lotman [1987] 1990b: 101)), achieves its full and complete development in analysis of the phenomenon of cultural memory. In this conceptual frame, the symbol is seen as a bearer of cultural information that it accumulates in its multiply layered, flexible structure, yet that opens out towards other symbols. A form of informational exchange takes place between the distinct elements that shape the 'genetic chain' of symbols, through which culture as a whole can be read as an open-ended multiplicity of communicative acts, accompanied by various rhetorical-semantic shifts, interlinguistic translations of that which cannot be adequately translated, and distinctive encoding mechanisms, overlaid one on top of another. The very optics of semiotic heterogeneity that underlies this vision of the semiosphere's functioning, in turn, brings us back once again to Lotman's understanding of the symbol as an 'informational paradox' of productive untranslatability, producing a rise in meaning as a result of the failure of completely successful translation.

The economy of the symbol, allowing it to archive in a compact form the extensive semantic volumes, as well as its structural autonomy and potential for incorporation in a variety of contexts, makes it a unique unit of exchange, ensuring not only the synchronic unity of the text but also the diachronic unity of culture itself: 'a symbol never belongs only to one synchronic section of a culture, it always cuts across that section vertically, coming from the past and passing on into the future. A symbol's memory is always more ancient than the memory of its non-symbolic text-context' (Lotman [1987] 1990a: 103). Stitching through the textual fabric, the symbol makes it possible for the text to achieve communication between disparate temporal layers, taking the form of 'an emissary from other cultural epochs (or from other cultures)' (Lotman [1987] 1990a: 104). It is its unvarying constancy that makes it possible to see the conceptual variations that arise in the interrelationship of the symbol with its non-symbolic context, in the course of which each undergoes mutual transformation: new experience receives ready symbolic forms for its articulation, while this articulation renews these ready symbolic forms (see also Chapter 17). Appearing as a marker of heterogeneity, as locus for the inscription and transgression of bounds between self and other, sacral and profane, mythological and historical, fixed and inconstant, the symbol carries out the function of semiotic catalyst, preventing the decomposition of culture into isolated synchronic layers whose monolinguistic systematicity makes it impossible to achieve or even imagine the step from one synchronic section to the next.

> Since symbols are important mechanisms of cultural memory, they can transfer texts, plot outlines and other semiotic formations from one level of a culture's memory to another. The stable sets of symbols which recur diachronically throughout culture serve very largely as unifying mechanisms: by activating a culture's memory of itself they prevent the culture from disintegrating into isolated chronological layers. (Lotman [1987] 1990a: 104)

Note that the temptation to interpret the cultural-mnemonic functionality of the symbol, as described earlier, in terms of intertextuality, contradicts the conceptions of Lotman himself, who made explicit note of the fundamental difference in nature between symbol and reminiscences, references and citations: 'They pass from the text into the depths of memory, whereas a symbol passes from the depths of memory into the text' (Lotman [1987] 1990a: 105). In distinction from a citation, a symbol is rooted not in the text, but in culture; it is equivalent in scale to the text as a whole, and not reducible to one of its parts.

Conclusion

In his text 'The Role of Typological Symbols in the History of Culture' (1990c), Lotman distinguishes between cultures founded on the conventionality of the sign and those founded on the motivated nature of the symbol, which on the level of social interaction leads to the domination of contract (the first cultural type) or of gift and service (the second type). Lotman classified Russian culture as belonging to the second type. Demanding that the subject offer itself up as gift, this culture not only became the object of analysis but also imposed an optics for its own investigation, simultaneously taking its position 'as a subject and its own object' (Lotman [1989] 2019). In Lotman's case, scholarly service to culture elicited an answering gift. His recognition in the symbol (in myth, in the poetic text) of a semiotic mechanism combining both the principle of preservation and that of transformation was itself carried out within a culture of the symbolic (mytho-poetic) type. His perception of transformative semiotic potential in syncretic cultural archaism was itself carried out from within a cultural context that was sequentially reproducing this same archaism. Access to comprehension of the mythological layers of culture, in the words of Lotman himself, grants nothing other than an internal experience made possible by the heterogeneous character of one's thought, preserving memory of archaic forms of semiosis, a cognition of which is 'tantamount to remembering' (Lotman and Uspenskij [1973] 1977: 240).

Notes

1. On the utopian connotations of this view and various projects for the creation of an ideal language, reproducing the structure of the world completely adequately and without contradiction, see Eco [1993] 1995.

2. A separate study could be devoted to the description of these latter terms in relation to metaphor and metonymy (as the 'poles' of language, in Jakobson's sense).

3. In this connection, in his notes from the 1990s concerning the semiotics of the 1960s, Alexander Piatigorsky, capitalizing on historical distance as a motivation for theoretical reflection, wrote, 'I now think that the reason culture became the universal object in semiotic research relates less to semiotics than to the concrete *Russian cultural context*. (We thought we were writing about culture from without, but in fact it was directing our hand from within all the time)' (Piatigorsky 1996: 54, my emphasis).

4. In the sense of this term articulated by Otto Jespersen, who conceptualized it as a limiting case, in which one and the same sign functions both as symbol and index, combining the functions of arbitrary signification and indexicality (deixis) (Jespersen 1924).

5. Lotman wrote about this dual articulation of the symbol in connection with the relationship between symbol and myth (Lotman and Uspenskij [1973] 1977: 240–1).

6. This comment is missing in the original English version of Lotman's book *Universe of the Mind* and appears only in the subsequent Russian publication (Lotman 1996: 367).

7. The Tartu scholars are quick to express solidarity with this position (Barsukov et al. 1987: 86).

8. The first publications of the works of Pavel Florensky after several decades of official oblivion, took place in *Trudy po znakovym sistemam*; among other texts, his 'Symbolarium (Dictionary of Symbols)' was published in this venue (Florenskij 1971).

9. The specificity of Lotman's understanding of symbol could not but bear an imprint of his wife, Zara Mints', research interests, which were strongly connected to Russian symbolism.

10. On the complex relations between Losev and representatives of the Tartu-Moscow school turning both on distinctions in theoretical standpoints and on ideological positions definitive for strategies of academic communication, see Stolovich 2009: 98–109.

11. Strikingly, only slightly earlier than Lotman, Victor Turner had articulated a structurally similar model of the mobile relationships between the symbol, its meaning ('the cultural theme') and its ritual (textual) function, in the process of working out his own version of symbolic anthropology. Turner writes of the unique economy of the symbol, which allows it to evoke a multiplicity of 'cultural themes'. The more fully a symbol is developed, the greater is its capacity for expression. This feature of the symbol (as a 'cultural condenser', Lotman would say) creates specific forms of communicative difficulty, but they may be resolved thanks to the contextual limitation of this polyvalent potential: 'since a ritual symbol may represent disparate, even contradictory themes, the gain of economy may be offset by a loss in clarity of communication. This would be inevitable if such symbols existed in a vacuum, but they exist in cultural and operational contexts that to some extent overcome the loss in intelligibility and to some extent capitalized on it' (Turner 1973: 1101). The shared interest of both scholars in liminal sociocultural states, situations of schism and disjuncture, and other phenomena that violate the principle of structural fixity is, in this light, unsurprising (see also Turner [1969] 1977).

References

Averintsev, S. S. 2001. *Sophia-Logos. Slovar*, Kiev: Dukh i Litera.

Barsukov, S. G., Grishakova, M. F., Grigorieva, E. G., Zajonc, L. O, Lotman, Ju. M., Ponomareva, G.M. and Mitroshkin, V. J. 1987. 'Predvaritel'nye zamechania po probleme "Emblema – simvol – mit' v kul'ture XVIII stoletia"', *Trudy po znakovym sistemam* 21: 85–94.

Barthes, R. [1970] 1982. *The Empire of Signs*, trans. R. Howard, New York: Hill & Wang.

Culler, J. 1976. *Saussure*, London: Fontana/Collins.

De Man, P. [1969] 1989. *Blindness and Insight: Essays in the Rhetoric of Contemporary Criticism*, 2nd edn, London: Routledge.

De Man, P. 1984. *The Rhetoric of Romanticism*, New York: Columbia University Press.

De Man, P. 1988. 'The Double Aspect of Symbolism', *Yale French Studies* 74: 3–16.

Eco, U. [1993] 1995. *The Search for the Perfect Language*, trans. J. Fentress, London: Fontana Press.

Florenskij, P. A. [1924] 1993. *Analiz prostranstvennosti i vremeni v khudozhestvenno-izobrazitel'nykh proizvedeniakh*, Moscow: Progress.

Florenskij, P. A. 1971. 'Symbolarium (Slovar' simvolov)', *Trudy po znakovym sistemam* 5: 521–7.

Grigorieva, E. 2006. 'Simvol, model' i mimesis po Lotmanu', in G. V. Obatnin and P. Pesonen (eds), *Istoria i povestvovanie*, 28–50, Moscow: Novoe Literaturnoe Obozrenie.

Ivanov, V. 1916. *Borozdy i mezhi*. Moscow: Musaget.

Jespersen, J. O. 1924. *The Philosophy of Grammar*, London: H. Holt & Company.

Kalinin, I. 2003. 'Semiotic Model of Historical Process. History: Between Grammar and Rhetoric', *Sign Systems Studies* 31 (2): 499–509.

Kalinin, I. 2009. 'Tartusko-moskovskaia semioticheskaia shkola: semioticheskaia model' kultury / kulturnaia model' semiotiki', *Novoe Literaturnoe Obozrenie* 98: 27–56.

Losev, A. F. [1927] 1993. 'Filosofia imeni', in A. F. Losev, *Bytie. Imya. Kosmos*, 613–801, Moscow: Mysl'.

Losev, A. F. [1930] 1993. *Ocherki antichnogo simvolisma*, Moscow: Mysl'.

Losev, A. F. [1973] 1991. 'Logika simvola', in A. F. Losev, *Filosofia. Mifologia. Kultura*, 247–74, Moscow: Izdatel'stvo politicheskoj literatury.

Losev, A. F. 1976. *Problema simvola i realisticheskoe iskusstvo*, Moscow: Iskusstvo.

Lotman, Yu. M. [1987] 1990a. 'The Symbol in the Cultural System', in Yu. M. Lotman, *Universe of the Mind: A Semiotic Theory of Culture*, trans. A. Shukman, 102–9, London and New York: I.B. Tauris.

Lotman, Yu. M. [1987] 1990b. 'The Symbol as Plot-Gene', in Yu. M. Lotman, *Universe of the Mind: A Semiotic Theory of Culture*, trans. A. Shukman, 82–101, London and New York: I.B. Tauris.

Lotman, J. [1989] 2019. 'Culture as a Subject and Its Own Object', in J. Lotman, *Culture, Memory and History: Essays in Cultural Semiotics*, trans. B. J. Baer, ed. M. Tamm, 83–93, Cham: Palgrave Macmillan.

Lotman, Yu. M. 1990c. 'The Role of Typological Symbols in the History of Culture', in Yu M. Lotman, *Universe of the Mind: A Semiotic Theory of Culture*, trans. A. Shukman, 254–68, London and New York: I.B. Tauris.

Lotman, Yu. M. 1990d. 'Iconic Rhetoric', in Yu. M. Lotman, *Universe of the Mind: A Semiotic Theory of Culture*, trans. A. Shukman, 54–62, London and New York: I.B. Tauris.

Lotman, Yu. M. 1990e. *Universe of the Mind: A Semiotic Theory of Culture*, trans. A. Shukman, London and New York: I.B. Tauris.

Lotman, Ju. M. [1992] 1997. 'Mezhdu emblemoi i simvolom', in E. V. Permiakov (ed.), *Lotmanovskii sbornik*, vol. 2, 416–23, Moscow: 'OGI'

Lotman, J. [1992] 2009. *Culture and Explosion*, trans. W. Clark, ed. M. Grishakova, Berlin and New York: Mouton de Gruyter.

Lotman, Ju. M. 1996. *Vnutri mysliashikh mirov*, Moscow: Jazyki russkoj kultury.

Lotman, Yu. and Uspenskij, B. [1973] 1977. 'Myth–Name–Culture', in D. P. Lucid (ed. and trans.), *Soviet Semiotics: An Anthology*, 233–52, Baltimore, MD: Johns Hopkins University Press.

Lotman, M. 1995. 'Za tekstom: zametki o filosofskom fone tartuskoj semiotiki', in E. V. Permiakov (ed.), *Lotmanovskii sbornik*, vol. 1, 214–22, Moscow: IC-Garant.

Lotman, M. 2002. 'Semiotika kultury v tartusko-moskovskoj semioticheskoj shkole', in Ju M. Lotman, *Istoriia i tipologiia russkoi kultury*, 5–20, Saint Petersburg: Iskusstvo–SPB.

Mamardashvili, M. K. and Piatigorsky, A. M. 1971. 'Tri besedy o metateorii soznania. (Kratkoe vvedenie v uchenie vidzhnianavady)', *Trudy po znakovym sistemam* 5: 345–76.

Mamardashvili, M. and Piatigorsky, A. 1997. *Simvol i soznanie. Metafizicheskie rassuzhdeniia o soznanii, simvole i iazyke*, Moscow: Jazyki russkoj kultury.

Mandelker, A. 1994. 'Semiotizing the Sphere: Organicist Theory in Lotman, Bakhtin, and Vernadsky', *Publications of the Modern Language Association* 109 (3): 385–96.

Mints, Z. [1979] 1999. 'Simvol u Aleksandra Bloka', in Z. Mints, *Poetika Aleksandra Bloka*, 334–61, Saint Petersburg: Iskusstvo–SPB.

Piatigorsky, A. M. 1996. 'Zametki iz 90-kh o semiotike 60-kh', in A. M. Piatigorsky, *Izbrannye trudy*, 53–60, Moscow: Shkola 'Jazyki russkoj kultury'.

Peirce, C. S. 1977. *Semiotics and Significs*, ed. C. Hardwick, Bloomington: Indiana University Press.

Saussure F. de [1916] 1959. *Course in General Linguistics*, ed. C. Bally and A. Sechehaye, trans. W. Baskin, New York: McGraw-Hill Book Co.

Stolovich, L. N. 2005. *Istoria russkoj filosofii. Ocherki*, Moscow: Respublika.

Stolovich, L. N. 2009. 'Iurii Mikhailovich Lotman. Vospominania i razmyshlenia', in V.K. Kantor (ed.), *Iurii Mikhailovich Lotman*, 82–131, Moscow: ROSSPEN.

Tamm, M. 2019. 'Introduction: Juri Lotman's Semiotic Theory of History and Cultural Memory', in J. Lotman, *Culture, Memory and History: Essays in Cultural Semiotics*, trans. B. J. Baer, ed. M. Tamm, 1–26, Cham: Palgrave Macmillan.

Todorov, T. [1977] 1984. *Theories of the Symbol*, trans. C. Porter, Ithaca, NY and London: Cornell University Press.

Turner, V. T. [1969] 1977. *The Ritual Proses: Structure and Anti-Structure*, Ithaca, NY, and London: Cornell University Press.

Turner, V. T. 1973. 'Symbols in African Ritual', *Science* 179 (4078): 1000–5.

Tynianov, J. 1924. *Problema stikhotvornogo iazyka*, Leningrad: Academia.

CHAPTER 16
IMAGE
Nikolay Poselyagin

Juri Lotman's approach to image (which can be defined in his terminology as visual sign) is not only semiotic in the strict sense but also phenomenological and narratological. Lotman's area of interest spread far beyond the issues of signs, sign systems and ways of transferring information through visual media. The main question he explored in his works on cinema and pictorial art related to the ways and modes of representing reality in a work of art. In general, it can be said that Lotman organized his research into image in visual texts on two levels: he analysed the inner structure of a text by semiotic and narratological means, although this very analysis was framed from the philosophical point of view, in which the image became a tool for gaining knowledge of our reality. However, Lotman was not trying to reflect this second – philosophical – level of his approach in a more developed way.

Conditional vs iconic signs

Lotman takes his lead from Ferdinand de Saussure's idea of two types of sign and, more specifically, from Saussurean distinction between an unmotivated, arbitrary sign and a relatively motivated one. In Lotman's terms, these two types of sign turn out to be conditional and pictorial, or iconic, respectively (Lotman [1973] 1981: 4). At the same time, the difference in Lotman's approach is far more profound than in Saussure's theory. Both Saussurean types of linguistic sign are equally isolated from any outer (extralinguistic) referent in reality and from human interpretation; relative arbitrariness here means that one sign can be partially motivated by other signs from which it is derived or by the whole sign system in which it is embedded (Saussure [1916] 1959: 131–4). All bonds between the sign and reality are unmotivated in Saussure's theory: any word form is a pure convention. Lotman retains this logic with regard to conditional signs, although in parallel, he adds another type the outer form of which can be associated with its referent, at least in part.

However, this very association strongly depends on cultural presuppositions. At first sight, iconic signs are more clear and comprehensible than conditional ones: we can intuitively understand an icon or a picture because we can automatically relate it to the object in the world around us that it designates. We rely upon external similarity between the sign and the object when we begin to establish references between them. But our perception is not linked directly with reality: it is restricted by the culture in which we are immersed. According to Lotman, national cultures as well as human culture as a whole form a kind of mediator between an individual consciousness and the world we live in; all the facts we can extract and all the interpretations we can produce depend on the cultural preconditions that exist before us and which are imposed upon us. We can distinguish any feature in an iconic sign just because surrounding culture creates our understanding of what is a fact (more precisely, what is considered as the fact) and what is not.

The iconic sign is no less conventional than the conditional one: cultural conventions governing the human perception of reality limit our comprehension of the iconic sign so it cannot be a universal transmitter of meaning. We interpret the same image in different ways according to which culture we belong to: 'The degree to which iconic signs are conventional will become clear if we recall that the ease of reading them is restricted to a single cultural area. Beyond the spatial and temporal boundaries of the area the signs cease to be understood' (Lotman [1973] 1981: 6). This logic applies to all kinds of visual information from traffic signs to masterpieces of pictorial art and cinema. Persons from one culture might be confused when they face a road sign in a foreign country made in a symbolic way unknown to them. People unfamiliar with impressionism, for instance, will look at a work of impressionist art 'as a collection of coloured blots which do not reproduce anything' (Lotman [1973] 1981).

The conditional sign, in turn, is universal: any sense that we are able to express can be transmitted and shared with other people through words that relate to conditional type. If a concept can be expressed at all, it can be expressed with words; natural language is the optimal translator and mediator between all humans and all spheres of culture including the sphere of the visual. We translate the meanings of iconic signs using the signs of natural languages; thus, we make pictorial images understandable to people not only from other cultures but also from our own culture. We make a connection between the iconic sign and its referent in the world around us using conditional signs, primarily words.

So, why do we need image? Would it perhaps be better to abandon pictorial signs all together? Moreover, why do we posit them as more 'natural' than the conditional signs?

The lie and the truth

The first reason for the necessity of the image in human culture is its relative independence from the problem of truth. The conventional sign can be true or false with, frequently, some effort required to test for truthfulness. The image is partly free of this: it is just presented before us, and we can rather contemplate its visual information than evaluate it. To be more accurate, we evaluate the information that we see behind the visual sign and transform this into words (i.e. information is always encoded in the conventional signs for us); but when we turn to the image itself, we rather prefer to check whether it succeeds in depicting its referent in the reality:

Depictive signs are perceived as 'signs in a lesser degree' than words. Therefore they already begin to oppose words in the situation: 'capable of being the means of a deception – not capable of being the means of a deception'. The Oriental proverb has it: 'Better to see it once than hear about it in a hundred times'. A word can be both true and false, and a picture contrasts with it, in this respect, to the same degree that a photograph contrasts with a picture. (Lotman [1973] 1981: 7)

Of course, this too is a convention. The image can be as false as the word. But the point is our belief: we are ready to believe that the pictorial sign exists in another coordinate system and not in the conventional one. We count image as a more or less exact and detailed depiction of reality; the lie could occur at the moment of correlating it with its referent in the real word, but not at the moment of our interpretation of this correlation. The visual sign exists here and now so we suggest that we operate not with a piece of pure conditionality but with a mimetic mould of nature.

The idea of mimesis is crucial. Ultimately, image aims to be like a mirror reflecting its object fully, coherently and in every detail. However, this is only an unattainable ideal: image is in balance between our trust in its ability to represent the object correctly and our comprehension that it is a kind of semiotic sign restricted by its internal characteristics. A category of correctness of reflecting the world replaces the category of truth inherent to the conditional sign systems.

Various types of visual sign approach that ideal to differing extents. Photography is the closest art to nature (because its audience is ready to think that it reflects the life 'as it is') while painting is far more conventional and dependent on the subjective vision of the artist:

In our cultural perception a photograph is a substitute for nature and as such we ascribe to it an identity with the object (such an evaluation does not define the real properties of a photograph but its place in the system of cultural signs, for everyone knows that a portrait of a person close to us painted by a good master can reveal a greater likeness to that person than a photograph; but when we are primarily concerned with accuracy of documentation, when the aim is to catch a criminal, for example, or in a newspaper report, then a photograph is preferable). Any individual photograph can be under suspicion of relative accuracy but The Photograph is a synonym for accuracy. (Lotman [1978] 1981: 36)

I extracted the aforementioned quotation from Lotman's 1978 article 'On the Language of Animated Cartoons'. Lotman repeated this idea in 1993 in his article 'Portrait', once again emphasizing that the similarity between an image and an object plays a less significant role than a 'formal ability *to be a sign of similarity*, to perform a certain conditional function' (Lotman [1993] 1998: 502). A little later he placed portrait and photograph in opposition as dynamic art and static evidence:

Oddly enough, dynamics is one of artistic dominants of a portrait. It becomes clear if anyone juxtaposes a portrait with a photograph. The last one indeed catches a static moment from moving world it reflects. A photograph has no past and future, it is always in the present time. The time of a portrait is dynamic, its 'present' is always full of memory about the previous state and of prediction about the future. (Lotman [1993] 1998: 502–3)

Thus, a mimetic image, a 'bare' reflection of reality, can be just a visual copy of an object, a documentation deprived of past and future. It cannot lie about the world, but at the same time it cannot be something more than evidence. On the contrary, a pictorial image is assigned more complex and profound semiotics. It begins to play a more important role not only as an image itself but also as a full-fledged, integrated semiotic system with its inner memory and ability to produce new meanings. Along with this, it takes all features of the conditional sign systems including the vulnerability to subjective interpretations and the necessity of a check for truthfulness.

Meanwhile, the idea of the truth about the world or the correctness of its reflection is only one aspect of image. Lotman discusses the problem of the representation of reality not only at the level of an isolated image/visual sign (even if it is a complete perceptive form or artistic work as with a picture or photograph) but also at the level of compound visual objects. He tests the visual sphere of human culture and its ability to discover the lines linking an image along with a visual work with reality through the dynamic membrane of culture.

Lotman's film phenomenology

The visual sphere is highly important to Lotman because it creates an illusion of penetration into the real world outside of culture, as well as of human perception in a world of Kant's things-in-themselves. We are restrained by the culture that surrounds us; we are detached from reality as such, which would be independent of cultural influence. Nevertheless, the visual sphere provides us with images that we attribute to reality and postulate as its (conventional) phenomena. Iconic signs create this illusion of going beyond the borders of culture to life as such, life in itself.

The art of cinema, among other visual arts, receives the greatest level of elaboration in Lotman's theory, so I will focus primarily on this. In 1973, Lotman begins his book *Semiotics of Cinema and Problems of Film Aesthetics* with a chapter meaningfully titled 'The Illusion of Reality' (Lotman [1973] 1981: 10–22). Here he still holds a semiotic position according to which a visual work of art (a film in this case) is an internally integrated sign system isolated from the outside world but linked with it in a plausible way. The question of the illusion of reality turns out to be a question of credibility: the real world stands behind films and films make direct references to it. The illusion remains, but plausible representation of reality is enough for spectators if they count it as credible. Here Lotman has not yet exceeded semiotics and does not care about the philosophical status of represented reality.

However, the very concept of plausibility later comes under question. In the early 1990s, Lotman starts work on a new book on cinema studies. He was not able to complete it before his death but his colleague Yuri Tsivian continued the work, publishing *Dialogue with Screen* in 1994. The theoretical basis of this book is Lotman's, so I can interpret it as an extension and evolution of Lotman's theory of the visual sign. *Dialogue with Screen* opens with a chapter called 'Cinema and Life' (Lotman and Tsivian 1994: 7–11) in which the authors ask what life is. Here the plausibility of film is already not just a synonym for its credibility (we believe that what we are seeing at any given moment is true in a certain sense). Now it implies an isomorphic model of reality duplicating the real world by means of cinema and creating a semblance of it on the screen. Plausibility becomes a degree of effectiveness of this model. Visual signs become material representations of cognitive phenomena, and real life in turn becomes material for visual art. Iconic signs now create not only an illusion of reality locked into a semiotic system but also the plausible model essentially related to it. So we need pictorial signs not only because they provide us with a specific kind of information (i.e. a visual mode of representing the world) but also because they help to link our process of cognition immediately with its primary object, specifically reality: 'Thus, the life around us as such is material of cinema art. It's like all the chain "things (people, landscapes) – optics – photography" is imbued with objectivity' (Lotman and Tsivian 1994: 11).

Nevertheless, this construction can work only if we have convenient technical tools such as optical instruments of photograph and film that make available an objective view on the world. Otherwise, we come back to the pictorial sign as a representation of an artist's point of view (painter, sculptor, etc.), but not of a representation of the world per se.

At this moment, Lotman's late view on visual art is closely similar to ideas of visual phenomenology in the early twentieth century. The first film scholars discovered that technically equipped media (photography and cinema) could presumably solve – or rather get around – one of the key problems of phenomenology, the problem of the relationship of phenomenological essences in the human mind with noumenal things. A practice of phenomenological reduction offered by Edmund Husserl was quite hard to implement in its entirety while technically equipped media supplied an objective view just because the 'creator' of their representation had been an optical mechanism instead of a human being. Visual theorists were convinced that they had found a truly objective way of knowing: a technical device, by definition, could not have subjectivity. They thought we would directly contemplate objects of the visible world depicted on film stock or in the photograph, thereby becoming immersed in reality. Some time after they realized that this solution to the question was generally illusory because people operate photographic and cinematographic apparatuses and used various techniques when shooting. Thus, the subjective human mind did not disappear from the process (for more see, e.g. Kracauer 1960; Iampolski 1993).

Lotman chooses another way. He presumes that the ultimate 'cognitive mechanism' is not just the mind of a private person but also the whole culture of humanity consisting of a network of every mind of every human being, resulting in the question of objective versus subjective cognition being meaningless. Images of reality are raw material which culture adopts and then retranslates to individual people. Human culture can be subjective within itself (we cannot independently check it) but it is objective to us. Its links between a depicted image and the real world are so far away from the private mind that it may postulate an objective nature of this image. The very category of objectiveness is being reformulated: according to Lotman's late theory, it depends on human culture, not on reality per se, and happens to be rather intersubjective:

> Semiotic space appears before us as the multi-layered intersection of various texts, which are woven together in a specific layer characterised by complex internal relationships and variable degrees of translatability and spaces of untranslatability. The layer of 'reality' is located underneath this textual layer – the kind of reality that is organised by a multiplicity of languages and has a hierarchical relationship with them. Together, both these layers constitute the semiotics of culture. That reality which is external to the boundaries of language lies beyond the limits of the semiotics of culture.
>
> The word 'reality' denotes two different phenomena. On the one hand, this reality is phenomenal, in the Kantian sense, i.e. it is that reality which correlates to culture, either resisting it, or merging with it. On the other, there is the noumenal sense (in Kantian terminology) in which we may refer to reality as a space which is forever beyond the limits of culture. However, the whole structure of these definitions and terms changes, if at the centre of our world we place not one isolate 'I' but a more complex organised space of the many mutually dependent correlative 'I's. (Lotman [1992] 2009: 23–4)

Lotman's visual narratology

Coming back to the visual arts, we can see that Lotman leaves phenomenological questions and focuses on ways and modes of work as they relate to visual art construction. Here he develops an all-embracing structuralist view on visual form, its techniques and the specificities of its composition. He does this in 1973 (in *Semiotics of Cinema and Problems of Film Aesthetics*) and in the early 1990s (in *Dialogue with Screen*) as well as in articles on other visual arts. Although Lotman's film theory is the most thorough and detailed, I think that Lotman's method can be called fully narratological only as it applies to cinema texts (see also Chapter 13). He researches the internal composition of an individual film frame and of a shot, principles of montage and plot construction, time and space in movies, distribution of diegetic points of view, use of sound, noise and human speech, screenplay, acting, shooting and editing film. Lotman defines this formal analysis as an analysis of film language and film style. It has to embrace the entire film form and reveal meanings related to all these details and techniques.[1]

In the meantime, the narratological analysis of the image can be quite difficult and complicated. First of all, narratology presumes that its main object of research is a continuing story told by a narrator. Furthermore, this story must be linear and discrete, separable into individual parts with their own meanings. But the image is a static and non-discrete object that requires some other way to analyse it. Lotman wrote about this in his article 'The Discrete Text and the Iconic Text:'

> Is a semiotic system without signs possible? This question taken by itself may seem absurd. If, however, we reformulate it as follows: 'Can meaning be conveyed by a message in which we cannot single out signs in the sense in which they are defined most often – as the words of natural language?' then, if we consider painting, music, and cinema, we cannot but answer in the affirmative. [. . .] The point is that the very concept of the sign is here difficult to isolate since the message does not apparently have the property of discreteness. (Lotman [1973] 1975: 333–4)

We cannot divide the image into smaller elements and look at parts of its message separately. In 1973, Lotman even allows that the integrated image cannot be considered as a sign at all (it appears rather as a specific inseparable kind of text): 'In the discrete verbal message, the text is made up of signs; in the second case, there are, essentially, no signs: the message is communicated by the text in its entirety' (Lotman [1973] 1975: 335). Nevertheless, according to Lotman, this does not mean that the image does not have any narrative function, but rather that its narration principles differ greatly:

> For the internally nondiscrete text-message of the iconic type, however, narration is a transformation, an internal transposition of elements. [. . .] the mechanism of the narration, at the basis of which lies not the syntagmatic combination of elements in space, which necessarily entails an increase in the size of the text, but an internal transformation and subsequent combination in time. One figure is transformed into another. Each of them constitutes a certain synchronically organized segment. These segments do not join in space, as would be the case if we were to draw a design; they are transformed one into another, becoming a summation in time. (Lotman [1973] 1975: 335)

An isolated image is raw material subject to transformation; and this transformation makes a story that can already be accessible for narratological methods. This logic underlies cinema and manifests itself in a sequence of frames and shots. Film constructs a text in which linear deployment from one shot to another is similar to deployment in a word text. In turn, literary text can take over the specificities of image:

> The verbal arts strive for freedom from the verbal principle of narration, and the iconic arts strive against automatically taking the type of narration dictated by the qualities of their material. As a consequence, verbal narrative is a revolutionizing element in immanently iconic narration, and vice versa. We find, then, on the one hand, the striving to construct film narrative like a sentence, Eisenstein's montage that is based on linguistic principles, the tendency to emphasize discrete signs on an analogy with words; and, on the other hand, the invasion of the iconic principle into the verbal arts, with the result that the word in poetry is not so perceptible

and recognizable as a unit, as it is in nonpoetry. We have already had occasion to note that it is not the word that acts as a unit in the poetic text, but the text as a whole – a phenomenon typical of the nondiscrete types of semiosis. (Lotman [1973] 1975: 337)

Inside the separate frame, we reveal not separate signs but rather techniques that can be studied using the methods of the Russian formalists.[2] This is why only cinema fits narratology well among other iconic arts: here we deal with forms that give structure in the same way that texts are made of conditional signs, especially signs of natural languages. Other types of image we can interpret only as an indivisible visual sign as a whole that cannot be dissected in a consistent way. Lotman's narratological method regarding image ends here.

Notes

1. Lotman's views on cinema have been the subject of previous research; see, first of all, Eagle 2006; Pezzini 2015; Konstantinov 2017. These works analyse aspects of Lotman's approach to film other than those analysed in this chapter.

2. By the way, other classics of cinema narratology describing their methodological principles prefer to address not Lotman but Russian formalists and French structuralists such as Tzvetan Todorov (who in turn was influenced by Russian formalism). See, for example, Chatman 1978; Bordwell 1989; Bordwell and Thompson 2008.

References

Bordwell, D. 1989. *Making Meaning: Inference and Rhetoric in the Interpretation of Cinema*, Cambridge, MA and London: Harvard University Press.

Bordwell, D. and Thompson, K. 2008. *Film Art: An Introduction*, 8th edn, New York: McGraw-Hill.

Chatman, S. 1978. *Story and Discourse: Narrative Structure in Fiction and Film*, Ithaca, NY and London: Cornell University Press.

Eagle, H. 2006. 'Bipolar Asymmetry, Indeterminacy, and Creativity in Cinema', in A. Schönle (ed.), *Lotman and Cultural Studies: Encounters and Extensions*, 229–47, Madison: The University of Wisconsin Press.

Iampolski, M. 1993. *Vidimyi mir: Ocherki rannei kinofenomenologii*, Moscow: NII kinoiskusstva; Central'nyi muzejikino; Mezhdunarodnaia kinoshkola.

Konstantinov, M. V. 2017. *Iu. Lotman i vizual'naia semiotika vtoroi poloviny XX veka (istoriko-filosofskii analiz)*, unpublished PhD thesis, Poltava.

Kracauer, S. 1960. *Theory of Film: The Redemption of Physical Reality*, Oxford: Oxford University Press.

Lotman, J. M. [1973] 1975. 'The Discrete Text and the Iconic Text: Remarks on the Structure of Narrative', trans. F. Pfotenhauer, *New Literary History* 6 (2): 333–8.

Lotman, J. [1973] 1981. *Semiotics of Cinema*, trans. M. E. Suino, Ann Arbor: University of Michigan.

Lotman, Yu. [1978] 1981. 'On the Language of Animated Cartoons', trans. R. Sobel, in L. O'Toole and A. Shukman (eds), *Film Theory and General Semiotics*, 36–9, Oxford: Holden Books.

Lotman, J. [1992] 2009. *Culture and Explosion*, trans. W. Clark, ed. M. Grishakova, Berlin and New York: Mouton de Gruyter.

Lotman, Ju. M. [1993] 1998. 'Portret', in Ju. M. Lotman, *Ob iskusstve*, 500–18, Saint Petersburg: Iskusstvo–SPB.

Lotman, Ju. and Tsivian, Ju. 1994. *Dialog s ekranom*, Tallinn: Aleksandra.

Pezzini, I. 2015. '*Ecce homo*: La riflessione di Lotman tra icone, caricature e ritratti', in M. Bertelé, A. Bianco and A. Cavallaro (eds), *Le Muse fanno il girotondo. Jurij Lotman e le arti: Studi in onore di Giuseppe Barbieri: Atti del convegno internazionale, Università Ca' Foscari Venezia, 26–28 novembre 2013*, 119–31, Venice: Terra Ferma.

Saussure, F. de. [1916] 1959. *Course in General Linguistics*, ed. Ch. Bally and A. Sechehaye in collaboration with A. Reidlinger, trans. W. Baskin, New York: Philosophical Library.

CHAPTER 17
MEMORY
Renate Lachmann

Memory and cultural semiotics

'Only that which has been translated into a system of signs can be appropriated by memory; in this sense, the intellectual history of mankind can be regarded as a struggle for memory' (Lotman [1970] 2000: 397). With this cardinal statement, Juri Lotman invites us to follow the historical formation of a concept which is vitally connected with the human mind and which is accompanied by or realized in different techniques of remembering. *Memoria* (the Greek *mneme*), the fourth of the five sections in classical rhetoric, comprises a system of rules (or devices) to help remember a speech or narration. These rules are described in rhetorical treatises dating from Aristotle to the end of the eighteenth century, when rhetoric as a discipline lost its importance. The notion and art of memory, however, were not confined to these rules, because from its advent *ars memoriae* decisively shaped an influential tradition in European culture serving as a pragmatic aid that helped to improve and sharpen recollection; beyond this it was established as a distinct part of the cultural domain (the social stock of knowledge), meaning that generation after generation could draw upon its contents.

From various treatises, one can conclude that in antiquity *memoria* was conceived as both *memoria naturalis* and *memoria artificialis*, the inborn ability and the skill acquired through learning. Not only was the perfect construction of speech or text at stake but also was the physical and intellectual perception of the world. The division between body and mind has accompanied the 'phenomenon' of memory ever since (phrenology/biology on the one hand and philosophy/sociology on the other).

Lotman canalizes this struggle of mankind with a new theory of memory which he develops as the essential part of culture conceived of as a semiotic system, a concept developed in the works of the Tartu-Moscow school. The latter operates with an inventory of categories for the analysis of cultural processes which are meant to totally describe the techniques of self-interpretation and self-modelling (transformation, translation, transcoding) by means of which a culture attempts to stabilize itself. Such categories are 'self-description', 'cultural metalanguage' or 'metatext', 'cultural grammar', 'dynamic mechanism' (e.g. Lotman [1974] 1977; Lotman and Uspensky [1971] 1978).

The typology of culture that Lotman proposes starts out with the cardinal question of what does 'to have meaning' mean. This typology is dependent on studies analysing the role of the text and the role of signs in individual cultures or in individual stages of a culture's development. The sign type (text type) preferred at a given time becomes a parameter for describing culture. This notion of culture (understood as a unified text governed by a unified code and as the sum total of all texts governed by such codes) develops specific modes of producing meaning (see Chapter 10). In general terms, it is thus necessary to ask how a culture functioning as a semiotic system relates to the sign and to semioticity. This relation to sign and semioticity is reflected, on the one hand, in the 'self-assessment' of a culture, in its descriptive system, that is, in the grammars it develops about itself, and, on the other hand, in the way the texts produced by the culture or relevant to it are evaluated with regard to their functionality. The questions about the character of the sign type and the text type are related, for both questions are concerned with the problem of 'semioticity' (*znakovost*). Text can be conceived of as an ordered sign sequence that can appear in different forms as literature, pieces of art, performances, and so on. The concept of text allows the interpretation of sign events as a kind of reading that follows the rules of cultural grammar (see Chapter 9).

Lotman's typological models are constructed as dichotomies. The duality of the cultural codes that he reconstructs and which can define both the diachrony and the synchrony of a culture is founded on the following criteria: how a culture models its relationship with extra-culture, what role a culture ascribes to texts and how a culture ascribes value to signs. To the extent a culture recognizes or denies semioticity, it draws a boundary line between itself and extra-culture, which it either defines as anti-culture (thus having a negative semioticity) or as non-culture (having no semioticity whatsoever). Cultural mechanism, that is, the displacement of one cultural type by another, takes place according to the same principle. Thus, in Lotman's concept, cultural dynamism reveals itself as based on the desemiotization of areas that have been accorded semioticity in the preceding stage of a culture and in the semiotization of new areas. Yet in Lotman's concept, mnemonic processes are closely connected with cultural types according to their changing semioticity (Lachmann 1995: 192–213).

The key element of cultural semiotics is a memory concept defined less by anthropology than by culturology. This emphasis allows us to grasp the following statement:

> We understand culture as the *nonhereditary memory of the community*, a memory expressing itself in a system of constraints and prescriptions. [. . .] Furthermore, insofar as culture is *memory* or, in other words, a record in the memory of what the community has experienced, it is, of necessity, connected to *past* historical experience. Consequently, at the moment of its appearance, culture cannot be recorded as such, for it is only perceived ex post facto. (Lotman and Uspensky [1971] 1978: 213)

Cultural semiotics describes more than just concepts such as storing cultural experience and cultural meaning and the indelibility of signs set by culture and kept available via its modes of reconstruction. The models essayed thus focus on the complex entanglement of a culture's attempts at self-description and its semiotic dynamics (whereby the metalanguage and modelling of cultural semiotics can themselves become the object of study). Cultural semiotics itself now advances compensating concepts to counter the idea – implicit in the assumption that meaning grows – that there is a certain indestructibility to the ever-increasing semantic potential of a culture that seems to reckon neither with the regulation provided by selection nor with the fact that meaning is suppressed and forgotten. The crucial factor is that which presupposes a mechanism of inclusion and exclusion of cultural meaning, which allows us to interpret forgetting as a pause for rest, in the sense of temporary inactivity in the system of meaning, and the shift between forgetting and remembering as an inherent movement of culture. In other words, cultural semiotics assumes a mechanism guaranteeing the stable functioning of cultural communication, a mechanism which, always legitimized and directed in different ways by a culture's model of self-description, serves to regulate the existing inventory of signs.

This mechanism is set in motion by specific techniques manifested as the de- and resemioticizing of cultural signs. Desemioticizing means that a sign vehicle loses its signifying quality, that is, both the semantic and the pragmatic function it fulfilled within the system and its institutions. If an element loses its signifying quality, this means it becomes culturally inactive, although not erased, since the 'vacant' signs remain within the culture in a kind of reserve that acts like a negative store. In a later phase in its development, due to changes in its self-description model that make certain exclusions appear problematic, culture can reinclude and thus resemioticize the forgotten elements. In other words, the signs whose relegation to latency creates cultural forgetting are taken up by the semiotic process and can be reactualized in the existing culture.

On the one hand, this mechanism guarantees semiotic invariance, preserving the identity of a culture, by means of certain constant texts and constant codes, by means of a certain lawlike regularity in the transformation of cultural information. On the other hand, however, this same mechanism also allows for a generative apparatus that calls attention to new mechanisms of transformation. In this context of cultural semiotics, the rivalry between texts functioning as accumulators and texts functioning as generators appear as the very subject of cultural description.

What is essential in this respect is that Lotman defines the semiotic structure of culture as language: 'Defining culture as a sign system subjected to structural rules allows us to view it as a language, in the general semiotic sense of the term. [. . .] Yet culture includes not only a certain combination of semiotic systems [languages], but the sum of all historically existent messages (texts) in these languages' ([1970] 2000: 396-7). Marek Tamm emphasizes this aspect, implicitly referring to other Lotmanian statements: 'Thus, from a semiotic perspective, culture is a multilingual system in which, side by side with natural languages, there exist cultural languages or secondary modelling systems (secondary to natural language as a primary modelling system) based on the former' (Tamm 2015: 130). Lotman stresses the mobility of culture as a semiotic system: 'Culture can be presented as an aggregate of texts; however, from the point of view of the researcher, it is more exact to consider culture as a mechanism creating an aggregate of texts and texts as the realization of culture' (Lotman and Uspensky [1971] 1978: 218). Texts in which culture is realized function, firstly, by 'accumulating' cultural meaning and, secondly, by generating it. A decisive element for the dynamic conception postulated by cultural semiotics is that the accumulated meaning is not merely 'stored' but 'grows' in the cultural memory.

Using constant texts common to the collective, constant codes and a certain regularity in the transmission of cultural information, this mechanism guarantees cultural invariance while also offering generative potential revealing new mechanisms of transformation (Lotman [1985] 2019: 136) The cultural space is defined as a space belonging to a 'common memory' in which certain common texts can be stored and updated. Culture seen from a semiotic perspective is conceived of as a collective intelligence and as collective memory interpreted as a supra-individual mechanism of preserving and transmitting information (texts) and of creating new ones (Lotman [1985] 2019: 133). This statement includes the assumption of a domain of common memory in which certain common texts can be stored and actualized according to a certain conceptual invariant (*smyslovogo invarianta*) that ensures, in the context of a new epoch, that the given text preserves its identity in spite of different variants of interpretation. This means that the common memory of a given culture can rely on the existence of some constant texts and on a unity of codes or their invariancy, or on the continuity and the legitimate character of their transformation. A second statement in this 'mnemonic-declaration' refers to the inherent multifoldedness of culture, that is, its unity exists only on a certain level and includes the existence of particular 'dialects of memory' (Lotman [1985] 2019: 133).

The concept of dividing culture-language into dialects corresponds to the statement that the existence of cultural substructures leads to elliptic texts which circulate in 'cultural sub-collectives' (*subkollektivy*) and to 'local semantics' (*lokal'nykh semantik*). Lotman admits that the tendency towards an individualization of memory represents the second pole of its dynamic structure. In other words: 'memory is not a passive storehouse for culture but a constitutive part of its text-generating mechanism' (Lotman [1985] 2019: 137).

To ensure the meaning of elliptic texts (having left the context of a given subcollective), they have to be replenished with meaning. Lotman illustrates this statement by referring to Gavriil Derzhavin, a prominent eighteenth-century poet who wrote a commentary on his odes so that he could recapture their lost meaning for a contemporary generation and to highlight the importance of genre. In this context, Lotman quotes Mikhail Bakhtin's famous idea of 'genre memory' (Bakhtin [1963] 1984: 106) – an idea that shattered concepts of literary history – emphasizing the aspect of supra-individuality (collectives alter, the genre persists). The appearance of commentaries and glossaries and the filling of gaps in texts shows in Lotman's view that the latter are reread by a (new, younger) collective with another capacity of memory. The recollection of forgotten texts means that even their former rejection is not final, there can always be a 'resurrection' on a later stage of cultural memory including essential changes in their semantic value. The history of icon painting, which earned its significance as an object of art only in post-Petrine Russian culture, serves as an example.

The formation of a new concept

The essence of culture is such that in it what is past does not 'pass away', that is, does not disappear as events do in the natural flow of time. By fixing itself in the memory of the culture the past acquires a constant, but at the same time potential, existence. This cultural memory, however, is constructed not only as a storehouse of texts, but also as a kind of generative mechanism. A culture which is united with its past by memory generates not only its own future, but also its own past, and in this sense is a mechanism that counteracts natural time. (Lotman and Uspensky [1977] 1984: 28)

In order to designate this new approach to the mnemonic conditions of culture Lotman coined the term 'cultural memory' (*kul'turnaia pamiat'*) (Lotman [1986] 2019], which he specified with the functional differentiation of memory as informative and as creative, addressing the complex process of inclusion and exclusion of cultural meaning (Lotman [1985] 2019: 134). Lotman clearly distinguishes two types of cultural self-modelling: on the one hand, a culture that selectively conceptualizes its involvement with the past and the available store of knowledge, and, on the other hand, a mechanism that regulates processes of storage and erasure in the service of a stable cultural communication. In this respect, the distinction between informative memory – which functions in linear terms and has a temporal dimension – and creative memory, which is conceived as panchronic and spatially continuous, and in which the entire textual body of a culture is potentially active is of decisive importance. Creative memory resists time. If it can be said that every culture develops a specific mechanism for storing and forgetting, a mechanism that is itself subject to change, then creative memory is characterized by a negative storage of the forgotten, the repressed, and that which has lost its semiotic quality. This means that there is no erasure in cultural memory; what is forgotten can be culturally reactivated and can take on its own (or a different) semiotic value.

Lotman does not discuss Maurice Halbwachs's theory of 'collective memory' (Halbwachs 1980); the frequent use of *kollektivnyi* (alternating with 'common'), however, presupposes a certain affinity especially concerning the concept of surpra-individuality and the presumption of certain schemes in mnemonic processes. Yet, Halbwachs's focus is on the mnemonic behaviour of a given society (or social group), Lotman's focus is on the dynamism of culture as memory (see also Chapter 28).

In Halbwachs's theory, one is led to understand that what he calls '*cadres sociaux*' function as instruments which are to capture the past, these frames being the language (as the most important instrument or rather factor, its loss, aphasia hinders recollection), time, space and experience. Collective memory is always, partial, not totalitarian; various groups of people have collective memories, which in turn give rise to different modes of behaviour; this idea of a fragmented memory resonates in Lotman's 'subcollective'. Whereas Lotman does not refer explicitly to Halbwachs's theory Jan Assmann does, in proposing two variants of memory, the communicative and the cultural, the latter being a quotation of Lotman's coinage.

The concept of cultural memory comprises that body of reusable texts, images, and rituals specific to each society in each epoch, whose 'cultivation' serves to stabilize and convey that society's self-image. Upon such collective knowledge for the most part (but not exclusively) of the past, each group bases its awareness of unity and particularity. (Assmann [1988] 1995: 132)

This concept of 'cultural memory' has a certain affinity to one of the two variants of cultural memory which Lotman distinguishes, namely the 'creative', whereas the 'informative' variant resonates in Assmann's 'communicative memory'.[1]

Aspects of the history of *memoria* as a concept and as a technique

If the function of memory is understood not just as an act of storing, but also as a structuring schema – one that both forms and represents a system – a connection to mnemotechnics in general is opened up. For in the latter, it is not simply a question of storage, but also of creating a figurative or schematic space:

> In rhetoric, memory craft is a stage in composing a work; presupposed is the axiom that recollection is an act of investigation and recreation in the service of conscious artifice. Its practitioners would not have been surprized to learn what was to them already obvious: that recollection is a kind of composition, and by its very nature is selective and formal. (Carruthers 2008: 138)

From a Lotmanian perspective one could argue, that a culture's semiotic mechanism consists in the alternation of its mnemonic paradigms, steering inclusion and exclusion, remembering and forgetting. 'Forgetting', as the exclusion of elements that have become passive (temporary desemiotization), is a necessary component of the cultural communication process that ultimately counteracts cultural forgetting in the sense of erasure.

Of these alternating, competing and interacting paradigms which always participate in different ways in the mnemonic construction of culture, especially those that have produced their own techniques, disciplines and consistent concepts are to be emphasized and examined in terms of their systematic place within cultural models. Such paradigms include the mnemotechnical, the diagrammatic and the diegetic. The argument is that mnemonic paradigms themselves are part (i.e. subjects) of cultural memory (the overarching metalanguage). Lotman's own mnemonic paradigm is subject to description and simultaneously the meta-paradigm. In this respect the following statement is telling:

> Every culture defines its own paradigm for what should be remembered, that is, preserved, and what should be relegated to oblivion. The latter is erased from the cultural memory and apparently 'ceases to exist'. But time changes along with systems of cultural codes and paradigms of remembering/forgetting. (Lotman [1985] 2019: 135)

The three historically different paradigms to be discussed in the following have a different focus. They are either arts or scholarly techniques, they either rely on imagination or on concepts. The *mnemotechnical paradigm* has a legendary source. The story of its invention by the Greek poet Simonides Melicus, passed down by Cicero and Quintilian, conceals an ancient myth narrating the development of the art of memory, at the threshold between an ancient epoch of ancestor cults from a later time when the deceased were mourned but not worshipped (Goldberg 1989: 43–66). The fundamental concepts of the art, place (*locus*) and image (*imago*) may be derived from the old cults. But the object of the disguised legend, mnemotechnics, has been handed down only in its postmythical form: as a prescription for acts of recollection and, on the other hand, as a tool for both the structuring and the presentation, open or encoded, of knowledge. Both aspects are central in Frances Yates's (1966) seminal history of the art of memory. No other art or scholarly method of antiquity has been legitimized through a detailed legend of its origin as that of the *ars memoriae*, and none is linked with an inventor whose name has been so emphatically inscribed in cultural memory as that of Simonides through the marble tablet of Paros.

Forgetting is the catastrophe; a given semiotic order is obliterated. It can only be restored by instituting a discipline that re-establishes semiotic 'generation' and interpretation. The mnemotechnical paradigm means that pictures stored in marked positions in a structured room help to remember a shattered order. Here, special rules are used to refine the transposition of the object of memory into its pictorial representation and its sequential placement in space. These rules regulate the semantic relations between that which is to be remembered (the signified) and the image (the signifier), determine the modes of their designation and guide the selection of the memory space. When the person doing the remembering turns an imagined architectural or other structured room into a memory space, the internal memory (what Plato described using the metaphor of the wax tablet) is externalized. The internal site of memory, the mind, the brain, is reproduced in an imagined external architecture (an early phrenological model?), as a space with passages, pillars and recesses.

The *diagrammatical paradigm* emerges with a new focus: the reproduction of knowledge, insight and finding truth. It is the transition from pictorial storage to systematics. Admittedly, deductive knowledge also requires 'reproduction'. This is performed by the diagram, which avails itself not of iconic signs, but of symbolic ones: geometric figures, letters, numbers or certain figures preformed by cultural semantics such as trees, wheels or ladders. Mnemonists work with schemas, insofar as they sketch diagrams to designate those themes that they wish to have at their disposal in the future. The diagrams are devices for use in a future where their own construction will already belong to the past. The formation of schemas, however, also refers to lost themes. In reference to the past, the formation of schemas entails the projection of a diagram, or, more precisely, the idea of a diagram, onto that which is absent – a diagram that bears as its first inscription the questions of the present. In the seventeenth century, the process of accumulating knowledge and of ordering it systematically reached its peak. The Baroque period is marked by the emergence of different modes governing the organization and transmission of knowledge. The programme underlying these modes originated with Raimundus Lullus. The German Jesuit Athanasius Kircher, scholar, linguist and founder of Egyptology, represents one model and Johannes Amos Comenius, philosopher in the Erasmian tradition, another. Kircher constructs a sophisticated edifice of erudition based on calculation and his *ars combinatoria* in order to reveal the inner structure of the world hidden in the accumulated data, Comenius formulates a lucid view of the nature of learning: things to be known and names to be remembered. Both strive for an exhaustive encyclopaedic summary of all knowledge to be remembered. Kircher's diagrams in his *Ars Magna Sciendi sive combinatoria* (1669) employ numeric and alphabetic devices derived from the Lullistic tradition. Comenius's *Orbis sensualium pictus* (1658) invites adolescents to enter the visible, perceptible world with the aid of *pictura* and *nomenclatura* that comprise all fundamental things, actions and notions of the world to be remembered.

The concept of accumulated sums of knowledge owing to deductive calculation trusts in the countability of the things constituting the world, both visible and invisible. All schemata, from those of Raimundus Lullus to those of Giordano Bruno and Leibniz, lay universal claim to knowledge of the world (Rossi 1983: 203). The diagrammatic paradigm does not refer to temporal and social categories; it is transindividually oriented, relying on definite procedures of reconstruction, with knowledge being the only object of recollection. To reactivate certain elements of knowledge means to remember the rules of their storage. This means the assumption of a human faculty to deal with it. In this sense, Lotman's *Lectures on Structural Poetics* (1964) is a book that lectures on the laws governing the interrelationship between textual elements, the rule of narration, the interdependence of the literary series of signs and the extraliterary. Such an analysis conveys not only the knowledge of the text as a structured object but also the memory of such a knowledge.

A shift towards an anthropological treatment of memory can be seen in Giambattista Vico's treatise *Szienza Nuova* (1744), in which Vico defines *phantasia*, *memoria* and *ingenium* as human faculties or capacities that are indivisible to each other (Trabant 1993: 406–24). Whereas fantasy transforms what memory offers, *ingenium* is the faculty that orders and registers what has been remembered. *Memoria* is what Vico calls '*un universale fantastico*', a coinage that combines the notion of a stable quantity of memorabilia with that of its imaginary quality. Marcel Danesi, comparing Vico's and Lotman's (the 'two ground-breaking thinkers') sign systems, emphasizes the *fantasia* aspect, imagination being the driving force in the mnemonic modelling of the world, an interpretation of Lotman's semiotics in which mind replaces the system (Danesi 2000).

The diegetic paradigm neither replaces nor competes with the two approaches mentioned earlier. In cultures that have developed neither a mnemotechnic nor a diagrammatic model, the diegetic paradigm features as the universal representation of *memoria*, which, however, functions as a semiotic matrix of all the guiding concepts of culture (its mythologemes and ideologemes). This matrix – which affects spheres of individual and social action, forms of social cohesion, organizations of life, practices of remembering and forgetting, or recalling – is a complex and controversial process of reconstruction that takes place in literal and oral genres: myth, epos, historiography and, of course, the historical novel. In societies without mnemotechnical concepts and without disciplines established for their cultivation, this paradigm represents the totality of memory reflecting the various ways in which collective life is organized. In the epic tradition, reproduction and repetition of oral texts (having recourse to certain schemes in metrics, *epitheta ornantia* and syntactic parallelisms) are such forms of memorizing. At the same time, they record events of the heroic past, which are constitutive of the way the epic community understands itself. The oral art of memorizing coexists with or is replaced by literal representation.

Literature appears to be the most prominent representative of the diegetic paradigm, the mnemonic art par excellence, not as a simple recording device but as a body of commemorative actions that include the knowledge stored by a culture, and virtually all texts a culture has produced and by which a culture is constituted. Writing is both an act of memory and a new interpretation, by which every new text is etched into memory space. Involvement with the extant texts of a culture, which every new text reflects (whether as convergence or divergence, assimilation or repulsion), stands in reciprocal relation to the conception of memory that this culture implies. The authors of texts draw on other texts, both ancient and recent, belonging to their own or another culture and refer to them in various ways. 'Intertextuality' is the term introduced by Julia Kristeva (based on Bakhtin's 'dialogicity of texts') to capture this interchange and contact, formal and semantic, between texts both literary and non-literary. Lotman expands this concept with the concept of 'transposition' (*transpozitsiia*) by including other non-linguistic sign systems in the dialogue of texts (Lotman 1969: 206–38). In her later works, Kristeva replaced the term *intertextualité*, which itself, incidentally, considers the transition of one sign system into another with *transposition* (Kristeva [1974] 1978: 69).

Intertextuality as the memory of the text demonstrates the process by which a culture continually rewrites and retranscribes itself. Every concrete text, as a sketched-out memory space, connotes the macrospace of memory that either represents a culture or appears as that culture. Furthermore, literature recovers and revives knowledge in reincorporating some of its formerly rejected unofficial or arcane traditions. (The particular mode of writing which deals with such knowledge is fantastic literature, especially in Romanticism. This mode of writing supported and nourished suppressed traditions of knowledge which ran as an undercurrent below the mainstream of the Enlightenment.) Authors of literary texts like to explicate their own memory concepts. The manifestos of avant-gardist movements (e.g. Italian and Russian futurism) proclaim the death of the established artistic–literary tradition in order to begin anew in its ruins. The corresponding literary theory, formulated by Russian formalism, sees literary (cultural) evolution as an alternation of systems, advocating discontinuity and disrupture as the moving force. Lotman describes changes in the annihilation of cultural heritage (referring to the futuristic formula 'thrown from the steamship of modernity' on the one hand and its veneration 'placed upon a pedestal' on the other hand) as having a sinus like character. Which is especially true of the Acmeists, who acquired a certain version of Henri Bergson's notions of *mémoire*, *durée irréversible* and *évolution créatrice* (Lachmann 1997: 231–61). Instead of defending the idea of a tabula rasa, the Acmeists 'yearn for the world culture' (Mandelshtam) as an imperishable thesaurus that they want to incorporate and to repeat, that is, to memorize, transforming it into a text.

In his readings of Nikolay Karamzin and Alexander Pushkin, Lotman not only applies diagrammatically his method of structural analysis, integrating a new interpretation of *Eugene Onegin*, but also follows the diegetic paradigm in those parts dedicated to biography (Lotman 1995 and 1997). This paradigm definitely dominates his work on the cultural history of Russian nobility (Lotman 1994). Here a definite sociological view accompanies his vivisection of certain parts of Russian society of the seventeenth to the nineteenth centuries. One reads this history, which he calls *Conversations about Russian Culture*, as the 'concretization' of his semiotic models – they are packed with social facts. His description of the Petrine reforms, especially of rank, as well as his narration of the habits of the nobility (balls, duels) are devoid of abstract terminology and deploy a definite literary quality. In this late work, Lotman relies on literature in addition to historical information. Literary texts (epic, dramatic, lyrical) serve as the memory place. Without explicitly referring to their artistic nature text fragments from prominent authors are quoted as witnesses of events and social conditions. One could say that in this comprehensive work Lotman applies his semiotically construed memory theory to perusing the vast complex of the Russian cultural cosmos, which was his perennial target.

Note

1. For a more detailed comparison of Assmann's and Lotman's approaches to memory, see Tamm 2015: 128, 133. A comparison between Lotman's culturological approach to memory with Alexander Luria's mnemonic concept shows a different striving for supra-individuality. Luria states that the progress of memory studies is 'bound up with the development of a new branch of technology, bionics, which has forced us to take a closer look at every possible indication of how the human memory operates', claiming that 'an analysis of an exceptional memory . . . should initiate this type of research' (Luria [1958] 1968: 6). Though he is interested in the interaction of memory and individual psychic 'behaviour', he, too, intends to discover a mechanism, a definite structure, a model, that is, supra-individual rules independent of social and even cultural conditions.

Literature

Assmann, J. [1988] 1955. 'Collective Memory and Cultural Identity', trans. J. Czaplicka, *New German Critique* 65: 125–33.

Bakhtin, M. [1963] 1984. *Problems of Dostoevsky's Poetics*, ed. and trans. C. Emerson. Minneapolis: University of Minnesota Press.

Carruthers, M. 2008. *The Book of Memory: A Study of Memory in Medieval Culture*, 2nd ed. Cambridge: Cambridge University Press.

Danesi, M. 2000. 'A Note on Vico and Lotman: Semiotics as a "Science of Imagination"', *Sign Systems Studies* 28: 99–114.

Goldmann, S. 1989. 'Statt Totenklage Gedächtnis: Zur Erfindung der Mnemotechnik durch Simonides von Keos', *Poetica* 21 (1/2): 43–66.

Halbwachs, M. 1980. *The Collective Memory*, trans. F. J. Ditter Jr. and V. Y. Ditter, New York: Harpers & Row.

Kristeva, J. [1974] 1978. *Revolution in Poetic Language*, trans. M. Waller, New York: Columbia University Press.

Lachmann, R. 1995. 'Tsennostnye aspekty semiotiki kul'tury/semiotiki teksta Iuriia Lotmana', in E. V. Permiakov (ed.), *Lotmanovskii sbornik 1*, 192–213, Moscow: IC-Garant.

Lachmann, R. 1997. *Memory and Literature. Intertextuality in Russian Modernism*, Minneapolis and London: University of Minnesota Press.

Lotman, Ju. M. 1964. *Lektsii po struktural'noi poetike, vyp. 1 (Vvedenie, teoriia stikha), vol. 1 of Trudy po znakovym sistemam*, Tartu: The University of Tartu.

Lotman, Ju. M. 1969. 'Stikhotvoreniia rannego Pasternaka i nekotorye voprosy strukturnogo izucheniia teksta', *Trudy po znakovym sistemam* 4: 206–38.

Lotman, Ju. M. [1970] 2000. 'Stat'i po tipologii kultury', in Ju. M. Lotman, *Semiosfera*, 391–459, Saint Petersburg: Iskusstvo–SPB.

Lotman, Yu. M. [1974] 1977. 'The Dynamic Model of a Semiotic System', *Semiotica* 21 (3/4): 193–210.

Lotman, J. [1985] 2019. 'Memory in a Culturological Perspective', in J. Lotman, *Culture, Memory and History: Essays in Cultural Semiotics*, trans. B. J. Baer, ed. M. Tamm, 133–7, Cham: Palgrave Macmillan.

Lotman, J. [1986] 2019. 'Cultural Memory', in J. Lotman, *Culture, Memory and History: Essays in Cultural Semiotics*, trans. B. J. Baer, ed. M. Tamm, 139–48, Cham: Palgrave Macmillan.

Lotman, Ju. M. 1994. *Besedy o russkoj kul'ture. Byt i tradiciii russkogo dvorjanstva (XVII–nachalo XIX veka)*, Saint Petersburg: Iskusstvo–SPB.

Lotman, Ju. M. 1995. *Pushkin. Biografia pisatelia. Stat'i i zametki. 1960–1990. Evgenii Onegin. Kommentarii*, Saint Petersburg: Iskusstvo–SPB.

Lotman, Ju. M. 1997. *Karamzin. Sotvorenie Karamzina. Stat'i i issledovaniia 1957–1990*, Saint Petersburg: Iskusstvo–SPB.

Lotman, Yu. M. and Uspensky, B. A. [1971] 1978. 'On the Semiotic Mechanism of Culture', trans. G. Mihaychuk, *New Literary History* 9 (2): 211–32.

Lotman, Yu. M. and Uspensky, B. A. [1977] 1984. 'The Role of Dual Models in the Dynamics of Russian Culture (Up to the End of the Eighteenth Century)', trans. N. F. C. Owen, in Yu. M. Lotman and B. A. Uspensky, *The Semiotics of Russian Culture*, ed. A. Shukman, 3–35, Ann Arbor: Department of Slavic Languages and Literatures, University of Michigan.

Luria, A. [1958] 1968. *The Mind of a Mnemonist: A Little Book about a Vast Memory*, trans. L. Solotaroff, Cambridge, MA and London: Harvard University Press.

Rossi, P. 1983. *Clavis universalis: Arti della memoria e logica combinatoria da Lullo a Leibniz*, Bologna: Il Mulino.

Tamm, M. 2015. 'Semiotic Theory of Cultural Memory: In the Company of Juri Lotman', in S. Kattago (ed.), *The Ashgate Research Companion to Memory Studies*, 127–41, Farnham: Ashgate.

Trabant, J. 1993. 'Memoria, Fantasia, Ingegno', in A. Haverkamp and R. Lachmann (eds), *Memoria: Erinnern und Vergessen*, 406–24, Munich: Fink.

Yates, F. 1966. *The Art of Memory*, London: Routledge and Kegan Paul.

CHAPTER 18
HISTORY
Taras Boyko

History is not a pursuit for those who have weak nerves. For a serious historian
this profession is rather sad, tense and painful. But at the same time this gives
hope. You see, where there is no danger, there is no hope.

– Juri Lotman (1993a)

In the winter of 1989, Juri Lotman prepared a short autobiographical note for BBC radio.
Unfortunately, the programme in question never aired, although four years later, after
Lotman's death, this note was published in the Russian and Estonian newspapers (Lotman
1993b). Describing the late 1930s and his high school years in this brief autobiographical
piece, Lotman mentions, in a somewhat casual manner:

We were waiting for historical events. We all had a feeling that we live in a historical
epoch . . . *we were Hegelians*, we knew that history follows completely untrodden
roads and that 'blessed is he who visits this life at its fateful moments of strife'[1].
We – me and my friends – felt ourselves to be [. . .] spectators of some sublime
performances. (Lotman 1993b, my emphasis)

The aforementioned quote can serve as a prelude to illustrate that Hegel and Hegelian
conception of history were constantly present in Lotman's thought, although with
academic maturity and his growing interest in semiotics, more often Hegelianism and
classic historicism acted as an in absentia opponent to his, as well as the Tartu-Moscow
school's per se, ideas on *history*. For example, in the mid-1960s Lotman elaborates on
the conception of cultural typology and the role of cultural universals, doing so in clear
opposition to Hegel's philosophy of history (see Lotman 1967; [1967] 1977; [1969] 1975).

For Lotman, Hegel's stress that the 'only possible history is *human* history and that the
only possible culture is *human* culture', while 'each separate stage of its development the
universal idea is realized only in a single national culture which, at that moment, appears
as the only one from the point of view of the universal historical process' (Lotman
[1969] 1975: 99) goes against the logic of the methodological foundation of a culture's
grammar (Lotman [1967] 1977: 216). Why? Because in the framework of the Tartu-
Moscow school describing any uniqueness, that is, being only one, necessarily requires
contrast with some other system. The Hegelian concept of history, in which differences
between epochs are the sole highlighted element and basically become absolutes, leaves
everything that is not a difference unmarked and thus not worthy of attention.

On the other hand, the 'historicism' of the Tartu-Moscow school and Lotman, in particular, stands on the opposite point. In his first semiotic monograph, while arguing against the juxtaposition of form and content, Lotman expresses hope that understanding the nature of structures within artistic texts will hasten the emergence of new research methods that could cover the entire complexity of a dynamic, multifactorial structure, that is, the history of human culture (Lotman 1964: 12; see also Chapter 25). For Lotman, that which is typologically common to all the epochs and civilizations should not remain neutral, that is, considered not to contain informational value elements, but instead it should become a crucial source of information about the specifics of human culture (Lotman 1967: 6). And what is the ultimate goal of this cultural typology? Lotman answers in his article 'Problems in the Typology of Culture':

(1) description of the main types of cultural codes on the basis of which the 'languages' of individual cultures, with their comparative characteristics, would take shape; (2) determination of the universals of human culture; (3) construction of a single system of typological characteristics relating to the fundamental cultural codes and universal traits that constitute the general structure of human culture. (Lotman [1967] 1977: 214)

According to Lotman, performing the aforementioned tasks and thus creating a grammar of cultural language 'will provide the basis for moving on to a *structural history* of culture' (ibid., 216, my emphasis). This ambitious agenda marks the crucial turn for the Tartu-Moscow school from narrow semiotic problems of particular disciplines (linguistics, myths studies, literature, etc.) to the study of the major and general issue of culture, that is, the turn to all-encompassing cultural semiotics (Lepik 2008: 26), with history obviously being its integral part (even though the place of history in the framework of cultural semiotics was not yet directly articulated by Lotman and his colleagues).

Hence, it is possible to conclude that the entire Tartu-Moscow school's (and Lotman's in particular) semiotics of history build-up basically starts around this time and around these anti-Hegelian ideas. On top of this, it is important to stress that the increasing focus on *history* here does not represent a radical 'historical turn' in the semiotics research programme; such attention coincides more with a logical extension within the ambitious cultural-semiotics project per se (Hałas 2013: 68). This entire thought about the gradual 'unification' of history and semiotics was highlighted on multiple occasions by Lotman himself (1992: 3) and also by later scholars (e.g. Grzybek 1994; Boyko 2014; 2015; Tamm 2017; 2019; Trunin 2017; Monticelli 2020).

History is . . . ?

When we speak about Lotman's scholarly contributions, it makes sense to highlight that it will be difficult for readers to find a clearly outlined theory of history in any one of Lotman's works or even a 'stable' definition across the different works of what *history* is for him and the Tartu-Moscow school in general.[2] Quite the contrary, Lotman's reflections on *history* are made up of rather scattered and often indirectly articulated theoretical observations which, for the most part, emerged from some particular empirical analyses of historical, cultural and literary phenomena (Monticelli 2020: 190). Hence, history-of-ideas-wise any reconstruction of what *history* is for Lotman is also bound to rely on a multiplicity of scattered notes. Lotman's definitions and understandings of *history* did tend to change depending on the context of the work it was articulated in, potential audience and even chronology of his academic interests. Nevertheless, it is possible to trace three key conceptions of *history* for Lotman, and this chapter will try to briefly reflect on each of these.

History as communication(al translation)[3]

In the programmatic 1971 article 'On the Semiotic Mechanism of Culture', Lotman and his co-author Boris Uspenskij rather boldly state that the fundamental 'task' of culture is to structurally organize the world around humans, to become the generator of structuredness and, in this way, to create a social sphere around humans which, just like the biosphere, makes life (not organic, in this case social) possible (Lotman and Uspensky [1971] 1978: 213), while the natural language in this context performs the necessary function of a 'structural "diecasting" mechanism' (*strukturnoie shtampuiushchiie ustroistvo*). Hence, it is the natural language that gives members of a group an intuitive sense of structuredness to the extent of forcing humans to treat as structures even such phenomena whose structuredness is not entirely apparent. Here Lotman and Uspenskij give an example of history:

> structuredness of history constitutes the initial axiom of our approach; otherwise there is no possibility of accumulating historical knowledge. However, this idea cannot be proved or disproved by evidence, as world history is incomplete and we are submerged in it. (Lotman and Uspensky [1971] 1978: 213)

For the scholars of the Tartu-Moscow school, it is sufficient that communication act participants regard communication as a structure and use it as such for it to begin to display structure-like qualities.

A few years later – in the 1974 article 'The Dynamic Model of a Semiotic System' – we can already see Lotman's first attempt to pinpoint what *history* is in the framework and overall context of the emerging semiotics of culture. Lotman notes here that the creation of a particular system of self-description reorganizes (*doorganizovyvaiet*) and simplifies (by cutting off what is 'superfluous') the object of research not only in its synchronic but also in its diachronic states, and, in doing so, in essence, such self-description creates a history of the object from its own point of view, while 'when a new cultural situation is formed and, with it, a new system of self-description, its past state is reorganized, i.e. a new conception of history is created [. . .] history as a whole begins from the moment that self-description of the given culture arises' (Lotman [1974] 1977: 200). While a decade later, in 1984, he would even go as far as to say that 'history is a necessary condition for a working semiotic system', while lack of thereof leads to the 'wave of myth-making' (Lotman 1984: 35–6). The key takeaways from 'The Dynamic Model of a Semiotic System' are that it is a (self-) description that creates history, and there is a constant and, to some extent, an inevitable need for reorganization. Description is a textual (in a wider semiotic meaning of the term 'text') phenomenon which is created as a communicative act with what is described (= past), while reorganization is nothing other than a translation (again, in a semiotic Tartu-Moscow school meaning of the term) of realia which happened back then into an understandable here and now, basically recoding due to some new needs, changes in 'language', form and so on.

In the aforementioned thoughts, we can already trace certain influences on Lotman of his friend and frequent co-author Boris Uspenskij, who presented and published his famous article '*Historia sub specie semioticae*' the very same year, that is, 1974, in Tartu. But on the other hand, it is somewhat surprising to see that no matter how similarly Lotman and Uspenskij were thinking about history in the mid-1970s, de facto the two got to the basic semantic discussion of the concept of *history* only much later. In the 1986 letters exchange, we find a discussion in which Lotman says to his Moscow colleague:

The meaning of the word 'history' is twofold (perhaps, not by accident): history as in historical events and history as a 'story about [these] events', a historical narrative. You must differentiate between the two when you talk about semiotic, retrospective and other qualities of history [. . .]. Today in a dream you told me that distinguishing between history as a chain of events and history as a story about this chain of events is superficial, since history as a fact of culture begins with a story about some event, and not when the event itself actually happens, and that as time goes by, real events develop according to the laws of storytelling (this dream of mine is proof of the identity of history and dreams). I agreed with you then. But now, in the light of day, I say that it would be best to look deeper into this issue. (Lotman and Uspenskij 2016: 595, 597, trans. in Trunin 2017: 352)

This 'deeper look' was indeed ongoing. For instance, in 1983, Lotman established a laboratory of history and semiotics at the University of Tartu (Tamm 2019: 17), while in 1986, when he was writing to Uspenskij about *res gestae* vs *historia rerum gestarum*, the last Soviet-era Summer School of Semiotics was held in Kääriku (it was heavily dominated by topics related to history and its place within cultural semiotics). The presentations delivered during this Kääriku gathering would later become the core of the twenty-fifth volume of the *Trudy po znakovym sistemam* with the famous foreword written by Lotman (see Tamm 2019: 15); however, as this text was a product of the year 1990, let us return to it a bit later in this chapter.

Meanwhile, another interesting piece which discussed the matter of history (and yet again appeared in cooperation between Lotman and Uspenskij with the latter being the editor who invited the former to contribute) is the short introduction to the 1987 volume *Iazyki kul'tury i problemy perevodimosti* (Languages of Culture and Problems of Translatability). Here, Lotman notes that any writing-based consciousness is characterized by attention to cause-and-effect relationships as well as what can be called effectiveness of actions, that is, what gets recorded in the chronicle is not when the crop was sown, but what the harvest was in a given year. This is also directly related to the particular attention to the concept of time and, as a consequence, the emergence of the concept of history. This leads Lotman to the expected conclusion that 'history is one of the by-products of the emergence of writing' (Lotman 1987: 4).

However, perhaps the first work of Juri Lotman dedicated entirely to discussing history is 'Clio at the Crossroads'. This 1988 piece was prepared for the newly established popular journal *Nashe Nasledie* (Our Heritage) (illustrating how the author did not have a purely academic audience in mind!) and had the subtitle 'The Idea of Law-governed Historical Development and Its Evolution in European and Russian Scholarship of the Seventeenth–Twentieth Centuries: In Correlation to the Current Situation'. From the very start, Lotman gives us a definition of history:

> History is a view of the past from the future, a view of what has already happened from the point of view of some concept of 'norm', 'law', or 'code' – which elevates that which has occurred to the level of historical fact, compelling us to perceive certain events as meaningful. (Lotman [1988] 2019: 178)

According to Lotman, the Renaissance-rooted scientific idea of the replicability of the process and the predictability of the result was transferred into history, and thus a 'link was established between a story about the past and an image of the "result"' (Lotman [1988] 2019: 179). Hence, the concept of an ideal model of historical development flourished in which there was a perception that humans are students attempting to solve one and the same problem, where 'some solved it in a way very close to the ideal algorithm, while others made mistakes', and the overall grand idea 'of a single historical staircase the upper steps of which were more advanced than the lower steps remained an unavoidable feature of the scholarly approach to history' (Lotman [1988] 2019: 179). Lotman questions such a concept of historical meaning in which history is seen as the movement from unconsciousness to consciousness. For him, the entire opposition of law-governed versus random created by classical historical scholarship does not exactly stand. He wittily notes that 'regularities in history [. . .] behave in somewhat unexpected ways and often present us with paradoxes that are very difficult to explain' (Lotman [1988] 2019: 181). In essence, developing over time the law-governed process is nothing more than a narrative text, and thus it's not surprising that the

> image of historical narrative has left its mark on our everyday understanding of history, for there exists a relationship of similitude between the chain of real

events organized in a cause and effect relationship that lies at the basis of historical regularity and the chain of narrative episodes organized according to the laws of language and the logic of storytelling. (Lotman [1988] 2019: 181)

But what does Lotman offer us instead? Firstly, he argues, we need to search for new models of causality. Secondly, accept that 'history stands before us not as a rolled-up ball of endless thread but as a cascade of spontaneous living matter', and within this cascade we inevitably have multiple colliding mechanisms with some designed to increase the entropy and thus limit choice by reducing alternative situations, while other mechanisms, on the contrary, create moments of choice and thus create situations in which it is impossible to predict the course of development (Lotman [1988] 2019: 184; see also Chapter 21).

Readers familiar with Lotman's late works, *Universe of the Mind* (1990a) and *Culture and Explosion* ([1992] 2009), will recognize here the clear influence of Ilya Prigogine's ideas about moments of bifurcation (see Prigogine and Stengers 1984), but Lotman wouldn't be himself if he didn't find a relevant reference within the Russian literary tradition. Therefore, the parallel comparison is mentioned earlier in this chapter, namely Fyodor Tyutchev's 'decisive/fateful moments' (*minuty rokovyie*). Lotman concludes his overall point on how the understanding of history changed by stating that 'history is not a unilineal process but a multi-factored stream. When a point of bifurcation is reached, movement appears to stop so as to permit contemplation over which path to take' (Lotman [1988] 2019: 184), all predictably leading to the somewhat poetic metaphor that 'Clio is no longer conceived as a passenger on a train that is travelling along a track from one point to another, but as a traveller moving from one crossroads to another and selecting which path to take' (Lotman [1988] 2019: 186).

The following year, Lotman published another important article, in *Wiener Slawistischer Almanach*, that often seems to be overshadowed by his better known 1990s books. This brief 1989 article – 'Culture as a Subject and Its Own Object' – is introduced by Lotman as a 'short exposition on some research principles' based on 'experience derived from researching specific facts in the history of culture' (Lotman [1989] 2019: 83). From the very start, Lotman states what he thinks to be the 'fundamental problem' in the semiotics of culture – the problem of meaning-making (*problema smysloporozhdeniia*), and by bringing up Roman Jakobson's model of communication basically explains the current hermeneutics-influenced (and obviously anti-Hegelian and anti-Darwinian) approach as:

The history of culture appears as the evolution of its interpretation by a contemporary audience, on the one hand, and by subsequent generations, including the tradition of scholarly interpretation, on the other. In the first case, the interpretation is carried out within the synchronic framework of a given culture and forms a part of it, while in the second case, it is studied diachronically and faces all the challenges of translating from one language into another. (Lotman [1989] 2019: 84)

Hence, yet again we can see even more clearly the stress on the communicative and interpretative nature of history as well as the inevitability of translation when dealing with the past. Perhaps on this point it makes sense to return to Lotman's previously mentioned introductory note to the theme issue of *Trudy po znakovym sistemam* in 1992, entitled 'Semiotics and History'. In this two-page preface, Lotman declares that 'during the past decades semiotics has changed. One achievement on its hard path was unification with history. The cognition of history became semiotic, but semiotic thinking obtained historic traits' (Lotman 1992: 3, trans. in Torop 2009: xxvii), and urges readers to stop seeing history as static matter and instead adopt a semiotic approach that is designed to avoid conventional halting of the historical process. Lotman directly argues the case for being 'historian-semioticians' (*istoriki-semiotiki*), for whom their own point of view must become one of the objects of their research and part of the historical process in its own right (Lotman 1992: 3).

The famous *Universe of the Mind* can perhaps be seen as Lotman's ultimate work when it comes to the discussion of 'history as a mechanism of intellectual activity'. It nicely gathers all the previously presented ideas on the problem of history, historicity and temporality into one long chapter entitled 'Cultural Memory, History and Semiotics' and, to some extent, reformulates those ideas for the better perception of a Western readership (e.g. Lotman's polemics with the *Annales* school when presenting the Tartu-Moscow school's semiotic approach to history) as the book was directly written for publication in the West. Thus, it is not surprising that when talking about Lotman's conception of history and historical fact, many scholars quote solely *Universe of the Mind*, for example the anti-Hegelian Marc Bloch's inspired comparison that 'history is an asymmetrical, irreversible process . . . history is a strange film because if we play it backwards we will not get back to the first shot' (Lotman 1990a: 230) or 'history is a process which takes place "with interference from a thinking being"' (Lotman 1990a: 232). But at the same time, *Universe of the Mind* is still a work where we can once again see Lotman's understanding of history not only as dialogue but also as communication(al translation) – for example 'the historian and history both are part of human culture but in principle they speak different languages and their relationship is an asymmetrical one' (Lotman 1990a: 271).

To give a brief summary, Lotman's conception of history as communication(al translation) stands on the premise that history is a multilayered and complex hierarchical structure with developments driven by laws and random choice, intertwined on different levels; hence, when we look ahead, we see various chances and randomicities, but when looking back, that is, into the past, these become governed by (historical) laws and based on patterns. This is why a historian only sees patterns and cause-and-effect relations governed by laws. He or she cannot write a story that did not happen, although, according to Lotman, the history of what did not happen is nevertheless great and a very important story to look into (Lotman 1990b: 2). The past is created according to laws and patterns which are predictable only from the point of view of the present, and hence history is always dynamic and open to dialogues and (mis)translations.

History as science (*nauka*)[4]?

Juri Lotman starts the *history*-related section of *Universe of the Mind* with somewhat provocative questions – 'What are the aims of historical science [*istoricheskoi nauki*]? Is history a science?' (Lotman 1990a: 217, on a similar matter, see also Lotman 1991) – and later, in one of the subsections, he accentuates how history-related scholarship is actually not that unique in terms of the obstacles it faces, because history, just as with many other areas of knowledge, faces the 'problem of language, the interaction between the metalanguage of description and the language being described' (Lotman 1990a: 269). Lotman is quite clear in his belief that we need to move away from existing naive faith in an 'absolute point of view' (i.e. the long-practised *wie es eigentlich gewesen* approach) towards historical semiotics and, as a result, be left to solve only the problem of translating the language of the source into the language of the researcher ('historian and history both are part of human culture but in principle they speak different languages and their relationship is an asymmetrical one' [Lotman 1990a: 271]).

Lotman's overall logic is that 'history is culture's memory' and 'memory is an instrument for thinking in the present although the content of the thought is the past', while the interrelationship between cultural memory and its self-reflection is nothing more than a constant dialogue where earlier texts are brought into culture and, in interaction with contemporary mechanisms, generate an image of the historical past (Lotman 1990a: 272). According to Lotman, this type of image of the historical past is neither anti-scientific, nor scientific. It simply exists alongside the scientific image of the past like another reality. But what then is this 'scientific image of the past'?

A few years earlier, in 'Clio at the Crossroads', Lotman emphasized the point that the whole foundation of historical science de facto rests on the idea that the historical process is governed by laws (*zakonomernosti*), while the very idea of law-governed events (which is also subject to change!) in essence belongs to scientific thought and was formulated under the influence of achievements in the natural sciences in the seventeenth and eighteenth centuries (Lotman [1988] 2019: 178). Thus, we have in parallel attempts at scientific reconstruction of the laws-governed events and language-biased images of the past related to 'culture's memory'. However, as Lotman continues on the same topic in *Culture and Explosion*, the overall complexity of culture with its multilayerdness and randomness of unpredictable collisions leads us to the conclusion that:

> harmonious picture sketched out by the researcher of an individual closed historical system is an illusion . . . we never encounter 'pure' historical processes, equivalent to the realisation of a theoretical schema. Moreover, it is precisely this disorderliness, this unpredictability, this 'spread' of history, which so grieves the researcher that represents the true value of history as such. Specifically, it is these things that fill history with unpredictability; collections of random events, i.e., information. Specifically, it is these things that transform the science of history from the domain of schoolroom boredom into the world of artistic variety. (Lotman [1992] 2009: 134–5)

At the same time, it is important to note that no matter the aforementioned theoretical suggestions, when it comes to Lotman's more empirical investigations into Russian literature and culture, readers can actually sense those *wie es eigentlich gewesen* vibes in Lotman's works quite often. A few examples in order to illustrate what is meant are the following: in one of his analyses of Alexander Pushkin's narrative poem 'Poltava', Lotman concludes that 'while the poem provides a poetic version of the plot, the sidenotes *reconstruct the historical* [version]' (Lotman 1970: 109, my emphasis); and, when investigating the everyday life of the Decembrists, Lotman notes that 'history is reconstructed [*vosstanavlivaetsia*] in this way' (Lotman 1975b: 54). Even in the programmatic 'On the Semiosphere', Lotman talks about 'real history' (*real'naia istoriia*), which gives 'another picture' (Lotman [1984] 2005: 217), while in the analysis of Nikolay Karamzin's *History of the Russian State*, Lotman goes even as far as to state that Karamzin's piece is undoubtfully a 'scientific work' (*nauchnyi trud*) and a wonderful literary work at the same time, and that, therefore, '*History of the Russian State* belongs to both science and literature. It belongs to Russian culture as a whole' (Lotman 1988a: 16).

History as actant

Aside from the aforementioned mainstream conceptions of history, an attentive reader of Juri Lotman's works might notice another minor, but nevertheless very interesting role history plays at times in the pages of his works. Lotman, as master of the word and passionate orator, occasionally tended to attribute to history qualities that are quite unusual in an academic context, that is, history became an actant in its own right. Obviously, in many instances, it was more of a metaphorical personification, although it feels important not to leave it behind.

History as actant is best visible in *Besedy o russkoi kul'ture* (Conversations on Russian Culture), as perhaps expected, as the volume represents a written version of the TV lectures delivered by Lotman in the late 1980s. To give a few examples: 'history again takes its course' (Lotman 1994: 13), tempestuous characters were born 'when history reached a tight turn' (ibid., 257), 'history drew Suvorov into a new war' (Lotman 1994: 283), 'history constantly creates myths about itself' (Lotman 1994: 288), 'riot in Moscow prevented it – history forced [Peter I] to change his plans' (Lotman 1994: 290) and so on. Aside from *Besedy*, we can often see history appearing as an actant in the publications where Lotman was somewhat less constrained with the tradition of academic publishing, for example in various conference papers, newspaper articles, afterwords. On the pages of such works, the reader might meet remarks like 'history is always right' (Lotman 1988b: 30) or 'with the close up observation history receded into the background' (Lotman 1988b: 31). For Lotman 'history is not free', but at the same time, 'we are also not free when studying it' (Lotman 1990c: 1), 'history gives neither fives [= excellent], nor twos [= fail], it does not say this is beneficial and this is not' (Lotman 1993a).

History here is alive ('history lives' in the volume of chronological spaces [ibid.]), it is a distinct character in the big picture, and it interferes. To correlate with Vladimir Propp's and Algirdas J. Greimas's narratological ideas, history constantly fulfils (either directly or through a particular actor) one or other character function in the grand narrative of things. The whole story is incomplete without history's contribution, because history is an integral element upon which the world and stories about this world revolve.

Concluding remarks

In 1990, the Polish translation of Lotman's biography of Alexander Pushkin was published, and to mark the occasion he wrote a new introductory article to accompany the book. However, just as with the BBC radio programme, for some unknown reason this introduction was not included in the volume, and was first printed only five years later in *Lotmanovskii sbornik 1* (Lotman 1995). This short piece is interesting for us because it is one of the rare works where Lotman replies to critics, luckily on a subject directly related to this chapter.

Lotman starts with a complaint that by that time (the introduction is dated 3 November 1984) he has repeatedly heard the accusations that in analysing texts, semiotics-based investigations overlook the complexity of the human being: 'history, the opponents of semiotics say, is the history of people, not of texts and codes.' In the critics' opinion, this human aspect of history remains beyond the capabilities of semiotics-based research. Lotman refutes such accusations by saying that he always believed that the human being, who can and should be an object of historical research, is a 'human being in communication with others, God, Nature, Culture, World'. *Homo communicatus* is in the communicative position even if he or she is in complete solitude and thus silent; then, it's just an instance of 'negative communication'. Hence, Lotman's conclusion: 'the human being as an object of humanities research is inevitably a semiotic human being' and thus studying him or her means researching the entire complexity of sociocultural codes which form the human being's self-determination and define him/her through the cultural, historical and social contexts (Lotman 1995: 85–6). But these definitions and contexts are neither static nor fully subjected to laws, that is, they are not laws-governed, because the thinking being does interfere and 'explosions' are inevitable (Lotman 1990a: 232), while history is nothing more than a dynamically temporal space of communication (and, if lucky, dialogue) where the codes collide, (mis)translation happens and (meta) texts are generated, immediately becoming part of culture.

Notes

1. The quote is a line from Fyodor Tyutchev's 1829 poem 'Cicero' (English translation by Frank Jude).

2. The dictionary of Tartu-Moscow school terminology (Levchenko and Salupere 1999) does not include an entry for history at all, while the entries 'Historical Process', 'Historical Fact' and 'Historical Description' are all based on Boris Uspenskij's work.

3. Why 'communication(al)' and not 'dialogue(cal)' as recently suggested by Daniele Monticelli (2020: 190)? Because 'dialogue' is actually a narrower concept that presupposes reciprocity based on code(s), language(s) and so on; the act of '(mis)communication' as transfer of information doesn't necessarily include reciprocal reaction (see Lotman [1984] 2005).

4. Although Russian is famous for not having a clear distinction between 'sciences' and 'studies', that is, every domain is called 'science' (*nauka*), in the case of Lotman it is definitely not just about a lack of semantic differentiation.

References

Boyko, T. 2014. 'Tartu-Moscow School of Semiotics and History', *Historein* 14 (2): 51–70.

Boyko, T. 2015. 'Describing the Past: Tartu-Moscow School Ideas on History, Historiography, and the Historian's Craft', *Sign Systems Studies* 43 (2/3): 269–80.

Grzybek, P. 1994. 'Semiotics of History – Historical Cultural Semiotics?', *Semiotica* 98 (3/4): 341–56.

Hałas, E. 2013. 'The Past in the Present: Lessons on Semiotics of History from George H. Mead and Boris A. Uspensky', *Symbolic Interaction* 36 (1): 60–77.

Lepik, P. 2008. *Universals in the Context of Juri Lotman's Semiotics*, Tartu: Tartu University Press.

Levchenko, J. and Salupere, S. (eds) 1999. *Materialy k slovariu terminov Tartusko-moskovskoi semioticheskoi shkoly*, Tartu: Tartu University Press.

Lotman, Ju. M. 1964. *Lektsii po struktural'noi poetike. Vyp. 1. Vvedenie, teoriia stikha*, Tartu: Izdatel'stvo Tartuskogo universiteta (*Trudy po znakovym sistemam*, 1).

Lotman, Ju. M. 1967. 'Ot redaktsii', *Trudy po znakovym sistemam* 3: 5–6.

Lotman, Yu. M. [1967] 1977. 'Problems in the Typology of Culture', in D. P. Lucid (ed. and trans.), *Soviet Semiotics: An Anthology*, 213–21, Baltimore, MD: The Johns Hopkins University Press.

Lotman, Yu. M. [1969] 1975. 'On the Metalanguage of a Typological Description of Culture', *Semiotica* 14 (2): 97–123.

Lotman, Ju. M. 1970. 'K strukture dialogicheskogo teksta v poemakh Pushkina: (Problema avtorskikh primechanii k tekstu)', *Uchenie zapiski Leningradskogo gosuderstvennogo pedagogicheskogo universiteta* 434: 101–10.

Lotman, Yu. M. [1974] 1977. 'The Dynamic Model of a Semiotic System', *Semiotica* 21 (3/4): 193–210.

Lotman, Ju. M. 1975. 'Dekabrist v povsednevnoi zhizni: (Bytovoie povedeniie kak istoriko-psikhologicheskaia kategoriia)', in V. G. Bazanov and V. E. Vatsuro (eds), *Literaturnoie naslediie dekabristov*, 25–74, Leningrad: Nauka.

Lotman, Ju. M. 1984. 'Simvolika Peterburga i problemy semiotiki goroda', *Trudy po znakovym sistemam* 18: 30–45.

Lotman, Y. [1984] 2005. 'On the Semiosphere', trans. W. Clark, *Sign Systems Studies* 33 (1): 215–39.

Lotman, Ju. M. 1987. 'Neskol'ko mys.lei o tipologii kul'tur', in B. A. Uspenskij (ed.), *Iazyki kul'tury i problemy perevodimosti*, 3–11, Moscow: Nauka.

Lotman, Ju. M. 1988a. 'Kolumb russkoi istorii', in N. M. Karamzin, *Istoriia Gosudartsvo Rossiiskogo*, vol. 4, 3–16, Moscow: Kniga.

Lotman, Ju. M. 1988b. 'Iz razmyshlenii nad tvorcheskoi evoliutsiiei Pushkina (1830 g.)', in M. O. Tchudakova (ed.), *Tynianovskii sbornik: Tret'i Tynianovskiie chteniia*, 29–49, Riga: Zinatne.

Lotman, J. [1988] 2019. 'Clio at the Crossroads', in J. Lotman, *Culture, Memory and History: Essays in Cultural Semiotics*, ed. M. Tamm, trans. B. J. Baer, 177–88, Cham: Palgrave Macmillan.

Lotman, J. [1989] 2019. 'Culture as a Subject and Its Own Object', in J. Lotman, *Culture, Memory and History: Essays in Cultural Semiotics*, ed. M. Tamm, trans. B. J. Baer, 83–93, Cham: Palgrave Macmillan.

Lotman, Yu. M. 1990a. *Universe of the Mind: A Semiotic Theory of Culture*, trans. A. Shukman, London and New York: I.B. Tauris.

Lotman, Ju. M. 1990b. 'O prirode iskusstva', *Alma Mater* 2 (4): 2–3.

Lotman, Ju. M. 1990c. 'Chem dlinneie proiden put', tem men'she veroiatnostey dlia vybora', *Alma Mater* 3: 1.

Lotman, Iu. 1991. 'Semiotics and the Historical Sciences', in B. Göranzon and M. Florin (eds), *Dialogue and Technology: Art and Knowledge*, 165–80, London: Springer.

Lotman, Ju. M. 1992. 'Ot redkollegii', *Trudy po znakovym sistemam* 25: 3–4.

Lotman, J. [1992] 2009. *Culture and Explosion*, trans. W. Clark, ed. M. Grishakova, Berlin and New York: Mouton de Gruyter.

Lotman, Ju. M. 1993a. 'Nam vse neobkhodimo. Lishnego nichego v mire net . . .', *Estoniia*, 13 February, 31.

Lotman, Ju. M. 1993b. '"Prosmatrivaia zhizn's ieio nachala . . .": Vospominaniia', *Nezavisimaia gazeta*, 11 November, 216 (640).

Lotman, Ju. M. 1994. *Besedy o russkoi kul'ture: Byt i traditsii russkogo dvorianstva (XVIII – nachalo XIX veka)*, Saint Petersburg: Isskustvo-SPB.

Lotman, Ju. M. 1995. 'Aleksandr Sergeevich Pushkin. Biografiia pisatelia', in E. V. Permiakov (ed.), *Lotmanovskii sbornik*, vol. 1, 85–8, Moscow: IC-Garant.

Lotman, Yu. M. and Uspenskij, B. A. [1971] 1978. 'On the Semiotic Mechanism of Culture', trans. G. Mihaychuk, *New Literary History* 9 (2): 211–32.

Lotman, Ju. M. and Uspenskij, B. A. 2016. *Perepiska 1964–1993*, eds. O. Kel'bert, M. Trunin, B. Uspenskij, Tallinn: Tallinn University Press.

Monticelli, D. 2020. 'Thinking the New After the Fall of the Berlin Wall: Juri Lotman's Dialogism of History', *Rethinking History* 24 (2): 184–208.

Prigogine, I. and Stengers, I. 1984. *Order out of Chaos: Man's New Dialogue with Nature*, Toronto: Bantam Books.

Tamm, M. 2017. 'Introduction: Semiotics and History Revisited', *Sign Systems Studies* 45 (3/4): 211–29.

Tamm, M. 2019. 'Introduction: Juri Lotman's Semiotic Theory of History and Cultural Memory', in J. Lotman, *Culture, Memory and History: Essays in Cultural Semiotics*, ed. M. Tamm, trans. B. J. Baer, 1–26, Cham: Palgrave Macmillan.

Torop, P. 2009. 'Foreword: Lotmanian Explosion', in J. Lotman, *Culture and Explosion*, trans. W. Clark, ed. M. Grishakova, xxvii–xxxix, Berlin and New York: Mouton de Gruyter.

Trunin, M. 2017. 'Semiosphere and History: Toward the Origins of the Semiotic Approach to History', *Sign Systems Studies* 45 (3/4): 335–60.

Uspenskij, B. A. 1974. 'Historia Sub Specie Semioticae', in Ju. M. Lotman (ed.), *Materialy vsesoiuznogo simpoziuma po vtorichnym modeliruiushchim sistemam I (5)*, 119–130, Tartu: State University of Tartu Press.

CHAPTER 19
BIOGRAPHY
Jan Levchenko

Biography was within Juri Lotman's research interest from at least the mid-1950s, when his first works about Russian culture were published, focusing on individual authors in their social and historical contexts. However, until the early 1970s there was no trace of any special concept of biography in Lotman's works. That concept was shaped in the course of the self-reflection that seized the intellectuals of the 1970s after a decade of social and cultural revival – whether youth movements in Europe and the United States or the so-called 'Thaw' in the USSR. For Soviet semiotics, the 1960s also became the era of Sturm und Drang,[1] while the next period heralded a transition to more specific topics and the development of 'ad hoc theories' (Torop 1992: 8). The concept of biography as a 'textualization' of life[2] took shape in the Tartu-Moscow Semiotic School during the 'long seventies', or the period from 1968 to the death of Leonid Brezhnev in 1982 (Bönker 2013: 210), or even Perestroika from 1985 (Lipovetsky and Berg 2011: 207).

The problematization of biography in Russian literary scholarship dates back to the 1920s, to the time of a brief blossoming of new cultural dimensions that responded to the challenges of the First World War and the Russian Revolution. The studies of Grigory Vinokur, Alexander Gabrichevsky and Ivan Rozanov (Brintlinger 2018) were too sophisticated and did not prove useful between the 1930 and 1950s, although this was the period when the genre of biography, the evolution and actions of a historical person, became the leading tune in the literary field. However, this type of biography was not operated by literary mechanisms but by administrative prohibitions and prescriptions, a convenient equivalent of ritual. First of all, biographies were written for the heroes of the revolutionary pantheon, with hagiographic templates coming into play. The other individuals approved by the censorship could only enjoy a lengthy and refined version of the genre, which was called 'autobiography' and 'characterization' in the bureaucratic language, complementing the diaries that were popular in the Stalinist era and imbued with self-censorship (see Jones 2018).

The stereotypical biographies were written in a monotonous style, had a limited subject matter and were uninformative in their description of the individual characteristics, contradictions and conflicts that are an integral part of an outstanding historical figure. At the same time, despite the political indulgences during the Thaw, a mechanical rejection of the biographical canon was impossible. Obviously, any changes in the dominant discourse and mindset happen slowly. Throughout the late Soviet era until the beginning of Perestroika in the mid-1980s, a single principle was preserved: the value of the historical person in question was determined by their connection with the 'revolutionary movement' that was essential to official Soviet history. Mihhail Lotman mentions that his parents humorously classified writers according to their degree of unreliability: some adhered to the 'reactionists', but could be saved ('rescued from the burning shed'), some were 'strong reactionists' themselves, but not as odious as others, and so on (M. Lotman 2015: 425).

Biography and/as historical description

The title of Lotman's first monograph is *Andrei Sergeevich Kaisarov i literaturno-obshchestvennaia bor'ba ego vremeni* (Andrei Sergeevich Kaisarov and the Literary and Social Struggle of His Time) (1958). It is the biography of a person whose validity had to be proved by organizing the facts of his life against the background of his time while taking into account ideological demands. The book was published five years after Stalin's death and emphasized thematic, substantive but certainly not discursive innovations. The attempt to deviate from the ritual exaltation of the character and the furious condemnation of his opponents of the most neutral description of the historical texture was already a step forward. The interest in Kaisarov's personality was a direct consequence of Lotman moving to Tartu and studying the history of Russian philology, which had existed at the local university for a century and a half by that time. Andrey Kaisarov briefly served as a professor of Russian literature at Dorpat University, which established him in the local context, and his thesis on releasing 'slaves' (i.e. 'peasants') in Russia (1807) served as a pass to Soviet historiography.

From the first page of the introduction Lotman presents Kaisarov through the optics of 'noble revolutionism' (in terms of Lenin) and mentions his loyalty using such concepts as 'vicious liberalism' (Lotman 1958: 5). Kaisarov falls into the category of the predecessors of the Decembrist revolt, something that Lotman emphasizes by quoting the opinion of official Soviet historian Militsa Nechkina on the 'ideological origins' of the Decembrists, dating back to the war of 1812. Kaisarov's local identity is also translated into the language of Soviet ritual: the position of the Russian professor in the Estonian university contributed to 'strengthening the ties of the progressive society of Russia and the Baltic states' (Lotman 1958: 7). In this regard, we may recall an aphorism by Boris Eikhenbaum: a history 'is a particular method of studying the present with the aid of facts from the past' (quoted in Any 1990: 239).

Kaisarov's biography has three key elements, which are (1) Andrei Turgenev's so-called 'Friendly Literary Society' in which Kaisarov supported the civic mission of literature, contrasting it with sentimentalism and emerging romanticism; (2) a dissertation on the emancipation of peasants, which Kaisarov prepared in Edinburgh and defended in Göttingen in 1806, (3) his activity as a Dorpat (Tartu) professor. Almost thirty years later, Lotman would write that the construction of a biographical narrative requires a choice of events, that is, moments when the routine course of things is disrupted (Lotman [1986] 1992: 367). Although the principles of organizing a biographical narration had not yet received separate interest here, the structure of the text suggested the replacement of events in chronological order by reflexive selection and combination (in the classical terms of Jakobson [1956] 1971: 74). A biography can be successful when its author knows what should be selected from the information about the character and for what purpose.

The next year Lotman published a short article titled 'Towards the Biography of Yakov Kozelsky' in the journal *Voprosy filosofii*, which was dedicated to a prominent figure of the Ukrainian Enlightenment of the eighteenth century, the author of treatises on arithmetic, mechanics and metaphysics. This publication was prompted by the release of the first Soviet book about Kozelsky (Kogan 1958). It could claim to be a novelty in comparison with the literature textbook of the eighteenth century that was published in 1938 by Grigory Gukovsky, who would be Lotman's teacher at Leningrad University a few years later. Gukovsky and other scholars, inspired by the works of Russian formalists in the 1920s, instilled in their students a tendency to cover phenomena in terms of typology. Therefore, Kogan's book with its ideological pressure and vulgar sociologism rather disappointed Lotman. In his article, he proposed a genetic analysis of Kozelsky's views and supplemented the biographical component with some details from letters found in Moscow archives. Biography in this work is construed as the accumulation of facts even to a greater extent than in the book about Kaisarov, probably because of the lack of information about the person. At that time, Lotman was just getting ready to read a new course on structural poetics[3] and considered himself a pure historian, which saved him from active participation in the ideological battles in which Soviet humanitarians were forced to engage.

Biography and/as secondary modelling

In the same year that Lotman's first structuralist course was published as *Lektsii po struktural'noi poetike* (Lectures on Structural Poetics) (1964), the summer schools on Secondary Modelling Systems were launched, contributing to a brief period in which Tartu flourished as a 'hub' for progressive Soviet intellectuals. It is hard to underestimate the role of this period, which ended in 1970, in Lotman's own biography. The volume and the variety of work he did in the 1960s can only be explained by the powerful motivation given by the community, which suddenly, albeit naturally rallied. In this sense, the 'short sixties' provided a resource for reflection and regrouping intrinsic to the 'long seventies'.

There are plenty of historical and literary works related to familiar topics among Lotman's works of the structuralist period, in particular articles about Alexander Radishchev (a PhD thesis about him was defended back in 1952) or biographical articles about Kaisarov and a number of other individuals for the *Short Literary Encyclopaedia* of 1966. But a theoretical interpretation of biography is not yet within their focus. Some traces of these reflections are seen in the short sketches, which, in the next decade, will be unfolded in the papers on the poetics of the everyday behaviour, as well as in Lotman's biography of Pushkin. For instance, the abstracts of the second summer school contain the title 'The Modelling Significance of the Concepts "End" and "Beginning" in Artistic Texts' ([1966] 1976) in which Lotman remarks on the special structural significance of these text elements and shows that culture can easily project them onto a human life. Certain epochs, such as romanticism or early modernism, saw a particularly active 'modelling' of life based on a textual form, and literary biographies compete with real ones or even supersede them ('live and die like a poet'). This does not mean that in more pragmatic periods (e.g. naturalism in painting and realism in literature) the categories of beginning and end did not make sense. Leo Tolstoy, describing the first phases of his life in *Childhood, Adolescence, Youth*, likewise ascribed the properties of a teleologically organized process to life and confirmed his sensitivity to its finale with such works as *Three Deaths* ([1966] 1976: 11) or, e.g. *The Death of Ivan Ilyich*.

The idea of organizing life as a literary text and its close connection with life was elaborated in the works of the mid-1970s on the semiotics of everyday behaviour. These studies on the history of culture have references to the biographical experience of Lotman himself. Like many other intellectuals, he was not a dissident in the literal sense, but frequently displayed opposing views, influenced by the sad changes in the USSR from the 1970s. Therefore, a number of articles on special types of behaviour in imperial Russia in the eighteenth and nineteenth centuries, which were written in the mid-1970s, regardless of the authors' conscious intentions, expose a search for identification models, ethical guidelines and templates for the thoughtful construction of a biography at a time of intensifying reaction.

Papers on cultures of behaviour, following the patterns of texts, do not form a complete research book. Speaking in Lotman's style, they form a 'bunch' of research, using different materials to work out the general idea – the creation of an 'abnormal', strange behavioural strategy against the background of a norm, rigidly imposed on society. That is the characteristic of the eccentric figures of the Russian Enlightenment in the eighteenth century when a quickly borrowed cultural language was added to the high degree of ritualization. Adherents to romanticist ideology, whether Decembrists (a sublime version) or Khlestakov (a low type of romanticism), implement their programme of play behaviour in their own way. The models of the first half of the nineteenth-century demonstrate evolutionary trajectories closely related to the social and political climate of the era. Thus, the work on Khlestakov demonstrates a slowdown in the development of Russian society under Nicholas I, its 'frozenness', which is a direct consequence of the despotic power (Lotman [1975a] 1985: 184). Khlestakov, with his self-contempt and obsessive desire to be someone else, appears as a tragic product of a society in which relationships rest on the presumption of guilt and the creation of the external in the absence of the internal. Readers of such an article could and undoubtedly did draw their own conclusions, sharing the author's experience of living in the Soviet Union in the 1970s. Studying Russian literature of the eighteenth and nineteenth centuries, as well as writing historical novels, traditionally granted options to show transparent historical analogies. The tzarist power, its despotism and lawlessness had to be condemned in the USSR, and this imperative led to parallels that did not require commentaries.

Lotman was a cultural historian who was not fascinated by theoretical concepts alone, but rather in the context of their ability to explain phenomena, the study of which required more than a simple description of sources (see also Chapter 25). In his article on the theatricality in Russian culture, which was the start of a series of works on behaviour ([1973] 1975), Lotman quoted the folklorist Petr Bogatyrev, who had been engaged in the total semiosis of the folk theatre back in the 1920s. Lotman needed the idea of human reincarnation and the transformation of things into 'signs of things' ([1973] 1975: 53) to project it onto his own historical material. In his article about Khlestakov in 1975, he unexpectedly mentioned Charles S. Peirce and his follower Charles Morris, who were needed to interpret the term 'pragmatics' (Lotman [1975b] 1985: 162), and, as researchers had already pointed out (Salupere 2017: 61), Lotman did not read American classics, being satisfied with some brief summaries. The theoretical message of Lotman's texts was based on generalizations of a colossal amount of historical material, which demonstrated the logic of preserved and changing views over extended periods of history. Lotman did not just borrow the terms that created the conceptual framework of the metalanguage but rethought them with a shift in meaning. This approach also shows that he did not see history as a self-sufficient continuum of information, but rather as a source of projections to understand what was here and now.

In his works on the semiotics of behaviour, Lotman did not so much move chronologically as he examined from different angles the phenomena that had had his constant interest throughout his scientific biography. One of Lotman's students wrote about this feature in a work devoted to a special course on the Decembrists, which had already been conceived in the late 1980s, but was never given. As a very young man, Lotman, in his correspondence with the literary historian Yulian Oksman, wittily wrote that his ideas flew before his eyes, and he only turned his head right and left, like a cat watching birds (Parsamov 2016). The Decembrists, who caught Lotman's interest when he was still a university student, engaged him throughout his life. His first publication in 1949 was devoted to Matvey Dmitriev-Mamonov's *Short Instruction to Russian Knights*, a forgotten monument to the Decembrist idea that triggered Lotman's correspondence with Oksman as a leading expert on the Decembrist movement. The studies of the works of Alexander Radishchev in the 1950s led Lotman, on the one hand, to Nikolai Karamzin's concept of history, which took shape in the fundamental book *Sotvorenie Karamzina* (1987) several decades later. On the other hand, Radishchev's prominent position in the revolutionary movement also accentuated his ties with the Decembrist theme, which were shown in a number of historical and literary works (e.g. about Vyazemsky and the Decembrist Movement (Lotman 1960)).

The article 'The Decembrist in Everyday Life' ([1975a] 1985), written in the same year as the voluminous text about Khlestakov, demonstrates the importance of optics through which one may look at a well-known subject from a new angle. It is this property of Lotman's texts that Richard Wortman noted in his review of a collection of translations, which, among other things, included articles on the semiotics of behaviour (Wortman 1986: 434). It is no coincidence that Lotman focuses on the growing importance of gesture in the behaviour of the Decembrists, who loved to speak and emphasized, above all, the importance of symbolism instead of the pragmatics of an action (Lotman [1975a] 1985: 105). Postulating that actions and words change places in the speech behaviour of the Decembrists, that the Decembrists tend to polarize evaluations and exclude the very possibility of a neutral perception of the surrounding life (Lotman [1975a] 1985: 107–8), Lotman offers a version of the cultural anthropology of Brezhnev's 'stagnation' with its endless kitchen conversations, disputes about spirituality, the role and mission of the intelligentsia along with its imposed social impotence. There are no direct analogies, but incomplete references in the mould of the allusions that Lotman analyses in his own historical material. Thus, for a paranoid member of a 'secret society', allusions are more important than words, and the people of the 1970s could say the same.

The intermediate result of the cycle was an article on the poetics of everyday behaviour ([1977] 1985) in which Lotman drew a detailed structuralist scheme of the behaviour of the nobility in the eighteenth century. It includes all 'basic types of behaviour which could be chosen by the eighteenth Russian nobleman from among alternate possibilities' ([1977] 1985: 76). As in the 1973 article on theatricality, examples and extensive excerpts from sources were strung together to illustrate the key thesis, which claimed that the forms of routine life were text-oriented and therefore experienced aesthetically. Lotman returned to the biography of Radishchev, and used theatrical codes to explain the reason for his death. That was facilitated by the assessment of Karamzin, who unambiguously 'read' Radishchev's action in an adequate coordinate system.

> Perceiving one's own life as a text organized according to the laws of a particular plot sharply emphasized 'unity of action', or life's movement toward an immutable goal. The theatrical category of the 'finale', the fifth act, became particularly significant. Structuring life as an improvized performance in which the actor must remain within the boundaries of his role created an open-ended text. One new scene after another could contribute and add variation to the flow of events. The presence of plot immediately introduced the idea of conclusion and simultaneously endowed this conclusion with decisive significance. Death, particularly tragic death, became the object of constant reflection and life's climactic moment. Naturally this attitude brought a focus on the heroic and tragic models of behaviour. Identifying oneself with the hero of a tragedy determined not only the type of behaviour but also the type of death. ([1977] 1985: 86)

The established rules of behaviour, inherent to noble culture of the eighteenth century, turned into a victory of literary optics in romanticism to perceive and describe life. The ecstatic creation of life by the romantics irritated the next generation of writers so much that they defiantly rejected any 'literariness' and chose instead a 'natural', 'artless', 'simple' path. In other words, they pretended that their biography was written *naturally*, that it did not expressly unfold in front of a shocked audience. It is remarkable that in his studies Lotman hardly ever turned to realist writers who gravitated towards this apparent simplicity.

The case of Pushkin

One of the brightest events in Lotman's historical and literary career was the publication of *Aleksandr Sergeevich Pushkin: Biografia pisatelia* (Alexander Pushkin: Biography of a

Writer) (1981), clearly recounting the studies of the literary process of the first half of the nineteenth century. The work conveys the idea of biography as a moving continuum of meanings, where a person's life turns into an instrument of observing the synchronized politics, social life and work of culture. Lotman studied Pushkin as the bearer of the typical features of the era, who simultaneously managed to overcome the inertia of cultural reproduction. Pushkin is the embodiment of the 'literary turn', in whose logic the culture of the nineteenth century will move forward. It began with a pure imitation of European literary models and ended with the works of Dostoevsky, Tolstoy and Chekhov, which transformed the landscape of world literature. In this sense, Pushkin's biography could be used as a code to the laws of the entirety of Russian nineteenth-century culture.

The historical life of the first quarter of the nineteenth century, from the beginning of the Napoleonic Wars to the Decembrist revolt, as Lotman postulated, was a part of Pushkin's personal biography and the biography of the people around him (fellow students, fellow writers). The book begins with the link between a 'historical life' and a 'personal biography' (Lotman [1981] 1995: 23); in other words, the author places this conceptual pair at the very beginning of the text, endowing it with a special meaning, according to his own earlier theory (Lotman [1966] 1976). One should probably not overestimate the conceptual message of the terms in a popular book, where the word 'biography' is often adjacent to the word 'reality' (e.g. Lotman [1981] 1995: 29, 42, 65, 181), which renders the everyday idea of a border between the 'real' (life) and the 'fictional' (literature). However, Lotman clearly values the initial significance of the Pushkin generation, which was the first to accept and spread in Russia the new romantic idea of the indispensable connection between an individual's life and actions. The first to be perceived as complete plots are the biographies of Napoleon and Byron. The mechanism of narrating human life is still fully functional today. The romanticist era sanctioned the connection of a person's activities with the details of his or her life path, which constitutes the resource of myth-making that determines the existence of mass culture. The model of a narrative plot with a string of incidents would be used for the romanticist biographies of Denis Davydov and Kondrati Ryleev, Mikhail Lermontov and, overcoming the romantic discourse, the biography of Pushkin himself (Lotman [1981] 1995: 57).

Two approaches were shaped in the biographical study of Pushkin, which began in the middle of the nineteenth century (Petr Bartenev, Pavel Annenkov, etc.), one deduced biography from creativity and the other, on the contrary, isolated the everyday life and the creative element. Lotman disagrees with both, proposing to deviate from the mechanical identifications and oppositions. In his opinion, the poet 'speaks to the world in many languages' (Lotman [1981] 1995: 63) and is involved in different contexts, according to which a strategy of behaviour is chosen. From the early 1960s, Lotman relied on the linguistic branch of semiotics (Saussure, Jacobson, the Prague School, etc.) based on the chance to present any material in terms of language and text. It is not surprising that Pushkin's biography focuses on communication (of the poet with the audience, people close him, himself) and self-reflection (about his place in the world, his role and mission). Only an effort of consciousness turns an event into a text, or at least a meaningful motif. Pushkin was indeed the first in Russian culture to proclaim literature his profession with its own identity, ethics and system of relations. Therefore, the core of the plot in his biography can be defined as 'the poet's coming-of-age'. Lotman argues that Pushkin deliberately created 'a second biography' in his works that would unite his works in a common context in the eyes of his readers (Lotman [1981] 1995: 71). This practice had no precedents in Russian culture.

However, Lotman's approach to Pushkin's biography had recent precedents. The mentioned works on a Decembrist and the poetics of everyday behaviour of the eighteenth century became a laboratory for the problematic description of historical facts, highlighting the intense interactions between individual behaviour and collective norms. In his work on behaviour, Lotman outlined a complex picture of contradictions and contrasts, which, at first glance, composed a strictly theatrical age of Russian Enlightenment.[4] In his turn, Lotman needed Pushkin, who was an example of an outstanding creative genius capable of breaking the system of rules, to show the battle of the individual with history. The personal will forcing a break in the norm, fighting the system and/or community, is able to induce a cultural revolution. Pushkin's biography is seen as one more trajectory leading Lotman to the theme of culture dynamics, the conflict of order and chaos, the unpredictability and voluntarist change in the 'natural' course of things.

The biography of a scholar: Way – story – mission

In 1986, Lotman summarizes his experience of understanding biography as a phenomenon of historical description and literary genre in an article on the birth of literary biography in Russian culture. The main ideas of the short paper in a 'home' scholarly series come down to the following. The 'right to a biography' is a consequence of an incident, a deviation from the cultural norm. The role of hero or saint, robber or God's fool, gypsy or sorcerer, recorded by the historical chronicle, gives birth to a biography as an 'incident of good or evil' depending on the orientation of cultural codes (Lotman [1986] 1992: 366–7). Later, Lotman switches to the theme of the creator of a biographical narrative, whose role he systematically plays himself. He talks about the right to write a biography and doubts this right, which is granted to the renderer of the norm, for example a medieval chronographer. In a secularized society, in particular in Post-Petrine Russia, the interest in the author's personality is growing, and his own biography becomes the benchmark for authoritative statements (Lotman [1986] 1992: 369). While in a medieval Russia holiness was endowed on a writer through the use of the Church-Slavic language, where no lie was possible, from the eighteenth century a writer didn't just receive a privileged position, he or she was expected to speculate on the eternal and preferably give advice. A writer 'had to prove his right to speak on behalf of the Higher Truth' (Lotman [1986] 1992: 374). Postulating the logic of the evolving literary role in Russian society, Lotman in fact does not look beyond the middle of the nineteenth century, although it was precisely the transformations of the writer's status in the Russian industrial era that destroyed post-romantic career standards.

Significantly, the next year sees the release of Lotman's second book dedicated to the cultural hero against the background of the era, *Sotvorenie Karamzina* (1987). The title of the book already paraphrases the genre invented for creative biography without fictional associations. Lotman called his Karamzin's biography 'a reconstruction novel', while 'co-creation' (*sotvorenie*)[5] is a dynamic term that defines the observation of a historical figure in its formation and its secondary shaping from today's perspective. Lotman hit the nerve of the time with 'his' Karamzin, instigating a surge of interest in his works and personality, which reached its peak in 1991 when the Russian intelligentsia widely celebrated the 225th anniversary of the birth of Karamzin, and the newly appointed President Boris Yeltsin wrote a welcoming letter for the anniversary conference.

This astonishing promotion of a once-forgotten historian in the national cultural hierarchy derived from the widely held belief that all contemporary questions have their answers in history and that knowing the truth about national history, which had been concealed from the country by the ill-meaning Communists, would resolve all existing problems. (Zorin 2007: 210)

In this article, Andrei Zorin elaborates on the connection between the figure of Karamzin and the mood of the liberal intelligentsia and the significance of Lotman's research, who concludes his book with a statement about the historian's civic duty to speak authoritatively about the country's future. The process of 'co-creation' showed that Lotman, like Karamzin, moved along the path of releasing creative energy and strengthening the author's presence in genres that were deemed academic, neutral and impersonal.

By the end of the 1980s, Lotman, directly influenced by Boris Uspenskij, who contributed to the steady growth of his interest in the semiotics of history, started referencing *l'École des Annales*, which he prefers to call *La Nouvelle Histoire*. But the school's scientific emphasis, which goes back to Hegel, does not satisfy Lotman, who knows this genealogy in its Soviet adaptation and realizes by the end of his life that he is closer to the Kantian paradigm (see M. Lotman [1995] 2000). In a posthumously published article on the natural and accidental in the historical process, Lotman gives examples of heroic biographies of historians who stuck to their beliefs under the pressure of circumstances. A few weeks before his suicide, Condorcet, who was sentenced to death by the Jacobins, had been working 'on a book of a historical progress that embodies all the optimism of the Enlightenment' (Lotman 1994: 358). A century and a half later, Marc Bloch, who wrote his last work in anticipation of his execution, never mentioned personal activity and responsibility. He was not interested in random biographical turns; he stubbornly transcended his object. In this regard, Lotman expresses an important thought that ideas are 'more conservative than personal behaviour and change more slowly under the influence of circumstances' (Lotman 1994). And yet, his own view is different. On the one hand, he is still the same, because he returns to cultural heroes whom he began to study in his university years. But he looks at them through the prism of a changing concept of history. And the further he goes, the more personal and unpredictable expression of will are manifested in it.

A dispute over the limitations of historical scientism coincides with tragic changes in Lotman's life. From the summer of 1989, Lotman could no longer read or write. After a stroke, all he can do is think and speak. This drastic turn in his own biography also modifies his research trajectory. Receiving no information from new and re-read texts, an intellect is limited by its own memory resources, which has to redistribute them vigorously in order to generate messages. Aided by secretaries and students, they acquire a relevant text form, but noticeably differ, if not by subject matter, then by genre and style. Shortly before his stroke, Lotman finishes working on the article 'Culture as a Subject and its Own Object', which became his unique experience of a philosophical reflection on the semiotics of culture. Influenced by the ideas of Ilya Prigogine about unbalanced systems, Lotman uses the Pythagorean term 'the monad', which was further developed in the writings of Leibniz and Husserl, to designate the human personality in terms of its role in cultural evolution.

While examining the development of 'monads' and their interaction with each other, Lotman concludes that the juxtaposition of subject and object in the cultural process is conventional. This separation makes sense in artificial statics and a synchronous section. It 'can arise only when an individual monad, having risen to the level of self-description, models itself as an isolated and solitary intellectual essence' (Lotman [1989] 2019: 91). The last lines of the article speak directly about the cultural historian, whose position is now much more complicated than before, but closer to 'reality' (Lotman [1989] 2019: 93). Unfortunately, Lotman kept silent about the status of this term, although he implied it in his book about Karamzin, where he meant that this construct is as textualized as the phenomenon of culture.

The ideas of violating the norm and destabilizing order, which determine the course of Lotman's later works, make the scholar think about the status of insanity, whose effect can be borne by such a positively perceived unpredictability. Insanity, according to Lotman, is an important cultural resource, confirming its intellectual character. Speaking easily, in order to lose senses, one must initially possess them. Therefore, the cultural mechanism includes the possibility and even the necessity of insanity in times of crisis. In an article written in 1977 which is the start of his later interests, Lotman refers to Herzen (history as 'the autobiography of a madman' ([1977] 1979: 88)) and interprets pathology as a challenge leading to the creation of a new language. But in 1991, in an interview with the Tartu newspaper *Edasi* (Forward), Lotman is already talking about the 'real' insanity into which the world is slipping, and about the mission of the intellectual, who is allegedly able to stop this process (Lotman [1991] 2005). The essence of the concept is morphing: it is no longer a counterpart of reason, subject to semiotic analysis, but a threat to life outside the semiotics of culture. A physically perceptible irreversibility forces the old historian to discard explanatory mechanisms and heuristic parallels. The book of life has been written, his loved ones begin to leave him, and the body almost refuses to function. Reality returns in the form of fear of the final hour. But this human weakness does not negate what is proven: a writing individual continues to work in the collective memory as a generator of metalinguistic descriptions of culture.

Notes

1. This period, named so by Alexander Zholkovsky (1995: 7) probably for the first time, has a number of features: (1) developing new descriptive languages while preserving the previous research field (for Lotman, it is the history of Russian literature, mainly of the eighteenth and nineteenth centuries), (2) a circle of intellectuals formed through connections in Moscow, Leningrad and a number of other centres in the USSR, and (3) the participants of the new transdisciplinary paradigm being divided by interest (the editorial classification of the *Trudy po znakovym sistemam* included at that time 'General Semiotics and Linguistics', 'Myth and Folklore', 'Semiotics of Art', etc.).

2. According to Mikhail Gasparov, Roman Timenchik, who is now a world-famous historian of Russian Acmeism, said at one unofficial seminar: 'If our life is not a text, then what is it?' (Gasparov 2001: 323).

3. For the first time in the 1960–1 academic year, judging by Lotman's letters to his colleague Boris Egorov: the autumn of 1960 witnesses a 'new course in theory' (Lotman 1997: 124), and at the end of August 1961 a book is being written which 'smells' of philosophy (Lotman 1997: 132). Lotman's self-irony is understandable: the positivist historian treads safely through the scepticism about theory.

4. The concept of role allocation within the structure of the noble ritual is clarified in more recent scholarship. For instance, in her work on gender extensions of the behavioural repertoire of the eighteenth century, Michelle Lamarche Marrese argues: 'Unlike Lotman, who emphasized the "consciously theatrical" behavior of the Europeanized nobility and only minimally addressed the experience of women, I maintain that the worldview of much of the Russian elite was characterized by unproblematic cultural bilingualism' (Maresse 2010: 705).

5. The conventional translation of this term ('creation') does not embrace the shades of meaning expressed in the Russian original. We should rather speak about *co-creation*, since Lotman implies a dialogical process, during which the author simultaneously traces the formation of his character's biography during the character's life, reconstructs it based on a modern perspective and, last but not least, constructs his author's identity. When writing someone else's biography, the author rethinks and re-creates facts that do not exist outside the text, which means that the author re-creates himself or herself.

References

Any, C. 1990. 'Boris Eikhenbaum's Unfinished Work on Tolstoy: A Dialogue with Soviet History', *Proceedings of Modern Language Association* 105 (2): 233–44.

Brintlinger, A. 2018. 'Lives and Facts: Biography in Russia in the 1920s', *The Slavonic and East European Review* 96 (1): 94–116.

Bönker, K. 2013. 'Depoliticalisation of the Private Life? Reflections of Private Practices and the Political in the Late Soviet Union', in W. Steinmetz, I. Gilcher-Holtey and H.-G. Haupt (eds), *Writing Political History Today*, 207–34, Frankfurt and New York: Campus Verlag.

Gasparov, M. 2001. 'Semiotika: vzgliad iz ugla', in M. Gasparov, *Zapisi i vypiski*, 329–32, Moscow: Novoe Literaturnoe Obozrenie.

Jakobson, R. [1956] 1971. 'Two Aspects of Language and Two Types of Aphasic Disturbances', in R. Jakobson and M. Halle, *Fundamentals of Language*, 69–96. Berlin and New York: Mouton de Gruyter.

Jones, P. 2018. '"Life as Big as the Ocean": Bolshevik Biography and the Problem of Personality', *The Slavonic and East European Review* 96 (1): 144–73.

Kogan, Ju. V. 1958. '*Prosvetitel' XVIII veka Iu. P. Kozelsky*, Moscow: Academy of Sciences.

Lipovetsky, M. and Berg M. 2011. 'Literary Criticism of the Long Seventies and the Fate of Soviet Liberalism', in E. Dobrenko and G. Tihanov (eds), *A History of Russian Literary Theory and Criticism*, 207–29, Pittsburg: University of Pittsburg Press.

Lotman, Ju. M. 1958. *Andrei Sergeevich Kaisarov i literaturno-obshchestvennaia bor'ba ego vremeni*, Tartu: Isdatel'stvo Tartuskogo universiteta.

Lotman, Ju. M. 1960. 'P. A. Vyazemsky i dvizhenie dekabristov', *Trudy po russkoi i slavianskoi filologii* 3: 24–142.

Lotman, Ju. M. 1964. *Lektsii po struktural'noi poetike. Vyp. 1. Vvedenie, teoriia stikha*, Tartu: Izdatel'stvo Tartuskogo universiteta (Trudy po znakovym sistemam, 1).

Lotman, Yu. M. [1966] 1976. 'The Modelling Significance of the Concepts "End" and "Beginning" in Artistic Texts', trans. W. Rosslyn, in L. M. O'Toole and A. Shukman (eds), *General Semiotics*, 7–11, Oxford: Holdan Books.

Lotman, Y. [1973] 1975. 'Theater and Theatricality in the Order of Early Nineteenth Century Culture', *The Soviet Review* 16 (4): 53–83.

Lotman, Iu. M. [1975a] 1985. 'The Decembrist in Daily Life (Everyday Behavior as Historical-Psychological Category)', trans. A. Beesing, in A. D. and A. S. Nakhimovsky (eds), *The Semiotics of Russian Cultural History: Essays by Iurii M. Lotman, Lidiia Ia. Ginzburg, Boris A. Uspenskii*, 95–149, Ithaca, NY and London: Cornell University Press.

Lotman, Iu. M. [1975b] 1985. 'Concerning Khlestakov', trans. L. Vinton, in D. and A. S. Nakhimovsky (eds), *The Semiotics of Russian Cultural History: Essays by Iurii M. Lotman, Lidiia Ia. Ginzburg, Boris A. Uspenskii*, 150–87, Ithaca, NY and London: Cornell University Press.

Lotman, Y. [1977] 1979. 'Culture as Collective Intellect and the Problems of Artificial Intelligence', trans. A. Shukman, in L. M. O'Toole and A. Shukman (eds), *Dramatic Structure: Poetic and Cognitive Semantics*, 84–96, Oxford: Holdan Books.

Lotman, Iu. M. [1977] 1985. 'The Poetics of Everyday Behavior in Russian Eighteenth Century Culture', trans. A. Beesing, in D. and A. S. Nakhimovsky (eds), *The Semiotics of Russian Cultural History: Essays by Iurii M. Lotman, Lidiia Ia. Ginzburg, Boris A. Uspenskii*, 67–94, Ithaca, NY and London: Cornell University Press.

Lotman, Ju. M. [1981] 1995. 'Pushkin. Biografia pisatelia', in Ju. M. Lotman, *Pushkin*, 21–184, Saint Petersburg: Iskusstvo–SPb.

Lotman, Ju. M. [1986] 1992. 'Literaturnaia biografia v istoriko-kul'turnom kontekste (K tipologicheskomu sootnosheniu teksta i lichnosti avtora)', in Ju. M. Lotman, *Izbrannye stat'i v trekh tomakh*, vol. 1, 365–76, Tallinn: Aleksandra.

Lotman, J. [1989] 2019. 'Culture as a Subject and its Own Object', in J. Lotman, *Culture, Memory and History: Essays in Cultural Semiotics*, trans. B. J. Baer, ed. M. Tamm, 83–94. Cham: Palgrave Macmillan.

Lotman, Ju. M. [1991] 2005. 'Mir soskal'zyvaet v bezumie', in Ju M. Lotman, *Vospitanie dushi*, 169–70. Saint Petersburg: Iskusstvo–SPb.

Lotman, Ju. M. 1994. 'Iziavlenie Gospodne ili azartnaia igra? (Zakonomernoe i sluchainoe v istoricheskom protsesse)', in A. D. Koshelev (ed.), *Iu. M. Lotman i tartusko-moskovskaia semioticheskaia shkola*, 353–63, Moscow: Gnozis.

Lotman, Ju. M. 1997. *Pis'ma*, ed. B. Egorov, Moscow: Iazyki slavianskoi kul'tury.

Lotman, M. [1995] 2000. 'A Few Notes on the Philosophical Background of the Tartu School of Semiotics', *S: European Journal for Semiotic Studies* 12: 23–46.

Lotman, M. 2015. '"Teper' my sosedi. Ustanovim druzhbu . . .": Pis'ma N. Ia. Mandelshtam Z. G. Mints i Ju. M. Lotmanu (1962–66)', in P. Nerler (ed.), *'Posmotrim, kto kogo pereupriamit . . .' Nadezhda Iakovlevna Mandel'shtam v pis'makh, vospominaniiakh i svidetel'stvakh*, 424–73, Moscow: AST.

Maresse, M. L. 2010. '"The Poetics of Everyday Behavior" Revisited: Lotman, Gender and Evolution of Russian Noble Identity', *Kritika* 11 (4): 701–39.

Parsamov, V. 2016. 'Ob odnom neprochitannom spetskurse Iu. Lotmana ("Epokha dekabristov")', *Novoe literaturnoe obozrenie* 139 (3), available online: https://www.nlobooks.ru/magazines/n ovoe_literaturnoe_obozrenie/139_nlo_3_2016/article/11960/ (accessed 30 January 2021).

Salupere, S. 2017. *O metaiazyke Iuriia Lotmana: problemy, kontekst, istochniki*, Tartu: Tartu University Press.

Torop, P. 1992. 'Tartuskaia shkola kak shkola', in G. Permiakov (ed.), *V chest' 70-leti'a professor Iu. M. Lotmana*, 5–19, Tartu: Eidos.

Wortman, R. 1986. 'Review on 'Iurii M. Lotman, Lidiia Ia. Ginzburg, Boris A. Uspenskii. The Semiotics of Russian Cultural History. Ed. by Alexander D. Nakhimovsky and Alice Stone Nakhimovsky. Ithaca, NY and London: Cornell University Press, 1985', *Russian History/ Histoire russe* 13 (4): 433–4.

Zholkovsky, A. 1995. *Inventsii*, Moscow: Gendalf.

Zorin, A. 2007. 'Lotman's Karamzin and the Late Soviet Liberal Intelligentsia', in A. Schönle (ed.), *Lotman and Cultural Studies*, 208–26, Madison: The University of Wisconsin Press.

CHAPTER 20
POWER
Pietro Restaneo

Introduction

The ideas of Juri Lotman have often caught the interest of researchers and scholars from a wide range of disciplines apart from semiotics and literary studies. Often these ideas have been employed in the analysis of social and cultural relations in situations of subalternity, in the study of hegemonic and counter-hegemonic formations, and in a broader sense in the context of power relations.[1] Interest in the *use* of Lotman's work in social and political analysis gained more momentum with the birth of the so-called political semiotics. Political semiotics is a transdisciplinary initiative aiming to exploit some innovative concepts of semiotic theory in the context of political analysis and political communication, often relying on Lotmanian concepts (e.g. Selg and Ventsel 2020). Use of Lotmanian concepts in the framework of political disciplines, however, warrants the question: What was the role of political concepts in Lotman's semiotic framework? In particular, seeing as many of these recent works, including those of political semiotics, are centred around the notion of power, the issues of what 'power' meant for Lotman, and whether for him the word had any special meaning, become relevant.

The answer to this question is in the negative. As far as we can tell from the study of Lotman's works, there never was, amidst the grand goals of his research, the aim to devise a theory of power, or even a theory of politics. Neither the concept of power nor that of politics were ever central elements to his meditations. Among the countless aspects of his scientific personality, such as *literaturoved* (literature scholar), historian and semiotician, we can confidently say that *political philosopher* or *political theorist* never had a place. The reader can rest assured that the goal of this chapter is not to attach a new label to Lotman's character, attributing him hitherto unheard of exploits in political theory, analysis or philosophy (see also Chapter 29).

What we aim to uncover instead is the *semiotic model of power* that exists and operates in Lotman's investigations of culture. At times explicitly, at others implicitly, such a model is present as the necessary framework to explain the contradictions, struggles and inequalities within any given culture and society as both context and engine of cultural, artistic and literary development. We call it a *semiotic* model of power not in the sense that it tries to reduce the explanation of power dynamics to a semiotic dynamic, but rather intending that it strives to explain the *semiotic aspect* of power from within the perspective of a semiotic theory. It is also not, properly speaking, distinct from Lotman's general model of culture. It is rather the latter that includes, as one of its dimensions of analysis, the aspect of power relations.

To the contemporary scholar, the term 'power' has an almost over-abundance of meanings, and the traditions from which these meanings came are many and complex.[2] To begin our enquiry, therefore, it is preliminarily necessary to clarify which of these traditions and meanings Lotman encountered during his studies: in other words, which meanings of the term 'power' he could have had in mind when he began his semiotic investigations.

Power in context

From his earliest studies, Lotman had a keen interest in the history of political theory, due to his specialization in the history of Russian literature, and in particular the life and work of the Russian writers Alexander Radishchev (Lotman 1951) and Alexander Pushkin (Lotman 2003). Lotman gives special attention to the reconstruction of the authors' ideas on the nature of power, exploring in great detail seventeenth- and eighteenth-century political discourse (e.g. Lotman 1962 and [1962] 2003).

Regarding 'social power as the delimitation of individual freedom' was characteristic of that time (Lotman [1965] 1992: 151). Such a 'premodern' notion sees power as 'a contractually regulated or forcibly acquired possession that justifies or authorizes the political sovereign in the exercise of repressive power' (Honneth 1991: 154). The discussion is often focused on determining the source of political legitimacy, and the characteristics and limits of the institutional procedures aimed at the exercise of repressive power.

Lotman's interest in political theory, however, was not purely historical. He followed closely the developments of 'bourgeois' sociology of his time. This interest is attested by the numerous books, collections and journals on, and by, Western sociologists that he kept in his personal library.[3] In particular, he collected and studied, as testified by his handwritten *marginalia*, a series of volumes exploring the contemporary developments in Western sociology and society edited by the Institute of Scientific Information on Social Sciences of the Soviet Academy of Science, with such titles as 'The Problem of Social Development in Contemporary Bourgeois Social Thought' and 'Contemporary Conceptions of Cultural Crisis in the West'.

The most important source of Lotman's idea of power, however, has to be traced to the discussions and ideas circulating in the USSR in his time. Lotman belonged to the first generation of Russians born in the USSR (he was born one month after ratification of the *Treaty on the Creation of the Union of Soviet Socialist Republics*, which created de jure the USSR), and through his education was well aware of Soviet intellectual reality. The term 'power' (*vlast'*), in Soviet common usage, mainly meant 'State power and its exercise by the ruling Bolshevik Party' (Fitzpatrick 1992: 1). This is also most probably the reason for its absence from Lotman's works. Soviet political discourse, however, within the elite circles of academics, behind the monolithic propaganda that the state fed to the masses, was complex and diverse. Almost immediately after the revolution, the party sought to impose on all parts of society its own view of the world. However, the canon of orthodoxy, at the whims of which careers and lives were often made and lost, rather than an immovable pillar was a constantly shifting battle line.

In this regard a crucial battleground was the discussion on the notion of *hegemony*. Popularized by Lenin (Shandro 2014), the notion had an important role in Soviet political discourse at least until the launch of the Five-Year Plan. At its core, this notion was understood as the leadership of the proletarian class – or of its vanguard elite, the party – over the allied classes (Buci-Glucksmann 1980: 178). In the first decades after the revolution, however, the idea gradually evolved to signify 'the proletariat's ideological, organisational, educational influence on the semi- and non-proletarian strata of the toiling masses' (Brandist 2015: 110). The Soviet Party came to see the construction of hegemony as a complex effort comprised of several dimensions – political, economic, cultural and linguistic – each to be dealt with using the necessary degree of knowledge and expertise in order to elaborate the 'subtle adjustments to policy that the proletarian leadership needed to make in order to lead the peasantry and national minorities according to shared interests' (Brandist 2015: 188).

This notion had numerous repercussions on the research priorities and theoretical positions of various disciplines, and few others were as deeply affected as linguistics and dialectology (akin to contemporary sociolinguistics). The most important linguists of the Soviet Union were involved in the implementation of the policy of *korenizatsia* ('nativization'), launched in 1923 at the Twelfth Party Congress as a tactical response to the centrifugal forces of the nationalist movements of the former Soviet empire. Congress' effort was aimed at creating new, inclusive, language and education policies (Smith 1998). At the front line of the early phases of *korenizatsia* were Leningrad linguists and dialectologists such as Polivanov, Jakubinsky and Zhirmunsky. The goal of these authors was to restructure the study of the social aspect of linguistics according to the principles of Marxism (Brandist 2003: 216). The dialectologists in their works focus especially on explaining the role of the struggle for the construction of individual or social group identity and position within the socio-economic field as a fundamental factor in the modification of languages (Jakubinskij 1930), and in the formation of a 'language hegemony' (Zhirmunskij 1936: 17).

The semiotic model of power

Lotman's model of power rests upon a small number of core notions: self-description, dominant, description, individuality. These are purely semiotic concepts that are also part of the essential framework of his culturological model of analysis, thus familiar to many semioticians and cultural theorists. As mentioned, the model of power is not separated from the model of culture, it is rather one of its aspects. In other words, by describing the former we will simply describe the main components of his idea of culture from the point of view of their role in power and political dynamics.

The first and most fundamental pillar of the model is the notion of *self-description*.

Self-description

The development of Lotman's model of power is a consequence of the shift of his interest from literary texts to the typology of culture. An analysis based on the individuation of structural types, characterized by a certain number of oppositional qualities, is bound to pose some questions in the course of the analysis of diachronic processes. Culture is by definition the sum of non-hereditary (i.e. not innate) information from the collective (*nenasledstvennaia pamiat' kollektiva*) (Lotman and Uspenskij 1971: 147), and the fundamental categories of culturological analysis are consequently *transmission* and *conservation* (Lotman 1970: 6). Since no individuals share the same identical sets of languages and codes, 'the act of communication [. . .] must be considered [. . .] as a *translation* of any text from the language of my "I" to the language of your "you"' (Lotman [1977] 2010: 563). Therefore, its results are always, to some degree, new and unpredictable.

A culture complex enough to show organizational differentiation in the form of a typological structure cannot simply rely for its own diachronic existence on spontaneous acts of transmission or on the memory of individuals, as the risk of loss of information and disaggregation is very high. In less complex cultures this would not be a problem, as a simpler structure allows for more flexible and fluid identities. More complex systems, however, that rely on the unity of their elements at a metalevel to continue functioning (e.g. a state, which relies on the concerted action of several heterogeneous institutions, each with its own different subsets of goals and needs) must delegate their own self-reproduction to more complex mechanisms in order to avoid the disaggregating effect of the unpredictability of communication. In other words, the mechanisms of *transmission* and *conservation* of culture must be embedded with other mechanisms the aim of which is to avoid unpredictability, normalize deviancy and '"remove" the diversity of the parts in the name of the order of the whole' (Lotman [1977] 2010: 564).

For those mechanisms to work, culture needs to elaborate its own metalanguage of description, based on the act of self-observation. Such metalanguage is embodied in an ensemble of texts that contain the model of that culture, that is, 'self-modelling texts' (*avtomodeliruiushchie teksty*) (Lotman 1971: 170): the so-called *self-description* (the term can be used interchangeably to refer to those texts and the metalanguage they are the embodiment of). Self-description can have different forms, as it can be structured as a set of norms (grammar) or as a group of exemplary texts (Lotman 1971: 168). From the immanent point of view of a culture, it can serve different functions, for example to change the culture towards an ideal model of culture or to preserve the current culture against change (Lotman 1971: 170). From a semiotic point of view, it is by virtue of the elaboration of self-description that the unity of culture arises (*voznikaet*) (Lotman 1971: 170) and is preserved: 'the stage of self-description is a necessary response to the threat of too much diversity within the semiosphere: the system might lose its unity and definition, and disintegrate' (Lotman 1990: 128).

Self-description is the main pillar of the model of power (and of the model of culture in general) as it is the embodiment of the two fundamental forces of development of cultural dynamics: *unity* and *exclusion*. *Unity* is the force that gives culture a *self*. As the preservation of the self is the ultimate goal of culture – for the simple reason that otherwise it would cease to exist – it is also the *final cause* of all its actions, that is, it motivates all the actions of a culture. *Exclusion* is a force of opposition and discrimination that proclaims deviancy and seeks normalization. It allows a culture to avoid dissolving into another, and as such it is the condition of possibility of unity.

A parallel with Leibniz's notions of *active* and *passive force* is here most appropriate, seeing as Lotman had a great interest in his philosophy (Restaneo 2018). According to Kuno Fischer, upon whose manual Lotman studied Leibniz, the active force is 'the same as life or life-principle, that is the inner principle of action [. . .] to which the external action corresponds' (Fischer 1905: 776). The passive force 'is that force through witch each substance defends its own fundamental boundaries [. . .] that make it in a way and not in another: it is an opposition force [. . .] through which the monad excludes from itself everything extraneous' (Fischer 1905: 371). The interplay between active and passive force by means of self-description is one of the most important dynamics in Lotman's model of power. The essence of the hegemonic struggle can be found here, in the attempt of each component of the semiosphere to preserve its own *unity* through the *exclusion* of the other.

We are however still describing a metapolitical dimension, as unity and exclusion can be seen more as laws of historical development than political categories. A more practical, political dimension is introduced through the notion of *dominant*, the second pillar of the model.

The dominant

Lotman borrows from Roman Jakobson the definition of dominant as 'the focusing component of a work of art: it rules, determines, and transforms the remaining components, it is the dominant which guarantees the integrity of the structure' (Jakobson [1935] 1981: 751). Lotman however extends the meaning of *dominant* to signify any substructure of a culture that, in the struggle for unity, manages to 'subjugate the other [sub-structures] to its own organisation and obtains the right to speak [for the others]' (Lotman [1984] 1985: 132). Within the semiosphere, the dominant structures reside in the *centre*, the area functionally farthest from the border, characterized by high structurality and low semiotic activity. It is spatially and functionally opposed to the periphery, areas of lower structurality and accelerated semiotic activity closer to the translational border of the semiosphere (Lotman 1984: 13).

Any meta-descriptive system, such as the self-description of a culture (grammar), also has a normative function. This is because as with any description, a self-description can't be a 1:1 representation of its object.[4] The selection of what to include – what is relevant – in the description determines the division of texts and languages into *proper* and *extraneous*, just as creating the grammar of a language means selecting only one *correct* variant of that language among countless others. The selection is a *political act* (Gramsci 1975: Q29 §2)[5] as it determines the dominance of one variant over others.

A dominant structure is *political* also in the sense that its reality – what it is actually made of – is the programmes of action for the modification of the surrounding space, regardless of whether the dominant has a mainly cultural and artistic character (Lotman 1985: 134) or is embodied in political institutions (Lotman 1971: 173). For example, we can think in the former case of all the quarrels between schools of thoughts, letters, debates, articles, manifestos and competitions for prestigious positions and funds in academic institutions. In the latter case, we can think of the emanation and execution of policies, reforms and laws by institutions, as exemplified by Lotman with the case of the 'regular [*reguliarnoe*] State' of Peter I (Lotman 1971: 171).

One must not therefore think of the *dominant* as a static configuration. The absolute opposition of unity and exclusion is a temporary abstraction of an otherwise fluid dynamic process (Lotman 1984: 10). The dominant is an activity rather than a result, an *energheia* rather than *ergon*: it could never completely and in a definitive way describe and subsume the whole of culture within its own language. Extraneous structures can never be fully translatable with a finite number of semiotic operations, as with any translation. The result of the activity of the dominant will therefore always be, to some degree, new and unpredictable (Lotman [1989] 1993: 369), and the struggle of the dominant to maintain its own unity against any disaggregating effect could never be complete.

This notion has, for Lotman, two important consequences. The first practical consequence is that when the dominant attempts to modify the periphery through its self-description, the process is not unidirectional but dialogical. The resulting texts will be the embodying of a metalanguage that accommodates elements of both the dominant and the periphery (Lotman 1984 [1992]: 19). To describe extraneous structures or texts in its own metalanguages, even the most uncompromising reforming endeavour would have to modify its own semiotic system in order to accommodate for the untranslatable elements of the periphery.[6]

For example, 'the nineteenth century literature, in order to powerfully influence painting, had to include in its language elements of the picturesque' (Lotman 1984 [1992]). Even the autocratic government of Peter I in Russia was not able to annihilate by decree the old traditions: 'the "regulations" could not transform society to their own image, rather they were diluted in the customs' (Lotman 1971: 173). The second consequence is that the very activity of the dominant structures contributes to the birth of new, counter-hegemonic structures that can threaten the centre itself. As the periphery attempts to adapt and respond to the norms of the centre, its semiotic activity sees a radical increase, due to the input of extraneous material from the centre. An increase in semiotic activity fosters the development of the periphery, that can in time acquire the functions of the centre, setting in motion a new process where the once-periphery can emerge to the stage of self-description and become the new centre (Lotman 1984: 13).

The world of culture described by Lotman is a world of contradictory forces committed to the continuing struggle to forge and preserve their own unity. Dominant centres perceive their environment as chaotic and constantly, 'aggressively' (Lotman [1983] 1985: 133) attempt to assimilate and normalize the 'other' in order to reduce such chaos and the risk of disaggregation it brings. The fundamental semiotic mechanism by which this continuous struggle plays out is that of the *description*, the third pillar of Lotman's semiotic model of power.

The description

If the self-description is the foundation of the unity of a structure, it is also but a specific case of a fundamental faculty of any culture: the faculty of description (*opisanie*) (Lotman 1984: 12; [1989] 1993: 372). A *description* is not a passive, observational act. It always has a performative force, as it has the effect of transforming the object of description (Lotman [1989] 1993: 369), and the subject with it. By analogy with the theory of speech acts, we could say that description has a perlocutionary effect (Austin 1962: 101), adding however that such effect extends to the subject itself as it enters a dialogical relationship with its object.

Describing something means subsuming its perceived structuredness (or non-structuredness, in the case that the culture considers the outside as a chaotic non-culture) within the parameters of our own languages in order to be able to *distinguish* the object from the subject. The markers of distinctiveness, however, do not exist as such prior to the operation of observation, in the sense that they do not carry a special significance in the immanent conscience of the subject and the object. When two cultures come into contact, they enter a state of 'reciprocal complementarity and structural antinomy and start to cultivate their own specificity and the reciprocal contrast' (Lotman [1989] 1993: 371). There can be the case of a culture considering itself as 'the bearer of a metalanguage of description and, consequently, without any specificity but the incarnation of its own neutral norm', or of a culture that 'aspires to the role of bearer of the norm for all cultures' (Lotman [1989] 1993: 371). The end result will often be a description of the *other* that is 'elaborated in the depths of the given culture [the subject of description] as its own ideal anti-structure' (Lotman [1989] 1993: 375). Such is often the case of the dominant structures, as they perceive the surrounding semiotic space as non-structured, rather than structured with a different grammar, and aggressively bringing their own structuredness (metalanguage of self-description) through an 'invasion' (*vtorzhenie*) (Lotman [1992] 2010: 116) of semiotic texts. These invasions will produce, in the invaded cultural space, an increase in semiotic activity, as the attempt to produce texts responding to the canon of the invading grammar, which is de facto an extraneous language, will produce in reality *new* texts (Lotman [1983] 1985: 134).

Lotman's focus on the productive aspect of hegemonic-subaltern formations must be understood by remembering that he is first and foremost an historian of literature and culture. In this he is in line with an important Russian comparatist tradition that sees the main engine of cultural development, understood as the passage from one type to the other, in the encounter between cultures. Lotman in this shares the thesis of his former professor V. M. Zhirmunsky 'that every external influence is only an accelerating factor in the immanent literary development' (Lotman [1983] 1992: 111). Lotman then goes further in specifying that, unlike the former comparative tradition, there is a vast array of factors to be considered in which the impulse of development is not given by the similarity between cultures, but by their difference.

Lotman is however not limiting himself to the description of literary development. As he is trying to construct a general model of culture (Lotman [1994/2010] 2013: 53), he sees the described processes as pertaining to *all* the different aspects of culture. For example, when discussing the process of self-description, he states: 'whether we have in mind language, politics or culture, the mechanism is the same' (Lotman 1990: 128).

The foundation of the subject

A model of power would not be complete without an answer to the fundamental question: Who are the *actors* that live those power relations? Who are the *subjects* of political-semiotic activity and how do they operate? We spoke so far of 'culture'; however, the recursive nature of the semiosphere allows for analogous structures to be found at any level. Lotman, in later works especially, opts for a more comprehensive notion: that of the 'semiotic individual', or 'semiotic personality' (*lichnost'*). This represents the last pillar of Lotman's model of power and sits in the background in relation to the others, as their foundation.

Giving a formal definition of the semiotic personality was a fundamental problem for Lotman. The methodology of typological linguistics disregards *time* and *space* in favour of *isomorphism*, and favours morphological necessity over empirical generalization (Jakobson [1958] 1962: 523); it therefore tends to disregard the role of the bearer of language as it is mainly an *historical* entity. What worked for the study of language, however, encountered immense difficulties when applied on the study of literature, art, and culture in general. The main problem was that of individuality: unlike in linguistics, in the field of culture, art and literature the individual, that is, the bearer of culture (be it a human being or a collective) strongly affirms his or her own existence, individuality, separation and diversity from others, and most of all his or her own capacity of choice as the fundamental reality (Lotman [1992] 2010: 119). Lotman, as a literary critic first and foremost, spent most of his time in close contact with the great authors of the past, geniuses and innovators whose identity and individuality could not, in any way, be disregarded. To define a 'semiotic personality' posed for Lotman a pressing problem to be solved: 'the characteristic of being a personality has an intuitive manifestation and is empirically indisputable; at the same time, it is very difficult to give a formal definition of the concept' (Lotman 1984: 8).

Lotman later elaborates on his definition of semiotic individuality through an exploration of the Leibnitian concept of *monad* (Restaneo 2018). The semiotic individuality has a double nature. On the one hand, it is embedded within a continuous semiotic space, the semiosphere, and is 'part of [another] intellectual whole' and at the same time 'a whole in relation to its parts' (Lotman [1989] 1993: 374). From this point of view, the individuality appears to be determined by the sum of the texts and languages it is a part of. On the other hand, the semiotic individual is capable of behaviour, described as 'the ability to independently choose programmes of activity' (Lotman 1984: 14). The semiotic individual has to be capable of *rational choice*, so that his or her actions are not simple reactions to external *stimuli* (mechanical causality) but purposeful and goal-oriented behaviour (teleological causality): 'one of the main features of human collective is the substitution of a circular movement with a directed [*napravlennoe*, in the sense of 'aimed at something'] one' (Lotman [1992] 2010: 58).

Lotman justifies the apparently contradictory nature of his model of individuality by turning to the Kantian concept of *transcendental unity of apperception* (Lotman [1992] 2010: 12). The fundamental act of self-reflecting activity of the individual, which is only possible as it operates to bring unity to the multiplicity of empirical representations, cannot in turn be a product of those same representations, that is, cannot be empirical in nature. In Lotman's terminology, the faculty of producing a self-description, the self-apperception, is not a product of the semiotic activity; rather, it is its necessary condition of possibility. Thus, the individual is not entirely governed by 'strict laws of determination' (Lotman [1989] 1993: 374), or by texts and signs of which he or she is made. For complex structures, 'possessing intellectual faculty [. . .] between cause and effect occurs an intellectual choice' (Lotman [1989] 1993: 373). Albeit Lotman is not interested in exploring further the philosophical foundation of free choice; his fundamental idea is that the possibility for a semiotic personality to possess autonomous behaviour is embedded in the very essence of the semiotic individual (Lotman [1989] 1993: 374; see also Lotman [1992] 2010: 59).

Final remarks

Through the fundamental category of self-description, the essence of Lotman's model of power revolves around the concept of identity, of the struggle of an individuality (be it a person, a group, an institution, etc.) to build, maintain and impose on the environment its own identity. The originality of the model lies in the fact that Lotman elaborates a series of traditions from the unique point of view of his semiotics of culture, thus acting as a translational border of sorts between different disciplines. It is perhaps this intrinsically transdisciplinary character of Lotman's work that attracted many researchers from neighbouring disciplines to explore the opportunities for cross-fertilization offered by his models.

The exploration of Lotman's model of power also appears to be relevant to the researcher in history of ideas. Through his work emerge diverse traditions and authors, some of which are very little known in contemporary non-specialist circles, and whose ideas however might be still relevant today. We wish in the conclusion to point out two of these traditions.

The most important and renowned is certainly the one that revolves around the notion of 'hegemony'. Albeit in Lotman's time the term had already fallen out of favour, the ideas and works of the authors who participated in that debate had a distinct effect on Lotman, thus justifying the numerous parallels that it is possible to make between him and Gramsci (Restaneo 2017).

A much-lesser-known tradition, which instead had a surprisingly significant role in many of his papers, is the Soviet critique of European Orientalism. Lotman's most direct link with this tradition is through the figure of Nikolai Konrad, whose works he cites on many occasions (e.g. in Lotman [1983] 1985: 135; [1989] 1993: 374; 1990: 244), through the works of Nikolai Marr,[7] and through his colleague Alexander Piatigorsky, who was actively involved in the debate (Piatigorsky 1971). This tradition often anticipated numerous critiques of Eurocentrism and the nexus power-knowledge that are well familiar to contemporary postcolonial and subaltern studies (see, e.g. Brandist 2018; Tolz 2011).

Notes

1. For example, in Carlo Ginzburg's account of witchcraft (Ginzburg 1989: xxxv), in the subaltern studies works of Ranajit Guha (1999: 277), in the works of anthropologists such as Christopher Pinney (1999: 203) as well as the collection of essays on Lotman and cultural studies edited by Andreas Schönle (2006).

2. For a brief overview of the different approaches to the study of power relations, see Selg and Ventsel 2020: 41–53. For a historical analysis of the idea of power in twentieth-century Europe, see Honneth 1991.

3. Juri Lotman Semiotics Repository in Tallinn University, see https://www.tlu.ee/en/taxonomy/term/194/juri-lotman-semiotics-repository (accessed on 17 December 2020).

4. 'In that Empire, the craft of Cartography attained such Perfection that the Map of a Single province covered the space of an entire City, and the Map of the Empire itself an entire Province' (Borges 1975: 131). 'Every 1:1 map of the empire decrees the end of the empire as such' (Eco 1994: 106).

5. References from Gerratana's 1975 edition of Gramsci's *Prison Notebooks* follow the traditional notation where Q# is the notebook and §# is the paragraph.

6. The idea of the unpredictability of dominant processes is also present in Gramsci, specifically related to a language policy aiming to impose a single idiom as the unitary language of a nation (1975: Q29 §3): 'one should not consider this intervention as "final", and imagine that the proposed goals will be achieved in all their details, in other words that a specific unitary language will be obtained [. . .]; which language would be obtained cannot be foreseen and planned'.

7. While criticizing Marr and Marrists for their abstruse linguistic theory, Lotman saw some value in their anthropological studies of culture and literature (Lotman [1992] 2010: 121).

References

Austin, J. 1962. *How to Do Things with Words*, Oxford: Oxford University Press.

Borges, J. L. 1975. 'Of Exactitude in Science', in J. L. Borges, *A Universal History of Infamy*, trans. N. T. de Giovanni, 131, London: Penguin Books.

Brandist, C. 2003. 'The Origins of Soviet Sociolinguistics', *Journal of Sociolinguistics* 7 (2): 213–31.

Brandist, C. 2015. *The Dimensions of Hegemony: Language, Culture and Politics in Revolutionary Russia*, Leiden and Boston: Brill.

Brandist, C. 2018. 'Nikolai Marr's Critique of Indo-European Philology and the Subaltern Critique of Brahman Nationalism in Colonial India', *Interventions*, available online: https://www.tandfonline.com/doi/abs/10.1080/1369801X.2017.1421043 (accessed 20 December 2020).

Buci-Glucksmann, C. 1980. *Gramsci and the State*, London: Lawrence and Wishart.

Eco, U. 1994. *How to Travel with a Salmon & Other Essays*, trans. W. Weaver, New York, San Diego and London: Harcourt Brace & Company.

Fischer, K. 1905. *Istoriia novoi filosofii. Trom tretii: Leibnits, ego zhizn', sochineniia i uchenie*, Saint Petersburg: Izdanie D. E. Zhukovskago.

Fitzpatrick, S. 1992. *The Cultural Front: Power and Culture in Revolutionary Russia*, Ithaca, NY and London: Cornell University Press.

Ginzburg, C. 1989. *Storia notturna: una decifrazione del sabba*, Turin: Einaudi.

Gramsci, A. 1975. *Quaderni del carcere*, ed. V. Gerratana, Turin: Einaudi.

Guha, R. 1999. *Elementary Aspects of Peasant Insurgency in Colonial India*, Durham and London: Duke University Press.

Honneth, A. 1991. *The Critique of Power: Reflective Stages in a Critical Social Theory*, Cambridge, MA: MIT Press.

Jakobson, R. [1958] 1962. 'Typological Studies and Their Contribution to Historical Comparative Linguistics', in R. Jakobson, *Selected Writings, Vol. 1: Phonological Studies*, 523–32, The Hague, Paris and New York: Mouton.

Jakobson, R. [1935] 1981. 'The Dominant', in R. Jakobson, *Selected Writings, Vol. 3: Poetry of Grammar and Grammar of Poetry*, 751–56, The Hague, Paris and New York: Mouton.

Jakubinskij, L. 1930. 'Stat'ia chetvertaia. "Klassovyi sostav sovremennogo russkovo iazyka. Iazyk krest'ianstva"', *Literaturnaia ucheba* 4: 80–92.

Lotman, Ju. M. 1951. *A. M. Radishchev v bor'be s obshchestvenno-politicheskimi vozzreminiami i dvorianskoi estetikoi Karamzina*, Tartu: Tartuskii Gosudarstvennyi Universitet.

Lotman, Ju. M. 1962. 'Istoki "tolstovskogo napravleniia" v russkoi literature 1830-kh godov', *Trudy po russkoi i slavianskoi filologii* 5: 3–77.

Lotman, Ju. M. [1962] 2003. 'Ideinaia struktura "Kapitanskoi dochki"', in Ju. M. Lotman, *Pushkin*, 212–27, Saint Petersburg: SPB-Iskusstvo.

Lotman, Ju. M. [1965] 1992. 'Otrozhenie etiki i taktiki revoliuzionnoi bor'by v russkoi literature kontsa XVIII veka', in Ju. M. Lotman, *Izbrannye stat'i v trekh tomakh*, vol. 2, 134–58, Tallinn: Aleksandra.

Lotman, Ju. M. 1970. 'Kul'tura i informatsiia', in Ju. M. Lotman, *Stat'i po tipologii kul'tury*, vol. 1, 3–6, Tartu: Tartuskii Gosudarstvennyi Universitet.

Lotman, Ju. M. 1971. 'Problema "obucheniia kul'ture" kak ee tipologicheskaia kharakteristika', *Trudy po znakovym sistemam* 5: 167–76.

Lotman, Ju. M. [1977] 2010. 'Kul'tura kak kollektivnyi intellekt i problemy iskusstvennogo razuma', in Ju. M. Lotman, *Semiosfera*, 557–67, Saint Petersburg: SPB-Iskusstvo.

Lotman, J. [1983] 1985. 'La dinamica dei sistemi culturali', in J. Lotman, *La semiosfera. L'asimmetria e il dialogo nelle strutture pensanti*, trans. S. Salvestroni, 131–45, Venice: Marsilio [original title: 'Dinamika kul'turnykh sistem', unpublished].

Lotman, Ju. M.[1983] 1992. 'K postroeniu teorii vzaimodeistviia kul'tur (semioticheskii aspekt)', in Ju. M. Lotman, *Izbrannye stat'i v trekh tomakh*, vol. 1, 110–20, Tallinn: Aleksandra.

Lotman, Ju. M.1984. 'O semiosfere', *Trudy po znakovym sistemam* 17: 5–23.

Lotman, Ju. M. [1989] 1993. 'Kul'tura kak sub'ekt i sama-sebe ob'ekt', in Ju. M. Lotman, *Izbrannye stat'i v trekh tomakh*, vol. 3, 368–75, Tallinn: Aleksandra,

Lotman, Yu. M. 1990. *Universe of the Mind: A Semiotic Theory of Culture*, trans. A. Shukman, London and New York: I.B. Tauris.

Lotman, Ju. M. [1992] 2010. 'Kul'tura i vzryv', in Ju. M. Lotman, *Semiosfera*, 12–149, Saint Petersburg: SPB–Iskusstvo.

Lotman, J. M. [1994/2010] 2013. *The Unpredictable Workings of Culture*, trans. B. J. Baer, ed. I. Pilshchikov and S. Salupere, Tallinn: TLU Press.

Lotman, Ju. M. 2003. *Pushkin*, Saint Petersburg: SPB–Iskusstvo.

Lotman, Ju. M. and Uspenskij, B. A. 1971. 'O semioticheskom mekhanizme kul'tury', *Trudy po znakovym sistemam* 5: 144–76.

Pinney, C. 1999. 'Indian Magical Realism: Notes on Popular Visual Culture', in G. Bhadra, G. Prakash and S. Tharu (eds), *Subaltern Studies: Writings on South Asian History and Society*, vol. 12, 201–33, Delhi: Oxford University Press.

Piatigorsky, A. M. 1971. 'O. O. Rozenberg i problema iazyka opisaniia v Buddologii', *Trudy po znakovym sistemam* 5: 423–36.

Restaneo, P. 2017. 'Governing the Word: Antonio Gramsci and Soviet Linguistics on Language Policy', *Language & History* 60 (2): 98–111.

Restaneo, P. 2018. 'Lotman, Leibniz, and the Semiospheric Monad: Lost Pages from the Archives', *Semiotica* 224: 313–36.

Schönle, A. (ed.) 2006. *Lotman and Cultural Studies: Encounters and Extensions*, Madison, WI: The University of Wisconsin Press.

Selg, P. and Ventsel, A. 2020. *Introducing Relational Political Analysis: Political Semiotics as a Theory and Method*, Cham: Palgrave Macmillan.

Shandro, A. 2014. *Lenin and the Logic of Hegemony: Political Practice and Theory in the Class Struggle*, Leiden and Boston: Brill.

Smith, M. G. 1998. *Language and Power in the Creation of the USSR, 1917–1953*, Berlin: Mouton de Gruyter.

Tolz, V. 2011. *Russia's Own Orient: The Politics of Identity and Oriental Studies in the Late Imperial and Early Soviet periods*, Oxford: Oxford University Press.

Zhirmunskij, V. 1936. *Natsional'nyi jazyk i social'nye dialekty*, Leningrad: Gosud. Izd. Khudozhestvennaia literatura.

CHAPTER 21
EXPLOSION
Laura Gherlone

Introduction

The concept of explosion in Juri Lotman's scientific thought originates from an existential experience – the vivid awareness that 'in life, unlike chess, we cannot predict even two moves ahead' (letter to Boris Uspenskij, end of January 1984; Lotman and Uspenskij 2016: 573). This conviction led him to investigate the ways in which humans culturally shape the experiences of randomness, unpredictability and creativity inherent in life.

Without doubt, Lotman's encounter in 1986 with Ilya Prigogine's theory of complex systems (Lotman [1989a] 2002: 135) was instrumental in his theorization of explosion, as demonstrated by his last two monographs, *Culture and Explosion* (Lotman [1992] 2009) and *The Unpredictable Workings of Culture* (Lotman [1994/2010] 2013), as well as a considerable and consistent body of essays. However, although it is a concept that essentially identifies the Lotman of the later years, we can find the roots of this horizon of reflection in his early writings. 'Explosion' is the tip of the iceberg of a community's intellectual path – the Tartu School's noosphere (see Lotman [1982] 2016) – marked by a strong internal evolution within the field of human communication studies: a change of vision that saw the transformation of 'static models of information theory [. . .] into a fascinating picture of interrelations, conflicts and transcoding', which, in turn, converted 'semiotic research into a dynamic portrait of the spiritual life of society' (Lotman [1983] 2005: 76).[1]

In this chapter I will address the concept of explosion in relation to two problem areas: *knowledge* and *evolution*.[2] I will make use of both theoretical writings and documents such as Lotman's letters, autobiographical interviews and television lectures for the general public. This array of sources will contribute to showing how his scientific thought, feeding on metaphorical images and 'explosive' insights, is inseparable from his aesthetic sensibility and, in general, from *real life* understood as ongoing creativity.

Human communication: Superfluous over-abundance or an engine of culture?

In the 1980s, Lotman postulated the idea that human semiotic activity is, in essence, an enormous communicative effort capable of generating a translation-driven intertextual sphere (or semiosphere) through which we can culturally and holistically know our surroundings (see Chapter 22).[3] In other words – as he pointed out in his unpublished article 'V otkrytom mire' (In an Open World) (Lotman 1992–93a) – in order to have access to a culturalized form of the world (or extracultural reality), we need to interact through an 'unstable, porous, non-reducible semiotic layer [which] immerses us in a world of different viewpoints. By crossing, colliding and contradicting each other, [these viewpoints] give us such a variety of different projections of the world' that they come 'to lend our knowledge a volumetric [obĕmnyi] character'. This would explain 'the wastefulness of culture in particular, and of human knowledge in general, which we cannot otherwise justify. [. . .] Why so many sciences? Why more and more new art forms? Why do we need cinema if there is theatre and novel if there is drama? Why this monstrous squandering of the best intellectual forces of humanity?'.

If it is true that the mutual translation of different ways of seeing things can offer us a multifaceted knowledge, will we ever come – Lotman wonders ([1990] 2005: 538) – to achieve 'a general encompassment [okhvat] of the reality'? Against the background of this question stands the issue of the unexpected; and 'the unexpected brings explosion' ([1992] 2009): 120).

The spark of the untranslatable

Despite the 'exuberance' of reality, human beings have become accustomed to thinking of knowledge as a space full of holes that must be progressively saturated. The holes represent untamed information, which is perceived as disorder, randomness, contradiction. They are under the illusion that achieving full knowledge is tantamount to *dominating information*, that is, to identifying an ordering principle and, together with it, 'unbending repetitions' (Lotman [1990] 2005: 521).

However, human beings' *real* experience of knowledge contradicts this ideal because – as mentioned earlier – life is not a chess game. While trying to model reality, giving it a sense and in some way an order, their semiotic action appears as a 'monstrous wastefulness' (*chudovishchnaia rastochitel'nost'*): an apparently entropic production of information. If human beings aspire to order knowledge, why then do they dissipate so much semiotic energy? And where does this redundancy of information go? Wouldn't it be less expensive and more 'efficient' (*rentabel'nyi*) to communicate through artificial language (Lotman [1993] 1994: 443–4)?

Lotman identified translation as the source of our knowledge of reality but included *the unexpected as a constituent element* of human communication and not as 'noise' to be ousted. He stressed that, paradoxically, translation is all the more effective the more it leaves a margin for untranslatability. This, in fact, is a symptom of the fact that the reality we mean to grasp is so semantically rich and/or culturally distant that it can only be expressed through *approximation*. The surplus of meaning that flows from the untranslatable is not actually a waste since it is never lost but rather 'hovers' in culture, entering a state of potential (meaning repository). We can picture the untranslatable like air filled with pollen: impalpable, ungraspable but potentially able to bear fruit in unpredictable times and places. When this happens, it can suddenly reveal new, unexpected, inconceivable, apparently illogical and inexpressible relationships between things.

Lotman calls this revealing moment an *explosion*, that is, 'the moment of supreme tension [which] removes all boundaries of untranslatability and unites the incompatible' ([1992] 2009: 22). The explosion, while taking place in a specific space–time frame, entails the suspension of the limits within which meaning is generated and the emergence of something radically new, the result of a non-synthetic unity of differences – 'a world of supreme clarity, which cancels out the contradictions in their particular deep-level unity' ([1992] 2009: 22). This is the instant in which a breakthrough (*proryv*) seems to happen between cultural reality and extracultural reality (or 'noumenal world', as Lotman defines it in his later writings), as if suddenly what is fatally unknowable presents itself to knowledge without the need for semiotic interpolation, although in reality the latter never disappears.

Focusing on explosion, Lotman inevitably has artistic inspiration in mind (poetry first and foremost), which sprung him into action from the very beginning. In his later writings, he speaks in general of the experience of 'unpredictable creativity' ([1992] 2009: 20; [1990] 2001: 101) that humans can potentially live – a way of opening up to the world with the mind and the senses that allows one to grasp, 'as if in a magnesium flare' (Lotman to Uspenskij, late April 1978; Lotman and Uspenskij 2016: 430), the profound meaning of heterogeneity and even of the contradictions of reality.

It is no coincidence that the monograph *The Unpredictable Workings of Culture* – the first version of which was titled *Physiology of Explosion: On Transitional Periods in History* (Kuzovkina and Shakhovskaia 2001: 26) – is basically a long reflection on the role of art in human history and on its epistemological significance. In Lotman's vision, art – as a form of thinking and modelling reality – is what gives life its inexhaustible randomness. While 'taking charge' of the culture within which it arises (i.e. material and immaterial limits such as constraining codifications), the artistic-creative thought is endowed with an intrinsic transcendent capacity that allows it to disarticulate the expected meanings. A thing as banal as a worn-out pair of boots (just think of Vincent van Gogh's *Shoes*, 1886) can become an uncanny subject precisely because in art objects 'constrained by the laws of reality acquire freedom' (Lotman [1994/2010] 2013: 172) and reveal an untranslatable vagueness that Lotman calls unpredictable explosion.

Such 'iridescent', 'twinkling' meanings, as Lotman ([1967] 2011: 264) guessed from the very beginning, are carriers of the unexpected because they shed light on facets of reality that would otherwise remain hidden or non-perceptible to most people. A depicted face can reveal, for example, the *co-presence* of mixed emotions, shifting expressions and different temporalities (Lotman [1990] 2005: 533–6; 1992–93c; [1993/1997] 2002; 2016): a glimmer of childhood can blossom between the wrinkles of a shrivelled face, thus revealing that time has a multiple, even 'ghostly' nature (Tamm 2015).

The 'essence of artistic cognition', Lotman sums up ([1994/2010] 2013: 84–5), 'is located in the explosion in meaning that arises at the intersection of non-intersecting (in other situations) images of reality'. We can deduce that this type of cognition is an indispensable component for humanity and, with its unpredictability, it is the closest there is to *real life*.

Otherness, freedom, imperfection

Three considerations may be drawn from what has been discussed so far. Firstly, the concept of explosion in its deepest meaning is a *thinking of otherness*. In fact, explosion implies that difference is a constitutive element of human life and knowledge, otherwise there would be no need for translation (i.e. the precondition of the explosive moment). If that were the case, we would be a mass of 'billiard balls', which can 'replace each other' without any margin for misunderstanding (Lotman [1988] 2005: 464). However, human beings' *real* experience of reality passes through the communicative exchange, where the need for incomprehension is paradoxically as relevant as the need for comprehension ([1990] 2005: 527). It is precisely because of the recognition of the other's diversity that human communication is so semiotically rich, redundant and contradictory – so much so that it generates thresholds of untranslatability but also, through the artistic cognition, moments 'of tension' which make 'the untranslatable translatable' (Lotman [1992] 2009: 23). The otherness is ultimately what makes reality knowable in its many facets.

Secondly, explosion maintains an indissoluble relation with *freedom*. Lotman writes ([1990] 2005: 532): 'as soon as we move on to real life, we enter a world where it is necessary not to get rid of contradictions or consider that contradictions are a mistake, but to understand that contradictions are our treasure.' Seeing contradictions as a treasure means thinking in an antinomic way, that is, accepting the *co-presence* of a thing and its opposite in the space of the semiosphere: for example, to recognize that past, present and future can simultaneously coexist. This refusal to compartmentalize is linked to Lotman's belief that freedom is, first and foremost, the possibility of tapping into information. Mutilating reality by dividing it into self-excluding oppositions actually results in giving up the wealth of information that a multi-perspective view can grasp: that is, depriving oneself of what can greatly influence the 'possibility of *choice*' ([1990] 2001: 226).

Thirdly, accepting the contradictions inherent in life means assuming that human semiotics is fundamentally imperfect and incomplete – Lotman speaks of *nepravil'nost'* (incorrectness, irregularity). But it is precisely this imperfection that enables the explosive moment to constitutively include a crisis of meaning, that is, what allows human beings to evolve. During an interview between Kalevi Kull and Lotman, the latter stated the following:

It happened to a Greek philosopher who was not from Athens. He arrived in Athens and there at the market a vendor told him: 'You are a foreigner'. Of course, he was Greek, but not from Athens. He said: 'How do you know?' 'Because your Greek is *too correct*', he replied. You see, so *too correct* is a clue that reveals the alien, while what is ours keeps a reserve for permissible incorrectness, admissible variants, uniqueness. So [. . .] this freedom of the system, its irregularity, is what ensures its survival, its possibility for evolution and, in general, makes it live. You see, life is incorrect by nature, but it is incorrect because it is profoundly correct. If it was only incorrect, it would be death. (Kull and Lotman [1992] 2015: 176–7)

Here we find the basis of Lotman's question: Can humans ever come to achieve a general comprehension of reality? The answer is no if the model of knowledge is the *too correct* one of a 'great teacher' (Lotman [1992] 2009: 158) who knows everything in advance, but it is yes if the model is that of a scientist open to unpredictability.

The arrow of time: Entropic death or creativity?

A model of knowledge that excludes the unexpected becomes, from a historical perspective, an interpretative framework through which humans self-describe their development over time, idealizing it as a path towards a state of predictability.[4] The movement of history takes on a predetermined character, thus affirming a vision of time in which life progressively takes possibilities away: 'a person comes into the world being able to choose many paths; as this opportunity for choice gradually runs out, to the extent that it is reduced, also the information decreases. The longer a person has lived, the easier it is to predict what will happen to him/her in the future' (Lotman [1990] 2005: 539).

It is a Weltanschauung based on the idea of irreversible time as 'entropic death': an idea that is, in humans' sociocultural life, continuously questioned by the daily experience of reality, where *instability* and *uncertainty* as well as the *need for choice* in conditions of *high improbability* and the *creative implications* of the decisions taken are commonplace, right up to the 'last exam', as Lotman defines death (Lotman [1983/1995] 2005). It follows that this vision hinged on predictability is extremely inconsistent and therefore lacerating for people.

When making this reflection, Lotman has in mind the work of Nobel laureate in chemistry Prigogine, who studied the so-called dissipative structures – typical of living organisms – that is, 'ordered systems maintained far from equilibrium by external constraints' (Lebon, Jou and Casas-Vázquez 2008: 136). Since they exist in a dynamic state, during their evolution these thermodynamic systems may encounter points of instability (or bifurcation) – which are also the most unpredictable and therefore only probabilistically treatable – and change direction *unexpectedly* and *irreversibly*, bringing to light their creative dynamic. In Lotman's vision, Prigogine's great teaching is to have highlighted that life stands out as a non-linear something and that the arrow of time (or irreversibility) is not necessarily synonymous with time-degradation (as the second law of classical thermodynamics postulates), but can manifest itself as time-creation.

The thought of the Belgian scientist of Russian origin had an explosive effect on Lotman, who had already been reflecting for some time on the role of chance in the dynamics of culture and, more generally, on the relationship between culture and history, which led him to question the structuralist-semiotic approach to culture oriented towards regularities (see also Chapter 25). Following Prigogine, he came to think – as he observed in his unpublished article 'Evoliutsiia: uslozhnenie ili uproshchenie?' (Evolution: Complexification or Simplification?, Lotman 1991–92) – that evolution is a cosmic extensive laboratory: something extremely *dynamic*, the result of the liminal position in which the human being finds himself 'situated in the boundary of the "dual abyss" (Tiutchev's expression) of the world that creates him and the world that he creates' (where the first one, Lotman writes in *Culture and Explosion*, 'is transformed into an inexhaustible source of information, like the Psyche, in which dwells the inherent self-growing Logos about which Heraclitus spoke', [1992] 2009: 159). This 'dual abyss' – the threshold between extracultural and cultural reality – is what coalesces the history of cosmos and the history of humanity in a single evolutionary-information process.

History, in Lotman's vision, is in fact the path of 'appropriation' (through the semiotic sphere) of the potentially infinite information contained in extraculture. This path advances with the development of thought (the precondition of the semiosphere; see Lotman [1990] 2001: 150), which 'is by no means direct and fatal and is not unambiguously predictable' as it includes 'a great deal of chance and disorder' (Lotman 1991–92). The randomness inherent in the evolutionary process continuously opens up the *possibility of choice* to human beings. And choice – as has already been partly highlighted – is what, on the one hand, extends the 'space of information' ([1992] 2009: 122) and, on the other, amplifies (i.e. enriches, refines and educates) thinking consciousness, without which this process would be a mechanical and uncreative movement.

Lotman's postulate is the 'translation' in historical-culturological terms of the Prigoginian idea of 'bifurcation', whereby periods of predictability are interrupted by explosions whose outcome is unpredictable – a translation that led him, like Pushkin, to see in 'Chance, the god of invention' (Lotman 1991a; [1992/1995] 2019: 123) but also to ask himself: Why is history often perceived and described as a 'train travelling at an unusually high velocity' ([1990] 2005: 519) when in fact it is 'an irreversible (unstable) process' (Lotman 1991b: 173), open to creativity?

How does explosion act?

From the second half of the 1980s, the discovery of Prigogine's thought stimulated Lotman to rethink his cultural theory from a historical perspective. Although this idea had been present since his linguistic-typological writings of the 1960s and 1970s, in the Lotman of the later years this perspective is amplified and bears an ethical-anthropological reflection on the triad *knowledge–memory–self-consciousness* caught in the individual-collective antinomy. This is a necessary and urgent reflection as it is only through the awareness of their action and 'performativity' in history that humans can learn to protect themselves from the blind alleys that have often characterized their historical-cultural journey. How? By learning to interpret *uncertainty* through different eyes. This alternative look is explosion.

We may synthetically say that explosion, in Lotman's history-oriented later writings, is a sort of breakthrough in humans' historical path, which is seen as a combination of gradual (or predictable) development and unexpected contingencies.[5] When it occurs, 'the moment of explosion breaks the chain of cause and effect, causing an entire area to rise up and a collection of identically probable events to come into view. Following from the logic of the preceding developments, it is essentially impossible to predict which of those events will actually occur' (Lotman [1994/2010] 2013: 64).

Explosion is that moment when humans, finding themselves at a crossroads (perceived as vagueness of information), choose a direction. What looked like a spatial-temporal force field, an 'array of possibilities' (Lotman [1992] 2009: 13), becomes retrospectively for the individual-collective self-consciousness 'the only possible option' (Lotman [1992] 2009: 154). It is as if the moment of explosion is variably (i.e. neither rigidly nor deterministically) articulated into two stages. In the first one, the space of the possibilities – the unpredictable – opens up in all its extension and informativity, thus bringing down the law of causality. In the second stage, which is 'the turning point of the process' (Lotman [1992] 2009: 15), the observers involved in the explosion are inclined to drive back to the starting point and to interpret the image of the explosion that took shape in their consciousness. This gives rise to a new, powerful process of description (and self-knowledge) able to 'explain what has occurred' (Lotman [1992] 2009: 15). Failing that, 'innovation would remain unnoticed, lessons from the explosion unlearned' (Torop 2009: xxxvi).

Reality presents itself as a *limit* (since choice necessarily implies the exclusion of other possibilities) but also as an opportunity to increase information through selection. The appearance of two divergent artistic paths, like Pushkin's and Gogol's, can be seen as the cut-off point for multiple potentialities ('why him and not others?') but, at the same time, as a selection that led humanity to take a huge leap forward: the moment when – Lotman writes (1993) in the unpublished article 'Odin: Ob iskhodnykh poniatiiakh' (One: On Basic Concepts) – the demon of art seemed to have raised Russian literature to the mountain top.

Explosion is presented by Lotman through three main properties. Firstly, he generally speaks of '*moment* of explosion', suggesting that it is a shifting, transitory temporal conformation. At the same time, it is spatial because it implies the existence of a (collective and individual) subject who perceives, interprets and evaluates it and who is inevitably situated in the geographic-social-symbolic location of a given culture. Secondly, rather than giving a definition of explosion, Lotman describes it through the actions it performs, that is, through its agency. If we consider the two main monographs mentioned earlier, we can observe that explosion 'breaks', 'changes', 'carries over', 'throws', 'involves', 'forces', 'occurs', 'renders', 'creates', 'generates', 'ends', 'results in', 'changes', 'expels', 'loses', 'penetrates', 'ruptures'. Thirdly, as an agent force – almost with its own intentionality, which encounters/clashes with the individual-collective subject's force – it seems to be a mnemonic-affective-sensory intelligence that makes use of familiar images-symbols from the past (something similar to archetypal schemas) to become present and graspable.

In light of these properties, the Lotmanian concept of explosion is very close to that of *atmosphere*, if we understand the latter as 'a contingent and fluid outcome of our perpetually configured surroundings, sensory perceptions, subjectivities and imaginations' (Sumartojo and Pink 2019, loc. 187; see also Trigg 2020) – an outcome that, in the *hic et nunc* of its manifestation, releases meanings able to 'move forward with people, continuing to shape [the] understandings of their experiences' (Sumartojo and Pink 2019, loc. 211) (different reminiscences and anticipatory insights into the future, pre-existing views of things, bodily capacities, cultural narratives via daily discourses and objects). Such 'atmospheric eruption' or explosion does not always present itself as the space of a free choice (and therefore bearer of newness and generator of original meanings), but can be conditioned by a mnemonic-cultural load that undermines the result. This is because 'the moment of explosion is not only the point at which new possibilities take shape but also the point at which one becomes conscious of another reality, a moment of dislocation and of the reinterpretation of memory' (Lotman [1994/2010] 2013: 69).

The agency of explosion, as mentioned earlier, can push towards the 'exhumation' of ancient experiences (symbolized by familiar images) which, instead of helping to embark on the path to novelty, *reproduce* a pernicious past in an apparent new guise: a sort of reinterpreted script. This may happen especially in those moments marked by high uncertainty, when '"historical memory" can lead to errors that are at times tragic in their consequences' (Lotman [1994/2010] 2013: 166). We may define such a situation as a *fallacious explosion* because, while presenting itself as a moment of suspension, it actually does not break the chain of cause and effect, nor does it generate substantially new information (or generates it at a very high cost, i.e. the cancellation of previous information). On the contrary, an authentic explosion, as Lotman underlines in the unpublished article 'Monostruktury i binarnost' (Monostructures and Binariness) (1991a), entertains a fertile bond with the past because it can awaken in it latent, unexploded forces with great information capacity – forces capable of *healing the past* itself.[6]

Starting from this vision, Lotman worked on two lines of research: the issues of (1) historical self-description and (2) collective emotion(s), with a particular focus on mass fear.

Binary and ternary systems

Those moments when historical memory proves to be a poor guide are the junctures in which the individual-collective self-consciousness thinks of binariness (cf. note 3) not in terms of coexistence of 'one's own' and 'the other' but in terms of exclusion of one of the two poles. Binariness turns into a way of interpreting historical development that absolutizes the (apparent) newness by declaring 'the alien' – namely what preceded it – non-existent.

In such sociocultural situations – called 'binary systems' – utopia prevails, that is, the conviction that the unrealizable ideal can be concretely actualized and that, in the name of such ideal, it is necessary to annihilate everything that exists as it is 'considered to be irremediably corrupt' (Lotman [1992] 2009: 166). The 'cleaning' – from circumscribed symbolic objects, such as religious images or books of poetry and literature, to entire peoples, with their language and their set of spiritual and material-cultural values – becomes the strategy to achieve the utopia.

Explosion entails a transforming effect in the sense that the binary system actually takes an *irreversible path*, but the 'bifurcation point' is retrospectively described as an *inevitable and necessary choice*, not as one among many possibilities. This feeds in the individual-collective self-consciousness a model of historical path as fatalism (or eschatologism) whereby the moments of suspension – when space–time 'is no longer' and 'is not yet' (Lotman 1994: 220) – are emptied of their creative possibilities.

In the so-called ternary systems, on the contrary, there is a sort of mediation between the ideal and the reality whereby 'certain values from the antecedent period' are preserved and transferred 'from the periphery to the centre of the system' (Lotman [1992] 2009: 166). In spite of not embarking into a deep analysis of the concept of ternariety (*ternarnost'*) from a historical viewpoint, Lotman succeeds in conveying that it is linked to his reflection on the need to think of reality in terms of a 'complex unity' (Lotman 1991a). The application of a complexity filter makes it possible to see the poles of binariness from a holistic perspective, that is, of grasping them in their reciprocity and unity, albeit the existing diversity – Lotman talks indistinctly about 'deep unity', 'higher unity' and 'dynamic unity', taking inspiration from the image of the Holy Trinity ([1994/2010] 2013: 80). The concept of ternary system in a historical sense is therefore an attempt (only sketched) to explain how in certain periods of transition *thinking ternarily* means identifying 'variable geometry' solutions to achieve a non-destructive change.

The dynamics of binary and ternary systems could not be explained, Lotman realized between 1988 and 1993, without considering an agent force that seems to have a collective face: fear.

The issue of mass fear

At transitory historical junctures – both in binary and ternary systems – society *feels* that the complex of discursive and material relations that sustains it has entered into crisis (in the etymological sense of the term, as an 'act of separating'). Objects (like a flag) or words (like 'roots'), which until recently had been constitutive elements of its unifying 'great narrative', are now perceived as something strange. Several reasons can trigger crisis: the emergence of a new and unpredictable threat, the conflictual nature of border areas (such as subcultures) that push towards a radical break, the unleashing of ancient pernicious experiences that act as a script, the change of image and function of the 'alien culture' (see the unpublished writing 'Chuzhoi mir, chuzhoe povedenie' [Alien World, Strange Behaviour], Lotman 1992–93b).

The void created in the *interim* (Lotman 1994: 220–3), that is, the shadow of *insignificance* over the meaning built up until that moment, releases cognitive, emotional and semiotic-pragmatic energies aimed at the reunification and reconstruction of meaning. These periods generally present themselves with a high degree of *vagueness*; it is difficult to decipher them, and the *nebulosity* they carry brings innovative forces, but also diffused affective waves (insecurity, fear, suspicion, etc.). These are periods when, according to Lotman (1989: 480–1), a 'psychology of the "fortress besieged"' may be more easily developed, a kind of spatial-temporal and sensorial configuration that pushes people to let themselves be carried away by an impalpable but real air of fear (Lotman speaks of an *atmosphere* of collective hysteria); to unearth 'atavistic myths', that is, to feed discursive plots soaked in fictional elements (which speak of ancient but living traumas); to search for 'dangerous but invisible enemies', by identifying a category or a sector of society often already persecuted in the past; to transfer to this dangerous figure the image-symbol of the 'culprit of all the troubles, the participant in an invisible conspiracy'; to extend this guilt to all those who, in some way, defend or are involved with the stigmatized subject; in the most extreme cases – as in the case of binary systems – to accept that legal guarantees be cancelled, legitimizing repressive actions (for further exploration, see Gherlone 2019). Lotman observes: 'it is not surprising then that a rigidly binary model is so conducive to displays of intolerance and destructive social emotions. Expressed with classic completeness in the formula "If you're not with us, you're against us", this model historically comes to the surface whenever creativity is pushed aside by destruction' (Lotman [1994/2010] 2013: 79–80)

This destructive emotional wave goes hand in hand with, and contributes to feeding, the construction of a *monolithic truth* (Lotman 1989: 479), which basically means loss of information as it severs a multi-perspective, creative look. Only the rehabilitation of such generative creativity can overturn the course of events.

Conclusions: On astonishment

All these reflections led Lotman (1991b: 175) to assert the need for a 'semiotics of history', that is, a science capable of providing 'an analysis of how [. . .] the human individual, in the process of making choices, imagines the world'. Interestingly, he does not talk about description but *imagination* of the world. This means that the process of making choices involves not only the realized occurrences but also the imaginable ones, namely the intuitive 'anticipation of potential "future states"' ([1992] 2009: 172). How? Lotman sees in art a form of thinking and modelling reality capable of (re)presenting to humans *pictures of the world of unrealized paths*. Art becomes a space of freedom because it is capable of opening up a range of possible choices (e.g. through the cognitive-emotional dialogical relationship with literary characters' voice) that real life inevitably limits.[7] Moreover, it shows that the 'history of *what-might-have-been* [*nesluchivshegosia*] is a great and fundamental history', offering us the chance to experiment 'an immense second life' (Lotman [1990] 2005: 522), an overcoming of the inevitability of death (see also Lotman 1992b).[8]

Finally, embracing artistic thought means *educating* ourselves to conceive reality as ongoing possibility, escaping from the temptation to evaluate the future through the lens of the past. When explosion occurs, art-educated thinking is able to see in uncertainty and even in crisis not closing routes but horizons that open up. After explosion, one 'discovers with astonishment that the most likely paths have been bypassed, and what was realized is the least probable or even considered impossible' (Lotman 1993). In other words, one discovers that a leap has been made in knowledge and evolution.

Notes

1. I quote Lotman describing Jakobson's intellectual path, which he deemed similar to his own.

2. For further reading, see Deotto et al. 1996; Avtonomova 2009, 2015; Torop 2009; Grishakova 2009; Lotman M. 2013; Pilshchikov 2013; Kim 2014; Kull 2015; Lorusso 2015; Semenenko 2016; Gramigna and Salupere 2017; Kull and Velmezova 2018; Restaneo 2018; Tamm 2019; the essays in Machado and Barei 2019; Demuru 2020; Monticelli 2020; Salerno and Lozano 2020; Zolyan 2020.

3. This idea is based on Lotman's belief that human thought is grounded on the fundamental opposition between 'one's own' [*svoi*] and 'the other' or 'the alien' [*chuzhoi*], specifically the *co-existence of two poles* 'simultaneously similar and functionally separate' (Lotman 1991a) or principle of binariness and asymmetry. This generates an infinite range of binary oppositions from a micro one between two languages modelling a text to a macro one between culture and extraculture (Lotman 1992–93b), whose mutual dynamism (or tension to translation) is at the basis of our knowledge of reality.

4. For an overview of this topic, see the essays included in Lotman 2019 as well as Lotman 1989; 1998; [1989b] 2002; [1992a] 2002; [1992b] 2002).

5. In *Culture and Explosion*, the process of gradual development is seen as an 'objective narrative of the third person' (Lotman [1992] 2009: 35), that is to say, something codified, consolidated and common to the observers, and therefore predictable – Lotman talks about 'space of common nouns' (Lotman [1992] 2009: 117). The explosion, on the contrary, is the realm of the 'first person' (or the 'space of proper names'), namely of uniqueness and particularity, a reason why it calls into play a tremendous collective effort of decoding and interpretation. Furthermore, 'it is no accident that historically explosive epochs push "great people" to the surface' (Lotman [1992] 2009: 136), by symbolizing the irreplaceability of 'individual creativity' (especially in art).

6. It is noteworthy that Lotman's theory offers a set of interesting ideas for nourishing a cultural affect theory and decoloniality (Gherlone, forthcoming).

7. In the realm of art, reality is transformed into the 'world of proper names', that is, a world 'experienced in an emotional and intimate way', where 'the "alien" is always our "own" but at the same time our "own" is also always "alien"' (Lotman ([1992] 2009: 118). In this way humans can live subjectively and personally even those experiences with which they might not in principle be familiar, such as the death of a son, a psychiatric illness, a situation of captivity or exile, and so on.

8. A detailed study of this topic can be found in Kuzovkina 1999.

References

Avtonomova, N. S. 2009. 'Pozdnii Lotman', in N. S. Avtonomova, *Otkrytaia struktura: Iakobson – Bakhtin – Lotman – Gasparov*, 215–23, Moscow: ROSSPEN.

Avtonomova, N. S. 2015. 'Le Lotman des derniers travaux: à l'arrière, au front ou tout simplement "en route"?', in E. Velmezova (ed.), *L'École sémiotique de Moscou-Tartu / Tartu-Moscou. Histoire. Épistémologie. Actualité*, 311–35 (Slavica Occitania 40), Toulouse: Université de Toulouse.

Demuru, P. 2020. 'Between Accidents and Explosions: Indeterminacy and Aesthesia in the Becoming of History', *Bakhtiniana: Revista de Estudos do Discurso* 15 (1): 83–109.

Deotto, P., Nortman, M., Pesenti, C. and Verch, I. (eds) 1996. *Slavica tergestina (Nasledie Ju. M. Lotmana: nastoiashchee i budushchee)*, 4, Trieste: Edizioni LINT.

Gherlone, L. 2019. 'Lotman Continues to Astonish: Revolutions and Collective Emotions', *Bakhtiniana: Revista de Estudos do Discurso* 14 (4): 163–83.

Gherlone, L., forthcoming. 'Semiotics and Cultural Affect Theory', in A. Biglari (ed.), *Open Semiotics*, Paris: Éditions L'Harmattan.

Gramigna, R. and Salupere, S. 2017. 'Umberto Eco and Juri M. Lotman on Communication and Cognition', in T. Thellefsen and B. Sørensen (eds), *Umberto Eco in His Own Words*, 248–57, Berlin, Munich and Boston: Walter de Gruyter.

Grishakova, M. 2009. 'Afterword: Around Culture and Explosion: J. Lotman and the Tartu-Moscow School in the 1980–90s', in J. Lotman, *Culture and Explosion*, trans. W. Clark, ed. M. Grishakova, 175–87, Berlin and New York: Mouton de Gruyter.

Kim, S.-H. 2014. 'Lotmanian Explosion: From Peripheral Space to Dislocated Time', *Sign Systems Studies* 42 (1): 7–30.

Kull, K. 2015. 'A Semiotic Theory of Life: Lotman's Principles of the Universe of the Mind', *Green Letters* 19 (3): 255–66.

Kull, K. and Lotman, Y. [1992] 2015. 'Au sujet de la sémiotique de la vie et de l'évolution. (Entretien de Kalevi Kull avec Youri Lotman. Tartu, juin 1992)', in E. Velmezova (ed.), *L'École sémiotique de Moscou-Tartu / Tartu-Moscou. Histoire. Épistémologie. Actualité*, 165–82 (Slavica Occitania 40), Toulouse: Université de Toulouse.

Kull, K. and Velmezova, E. 2018. 'O paradokse "semiotiki zhizni": raboty poslednikh let Iuriia Lotmana', *Slovo.ru: Baltiiskii aktsent* 9 (4): 6–14.

Kuzovkina, T. 1999. 'Tema smerti v poslednikh stat'iakh Ju. M. Lotmana', in B. Egorov, *Žizn' i tvorchestvo Iu. M. Lotmana*, 259–70, Moscow: Novoe literaturnoe obozrenie.

Kuzovkina, T. and Shakhovskaia, T. 2001. 'Lotman, Juri. Fond 136. Inventarinimistu'. Available online: http://dspace.ut.ee/bitstream/handle/10062/46412/f136_lotman.pdf (accessed 21 November 2020).

Lebon, G., Jou, D. and Casas-Vázquez, J. 2008. *Understanding Non-Equilibrium Thermodynamics: Foundations, Applications, Frontiers*, Berlin and Heidelberg: Springer.

Lorusso, A. M. 2015. 'Unity and Pluralism: The Theory of Jurij Lotman', in A. M. Lorusso, *Cultural Semiotics: For a Cultural Perspective in Semiotics*, 67–115, Basingstoke: Palgrave Macmillan.

Lotman, J. [1967] 2011. 'The Place of Art Among Other Modelling Systems', trans. T. Pern, *Sign Systems Studies* 39 (2/4): 249–70.

Lotman, Ju. M. [1982] 2016. 'Universitet – nauka – kul'tura', in Ju. M. Lotman and B. A. Uspenskij, *Perepiska 1964–1993*, 679–88, Tallinn: Tallinn University Press.

Lotman, Ju. M. [1983] 2005. 'Poslednii ekzamen, poslednii urok . . . (Neskol'ko slov o Romane Osipoviche Iakobsone)', in Ju. M. Lotman, *Vospitanie dushi*, 74–7, Saint Petersburg: Iskusstvo–SPB.

Lotman, Ju. M. [1988] 2005. 'Besedy o russkoi kul'ture. Televizionnye lektsii – Tsikl vtoroi. Vzaimootnosheniia liudei i razvitie kul'tur', in Ju. M. Lotman, *Vospitanie dushi*, 414–69, Saint Petersburg: Iskusstvo–SPB.

Lotman, Ju. M. 1989. 'Vykhod iz labirinta', in U. Eco, *Imia rozy*, 468–81, Moscow: Knizhnaia palata.

Lotman, Ju. M. [1989a] 2002. 'O roli sluchainykh faktorov v literaturnoi evoliutsii', in Ju. M. Lotman, *Istoriia i tipologiia russkoi kul'tury*, 128–35, Saint Petersburg: Iskusstvo–SPB.

Lotman, Ju. M. [1989b] 2002. 'V perspektive Frantsuzskoi revoliutsii', in Ju. M. Lotman, *Istoriia i tipologiia russkoi kul'tury*, 371–5, Saint Petersburg: Iskusstvo–SPB.

Lotman, Yu. M. [1990] 2001. *Universe of the Mind: A Semiotic Theory of Culture*, trans. A. Shukman, London and New York: I.B. Tauris.

Lotman, Ju. M. [1990] 2005. 'Besedy o russkoi kul'ture. Televizionnye lektsii – Tsikl chetvertyi: Chelovek i iskusstvo', in Ju. M. Lotman, *Vospitanie dushi*, 515–44, Saint Petersburg: Iskusstvo–SPB.

Lotman, Ju. M. 1991a. 'Monostruktury i binarnost', Tartu University Library, Collection 136, n. 268, 6 pages.

Lotman, Ju. M. 1991b. 'Semiotics and the Historical Sciences', in B. Göranzon and M. Florin (eds), *Dialogue and Technology: Art and Knowledge*, 165–80, London: Springer.

Lotman, Ju. M. 1991–92. 'Evoliutsiia: uslozhnenie ili uproshchenie?', Tartu University Library, Collection 136, n. 271, 14 pages.

Lotman, Ju. M. 1992a. 'Povtoriaemost' i vzryv v dinamicheskikh protsessakh', Tartu University Library, Collection 136, n. 279, 15 pages.

Lotman, Ju. M. 1992b. 'V ozhidanii iazyka (nakanune vzryva)', Tartu University Library, Collection 136, n. 272, 21 pages.

Lotman, Ju. M. [1992a] 2002. 'Povtoriaemost' i unikal'nost' v mekhanizme kul'tury', in Ju. M. Lotman, *Istoriia i tipologiia russkoi kul'tury*, 67–70, Saint Petersburg: Iskusstvo–SPB.

Lotman, Ju. M. [1992b] 2002. 'Iskusstvo na peresechenii otkrytykh i zakrytykh struktur', in Ju. M. Lotman, *Istoriia i tipologiia russkoi kul'tury*, 174–88, Saint Petersburg: Iskusstvo–SPB.

Lotman, J. [1992] 2009. *Culture and Explosion*, trans. W. Clark, ed. M. Grishakova, Berlin and New York: Mouton de Gruyter.

Lotman, Ju. M. 1992–93a. 'V otkrytom mire', Tartu University Library, Collection 136, n. 273, typewritten version, 10 pages.

Lotman, Ju. M. 1992–93b. 'Chuzhoi mir, chuzhoe povedenie', Tartu University Library, Collection 136, n. 289, 4 pages.

Lotman, Ju. M. 1992–93c. 'Ogon' v sosude', Tartu University Library, Collection 136, n. 278, 26 pages.

Lotman, J. [1992/1995] 2019. 'The Role of Art in the Dynamics of Culture', in J. Lotman, *Culture, Memory and History: Essays in Cultural Semiotics*, trans. B. J. Baer, ed. M. Tamm, 115–30, Cham: Palgrave Macmillan.

Lotman, Ju. M. 1993. 'Odin. Ob iskhodnykh poniatiiakh', Tartu University Library, Collection 136, n. 294, pages 4 of 174.

Lotman, Ju. M. [1993] 1994. 'Nam vsë neobkhodimo. Lishnego v mire net . . .' in A. D. Koshelev (ed.), *Iu. M. Lotman i tartusko-moskovskaia semioticheskaia shkola*, 442–51, Moscow: Gnozis.

Lotman, Ju. M. [1993/1997] 2002. 'Portret', in Ju. M. Lotman, *Stat'i po semiotike kul'tury i iskusstva*, 349–75, Saint Petersburg: Akademicheskii proekt.

Lotman, Yu. 1994. 'Theses Towards a Semiotics of Russian Culture', *Elementa* 1 (3): 219–27.

Lotman, Ju. M. 1998. 'Okhota za ved'mami. Semiotika strakha', *Sign Systems Studies* 26: 61–82.

Lotman, J. [1994/2010] 2013. *The Unpredictable Workings of Culture*, trans. B. J. Baer, ed. I. Pilshchikov and S. Salupere, Tallinn: Tallinn University Press.

Lotman, J. 2016. *Juri Lotmani autoportreed. Avtoportrety Iu. M. Lotmana. Juri Lotman's Self-Portraits*, trans. P. Peiker, ed. T. Kuzovkina and S. Daniel, Tallinn: Tallinn University Press.

Lotman, J. 2019. *Culture, Memory and History: Essays in Cultural Semiotics*, trans. B. J. Baer, ed. M. Tamm, Cham: Palgrave Macmillan.

Lotman, Ju. M. and Uspenskij, B. A. 2016. *Perepiska 1964–1993*, Tallinn: Tallinn University Press.

Lotman, M. 2013. 'Afterword: Semiotics and Unpredictability', in J. Lotman, *The Unpredictable Workings of Culture*, trans. B. J. Baer, ed. I. Pilshchikov and S. Salupere, 239–78, Tallinn: Tallinn University Press.

Machado, I. and Barei, S. (eds) 2019. *Bakhtiniana: Revista de Estudos do Discurso* 14 (4), available online: https://revistas.pucsp.br/index.php/bakhtiniana/issue/view/2280/showToc (accessed 21 November 2020).

Monticelli, D. 2020. 'Thinking the New After the Fall of the Berlin Wall: Juri Lotman's Dialogism of History', *Rethinking History* 24 (2): 184–208.

Pilshchikov, I. (ed.) 2013. *Sluchainost' i nepredskazuemost' v istorii kul'tury: Materialy Vtorykh Lotmanovskikh dnei v Tallinnskom universitete (4–6 iiunia 2010 g.)*, Tallinn: Tallinn University Press.

Restaneo, P. 2018. 'Lotman, Leibniz, and the Semiospheric Monad: Lost Pages from the Archives', *Semiotica* 224: 313–36.

Salerno, D. and Lozano, J. 2020. 'Future: A Time of History', *Versus: Quaderni di studi semiotici* 2: 189–205.

Semenenko, A. 2016. '*Homo polyglottus*: Semiosphere as a Model of Human Cognition', *Sign Systems Studies* 44 (4): 494–510.

Sumartojo, S. and Pink, S. 2019. *Atmospheres and the Experiential World: Theory and Methods*, Abingdon and New York: Routledge (Kindle File Format).

Tamm, M. (ed.) 2015. *Afterlife of Events: Perspectives on Mnemohistory*, Basingstoke: Palgrave Macmillan.

Tamm, M. 2019. 'Introduction: Juri Lotman's Semiotic Theory of History and Cultural Memory', in J. Lotman, *Culture, Memory and History: Essays in Cultural Semiotics*, trans. B. J. Baer, ed. M. Tamm, 1–25, Cham: Palgrave Macmillan.

Torop, P. 2009. 'Foreword: Lotmanian Explosion', in J. Lotman, *Culture and Explosion*, trans. W. Clark, ed. M. Grishakova, xxvii–xl, Berlin and New York: Mouton de Gruyter.

Trigg, D. 2020. 'The Role of Atmosphere in Shared Emotions', *Emotion, Space and Society* 35: 1–7.

Zolyan, S. 2020. *Iurii Lotman: O smysle, tekste, istorii. Temy i variatsii*, Moscow: Izdatel'skii Dom IASK.

CHAPTER 22
SEMIOSPHERE
Peeter Torop

Semiosphere is one of Juri Lotman's most famous concepts, which he introduced in his 1984 article 'On the Semiosphere' ([1984] 2005) and which he had first presented orally in 1982 (Kull 2006). This concept is not constantly used in Lotman's late work, but it marks his move towards dynamic cultural analysis. As a result, we can also observe the dynamics of this concept in Lotman's personal development, as well as in its elaborations and interpretations by researchers from different disciplines and traditions. Since 1984, this concept has travelled from one terminological field to another. In the disciplinary terminological field of the Tartu-Moscow school, 'semiosphere' is connected with the linked terms 'language – secondary modelling system – text – culture'. In the interdisciplinary terminological fields, the association, on the one hand, with biosphere and noosphere, and on the other hand with logosphere, is perhaps the most important. As a metadisciplinary concept, 'semiosphere' belongs to the methodology of cultural research and is associated with the concepts of holism and the part and the whole. And finally, as a transdisciplinary concept, 'semiosphere' is very close to the concept of symbol in symbolism: 'symbol' as an indefinable term is suitable to convey the cognition of the non-cognizable, and at the same time symbol can have enormous semantic volume as a reduced myth (see also Chapter 15). In this context, 'semiosphere' marks the complementarity of disciplines studying culture, the movement towards the creation of general theory of culture and flexible methodology (Torop 2005: 161).

Anatomy of semiosphere

'Spherical' thinking existed in Lotman's works before 1984. In 1971, he published, together with Boris Uspenskij, the article 'On the Semiotic Mechanism of Culture', in which they introduced the notion of social sphere:

> As a methodological abstraction, one may imagine language as an isolated phenomenon. However, in its actual functioning, language is molded into a more general system of culture and, together with it, constitutes a complex whole. The fundamental 'task' of culture, as we will try to show, is in structurally organizing the world around man. Culture is the generator of structuredness, and in this way it creates a social sphere around man which, like the biosphere, makes life possible; that is, not organic life, but social life. (Lotman and Uspensky [1971] 1978: 213)

Implicitly Lotman and Uspenskij fixed in this article some basic binary oppositions: nature–culture, life–social life, biosphere–social sphere. The relations between different spheres are explained more closely in 'On the Semiosphere':

> Such a continuum we, by analogy with the concept of 'biosphere' introduced by V. I. Vernadsky, will call the 'semiosphere'. We must, however, warn against any confusion between the term 'noosphere' used by V. I. Vernadsky and the concept of 'semiosphere' here introduced. The noosphere – is a specific stage in the development of the biosphere, a stage connected with human rational activity. Vernadsky's biosphere is a cosmic mechanism, which occupies a specific structural place in planetary unity. (Lotman [1984] 2005: 206–7)

Lotman emphasizes that both biosphere and noosphere are material spaces, meaning that in both cases we can talk about real boundaries. Noosphere as a biosphere developed or changed by people diverges from semiosphere as a sphere of communication and self-communication:

> If the noosphere represents the three-dimensional material space that covers a part of our planet, then the space of the semiosphere carries an abstract character. This, however, is by no means to suggest that the concept of space is used, here, in a metaphorical sense. We have in mind a specific sphere, possessing signs, which are assigned to the enclosed space. Only within such a space is it possible for communicative processes and the creation of new information to be realised. (Lotman [1984] 2005: 207)

Therefore, semiosphere is not only a semiotic but also a semiosic space: 'The semiosphere is that same semiotic space, outside of which semiosis itself cannot exist' (Lotman [1984] 2005: 208). Whereas the biosphere is a planetary phenomenon and thus a finite structural part of the planet, the semiosphere is an indefinite whole denoting human culture at the global level, which creates within itself cultural and thus structural diversity. The semiosphere includes territorial, social, cultural and individual identities, which in turn are represented by semiospheres of different levels.

Lotman stresses in 1984 that one of the most important attributes of the semiosphere is the boundary. In his earlier work on text as the central notion of cultural semiotics Lotman accentuated delimitation, that is, the text has a frame, a beginning and end, and a structure as an object of immanent interpretation or close reading (see Chapter 9). Of course, together with textual meanings functional meanings, the functions of texts in a culture were also important. The structural identity of the semiosphere is, however, more complicated. In 'On the Semiosphere', Lotman explains that the boundary of the semiosphere is the contact zone between the 'own' and the 'other', between the internal and the external. It is a sphere of semiotization:

> One of the fundamental concepts of semiotic delimitation lies in the notion of boundary. Insofar as the space of the semiosphere has an abstract character,

its boundary cannot be visualised by means of the concrete imagination. Just as in mathematics the border represents a multiplicity of points, belonging simultaneously to both the internal and external space, the semiotic border is represented by the sum of bilingual translatable 'filters', passing through which the text is translated into another language (or languages), situated *outside* the given semiosphere. (Lotman [1984] 2005: 208–9)

In his later book, *Universe of the Mind* (1990), Lotman describes the functions of a boundary in the spirit of the sphere of semiotization: 'On the level of the semiosphere it implies a separation of "one's own" from "someone else's", the filtering of what comes from outside and is treated as a text in another language, and the translation of this text into one's own language. In this way external space becomes structured' (Lotman 1990: 140). Only in some cases can a boundary be real: 'When the semiosphere involves real territorial features as well, the boundary is spatial in the literal sense' (Lotman 1990: 140). Thus, while at the territorial level semiospheres can be easily delineated, at the cultural level the boundaries of the semiospheres are communicative and functional. The semiosphere as a meaningful whole can function only in relation to meaningfully different wholes and in communication with 'others'. Therefore, the boundary of the semiosphere as a meeting place of one's own and someone else's is changeable and dynamic, including both sustained self-defence from the foreign and the desire to receive innovative input from outside.

Although the semiosphere is, in Lotman's view, an abstract space, it is possible to identify within it the specific finite elements that relate to the concept of text. The text is a delimited whole according to its beginning, end and frame, although its meaning may vary depending on the way the text is interpreted. Lotman distinguishes between subtextual, textual and functional meanings. The complementarity of the text and the semiosphere and the importance of the holistic dimension is reflected in the use of the philosophical concept 'monad' in Lotman's later works. In the article 'Culture as a Subject and Its Own Object' ([1989] 2019), for example, Lotman uses the notion of monad in a sense that can be compared to the concept of text in his earlier writings:

The invariant model of a meaning-making entity assumes, first and foremost, its definitive delineation and self-sufficiency, and the presence of a border between it and the semiotic space outside it. This makes it possible to define meaning-making structures as their own form of semiotic monad, functioning at all levels of the semiotic universe. Such monads are represented by the culture as a whole as well as by every sufficiently complex text within it, including individual humans viewed as texts. ([1989] 2019: 85)

Lotman describes the behaviour of monads in similar terms to the behaviour of semiospheres within the semiophere:

However, no semiotic mechanism can function as an isolated system within a vacuum. A necessary condition for its functioning is its location within the semiosphere – that is, in semiotic space. Every semiotic monad, due precisely to its independence and semiotic autonomy, is capable of entering into a convergent relationship with another (or other) monad (monads), forming a bipolar unity at a higher structural level. ([1989] 2019: 86)

It is possible to explain these examples as complementarity between static and dynamic understanding on the one side and partial and holistic understanding on the other. However, there is also a third complementary in understanding semiosphere. In his 1984 article, Lotman provides an example from the history of ancient Rome, in which spatial dynamics is transformed into temporal: 'The opposition of centre/periphery is replaced by the opposition of yesterday/today' (Lotman [1984] 2005: 212). Lotman actualized this temporal aspect later in his *Culture and Explosion*, where the notion semiosphere is used only once: 'One of the foundations of the semiosphere is its heterogeneity. Sub-systems with variable speeds of cyclic motion are drawn together on a temporary axis' (Lotman [1992] 2009: 114). This means that spatial dynamics between centre and periphery actualizes boundary as a sphere of semiotization not only on the level of space but also on the level of time. The level of time relates to not only diachrony and synchrony but also different parallel cultural languages with different dynamics.

Reception of the concept of 'semiosphere' *post factum*

When we observe the scholarly reception of the concept of semiosphere, we notice the emergence of some dominants in the various interpretations. The first dominant is related to semiosphere as a universal research level. For instance, Irene Portis-Winner in her last book remarks that Lotman's concept of semiosphere creates a perspective of holistic analysis: 'Lotman's concept of the semiosphere subsumes all aspects of the semiotics of culture, all the heterogeneous semiotic systems or "languages" that are constantly changing and that in an abstract sense, have some unifying qualities' (Portis-Winner 2002: 63; see also Portis-Winner 1999). Edna Andrews, in turn, argues that the concept of semiosphere is helpful in better understanding semiosis: 'Lotman's extensive work on the semiosphere and the semiotics of communication provide some invaluable concepts and categories that offer insights into the structural principles of semiosis' (Andrews 1999: 8). Whereas in Neil Cornwell's opinion, the quality that the semiosphere has of binding diachrony and synchrony, organize memory and transform systems turns it into a very functional mechanism that has been connected even with the Jungian term of 'collective unconscious' (Cornwell 1992: 166).

From the collective unconscious it is convenient to proceed to the next dominant, dynamism. Bogusław Żyłko stresses, from the perspective of Lotman's evolution, that the concept of semiosphere signifies transfer from static to dynamic analysis, and the basis of this transfer is understanding the relationship between holism and heterogeneity:

The shift, from the conception of culture as a bundle of primary and secondary modelling systems to the notion of semiosphere, is also a shift from static to dynamic thinking. If we took the former approach, culture would resemble a motionless unit made up of semiotic systems; whereas if we follow the semiospheric approach, culture takes the shape of a heterogeneous whole bustling with multiple rhythms of development and transient dominants. (Żyłko 2001: 400)

Dynamism is also stressed by Floyd Merrell in his comparison of Peirce and Lotman and in his theory of biosemiosphere: 'Cultures are processes, never products' (Merrell 2001: 400). Biosemiotically oriented research forms highly diverse complexes in its interpretations of semiosphere (see Alexandrov 2000).

In addition to the identification of the biosphere and the semiosphere (Yates 1998), the other aspect is the global approach, represented by Jesper Hoffmeyer. For him, the semiosphere is an 'autonomous sphere of communication': 'The semiosphere is a sphere like the atmosphere, the hydrosphere or the biosphere. It penetrates these spheres and consists in signification and communication' (Hoffmeyer 1997: 934; see also Chang 2003). Between them lie dualistic approaches that create distinctions within the concept of semiosphere. Examples include the statement by Augusto Ponzio and Susan Petrilli that 'the semiosphere is part of a far broader semiosphere, the semiobiosphere' (Ponzio and Petrilli 2001: 265), or the methodological position of Kaie Kotov and Kalevi Kull: 'Semiosphere is both a semiotic model, and an object of semiotics. This is the approach used by Juri Lotman, simply extended to cover all forms of semiosis, as biosemiotics has been doing. In this way, the theory of the semiosphere can be seen as a basis for general semiotics' (Kotov and Kull 2011: 191; see also Kull 1998 and 2005). A separate tendency is the reference to complementarity in the concepts of Uexküll and Lotman (e.g. in the work of Mihhail Lotman, 2002).

The ability of the semiosphere concept to participate in the development of both theoretical and empirical toolboxes is worth noting. One of the first active implementers of the concept of the semiosphere was John Hartley, from whose works we know the concepts of 'mediasphere', 'Australian semiosphere' and 'digital semiosphere' (Hartley 1999; 2004; Hartley, Ibrus and Ojamaa 2021; see also Chapter 30). While Irene Machado interprets semiosphere as a critical theory of communication, Pieter J. Fourie sees it as a tool for mass communication research (Fourie 2010). Massimo Leone seeks to establish a method for the analysis of different kinds of symmetry in the semiosphere on the basis of the topological theory of fractals (Leone 2018). Jacques Fontanille uses the concept of the semiosphere as a tool for a comparative analysis of Lotman, Greimas and others. He tries to 'update' the semiosphere model in the context of anthropo-semiotics (Fontanille 2019). Edna Andrews and Elena Maksimova consider the concept of the semiosphere productive to modelling translation (Andrews and Maksimova 2008).

We used these examples of the reception of semiosphere in order to emphasize one of Lotman's methodological principles, on which his own treatment of semiosphere is based. This is the principle of dialogism. Usually the term 'dialogue' is associated with the name of Mikhail Bakhtin, and Lotman's treatment certainly has its connections to

Bakhtin's approach. Several works have been dedicated to the comparison of Bakhtin's and Lotman's dialogisms (see Chapter 5), but the simultaneity of the dual understanding has not been stressed much. In essence, this is a situation in which understanding is a process that on the one hand creates differences (word and the counterword) and, on the other hand, similarities (word and its translation). Dialogue as complementarity between answering and translating helps better understand how semiosphere functions. Alongside the importance of Bakhtin for the concept of the semiosphere (see Mandelker 1994; 1995), Roman Jakobson's communication model must be also mentioned (Torop 2003). Against this background, Winfried Nöth's reference to the autocommunicative aspect of the semiosphere that accompanies every act of communication is important (Nöth 2014; see also Chapter 11).

Dialogic semiosphere

In Lotman's opinion, in order to understand dialogue, it is not enough to understand the language that is used in the dialogue. In 'On the Semiosphere', he wrote:

> Meaning without communication is not possible. In this way, we might say, that dialogue precedes language and gives birth to it. And this also lies at the heart of the notion of semiosphere: the ensemble of semiotic formations precedes (not heuristically but functionally) the singular isolated language and becomes a condition for the existence of the latter. Without the semiosphere, language not only does not function, it does not exist. (Lotman [1984] 2005: 218–9)

In the next stage of discussion on semiosphere, in his book *Universe of the Mind*, Lotman emphasized that the dialogic situation has to be understood before any dialogue: 'the need for dialogue, *the dialogic situation*, precedes both real dialogue and even the existence of a language in which to conduct it: the semiotic situation precedes the instruments of semiosis' (Lotman 1990: 143–4). Thus, 'dialogue' becomes a term closely related to not only semiosphere but also one of its ontological characteristics. The concept of a dialogical model of culture appeared in Lotman's work in 1983, with the discussion on semiosphere developing this model first of all on the level of dynamics between the part and the whole:

> Since all levels of the semiosphere – from human personality to the individual text to the global semiotic unity – are a seemingly inter-connected group of semiospheres, each of them is simultaneously both participant in the dialogue (as part of the semiosphere) and the space of dialogue (the semiosphere as a whole). (Lotman [1984] 2005: 225)

The understanding of dialogue as an ontological characteristic of semiosphere in turn means that the outer and inner borders of semiosphere are seen as bilingual. Therefore, for Lotman the most important feature of the borders of semiosphere is their role as translation mechanisms. Human consciousness, too, is related to the same mechanisms since in determining one's identity, a person needs first to describe it to himself or herself. Translation mechanisms also form the basis for this thinking activity. And thus Lotman reaches the conclusion 'that the elementary act of thinking is translation' and 'the elementary mechanism of translation is dialogue' (Lotman 1990: 143).

It is important to keep in mind that semiosphere is simultaneously an object- and a meta-concept. Semiosphere is what is being studied in or as culture, while at the same time semiosphere is the conceptual tool that is being used to study culture. The idea that *semiosphere is studied by means of semiosphere* is not a paradox but points to the dialogue between the research object and its description language. The dynamism of culture as a research object forces science to search for new description languages, while the new description languages in turn influence cultural dynamics as they offer new possibilities for self-description. Often, however, from a historical perspective, a new description language is nothing but a methodological translation. Thus, the term 'semiosphere' also joins several concepts that are related to semiotics of culture and which have gained new relevance against the background of the developmental dynamics of culture.

Semiosphere is a concept that allows semiotics of culture to reach a new understanding of holism, a holistic analysis of dynamic processes. In semiotics of culture, the term 'semiosphere' bring together all that has recently converged, in the disciplines studying culture, in semiotics: a wish to find a description language that could be translated into and which could unify different disciplinary and interdisciplinary languages. In elaborating the general principles of cultural analysis in the interests of an understanding methodology, science needs to search for possible ways to interpret as diverse and non-trivial cultural phenomena and texts as possible and to promote cultural self-description. At the same time, from the historical perspective, the metalinguistic and conceptual heterogeneity of our contemporary science is much more homogeneous.

Therefore, it has to be said that the concept of semiosphere brings semiotics of culture again into contact with its own history, in the same way that it brings applicational cultural analysis into contact with the history of culture and with the newest phenomena in culture. The science of signs comes into contact with the art of signs. These contacts determine the place of the semiotics of culture among the sciences studying culture. And, as already was mentioned, it is not paradoxical that semiosphere studies semiosphere and culture studies culture. This is so because all this takes place within one single semiosphere of human culture, and each attempt to describe culture from any scientific position proves, on a different level, to be a self-description of culture.

From text to semiosphere

Textuality as a methodological principle has a significant role in the development of the Tartu-Moscow school. One of the most renowned members of the school, Alexander Piatigorsky, has post factum observed that this tradition started out with an undelimited research object. While in the first works at the beginning of the 1960s the object of semiotics was 'anything', then after the publication of Lotman's first semiotic book *Lectures on Structural Poetics* (1964) the object became specified as literature:

> In Lotman's *Lectures*, a huge role was played by the introduction of the term 'text' as a fundamental concept of semiotics and at the same time, as a *neutral* concept with respect to its object, literature. It was precisely the concept of 'text' which made it possible for Juri Mikhailovich to pass from literature over to culture as a *universal* object of semiotics. (Piatigorsky 1996: 54–5)

'Theses on the Semiotic Study of Cultures', the programmatic work of the Tartu-Moscow school, defines semiotics of culture as a science investigating the functional correlation of different sign systems, which proceeds from the position that 'none of the sign systems possesses a mechanism which would enable it to function culturally in isolation' (Lotman et al. [1973] 2013: 41). Text has been defined in 'Theses' as a bridging link between a general semiotic and a concrete empirical investigation:

> The text has integral meaning and integral function (if we distinguish between the position of the investigator of culture and the position of its carrier, then from the point of view of the former the text appears as the carrier of integral function, while from the position of the latter it is the carrier of integral meaning). In this sense it may be regarded as the primary element (basic unit) of culture. The relationship of the text with the whole of culture and with its system of codes is shown by the fact that on different levels the same message may appear as a text, part of a text, or an entire set of texts'. (Lotman et al. [1973] 2013: 57–8)

In the tradition of the Tartu-Moscow school, the concept of text is, above all, dynamic: text can be an integral sign or a sequence of signs; it can be a part or a whole. On the other hand, a text can be a linguistically concrete *text of language* or a culturally concrete *text of culture*: 'In defining culture as a certain secondary language, we introduce the concept of a "culture text", a text in this secondary language. So long as some natural language is a part of the language of culture, there arises the question of the relationship between the text in the natural language and the verbal text of culture' (Lotman et al. [1973] 2013: 62).

As three subtypes of this relationship the authors mention cases in which (1) a text in a natural language is not a text of a given culture (e.g. oral texts in a writing-oriented culture); (2) a text in a secondary language, that is, a cultural text, is at the same time also a text of language, that is, a text in a natural language (e.g. a poem that is expressed simultaneously in a secondary, poetic language and in a primary language, for instance, in the poet's mother tongue); (3) a verbal cultural text is not a text in a natural language (e.g. a Latin prayer for Slavs).

From the contemporary perspective, 'Theses on the Semiotic Study of Cultures' touched upon an important aspect, that of virtuality: 'The place of the text in the textual space is defined as the sum total of potential texts' (Lotman et al. [1973] 2013: 64). In the *Universe of the Mind*, expanding upon the ideas of Ferdinand de Saussure, Lotman claimed that 'synchrony is homeostatic while diachrony is made up of a series of external and accidental infringements of it, in reacting against which synchrony re-establishes its integrity' (Lotman 1990: 6). Against the background of cultural homeostasis, the advance towards semiosphere appears natural. Let us recall once again the well-known thought of Vyacheslav Ivanov: 'The task of semiotics is to describe the semiosphere without which the noosphere is inconceivable' (Ivanov 1998: 792). As noosphere is the future living environment of humankind, created in mutual agreement and on rational principles, it follows from this definition that semiotics must assist mankind in understanding both history and the future. Hence, in addition to the relationship with the present, semiosphere also has its dimensions of history and future. What is more important, however, is that semiosphere establishes the dynamics between the part and the whole. And this whole–part relationship is joined, in turn, by the dynamics between the subjective and the objective: 'The structural parallelism of textual and individual semiotic characteristics allows us to define a text at any level as a semiotic entity, and to view an entity at any socio-cultural level as a text' (Lotman [1983] 2019: 75).

The notion of semiosphere stems from the dynamic nature of the notion of text. For Lotman, it helped to make closer contacts between space (textual, cultural, semiotic) and time (synchrony, diachrony, achrony). The last books by Lotman are about dynamics and processuality. However, the ambiguity of the boundary of the terminological field of semiosphere (biosphere, social sphere, semiosphere, noosphere, semiotic space) is a reason why the development of this concept is important.

From culture to semiosphere

In his late article 'Text and Cultural Polyglotism', Lotman wrote about the model of space as one of the primary languages of culture: 'Genetically speaking, culture is built upon two primary languages. One of these is the natural language used by humans in everyday communication. [...] The nature of the second primary language is not so obvious. What is under discussion is the structural model of space' (Lotman 1992: 142). On this general level, there are two complementary interpretations of semiosphere. Firstly, semiosphere as abstract space is a global model of human culture and global semiosis. Secondly, semiosphere as subsemiosphere, which is the dynamic element of human culture and which can be described as a whole, as a part of a greater whole (semiospheres within the semiosphere) or as the constellation of entangled semiospheres. At the same time, these dynamic semiospheres are describable as independent texts or monads with fixed and relatively static boundaries. This means, 'In a sense, the semiosphere can be understood as an elaboration of the notion of "culture" to its logical limits, producing an isomorphic chain: text–culture–semiosphere' (Tamm 2019: 8).

If Lotman described culture as both a text and a combination of texts, it means that text was a functional concept for him. At the empirical level of culture, a text is an artefact, a delimited whole that is made dynamic by its use. At a more abstract level, a text can be an operational concept that contributes to the analysability of culture by delimiting and, for the sake of analysis, by making static inherently dynamic and procedural phenomena. In this vein, Lotman has studied a human life or a historical era as a text. However, in linking the concept of text to culture, Lotman has remained faithful to his credo to ground theoretical approaches in empirical analysis. And for him, empirical analysis was related to Russian culture. He set out his creed in one of his latest articles, published shortly after his death:

> The study of Russian culture from a semiotic perspective may take two directions. On the one hand, the researcher may utilize the broad achievements of semiotic studies and describe Russian culture on their foundation. The other approach implies a certain dissatisfaction with existing semiotic studies of culture and a desire to find a basis for other methods and approaches in the material of Russian culture. Our approach is precisely the latter. We propose that the study of the material of Russian culture from this angle may provide new impetus to the general methodology of the semiotics of culture. The dynamism, instability and persistent internal contradictions of Russian culture cause it to be a sort of historical and theoretical proving ground, leading both to unavoidable losses and, at times, prophetic insight into this inherently experimental field of study. (Lotman 1994: 219)

Through the concept of the semiosphere, Lotman continues the same logic. On the one hand, he seeks to make empirical cultural analysis more dynamic by valuing the so-called parametric description and complementarity between the partial description and the full description as well as the static and dynamic description. The semiosphere as an operational and global concept contributes to the possibility of seeing general cultural problems (in relation to the global semiosphere as a model of human culture) in the analyses of cultural phenomena such as, for example, global connections between the East and the West or universal connections between the right and left hemisphere. Using the concept of the semiosphere, Lotman sought to explore culture as a process in historical development; using this concept, it is useful to distinguish, as in the case of the concept of text, the empirical and operational levels. The concept of the semiosphere naturally includes the importance of the observer in the processes of interpretation, and in using this concept it is also important to determine one's position as the observer.

References

Alexandrov, V. E. 2000. 'Biology, Semiosis, and Cultural Difference in Lotman's Semiosphere', *Comparative Literature* 52 (4): 339–62.

Andrews, E. 1999. 'Lotman's Communication Act and Semiosis', *Semiotica* 126 (1/4): 1–15.

Andrews, E. and Maksimova, E. 2008. 'Semiospheric Transitions: A Key to Modelling Translation', *Sign Systems Studies* 36 (2): 259–69.

Chang, H. 2003. 'Is Language a Primary Modeling System? On Juri Lotman's Concept of Semiosphere', *Sign Systems Studies* 31 (1): 9–23.

Cornwell, N. 1992. 'Lotman's Semiosphere', *Irish Slavonic Studies* 13: 163–7.

Fontanille, J. 2019. 'Semiosphere Challenged by Anthropo-Semiotic Enunciation', *Bakhtiniana: Revista de Estudos do Discurso* 14 (4): 61–82.

Fourie, P. J. 2010. 'An Examination of the Value of the Concept of the "Semiosphere" in the Study of Mass Communication: Testing the Value and Feasibility of a Proposed Research Project', *Razón y Palabra* 15 (72), available online: https://www.redalyc.org/articulo.oa?id=199514 906010 (accessed 15 January 2021).

Hartley, J. 1999. *Uses of Television*, London and New York: Routledge.

Hartley, J. 2004. 'Television, Nation, and Indigenous Media', *Television & New Media* 5 (1): 7–25.

Hartley, J., Ibrus, I. and Ojamaa, M. 2021. *On the Digital Semiosphere: Culture, Media and Science for the Anthropocene*, London and New York: Bloomsbury Academic.

Hoffmeyer, J. 1997. 'The Global Semiosphere', in I. Rauch and G. F. Carr (eds), *Semiotics around the World: Synthesis in Diversity. Proceedings of the Fifth Congress of the International Association for Semiotic Studies, Berkeley 1994*, 933–6, Berlin: Mouton de Gruyter.

Ivanov, V. V. 1998. *Izbrannye trudy po semiotike i istorii kul'tury*, vol. 1, Moscow: Iazyki russkoi kul'tury.

Kotov, K. and Kull, K. 2011. 'Semiosphere Is the Relational Biosphere', in C. Emmeche and K. Kull (eds), *Towards a Semiotic Biology: Life is the Action of Signs*, 179–94, London: Imperial College Press.

Kull, K. 1998. 'On Semiosis, Umwelt, and Semiosphere', *Semiotica* 120 (3/4): 299–310.

Kull, K. 2005. 'Semiosphere and a Dual Ecology: Paradoxes of Communication', *Sign Systems Studies* 33 (1): 175–89.

Kull, K. 2006. '"Semiosfäär", 1982: Kommentaariks' ['Semiosphere', 1982: A Comment]', *Acta Semiotica Estica* 3: 222–4.

Leone, M. 2018. 'Symmetries in the Semiosphere: A Typology', *Wenyi Lilun Yanjiu* 38 (1): 168–81.

Lotman, J. [1983] 2019. 'Toward a Theory of Cultural Interaction: The Semiotic Aspect', in J. Lotman, *Culture, Memory and History: Essays in Cultural Semiotics*, trans. B. J. Baer, ed. M. Tamm, 67–81, Cham: Palgrave Macmillan.

Lotman, J. [1984] 2005. 'On the Semiosphere', trans. W. Clark, *Sign Systems Studies* 33 (1): 205–29.

Lotman, J. [1989] 2019. 'Culture as a Subject and Its Own Object', in J. Lotman, *Culture, Memory and History: Essays in Cultural Semiotics*, ed. M. Tamm, trans. B. J. Baer, 83–93, Cham: Palgrave Macmillan.

Lotman, Yu. M. 1990. *The Universe of the Mind: A Semiotic Theory of Culture*, trans. A. Shukman, Bloomington, IN: Indiana University Press.

Lotman, Ju. M. 1992. 'Tekst i poliglotizm kultury', in Ju. M. Lotman, *Izbrannye stat'i v trekh tomakh*, vol. 1, 142–7, Tallinn: Aleksandra.

Lotman, J. [1992] 2009. *Culture and Explosion*, trans. W. Clark, ed. M. Grishakova, Berlin and New York: Mouton de Gruyter.

Lotman, J. 1994. 'Theses Towards a Semiotics of Russian Culture', *Elementa* 1 (3): 219–27.

Lotman, J. M., Ivanov, V. V., Pjatigorskij, A. M., Toporov, V. N. and Uspenskij, B. A. [1973] 2013. 'Theses on the Semiotic Study of Cultures (as Applied to Slavic Texts)', in S. Salupere, P. Torop and K. Kull (eds), *Beginnings of the Semiotics of Culture*, 53–77, Tartu: University of Tartu Press.

Lotman, Y. M. and Uspensky, B. A. [1971] 1978. 'On the Semiotic Mechanism of Culture', trans. G. Mihaychuk, *New Literary History* 9 (2): 211–32.

Lotman, M. 2002. 'Umwelt and Semiosphere', *Sign Systems Studies* 30 (1): 33–40.

Machado, I. 2011. 'Lotman's Scientific Investigatory Boldness: The Semiosphere as a Critical Theory of Communication in Culture', *Sign Systems Studies* 39 (1): 81–103.

Mandelker, A. 1994. 'Semiotizing the Sphere: Organicist Theory in Lotman, Bakhtin, and Vernadsky', *Publications of the Modern Language Association* 109 (3): 385–96.

Mandelker, A. 1995. 'Logosphere and Semiosphere: Bakhtin, Russian Organicism, and the Semiotics of Culture', in A. Mandelker (ed.), *Bakhtin in Contexts Across the Disciplines*, 177–90, Evanston: Northwestern University Press.

Merrell, F. 2001. 'Lotman's Semiosphere, Peirce's Categories, and Cultural Forms of Life', *Sign Systems Studies* 29 (2): 385–415.

Nöth, W. 2014. 'The Topography of Yuri Lotman's Semiosphere', *International Journal of Cultural Studies* 14 (4): 1–17.

Piatigorsky, A. M. 1996. 'Zametki iz 90-kh o semiotike 60-kh godov', in A. M. Piatigorsky, *Izbrannye trudy*, 52–7, Moscow: Iazyki russkoi kul'tury.

Ponzio, A. and Petrilli, S. 2001. 'Bioethics, Semiotics of Life, and Global Communication', *Sign Systems Studies* 29 (1): 263–76.

Portis-Winner, I. 1999. 'The Dynamics of Semiotics of Culture; Its Pertinence to Anthropology', *Sign Systems Studies* 27: 24–45.

Portis-Winner, I. 2002. *Semiotics of Peasants in Transition: Slovene Villagers and Their Ethnic Relatives in America*, Durham: Duke University Press.

Tamm, M. 2019. 'Introduction: Juri Lotman's Semiotic Theory of History and Cultural Memory', in J. Lotman, *Culture, Memory and History: Essays in Cultural Semiotics*, ed. M. Tamm, trans. B. J. Baer, 1–26, Cham: Palgrave Macmillan.

Torop, P. 2003. 'Semiospherical Understanding: Textuality', *Sign Systems Studies* 31 (2): 323–39.

Torop, P. 2005. 'Semiosphere and/as the Research Object of Semiotics of Culture', *Sign Systems Studies* 33 (1): 159–73.

Yates, F. E. 1998. 'Biosphere as Semiosphere', *Semiotica* 120 (3/4): 439–53.

Żyłko, B. 2001. 'Culture and Semiotics: Notes on Lotman's Conception of Culture', *New Literary History* 32 (2): 391–408.

PART III
LOTMAN IN DIALOGUE

CHAPTER 23
LOTMAN AND FRENCH THEORY
Sergey Zenkin

Juri Lotman was a contemporary of the so-called French Theory, constituted in the 1960s–80s through cooperation between different disciplines (philosophy, literary theory, psychoanalysis, semiotics, sociology) and commonly subsumed under the rather vague name of 'post-structuralism' (Cusset 2003). Lotman was aware of this intellectual movement, and his own research converged in more than one regard with that of the French authors; however, his relationship with them was distant and rarely manifested.

Lotman understood French. He held in esteem the historiographical school of the *Annales* (Lotman [1994] 2010: 65–6) and the classics of French structuralism, from Ferdinand de Saussure to Claude Lévi-Strauss and Algirdas Julien Greimas; he read and cited Tzvetan Todorov's and Claude Bremond's works on structural poetics and included a translation of Bremond's article on the logic of narrative possibilities in the volume *Semiotika i iskusstvometria* (Semiotics and Computing of Art) published under his direction in 1972. As for the new theorists who revised structuralism, he has read Roland Barthes and the first publications by Barthes's disciple Julia Kristeva. Kristeva was the only French post-structuralist to be acquainted with him in the late 1960s (Waldstein 2008: 112) and to exchange texts with him. In a letter of 1970 Lotman referred to her advice when thinking of reforming the editorial board of *Trudy po znakovym sistemam* (Lotman 1997: 678), and in 1969 Kristeva entitled her own book using the Greek word Σημειωτική, which features on the cover of the Tartu periodical collection (Kristeva 1969). She offered her book to Lotman '*avec l'admiration et l'amitié*' ('with admiration and friendship' – Lotman [1967a] 2018: 162, quoted in notes). Lotman in a letter to another person playfully commented on her borrowing of the term as 'a diurnal theft of our title' (Lotman 1997: 656).

Lotman never had occasion to make the acquaintance of other representatives of the French Theory: the Soviet authorities forbade him to go abroad; as a result he was able to participate neither in 1967 in the organizational meetings of the International Association for Semiotic Studies in Paris, where he was invited by Greimas (Lotman [1968a] 2018: 192, notes), nor in the first congress of that association, which took place in Warsaw in 1968; he was elected its vice president in absentia (Lotman 1997: 497–8).

Julia Kristeva, who read Lotman's works in Russian, attempted to introduce them in France. In 1968, she presented a collection of articles by the Soviet semiotic school in the avant-garde Parisian review *Tel Quel* (no. 35) (see Kristeva 1968), including Lotman's text 'Semantics of Number and Typology of Culture' (Lotman 1968); and the next year she published a translation of Lotman and Piatigorsky's essay 'Text and Function' in the international review *Semiotica* (Lotman and Piatigorsky 1969). Many years later, after

Lotman's death, she wrote a necrology 'On Yury Lotman' in which she praised his work as 'testifying to those shoots of modest but tenacious vitality that sometimes – indeed, more often than one might think – grow under the snows of Russian winter and that the West is not always alert or sensitive enough to detect' (Kristeva 1994: 376). Significantly, her text was published in English, in the United States; in France, Lotman's work never obtained wide renown. Even though several of his books were translated into French in his lifetime (Lotman 1973; 1977; Lotman and Ouspenski 1990), they did not grant him a reputation comparable, say, to Mikhail Bakhtin's.

Lotman's own opinion of contemporary French Theory was sceptical on the whole. An exemplary case might be his variable attitude towards Roland Barthes, the most renowned French theoretician of literature and semiotics. In the 1960s, he welcomed Barthes's works and tried to use them in his own research: so the title *Writing Degree Zero* (Barthes [1953] 1993) converged with Lotman's idea of 'zero elements' that function within semiotic structures (Lotman [1970] 1998: 61), and the critical analysis of contemporary 'myths' provided by the French author in *Mythologies* (Barthes [1957] 1993) seemed to continue the structural studies of ancient myths initiated by Lévi-Strauss. In 1968, Lotman praised Barthes for having 'applied the principles of contemporary structural ethnography to the study of the world of everyday French life which surrounded him' (Lotman [1968a] 2018: 176). He also favourably mentioned Barthes's study of fashion, critical essays on literature and, above all, 'the most complete in French and generally one of the best accounts of the main principles of semiotics' (Lotman [1968a] 2018: 176), that is, Barthes's theoretical treatise *Elements of Semiology* (Barthes [1964] 1993), afterwards rather underestimated by its author.[1] Moreover, Lotman annotated this treatise and began to translate it into Russian – a draft of the first pages has been conserved (Lotman [1968a] 2018: 194, notes). But a little later, after having named Barthes in the first version (1968–69) of his article on structuralism in literary studies (for the *Short Literary Encyclopaedia*, published in Moscow in the 1960s and 1970s), he withdrew this credit in two amended versions (Lotman [1968b] 2018: 237, 243, 250). The reason was probably not the ideological censorship, because of which his article was finally refused by the editorial board, but rather changes in Barthes's purposes and in Lotman's appreciation of him. Indeed, exactly in the late 1960s Barthes abandoned rigorous structural poetics and declared his shift 'from scholarship to literature' (the title of his 1967 article), while Lotman remained committed to the academic style of thought and writing. Later on, in 1988, Lotman referred for the last time to Barthes's *Mythologies*, but on a symptomatically frivolous occasion, discussing different ways to use alcoholic drinks (Lotman [1988] 2012: 671).

In his letters Lotman confessed to being 'irritated' by the Parisian review *Tel Quel*, in which Kristeva had published his own text,[2] scornfully characterizing it with a quotation from Pushkin: 'amusements for naughty adult children' (Lotman 1997: 658). His texts of the 1970s and 1980s contain very few references to contemporary French theorists: one hardly finds in them any mention of Jacques Lacan, Jacques Derrida, Jean Baudrillard, Jean-François Lyotard or Gilles Deleuze, and if he quoted Michel Foucault's *The Order of Things* (Foucault 1966) twice, it's only for the analysis of Velasquez' painting *Las*

Meninas, with which Foucault's book began (Lotman [1973] 1998: 336; [1981] 1998: 412). In 1978, he wrote to Natalia Avtonomova, one of the Russian translators of that book: 'Lévi-Strauss is a great researcher in a particular field (this is always the most worthwhile), Foucault is an acute and gifted *philosophe* in the French sense of this word, and Barthes and Kristeva (God forgive me, the sinner!) are of a petty interest. They are literary essayists, not of a higher range' (Avtonomova 2009: 469).

So, on the biographic and anecdotal level the relationship of Lotman (and, more generally, of the Tartu-Moscow school) with the French Theory appears 'as a series of misunderstandings and mismatches piling up one upon another' (Waldstein 2008: 113). They knew each other insufficiently, and their rare attempts to assimilate and use their respective discoveries usually ended in failure. Nevertheless, working at the same time (albeit in quite different sociopolitical conditions), they challenged the same scholarly and philosophical endeavours, and their main intellectual options display some points of similarity as well as significant divergences.

1. *Disciplinary context.* Russian and French theorists defined the place of their researches in the multidisciplinary field of the sciences differently. They all draw ideas from the structural linguistics – a leading human science of the twentieth century. Lotman also used concepts taken up from cybernetics, formal logic, physics (cf. his concept, originating from molecular physics, of meaningful 'holes' within a structure). Saussurian linguistics remained a reliable basis for his theory of culture (see Chapter 2), while the French theorists tended to deconstruct it (Jacques Derrida) or to replace it with methodological alternatives, for example Saussure's own research on anagrams (Julia Kristeva, Jean Baudrillard). Lotman would sometimes cite the notion of 'organic unity' (Lotman [1968b] 2018: 233), a biological metaphor borrowed through Russian traditional aesthetics, and serving to approximately account for the idea of structure (Sériot 2016: 12). Later, and more importantly, he resorted to a biological model, comparing the functioning of the semiosphere to the functional asymmetry of the brain. Among the French theorists, one encounters a biological model in Deleuze and Guattari's concept of the rhizome, which differs from 'organic unity' in its essential decentralization. French Theory privileged sociological, rather than biological, models: *la langue* as an imperative social instance (Roland Barthes), the idea of 'symbolic exchange' taken up by Jean Baudrillard from the anthropology of Mauss and Lévi-Strauss. As a final point, several French theorists – Deleuze, Derrida, Foucault, Lyotard – were professional philosophers. In contrast, Lotman, even in his most abstract theoretical concepts, avoided any reference to the twentieth century's philosophy, partly because of the censorship that it was subjected to in the Soviet Union.

2. *Semiotics.* Lotman was committed to the positive and 'scientific' understanding of semiotics, defined as a science of communication, and he particularly privileged the semiotic processes taking place in literature and art. He distinguished between different forms of communication (oral and written, external and internal, poetic and prosaic speech) and attempted to explain the aesthetic effect of art by its informational capacity: 'Beauty is information' (Lotman [1964] 1994: 132). A number of the terms Lotman used were taken from information theory: 'code', 'model', 'noise'. In France, the advanced

theory considered semiotics/semiology another way: in 1974, Roland Barthes denied the scientific nature of semiology, since 'there [was] no extraterritoriality of the subject – be it a scholar – in relation to his discourse' (Barthes [1974] 1995: 39). Semiotics, he claimed, had to engage in an all-embracing critique of the Western civilization, a 'semioclastic' deconstruction of sign systems. As early as the 1960s, Julia Kristeva put forward a programme of 'semanalysis', endeavouring to trace the global movement of intertextuality, that is, a circulation of signs which does not depend, in principle, on particular acts of communication (Kristeva 1969).

3. *Sign*. Lotman focused on the function of signs not in language, as Saussure did, but primarily in artistic communication, comparing different kinds of sign (visual and verbal, ideographic and symbolic) in literature, cinema and so on, hence the global character of the signs he studied. These are not minimal constructive units of a linguistic structure, but rather integral texts/works of art ('a sign, a carrier of meaning, is not here a word, but the whole text', Lotman [1964] 1998: 378). Lotman's preference in moments of heightened, accentuated semiotic effect resulted from the aesthetic specificity of the material, such as 'signs of signs' in animation cinema, puppets, rhetorical figures, 'the text within the text', 'the movie within the movie'.

French theorists converged with him in their interest in the nomination and the particular semiotic structure of proper names. Lotman wrote about the 'world of proper names' in his *Culture and Explosion* (1992), and Barthes – about the proper names in Proust, and Foucault – wrote about the history of the classical idea of essential signs, which was to be deconstructed in modern culture. Unlike Lotman, the French tried to delve into the internal structure of the ordinary, not necessarily artistic, sign. They discerned its different levels of signification, including that of external referent (Barthes's 'reality effect'); they deconstructed the sign taken as such, reducing it to a 'trace' (Derrida), introducing it not in stable structures, but in mobile 'series' (Deleuze). A parallel can be established between Lotman's dynamic opposition *prose/poetry* and Derrida's contrariety of the writing and the oral speech. Both theorists tend to ascribe to the first term (apparently poorer than the second) a greater ability to produce and transform meaning, but they do so in quite different intellectual contexts (Derrida in general philosophy of sense-making, Lotman in the historical typology of literary expression; see also Chapter 24).

4. *Secondary systems*. Lotman and Barthes both attached great importance to the secondary processes of sense-production, although they defined them in different ways (Monticelli 2016). In *Mythologies* (1957), Barthes described in detail connotation (designated then by the terms 'myth' and 'metalanguage'), an additional meaning that culture attributes to primary semiotic objects (e.g. to visual images). This meaning is introduced into the message unknowingly for the addressee and serves the purposes of seduction in advertising or propaganda in politics. Later, in his 'post-structuralist' book *S/Z* (Barthes [1970] 1994), Barthes acknowledged the leading role of connotation in the formation of the limited multiplicity of meanings in the classical narrative. Although Lotman knew Barthes's *Mythologies*, one cannot claim that he took into account its theory of connotation; however, in his own works he used a somewhat similar notion,

common to the Tartu school, that of 'secondary modelling systems'. These are 'systems based on natural language and acquiring additional superstructures, creating languages of the second degree' (Lotman [1967] 1998: 387). Lotman is speaking here of systems, not of isolated, weakly related meanings as Barthes has described his 'myths'. Systems are built over the language as a whole, and not over a particular text or image, and their main function – especially that of art – is cognitive; they produce models of the world and its cultural representations ('Art is a means of the cognition of life' Lotman [1964] 1994: 33).

5. *Text.* In opposition to the linguistic understanding of text as an element of Saussurian *parole*, that is, a manifestation of the general laws of language, Lotman put forward its 'literary' definition – as a single and unique product of culture, serving not only to transmit information but also as a 'generator of sense' (Lotman [1969] 2002: 189), capable even of selecting and shaping its own audience (see also Chapter 9). From this point of view, 'being a text' is not an immanent property of a symbolic complex, but a function attributed to it: culture assigns some particular statements as texts and conserves them as valuable monuments (Zolyan 2020: 13–58). To be recognized as a text, a verbal utterance must be materially expressed, structured, limited (in particular with a beginning and an end), meaningful (subject to interpretation); a complex of texts united by a common code can be considered as a single text. Representatives of the French Theory (Barthes, Kristeva, Derrida) treated the text rather in the linguistic way, as an unlimited activity of language, 'felt only in the process of operation' (Barthes [1971] 1994: 1212), as a discourse covering the entire space of semantic production (Derrida: 'there is nothing outside the text' Derrida 1967: 227). They agreed with Lotman in recognizing the plurality of meanings of the text, but if Barthes considered a variable text richer than a fixed work, then for Lotman the situation was the opposite: a work of art is richer than its own text, since it includes also 'extratextual structures' determined by context (Lotman [1970] 1998: 59–61).

6. *Semiosphere.* Lotman defined the semiosphere as a global space of semiotic communication, but immediately recognized the necessity of a border separating it from the outer, non-semiotic space or from other semiospheres (Lotman [1984] 1992; see also Chapter 22). The elements of semiosphere are cultural codes – multiple languages of culture used in that area, and united by the typical relationship of translation – something that was rarely conceptualized by the French theorists. They did not have a general concept similar to semiosphere; instead, they described an unlimited text (Derrida) or distinguished between languages of power and non-power opposing each other in social life and in a particular text ('*text, textile* and *tress* are the same thing', Barthes [1971] 1994: 663). An analogue of the semiosphere might also be intertextuality, an all-embracing process in which it is not cultural codes that interact, but rather particular texts that endlessly 'quote' each other (Kristeva).

7. *Inner speech.* One of the sources of French Theory was psychoanalysis. Since Lacan gave Freudian psychoanalysis a structural interpretation, pointing out the symbolic register of the unconscious, 'structured as a language', psychoanalytic patterns were widely used in the analysis of texts (Barthes), deconstructed through the concept of 'différance' (Derrida) and radicalized within the framework of general critique of the

sign (Baudrillard) and of the thinking subject. Lyotard, Deleuze and Guattari, criticizing the Freudian concept of the Oedipus complex, outlined instead a 'libidinal economy' of flows organizing the subject's semantic activity. Lotman was generally sceptical about Freud's theories and considered his schemes of the infantile unconscious as secondary phenomena which result from '*translating* complex texts received by a child from the adult world into a much simpler language of children's ideas' (Lotman [1974] 2002: 142). From this point of view, one should make 'not culture a metaphor of sex, as Freud claims, but sex a metaphor of culture' (Lotman 1992: 256). Lotman had another theory of mental life, based on Lev Vygotsky's idea of inner speech. He constructed upon it his own concept of autocommunication, a silent discourse in which the code encrypting the message becomes enriched: 'the information grows by being transformed and reformulated in other categories' (Lotman 1992: 84), and things go the same way in artistic creativity.

8. *Simulacra.* From the 1970s, French philosophers were thinking about *simulacra*, semiotic or mimetic figures of real institutions, social movements, and so on, that function in modern society along with or instead of the real ones they imitate. According to Jean Baudrillard, in the mind of their contemporaries the simulacra can 'precede' their originals (Baudrillard 1981). Derrida introduced in philosophy the concept of 'economimesis' (Derrida 1975) and the idea of the 'ghostly' existence of certain historical facts (Derrida 1993). Lotman did not conceptualize such phenomena *in abstracto*, but provided a historical study of the cultural pseudomorphosis in a series of articles on the poetics of everyday behaviour and sociopolitical action. He showed how aesthetic models (literary, pictorial, theatrical) could encode the real acts of people, thereby acquiring a 'ghostly' existence in the real world. Significantly, he localized these phenomena not in a 'post-modern' society as the French thinkers did, but in Russian culture of the eighteenth and nineteenth centuries, especially after the reforms of Peter the Great, who forced the Russian nobility to mimetically reproduce Western cultural patterns.

9. *Dialectics.* French Theory was generally reluctant to the dialectical idea of creative negativity. Jacques Derrida criticized Hegel's dialectics, considering it incompatible with deconstruction: the former seeks to reconcile the contradictions in synthesis, the latter reveals their irreconcilability. Derrida and Foucault interpreted negativity in terms not of dialectics, but rather of transgression, a unilateral negation without resolving contradictions and without dialectical sublation (*Aufhebung*). In the 1960s and 1970s, Kristeva and Baudrillard attempted to renew the Marxist dialectic by introducing concepts of 'productivity' and 'negativity of poetry' (Kristeva 1969; Baudrillard 1976), which presupposed a sacrificial extermination of language and its meanings without any rational synthesis (the idea had been inherited from Georges Bataille, together with the concept of transgression). As for Lotman, his attitude towards dialectics was partly due to the place it occupied in the doctrine of Soviet Marxism: he often used the word 'dialectic' in his early works, but preferred to avoid it in his last years, when the communist regime collapsed. But independently of its ideological connotations, he took the idea of dialectics, seriously acknowledging it to be 'the methodological basis of structuralism' (Lotman [1967b] 2018: 71), allowing

one to consider 'the structure as a dialectical unity' (Lotman [1994] 2018: 366). A dialectical state of mind manifested itself in Lotman's interest in structural negativity, in phenomena such as the presence/absence of 'zero elements' and 'holes' in literary structures. Dialectics served him to explain the relationship between the elements of structure, between part and the whole, between different languages of culture, between reality and its artistic representation ('The resemblance between art and life is not a mechanical identity but a dialectical approximation' Lotman [1964] 1994: 41). Implicitly, dialectic was also used to account for the development of art and literature, justifying, for example, the historical interchange of poetry and prose, and the great alternation of two contradicting but mutually indispensable phases of the historical evolution, 'culture' and 'explosion'.

10. *Typology of cultures*. More than other French theorists, Michel Foucault was interested in the problem of historical types of culture. He formulated (Foucault 1966; 1969) the concept of *episteme*, the historical configuration of knowledge characterizing a particular epoch and determined by the practices of obtaining, institutionalizing and disseminating knowledge (later he called it 'the regime of truth'). Units of episteme are, according to Foucault, utterances, also determined by the pragmatics of their production. This theory can be compared to Lotman's concept of the type of culture, although it does not mean that Lotman had been influenced by his acquaintance with the works of the French philosopher (he was rather familiar with Oswald Spengler's morphology of cultures). Describing a historical type of culture, Lotman defined it both on pragmatic grounds (e.g. by the dominant method of teaching culture, i.e. through grammar or through texts, and by the predominance of external or internal communication within that culture) and also by the inner structure of its language (e.g. its prevalent orientation on 'proper nouns' or 'pronouns'). A feature of Lotman's theory of culture that has no analogue in Foucault is his analysis of the interaction of different cultures, each of them determining its 'own other', shaping its own non-culture. Thus, in contrast to the episteme defined by Foucault, culture according to Lotman functions not only as a descriptive notion but also as a real agent of the historical process, engaged in dynamic relationships with other cultural formations. While some French theorists were inclined to seek the cultural otherness of the West in the postcolonial Orient, Lotman's typology of culture apparently followed the traditional track of Russian philosophical thought, opposing 'Russia' and 'the West' (Gasparov 1998: 233–6). However, his assessments of these two cultural types were complex and unequivocal: even if sometimes their distinction could be read as the one of 'organic tradition' versus 'rationality', in his late texts, Lotman applied another criterion of value to the same opposition. Western culture, he claimed, practices a ternary (dialectical) mode of thinking and of self-formation, whereas Russia has to embrace this mode and to get out of her traditional 'dual models' blocking her sociopolitical progress (Lotman 1992: 267–70).

11. *Philosophy of history*. Lotman never called himself a 'philosopher', but nevertheless outlined an original concept of historical evolution (see Chapters 18 and 25), which had no analogues in France, despite the profound interest of some French theorists (Barthes, Foucault) in the problems of cultural history. He proclaimed this

task in one of his last works: 'it is possible to consider semiotics as a science studying the theory and the history of culture' (Lotman [1994] 2010: 37). The unpredictability of historical development, seen as uncertain by contemporaries and as predetermined by posterity, as well as the necessary alternation of periods of 'culture' and 'explosion' in the historical process – all these ideas correspond to different moments of dialectical self-regulation of history, that Lotman wanted to rely on the mathematical model of 'order from chaos' proposed by Ilya Prigogine and Isabelle Stengers (Prigogine and Stengers 1986). Their works refer to the natural, rather than social, sciences; they have nothing to do with post-structuralism and are therefore usually not included in the 'French Theory'.

12. *Politics*. Last but not least, divergence between Lotman and French Theory was due to the fact that their scholarly ideas had different, partly opposing political implications because they had developed in fundamentally different political environments (see also Chapter 20). French theorists lived in a democratic society and openly criticized its flaws; many of them participated in political protests and occupied more or less clear positions on the left flank of the political struggle. Lotman and his Soviet fellows were facing a totalitarian state that censored any deviations from the tenets of official Marxism. Until the fall of censorship in the late 1980s, this led Lotman, firstly, to avoid any open political conclusions from his theory (although, e.g. his idea of at least two different codes needed for the fruitful development of a semiotic system could be interpreted as an indirect claim for a multiparty system) and, secondly, to mistrust the Marxist and leftist convictions of his foreign colleagues. The incompatibility of political conditions and of current political tasks was one of the main reasons that Lotman's interaction with the French Theory turned out to be an 'impossible dialogue' (Landolt 2012).

To conclude, in his theoretical works Lotman addressed the same great problem as the French scholarship of the 1960s–80s: they both had to account for the dynamic organization of culture, and not only for its static structure. However, they chose different approaches to this problem. In France, the theory was critical, characterized by 'an eternal struggle between theory and the common sense' (Compagnon 1998: 24). The French intellectuals emphasized the demystification of culture, putting it in motion from the outside through their analytical efforts. As for Lotman, he shared in his own way a belief in the cognitive task of art characteristic of Russian aesthetics. In his mind, art and culture have a dynamic principle in themselves, so they are not subject to critical demystification or deconstruction, but to objective scholarly inquiry revealing this principle. Their ability to self-develop guarantees the growth of their diversity and an enrichment of their semantic content.

Notes

1. First published in *Communications*, 1964, no. 4. Lotman provided the wrong date: 'no. 4, 1966'.

2. He had a somewhat more positive opinion on another avant-garde French theoretical review, *Change*, which published three short translations of his work in the early 1970s.

References

Avtonomova, N. 2009. *Otkrytaia struktura: Iakobson – Lotman – Bakhtin – Gasparov*, Moscow: ROSSPEN.

Barthes, R. [1953] 1993. 'Le Degré zéro de l'écriture', in R. Barthes, *Œuvres complètes*, vol. 1, 157–90, Paris: Seuil.

Barthes, R. [1957] 1993. 'Mythologies', in R. Barthes, *Œuvres complètes*, vol. 1, 561–724, Paris: Seuil.

Barthes, R. [1964] 1993. 'Élements de sémiologie', in R. Barthes, *Œuvres complètes*, vol. 1, 1465–26, Paris: Seuil.

Barthes, R. [1970] 1994. 'S/Z', in R. Barthes, *Œuvres complètes*, vol. 2, 555–42, Paris: Seuil.

Barthes, R. [1971] 1994. 'De l'œuvre au texte', in R. Barthes, *Œuvres complètes*, vol. 2, 1211–17, Paris: Seuil.

Barthes, R. [1974] 1995. 'L'aventure sémiologique', in R. Barthes, *Œuvres completes*, vol. 3, 36–40, Paris: Seuil.

Baudrillard, J. 1976. *L'Échange symbolique et la mort*, Paris: Gallimard.

Baudrillard, J. 1981. *Simulacres et simulation*, Paris: Galilée.

Compagnon, A. 1998. *Le Démon de la théorie: Littérature et sens commun*, Paris: Seuil.

Cusset, F. 2003. *French Theory: Foucault, Derrida, Deleuze & Cie et les mutations de la vie intellectuelle aux États-Unis*, Paris: La Découverte.

Derrida, J. 1967. *De la grammatologie*, Paris: Minuit.

Derrida, J. 1975. 'Economimesis', in S. Agacinski, J. Derrida, S. Kofman, Ph. Lacoue-Labarthe, J.-L. Nancy and B. Pautrat, *Mimesis des articulations*, 57–93, Paris: Aubier – Flammarion.

Derrida, J. 1993. *Les Spectres de Marx*, Paris: Galilée.

Foucault, M. 1966. *Les Mots et les choses*, Paris: Gallimard.

Foucault, M. 1969. *L'Archéologie du savoir*, Paris: Gallimard.

Gasparov, B. 1998. 'V poiskakh "drugogo" (Frantsuzskaia i vostochnoevropeiskaia semiotika na rubezhe 1970-kh godov', in S. Nekliudov (ed.), *Moskovsko-tartuskaia semioticheskaia shkola*, 213–36, Moscow: Iazyki russkoi kul'tury.

Kristeva, J. 1968. 'Linguistique et sémiologie aujourd'hui en U.R.S.S.', *Tel Quel* 35: 3–8.

Kristeva, J. 1969. *Σημειωτική: Recherches pour une sémanalyse*, Paris: Seuil.

Kristeva, J. 1994. 'On Yury Lotman', *PMLA* 109 (3): 375–6.

Landolt, E. 2012. 'Histoire d'un dialogue impossible: J. Kristeva, J. Lotman et la sémiotique', *Langage et société* 141: 121–40.

Lotman, Ju. M. [1964] 1994. 'Lektsii po struktural'noi poetike', in A. D. Koshelev (ed.), *Iu. M. Lotman i tartusko-moskovskaia semioticheskaia shkola*, 10–263, Moscow: Gnozis.

Lotman, Ju. M. [1964] 1998. 'Problema znaka v iskusstve', in Ju. M. Lotman, *Ob iskusstve*, 377–8, Saint Petersburg: Iskusstvo–SPb.

Lotman, Ju. M. [1967] 1998. 'Tezisy k probleme "Iskusstvo v riadu modeliruyutshikh system"', in Ju. M. Lotman, *Ob iskusstve*, 387–400, Saint Petersburg: Iskusstvo–SPb.

Lotman, Ju. M. [1967a] 2018. 'O printsipakh strukturalisma v literaturovedenii', in Ju. M. Lotman, *O strukturalizme. Raboty 1965–1970 godov*, ed. I. A. Pilshchikov, with N. V. Poselyagin and M. V. Trunin, 60–97, Tallinn: TLU Press.

Lotman, Ju. M. [1967b] 2018. 'Semiotika i gumanitarnye nauki', in Ju. M. Lotman, *O strukturalizme. Raboty 1965–1970 godov*, ed. I. A. Pilshchikov, with N. V. Poselyagin and M. V. Trunin, 156–66, Tallinn: TLU Press.

Lotman, Ju. M. [1968a] 2018. 'Sovremennye perspektivy semioticheskogo izuchenia iskusstva', in Ju. M. Lotman, *O strukturalizme. Raboty 1965–1970 godov*, ed. I. A. Pilshchikov, with N. V. Poselyagin and M. V. Trunin, 166–206, Tallinn: TLU Press.

Lotman, Ju. M. [1968b] 2018. 'Strukturalism v literaturovedenii', in Ju M. Lotman, *O strukturalizme. Raboty 1965–1970 godov*, ed. I. A. Pilshchikov, with N. V. Poselyagin and M. V. Trunin, 232–81, Tallinn: TLU Press.

Lotman, I. M. 1968. 'Sémantique du nombre et type de culture', *Tel Quel* 35: 24–7.

Lotman, Ju. M. [1969] 2002. 'K sovremennomu poniatiu teksta', in Ju. M. Lotman, *Istoriia i typologiia russkoi kul'tury*, 188–91, Saint Petersburg: Iskusstvo–SPb.

Lotman, Ju. M. [1970] 1998. 'Struktura khudojestvennogo teksta', in Ju. M. Lotman, *Ob iskusstve*, 13–285, Saint Petersburg: Iskusstvo–SPb.

Lotman, Ju. M. [1973] 1992. 'O dvukh modeliakh kommunikatsii v sisteme kul'tury', in Ju. M. Lotman, *Izbrannye stat'i v trekh tomakh*, vol. 1, 76–89, Tallinn: Aleksandra.

Lotman, Ju. M. [1973] 1998. 'Semiotika kino i problemy kinoestetiki', in Ju. M. Lotman, *Ob iskusstve*, 287–372, Saint Petersburg: Iskusstvo–SPb.

Lotman, Y. 1973. *La structure du texte artistique*, trans. A. Fournier, B. Kreise, E. Malleret, J. Young, sous la dir. de H. Meschonnic, Paris: Gallimard.

Lotman, Ju. M. [1974] 2002. 'O reduktsii i razvertyvanii znakovykh sistem', in Ju. M. Lotman, *Istoriia i typologiia russkoi kul'tury*, 141–6, Saint Petersburg: Iskusstvo–SPb.

Lotman, Y. 1977. *Sémiotique et esthétique du cinéma*, trans. S. Breuillard, Paris: Éditions sociales.

Lotman, Ju. M. [1981] 1998. 'Ritorika', in Ju. M. Lotman, *Ob iskusstve*, 404–22, Saint Petersburg: Iskusstvo–SPb.

Lotman, Ju. M. [1984] 1992. 'O semiosfere', in Ju. M. Lotman, *Izbrannye stat'i v trekh tomakh*, vol. 1, 11–24, Tallinn: Aleksandra.

Lotman, Ju. M. [1988] 2012. 'O Khlestakove', in Ju. M. Lotman, *O russkoi literature*, 659–88, Saint Petersburg: Iskusstvo–SPb.

Lotman, Ju. M. 1992. *Kultura i vzryv*, Moscow: Gnozis.

Lotman, Ju. M. [1994] 2010. *Nepredskazuemye mekhanizmy kul'tury*, Tallinn: TLU Press.

Lotman, Ju. M. [1994] 2018. 'Jan Mukařovský – teoretik iskusstva', in Ju. M. Lotman, *O strukturalizme. Raboty 1965–1970 godov*, ed. I. A. Pilshchikov, with N. V. Poselyagin and M. V. Trunin, 356–411, Tallinn: TLU Press.

Lotman, Ju. M. 1997. *Pis'ma*, ed. B. Egorov, Moscow: Iazyki russkoi kul'tury.

Lotman, I. and Ouspenski, B. 1990. *Sémiotique de la culture russe: études sur l'histoire*, trans. F. Lhoest, Lausanne: L'Âge d'Homme.

Lotman, Ju. M. and Piatigorsky, A. M. 1969. 'Le texte et la fonction', *Semiotica* 1/2: 205–17.

Monticelli, D. 2016. 'Critique of Ideology or/and Analysis of Culture? Barthes and Lotman on Secondary Semiotic Systems', *Sign Systems Studies* 44 (3): 432–51.

Prigogine, I. and Stengers, I. 1986. *La Nouvelle alliance: metamorphose de la science*, Paris: Gallimard.

Sériot, P. 2016. 'Barthes and Lotman: Ideology vs Culture', *Sign Systems Studies* 44 (3): 402–14.

Waldstein, M. 2008. *The Soviet Empire of Signs*, Saarbrücken: VDM Verlag.

Zolyan, S. 2020. *Iurii Lotman: O smysle, tekste, istorii. Temy i variatsii*, Moscow: Izdatel'skii Dom IASK.

CHAPTER 24
LOTMAN AND DECONSTRUCTIONISM
Daniele Monticelli

Any comparison of deconstructionism with Juri Lotman's semiotics of culture has to start from two evident problems. Firstly, the absence of any theoretical dialogue between Lotman and Jacques Derrida. The two thinkers never referred to one another and were probably only very superficially, if at all, acquainted with one other's work. It is very rare to encounter Lotman's name in scholarship on Derrida, and the same can be said of Derrida's name in scholarship on Lotman (see Monticelli 2012).

This 'missed encounter' is more significant if we consider that Derrida's deconstruction matures in an environment in which the theoretical insights of Lotman and the Tartu-Moscow School of Semiotics were not only known but actively promoted, interpreted and applied. In the second half of the 1960s, Julia Kristeva engaged in a thorough work of mediation of Lotman's work to the Parisian intellectual milieu (see Landolt 2012). In 1968, the journal *Tel Quel*, a fundamental venue in the exchange of ideas which gave birth to post-structuralism and deconstruction, published (no. 32) the groundbreaking essay 'La pharmacie de Platon' by Jacques Derrida as well as a special issue (no. 35) edited by Kristeva on 'La sémiologie aujourd'hui en U.R.S.S.' with translations of articles by Lotman and other representatives of the Tartu-Moscow school. The same year, in an article published in the Estonian journal *Keel ja Kirjandus* (Language and Literature), Lotman (1968) presents an overview of contemporary results in the semiotic analysis of art in which he expresses his interest in Barthes's seminal analyses of mode and mass culture, while at the same time manifesting his disappointment in the frivolity and superficiality of French semiology. In the following years, Lotman (e.g. 1997: 528, 656) will repeatedly confirm this negative opinion of post-structuralist French thinkers (he usually mentions Barthes and Kristeva, never Derrida) in his correspondence with the other members of the Tartu-Moscow school (see Chapter 23). Such fragments of opinions about French thinkers contain many elements of the widespread critical attitude which sees deconstruction as a dangerous attempt to replace serious thinking and argumentative discourse with wild stylistic and rhetoric play in philosophy and literary criticism.

This brings us to the second and thoroughly theoretical problem for a comparative analysis of Lotman and deconstructionism. As Jonathan Culler (1979: 137) has claimed, deconstruction represented a radical critique of 'the scientific pretensions of semiotics'. Lotman, on the contrary, will enthusiastically defend such 'pretensions' until the end of his life. In 1990, while prefacing the series of essays gathered in the *Universe of the Mind*, he describes semiotics as a 'scientific discipline' and a 'method of the humanities' (Lotman 1990: 4).

However, it would be wrong to interpret deconstruction as a movement of simple reversal that destroys the old in order to replace it with the new. The issue for Derrida is never to 'definitely overcome' traditions of thought such as semiotics, but rather to approach them with a critical vigilance that aims to constantly expose their limits and internal contradictions. It is therefore not a question of abandoning semiotics, but of developing a 'special practice within it' (Culler 1979: 141). This is particularly clear in Derrida's critique of Saussure (Derrida [1967] 1997: 1–93), which is at the origin of the notions of *différance* and grammatology. Through that critique, Derrida takes leave of structuralism by mobilizing Saussure's own idea of the differential character of the sign against the self-enclosure of the linguistic system and moving in the direction of an unbounded understanding of textuality.[1]

It is in its quality of 'special practice' within semiotics that deconstruction can be fruitfully compared with Lotman's semiotic theory. In his preface to the *Universe of the Mind*, while recognizing the persisting importance of Saussurean conceptuality for contemporary semiotics, Lotman (1990: 6) stresses the transformations that 'even the fundamental propositions and the whole cast of semiotics have undergone in the second half of the twentieth century'. As Umberto Eco (1990: ix) explains in his introduction to the same book, Lotman 'started from structuralism' but 'does not remain bound to it'. The development of Lotman's semiotics, from the 1960s–70s' focus on 'secondary modelling systems' to the 1980s–90s' theories of the semiosphere and explosion, has been often described (e.g. Schönle 2006; Nöth 2014; Pilshchikov and Trunin 2016; Monticelli 2016; Epstein 2018) in terms of a shift from a structuralist to a post-structuralist understanding of languages and texts which parallels the turn of the late 1960s in Western semiotics.[2] A preliminary comparison of later Lotman theory and Derrida's *différance* is elaborated in Monticelli 2012. An entire panel of the 2014 World congress of semiotics was dedicated to a 'dialogue between Lotman's semiotics and Derrida's philosophy of religion' (Ethical aspects 2014).

Deconstruction is a complex phenomenon with many internal differences and styles that vary from wild 'rhetorical juggling' (Norris 2002: 98) to rigorous philosophical argumentation. In what follows, I will mainly focus on the theoretical foundations of deconstruction in the works of Derrida with some references to its developments by Yale literary scholars, who found in Derrida's work a powerful ally in the struggle against American New Criticism. The Paris-Yale connection interestingly evokes the Tartu-Moscow one, though the characterization of the former in the institutional terms of a 'school' is out of the question, running against the very same principles of deconstruction. Such principles also make it impossible to define deconstruction as a 'method', which is along with 'science' the other recurring way in which Tartu-Moscow semioticians were familiar with describing semiotics. According to Culler (1994: 85), scholars have variously presented deconstruction as 'a philosophical position, a political or intellectual strategy and a mode of reading'. I will use such characterizations to structure the following reflections on deconstruction and Lotman. Starting from general philosophical issues, I will then proceed to consider deconstruction as a strategy for the critique of self-enclosed and self-identical structural totalities and, finally, I will discuss the deconstructionist understanding of the text and criticism. Each of these aspects of the deconstructionist project will be compared with Lotman's semiotic theory with particular attention to the post-semiosphere period of his thought. The comparison with deconstruction will help to highlight some aspects of Lotman's theory that deserve particular attention today.

Philosophical grounds

Derrida elaborates the notion of deconstruction drawing on Martin Heidegger's notion of *Destruktion* (Heidegger [1927] 1962: 94). He endorses the German philosopher's idea that an authentically radical philosophical position can be developed only on the basis of a systematic revision of the tradition of Western metaphysics. This tradition culminates in Kant's and the Enlightenment's trust in knowledge and its validity as rooted in the structure of human consciousness. Derrida subjects this to a thorough critique mobilizing, in addition to Heidegger's destruction of tradition, the disruptive effect of the linguistic turn on any naïve understanding of the relationship between the world of phenomena and the capacity of our reason to transparently grasp and comprehend them. As Christopher Norris (2002: 5) observes, 'there is simply no access to knowledge except by way of language and other, related orders of representation.' A consequence of this is the notorious Nietzschean reduction of truth to a matter of rhetoric, substantiated in the claim that 'there are no facts, only interpretations' (Nietzsche [1901] 1967: § 481).

Deconstruction paradoxically lies and relies on this ungrounding of the fundaments of Western thought and its rationality. As the abundance of traditional ontological jargon in Heidegger's texts show, *Destruktion* does not finally abandon the concepts of the tradition it criticizes. It rather remains within the limits of that tradition but submits its concepts to thorough revision. Derrida takes a step forward when he claims that these concepts can be used only 'under erasure' – something inadequate, but at the same time necessary, something which must be used in order to get out of its orbit (Harvey 2004: 60). Leaving aside the certainties of truthful knowledge unaffected by language, deconstruction exposes the realm of philosophy to contamination by the playfulness and creativeness of other orders of knowledge such as literature and art. The blurring of the boundaries between literature and theoretical thinking, which can be considered the most pre-eminent intellectual strategy and stylistic feature of deconstructionism, is therefore a direct consequence of its philosophical (non-)grounds.

Lotman never stopped to consider the quest for truthful knowledge as the foundation of semiotic theory, an index of its scientificity. It is therefore not a surprise that scholars (e.g. Lotman M. 1995; Restivo 1999; Steiner 2003) have often positioned the philosophical bases of Lotman's thought in Kant and the Enlightenment. Lotman's semiotics of culture can in this respect be understood as describing *a priori* (transcendental) semiotic principles that are universal conditions of intelligibility for cultural phenomena (Shukman 1977: 1). While this notion of semiotics as a body of scientific knowledge that describes universal mechanisms in the functioning of culture and consequently aspires to the role of overarching method for the humanities may seem the most remote philosophical position from deconstruction, it is important to integrate it with two other essential aspects of Lotman's theory that mark an important difference with the philosophical tradition represented by Kant and the Enlightenment.

As Giuseppina Restivo (1999: 27) remarks, Lotman's semiotics is based on an 'epistemology of intersection' that could also be defined as a 'dialogical epistemology'. This means that any comprehensive explanation of the workings of the human intellect and culture must include, along with a priori principles and universal regularities, heterogeneity, exceptions and idiosyncrasies. In Lotman's late theory history and culture as dynamic processes are consequently characterized by the tension and interaction between regular laws and unpredictable explosions. This ineliminable pluralism is extended by Lotman to cover the whole sphere of human cognition and meaning-making, where conceptual reason is considered in interaction with irrational acts like artistic creation, dreams, and so on. These are the elements of a Lotmanian 'romantic epistemology', which Lina Steiner (2003: 49, 51) compares to the 'critique of instrumental rationality' developed by critical theorists in the twentieth century and shared by deconstructionist such as Derrida. However, in Lotman's thought 'romantic epistemology' does not replace 'enlightened epistemology'; rather, it interacts with it.

Contrary to deconstruction, Lotman never blurs in his work the boundaries between theoretical thinking and artistic creation. What interests him is rather their tense interaction (dialogue and conflict) in the generation of meanings within culture and the historical process. He remains confident in semiotics as a scientific metalanguage capable of describing the dialogical epistemology. Nevertheless, such metalanguage more than often emerges in Lotman's works from a full immersion in artistic texts, which far from being frozen by theory, become themselves a living generator of theoretical ideas.

The deconstruction of self-enclosed totalities: Identity and difference

Derrida develops the crucial deconstructionist notion of writing as difference through a critical analysis of Saussure's theory of the linguistic system (langue). For Derrida, Saussure's semiology is characterized by an incurable fracture between a positive notion of the sign as based on the natural bond between the signifier and the signified in speech and presence, and a negative, differential conception of the sign, based on the notion of value. The former echoes the long history of Western metaphysics from Plato (Derrida 1968) to Husserl (Derrida [1967] 1973), presupposing an inner, pregiven and stable (transcendental) meaning transparently accessible through the full presence of the signifier in speech. Such a history shares the idea of the derivative and lower status of writing as a sign system that removes utterances from their immediate presence in the context of uttering, thus bringing a deranging difference and absence into language and communication. If writing is what the metaphysical tradition conceals and excludes in favour of speech, the first move of deconstruction is to reverse the hierarchy (Derrida

[1972] 1981: 65), bringing writing to the centre of reflection on language. But such writing is something other than the opposite of speech, because the second move of deconstruction is to challenge binary opposition itself. Writing thus becomes 'arche-writing', the general principle of difference that underlines every writing as well as speech in their usual meaning: 'therefore one has to admit, before any dissociation of language and speech, code and message, etc. (and everything that goes along with this dissociation) a systematic production of differences, the production of a system of differences' (Derrida [1972] 1981: 28). Having established this new meaning of writing, Derrida comes to define deconstruction, possibly with a certain irony, as a 'science of writing' that he names 'grammatology' (Derrida [1967] 1997: 4). 'Arche-writing' and 'grammatology' push to its ultimate consequences Saussure's differential definition of the sign, replacing Saussure's *'langue'* and 'linguistics' as notions that remained too close to the core of Western metaphysics.

Derrida's notion of *différance* ([1972] 1982: 1–28) is the point at which the deconstruction of identity and the deconstruction of presence come notoriously to coincide. The first conceptual side of *différance* is 'differing': to be not identical, to be other, discernible. The second conceptual side of *différance* is deferral in the fixation of meaning, the never-ending play of difference which always haunts the plenitude of the present with the ghosts of the past and the future to come (Derrida [1993] 2006). This is the core tool of deconstruction that Derrida put to work in 'cracking nutshells' (Caputo 1997: 31–2), that is, all those systems which present themselves as self-enclosed and self-identical: 'in the case of culture, person, nation, language, identity is a self-differentiating identity, an identity different from itself, having an opening or a gap within itself' (Caputo 1997: 14). Far from being driven by a simple 'taste for destruction', *différance* is an ethical imperative insofar as it makes openness and dialogue possible (Derrida [1993] 2006: 36). As Derrida explains (in Caputo 1997: 14), 'It is because I am not one with myself that I can speak with the other and address the other'.

Lotman opens *Culture and Explosion* with a critique of Roman Jakobson's model of communication ([1992] 2009: 4–6). For him, Jakobson's model is based on a mistaken 'abstraction', because it presupposes the self-identity of the sender and the receiver as well as the identity of the language they share. Lotman rather aligns with Derrida and grounds communication in difference, the non-self-identity of language and the participants in communication:

> The dialogue partner is located within the 'I' as one of its components or, conversely, the 'I' is part of the constitution of the partner [. . .]. The need for the 'other' is the need for the origin of the self; a partner is needed insofar as he presents a different model of the familiar reality, a different modelling language, a different interpretation of the familiar text. (Lotman [1981] 2000: 589)

This Lotmanian version of 'self-differentiating identity' is developed in the theory of the semiosphere by the idea that semiosis presupposes at least two languages and heterogeneous systems, and our understanding of reality can never be reduced to a single, universal and monolingual principle of explanation such as Kant's 'pure reason'. In 'Statement of the Problem' at the beginning of *Culture and Explosion*, Lotman explicitly opposes the Kantian idea of 'the transcendental unity of self-consciousness' with his own dialogical epistemology:

> The idea of the possibility for a single ideal language to serve as an optimal mechanism for the representation of reality is an illusion. A minimally functional structure requires the presence of at least two languages and their incapacity, each independently of the other, to embrace the world external to each of them. This incapacity is not a deficiency, but rather a condition of existence, as it dictates the necessity of *the other* (another person, another language, another culture). (Lotman [1992] 2009: 2)

Difference is the ontological ground of Lotman's dialogical epistemology. As Lotman states, in a very well-known passage of his essay 'On the Semiosphere', 'dialogue precedes language and gives birth to it. [. . .] Since all levels of the semiosphere – from human personality to the individual text to the global semiotic unity – are a seemingly interconnected group of semiospheres, each of them is simultaneously a participant in both the dialogue (as part of the semiosphere) and the space of the dialogue (the semiosphere as a whole)' (Lotman [1984] 2005: 218).[3] Difference, which Lotman variably calls 'binarism', 'heterogeneity', 'polyglotism', can thus be considered the foundation of Derrida's as well as Lotman's understandings of language and communication. If for Derrida grammatology was the science of writing as difference, in 1981, at the threshold of the semiospheric turn, Lotman describes the semiotics of culture as 'the research area which studies the mutual interaction of semiotic systems with different structures, the internal heterogeneity of semiotic space, the inevitability of cultural and semiotic polyglotism' (Lotman 1981a: 3).

As the aforementioned quote clearly shows, Lotman's understanding of difference takes as its basis semiotic systems, while Derrida and deconstructionists rather work on the more basic level of single signs or even their constitutive components, the signifier and the signified. This is an important divergence. While Derrida ([1972] 1981: 27) claims that '*différance* is incompatible with the static, synchronic, taxonomic, ahistoric motifs in the concept of "structure"', Lotman continues to employ the notion of structure (system), transforming it in the very site of 'self-differentiating identity'. What he defines as 'the smallest functioning semiotic mechanism' 'includes at least two semiotic mechanisms (languages) which are in a relationship of *mutual untranslatability*, yet at the same time *being similar*, since by its own means each of them models one and the same extrasemiotic reality' (Lotman [1989] 1997: 10).

In Lotman's later texts, the issue of translation and untranslatability acquires an increasingly important role, because the two notions offer an adequate tool to describe the effects of difference on communication. Instead of seeing translation and untranslatability as opposed categories, Lotman is interested in their co-occurrence in what he calls the 'translation of the untranslatable' where radical difference (untranslatability) sets into motion a process of interpretation (translation). The result is, according to Lotman ([1992] 2009: 23), a 'semantic explosion' with the generation of 'information of the highest value' ([1992] 2009: 6), that is, new, unpredictable meanings. This is why, for Lotman, any meaningful act of communication implies a certain degree of untranslatability and tension between the different systems involved. Total untranslatability makes communication impossible, while total translatability, based on a pregiven, exhaustive set of equivalences between the elements of the systems involved, makes communication predictable and, therefore, trivial ([1992] 2009: 4).

This is possibly the point at which Lotman's and Derrida's thoughts more clearly converge. Derrida ([1993] 2006: 42) also claims that 'guaranteed translatability, given homogeneity, systematic coherence in their absolute forms [. . .] is surely (certainly, a priori and not probably) what renders [. . .] the other impossible'. And for Derrida too, the coexistence of translation and untranslatability is the condition of possibility for meaningful communication and interpretation: 'A text lives only if it lives on, and it lives on only if it is at once translatable and untranslatable (always "at once . . . and . . .", at the "same" time). Totally translatable, it disappears as a text, writing, as a body of language. Totally untranslatable, even within what is believed to be one language, it dies immediately' (Derrida 1991: 17).

What distinguishes Lotman from Derrida and deconstruction is that Lotman's understanding of culture postulates a further layer in the play of difference that escaped the grasp of Derrida and deconstruction. The theory of the semiosphere as well as *Culture and Explosion* describe a metadialogical level at which heterogenizing forces (dialogue, translation of the untranslatable and explosion) are counterbalanced in culture by that homogenizing mechanism which Lotman defines as 'self-description', a metalanguage aimed at constructing a single, self-identical image of culture and closing the boundaries of the semiotic space. Now, while for Derrida this coincides with that kind of philosophical, ethical, political move that is at the origin of Western metaphysics and needs to be relentlessly deconstructed, for Lotman self-description is a fundamental mechanism of culture itself that lays at the origins of what he calls a 'semiotic homogeneity and individuality' (Lotman [1984] 2005: 208). Consequently, cultural dynamism is not exclusively rooted in heterogeneity and polyglotism (difference), but emerges from the incessant clash and interaction between heterogenizing (translation of the untranslatable, explosion) and homogenizing (self-description, integration) forces. Lotman also captures this dialectic in the topological terms of the centre versus the periphery of the semiotic space, their interaction and exchange of places in the history of a given culture.[4]

Mode of reading: The text and criticism

Deconstruction is often considered *in primis* as a particular way of reading literary and philosophical texts and other cultural artefacts as texts. Renouncing the possibility of an ordered knowledge about the text – the 'rational ordering of literary studies' and the 'happy positivism' characterizing, according to Joseph Hillis Miller (1976: 335), old 'Socratic critics' – deconstructionists consider logical failure and aporia as the deepest truth of a text; their readings focus on the tensions, contradictions and heterogeneity that take place in the text. This can be considered the generic common ground of deconstructive reading, which for the rest is intended to grant 'high speculative freedom for the critic' (Norris 2002: 15). The results may vary from the unbounded playfulness and 'anything goes' of above mentioned 'wild deconstruction' to the rigorous philosophical exegesis in many critical pieces by Derrida or Paul de Man.

While traditional criticism starts from the presupposition of a meaning which is to be exposed through a systematic interpretative act by the critic, deconstructionists are much more focused on the activity of writing in the text under investigation as well as in their own text. The encounter between the two sets the play of meaning into a movement that aims to lose any point of origin or destination. As Gayatri Spivak (1997: xii) observes in her introduction to Derrida's *Grammatology*, in deconstructive criticism 'the text has no stable identity, no stable origin . . . each act of reading "the text" is a preface to the next'. In the intellectual strategy of deconstruction, the abovementioned blurring of the boundaries between literature and philosophy is thus doubled by the blurring of the boundaries between literature and criticism. The open, decentered, unhinged, never departed and never arriving, constantly moving text is an effect of the play of writing as *différance* and becomes the model of every deconstructionist understanding of literature as well as criticism and philosophical reflection.

The notion of the text is 'one of the cornerstones of Lotman's theory', being 'much broader than the concept of literary work' (Semenenko 2012: 75); so broad that even culture itself is defined by Lotman as a 'text' (see also Chapter 9). Lotman's understanding of the text seems very distant from the deconstructionist view described earlier. We can, however, distinguish two different moments in Lotman's approach to the study of the text and criticism that corresponds, respectively, to the structural phase of the 1960s–early 1970s and the later works of the 1980s–early 1990s. Commenting at the end of the 1980s on the development of the Tartu-Moscow School over the previous twenty-five years, Lotman writes of 'a movement away from general structures (languages, codes) to the issue of textuality and the analysis of individual texts, and from a strictly synchronic approach to a historical one' (Lotman 1987b: 13, quoted in Trunin 2017: 354).

In *The Structure of the Artistic Text* (1970 [1977]), Lotman still considers as defining characteristic of the artistic text its closure, the fact that it is delimited, it has a beginning and an end, and its meaning derives from its hierarchical structure. In the *Analysis of the Poetic Text* (1972) he consequently understands the task of literary analysis as separating the essential from the inessential in order to grasp the artistic reality of the text, which 'is created by its systemic relationships, by its meaningful antitheses, that is, by what enters into *the structure of the work*' (Lotman [1972] 1976: 11). However, already in this work, Lotman introduces the idea that the relationship between text and system cannot be properly understood as 'the automatic realization of an abstract structure in concrete form' and the text should rather be considered the site of tension and conflict (Lotman [1972] 1976: 123–4).

In his later work, Lotman will fully embrace an understanding of the text as a polyglottic device by which different languages are made to interact, with transformative results. As he explains in the programmatic article 'Cultural Semiotics and the Notion of the Text', 'the text does not appear to us as the realization of a message in a single language, but as a complex construction including various codes which is able to transform existing messages and generate new ones' (Lotman 1981a: 7). The notion of 'text' as a transformer of existing meanings and generator of new ones is another example of polyglottic communication and translation. The Lotmanian equation of culture with the text thus aims to extend to culture the textual conditions for the transformation and generation of meanings: 'one might say that what turns a culture into a Text is internal polyglotism' (Lotman 1979: 507). It is interesting to observe here that the abovementioned distinction and interaction between the translation of the untranslatable and metalinguistic self-description is paralleled in Lotman's distinction and interaction between 'myth-texts' and 'plot-texts', the former characterized by the stability of meaning which maintains a certain world view, the latter introducing 'revolutionary elements' through events which imply the crossing of forbidden boundaries and challenge established world views (Semenenko 2012: 83–4).

The Lotmanian shift from an understanding of the text as a system of relations (a closed structure) to a transformative/generative mechanism is fuelled by difference (internal polyglotism) and opens the text to ever new interpretations; the result of the encounter of an artistic text with its interpreters consequently remains unpredictable. While this makes Lotman's understanding of the text a bit closer to deconstruction, the critical practice developed by Lotman in his later works partly continued to be based on topological modelling and binary oppositions (see, for instance, the analysis of Russian medieval texts, Dante's *Divine Comedy* and Bulgakov's *The Master and Margarita* in his *Universe of the Mind*). Nevertheless, Lotman also employed literary texts to illustrate the explosive results of the encounter between different systems of meaning (see, for instance, the analysis of Aleksander Blok's *The Artist* in his *Culture and Explosion*).

Another pre-eminent line of Lotman's literary semiotics since the 1980s is well illustrated in the series of monographic studies on Pushkin and Karamzin (Lotman 1980; 1981b; 1987), where textual analysis is paralleled by a particular attention to the relations between the literary world and the surrounding intellectual milieu, the construction of the poetic personality in the texts and the 'poetic of everyday behaviour' (Lotman [1994] 1997). In these works, Lotman focuses on the conformist pressure of closed cultural codes on individual lifestyle and artistic creation as well as the disruptive challenges that the latter pose to the former (see Bethea 1997: 5–11).

Lotmanian literary analyses share the absence of a rigid method and critical metalanguage to be constantly applied to any single case, as happened in the tradition of literary semiotics from the golden age of semiological structuralism (e.g. Greimas 1966) to the interpretative approach of Umberto Eco (1979). Lotman proceeds ad hoc, setting his tasks and tools according to the specificity of the texts he is going to analyse, free from a drive to overarching systematization and rather inclined to intertwine literary analysis with theoretical reflection and historical digression. This certainly doesn't bring Lotman to that abandonment of any 'distance between the literary text and the discourse which seeks to comprehend it' (Norris 2002: 16), which is characteristic of deconstruction. Lotman's criticism is rather based on 'the absence of adequate language and the need to replace it with a multiplicity of mutually conflicting languages' (Lotman [1992] 2009: 22). Metalinguistic monologism thus gives way to the dialogical plurality of the different languages of criticism.[5]

Conclusion

This comparison of Lotman's semiotics with deconstruction as it is theoretically delineated in the works of Derrida allowed me to draw particular attention to the grounding function of difference in Lotman's understanding of all semiotic mechanisms from the semiosphere, culture and the text to single languages and the human intellect. Lotmanian difference does not coincide with the stable, static binary oppositions of structuralism, but is always an 'at least two' wherein binarism 'must be understood as a principle which is realized in plurality' (Lotman 1990: 214). This prevents the reduction of binarism to a structuring, stabilizing device, and makes it instead into an instrument of dynamism, transformation and generation of meaningful novelty.

While this can be considered an important convergence between Lotman's semiotics of culture and Derrida's deconstruction, important divergences emerge on this very same ground. For Lotman, a fundamental, possibly the most fundamental, level of difference in the study of texts, cultures, history is the difference between homogenizing and heterogenizing semiotic mechanisms, integration and explosion, self-description and translation of the untranslatable, myth-text and plot-text, and so on. The acknowledgement and analysis of the tense interaction (conflict and dialogue) between these different poles of semiotic activity is for Lotman an indispensable prerequisite for a scientific study of culture. Deconstructionists seem much more unilateral in this respect and generally acknowledge only the disruptive and heterogenizing side of difference; thus, approaching a text they rather expose the illusion of its unity and self-identity, looking for the cracks in the textual tissue and the traces of the absent and removed, what give access to a space where the textual signifiers and signifieds lose their anchorage in a pre-given system of meaning and start to drift in the play of difference. This is the reason for the evident divergence in deconstructionist and Lotman's approach to criticism. For the latter, the meaningfulness of the text continues to be essentially related to its limitedness, hierarchical structure, relation to existing cultural codes. However, the Lotmanian text is always more than this, due to the heterogeneity that crosses it and makes it into a semiotic device that not only transmits existing meanings but also transforms them and creates new ones.

While my reading has focused on the 'dialogical epistemology' of Lotman's later thought through the lens of deconstruction, we might in future research reverse this focus looking at deconstruction through the lens of Lotman's later thought. Perhaps we would discover in this way that, despite the unilateral extremism of many later deconstructionists, Derrida's original text was closer to Lotman than one might expect. The next, 'Lotmanian', passage by Derrida (in Caputo 1997: 6) is a good example of this possible proximity and a good way of concluding our comparison: 'That is what deconstruction is made of: not the mixture but the tension between memory, fidelity, the preservation of something that has been given to us, and, at the same time, heterogeneity, something absolutely new and a break.'[6]

Notes

1. For a critical discussion of Derrida's relations with Saussure, see Strozier 1988 and Daylight 2012.

2. For a reconstruction of the different stages of this shift, see Monticelli 2017. This interpretation of Lotman's intellectual trajectory remains controversial, and some scholars have taken issue with it, stressing rather the continuities in Lotman's semiotics from the 1960s to the 1990s (e.g. Żyłko 2014; Trunin 2017) or important differences between the assumptions of the Tartu-Moscow School and those of Anglo-American cultural studies and French post-structuralism (e.g. Waldstein 2008).

3. Steiner (2003: 50) describes this characteristic of Lotman's thought as the 'priority of semioticity over every individual semiotic subject and event'. Such 'semioticity' resembles in this respect Derrida's 'arche-writing'.

4. One of the favourite Lotmanian examples is the tension between mannerism/academicism (centre) and avant-garde (periphery) in the history of the arts. When avant-garde becomes dominant, it comes to occupy the centre of the cultural space and progressively turns into a new mannerism to be challenged by the periphery (a new avant-garde) and so on and so forth.

5. I have argued elsewhere (Monticelli 2016) that this brings Lotman closer to the Roland Barthes of *S/Z* than to the Derrida of *Acts of Literature*.

6. This work was supported by the European Research Council under ERC Grant [757873] BETWEEN THE TIMES – Embattled Temporalities and Political Imagination in Interwar Europe.

References

Bethea, D. 1997. 'Bakhtinian Prosaics versus Lotmanian "Poetic Thinking": The Code and Its Relation to Literary Biography', *Slavic and East European Journal* 41 (1): 1–15.

Caputo, J. (ed.) 1997. *Deconstruction in a Nutshell: A Conversation with Jacques Derrida*, New York: Fordham University Press.

Culler, J. 1979. 'Semiotics and Deconstruction', *Poetics Today* 1 (1/2): 137–41.

Culler, J. 1994. *On Deconstruction: Theory and Criticism after Structuralism*, London and New York: Routledge.

Daylight, R. 2012. *What if Derrida was Wrong About Saussure?*, Edinburgh: Edinburgh University Press.

Derrida, J. 1968. 'La pharmacie de Platon', *Tel Quel* 32: 3–48; 33: 18–59.

Derrida, J. [1967] 1973. *Speech and Phenomena and Other Essays on Husserl's Theory of Signs*, trans. D. B. Allison, Evanstone, IL: Northwestern University Press.

Derrida, J. [1967] 1997. *Of Grammatology*, trans. G. C. Spivak, Baltimore, MD, and London: The Johns Hopkins University Press.

Derrida, J. [1972] 1981. *Positions*, trans. A. Bass, Chicago and London: The University of Chicago Press.

Derrida, J. [1972] 1982. *Margins of Philosophy*, trans. A. Bass, Chicago and London: The University of Chicago Press.

Derrida, J. 1991. *Acts of Literature*, ed. D. Attridge, New York and London: Routledge.

Derrida, J. [1993] 2006. *Specters of Marx: The State of the Debt, the Work of Mourning and the New International*, trans. P. Kamuf. New York and London: Routledge.

Eco, U. 1979. *Lector in Fabula*, Milan: Bompiani.

Eco, U. 1990. 'Introduction', in Yu. M. Lotman, *The Universe of the Mind: A Semiotic Theory of Culture*, trans. A. Shukman, vii–xiii, Bloomington: Indiana University Press.

Epstein, M. 2018. 'Yuri Lotman (1922–1993)', in *Filosofia: An Encyclopedia of Russian Thought*, available online: http://filosofia.dickinson.edu/encyclopedia/lotman-yuri/ (accessed 3 January 2021).

Ethical Aspects. 2014. 'Ethical Aspects: How to Think Semiotically a Present Time at the Epoch of Explosion', Panel at the World congress of semiotics, Sofia, available online: https://semio20 14.org/fr/how-to-think-semiotically-a-present-time-at-the-epoch-of-explosion (accessed 3 January 2021).

Greimas, A. J. 1966. *Sémantique structurale: recherche de méthode*, Paris: Larousse.

Harvey, I. E. 2004. 'Derrida, Kant and the Performance of Parergonality', in H. Silverman (ed.), *Continental Philosophy II: Derrida and Deconstruction*, 57–74, New York and London: Routledge.

Heidegger, M. [1927] 1962. *Being and Time*, trans. J. Macquarrie and E. Robinson, New York: Harper & Row.

Kristeva, J. (ed.) 1968. Special Issue 'La sémiologie aujourd'hui en U.R.S.S.', *Tel Quel* 35.

Landolt, E. 2012. 'Histoire d'un dialogue impossible: J. Kristeva, J. Lotman et la sémiotique', *Langage et société*, 141: 121–40.

Lotman, J. 1968. 'Kunsti semiootilise uurimise tulemusi tänapäeval' [Results of the Contemporary Semiotic Analysis of Art], *Keel ja Kirjandus* 10: 577–85.

Lotman, J. [1970] 1977. *The Structure of the Artistic Text*, trans. R. Vroon, Ann Arbor, MI: University of Michigan, Department of Slavic Languages and Literatures.

Lotman, Yu. M. [1972] 1976. *Analysis of the Poetic Text*, ed. and trans. D. B. Johnson, Ann Arbor: Ardis.

Lotman, Yu. 1979. 'The Future for Structural Poetics', trans. L. M. O'Toole, *Poetics* 8: 501–7.

Lotman, Ju. M. 1980. *Roman A. S. Pushkina Evgenii Onegin, kommentarii: posobie dlia uchitelia*, Leningrad: Prosveshchenie.

Lotman, Ju. M. 1981a. 'Semiotika kul'tury i poniatie teksta', *Trudy po znakovym sistemam* 12: 3–7.

Lotman, Ju. M. 1981b. *Aleksandr Sergeievich Pushkin: Biografia pisatelia*, Leningrad: Prosveshchenie.

Lotman, Ju. M. [1981] 2000. 'Mozg – tekst – kul'tura – iskusstvennyi intellekt', in Ju. M. Lotman, *Semiosfera*, 580–9, Saint Petersburg: Iskusstvo–SPB.

Lotman, J. [1984] 2005 'On the Semiosphere', trans. W. Clark, *Sign Systems Studies* 33 (1), 205–29.

Lotman, Ju. M. 1987. *Sotvorenie Karamzina*, Moscow: Kniga.

Lotman, Ju. M. 1987b. 'Ob itogakh i problemakh semioticheskikh issledovanii', *Trudy po znakovym sistemam* 20: 12–6.

Lotman, J. [1989] 1997. 'Culture as Subject and Object of Itself', *Trames* 1 (51/46): 7–16.

Lotman, Yu. M. 1990. *The Universe of the Mind: A Semiotic Theory of Culture*, trans. A. Shukman, Bloomington: Indiana University Press.

Lotman, J. [1992] 2009. *Culture and Explosion*, trans. W. Clark, ed. M. Grishakova, Berlin and New York: Mouton de Gruyter.

Lotman, J. [1994] 1997. 'Conversations on Russian Culture: Russian Noble Traditions and Lifestyle in the Eighteen and Early Nineteenth Centuries', *Russian Studies in History* 35 (4): 6–34.

Lotman, Ju M. 1997. *Pis'ma*, ed. B. Egorov, Moscow: Iazyki russkoj kul'tury.

Lotman, M. 1995. 'Za tekstom: zametki o filosofskom fone tartuskoi semiotiki (Stat'ia pervaia)', in E. V. Permiokov (ed.), *Lotmanovskii sbornik*, vol. 1, 214–22, Moscow: IC-Garant.

Miller, J. H. 1976. "Stevens' Rock and Criticism as Cure. Part II', *Georgia Review* 30: 330–48.

Monticelli, D. 2012. 'Challenging Identity: Lotman's "Translation of the Untranslatable" and Derrida's *Différance*', *Sign Systems Studies* 40 (3/4): 319–39.

Monticelli, D. 2016. 'Critique of Ideology or/and Analysis of Culture? Barthes and Lotman on Secondary Semiotic Systems', *Sign Systems Studies* 44 (3): 432–51.

Monticelli, D. 2017. 'From Modelling to Untranslatability: Translation and the Semiotic Relation in Y. Lotman's Works (1965–1992)', *Acta Slavica Estonica* 9: 15–35.

Nietzsche, F. [1901] 1967. *The Will to Power*, trans. W. A. Kaufmann and R. J. Hollingdale, New York: Random House.

Nöth, W. 2014. 'The Topography of Yuri Lotman's Semiosphere', *International Journal of Cultural Studies* 18 (1): 11–26.

Norris, C. 2002. *Deconstruction, Theory and Practice*, London and New York: Routledge.

Pilshchikov, I. and Trunin, M. 2016. 'The Tartu-Moscow School of Semiotics: A Transnational Perspective', *Sign Systems Studies* 44 (3): 368–400.

Restivo, G. 1999. 'The Enlightenment Code in Yuri Lotman's Theory of Culture', *Slavica tergestina* 7: 5–31.

Schönle, A. (ed.) 2006. *Lotman and Cultural Studies. Encounters and Extensions*, Madison, WI: The University of Wisconsin Press.

Semenenko, A. 2012. *The Texture of Culture: An Introduction to Yuri Lotman's Semiotic Theory*, New York: Palgrave Macmillan.

Shukman, A. 1977. *Literature and Semiotics: A Study of the Writings of Yu. M. Lotman*, Amsterdam: North-Holland Publishing Company.

Spivak, G. C. 1997. 'Translator's Preface', in J. Derrida, *Of Grammatology*, ix–lxxxviii, Baltimore, MD and London: The Johns Hopkins University Press.

Steiner, L. 2003. 'Toward an Ideal Universal Community: Lotman's Revisiting of the Enlightenment and Romanticism', *Comparative Literature Studies* 40 (1): 37–53.

Strozier, R. 1988. *Saussure, Derrida and the Metaphysics of Subjectivity*, Berlin and New York: Mouton de Gruyter.

Trunin, M. 2017. 'Semiosphere and History: Toward the Origins of the Semiotic Approach to History', *Sign Systems Studies* 45 (3/4): 335–60.

Waldstein, M. 2008. *The Soviet Empire of Signs: A History of the Tartu School of Semiotics*. Saarbrücken: VDM Verlag.

Żyłko, B. 2014. 'Notes on Yuri Lotman's Structuralism', *International Journal of Cultural Studies* 18 (1): 27–42.

CHAPTER 25
LOTMAN AND CULTURAL HISTORY
Marek Tamm

Cultural-semiotics and cultural history are kindred spirits, at least the Lotmanian cultural semiotics and the so-called New Cultural History (Hunt 1989). Like cultural historians, cultural semioticians are not interested in the whole reality, but mainly in its semiotic models – systems of representations. They both study the *homo culturalis* – the meaning-seeking human species 'whose hunger and search for *meaning* to its existence has led it to invent myths, art, ritual, language, science and all other cultural phenomena that guide its search' (Danesi and Perron 1999: ix). For Lotman, historical and semiotic approaches are closely intermingled. In 1990, he admits: 'Personally, I cannot draw a sharp line where a historical description ends for me, and semiotics begins. There is neither opposition nor gap. For me, these areas are organically linked' (Lotman [1990] 1994: 296). According to Lotman's older sister Lidia Lotman, he was quite comfortable being called a cultural historian (Andrews 2003: xiii–xiv). One of his closest colleagues, Vyacheslav Ivanov, has admitted that 'Lotman was not only one of the founders of the contemporary semiotics [. . .]. He was an historian and a cultural historian in the most general and in the most concrete sense, at the same time' (Ivanov 1996: XI). And one of Lotman's earliest students and closest collaborators, Igor Chernov, stated in 1982: 'By his very nature, way of thinking and approaching – not to mention his almost phenomenal memory – Lotman is a historian' (Černov 1982: 272).

Without underestimating Lotman's strong penchant for theorizing, one has to admit indeed that he never gave up his early vocation to meticulous archival and library work. He proposed many new theoretical concepts and models, but also enriched our knowledge of particular historical periods and phenomena. The two scholarly *personae* – cultural theorist and cultural historian – lived happily together in Lotman. Another of his colleagues, Boris Gasparov (1994: 739), captures this very aptly in his obituary to the Tartu scholar: 'His theory never becomes a pure theory, while his research in the minutiae of cultural history, however detailed and idiosyncratic, never loses contact with the ideal plane of an all-encompassing vision.' Andreas Schönle (2020: xiv) has recently reached the same conclusion: 'Lotman was both a theorist and a historian. [. . .] Indeed, perhaps his greatest asset was the ability to underpin history with theory and substantiate theory with history, casting a new light on everything he touched' (see also Avtonomova 2009: 32; Semenenko 2012: 7).

This chapter will not be so much a portrait of Lotman as a cultural historian, but more an attempt to elucidate some of the most promising cultural-historical ideas and concepts from his academic legacy and to show their relevance in the context of contemporary cultural history. I find this an important task, considering that Lotman's semiotic engagement with cultural history has not seen many followers. We do not find his texts included in anthologies of cultural history or discussed in general introductions to this blooming field (with some exceptions, see Burke 2004: 35–6; Arcangeli 2012: 64, 103). Apart from Lotman's important influence within Russian cultural-historical studies, the cultural historians who have entered into dialogue with his thinking are few and far between, especially in the English-speaking world. Without aiming to cover every potential of Lotman's work for today's cultural-historical research, I shall focus on four themes: epistemology of cultural history, poetics of everyday behaviour, semiotics of cultural emotions and analysis of self-creation practices.

Epistemology of cultural history

Lotman's interest in methodological questions of cultural history dates back to the early days of his academic career, but in a more systematic way he developed his programme of historical epistemology only in the late 1980s–early 1990s (see also Chapter 18). The turn towards semiotics and structural poetics in the 1960s somewhat eclipsed his previous cultural-historical studies, but it is still highly revealing that in the introduction to his first semiotic monograph, *Lectures on Structural Poetics*, he connects the structural study of literature with a more ambitious programme of developing a new methodology for the historical study of human culture: 'we hope that understanding the nature of the artistic text brings us closer to a time when new research methods will emerge that can comprehend the whole complexity of human cultural history as a dynamic and multifaceted structure' (Lotman 1964: 12). With the wisdom of hindsight, we could say that at the end of his life, Lotman returned to this major task.

In his ultimate book, *The Unpredictable Workings of Culture*, Lotman notices that there is a major discrepancy between traditional historical epistemology and our contemporary understanding of the historical process. He declares that 'contradictions between the philosophical presumptions and historical reality knock at the door of the cultural historian', but only to conclude that 'historians, however, continue to be interested in these questions only to the extent that they disturb or do not disturb their specific research' (Lotman [1994/2010] 2013: 41). In this book and some other late writings, Lotman proposes a new semiotic model for cultural history that still needs to be digested and tested by historians. Heralding the joining of history and semiotics, Lotman declares that 'at this stage it is possible to define semiotics as the study of the theory and history of culture' (Lotman [1994/2010] 2013: 53). Elsewhere he introduces the concept of 'historical semiotics' (or sometimes also 'historical semiotics of culture' – Lotman [1992b] 2019: 195), which can be seen as an alternative term for cultural history. In Lotman's definition the task of historical semiotics is 'to analyse how that human individual who has to make a choice looks at the world' (Lotman 1990a: 232), which is very close to the traditional understanding of new cultural history or history of mentalities. Lotman is very much aware of this, admitting that 'this approach is not too different from what the *nouvelle histoire* calls *mentalité*' (Lotman 1990a: 232). 'However', he continues, 'the results of researches in this field and a comparison of what Soviet scholars have achieved [. . .] in the reconstruction of different ethno-cultural types of consciousness leads us to the conclusion that historical semiotics is the most promising way forward' (Lotman 1990a: 232–3).[1]

Lotman's new semiotic model for (cultural) history relies on three main arguments. Firstly, history is not a homogenous stream, but a polychronic process, not a 'rolled-up ball of endless thread but as a cascade of spontaneous living matter' ([1988a] 2019: 184). History is made up of temporal layers that develop at different speeds (Lorusso 2019). This stance stems from the work of Juri Tynianov on cultural evolution. According to Tynianov, culture is a system that consists of various 'cultural orders' (literary order, the order of everyday life, etc.) which develop in different tempos. The study of cultural evolution presupposes the investigation of connections between the closest neighbouring orders (Tynianov 1977: 281; see also Torop 2017: 319–20). For example, Lotman argues in the vein of Tynianov, tempestuous developments in one sphere of science may not be chronologically or causally connected with corresponding explosive movements in the spheres of everyday life (Lotman [1992a] 2019: 97). It is interesting to note that Lotman's idea that 'real historical processes are multi-layered and poly-functional' ([1992a] 2019: 98) comes very close to Reinhart Koselleck's influential theory of *Zeitschichten*, 'layers or sediments of time', developed in the 1990s (Koselleck 2000). Arguing that time is not linear, progressing from one period to another, Koselleck proposed that, instead, there are multiple historical times present at the same moment, layer upon layer pressed together; 'historical times consist of multiple layers that refer to each other in a reciprocal way, though without being wholly dependent upon each other' (Koselleck [1995] 2018: 4). Lotman writes in the same vein that from a historical perspective, culture is a complex whole, but it is 'created from elements which develop at different rates, so that any one of its synchronic sections reveals the simultaneous presence of these different stages'. 'Explosions in some layers', Lotman asserts, 'may be combined with gradual development in others. This, however, does not preclude the interdependence of these layers' (Lotman [1992] 2009: 13).

Cultural evolution can vary from the slowness of gradual development to the explosiveness of an unforeseen change. For the sake of simplicity, Lotman elaborates the model of two main types of historical change: gradual, and dynamic or explosive. He argues that the French historians of the so-called *Annales* school focused on the study of slow-processes, gradual, unnoticeable changes, whereas Lotman himself and the Tartu-Moscow school took the opposite path, paying attention to the unpredictable and explosive changes in history (Lotman [1994/2010] 2013: 86–7). However, it is important to emphasize that these two aspects of historical process can only be conceived of as one against the background of the other. Lotman asks: 'Does cultural evolution take place gradually and principally as a process devoid of the unexpected or as a chain of unpredictable explosions?' But answers immediately: 'It is worth formulating the question in this way so as to make the error of this formulation readily apparent. Before us lie two aspects of one inseparable unity' (Lotman [1994/2010] 2013: 130–1; see also [1992] 2009: 7).

Next to distinguishing conceptually *gradual* and *explosive* aspects of cultural history, Lotman also proposes, as his second main epistemological argument, a distinction between *external* and *internal* factors in the dynamics of culture. He elaborates on this in his *Culture and Explosion*: 'The history of the culture of any population may be examined from two points of view: firstly, as an immanent development; secondly, as the result of a variety of external influences.' In other words, culture transforms by continual self-renewal, by reinterpreting itself and providing new self-descriptions, but also by receiving foreign impulses and effects. The extent to which cultural situation is transformed depends on the degree of the semiotic shift. Cultural history knows several radical turns which Lotman terms 'cultural explosions'. According to him, there are two main types of cultural explosion. The first is caused by an invasion of new cultural texts, whereas the second arises from an arrival of new texts for which the culture's internal tradition has no adequate codes to decipher (Lotman [1985] 2019: 136). But once again, Lotman reminds us that both external and internal factors 'are closely intertwined and their separation is only possible in the modality of scientific abstraction' (Lotman [1992] 2009: 65). 'Thus', he concludes, 'the dynamic development of culture is accompanied by the constant transposition of internal and external processes' (Lotman [1992] 2009: 137)

Finally, Lotman's third argument is to reintroduce the moment of unpredictability in the historical interpretation. He argues that historical research cannot be reduced to merely investigating the circumstances and the inevitability of the historical phenomena. 'By removing the moment of unpredictability from the historical process, we make it totally redundant', Lotman contends (Lotman [1992] 2009: 14). He considers it 'obvious that the historian must study not only the events that actually took place and that were retrospectively canonized but also all the potential paths that remained unrealized' (Lotman [1992c] 2019: 230). According to Lotman, random events or elements in the historical process, be they internal or external, can cause unpredictable situations, but these accidental elements can also act as a reserve for future reorganizations of the culture. In line with some contemporary 'counterfactual' cultural historians (Gallagher 2018), Lotman points out that the retrospective gaze of the historian creates the illusion of a linear and causal stream of time and excludes all unpredictable and random elements from the past (Zolyan 2020). Historian's dependence on textual mediation of the past leaves history writing facing a double distortion: 'On the one hand, the syntagmatic directionality of the text transforms the event by placing it into a narrative structure while, on the other hand, the contradictory directionality of the historian's gaze deforms the written object' (Lotman [1992b] 2019: 198). To sum up, Lotmanian epistemology of cultural history requires an understanding of history as a polychronic process, made up of many temporal layers that develop at different speeds; cultural dynamics is to be conceived of as a constant transposition of internal and external processes, and historical interpretation also has to consider the potential paths in the past that remained unrealized.

Poetics of everyday behaviour

In Lotman's legacy, his work on the 'poetics of everyday behaviour' (*poetika bytovogo povedeniia*) has been without doubt the most influential among cultural historians. This can be explained, on the one hand, by a deeply rooted interest in everyday life in cultural history and, on the other hand, by Lotman's emphasis on human agency and self-fashioning, in accordance with the agenda of new cultural history and new historicism (Waldstein 2008: 166). Lotman started to work more systematically on the history of everyday life in the early 1970s. He held special courses at the University of Tartu and published a series of innovative articles on the everyday behaviour of the eighteenth- and the nineteenth-century Russian noblemen. For Lotman, attention to daily detail is a genuine part of cultural history, 'without a knowledge of ordinary lives and the seeming "trivialities" thereof, there can be no *understanding* of history', he writes in the introduction to his *Conversations about Russian Culture*. 'I emphasize *understanding* because in history, knowing certain facts and understanding them are quite different things' (Lotman [1994] 1997: 16; original emphasis). In the same text, Lotman formulates felicitously the very reason for combining semiotics with cultural history: 'in order to understand the *meaning* of the behaviour of living persons and the literary heroes of the past, one must know their culture, their simple and ordinary lives, their customs, their conceptions of the world, and so forth' (Lotman [1994] 1997: 11; original emphasis). During his last years, he was engaged in many major projects of everyday history, in addition to *Conversations about Russian Culture*, a study of the daily lifestyle of Russian nobles in the eighteenth and early nineteenth centuries (Lotman 1993), also in a joint project with his student Jelena Pogosjan, published posthumously under the title of *High Society Dinners: Dining in Tsarist Russia* (Lotman and Pogosjan [1996] 2014). The book offers an insight into the domestic arrangements of the Russian aristocracy, presenting nine months' worth of menus served in Saint Petersburg to the guests of Petr Durnovo (1835–1918), adjutant general of the tzar's Imperial Suite.

Lotman's main conceptual innovation in the study of everyday behaviour is his theory of 'theatricality' (*teatral'nost'*). He introduced this concept in the early 1970s, probably inspired by the work of Nikolay Evreinov, the early twentieth-century Russian director, dramatist, and theoretician, who proposed theatricality as an all-subsuming category of human behaviour and interaction (Buckler, Cassiday and Wolfson 2018: 8). Lotman developed the notion of 'theatricality' to describe the highly 'semioticized' behaviour of the Westernized Russian elite in the post-Petrine period. Theatricality, in Lotman's understanding, is 'a change in the degree of conventionality in behaviour' (Lotman [1973a] 1984: 150). It is precisely in this change that the individuality of the self comes to the fore and establishes itself. As Lotman explains, Russian nobles constructed their everyday behaviour in accordance with literary works, as a kind of theatrical play:

> In the everyday behaviour of the Russian gentlemen of the end of the eighteenth and early nineteenth centuries it is characteristic both for a certain type of behaviour to be bound to a particular 'stage area' and for there to be an inclination towards

the 'entr'acte', the intermission during which the semiotic value of behaviour is reduced to a minimum. (Lotman [1973a] 1984: 151)

Poetika bytovogo povedeniia refers to cases of historical actors deliberately turning their everyday lives into a text arranged according to the laws of specific plots, thus making their lives' codes decipherable by means of reconstructing these plots. 'To speak of the poetics of everyday behaviour amounts to claiming [. . .] that certain forms of ordinary daily activity were consciously oriented towards the laws and norms of literary texts and were lived through as direct aesthetic experiences' (Lotman [1977] 1984: 231). Analysing the everyday behaviour of Decembrists, Lotman concludes that 'the real-life behaviour of an individual of the Decembrist circle takes the form of an encoded text, and a literary plot is the code which enables us to penetrate its hidden meaning' (Lotman [1975] 1984: 93). To generalize, we can see how Lotman conceives individual behaviour as a historical category moving away from impersonal approaches to history and demonstrating how semiotic models can exercise influence on everyday life (Nascimento 2019: 216). In his article 'The Decembrist in Everyday Life', Lotman proposed the concept of 'behaviour-text' as a 'completed chain of meaningful acts that runs between intention and result' (Lotman [1975] 1984: 85). A behaviour-text (*povedencheskii tekst*) is Lotman's term for the way in which one's everyday actions may be guided and interpreted with reference to assimilated literary topoi (Kliger and Maslov 2016: 13). In addition to theatre, Lotman also focuses on the role of painting in shaping the ways to self-introduce and act in the everyday of the Russian nobility. 'There are epochs when art intrudes imperiously upon everyday life, making its day-to-day course aesthetic in the process. Such were the Renaissance, the ages of Baroque and Romanticism, the art of the early twentieth century', Lotman writes ([1973b] 1984: 159). In his essay 'Painting and the Language of Theatre: Notes on The Problem of Iconic Rhetoric', he addresses, among other issues, the theatricalization of the costumes of characters portrayed in eighteenth century's paintings and how this had influence on the clothes of the Russian aristocracy. He argues that life and painting communicate in various ways through the theatrical medium, which 'functions in this process as the intermediate code, the translator-code' (Lotman [1979] 1993: 51).

Lotman's project of the 'poetics of everyday behaviour' has been briefly discussed by quite a few leading cultural historians. For instance, Peter Burke refers to Lotman's approach in many of his writings (Burke 1997: 194; 2001: 10; 2004: 35–6), connecting this with the methods of historical anthropology. Burke also notes that if Lotman treats his project as exceptional, limited to a certain period of Russian history, then 'this approach can be and has been employed more generally' (Burke 2004: 36). A good example of a more general approach is Stephen Greenblatt's influential theory of the 'poetics of culture', directly inspired by Lotman (Greenblatt 1989: 14n10; see Chapter 27). Lotman's work on the poetics and theatricality of everyday behaviour has inspired a great amount of research in Russian cultural-historical studies. Richard Wortman, in particular, has emphasized how the interaction with Lotman's writings enabled him to develop his well-known interpretation of Russian monarchy's 'scenarios of power' that he set forth in his two-volume study of Russian imperial myths and representation (Wortman 1995; 2000, for Lotman's influence, see Wortman 2014: 370). Many scholars have applied and expanded Lotman's notion of theatricality to various spheres of Russian social and cultural life, demonstrating its great explanatory potential (e.g. Paperno 1988; Roosevelt 1991; 1995; Perlinska 1992; Reyfman 1999; Engelstein 2000; Ransel 2000; Stites 2005; Norimatsu 2018; Schönle and Zorin 2018). But Lotman's thesis that, in the wake of the collision of European culture and Russian tradition, art invaded the everyday behaviour of the nobility, has also been challenged and criticized, most notably by Michelle Lamarche Marrese (2010), who argues that Lotman overstated the degree of self-determination available to noblemen in pre-reform Russia and simultaneously underestimated the opportunities that women enjoyed; however, she does not question the utility of Lotman's conceptual tools, rather, she asserts that cultural bilingualism – like theatricality – was not unique to Russia but a feature of aristocratic life throughout eighteenth- and early nineteenth-century Europe.

Semiotics of cultural emotions

Emotions and affects have, in recent years, become the subject of a rising tide of study in cultural history (see, for example, Plamper 2015; Bodice 2018; 2019; Nagy 2018; Rosenwein and Cristiani 2018). In this context, Lotman's attempts to elaborate in the 1980s a semiotics of cultural emotions, especially of fear, is worth particular attention. Lotman's interest in affectional phenomena in culture goes back at least to 1970, when he published his short article 'On the Semiotics of the Concepts of "Shame" and "Fear" in the Mechanism of Culture' ([1970] 2000). However, the real turn towards the affective mechanisms of cultural dynamics happened in 1983, with the article 'On Lomonosov's "Ode Paraphrased from Job"' ([1983] 1992), in which Lotman seeks to show that rational and irrational processes in history are closely intertwined and often stem from the same sources, or even more, how rationalism can give birth to irrationality (M. Lotman 2007: 151). This article was followed by a whole series of studies of the semiotics of the irrational and affective mechanisms of culture, most notably 'Technological Progress as a Culturological Problem' ([1988b] 2019), 'Witch Hunts: Semiotics of Fear' ([1988] 1998) and 'The Time of Troubles as a Cultural Mechanism' ([1992c] 2019). Inspired partly by the work of French cultural historian Jean Delumeau (1978), Lotman shows how social instability creates fear and how in times of rapid change fear can spread as an epidemic, without any real reason, except semiotic. 'In this situation [of instability], mystified, semiotically constructed addressees arise – it is not the threat which causes the fear, but fear that constitutes the threat. The object of fear turns out to be a social construction, the product of semiotic codes, through which the society encodes itself and the world around it' (Lotman [1988] 1998: 63–4). Lotman focuses his attention especially on the mass hysteria that gripped Western Europe from the end of the fifteenth century to the middle of the seventeenth:

The rapid change that took place in all aspects of life, in its basic social, moral, and religious values, over the course of two to three generations, which historically speaking is a paltry amount of time, engendered feelings of uncertainty and disorientation in the vast majority of the population, resulting in a sense of fear and encroaching danger. (Lotman [1988b] 2019: 209)

We can notice here the deep connection between Lotman's late interest in the unpredictable and explosive workings of culture, on the one hand, and his explorations in the semiotics of fear, on the other. Lotman sees the semiotics of emotion as an object of study primarily to understand the dynamics of culture, especially during periods perceived as revolutionary or transitional (Gherlone 2019). He explains himself that he wants to study the phenomena of collective fear 'as a mean of gaining an idea of the semiotic mechanism of culture as such' (Lotman [1988] 1998: 63). Concluding elsewhere that 'the study of the semiotics of culture therefore leads us to the semiotics of "cultural emotions"' (Lotman [1984] 1985: 145).

Andrei Zorin in his research has suggested another interesting potential to connect various strands of Lotman's cultural-historical research, more precisely his semiotics of cultural emotions and the poetics of everyday behaviour. Zorin combines these approaches in his study of the role of 'canonic' literary texts in the formation of the psychological reactions and behaviour of eighteenth- and early nineteenth-century Russian nobles. He proposes the existence of various 'emotional patterns', taken from European literature, which shaped the psychological profile of educated people:

Each culturally significant part of everyday life had its own European classic that set the mode of emotional reaction and subsequent behaviour. The European public learned how to fall in love while reading *La Nouvelle Héloïse* and *Werther* . . . how to go to the countryside with Thomson and Rousseau, how to visit cemeteries with Young and Gray, and how to escape from the world with Zimmerman. (Zorin 2011a: 34)

Zorin emphasizes that this type of reading was by no means confined to Russia but was typical of the European public of the time. 'But in Russia this type of relationship between literature and its audience was even more manifest as the role of literature as a manual of correct feelings was greatly strengthened by the efforts to appropriate the new Western type of culture', Zorin (2011b: 46) concludes, in a clearly Lotmanian spirit. But Zorin's research also points in another promising direction in Lotman's academic interests, towards studying 'the emotional world of the person in its historical development' (Zorin 2006: 25).

Life-creation and cultural isomorphism

Relations between individual psychology and collective mentality is one of the thorniest issues in cultural history. Traditionally, cultural history has emphasized the primacy of collective attitudes over individual thinking. French cultural historian Lucien Febvre argued influentially that each epoch supplies people with a specific *outillage mentale* ('mental equipment') that shapes their way of thinking and feeling (Febvre 1942). New cultural historians and new historicists have taken a slightly different path: instead of simply reconstructing the collective *outillage mentale*, they are also interested in individual agency and forms of self-fashioning. For example, Stephen Greenblatt analysed in his *The Renaissance Self-Fashioning* the increase of the self-consciousness in the sixteenth century 'about the fashioning of human identity as a manipulable, artful process' (1980: 2), and Natalie Zemon Davies showed in her classic *The Return of Martin Guerre* (1983) that early modern 'self-fashioning' was not just an elite and courtly practice, but also one that could flourish in a remote mountain village.

Lotman brings to this debate his own original approach, departing from the work of early twentieth-century Russian literary scholars, especially Alexander Veselovsky and Juri Tynianov. Veselovsky developed in the 1900s an original 'poetics of psychological biography' in which the emotional world of an individual is approached as the product of a given cultural-historical moment (Vinitsky 2016). His aim was to trace the ways in which a historical individual is able to fashion 'alien' cultural goods (like literary texts) into an authentic expression of his emotional life. Tynianov, in turn, elaborated in 1920s a theory of 'literary personality', in order to deal 'with the problem of the reverse expansion of literature into actual life' (Tynianov [1927] 2019: 279). This principle of fusing art and life is a well-known motif in Russian culture, practised especially by Russian Symbolists, and known generally under the name of *zhisnetvorchestvo* (life-creation) or *zhiznestroitel'stvo* (life-building), that is, a deliberate aesthetic organization of one's behaviour (see Paperno and Grossman 1994).

Lotman's biographical studies rely on his earlier work on poetics of everyday behaviour (see also Chapter 19). In the article 'The Writer's Biography as a Creative Act', written in the late 1980s, he distinguishes between the writer's *poetic behaviour* and *ordinary behaviour*, comparing it to the relationship between poetry and spoken language. The poetic behaviour concerns not only the public reception of the writer; it can also have an effect on the writer's behaviour, 'thus acting as a factor of real biography': 'Following the stereotype or ignoring it deliberately, the writer consciously begins to shape his biography. In extreme cases, such as Pushkin's or Byron's, one can speak of life as a creative form and biography as a work of art' (Lotman 1990b: 357).

Lotman was particularly intrigued by these extreme cases of 'life-creation'. In the 1980s, he authored two historical biographies, the first on Pushkin (1981) and the second on Nikolay Karamzin (1987), both developing a model of individual self-fashioning in specific cultural-historical contexts. Pushkin's life was in Lotman's interpretation a succession of 'poetic roles', of particular types of poetic behaviour that he changed according to the new situations. In his youth he espoused the Romantic model of life, 'which at that time was not yet a tradition, but a living literary (and, more broadly, cultural) experience floating in the air' and which 'served as a fulcrum for Pushkin at the new stage of his artistic life'. Departing from this Romantic model, Pushkin moved further, 'creating not only a completely unique art of the written word, but also a completely unique art of life' (Lotman [1981] 1995: 56–7). After his Mikhailovsky period, in the second half of the 1820s when Romanticism asserted that the poet is completely different from other people, Pushkin started to cultivate the ordinary model of behaviour, following the idea 'that the poet is "just a man"' (Lotman [1981] 1995: 99). What is striking in Lotman's interpretation is that Pushkin switched from poetic to prosaic behaviour in his life a few years earlier than he moved from poetry to prose in his writings (Lotman [1981] 1995: 100). Put differently, Pushkin's art imitated his life, not vice versa.

Karamzin is another excellent example of self-creation, in Lotman's reading. Firstly, he was constantly refashioning himself, developing new roles and masks. But secondly, Karamzin created various masks or models of behaviour in his writings, especially in *Letters of a Russian Traveller* (1797). According to Lotman, Karamzin's travelogue was not only one of the most popular Russian novels at the time, but it also proposed a pattern for individual self-fashioning for Russian readers: 'Karamzin created Karamzin. Created during all his life as a writer. Created consciously and persistently. By producing works and producing the image of their author for the reader, he simultaneously produced the reader. He produced a type of a new Russian cultured person. The value of this creation is inestimable' (Lotman 1987: 29).

In his biography of Karamzin, Lotman compares the human life to building a temple; firstly, the walls are erected, then decoration is selected and so on. A little later, there emerges a need to build something completely new, something different, so one starts all over again, and, ultimately, the human being 'is the temple that s/he has built all his life and which gave unity and meaning to his/her work' (Lotman 1987: 12). But it is important to underline that while the model (the 'code') of this life-building is given in advance, the process of creation itself is free and the outcome unpredictable. David Bethea has considered with good reason this to be one of Lotman's most profound insights in his biographical studies:

> For the genuinely creative personality the 'code' exists only as precondition, firm footing from which to push off, but after that it exists *to be overcome*. [. . .] It is not a totalizing model to follow. Rather it is a formal occasion that guarantees *in advance* that the emerging plot [. . .] will produce a change, *but one that is itself not necessarily predictable*. Signifying turning-points in a biography, which to a literary sensibility always evoke the spectre of pre-existing codes, are perceived as belonging more to the authoring personality than to the modelling codes. Pushkin and Karamzin were creative precisely because the literary roles / masks they routinely donned at various stages of their careers [. . .] allowed them freedom in the privacy of their own thoughts to develop personalities that had little to do with those masks and indeed could be seen in retrospect to actually oppose them. (Bethea 1997: 8)

The potentiality of Lotman's biographical model has been tested and developed many times, for instance, by Irina Paperno in her study of Nikolay Chernyshevsky, an influential Russian journalist and literary critic of the nineteenth century

(Paperno 1988). Like Lotman, Paperno is not interested only in how cultural codes shape individual behaviour, but she also explores how individuals can influence the cultural codes. Through an examination of Chernyshevsky's life and works, Paperno traces the transformation of personal experience into literary structure, and then, how his work's ensuing influence structured the experience and behaviour of others, including, most famously, Vladimir Lenin. In a similar way, Angela Brintlinger has studied how Alexander Griboedov, a Russian diplomat, playwright and poet, lived his life and wrote about it for his friends, 'creating not only a kind of literary text, but also performing what were functionally literary acts, for Griboedov felt himself to be living a paradigmatically artistic and emplotted life on a literary model' (Brintlinger 2003: 374).

However, Lotman has another answer in reserve to the thorny question of relations between the individual and the collective in history. In *Creating Karamzin* he writes: 'Just as the fate of Hamlet or Othello, which takes only a few hours of stage time, is similar and equivalent to the fate of all humankind, so the fate of one cultural figure is equal in significance to the fate of the entire culture as a whole' (Lotman 1987: 14). In this sentence, Lotman formulates his principle of cultural isomorphism, 'the main ethos of Lotman's works on Russian cultural history' (Semenenko 2012: 87). Probably the most concise definition of this principle is provided in *The Unpredictable Workings of Culture*: 'The isomorphism between the whole and all its parts means that any part in isolation and all the parts together are to a certain degree alike' (Lotman [1994/2010] 2013: 76; see also [1992b] 2019: 192). In the context of cultural history, the idea is expressed in the final paragraph of his *Conversations about Russian Culture*: 'History, reflected in one person, in his life and gesture, is isomorphic to the history of humankind. They are reflected in one another and are comprehended through one another' (Lotman 1994: 389).

Conclusion

'At the inception of semiotic studies, the isolation of the field of culture from the sphere of history was in part necessary and in part polemical in nature', Lotman dictated a few months before his death (Lotman [1994/2010] 2013: 53). A couple of years earlier, he had admitted that 'abandoning the historical study was necessary in order *to return* to it later. It was necessary to break the ties with tradition in order to restore them later on a completely different basis' (Lotman [1990] 1994: 296). One can only agree that attention to history is a logical extension of cultural semiotics. The semiotic modelling of the world is constitutive for culture. Thus, conceptually elaborating the temporal dimension of semiotic modelling proves to be a consistent extension of the semiotic analysis of culture (Hałas 2013; Tamm 2017). Lotman's semiotic reconceptualization of history in general and cultural history in particular has not yet attracted much attention among historians. I hope that this chapter succeeds in demonstrating how current discussions in cultural history would benefit from engaging with Lotman's writings.[2]

Notes

1. Lotman's late interest in the historiographic tradition of the French *Annales* School played an important role in formulating his semiotic model of cultural history. He has read quite a few books by French cultural historians (especially Jean Delumeau, Jacques Le Goff and Michel Vovelle), but one can suppose that he also learned a great deal about French *nouvelle histoire* from Aron Gurevich, the main promoter of the French historiography in Russia, and close colleague to Lotman. In his autobiography, Gurevich emphasizes the significant role of Lotman in his intellectual development and his participation in the activities of the Tartu-Moscow school (Gurevich [2004] 2012: 170–2; see also Gurevich 2017: 355).

2. This chapter was written with the support of the Estonian Research Council (PRG1276). I am grateful to Igor Pilshchikov and Peeter Torop for their comments to the first version of the chapter.

References

Andrews, E. 2003. *Conversations with Lotman: Cultural Semiotics in Language, Literature, and Cognition*, Toronto, Buffalo and London: University of Toronto Press.

Arcangeli, A. 2012. *Cultural History: A Concise Introduction*, London and New York: Routledge.

Avtonomova, N. S. 2009. 'History, Structure, Explosion. (Contexts of Our Memory of Lotman)', *Russian Studies in Philosophy* 48 (2): 28–46.

Bethea, D. M. 1997. 'Bakhtinian Prosaics versus Lotmanian "Poetic Thinking": The Code and Its Relation to Literary Biography', *The Slavic and East European Journal* 41 (1): 1–15.

Boddice, R. 2018. *The History of Emotions*, Manchester: Manchester University Press.

Boddice, R. 2019. *A History of Feelings*, London: Reaktion Books.

Brintlinger, A. 2003. 'The Persian Frontier: Griboedov as Orientalist and Literary', *Canadian Slavonic Papers / Revue Canadienne des Slavistes* 45 (3/4): 371–93.

Buckler, J. A., Cassiday, J. A. and Wolfson, B. 2018. 'Introduction: Thinking through Performance in Modern Russian Culture', in J. A. Buckler, J. A. Cassiday and B. Wolfson (eds), *Russian Performances: Word, Object, Action*, 3–20, Madison and London: The University of Wisconsin Press.

Burke, P.1997. *Varieties of Cultural History*, Cambridge: Polity Press.

Burke, P. 2001. 'Ouverture. The New History: Its Past and its Future', in P. Burke (ed.), *New Perspectives on Historical Writing*, 2nd edn, 1–24, University Park: The Pennsylvania State University Press.

Burke, P. 2004. *What is Cultural History?* Cambridge: Polity Press.

Černov, I. 1982. 'Juri Lotman ja kirjandusteadusliku mõtte areng' [Juri Lotman and the Development of the Literary-Historical Thought], *Looming* 2: 270–6.

Danesi, M. and Perron, P. 1999. *Analyzing Cultures: An Introduction and Handbook*, Bloomington: Indiana University Press.

Davies, N. Z. 1983. *The Return of Martin Guerre*, Cambridge, MA: Harvard University Press.

Delumeau, J. 1978. *La Peur en Occident (XIVe–XVIIIe siècles): Une cité assiégée*, Paris: Fayard.

Engelstein, L. 2000. 'Personal Testimony and the Defense of Faith: Skoptsy Telling Tales', in L. Engelstein and S. Sandler (eds), *Self and Story in Russian History*, 330–50, Ithaca, NY and London: Cornell University Press.

Febvre, L. 1942. *Le problème de l'incroyance au XVIe siècle. La religion de Rabelais*, Paris: Albin Michel.

Gallagher, C. 2018. *Telling It Like It Wasn't: The Counterfactual Imagination in History and Fiction*, Chicago and London: The University of Chicago Press.

Gasparov, B. 1994. 'In memoriam: Iurii Mikhailovich Lotman (1922–1993)', *The Slavic and East European Journal* 38 (4): 731–9.

Gherlone, L. 2019. 'Lotman Continues to Astonish: Revolutions and Collective Emotions', *Bakhtiniana: Revista de Estudos do Discurso* 14 (4): 163–83.

Greenblatt, S. 1980. *The Renaissance Self-Fashioning: From More to Shakespeare*, Chicago and London: The University of Chicago Press.

Greenblatt, S. 1989. 'Towards a Poetics of Culture', in H. A. Veseer (ed.), *The New Historicism*, 1–14, New York: Routledge.

Gurevich, A. [2004] 2012. *Istoriia istorika*, Moscow and Saint Petersburg: Tsentr gumanitarnykh initsiativ.

Gurevich, A. 2017. *Izbrannoe. Medievistika i skandinavistika*, Moscow and Saint Petersburg: Tsentr gumanitarnykh initsiativ.

Hałas, E. 2013. 'The Past in the Present: Lessons on Semiotics of History from George H. Mead and Boris A. Uspensky', *Symbolic Interaction* 36 (1): 60–77.

Hunt, L. (ed.) 1989. *The New Cultural History*, Los Angeles and Berkeley: The University of California Press.

Ivanov, V. V. 1996. 'Semiosfera i istoriia', in Ju. M. Lotman, *Vnutri mysliashchikh mirov: Chelovek – Tekst – Semiosfera – Istoriia*, vii–xiv, Moscow: Iazyki russkoi kultury.

Kliger, I. and Maslov, B. 2016. 'Introducing Historical Poetics: History, Experience, Form', in I. Kliger and B. Maslov (eds), *Persistent Forms: Explorations in Historical Poetics*, 1–36, New York: Fordham University Press.

Koselleck, R. [1995] 2018. 'Sediments of Time', in R. Koselleck, *Sediments of Time: On Possible Histories*, trans. S. Franzel and S.-L. Hoffmann, 3–9, Stanford, CA: Stanford University Press.

Koselleck, R. 2000. *Zeitschichten: Studien zur Historik*, Frankfurt am Main: Suhrkamp.

Lorusso, A. M., 2019. 'Between Times and Spaces: Polyglotism and Polychronism in Yuri Lotman', *Bakhtiniana: Revista de Estudos do Discurso* 14 (4): 83–98.

Lotman, Ju. M. 1964. *Lektsii po struktural'noi poetike. Vyp. 1. Vvedenie, teoriia stikha*, Tartu: Izdatel'stvo Tartuskogo universiteta (*Trudy po znakovym sistemam*, 1).

Lotman, Ju. M. [1970] 2000. 'O semiotike poniatii "styd" i "strakh" v mekhanizme kul'tury', in Ju. M. Lotman, *Semiosfera*, 664–6, Saint Petersburg: Iskusstvo–SPB.

Lotman, Ju. M. [1973a] 1984. 'The Theater and Theatricality as Components of Early Nineteenth-Century Culture', trans. G. S. Smith, in Ju. M. Lotman and B. A. Uspenskij, *The Semiotics of Russian Culture*, ed. A. Shukman, 141–64, Ann Arbor: The University of Michigan.

Lotman, Ju. M. [1973b] 1984. 'The Stage and Painting as Code Mechanisms for Cultural Behavior in the Early Nineteenth Century', trans. J. Armstrong, in Ju. M. Lotman and B. A. Uspenskij, *The Semiotics of Russian Culture*, ed. A. Shukman, 165–76, Ann Arbor: The University of Michigan.

Lotman, Ju. M. [1975] 1984. 'The Decembrist in Everyday Life: Everyday Behavior as Historical-Psychological Category', trans. C. R. Pike, in Ju. M. Lotman and B. A. Uspenskij, *The Semiotics of Russian Culture*, ed. A. Shukman, 71–123, Ann Arbor: The University of Michigan.

Lotman, Ju. M. [1977] 1984. 'The Poetics of Everyday Behavior in Russian Eighteenth Century Culture', trans. N. F. C. Owen, in Ju. M. Lotman and B. A. Uspenskij, *The Semiotics of Russian Culture*, ed. A. Shukman, 231–56, Ann Arbor: The University of Michigan.

Lotman, Ju. M. [1979] 1993. 'Painting and the Language of Theatre: Notes on The Problem of Iconic Rhetoric', in A. Efimova and L. Manovich (eds), *Tekstura: Russian Essays on Visual Culture*, 45–55, Chicago and London: University of Chicago Press.

Lotman, Ju. M. [1983] 1992. 'Ob "Ode, vybrannoi iz Iova" Lomonosova', in Ju. M. Lotman, *Izbrannye stat'i v trekh tomakh*, vol. 2, 29–39, Tallinn: Aleksandra.

Lotman, Yu. [1984] 1985. 'La dinamica dei sistemi culturali', in Yu. Lotman, *La semiosfera: l'asimmetria e il dialogo nelle strutture pensanti*, 131–45, Venice: Marsilio Editori.

Lotman, J. [1985] 2019. 'Memory in a Culturological Perspective', in J. Lotman, *Culture, Memory and History: Essays in Cultural Semiotics*, trans. B. J. Baer, ed. M. Tamm, 133–7, Cham: Palgrave Macmillan.

Lotman, Ju. M. 1987. *Sotvorenie Karamzina*, Moscow: Kniga.

Lotman, Ju. M. [1988] 1998. 'Okhota za ved'mami. Semiotika strakha', *Sign Systems Studies* 26: 61–82.

Lotman, J. [1988a] 2019. 'Clio at the Crossroads', in J. Lotman, *Culture, Memory and History: Essays in Cultural Semiotics*, trans. B. J. Baer, ed. M. Tamm, 177–88, Cham: Palgrave Macmillan.

Lotman, J. [1988b] 2019. 'Technological Progress as a Culturological Problem', in J. Lotman, *Culture, Memory and History: Essays in Cultural Semiotics*, trans. B. J. Baer, ed. M. Tamm, 201–23, Cham: Palgrave Macmillan.

Lotman, Yu. M. 1990a. *Universe of the Mind: A Semiotic Theory of Culture*, trans. A. Shukman, Bloomington: Indiana University Press.

Lotman, J. 1990b. 'Kirjaniku biograafia kui loomeakt', trans. I. Soms, in J. Lotman, *Kultuurisemiootika [Cultural Semiotics]*, 347–64, Tallinn: Olion [the article was translated into Estonian from a Russian manuscript, titled 'Biografiia pisatel'ia kak akt tvortchestva'; the original text has not been published in print].

Lotman, Ju. M. [1990] 1994. 'Zimnie zametki o letnikh shkolakh', in A. D. Koshelev (ed.), *Iu. M. Lotman i tartusko-moskovskaya semioticheskaya shkola*, 295–8, Moscow: Gnozis.

Lotman, J. [1992] 2009. *Culture and Explosion*, trans. W. Clark, ed. M. Grishakova, Berlin and New York: Mouton de Gruyter.

Lotman, J. [1992a] 2019. 'On the Dynamics of Culture', in J. Lotman, *Culture, Memory and History: Essays in Cultural Semiotics*, trans. B. J. Baer, ed. M. Tamm, 95–113, Cham: Palgrave Macmillan.

Lotman, J. [1992b] 2019. 'A Divine Pronouncement or a Game of Chance? The Law-Governed and the Accidental in the Historical Process', in J. Lotman, *Culture, Memory and History: Essays in Cultural Semiotics*, trans. B. J. Baer, ed. M. Tamm, 189–99, Cham: Palgrave Macmillan.

Lotman, J. [1992c] 2019. 'The Time of Troubles as a Cultural Mechanism', in J. Lotman, *Culture, Memory and History: Essays in Cultural Semiotics*, trans. B. J. Baer, ed. M. Tamm, 225–43, Cham: Palgrave Macmillan.

Lotman, Ju. M. 1994. *Besedy o russkoi kul'ture: Byt i traditsii russkogo dvorianstva (XVIII–nachalo XIX veka)*, Saint Petersburg: Iskusstvo–SPB.

Lotman, J. [1994] 1997. 'Conversations on Russian Culture', *Russian Studies in History* 35 (4): 6–34.

Lotman, J. [1994/2010] 2013. *The Unpredictable Workings of Culture*, trans. B. J. Baer, ed. I. Pilshchikov and S. Salupere, Tallinn: Tallinn University Press.

Lotman, Ju. M. 1995. *Pushkin. Biografia pisatelia. Stat'i i zametki. 'Ievgenii Onegin'. Kommentarii*, Saint Petersburg: Iskusstvo–SPB.

Lotman, Y. and Pogosjan, J. [1996] 2014. *High Society Dinners: Dining in Tsarist Russia*, trans. M. Schwartz, ed. D. Goldstein, Devon: Prospect Books.

Lotman, M. 2007. 'Hirm ja segadus. Irratsionaalse semioosi poole' [Fear and Confusion: Toward the Semiosis of the Irrational]', in J. Lotman, *Hirm ja segadus: Esseid kultuurisemiootikast [Fear and Confusion: Essays in Cultural Semiotics]*, ed. M. Lotman, trans. K. Pruul, 141–58, Tallinn: Varrak.

Marrese, M. L. 2010. '"The Poetics of Everyday Behavior" Revisited: Lotman, Gender, and the Evolution of Russian Noble Identity', *Kritika: Explorations in Russian and Eurasian History* 11 (4): 701–39.

Nagy, P. 2018. 'History of Emotions', in M. Tamm and P. Burke (eds), *Debating New Approaches to History*, 189–202, London: Bloomsbury Academic.

Nascimento, R. A. do 2019. 'Yuri Lotman and the Semiotics of Theatre', *Bakhtiniana: Revista de Estudos do Discurso* 14 (3): 208–29.

Norimatsu, K. 2018. 'Within or Beyond Policing Norms: Yuri Lotman's Theory of Theatricality', in C.-A. Mihăilescu and T. Yokota-Murakami (eds), *Policing Literary Theory*, 111–34, Leiden: Brill.

Paperno, I. 1988. *Chernyshevskii and the Age of Realism: A Study in the Semiotics of Behavior*, Stanford, CA: Stanford University Press.

Paperno, I. and Grossman, J. D. (eds) 1994. *Creating Life: The Aesthetic Utopia of Russian Modernism*, Stanford, CA: Stanford University Press.

Perlinska, A. 1992. 'A Semiotic Analysis of Eighteenth-Century Russian Culture: Discovering the Past and Modeling the Present', *Historical Reflections / Réflexions Historiques* 18 (3): 45–57.

Plamper, J. 2015. *The History of Emotions: An Introduction*, Oxford: Oxford University Press.

Ransel, D. L. 2000. 'Enlightenment and Tradition: The Aestheticized Life of an Eighteenth-Century Provincial Merchant', in L. Engelstein and S. Sandler (eds), *Self and Story in Russian History*, 305–29, Ithaca, NY, and London: Cornell University Press.

Reyfman, I. 1999. *Ritualized Violence Russian Style: The Duel in Russian Culture and Literature*, Stanford, CA: Stanford University Press.

Roosevelt, P. R. 1991. 'Emerald Thrones: Theater and Theatricality on the Russian Estate', *The Russian Review* 50: 1–23.

Roosevelt, P. 1995. *Life on the Russian Country Estate: A Social and Cultural History*, New Haven and London: Yale University Press.

Rosenwein, B. H. and Cristiani, R. 2018. *What Is the History of Emotions?* Cambridge, UK: Polity Press.

Semenenko, A. 2012. *The Texture of Culture: An Introduction to Yuri Lotman's Semiotic Theory*, New York: Palgrave Macmillan.

Schönle, A. 2020 'Introduction', in A. Schönle (ed.), *Culture and Communication: Signs in Flux. An Anthology of Major and Lesser-Known Works by Yuri Lotman*, trans. B. Paloff, xiii–xxiv, Boston: Academic Studies Press.

Schönle, A. and Zorin, A. 2018. *On the Periphery of Europe, 1762–1825: The Self-Invention of the Russian Elite*, DeKalb: Northern Illinois University Press.

Stites, R. 2005. *Serfdom, Society, and the Arts in Imperial Russia: The Pleasure and the Power*, New Haven: Yale University Press.

Tamm, M. 2017. 'Introduction: Semiotics and History Revisited', *Sign Systems Studies* 45 (3/4): 211–29.

Torop, P. 2017. 'Semiotics of Cultural History', *Sign Systems Studies* 45 (3/4): 317–34.

Tynianov, Y. [1927] 2019. 'On Literary Evolution', in Y. Tynianov, *Permanent Evolution: Selected Essays on Literature, Theory and Film*, ed. and trans. A. Morse and P. Redko, 267–82, Boston: Academic Studies Press.

Tynianov, Ju. 1977. *Poetika, istoriia literatury, kino*, Moscow: Nauka.

Vinitsky, I. 2016. 'Breakfast at Dawn: Alexander Veselovsky and the Poetics of Psychological Biography', in I. Kliger and B. Maslov (eds), *Persistent Forms: Explorations in Historical Poetics*, 314–38, New York: Fordham University Press.

Zolyan, S. 2020. 'O nepredskazuemosti proshlogo: Iurii Lotman ob istorii i istorikakh', in S. Zolyan, *Iurii Lotman: O smysle, tekste, istorii. Temy i variatsii*, 59–95, Moscow: Izdatel'skii Dom IASK.

Zorin, A. L. 2006, 'Poniatie "literaturnogo perezhivaniia" i konstruktsiia psikhologicheskogo protonarrativa', in G. B. Obatnin and P. Pesonen (eds), *Istoriia i povestvovanie*, 12–27, Moscow: Novoe literaturnoe obozrenie.

Zorin, A. 2011a. 'Feeling across Borders: The Europeanization of Russian Nobility through Emotional Patterns', in D. Adams and G. Tikhanov (eds), *Enlightenment Cosmopolitanism*, 31–43, Abington: Routledge.

Zorin, A. 2011b. 'Leaving Your Family in 1797: Two Identities of Mikhail Murav'ev', in M. D. Steinberg and V. Sobol (eds), *Interpreting Emotions in Russia and Eastern Europe*, 44–60, DeKalb, IL: Northern Illinois University Press.

Waldstein, M. 2008. *The Soviet Empire of Signs: A History of the Tartu School of Semiotics*, Saarbrücken: VDM Verlag.

Wortman, R. S. 1995. *Scenarios of Power: From Peter the Great to the Death of Nicholas I*, Princeton: Princeton University Press.

Wortman, R. S. 2000. *Scenarios of Power: From Alexander II to the Abdication of Nicholas II*, Princeton: Princeton University Press.

Wortman, R. 2014. *Visual Texts, Ceremonial Texts, Texts of Exploration: Collected Articles on the Representation of Russian Monarchy*, Boston: Academic Studies Press.

CHAPTER 26
LOTMAN AND LITERARY STUDIES
Katalin Kroó

A chapter reflecting upon the relationship between Juri Lotman's oeuvre and literary studies, and the perspectives of the application of his ideas in this field, must, self-evidently, be structured in a specific way within the major topic of 'Lotman and other disciplines'. Here the main purpose does not lie in discovering general (semiotic or semiotically rooted) theories and concepts related to *another* discipline, when the argumentation may run through two kinds of logic. On the one hand, it is possible to demonstrate the way the 'application' or further development of Lotman's ideas appear in a given inter- or transdisciplinary context (frequently with overt references to relevant works). On the other, similar trends can be revealed between kernel components in Lotman's thinking and the 'stock' ideas, the basic postulations in a certain field (an independent discipline or an intellectual trend or paradigm representing a particular mode of thought). As opposed to such approaches, the research task motivating this chapter is set to contextualize Lotman's literary critical oeuvre within the same disciplinary domain to which it originally belonged. At the same time, such general paradigms, having significant links to and implications for literary studies, as post-structuralism, deconstruction or new historicism are treated elsewhere in this *Companion* (Chapters 23, 24 and 27).

The shift in the dominant field of Lotman's reception

If we remain within literary criticism, emphasizing that Lotman was, by education, a philologist specialized in the history of Russian literature with a primary interest in the eighteenth and nineteenth centuries, to judge his influential role, first of all, we have to repay an old debt to the meta-history of literary science. This requires a radical change of viewpoint to be taken for the definition of Lotman's productivity as a scholar, projected upon the problem of his visibility on the international map of sciences and literary criticism in particular. After Lotman's death, there was increasing demand to approach his personality as a scholar, through the reconstruction of the history of his international reception (e.g. Kristeva 1994) showing traits of confinements and conspicuous unevenness in the various geographical areas. Artur Blaim, presenting a whole system of arguments to explain 'Lotman's failure to receive wider recognition in England and America' (1998: 333), suggested that, as Anna Maria Lorusso (2019) puts it, 'a negative role was played by the Slavic field where Lotman started to circulate, and where he remained to a certain extent confined', so his reputation remained within Russian studies, resulting in a lack of due attention to 'the importance of his general theory of culture and semiosis'. We have nevertheless to note that thanks to the relatively early translations of his two famous books on the artistic text, Lotman's achievement in literary theory was evaluated and creatively interpreted in separate works and reviews (e.g. Shukman 1977; Thompson 1977; Champagne 1978; on the basis of the French translation [1973], with Uspenskij's book: De Jean 1977) at a time quite close to the original Russian publications. What, at that time, could primarily be seen and interpreted from Lotman was his structuralist-semiotic-oriented theory, without the wider range of that basic (according to its function: pivotal) 'hinterland' of poetological and cultural-historical literary research which brings to the fore a whole complex of text interpretations and literary-historical studies. When later *Universe of the Mind* (1990) became well-known, its influence on various disciplines was much wider than literary criticism. This can be explained by the focus of the volume, which is more distant from literary text research both within the framework of theory and text explanation.

However, if we question Lotman's influence on literary studies at the beginning of the twenty-first century, it can be stated, unequivocally, that, first of all, we have to return with our evaluation to the field of Russian literary culture. This does not mean we should restrict appreciation of Lotman's influence on literary criticism, again, to the limits of the 'Slavic field', as it was problematized two decades ago by Blaim, but we should also give due international recognition to his literary scholarship in Russian philology as a discipline cultivated worldwide (see Polukhina, Andrew and Reid 1993). In this international cultural space, achievement of Lotman's research, in interpreting medieval (Old Russian), eighteenth- and nineteenth-century Russian literature (Pliukhanova 1994; Crow 1994; Steiner 2003), Karamzin's (Garrard 1967: 464–6) and Pushkin's (Reyfman 1999; Bethea 2009) entire oeuvres, the lyrical work of numerous Russian poets, and his contribution to a new conceptualization of Russian literary history through the examination of the genre-specific and cultural-historical aspects of certain literary-historical periods, can no longer be ignored. No Karamzin, Pushkin or Gogol scholar can do research without taking into account Lotman's text interpretations and literary-historical studies. We should be developing awareness of his tremendous influence on Russian philology, where the creative development of this literary critical heritage, in new text interpretations representing multifaceted textual dialogues, corresponds to Lotman's own understanding of cultural dynamics in a polyglot semiospheric cultural system. In this sense, Lotmanian post-metatexts on Pushkin, nineteenth-century and so on studies prove *in actu* the force of his cultural-theoretical postulations. At the same time, his productive cultural assimilation reminds us that Russian literature and literary philology are the major spheres within the complex research field in which the phenomena of texts and cultural dynamics were investigated and the 'Theses on the Semiotic Study of Cultures' were formulated 'As Applied to *Slavic* Texts' (Lotman et al. 1973; my emphasis). Consequently, the reinterpretation of Lotman in the Russian context, not only from the perspective of his Russian sources (Russian Formalists, Bakhtin etc., and the whole collective of the TMS) but also from that of the relation of his literary scholarship to contemporary Russian philology worldwide, is a scientific-historical necessity for the future in depicting an objective picture.

Synergy, synthetized knowledge and modelling force

Further considering Lotman's inspirational energy within literary criticism, it is essential to discuss three other phenomena: synergy, synthetized knowledge and the influential model. These are interlinked within the methodological perspective taken to nuance the concept of influence. Julia Kristeva (1994), relating the French academic context of the 1960s, with its (post)structuralist orientation, to the intellectual activity of which Lotman was among the forerunners, calls attention to the possible historical simultaneity of scholarly evolutionary processes, stating that 'parallel with [her] concept of intertextuality, Lotman elaborated a notion of art as a "secondary modeling system"' (Kristeva (1994): 376). Acknowledging in the history of science examples of the parallel development of congenial ideas or intellectual tendencies, we should bear in mind the emergence of structuralism (structural semiotics) as an overall paradigm (Grishakova 2018) also in terms of *synergy*. The phenomenon of synergy, in the long run, usually leads to *synthesized knowledge*, consisting, though, of heterogeneous, sometimes controversial elements, in their variants potentially exhibiting features of individuality (Smirnov 2001: 8; Konstantinov 2016). Nevertheless, this kind of 'global' knowledge, in its internal diversity, can articulate a well-outlined scientific paradigm. In this spirit, regarding the effect of Lotman's semiotic poetics, we cannot be restricted to the question of the influence exercised on literary studies exclusively by his relevant structural-semiotic works. The issue requires the consideration of the synthetized influence of (post-)structuralist poetics, including Czech structuralism, American New Criticism, structural semiotics in general, that is, each scholarly experience contributing to the shaping of an overall episteme throughout a long process of evolution.

This is in accordance with the complex nature of Lotman's scientific heritage source itself, emerging partly from the harmonization, through creative reception, with well-defined literary/cultural-theoretical frameworks. In the first place, the active (re) explanation by Lotman and the TMS of Russian Formalist theory should be underlined, including the dialogue with the Czech structuralist theoretical tradition (primarily Jakobson and Mukařovský, see Lotman [1970] 2018; Lotman and Malevich [1994–6] 2018; Pilshchikov and Trunin 2018). The Russian Formalist heritage, with Tynianov's recognized role in the transition to the presentation of the functional nature of the artistic system (Lotman 1964: 23, 26; see Chapter 3), however, also means its cultural metatexts – Bakhtin, Vygotsky and their intellectual material, which constitutes a 'kind of general theoretical discourse' belonging to the 1920s and 1930s, and have a synthetic character conceptualized by Sergey Zenkin as 'Russian theory' (Zenkin 2004). This represents 'a cultural scientific phenomenon comprising, on the one hand, literature and art, and on the other hand, philosophy, religion and ideology' (Torop 2019); we can add the Russian Neo-Kantian philosophical roots (e.g. West 1995) and phenomenological implications. At the same time, Lotman stressed on more than one occasion the importance of a more extensive range of heritage – in cases, with a polemical stance (see, e.g. Gukovsky) – among others stemming from Freidenberg, Zhirmunsky, Veselovsky and so on (Lotman [1964] 1994: 26–7).

There is a third aspect when weighing the influential role of Lotman's work in literary science. This stems from the modelling capacity of his literary scholarship taken as an entire oeuvre. In the next parts of this chapter, we will provide a brief overview, attempting to grasp Lotman's concentration on *creative openness*. Our intention is to grasp this orientation, making a clear distinction between its functioning in the research methodology and in the definitions of the principles of meaning generation in literature, and demonstrating its presence in both spheres. The interpretation of this kind of isomorphism may result in the understanding of how Lotman's reading becomes a part of literary culture, sharing the quality of the research object according to the tenet formulated in the 'Theses' (Lotman et al. [1973] 2013: 77): 'Scientific investigation is not only an instrument for the study of culture but is also part of its object.' This explains why all of the basic features of culture, identified by Lotman, show themselves in his own literary scholarship, which behaves as a spacious semiosphere (Lotman [1984] 2005). It is able to model, through its own activity, interpretative meaning creation processes, which, at the same time, represent the major issue that the entire oeuvre investigates. Hence arises the intensive force radiating from Lotman's literary studies. Its implied telos of creative openness, coming to light as a research methodological trait and the characteristic feature of the studied object, addresses posterity with an invitation to supply open forms of continuation.

This is also an argument for the *internal coherence* of the whole oeuvre (Kvan 2003). Following the methodological and analytical orientation towards creative openness, interlinked with the explanation of some basic Lotmanian concepts within and beyond his literary criticism, we become aware, for example, of how one of the most productive elements of Lotman's theoretical legacy, the *spatial conceptualization of text and culture*, develops into the notion of the *semiosphere* with all the shared further concepts and ideas (e.g. centre, periphery, border, transgression, dominance, hierarchy, part–whole, evolution, translation and dynamics). They can all be traced back to Lotman's earlier literary critical work where they emerged either at the level of theory (regarding the structure of the artistic text), or were demonstrated through the methodological 'spirit' of the scientific reading mode of literary culture. Consequently, it would not be correct to state that, in the field of literary studies, we are confronted with a narrower scope of the continuous productivity of Lotman's theoretical thinking. We should rather insist that what, at the start, was interpreted *in the language of structurual-semiotic poetics*, gradually gained more abstract and general conceptualizations, primarily through the notion of the semiosphere (the definition and characterization of which progress alongside many other crucial basic semiotic, or semiotized, notions). It is, therefore, natural that the transdisciplinary effect of Lotman's theory draws from the more abstract, general notions, valid for the interpretation of cultural phenomena beyond, but also including, literary culture. If this is so, then it is absolutely necessary to keep alive the memory of the literary investigations that served as the basis of later abstractions and transdisciplinary applications. Within this perspective, however, first of all, it is not Lotman's interpretational achievements regarding literary works which should be remembered, as in the Russian philological context, but the characteristic features of his research methodology in the light of its isomorphism with the research material.

The aims set for the following brief overview of some crucial aspects of Lotman's literary criticism, at the same time, rely on one of Lotman's ([1971] 2009: 18) challenging ideas, according to which 'the examination of culture as a language and the sum total of texts in this language naturally poses the question of teaching'. The question is, what Lotman's literary scholarship, with its texts written in *his* language, teaches to its professional readers, in terms of effect. This question needs to be answered at both the object level (the understanding of, the knowledge acquisition from, the examined literary culture) and the metalevel (the process of arriving at this understanding, in other words, scientific methodology). In the course of the next parts, some points and domains of relevance to certain fields or aspects of general literary studies will be mentioned. These fields, such as hermeneutics, reception theory, generative poetics, narratology, possible world theory and so on, have obvious potential to assimilate Lotman's ideas. In the last section of the chapter, two major and complex spheres of influence will be treated separately.

Flexible contexts for cultural history

Lotman read and interpreted literature from early on with a methodological orientation of setting or implying cultural contexts. In the 1960s and 1970s, the problem of context becomes, on theoretical grounds, an explicit research issue during the search for a conceptual definition of the artistic text regarded as a complex structure. In the great bulk of Lotman's writings on literary history, however, the relevant theoretical aspects of the various facets of cultural contexts to which the interpretation of literature is linked, emerge implicitly within the framework of a chosen perspective from which literary history is viewed, that is, how a particular topic is posed, be it the explanation of the prose writers' or poets' literary works or the description of a whole period as a literary-cultural paradigm.

Examples offer themselves in abundance from the 1960s, testifying as to how cultural contexts are heavily implied within the demonstration of specific literary-historical processes or the interpretation of (corpuses of) literary works. A significant early article ([1962a] 2005) can be our first reference, raising the problem of the originality of *The Tale of Igor's Campaign*, where Lotman clearly touches upon the history of social ideas and the political mentality of medieval Russia and the eighteenth and nineteenth centuries, and evaluates their importance in the understanding of the reception of one cultural epoch by another. This cultural context is as important as the detection of a literary-style system or the background history of genre transformations, which are also discussed in the paper. Similarly, the differentiation of the notions of '*chest*' [honour] and '*slava*' [glory] in the secular texts of the Kiev period ([1967] 2005) relies on the elucidation of the historical cultural-behavioural context of forms of semiotization and desemiotization within the given period. The notion of geographic space in Old Russian literature is set in the context of the religious Weltanschauung ([1965a] 2005), and the famous article on eighteenth-century Russian literature, already in its title, comprises the idea of an overview to be given '*in the context* of eighteenth-century Russian culture' ([1966] 2005, our emphasis), treating such issues as the cultural consciousness of the epoch, the relationship between life and artistic forms and their cultural patterns concerning organizations through private and official channels, and literature as tradition. Ethics, a philosophical system, and the strategic patterns (tactics) of revolutionary struggle supply the cultural contexts in which eighteenth-century poetry is discussed in another writing ([1965b] 2005).

Cultural contexts can be identified as systems. Literature as a system and subsystem (concrete text, corpus, the literary specificity of an epoch, author poetics, tradition) is interpreted in relation to other systems (ideology, philosophy, social-political trends, historical movements, ethics, behaviour patterns, cultural organizations, abstract forms of semiotization etc.). What matters in the examination of the scrutinized literary phenomenon as a system – further: literary personality, oeuvre, generic construction, characteristic features of the poetry of an epoch and so on – is the interaction of cultural systems drawn into relationality not in a simple cause–effect network, but through dynamic correlations showing themselves in a wide range of functions. They can be projected onto the postulation of intra- and extratextual relations, assuming a culturally conditioned hierarchy of structures 'through hypersystems of extratextual character' (Eimermacher [1995b] 2001: 330). Without doubt, Lotman's early literary scholarship on the most diversified topics can be traced back to a structuralist-semiotic code of research methodology, relying on the demonstration of meaning-emergence based on the relationality of semiotic systems, organized within the cultural hierarchy and relying on part–whole relationships.

Methodological part–whole: Progressive reading spiral

One could conclude that Lotman's structural poetics at the end of the 1950s and in the 1960s was methodologically 'bilingual', manifesting itself *in an implicit form* (literary history-oriented research with the emergence of a structural-semiotic approach) and *in an explicit form* (theory-oriented scholarship accompanied by a conscious search for a new methodological culture engendering an objective and precise scientific metalanguage [Lotman 1967]) *of structural-semiotic suggestions and conceptualizations*. This double methodological trajectory remained characteristic throughout the following decades, in the 1970s and 1980s, when Lotman went on discussing major issues of Russian literary history and theory linked to the problem of text and textuality. Both analytical languages include text interpretations. The literary text stands at the intersection of literary history and explicit or implicit theory, projected upon one another in a process of formulations and reformulations. Lotman, in his research, proceeds with an ever-extending empirical and theoretical experience through an upgrading scientific reading 'spiral', interpreting literary culture as a whole.

Such a scientific reading method is analogous to the 'spiral' about which Lotman speaks in his article 'On the Differentiation of the Linguistic and Literary Concept of Structure' (1963: 50), where he reflects on interpretational dynamics revealing itself in fitting the parts to the whole, in a process where they are presupposed and determined by one another, in their mutual projections, in the various phases of the semantic text explanation. This is defined as the specific trait of the reception of structures realized through language (1963: 50). The structural semantics (in contexts) of the word (details) and the overall meaning of the literary text as a whole interact in a process of the systematic recurrences, returns to the same textual elements.

This methodological principle, from a functional point of view interpretable with reference to the 'hermeneutic circle', is far from representing a self-contained circularity. The permanent return to the word (as part and detail) necessary to define the semantic universe of the text as a whole discloses the continuously updated internal structural aspects which can be interpreted as contexts. The more contexts for a word can be defined, the richer in its semantic aspects that particular unit will become. In this process the general linguistic meaning of the word (its polysemantic nature (*polisemantizm*) discernable in various linguistic contexts) will be metamorphosed into a multivalent semantic nature (*mnogoznachitel'nost'*) as a result of the ever-enlarging range of separate internal structural contexts in the course of interpretation. This entails an increasing degree of semantic individualization of the word and the overcoming of its ambiguity. The more complex the literary structure, as the sum of internal microstructural contexts, the more multivalent, multilayered and, at the same time, unambiguous the literary semantics of the word is (Lotman 1963: 49), since it is presupposed that the variety of semantic aspects of the word (defined in multiple internal structural contexts) will find its place in its complex artistic meaning (Lotman [1970] 1977: 72). The intersection points of meanings and systems function as semantic–semiotic high-density points of the emergence of creativity.

What Lotman articulates in the referenced paper is a very clear tenet for defining the *interpretation of the literary text* as searching for the understanding of the dynamics of meaning-creation, metaphorized as a progressive, upgrading spiral. The methodological starting point is the 'pulsation of the part and the whole' (Lotman 1963: 50), which is examined from the point of view of identifying the artistic forms of internal semanticization, when contexts are implicitly interpreted in their semiotic nature (defining various signifying conditions for the same signifier). Lotman's main focus is what the Russian Formalists called *literariness* (Eichenbaum [1925] 2001: 1065–6; cf. e.g. Balcerzan 2016), which emerges in his research as the *semiotic conditions for literary meaning creation*. Here, we can detect the potential to rename the phenomenon as 'semiotic literariness' (on the introduction of the term see Kroó and Torop 2018: 144). The definition of the scope of semiotic literariness and the examination of its concrete realization can be regarded as one of the most prolific theoretical and practical research questions. It has enormous potential regarding the understanding of the formation and the development of semantic units in the literary text. The various 'semantic events' there can be identified and classified taking into consideration various signifier-signified configurations. This may include the examination of composition, points of view, syntactic structures, the phonic organization of lyrical and prose texts, and the investigation into discourse, as a linguistic achievement, through and within various types of literary narrative and discourse poetics (see in this field important works by J. Faryno, W. Schmid, M. Freise, I. Smirnov, E. de Haard, Á. Kovács, A. Faustov etc.). Text-coherence, text-cohesion can also be posed as crucial complementary problems to be researched in the relevant linguistically centred literary critical subfield (see also literary text linguistics). The specification of the signifier–signified configurations can require the definition of the role of the reader who creates interpretations within the literary work as a semantic figure and/or as a recipient taking an external position to the poetics of the text (narratology).

The integrative openness of literary semiotics

The methodological complementarities, the parts gravitating towards a whole in Lotman's literary scholarship – the alternation of implicit and explicit semiotic conceptualizations; terminological approximations through analogous notions and their exact differentiations; theoretical and empirical orientations; the dialogue of the discussion of particular/partial issues and holistic approaches; the analysis of concrete texts and generalizations about their cultural contexts – paved the way for and entered that polyglot research space of the semiotics of culture which Karl Eimermacher ([1995c] 2001: 349) identified as 'the semiotic variant of integrative culturology'. The quality of being 'integrative' in its relevance to Lotman's literary scholarship reveals itself in several characteristic traits.

Regarding the *disciplinary complexity* of the literary critical methodological approach, in itself ensuring transdisciplinary perspectives, the integrative aspect consists of the inclusive nature of an interdisciplinary complex of *conceptual and methodological stock knowledge*. Initially this comes mainly from linguistics, philosophy, logic, mathematics, cybernetics, information theory and literary and cultural studies, with its interactive notional elements crossing disciplinary borders and the limits of singularized research objects, moving towards semiotic generalizations (Eimermacher [1995a] 2001: 109–14). Relating to the contextualization of literary texts in culture, the integrative nature is represented by discussing literature in the complex cultural space of communication. The conceptual and practical interpretational analogy between text and culture provides a solid base for interpreting integrational processes through diverse forms of cultural memory.

The integrative nature of Lotman's literary semiotics, consequently, is organically linked with its open perspectives. At the same time, finding ever newer contexts in which literary cultural phenomena are discussed testifies to the coherence of the project of exploring literary culture with an expanding and enriched knowledge. That is the reason why any results are ambiguous if we try to draw radical borderlines between the major periods in Lotman's literary research. The organic link between his first three books has been clarified (Gasparov 1994: 11). Lotman remained, throughout his life, a literary historian (Mayenowa 1977). The spatial essence of text and culture (Škulj 2004) is systematically reinterpreted within the notion of the polyglot semiosphere (Nöth 2015), the languages of which show features of asymmetry, with their positions in the centre or periphery. The communication between them excludes reliance on their total equivalence, in the same way as previously assumed in the literary text.

Further facets of creative openness

In the long and systematic process of Lotman's investigations into the nature of the literary text, the notion of the text-generator appears as entirely opposed to the code-based 'meaning-text', this latter embodying a 'passive package' of ready-made information. The text-generator transforms the recipient into a 'historian', who has to follow the meaning-engendering processes through the emergence (both in verse and in prose texts) of yet non-existent or unknown codes, in a plural system, requiring creative power even in the process of understanding.

This idea of the generative text as the kernel mechanism of dynamic cultural functioning constitutes the centre of Lotman's structural-semiotic poetics with the stable nucleus of his search for literary meaning-emergence linked to creativity (Żyłko 2015: 31). His literary critical oeuvre, from this perspective, may be defined as representing *generative semiotic poetics* – this term carrying a much broader sense than the notion of generative poetics based either on literary discourse analysis on the analogy with or having inspiration from Chomsky's generative grammar (on deep structures, see, e.g. van Holk 1994), or on the principles of generative poetics (for its reinterpretation, see Zolyan 2020: 239–42), defined as the 'poetics of expressiveness' by Shcheglov and Zholkovsky (1987). The idea of creativity related to semantic dynamics and interpreted in terms of openness (Avtonomova 2009: 203–68) is present from the very beginning of Lotman's literary semiotics. Its continuous reformulation defies a mechanical explanation by a simple shift from structuralism to post-structuralism. Through time, it involves and relies on the conceptualization of translation (initially: internal and external recoding, Thompson 1977: 232–3; Shukman 1977: 72–82) with shared features of its dynamics within or between texts. Lotman's interpretative metatexts can also be regarded as ever newer translations of ideas and concepts proceeding through the reading spiral.

The creative nature of transgression

Translation also raises the problem of 'going beyond', leading to semantic innovation. Lotman's reading of *Eugene Onegin* offers significant perspectives for the interpretation of the transgression of borders/limits. He illustrates how Pushkin's work places in centre stage the problem of literary expectations and the violation of the norms in a specific way, with the poetic intention to overcome not a concrete literary cultural tradition but literary conditionality (*uslovnost'*) as such, transgressing any kind of fixed (ritualistic) forms, through creating the illusion of the immediacy of real life (Lotman 1988: 47). Paradoxically, this could be achieved by the poetic strategy of the strengthening of the complexity of literary conditionality. As a result, a plural system of conflicting elements is created with none reaching the status of a final authentic conditionality. Lotman's research interest in the poetics of conflict, contradiction (its criticism: Kibalnik 2011) represents not a simple structuralist focus in the given interpretation (Faritov 2017: 2), but arrives at a final explanation through the idea of plurality, implying complementarity and also creative meaning-transfigurations (transgressions at points of intersection). This idea, on the other hand, is linked to the problematization of literary conditionality overcome by the semanticization of 'natural', that is, non-literary reality (within the poetic framework of norm transgressions). On this track, Lotman also opens up a wide range of flexible research perspectives, adjustable to literary and philosophical investigations into the phenomena of 'possible worlds' (e.g. Doležel 1998), fictionalizations and further forms of virtualization.

Transgression proves a crucial criterion for the evaluation of the scope of freedom characterizing the literary hero in the plot (see their choice against the deterministic factors of reality: Lotman [1987] 2005: 717; the 'normativity of the approach to personality': [1962b] 2005: 557; 'metaphysical normativity': Lotman, Egorov and Mints [1960] 2005: 531, 536). Transgression also serves as a semiotic requirement for the event as 'the shifting of a persona across the borders of a semantic field' ([1970] 1977: 233). The literary character's function as a 'plot-creator' ([1987] 2005: 717) is linked to the specificity of the Russian novel, from Gogol onwards 'raising the problem which is not the change of the hero's state but the metamorphosis of his internal essence, or the transformation of life forces surrounding him' ([1987] 2005: 719). This potentiality fits into the openness of the novel which, unlike folklore genres (especially the fairy tale), enters a wide range of extratextual social and everyday semiotic material of its epoch, giving rise to a great variety of plot opportunities. From this follows Lotman's criticism on the narratological application of Propp's model to the novel ([1987] 2005: 712), suggesting a polemic stance against certain narratological approaches. In the novel unforeseen combinations may also emerge through symbolic objects. The plot for Lotman becomes a significantly enlarged notion interpreting heterogeneous elements from the semantics of the word up to the most complex cultural symbols, all of them being transformed through poetic play into a plot fact ([1987] 2005: 714; see also Chapter 13).

Multiplying text boundaries and descriptions

The possibility of the dynamic rearrangement of borders in the various forms of textual interaction and transfiguration – intertextuality, text–metatext, text within the text, text-internalization and so on – offer an unrestricted openness for creativity, all the more so that culture generates an unlimited range of communicating text types. Social-cultural behaviour patterns are seen as traditions in the sense of texts (Lotman 1980; 1994), and an artist's biography can be conceived of as the model of an extended behavioural text and the model of Lotman's own life (Kliger 2010: 270; Reyfman 1999: 441–3). In the same way as a literary oeuvre is created by the artist, a whole life – such as Pushkin's – may arise as an artistic text (Lotman 1981), and, accordingly, the individual, unprecedented personality as an identity construction may be shaped by the writer ('Karamzin creates Karamzin'). Such an approach gives the literary critic the right to reconstruct, following his 'archeological project', 'the integral ideal of personality [. . .] which the hero of the biography created in his soul' (Bethea 2005: 3–4). The result is, in the book on Karamzin (1987), as Boris Egorov states, the 'biography of the soul' (Bethea 2005: 3–4: 7). The literary research innovation emerges on a whole range of crossings across textual borders: those of the realized and non-realized (but potential) texts; the actually or supposedly present and the reconstructed; the biographical (life as extratextual) and the poetic (the artistic work, the intratextual); external and internal discourses (in this case, concerning letters as genre variants); history as biographical or historiographical text and as artistic text. Within Lotman's oeuvre itself the reconstruction-novel functions in one semiosphere with all of his other works on Karamzin, including his dissertation (Kliger 2010: 263; Egorov 1999: 8, 52–9).

Shifting borders entailing changing textual identities within literary/cultural texts and between them create the need for an open-ended multiple description that seems to be adequate to follow various structures and meaning-engendering processes (e.g. text layers or readers' expectations and their violations, cf. the idea from and for reception aesthetics: Pilshchikov, Poselyagin and Trunin 2018: 18). This also works for the multiplication of synchronic states (Pilshchikov, Poselyagin and Trunin 2018: 35–6, 45; Żyłko 2015: 7), reaching a model of dynamic processes.

Literary comparatistics and semiotics

In the final part of this chapter outlining some major perspectives from which Lotman's effect and influential potential in literary studies can be evaluated, two complex domains should be given special focus: *comparative literary studies* (cf. Tötösy de Zepetnek 2017) and the *semiotics of literature*. Both realms study as their focal point *literary dynamics* (including the issues of literary evolution; textual interactions in the world-literary space; the problem of meaning-emergence and poetic innovation). Similarly, they bring to the fore, in their interpretational methodology, the phenomenon of relationality. Traditionally, relationality is regarded as a marked constituent of structuralist approaches; however, this perspective provides a basic operational tool for any comparative research (see, in the Central and Eastern European context, on 'the advancement of comparatism as a value, a principle and a methodology', Sywenky 2011; cf. Mitterbauer and Smith-Prei 2017). The function of relationality works in the identification, based on equivalences and projections, of both simultaneous conditions and evolutionary phases, literary phenomena or meaning-developmental processes, with the demarcation lines between the older and newer stages and meanings. The productivity of Lotman's thought in these two complex fields of literary criticism, sharing implicitly or explicitly the relational comparative methodological point of view, testifies to the interpretability of his overall 'structural-semiotic' approach to literature as representing a general mode of reading and interpretation, going far beyond the narrow technology of structuralist analysis.

Lotman's treatment of literature as a significant semiospheric part of culture (culture conceived as a larger semiosphere with an unbounded range of potentially interacting internal boundaries delimiting sub-semiospheric organizations of various types at different hierarchical levels), in which the interpretation of the dynamics of semiotic processes cannot be separated from the central and peripheral positions, establishes solid grounds for the investigations into 'literature as a world system' (Kliger 2010: 259), that is, into 'a holistic conception of world literature as a megasystem made up of systems, subsystems, and the network of its interrelations' (Domínguez 2006: 5; cf. Moriarty 1996). The theoretical methodological framework involved offers the means to transcend 'national literature' as a central category (a crucial unit in the 'megasystem'), taking the problem of 'literary emergence' in terms of a 'hegemony crisis'. The examination of the transformations of the 'dominant system' as 'contemplated from both an intra- and intersystemic standpoint' can entwine a reliance on the logic of 'a linear sequence of phases' 'in a continuity according to the model of developmentalism' and the analysis of facts relating to unpredictability and explosive emergence (Domínguez 2006). Lotman's position in this field may find its place in a complex context of elements of theoretical approaches, among others represented by Even-Zohar and the Tel-Aviv school, 'the interliterary theory of the school of Bratislava, the cultural materialism approach of Birmingham School' and so on (Domínguez 2006: 4). Kliger also insists that when calculating 'the mode of local response to foreign interference, one must include, in the mapping of world-literary interactions, something like an account of the semiotic disposition of the core–periphery relations within the target culture as a whole' (Kliger 2010: 267), as in the source culture. To suggest that both cultures have their multiple internal asymmetries may lead to outlining a more sophisticated picture of the mechanism of the spread and reception of literary influence (see Juvan 2000) in a world-literary space, which cannot be restricted to a simple interpretation of hegemony or its change, since processes cannot be predicted (see also a relevance to postcolonial poetics). This kind of interpretation of textual interaction within a comparative framework implies the conceptualization of literary evolution, that is, literary history. Linked to this, the most intensive research sphere in literary studies, with its interpretative achievements significantly influencing and constantly nuancing our comprehension and the writing of literary history, is intertextuality, with an intensifying orientation towards transmedial studies.

These fields must also be ranked among the main issues of contemporary literary semiotics, where Lotman's heritage is the most active. There are many critical works which interpret literary semiotics as a discipline or subdiscipline within literary criticism or general semiotics, or outline it as a reading method. Such approaches offer empirical literary text analyses (e.g. from the point of view of spatial or chronotopic systems, Veivo 2001; see in space poetics the legacy of Lotman, e.g. van Baak 1983), or elaborate theoretical assumptions (e.g. in the field of narratology, Pier 2018). The exact definition of literary semiotics in terms of its disciplinary identity proves to be a complex task (Kroó 2020) which hasn't yet reached a state of completion. One important step was made by taking and interpreting the new orientation which develops within the context of Peircean semiotics (e.g. Johansen 2002, 2007; Veivo 2007; Veivo and Ljungberg 2009). Another current trend functions within cultural semiotics, extending literary investigation towards transmedia studies (labelled, e.g. as 'literature on screen', Milyakina et al. 2019). Both trends represent significant fields of exploration, enabling us to comprehend the complexity of literary culture. Lotman's literary criticism, in the light of these contemporary semiotic achievements, remains topical. In the spirit of the intention aiming at the 'reconciliation' of structuralist and Peircean semiotics, there are signs raising the expectations that the evaluation of Lotman's literary semiotics can also be drawn into that larger interpretative space, where such a harmonization may take place (Kiryushchenko 2012). In Peirce's understanding of the 'interpretant', we can discern one of the most productive sources for such a reassessment, potentially leading to knowledge about more complex parallels.

Lotman's polyglot and dynamic literary critical semiosphere invites us to assume its further growth through effects both in predictable and unpredictable directions.

References

Avtonomova, N. 2009. *Otkrytaia struktura: Iakobson–Bakhtin–Lotman–Gasparov*, Moscow: ROSSPEN.

Van Baak, J. J. 1983. *The Place of Space in Narration: A Semiotic Approach to the Problem of Literary Space, with an Analysis of the Role of Space in Babel's Konarmija*, Amsterdam: Rodopi.

Balcerzan, E. 2016. *Literariness: Models, Gradations, Experiments. Studies in Modern Polish Literature and Culture*, Frankfurt am Main: Peter Lang.

Bethea, D. 2005. 'Whose Mind Is This Anyway? Influence, Intertextuality, and the Boundaries of Legitimate Scholarship', *The Slavic and East European Journal* 49 (1): 2–17.

Bethea, D. 2009. 'Of Pushkin and Pushkinists', in D. M. Bethea (ed.), *The Superstitious Muse: Thinking Russian Literature Mythopoetically*, 185–204, Boston: Academic Studies Press.

Blaim, A. 1998, 'Lotman in the West: An Ambiguous Complaint', in J. Andrew and R. Reid (eds), *Neo-formalist Papers: Contributions to the Silver Jubilee Conference to Mark 25 Years of the Neo-formalist Circle*, 329–37, Amsterdam: Rodopi.

Champagne, R. A. 1978. 'A Grammar of the Languages of Culture: Literary Theory and Yury M. Lotman's Semiotics', *New Literary History* 9 (2): 205–10.

Crowe, N. J. 1994. 'Jurij Lotman and the Re-presentation of Eighteenth-century Russian Literature', *Russian Literature* 35: 277–84.

DeJean, J. 1977. 'In Search of the Artistic Text: Recent Works by Lotman and Uspensky', *SubStance* 6/7 (17): 149–58.

Doležel, L. 1998. *Heterocosmica: Fiction and Possible Worlds*, Baltimore, MD and London: The Johns Hopkins University Press.

Domínguez, C. 2006. 'Literary Emergence as a Case Study of Theory in Comparative Literature', *CLCWeb: Comparative Literature and Culture*, 8 (2), available online: https://docs.lib.purdue.edu/clcweb/vol8/iss2/1/ (accessed 15 October 2020).

Egorov, B. 1987. 'Biografiia dushi', in Ju. M. Lotman, *Sotvorenie Karamzina*, 7–10, Moscow: Kniga.

Egorov, B. 1999. *Zhizn' i tvorchestvo Iu. M. Lotmana*, Moscow: Novoe literaturnoe obozrenie.

Eichenbaum, B. [1925] 2001. 'The Theory of the "Formal Method"', trans. L. T. Lemon and M. J. Reis, in V. B. Leitch (ed.), *The Norton Anthology of Theory and Criticism*, 1062–80, New York: W. W. Norton & Company.

Eimermacher, K. [1995a] 2001. 'Semiotika i literaturovedenie', in K. Eimermacher, *Znak, tekst, kul'tura*, trans. S. Romashko, 96–114, Moscow: Rossiskii gosudarstvennyi gumanitarnyi universitet.

Eimermacher, K. [1995b] 2001. 'Metodologicheskie aspekty nauchnoi deiatel'nosti Iu. M. Lotmana (50-e i 60-e gody)', in K. Eimermacher, *Znak, tekst, kul'tura*, trans. S. Romashko, 325–48, Moscow: Rossiskii gosudarstvennyi gumanitarnyi universitet.

Eimermacher, K. [1995c] 2001. 'Iu. M. Lotman: Semioticheskii variant integrativnoi kul'turologii', in K. Eimermacher, *Znak, tekst, kul'tura*, trans. S. Romashko, 349–64, Moscow: Rossiskii gosudarstvennyi gumanitarnyi universitet.

Faritov, V. T. 2017. 'Semiotika transgresii: Iu. M. Lotman kak literaturoved i filosof', *Vestnik gosudarstvennogo universiteta* 419: 60–6.

Garrard, J. G. 1967. 'Karamzin in Recent Soviet Criticism: A Review', *The Slavic and East European Journal* 11 (4): 464–72.

Gasparov, M. 1994. 'Predislovie', in A. D. Koshelev (ed.), *Iu. M. Lotman i tartusko-moskovskaia semioticheskaia shkola*, 11–16, Moscow: Gnozis.

Grishakova, M. 2018. 'Structuralism and Semiotics', in D. H. Richter (ed.), *A Companion to Literary Theory*, 48–59, Hoboken: John Wiley & Sons Ltd.

Van Holk, A. G. F. 1994. 'On the Deep Structure of Ostrovskij's "Dark Realm"', *Russian Literature* 36 (3): 301–16.

Johansen, J. D. 2002. *Literary Discourse: A Semiotic-pragmatic Approach to Literature*, Toronto, Buffalo and New York: University of Toronto Press.

Johansen, J. D. 2007. 'A Semiotic Definition of Literary Discourse', *Semiotica* 165 (4): 107–31.

Juvan, M. 2000. 'On Literariness: From Post-Structuralism to Systems Theory', *Comparative Literature and Culture* 2 (2), available online: https://docs.lib.purdue.edu/clcweb/vol2/iss2/1/ (accessed 15 September 2020).

Kibalnik, S. 2011. '"Ievgenii Onegin" ili "Ievgenii Lotman", ili mif o "Poetike protivorechii" v pushkinskom romane', *Kul'tura i tekst* 12, available online: https://cyberleninka.ru/article/n/ evgeniy-onegin-ili-evgeniy-lotman-ili-mif-o-poetike-protivorechiy-v-pushkinskom-romane (accessed 16 January 2021).

Kiryushchenko, V. 2012. 'Peirce's Semiotics and the Russian Formalism: Points of Convergence', in *Proceedings of the 10th World Congress of the International Association for Semiotic Studies (IASS/AIS)*, 1317–22, Universidade da Coruña, Spain.

Kliger, I. 2010. 'World Literature Beyond Hegemony in Yuri M. Lotman's Cultural Semiotics', *Comparative Critical Studies* 7 (2–3): 257–74.

Konstantinov, M. V. 2016. 'Poniatie struktury Iu. Lotmana i R. Barta', *Visnik Dnipropetrovs'kogo universitetu* 1: 92–8.

Kristeva, J. 1994. 'On Yury Lotman', *PMLA*, 109 (3): 375–6.

Kroó, K. 2020. *Korunk hőse – Korunk irodalomszemiotikája? Karakterpoétika és olvasásszemiotika Lermontov regényében* [*A Hero of Our Time – Literary Semiotics of Our Time. Character Poetics and Semiotics of Reading in Lermontov's Novel*], Budapest: L'Harmattan.

Kroó, K. and Torop, P. 2018. 'Text Dynamics: Renewing Challenges for Semiotics of Literature', *Sign Systems Studies* 46 (1): 143–67.

Kvan, K. S. 2003. *Osnovnyie aspekty tvorcheskoi evoliutsii Iu. M. Lotmana. Ikonichnost' – prostranstvennost' – mifologichnost' – lichnostnost'*, Moscow: Novoe literaturnoe obozrenie.

Lorusso, A. M. 2019. 'Jurij Lotman', in *Oxford Bibliographies in Literary and Critical Theory*, available online: https://www.oxfordbibliographies.com/view/document/obo-97801902219 11/obo-9780190221911-0074.xml (accessed 19 January 2021).

Lotman, Ju. M. [1962a] 2005. '"Slovo o polku Igorove" i literaturnaia traditsiia XVIII – nachala XIX v.', in Ju. M. Lotman, *O russkoi literature*, 14–79, Saint Petersburg: Iskusstvo–SPB.

Lotman, Ju. M. [1962b] 2005. 'Istoki tolstovskogo napravleniia v russkoi literature 1830-kh godov', in Ju. M. Lotman, *O russkoi literature*, 548–93, Saint Petersburg: Iskusstvo–SPB.

Lotman, Ju. M. 1963. 'O razgranichenii lingvisticheskogo i literaturovedcheskogo poniatiia struktury', *Voprosy iazykoznaniia* 3: 44–52.

Lotman, Ju. M. [1964] 1994. 'Lektsii po struktural'noi poetike', in A. D. Koshelev (ed.), *Iu. M. Lotman i tartusko-moskovskaia semioticheskaia shkola*, 17–263, Moscow: Gnozis.

Lotman, Ju. M. [1965a] 2005. 'O poniatii geograficheskogo prostranstva v russkikh srednevekovykh tekstakh', in Ju. M. Lotman, *O russkoi literature*, 112–17, Saint Petersburg: Iskusstvo–SPB.

Lotman, Ju. M. [1965b] 2005. 'Otrazheniie etiki i taktiki revoliutsionnoi bor'by v russkoi literature kontsa XVIII veka', in Ju. M. Lotman, *O russkoi literature*, 211–38, Saint Petersburg: Iskusstvo–SPB.

Lotman, Ju. M. [1966] 2005. 'Literatura v kontekste russkoi kul'tury 18 veka', in Ju. M. Lotman, *O russkoi literature*, 118–67, Saint Petersburg: Iskusstvo–SPB.

Lotman, Ju. M. 1967. 'Literaturovedeniie dolzhno byt' naukoi', *Voprosy literatury* 1: 90–100.

Lotman, Ju. M. [1967] 2005. 'Ob oppozitsii "chest" – "slava" v svetskikh tekstakh kiievskogo perioda', in Ju. M. Lotman, *O russkoi literature*, 84–94, Saint Petersburg: Iskusstvo–SPB.

Lotman, J. [1970] 1977. *The Structure of the Artistic Text*, trans. R. Vroon, Ann Arbor, MI: University of Michigan, Department of Slavic Languages and Literatures.

Lotman, Ju. M. [1970] 2018. 'Ian Mukarzhovskii – teoretik iskusstva', in Ju. M. Lotman, *O strukturalizme. Raboty 1965-1970 godov*, ed. I. A. Pilshchikov, with N. V. Poselyagin and M. V. Trunin, 356–90, Tallinn: TLU Press.

Lotman, Ju. M. [1971] 2009. 'Problema "obucheniia kul'ture" kak tipologicheskaia kharakteristika', in Ju. M. Lotman, *Chemu uchatsia liudi. Stat'i i zametki*, ed. P. Torop, 18–32, Moscow: Tsentr Knigi – BGBIL im M. I. Rudomino.

Lotman, Ju. M. 1980. *Roman A. S. Pushkina "Ievgenii Onegin". Kommentarii*, Leningrad: Prosveshchenie.

Lotman, Ju. M. 1981. *Aleksandr Sergeevich Pushkin. Biografiia pisatelia: Posobie dlia uchashchikhsia*, Leningrad: Prosveshchenie.

Lotman, J. [1984] 2005. 'On the Semiosphere', trans. W. Clark, *Sign Systems Studies* 33 (1): 205–29.

Lotman, Ju. M. 1987. *Sotvorenie Karamzina*, Moscow: Kniga.

Lotman, Ju. M. [1987] 2005. 'Siuzhetnoie prostranstvo russkogo romana 19 stoletiia', in Ju. M. Lotman, *O russkoi literature*, 712–29, Saint Petersburg: Iskusstvo–SPB.

Lotman, Ju. M. 1988. *V shkole poeticheskogo slova*. Pushkin, Lermontov, Gogol, Moscow: Prosveshchenie.

Lotman, Yu. M. 1990. *Universe of the Mind: A Semiotic Theory of Culture*, trans. A. Shukman, Bloomington, IN: Indiana University Press.

Lotman, Ju. M. 1994. *Besedy o russkoi kul'ture. Byt i traditsii russkogo dvorianstva (XVIII – nachalo XIX veka)*, Saint Petersburg: Iskusstvo–SPB.

Lotman, Ju. M. and Malevich, O. [1994–1996] 2018. 'Prilozhenie. "Issledovaniia po teorii iskusstva" Iana Mukarzhovskogo v dvukh tomakh (sostav i struktura)', in Ju. M. Lotman, *O strukturalizme. Raboty 1965-1970 godov*, ed. I. A. Pilshchikov, with N. V. Poselyagin, and M. V. Trunin, 350–5, Tallinn: TLU Press.

Lotman, Ju. M., Egorov, B. F. and Mints, Z. G. [1960] 2005. 'Osnovnyie etapy razvitiia russkogo realizma', in Ju. M. Lotman, *O russkoi literature*, 530–47, Saint Petersburg: Iskusstvo–SPB.

Lotman, J., Ivanov, V., Piatigorsky, A., Toporov, V. and Uspenskij, B. [1973] 2013. 'Theses on the Semiotic Study of Cultures (as Applied to Slavic Texts)', in S. Salupere, P. Torop and K. Kull (eds), *Beginnings of the Semiotics of Culture*, 53–77, Tartu: University of Tartu Press.

Mayenowa, M. R. 1977. 'Lotman as a Historian of Literature', *Russian Literature* 5 (1): 81–90.

Milyakina, A., Ojamaa, M., Pilipovec, T. and Rickberg, M. 2019. 'Literature on Screen: Teaching Adaptations in a Multimodal Course', *Media Practice and Education* 21 (3): 1–11.

Mitterbauer, H. and Smith-Prei, C. 2017. *Crossing Central Europe: Continuations and Transformations, 1900 and 2000*, Toronto, Buffalo and London: University of Toronto Press.

Moriarty, M. E. 1996. *Semiotics of World Literature*, Lewiston, Quenston and Lampeter: The Edwin Mellen Press.

Nöth, W. 2015. 'The Topography of Yuri Lotman's Semiosphere', *International Journal of Cultural Studies* 18 (1): 11–26.

Pier, J. 2018. 'Monde narratif et sémiosphère', *Communications* 103: 265–86.

Pilshchikov, I. and Trunin, M. 2018. 'Vokrug podgtovki i zapreta russkogo izdaniia rabot Iana Mukarzhovskogo pod redaktsiei Iu. M. Lotmana', in Ju. M. Lotman, *O strukturalizme. Raboty 1965–1970 godov*, ed. I. A. Pilshchikov, with N. V. Poselyagin, and M. V. Trunin, 315–49, Tallinn: TLU Press.

Pilshchikov, I., Poselyagin, N. and Trunin, M. 2018. 'Problemy genezisa i evoliutsii tartusko-moskovskovskogo strukturalizma v rabotakh Iu. M. Lotmana 1960-kh i nachala 1970-kh godov (Vstupitel'naia stat'ia)', in Ju. M. Lotman, *O strukturalizme. Raboty 1965–1970 godov*, ed. I. A. Pilshchikov, with N. V. Poselyagin, and M. V. Trunin, 7–62, Tallinn: TLU Press.

Pliukhanova, M. 1994. 'Iurii Lotman on Old Russian Literature and the Eighteenth Century', *The Slavonic and East European Review* 72 (4): 601–8.

Polukhina, V., Andrew, J. and Reid, R. (eds) 1993. *Literary Tradition and Practice in Russian Culture: Papers from an International Conference on the Occasion of the Seventieth Birthday of Yury Mikhailovich Lotman*, Rodopi: Amsterdam.

Reyfman, I. 1999. 'Iurii Lotman's Pushkiniana', *Slavic Review* 58 (2): 440–4.

Shcheglov, Y. and Zholkovsky, A. 1987. *Poetics of Expressiveness: A Theory and Application*, Amsterdam: John Benjamins Publishing Company.

Shukman, A. 1977. *Literature and Semiotics: A Study of the Writings of Yu. M. Lotman*, Amsterdam, New York and Oxford: North-Holland Publishing Company.

Škulj, J. 2004. 'Literature and Space: Textual, Artistic and Cultural Spaces of Transgressiveness', in J. Škulj and D. Pavlič (eds), *Literature and Space: Spaces of Transgressiveness*, 21–37, Ljubljana: Slovenian Comparative Literature Association, available online: http://sdpk.zrc-sazu.si/PKrevi ja/2004-Literature&Space.htm (accessed 10 November 2020).

Smirnov, I. 2001. *Smysl kak takovoi*, Saint Petersburg: Akademicheskii proekt.

Steiner, L. 2003. 'Toward an Ideal Universal Community: Lotman's Revisiting of the Enlightenment and Romanticism', *Comparative Literature Studies* 40 (1): 37–53.

Sywenky, I. 2011. 'Back to the Beginnings: Notes on Comparative Literature in Central and Eastern Europe', *Inquire: Journal of Comparative Literature* 1 (2), available online: http://inquire.streetmag.org/articles/37 (accessed 15 December 2020).

Thompson, E. M. 1977. 'Jurij Lotman's Literary Theory and its Context', *The Slavic and East European Journal* 21 (2): 225–38.

Torop, P. 2019. 'Russian Theory and Semiotics of Culture: History and Perspectives', *Bakhtiniana: Revista de Estudos do Discurso* 14 (4): 19–39.

Tötösy de Zepetnek, S. 2017. 'About the Situation of the Discipline of Comparative Literature and Neighboring Fields in the Humanities Today', *Comparative Literature: East & West* 1 (2): 176–203.

Veivo, H. 2001. *The Written Space: Semiotic Analysis of the Representation of Space and its Rhetorical Functions in Literature*, Imatra: International Semiotics Institute.

Veivo, H. 2007. 'The New Literary Semiotics', *Semiotica* 165 (3/4): 41–55.

Veivo, H. and Ljungberg, C. 2009. 'Introduction', in H. Veivo, C. Ljungberg and J. D. Johansen (eds), *Redifining Literary Semiotics*, 1–9, Newcastle upon Tyne: Cambridge Scholar Publishing.

West, J. 1995. 'Art as Cognition in Russian Neo-Kantianism', *Studies in East European Thought* 47 (3/4): 195–223.

Zenkin, S. 2004. 'Vvedenie', in S. Zenkin (ed.), *Russkaia teoriia: 1920–1930-e gody*, 7–10, Moscow: RGGU.

Zolyan, S. 2020. *Iurii Lotman. O smysle, tekste, istorii. Temy i variatsii*, Moscow: Iazyki slavianskikh kul'tur.

Żyłko, B. 2015. 'Notes on Yuri Lotman's Structuralism', *International Journal of Cultural Studies* 18 (1): 27–42.

CHAPTER 27
LOTMAN AND NEW HISTORICISM
Andreas Schönle

The works of Juri Lotman and the ill-defined corpus of New Historicist cultural analysis and theoretical self-reflection share a number of superficial similarities. Lotman and New Historicists approach literature within a broad space of discursivity that undermines the distinction between the literary and the social, or text and context. They conceive of culture semiotically as a contested field of competing discourses subject to more or less rigid constraints and boundaries. Within culture, they identify forces that drive towards centralization and homogeneity along with mechanisms that produce difference and alterity. They conceive of power as an energy manifested first and foremost discursively, though they differ in the ways in which they conceptualize the ultimate causes of such power. They share an interest in delineating the fashioning of behaviour and subjectivity and in testing the potentialities and limits of individual agency. They aim to resist totalizing master narratives, perhaps not always successfully, and are alive to the role of serendipity in cultural life, though they are also prone to erecting homologies between phenomena belonging to various social and cultural orders, suggesting some overall structural coherence.[1]

Their scholarly practice reflects these interests. The periods they explore, such as Renaissance England or late eighteenth- and early nineteenth-century imperial Russia, were marked by profound change and the rapid emergence of new paradigms out of more homogenous and integrated cultural models, leading to polarized and violent interactions between cultural agents. Lotman and New Historicists alike reinvigorate the study of canonical literature from Shakespeare to Pushkin by placing it in contact with seemingly anodyne and marginal narratives procured in the archives. Stephen Greenblatt's signature method of unfurling his analysis of a cultural phenomenon from a seemingly inconsequential anecdote illustrates the aspiration to embrace the multilayeredness of culture and to track the circulation and intrinsic energy of stories across the dense field of social life.[2] New Historicists and Lotman also manifest a strong scholarly interest in silenced or forgotten voices, the cultural production and socially significant behaviour of women, for example. Their overriding interest in the constitution of subjectivity manifests itself in the return of biography as a scholarly genre. And in their scholarly practice, cultural analysis is never insulated from self-reflexive introspection, just as an engagement with theory underpins and cross-fertilizes their interpretations of particular texts.

In juxtaposing the writings of Lotman and New Historicists, this contribution will aim to reread Lotman in the light of New Historicism, creating a foil that will help to throw into relief what makes Lotman's works distinctive, whether that points to advantages or limitations in his approach. There is, of course, no evidence of influence in either direction. There are no reasons to believe that Lotman ever read Greenblatt, for example, and Greenblatt quotes Lotman only once, in an article in which he acknowledges that he borrows the concept of 'poetics of culture' from Lotman (Greenblatt 1989: 14n10).[3] In staging an encounter between Lotman and New Historicism, this contribution will focus on three core aspects: mapping the aesthetic sphere and its relations to social life; the inscription of power; and the fashioning of subjectivity. The focus will be on Lotman's later works, where he more explicitly sheds the rigidities of Saussurean linguistics, for example the distinction between code and message, even though the distinction between an 'early' and a 'late' Lotman is a superficial periodization that would not fully survive stringent analysis.[4] In my treatment of New Historicism, the focus will be on Greenblatt, who has served the role of unwitting flagbearer, but I will also reference a few other practitioners of this loosely affiliated intellectual community.

It is worth noting that New Historicism is not in fact historical or historicist in the sense of aiming to think through historical change or the relations between the past, present and future on a theoretical level.[5] In contrast, Lotman spent the last few years of his scholarly life pondering precisely these issues, which for him came to the fore as he witnessed the collapse of the Soviet Union (see Chapter 18). Accordingly, this chapter will not directly consider Lotman's historiographic thinking, which Daniele Monticelli (2020) has recently put in relation with (mainly) French cultural theory of the 1990s. Of course, New Historicist ideas about human subjectivity, agency and choice have implications for conceptualising the historical process, which will occasionally provide us with an opportunity to briefly reference Lotman's meta-historical ideas. Indeed, one of the main differences between New Historicism and Lotman is precisely the latter's diachronic frame, his emphasis on the constructive and fluid entanglement between the past and the present, on the continuities and discontinuities between the two that make the future unpredictable, whereas Catherine Gallagher and Greenblatt approach literature in what we could call a 'presentist' mode, as traces of 'real bodies and living voices' that could be experienced as if they were present, so as to afford 'a confident conviction of reality' or 'the touch of the real' (Gallagher and Greenblatt 2000: 30–1).[6]

Analogies between Lotman and New Historicism have been explored in my earlier article (Schönle 2001) and chapter (Schönle 2006). This present chapter will update, extend and deepen the argument presented in these pieces. Subsequently, Schamma Shahadat (2012) focused particular attention on the ways in which Lotman and Greenblatt conceived, respectively, of the 'poetics of behaviour' and 'self-fashioning'. Juxtaposing two specific essays by the two scholars, Shahadat foregrounded Lotman's literature-centric approach, in which literature shapes social behaviour, in contrast with Greenblatt's way of unpacking literature as a record encapsulating and mirroring social norms. Finally, Kyohei Norimatsu (2018: 126–7) briefly contrasted Lotman and Greenblatt in a chapter that explores the implications of Lotman's notion of theatricality and life-construction for his stance within Soviet public discourse. There is more extensive secondary literature on the subject of Lotman's underlying historical paradigm and its evolution. Mikhail Gasparov (1996: 8–10) maintained somewhat facetiously that in its method Lotman's structuralism was more genuinely Marxist than the scholarship of his communist contemporaries. B. F. Egorov (1999: 87–92) wrote more narrowly about the endurance of basic Hegelian/early Marxian premises, but accompanied by a rejection of the primacy of class consciousness and a greater sense of the complexity of cultural phenomena. Taras Boyko (2015) emphasized that Lotman's treatment of history is first and foremost semiotic in nature, which manifests itself in his call for attention to the specific conventions that govern historical documents, a move that prefigures the 'linguistic turn' in historiography. Lotman's late conceptualization of history has received scholarly elaboration more recently. In addition to Monticelli (2020), Laura Gherlone (2017) drew attention to Lotman's yet unpublished works on this subject. Marek Tamm (2019) offered a succinct overview of the evolution of Lotman's views on memory and history. And earlier, Lina Steiner (2003) juxtaposed Lotman's meta-historical works with the early German romantics, emphasizing the importance of *Bildung*, that is, moral education, as a conduit towards the creation of a universal community.

Mapping the aesthetic sphere

Neither Lotman nor Greenblatt conceives of the literary text as a self-contained, neatly bounded entity. Both see the text as the material sediment of a communicative exchange that unfolds within a larger communicative context and draws its meaning from it. For Lotman, it is primarily the reader who defines a particular text as an aesthetic composition. The aesthetic effect arises when a text is read as a code and then projected onto the inner stage of the reader's consciousness, where this code informs the reader's inner dialogue with him or herself. The aesthetic effect, then, stems from an ambivalence as to the status of a text, as code or as message, and hence from the indeterminacy of its referent (Lotman 1990: 30–2). For Lotman, art is a sphere of free experiment outside the parameters of cultural norms. More poignantly, art functions as culture's central mechanism for the generation of novelty. 'The artistic work', he maintains, 'is a thinking structure, a generator of new information. Art is one of the hemispheres of the collective brain of humankind' (Lotman [1994/2010] 2013: 220). Yet if art violates established values and norms, it does so with an eye towards an audience that is preoccupied with ethical questions. Hence, art is not immune from cultural norms, even though it appears to negate their validity. Ethics and aesthetics are as inseparable as they are opposite (Lotman [1992] 2009: 150–9).

Greenblatt also problematizes the text, rejecting the New Critical notion of organic unity and preferring to speak in terms of masses of textual traces. He does so partly in order to recognize contingency in the production, performance and reception of texts, and partly in light of the historical record showing that cultural agents in the Renaissance had little stake in, and care for, the integrity and presumed notional totality of a literary text (Greenblatt 1982: 4; 1988: 3–4). However, New Historicism has been keen to challenge the notion that an aesthetic text, once demarcated, constitutes an arena for the free contestation of social norms. Gallagher, one of Greenblatt's closest interlocutors, maintains, for example, that 'it was against such claims for the automatic subversiveness of art [. . .] that many new historicists directed their critiques'. For her, one of the main contributions of New Historicism was the demonstration that 'the display of ideological contradictions is completely consonant with the maintenance of oppressive social relations', highlighting instead how 'the very antagonism between literature and ideology becomes, in specific historical environments, a powerful and socially functional mode of constructing subjectivity' (Gallagher 1996: 51). For Greenblatt, texts are embedded in social life, so much so that they become 'signs of contingent social practices' (1988: 4–5). While literature does not fully dissolve in social life and draws specific energy from its unique status, it cannot but encapsulate and represent the full density of social contradictions, which it projects into the ways in which it constitutes subjectivity.

While Greenblatt seems to posit that texts gain their relevance mainly from their position within the broader field of social practice, Lotman also underscores that texts draw an intrinsic power from the history of their past entanglements. Literary texts (or rather texts construed as such) are endowed with a complex structure that reveals itself only over time. They accumulate a memory of their past significations which shores up their distinctiveness (Lotman 1990: 18–9). Such texts thus exhibit an ever-changing intersection between the past and the future, mediating between the two. They are engaged in a process of becoming which unfolds both synchronically and diachronically, and they contain within themselves a richer repository of alterity than that assumed by Greenblatt. In short, for Lotman it is the structural density of literary texts that confers them a degree of relative autonomy which enables historically variable interpretations and licenses the readers' meaning-generating activity.

This difference between a presentist and a historically attuned construction of the latent power of literature is reflected in the metaphors Lotman and Greenblatt use to describe the way literature interacts with the social environment. For Greenblatt literature transmits values conceived broadly: economic, ideological and emotional goods are exchanged through processes of translation and negotiation between non-homologous fields. The exchanges between culturally demarcated spheres represent a 'process of movement across the shifting boundaries between them' (Greenblatt 1988: 7).[7] Economics becomes the master discourse, as what Greenblatt ultimately seeks to describe is the circulation of value through unstable conversions between various currencies. As a metaphor, economics here signals not so much that culture is quantifiable, but more that it disseminates values that are fluid and fungible.

Lotman, in contrast, draws his metaphors from geology, which witness the image of the semiosphere, the semiotic environment that enables and sustains semiotic exchanges – seething like the sun where 'centers of activity boil up in different places, in the depths and on the surface, irradiating relatively peaceful areas with its immense energy' (Lotman 1990: 150). Circulation of energy, layering in strata, cataclysmic events are some of the qualities a geological formation shares with the semiosphere. What interests Lotman most in this geospherical framework is the idea that the earth's complex layers of mineral matter enable and support organic life. The superimposition of live and dead matter serves as an analogy to the ways in which cultural memory operates in the semiosphere, presenting an ever-changing repository of dormant texts that can be returned to life (Lotman 1990: 127). The boundary between the mineral and the organic is really a filter promoting constant exchange and enriching the circulation of semiotic activity within the semiosphere.

Yet for both of them, meaning is tightly interwoven with movement. In his definition of culture, Greenblatt underscores the role of culture as a mechanism that both enables and necessitates mobility: 'If culture functions as structure of limits, it also functions as the regulator and guarantor of movement. Indeed the limits are virtually meaningless without movement; it is only through improvisation, experiment, and exchange that cultural boundaries can be established' (Greenblatt 2005: 14). Works of art, he adds, 'do not merely passively reflect the prevailing ratio of mobility and constraint; they help to shape, articulate, and reproduce it through their own improvisatory intelligence' (Greenblatt 2005: 15). If art is a sphere of improvisation and experiment, it is telling here that Greenblatt emphasizes more the ways in which such commotion erects, rather than deflects boundaries. Play seems dialectically to institute rules that underpin a degree of mobility that is at once necessary, hidden and limited (Greenblatt 2009: 251).

For Lotman, cultural innovation and experimentation manifest as a crossing across the semiosphere. In *Universe of the Mind* he introduces a division between two kinds of discourse, those on the centre and those on the periphery. The centre creates a master plot that seeks to absorb all incidental messages under its logic. This master plot features a highly integrated structure and assumes a normative function with regard to the discourses circulating in the semiosphere. It thus serves as a kind of metalanguage that both enables and restricts communication. Semiotic activity and creativity are relegated to the margins of the semiosphere, where the hegemony of the centre's master plot subsides. The periphery is the place where discourses clash, where improvisation and innovation take place, where alien discourses trickling in from contiguous semiospheres have an effect. Multiplicity, heterogeneity, disorder, disjunction and chance characterize the periphery. The periphery challenges the centre, and particular discourses in it seek to supplant the master plot the centre aims to impose. Thus, the semiosphere presents an asymmetric paradigm of competing narratives (Lotman 1990: 127–30, 134–5, 162). Where Lotman posits an agonistic relationship between norm and event, centre and periphery, Greenblatt emphasizes their interdependency. For Lotman, movement implies contestation, and, for Greenblatt, it offers confirmation. Yet both also emphasize the formative, generative power of culture – rather than its mere mimetic function – that is, the way it actively shapes subjectivities. But as we will see in the following text, what is being shaped is different.

The inscription of power

Lotman's semiosphere makes for a framework well-equipped to account for the ways in which languages shape our consciousness and constitute our reality, rather than mirroring it. In good cultural studies fashion, this framework tells us that discourse is power, more than it transmits power (Lotman 1990: 233). The distinction between centre and the periphery presupposes a differentiation between a homogeneous discursive practice that has normative force and heterodox discursive events. While the former displays a high level of semiotic integration, the latter are avowedly disjoined and haphazard. Integration, one could say, is the semiotic expression, albeit not the cause, of what makes a particular discourse hegemonic. The cause is obviously external to the process of communication, and so the semiotician does not need to conceptualize it. Of course, Lotman could not be oblivious to the political and social realities underpinning communicative acts, as under the Soviet regime, attention to such constraints on discourse was a matter of survival, but these enter the semotician's purview only to the extent that they manifest themselves semiotically.[8]

In *Culture and Explosion*, Lotman refines the notion that power is predicated on the imposition of a consistent, integrated ideological master plot, acknowledging the import of political unpredictability. Through the figure of Ivan the Terrible, whose erratic actions in the second half of his reign defied all logic, he seems to explore the semiotic consequences of raw acts of power, which provoke what he calls a semiotic 'explosion', leading to a radical semiotic disjunction and a complete reconfiguration of the semiosphere (Lotman [1992] 2009: 82–5). He thus envisions two technologies of power: one enforcing an orderly, continuous normative master discourse, the other deploying unpredictable behaviour that tears into the semiotic order and reorders it. In both cases, however, power is concentrated within a single source, sitting at the centre of the semiosphere. And in both cases, power draws on semiotic means to express itself. For Lotman, there is no life outside semiosis.

Greenblatt, in contrast, seeks ways to harness semiotic and asemiotic manifestations of power together. He underscores the ways in which messages express desires and articulate power, both of which partly pre-exist the emergence of a given communication act and manifest through asemiotic means. As he analyses the discourse deployed by the Spanish to legitimate the conquest of America, for example, Greenblatt concludes that 'words in the New World seem always to be trailing after events that pursue a terrible logic quite other than the fragile meanings that they construct'. And yet he is unwilling to dismiss words completely, for he sees them as components and symptoms of a larger symbolic system that motivates and enables the conquest (Greenblatt 1991: 63–4). Greenblatt is careful to have it both ways, endowing artistic discourse with considerable agency of its own – he calls it energy – while also tying literature back to its institutional embedding and, further, to the social practices that it depicts. Literature is all the more successful at transmitting pre-existing social values and interests because within its boundaries it claims to suspend the real world. So it circulates all kinds of social energy in a seemingly playful manner. 'Power, charisma, sexual excitement, collective dreams, wonder, desire, anxiety, religious awe' are conveyed haphazardly, without being subject to a controlling, totalizing system (Greenblatt 1988: 18–9). Greenblatt shares Lotman's sense that cultures gain stability only by foisting a master discourse on their constituent spheres. He describes a mechanism he calls blockage – 'the social imposition of an imaginary order of exclusion' – by which cultures control the influx of texts and ascribe a given order to their central representations (Greenblatt 1991: 121).

Contrary to Lotman, Greenblatt avoids positing a centre of authority which seeks to draw all cultural phenomena under its homogenizing blanket. As he discusses the position of culture in a capitalist society, he turns against two opposite views: the Marxist argument that capitalism promotes culture as a private and therefore inauthentic sphere walled off from underlying economic relations and the post-structuralist argument that charges capitalism with levelling differences and ultimately destroying individuality. Greenblatt is convinced that both views fail, because capitalism's relationship to culture does not lend itself to a monolithic theoretical treatment (Greenblatt 1989). While New Historicism refuses to theorize a fixed relationship between culture and politics (Gallagher 1996: 45), it tends to assume that power is diffused and refracted through all cultural practices. Gallagher, for example, maintains 'that power cannot be equated with economic or state power, that its sites of activity, and hence of resistance, are also in the micro-politics of daily life'. 'The traditionally important economic and political agents and events', she continues, 'have been displaced or supplemented by people and phenomena that once seemed wholly insignificant, indeed outside of history: women, criminals, the insane, sexual practices and discourses, fairs, festivals, plays of all kinds' (Gallagher 1996: 50–1). As H. Aram Veeser puts it, New Historicism is steeped in Foucault's 'microphysics of disciplinary society' (1994: 6), and in positing such pervasive manifestation of power, it takes the wind out of any possibility of resistance. Critiques on the left have taken New Historicism to task for representing any form of resistance as a delusion that only reinforces power structures. Catherine Belsey goes so far as to claim that in New Historicist practice 'texts are understood as homogeneous, monologic, in the last instance non-contradictory, because the uncertainties they formulate are finally contained by the power they might seem to subvert' (1996: 88).

In short, while Lotman operates with a centripetal view of culture, he makes room for the possibility of innovation and contestation. In contrast, the New Historicist assumption of ubiquitous power and the harnessing of literary energy to asemiotic social practices ultimately seem to deprive culture of its intrinsic force and its ability to effect change.

Selfhood and autonomy

What is the fate of the self in the discursive fields described by Greenblatt and Lotman? For Greenblatt, individuals are enmeshed in various networks of sociocultural and discursive practices which constrict their options and subvert their intentions (Greenblatt 1990: 74–5). Both *Renaissance Self-Fashioning* and *Shakespearean Negotiations* exemplify the drastic limits placed on the self's autonomy and ability to resist social forces. The linchpin of the former, the much-abused notion of self-fashioning, derives its potency from its ambivalence. It is clear that this concept concerns the fashioning of a self, but by whom: social forces or the individual? Greenblatt uses the term in both senses. And yet, when he writes that self-fashioning 'involves submission to an absolute power or authority situated at least partially outside the self', one wonders what has happened to individual agency (Greenblatt 1980: 9). However in a later piece, Greenblatt refuses to grant this dismissal of individual agency universal validity (Greenblatt 1990: 75), while in *Cultural Mobility: A Manifesto*, he submits that 'mobility studies should account in new ways for the tension between individual agency and structural constraint'. 'This tension', he continues, 'cannot be resolved in any abstract theoretical way, for in given historical circumstances structures of power seek to mobilize some individuals and immobilize others'. Yet even in this statement, it is characteristic that instances of individual mobility are, as it were, authorized, if not enabled, by structures of power. Nonetheless, he proposes that mobility studies should explore 'the way in which seemingly fixed migration paths are disrupted by the strategic acts of individual agents and by unexpected, unplanned, entirely contingent encounters between different cultures' (Greenblatt 2009: 250–1). In the conclusion to *Renaissance Self-Fashioning*, speaking about his own times, he suggests that the presumption of autonomy is a sustaining illusion that is as necessary as it is futile (Greenblatt 1980: 257). While he allows for the theoretical possibility of resistance, autonomy and freedom, his analysis of specific cases tends to show how the longing for freedom is ultimately part of the matrix of social control (Brannigan 1998: 8–9). As discussed earlier, one of the ways New Historicism demonstrates the pervasive (and intrusive) reach of power structures is by insisting that structural contradictions – the antagonism between improvisation and constraint, literature and ideology – are inherent to the human self and represent 'a powerful and socially functional mode of constructing subjectivity' (Gallagher 1996: 51).

Lotman grants the self greater autonomy and creativity. His semiotic analysis of the constitution of subjectivity has two parts, one dealing with the way the self forges its own narratives, the other with how it interacts with social codes (see also Chapter 25). The self develops its subjective identity by absorbing a message coming from outside and projecting it upon a supplementary code coming from within (Lotman 1990: 22). To keep it simple, suffice it to say that the self is endowed with an ability to recode messages it receives and to restructure its own identity in the process. This restructuring results from the creative intersection between two non-homologous, mutually untranslatable codes. A diary would be an example of this restructuring, in which discourses from everyday life are being introjected and refashioned according to the rhythms, inflections and nuances of first-person narration.

Now, this self needs to publicize its reconfigured identity, and here matters become more complex. In keeping with his spatial modelling, Lotman views the social assertion of identity as a drawing of boundaries. 'One of the primary mechanisms of semiotic individuation', as he puts it, 'is the boundary, and the boundary can be defined as the outer limit of a first-person form' (Lotman 1990: 131). Yet, this boundary needs to be recognized socially. As Lotman concedes, boundaries belong to both frontier systems, the one inside and the one outside (Lotman 1990: 136). Lotman never explores the implications of this state of affairs for the individual self, and it is clear that society's failure to recognize an individual boundary would lead to a confrontation. Whereas

Greenblatt and other New Historicists describe power mechanisms that are at once pervasive and invisible, and thus shape individuals in surreptitious and unnoticeable ways, Lotman's model of boundary-setting posits a more rational process of explicit negotiation or contestation. Yet Lotman plays down the antagonistic ramifications of his model by suggesting that an individual self is always also an isomorphic image of society as a whole, depending on the semiotic vantage point one chooses. On the micro level, the self appears as distinct from the collectivity, and yet from a more distanced external point of view, the self looks like a small-scale replica of the collective body it inhabits. Lotman's example is dandyism, which is a mass phenomenon to the cultural historian, but a form of individualization to a dandy (Lotman 1990: 226). The actual notion of individuality, Lotman maintains, 'is not primary or self-evident but depends on the means of encoding' (Lotman 1990: 234).

While this semiotic view of the self allows for easy creative re-coding – one can readily tell oneself individualizing narratives – the larger social import of these micro-stories seems limited, as they become socially relevant only when they prompt new patterns of behaviour. Yet Lotman's conceptualization of the 'poetics of behaviour' invariably emphasizes conformity with established conventions, whether social or literary, and a dichotomy between public, that is, conformist, and private, that is, self-driven forms of behaviour.[9] In a passage in *Culture and Explosion*, Lotman opposes the fool, the madman and the wise man. The only unpredictable one of the three is the madman, for the fool displays *patterns* of inappropriate behaviour, while the wise man's behaviour 'corresponds to customary rules and regulations' (Lotman [1992] 2009: 38). Lotman similarly marks public behaviour as norm-compliant in his studies of the Russian nobility where he opposes the Westernized forms of behaviour deployed by the nobility in public settings to the domestic behaviour and identities they reverted to when away from the public eye (Lotman [1973] 1984, [1977] 1985). Yet, this dichotomy between the public sphere and private life was alien to the life of the nobility (Schönle 1998), which often discharged codes of behaviour and forms of expression in syncretic and macaronic ways (Marrese 2010).

Lotman's abidance by a dichotomy between the public and the private underpins his thinking about individual agency.[10] Referring to Kant's concept of rational autonomy of the Enlightened self, Lotman explains that 'a culture oriented towards a person's capability to choose his or her own behaviour strategy requires rationality, caution, circumspection and discretion, since each event is regarded as "happening for the first time"' (Lotman 1990: 248). The language in this quotation is revealing, implying as it does that autonomy is relegated to the carefully protected sphere of private life. Why else would 'caution, circumspection, and discretion' be required if not to deflect or elude impositions from public authorities? Lotman's existential stance in his own life confirms this premise. In 1985, he confessed to his friend Egorov that his yearning to set up his own laboratory and form his disciples was nothing but a 'soap bubble', an 'illusion' which he needed to shed to recover his freedom. The main illusion here is that a public role and effect would fulfil his life aspirations. As he put it, 'liberty is the freedom from illusions', and it is only by experiencing disappointment in his public endeavours that he could reclaim his freedom

(Lotman 1997: 341–2).[11] Lotman's political stance was likewise predicated on a withdrawal from engagement with political issues in favour of the cultivation of private virtues (Zorin 2006). Thus, it becomes clear that Lotman's upbeat views of individual autonomy and creativity hinge on his deep commitment to Enlightenment ideas of rational autonomy, that is, to what is often called the liberal self, defined as the capacity to formulate and pursue various goals independent from collective impositions. But for him, this ability depends on the distinction between the private and the public and is relegated to the former, while the latter requires abidance by collective norms of behaviour.

Notes

1. The literature on New Historicism is vast, but Veeser's short overview remains handy (1994). For a more extensive critical introduction, see Brannigan 1998. Gallagher and Greenblatt reflect interestingly on the emergence of New Historicism and on its methodologies in the Introduction to their *Practicing New Historicism* (2000: 1–19).

2. On the rationale behind the New Historicist use of the anecdote, see Gallagher and Greenblatt 2000: 20–74.

3. For a preliminary study of Lotman's international networks and sources, see Pilshchikov and Trunin 2016, and Chapter 7 in this volume.

4. On Lotman's theory of the semiosphere as post-structuralist semiotics, or post-post-structuralism, see Mandelker 1995: 178–9.

5. For a sustained analysis of Greenblatt's 'historicism', see Pieters 2000.

6. Louis A Montrose writes that the New Historicist project 'reorients the axis of inter-textuality, substituting for the diachronic text of an autonomous literature history the synchronic text of a cultural system' (1989: 17). Veeser links this presentism to the influence of Clifford Geertz's notion of thick description and the ambition to recreate an integrated setting in detail, thereby letting 'organicism eclipse their historism' (1994: 10).

7. Greenblatt's language, here, recalls Lotman's definition of an event as the shifting of a character across the borders of a semantic field (Lotman [1970] 1977: 233).

8. In contrast to much French and US cultural theory, Lotman sees his role primarily as reconstructing past cultures, rather than exposing the ideological blind spots of discursive formations. See Monticelli 2016 and Schönle 2020: xix–xx.

9. For a discussion of the question of 'life-creation' and of the two modes of life emplotment which Lotman differentiates and of the creative role of codes, see Bethea 1997.

10. Norimatsu (2018) discusses in greater detail the ways in which Lotman articulates the relationship between the public and the private in his studies of nobility culture, as well as in his own public stance.

11. I explore in greater detail Lotman's metaphor of the soap bubble in Schönle 2006: 201–3.

References

Belsey, C. 1996. 'Towards Cultural History – in Theory and Practice', in K. Ryan (ed.), *New Historicism and Cultural Materialism: A Reader*, 82–91, London: Arnold.

Bethea, D. 1997. 'Bakhtinian Prosaics versus Lotmanian "Poetic Thinking": The Code and Its Relation to Literary Biography', *Slavic and East European Journal* 41 (1): 1–15.

Boyko, T. 2015. 'Describing the Past: Tartu-Moscow School Ideas on History, Historiography, and the Historian's Craft', *Sign Systems Studies* 43 (2/3): 269–80.

Brannigan J. 1998. *New Historicism and Cultural Materialism*, London: Palgrave.

Egorov, B. F. 1999. *Zhizn' i tvorchestvo Iu. M. Lotmana*, Moscow: Novoe literaturnoe obozrenie.

Gallagher, C. 1996. 'Marxism and the New Historicism', in K. Ryan (ed.), *New Historicism and Cultural Materialism: A Reader*, 45–55, London: Arnold.

Gallagher C. and Greenblatt, S. 2000. *Practicing New Historicism*, Chicago: The University of Chicago Press.

Gasparov, M. 1996. 'Lotman i marksizm', *Novoe literaturnoe obozrenie* 19: 7–13.

Gherlone, L. 2017. 'Waiting for History: At the Eve of Explosion', in K. Bankov (ed.), *New Semiotics Between Tradition and Innovation. Proceedings of the 12th World Congress of the International Association for Semiotic Studies (IASS/AIS)*, 97–103, Sofia: NBU Publishing House & IASS Publications.

Greenblatt, S. 1980. *Renaissance Self-Fashioning: From More to Shakespeare*, Chicago: The University of Chicago Press.

Greenblatt, S. 1982. 'Introduction', in S. Greenblatt (ed.), *The Power of Forms in the English Renaissance*, 3–6, Norman: Pilgrim Books.

Greenblatt, S. 1988. *Shakespearean Negotiations: The Circulation of Social Energy in Renaissance England*, Berkeley: University of California Press.

Greenblatt, S. 1989. 'Towards a Poetics of Culture', in H. A. Veseer (ed.), *The New Historicism*, 1–14, New York: Routledge.

Greenblatt, S. 1990. 'Resonance and Wonder', in P. Collier and H. Geyer-Ryan (eds), *Literary Theory* Today, 74–90, Cambridge: Polity Press.

Greenblatt, S. 1991. *Marvelous Possessions: The Wonder of the New World*, Chicago: The University of Chicago Press.

Greenblatt, S. 2005. 'Culture', in M. Payne (ed.), *The Greenblatt Reader*, 11–17, Oxford and Malden: Blackwell Publishing.

Greenblatt, S. 2009. 'A Mobility Studies Manifesto', in S. Greenblatt et al., *Cultural Mobility: A Manifesto*, 250–3, Cambridge: Cambridge University Press.

Lotman, J. [1970] 1977. *The Structure of the Artistic Text*, trans. R. Vroon, Ann Arbor, MI: University of Michigan, Department of Slavic Languages and Literatures.

Lotman, Yu. M. [1973] 1984. 'The Theatre and Theatricality as Components of Early Nineteenth-Century Culture', trans. G. S. Smith, in Yu M. Lotman and B. A. Uspenskij, *The Semiotics of Russian Culture*, ed. A. Shukman, 141–64, Ann Arbor: Michigan Slavic Contributions.

Lotman, Yu. M. [1977] 1985. 'The Poetics of Everyday Behavior in Eighteenth-Century Russian Culture', in A. D. Nakhimovsky and A. S. Nakhimovsky (eds), *The Semiotics of Russian Cultural History*, 67–94, Ithaca, NY and London: Cornell University Press.

Lotman, Yu. M. 1990. *Universe of the Mind: A Semiotic Theory of Culture*, trans. A. Shukman, Bloomington: Indiana University Press.

Lotman, J. [1992] 2009. *Culture and Explosion*, trans. W. Clark, ed. M. Grishakova, Berlin and New York: Mouton de Gruyter.

Lotman, J. M. [1994/2010] 2013. *The Unpredictable Workings of Culture*, trans. B. J. Baer, ed. I. Pilshchikov and S. Salupere, Tallinn: Tallinn University Press.

Lotman, Ju M. 1997. *Pis'ma*, ed. B. Egorov, Moscow: Shkola 'Iazyki russkoi kul'tury'.

Mandelker, A. 1995. 'Logosphere and Semiosphere: Bakhtin, Russian Organicism, and the Semiotics of Culture', in A. Mandelker (ed.), *Bakhtin in Contexts Across the Disciplines*, 177–90, Evanston, IL: Northwestern University Press.

Marrese, M. L. 2010. '"The Poetics of Everyday Behavior" Revisited: Lotman, Gender, and the Evolution of Russian Noble Identity', *Kritika* 11 (4): 701–39.

Monticelli, D. 2016. 'Critique of Ideology or/and Analysis of Culture? Barthes and Lotman on Secondary Semiotic Systems', *Sign Systems Studies* 44 (3): 432–51.

Monticelli, D. 2020. 'Thinking the New after the Fall of the Berlin Wall: Juri Lotman's Dialogism of History', *Rethinking History: The Journal of Theory and Practice* 24 (2): 184–208.

Montrose, L. A. 1989. 'Professing the Renaissance: The Poetics and Politics of Culture', in H. A. Veeser (ed.), *The New Historicism*, 15–36, New York: Routledge.

Norimatsu, K. 2018. 'Within or Beyond Policing Norms: Yuri Lotman's Theory of Theatricality', in C.-A. Mihăilescu and T. Yokota-Murakami (eds), *Policing Literary Theory*, 111–34, Leiden and Boston: Brill.

Pieters, J. 2000. 'New Historicism: Postmodern Historiography between Narrativism and Heterology', *History and Theory* 39 (1): 21–38.

Pilshchikov, I. and Trunin, M. 2016. 'The Tartu-Moscow School of Semiotics: A Transnational Perspective', *Sign Systems Studies* 44 (3): 368–401.

Schahadat, S. 2012. 'Russische Poetik des Verhaltens und amerikanische Poetics of Culture: Jurij Lotman und Stephen Greenblatt', in S. K. Frank, C. Ruhe and A. Schmitz (eds), *Explosion und Peripherie. Jurij Lotmans Semiotik der kulturellen Dynamik revisited*, 153–73. Bielefeld: Transcript.

Schönle, A. 1998. 'The Scare of the Self: Sentimentalism, Privacy, and Private Life in Russian Culture, 1780–1820', *Slavic Review* 57 (4): 723–46.

Schönle, A. 2001. 'Social Power and Individual Agency: The Self in Greenblatt and Lotman,' *Slavic and East European Journal* 45 (1): 61–79.

Schönle, A. 2006. 'The Self, its Bubbles, and Illusions: Cultivating Autonomy in Greenblatt and Lotman,' in A. Schönle (ed.), *Lotman and Cultural Studies: Encounters and Extensions*, 183–207, Madison: The University of Wisconsin Press.

Schönle, A. 2020. 'Introduction', in A. Schönle (ed.), *Culture and Communication: Signs in Flux: An Anthology of Major and Lesser-Known Works by Yuri Lotman*, xiii–xxiv, Boston: Academic Studies Press.

Steiner, L. 2003. 'Toward an Ideal Universal Community: Lotman's Revisiting of the Enlightenment and Romanticism', *Comparative Literature Studies*, 40 (1): 37–53.

Tamm, M. 2019. 'Introduction: Juri Lotman's Semiotic Theory of History and Cultural Memory', in J. Lotman, *Culture, Memory and History: Essays in Cultural Semiotics*, ed. M. Tamm, trans. B. J. Baer, 1–25, Cham: Palgrave Macmillan.

Veeser, H. A. 1994. 'The New Historicism', in H. A. Veeser (ed.), *The New Historicism Reader*, 1–32, New York: Routledge.

Zorin, A. 2006. 'Lotman's Karamzin and the Late Soviet Liberal Intelligentsia', in A. Schönle (ed.), *Lotman and Cultural Studies: Encounters and Extensions*, 208–26, Madison: The University of Wisconsin Press.

CHAPTER 28
LOTMAN AND MEMORY STUDIES
Nutsa Batiashvili, James V. Wertsch and Tinatin Inauri

Introduction

The field of memory studies is a reflection of the 'memory boom' (Winter 2001) of the past few decades. The upshot is a vibrant interdisciplinary discussion that includes the appearance of widely cited journals (e.g. *Memory Studies*) and a Memory Studies Association whose membership has more than doubled during each of the past several years. An especially active part of this discussion has been directed at national memory, which comes as no surprise in the age of the 'new nationalism' (Rose 2019). Given this, national memory will be the focus of our remarks, which is not to say, however, that our comments are not also relevant to other forms of collective and individual memory.

Of course, Juri Lotman did not write in order to inform today's field of memory studies, and his comments that directly addressed memory are not necessarily the ones we take up here (see Chapter 17). Instead, we see a much broader array of insights for memory studies that can be gleaned from his semiotic analyses. Indeed, his writings offer a plethora of 'thinking devices' for this budding field to consider, and we shall examine this by focusing on a few key constructs. These include his notions of the 'semiosphere', 'plot genes' and the idea of symbols as 'semiotic condensers'.

Semiosphere and autocommunication

A starting point for understanding Lotman's ideas is that he views culture as a 'vast example of autocommunication' (Lotman 1990: 32) and his understanding that all forms of communication are grounded in the notion of the semiosphere (see Chapter 22).

Lotman developed the concept of the semiosphere under the influence of a Russian mineralogist, Vladimir Vernadsky (1886–1943). Vernadsky thought that the creation of life is possible only from life and not from an inanimate object or inert matter (see Lotman 1990: 123–43). Building on this, Lotman suggested that every text is a precondition for a new text, much the same way one civilization is a precondition for another. The semiosphere is a cultural space that generates structure and social life, but is nevertheless defined by its heterogeneity, multiplicity of languages and by irreducibility of its structural logic.

> The semiosphere, the space of culture, is not something that acts according to mapped out and pre-calculated plans. It seethes like the sun, centres of activity boil up in different places, in the depths and on the surface, irradiating relatively

peaceful areas with its immense energy. But unlike that of the sun, the energy of the semiosphere is the energy of information, the energy of Thought. (Lotman 1990: 150)

A crucial aspect of Lotman's account of the semiosphere is the primacy he gave to dialogue in the creation of meaning. The idea is that the activation of semiosphere always takes place at the level of communicative practices through which information is coded, translated and recoded. For Lotman, 'dialogue precedes language and gives birth to it. And this also lies at the heart of the notion of semiosphere: the ensemble of semiotic formations precedes (not heuristically but functionally) the singular isolated language and becomes a condition for the existence of the latter. Without the semiosphere, language not only does not function, it does not exist' (Lotman [1984] 2005: 218–9). Lotman warns us that we should not think of the semiosphere as a unity of languages, but rather as of the polysemic net through which generation of meaning can take place. Thus, semiosphere is not 'a single coding structure but a set of connected but different systems' (Lotman 1990: 125).

One point where Lotman's account of the semiosphere has implications for memory studies concerns the relationship between individual mental processes and social processes. These two realms have been part of the discussion of collective memory since Maurice Halbwachs's early formulation, but the tendency has been to elaborate them in distinct, often isolated ways in different disciplines, resulting in what Jeffrey Olick (1999) called 'the two cultures' of collective memory studies. Related distinctions surface in the writings of figures such as Jan Assmann ([1992] 2011), Aleida Assmann ([1999] 2011) and Astrid Erll (2011), suggesting the need to address the dynamic interconnections between individual and social processes in accounts of collective memory. Lotman's formulation of the semiosphere as 'a set of connected but different systems' (Lotman 1990: 125) has the potential to bring these strands of inquiry together into an overarching conceptual approach, giving rise to formulations by Erll (2011) and Marek Tamm (2015) of 'cultural memory' as a more comprehensive and inclusive notion than collective memory. Indeed, in the view of Tamm (2015: 127), cultural memory 'is largely synonymous with the concept of "culture" itself, stressing its mnemonic functions'.

Along with the internal interconnectedness of the elements of a semiosphere, Lotman emphasized the importance of boundaries that separate one semiosphere from another, a point that points to a notion of culture as 'a bounded and organized entity' (Tamm (2015: 130). This has major implications for understanding collective memory, especially national memory, where communities can live in isolated worlds where they are deeply and emotionally committed to different accounts of the past. For Lotman, boundaries between semiospheres serve as points for exchange and creativity, but they also serve as borders that separate one community from another. These boundaries, which are 'the hottest spots for semioticizing processes' (Lotman 1990: 136), are complex, reflecting the fact the 'notion of boundary is an ambivalent one: it both separates and unites. It is always the boundary of something and so belongs to both frontier cultures, to both contiguous semiospheres' (Lotman 1990: 136).

As an illustration of the power of boundaries to separate the semiospheres of national communities, consider the differences between standard American and Russian versions of the United States's atomic bombing of Japan in 1945 (Wertsch 2021). Whereas American national memory has it that the atomic bombs were intended to shock the Japanese into surrender and succeeded in doing so, the Russian account views Truman's use of atomic bombs as motivated by a desire to intimidate Stalin. In reality, there is historical scholarship to support both of these interpretations, but each national community (as seen in history textbooks, commemorative activities etc.) remains confident in the truth of its own account and finds the other risible. The resulting 'mnemonic standoff' separates the two national communities' memory and identity and can lead them to dismiss other accounts of the past as products of ignorance, lack of information or brainwashing. As James Wertsch (2021) has argued, the confidence and tenacity with which the two accounts of the past are held in this case suggest different underlying codes and habits in the form of schematic 'narrative templates', a notion that once again can be expanded upon by employing Lotman's rich notions of semiosphere and accounts of cultural memory consistent with it.

Along with semiosphere, Lotman's notion of autocommunication can provide major insights into national memory. For him, 'autocommunication is the dominant mode of communication in culture, as well as the basis of its mnemonics' (Tamm 2015: 129). Communicative practices that involve the use of collective memory narratives and symbols reflect the publics that already have knowledge or memory of the meanings that are entrenched in these symbols. For example, when Georgians mention their medieval king David the Builder, the possible meanings of his invocation are easily identifiable (see Batiashvili 2012; 2020). Similarly, the American Civil War to the American public is not merely a name for the events that took place some 150 years ago, but is a symbolic story of what America is about (see Wertsch 2021). Crucially, David the Builder and the American Civil War both are contested symbols in that their use not only refers to a specific story of the past but also indexes several additional variants of a general historical narrative. They function not merely as oratory about particular episodes in the past but as semiotic tools, as instruments in a more elaborate grammar that organizes a broader set of meanings, and as such, these semiotic means anchor thinking by mobilizing affect and emotion.

For Lotman, this autocommunicative nature of culture is revealed in various forms of addressivity that are embedded in any cultural text. In his view, any text involves a 'complex game of positions' reflecting the embedded image of its audience (Lotman 1990: 36). This point on the 'semiotic unity' within a semiosphere, between addresser and addressee is vividly expressed in Lotman's emphasis of how semantically rich exchanges can be carried out through mere 'hinting'. Lotman's discussion on this issue is reminiscent of Clifford Geertz's use of the winking example to demonstrate how a complex web of meanings can be condensed into simple icons, images or acts (Geertz 1973). This is why 'a hint is enough to activate memory', and hence, 'orientation towards one or the other type of memory will make the addresser use either "a language for others," or "a private language"' (Lotman 1990: 64).

Taking a cue from these discussions, our focus is on ways that memory is employed in social discourse and political rhetoric through mere hinting. This includes instances in which historical figures, events or processes are brought into a discussion not through the recitation of full narratives, but through implication that merely uses narrative tags such as *the American Civil War, Abraham Lincoln, David the Builder, the Mongol Invasion* and so forth. In everyday discourse, these tags function as condensed symbols of memory, and they are part of a more frequent form of national remembering. Such use of symbols in everyday rhetoric demonstrates the kind of autocommunication that Lotman described in his works and provides a good starting point to reflect not only on how nations remember but also on how national memory symbols structure discourse and shape thinking patterns.

The attempt to understand 'how nations remember' (Wertsch 2021) involves an emphasis on the collective 'memory as a process' (Dudai 2002: 51), meaning that memory is understood not as a body of knowledge, but as a 'constant dialogue between individuals and social groups' (Dudai 2002: 51). In some instances, this dialogue involves an intense debate – a mnemonic struggle (Wertsch, 2021) on the possible interpretations of the past events. For instance, in American national memory a crucial point of mnemonic struggle involves competing readings of the American Civil War over the motives behind Lincoln's words and deeds (cf. Blight 2001). These concern an opposition between a version that emphasizes the desire to preserve the Union, on the one hand, and a desire to eliminate slavery, on the other.

As part of Lotman's autocommunicative process, such dialogue relies on a reservoir of semiotic formations that individuals and groups make use of in their communication, where this reservoir is itself fundamentally grounded in dialogism as a constitutive principle of semiosis. When viewed in light of the semiosphere, then, national memory functions both as a dialogic sphere and as a pool of symbols that generate and acquire meaning through dialogic encounters.

Lotman's emphasis on the role of autocommunication, his definition of semiosphere and the presence of both dialogism and multiple languages within a single semiotic realm provide insight into how national remembering can be sealed off and insulated from information or meanings outside the realm of cultural semiosis. Lotman's perspective on the boundaries of the semiosphere also helps explain the self-centred narcissism that typically characterizes national remembering. Lotman's notion of border (*granitsa*) implies a structurally and functionally marginal point of the semiotic space. It is a bilingual position at which translation of the external – extra-semiotic or non-semiotic – information takes place (Lotman [1984] 2005: 210). Lotman uses analogy to sensory receptors to explain 'translation' as a process by which readjustment of the meaning takes place so that the external codes are recoded in the familiar language: 'the border points of the semiosphere may be likened to sensory receptors, which transfer external stimuli into the language of our nervous system, or a unit of translation, which adapts the external actor to a given semiotic sphere' ((Lotman [1984] 2005: 209). The border is an ambiguous, hybrid and bilateral position of the semiosphere, it serves both as a point of contact and as a point of separation between distinct semiotic spaces. The crucial significance of dialogism in semiosis is once again emphasized in Lotman's point that 'the extreme edge of the semiosphere is a place of incessant dialogue' (1990: 142), suggesting constant dynamism between distinct languages functioning within a semiosphere and a perpetually shifting relations between the centre and the periphery.

When viewed in light of national memory, semiosphere, autocommunication and the phenomenon of the semiotic border can provide important insights into the question of how national perspectives remain so committed to their self-centred narratives, even when information suggesting alternative truths is readily available. Among many examples that can serve to demonstrate both the dialogism and the self-centredness of the national memory, one can consider narrative standoffs in the Armenian–Azerbaijani, the Armenian–Turkish and the Russian–Georgian conflicts (see Garagazov 2008; 2014; Wertsch and Batiashvili 2011; Batiashvili 2020). In all of these cases, memory serves in the practice of semiosis that involves the hidden polemic with the memory frames of the enemy. As such, narratives about the national past embody this incessant dialogue with another and are almost always construed at the extreme edge of the semiosphere. At the same time, memory narratives serve distinctly autcommunicative function, because through their use national communities not only conjure up the past upon which collective identities are based but also produce the language through which national public is demarcated.

Symbols as mechanisms for ordering consciousness

In everyday cultural practices, national memory surfaces most often as part of political speeches, public polemic or private conversation, where references to the past serve as rhetorical tactics for speakers. In these communicative acts, historical events or figures appear as symbolic tropes through which meaning is organized in discourse. Usually we take these instances as expressions of cultural stances where prefixed meanings are merely revoiced and reiterated. But Lotman treats rhetoric as a mechanism of meaning generation within which tropes are understood as 'means of forming a special ordering of consciousness' (Lotman 1990: 43). This has several implications. Firstly, symbolic tropes have a performative function. They serve in the construction of persuasive rhetoric, and as such are part of the practice of power. Secondly, the use of the symbols is part of an interpretive attempt. In other words, symbols in discourse function as framing mechanisms through language and can impose a certain order on an experience.

Lotman's emphasis on rhetorical discourse as a meaning-generating mechanism suggests that this genre is a communicative realm within which semiosis takes place. With each use of a trope rhetorical utterances do not merely reiterate previously fixed meanings, but construct new ones. In Lotman's own words 'a trope [. . .] is not an embellishment merely on the level of expression, a decoration on an invariant content, but is a mechanism for constructing a content which could not be constructed by one language alone' (1990: 44).

The implications of these ideas for the national memory are several. Empirical cases of national remembering have shown that it takes various forms, ranging from quotidian conversations around the kitchen table to the official rhetoric of leaders, as well as institutional practices that involve the work of the historians, public intellectuals, teachers and educators. In all cases, national remembering and memory-making involve the use of symbols in a way that suggests repetition and reiteration as well as redefinition and readjustment of their meanings. In other words, when it comes to national memory what we persistently observe is that memory narratives can be recycled and remade to fit current political needs, but they also retain certain semantic rigidity that makes them resist radical change.

One reason for the conservative nature of memory (Wertsch 2002: 90) is that symbolic forms such as narrative give rise to habits shared by members of the national community. In the use of memory as part of the 'effort after meaning' (Bartlett 1977: 41), symbols are persistently reused and re-employed. But as Wertsch (2002) notes, mnemonic communities are not so much united by 'specific narratives' but by more general habits of thinking based on schematic 'narrative templates' – symbolic forms that frame conceptions of the reality. These are above all sense-making instruments that help organize meaning in the discourse by way of eliciting and imposing a schematic template on the argumentative logic of an interlocutor. Their use is inherently dialogic or multivoiced because the effect of memory symbols involves schematic shared knowledge that is animated in particular ways in unique speech events.

A key takeaway from Lotman is that memory symbols function not only as tropes in particular rhetorical encounters but as mechanisms for organizing consciousness across discursive episodes more generally. In this view, a trope has meaning-generating capacity stemming from the fact that it is 'a figure born at the point of contact between two languages' (Lotman 1990: 44). It juxtaposes two or more distinct segments of meaning. Lotman's emphasis here and elsewhere on the constant presence of multiple languages in any single text has great significance when it comes to understanding how the use of memory symbols, which are polysemic in their own right, generate new meanings, while at the same time reinforcing and reinstating schematic frames and templates. This is the question that we address in the following section on the polysemic nature of symbols as outlined in Lotman's account of a plot-gene.

Variability and invariance of symbols

A starting point for conceptualizing memory symbols as both being malleable and resistant to change is Lotman's suggestion that a symbol's 'invariable essence is realized in its variations' (Lotman [1987] 2019: 164). The groundwork for this assumption is laid in Lotman's analysis of the symbol as a 'semiotic condenser' that reveals its potential for both variability and invariance (see also Chapter 15). To that end, Lotman distinguishes between the textual content of the symbol and its expression. The textual content always belongs to a more multidimensional conceptual field, while expression is an abbreviated version of these texts. Hence, any expression of the symbol does not convey its entire content but merely alludes to it. In Lotman's own words:

> the meaning potential of a symbol is always greater than any given manifestation; that is, the connections a symbol makes to this or that semiotic context with the help of its expression do not exhaust its meaning potential. This is what constitutes its meaning repository, which allows a symbol to enter into unexpected associations that can alter its essence and deform its textual surroundings in unexpected ways. (Lotman [1987] 2019: 164)

Two important things are revealed here. Firstly, elaborate texts, distinct interpretations and variants of the past can become sedimented in the polysemic conceptual field of a symbol, and, secondly, the nature of symbolic expression is such that it always leaves some space for redesignation of meaning. This idea is vividly expressed in Lotman's discussion of how hinting works through symbolic expression, as in his analysis of Dostoevsky's texts, where 'the words do not designate things and ideas but only hint at them while also suggesting the impossibility of arriving at an exact designation' (Lotman [1987] 2019: 167).

This line of reasoning on the relationship between a symbol's expression and its content extends to the distinction Lotman makes between representation and a symbol. Representation in his view embodies the basic features of a thing represented. A thing then can be judged based on its representation. A symbol on the other hand never exhausts the content of its referent. A symbol of a thing 'expresses' its 'essence' to some extent, but it remains 'not entirely exposed' (Lotman [1987] 2019: 167). This is significant for understanding memory discourse as a semiotic practice in which logic and conceptual frames, as well as the emotive nature of interaction, are shaped by the 'referencing' and 'hinting' done by words, phrases or narrative structures that function as memory symbols.

Lotman finds another instantiation of 'hinting' in what he calls the iconic aspect of the symbol. In the icon (which in Lotman's writings can mean religious icons as well as any image-based representation of the meaning), 'content only glimmers through the expression and the expression only hints at the content' (Lotman [1987] 2019: 172). Symbolic expressions therefore operate as intermediaries between distinct conceptual fields, between the textual realm that it alludes to and the reality in which it is referenced. And further, the function of a symbolic expression is that of a 'semiotic condenser' (Lotman [1987] 2019: 172):

> As an important mechanism of cultural memory, symbols carry over texts, plotlines and other semiotic formations from one cultural stratum to another. An immutable set of symbols passing diachronically through a culture assumes to a significant degree the function of unifying that culture; as a culture's memory of itself, symbols prevent a culture from disintegrating into isolated temporal strata. (Lotman [1987] 2019: 163)

Thus, the symbol has a dual nature. On the one hand, it has the ability to permeate various layers of culture and serve as a unifying cultural code across distinct historical and social contexts. This is due to its inclination towards invariancy, its inherent conservatism and echoes what Bakhtin outlined in connection with the centripetal forces acting upon the language ([1934–35] 1981: 270–5), or what Shpet means by the 'inner form of the word' (1927). On the other hand, symbols have the capacity to adapt to novel contexts and generate new layers of meaning without necessarily abandoning the 'inner form' that is part of their patterning faculty. Lotman maintained that because of its 'invariable essence' and its 'iterability', a symbol will perform as a messenger, as a semiotic node bridging alien cultural contexts of the past and present, and thus will act 'as something alien to the textual field surrounding it' (Lotman [1987] 2019: 163). But on the other hand, any symbolic expression implies active alignment with the context in which it is used, and its meaning is 'transformed under its influence while at the same time transforming it' (Lotman [1987] 2019: 163). Before dwelling on the reasons behind this dual nature of symbols, Lotman concludes: 'It is precisely in the variations to which the "eternal" meaning of a symbol is subjected in a given cultural context that this context most vividly displays its own variability' (Lotman [1987] 2019: 163).

To some degree, the mechanism that underlies a symbol's potential for variability has to do with the 'indeterminacy in the relationship between textual expression and textual content' (Lotman [1987] 2019: 164). This is why hinting is an important aspect of this discussion. As Lotman himself notes: 'Textual content always belongs to a more multidimensional conceptual field, and so expression does not entirely contain content but only hints at it' (Lotman [1987] 2019: 164). In addition, he makes a point about the simplicity of symbols: 'Symbols that are elementary in terms of their expression possess a greater capacity for cultural meaning than complex symbols' (Lotman [1987] 2019: 164), and this has direct relevance for understanding both iterability and variability of the mnemonic forms. The structures – schematic narrative templates – that underlie mythic representations of the past are usually composed of simple repetitive motifs. Because of their simplicity, they can be easily adjusted to a variety of contexts, and at the same time can absorb multiple layers of meaning. The analysis of different national narratives (Batiashvili 2018; Garagozov 2008; Wertsch 2002) suggests that these schemas are made up of simple fabulas of action – the kinds we see in fairy tales, myths, folktales and legends of all kinds – that move the plot line towards its closure. For Lotman, elementary symbols not only 'form the symbolic core of a culture' but are 'voluminous' (Lotman [1987] 2019: 170) because of their capacity to condense vast amounts of content.

Symbol as a plot-gene

Lotman examined the inverse version of this paradigm in his essay 'The Symbol as Plot-Gene' (1990: 82–102), where he suggested that the symbol embodies the potential for a new semiosis and in this way performing as a hidden script for the unfolding of meaning. The idea of a plot-gene concerns the ability of a symbol to organize consciousness and thus to impose order or fit the textual content in which it is used in some kind of a structured schema. At the same time, it suggests that a symbolic expression has the potential not just to hint at, or allude to the voluminous content hidden behind its expression, but to generate plot lines that are expressive of the prefixed meanings, while at the same time having variability in the ways in which they reconfigure these prefixed meanings.

Hence, in everyday discourse and in political rhetoric, symbols perform not as passive referents of a *given* meaning, but as active agents through which meaning can be *posited*. This means that certain uses of symbols, even of old symbols can destabilize old meanings. Lotman's concluding remarks in his essay on the symbol as plot-gene are instructive in this sense:

> [T]he symbol serves as a condensed programme for the creative process. The subsequent development of a plot is merely the unfolding of a symbol's hidden possibilities. A symbol is a profound coding mechanism, a special kind of 'textual gene'. But the fact that one and the same primary symbol can be developed into different plots, and the actual process of this development is irreversible and unpredictable, proves that the creative process is asymmetrical. (Lotman 1990: 101)

Lotman's point was to show – mainly through his analysis of Pushkin's creative symbolism – that symbols not only are complexly polysemic but also are condensed mechanisms for transmitting and expressing multiple layers of meaning. Symbols can unfold in myriad ways, meaning they index copious texts in a cultural reservoir; their use in novel contexts can engender narratives in newly creative ways.

This implication on the asymmetrical creative process has significance, especially when trying to understand how semantic shifts in national memory can occur even when the arsenal of symbols (with their referents) remains unchanged. Members of the Georgian mnemonic community, for example, may continuously use the Golden Age as a model for political imagination, a symbol will retain its capacity to index, or hint at specific narratives. It will also retain its capacity to activate a schematic narrative template that underlies the representations of the Georgian Golden Age (Batiashvili 2020). But this is not the sole reason why Lotman calls symbol a plot-gene. The gene has the capacity to 'express' the information that is coded in it, but at the same time this involves a process of creation, of engendering and not solely of repeating or reiterating. In part this is due to the fact that what symbol engenders has a new context of articulation with every iteration. So while it hints at the narratives it has condensed within it, these narratives are harnessed in new contexts of specific times and settings.

Lotman's remarks on the syntagmatic nature of myths shed more light on how symbols function as plot-genes. In his discussion of autocommunication, he cited Lévi-Strauss and emphasized the 'tendency of myths to become purely syntagmatic, a-semantic texts, not records of particular events, but schemas for organizing messages' (Lotman 1990: 34). These remarks offer a key to understanding how national memory functions in the sphere of social poiesis. In particular if we apply Lotman's ideas, we can see how memory symbols appear in everyday discourse or in the political rhetoric as codes, rather than as messages. When evoked, the primary function of David the Builder, the American Civil War or the Georgian Golden Age is not so much to convey information about past events, and in that sense they are a-semantic messages. Their primary effect is in their syntagmatic function, in their ability to generate schemas for organizing conceptions of a present reality.

Conclusion

Lotman's works can be mined endlessly for insights into various mechanisms through which symbols function in daily life, political rhetoric or social discourse. Our emphasis has been on a line of Lotman's thought that has rarely been explored in relation to contemporary memory studies. His notion of a plot-gene affords an inexhaustible potential to theorize the nature and function of semiotic structures, something that undoubtedly has much broader applicability than we explore here. Nevertheless, plot-gene offers an insight not only into how or why memory symbols retain validity across spatial and temporal boundaries of culture, or how a symbol's invariable essence is realized in its variability, but also on a more general level into how narratives and plot-structures persist as invaluable communicative instruments across human cultures.[1]

Note

1. Nutsa Batiashvili's work for this chapter was supported by Shota Rustaveli National Science Foundation of Georgia (SRNSFG) grant number YS-19-2485.

References

Assmann, J. [1992] 2011. *Cultural Memory and Early Civilization: Writing, Remembrance, and Political Imagination*, Cambridge: Cambridge University Press.

Assmann, A. [1999] 2011. *Cultural Memory and Western Civilization: Functions, Media, Archives*, Cambridge: Cambridge University Press.

Bakhtin, M. [1934–35] 1981. 'Discourse in the Novel', in M. Bakhtin, *The Dialogic Imagination*, eds and trans. C. Emerson and M. Holquist, 259–422, Austin: University of Texas Press.

Bartlett, F. C. 1977. *Remembering: A Study in Experimental and Social Psychology*, Cambridge: Cambridge University Press.

Batiashvili, N. 2012. 'The "Myth" of the Self: The Georgian National Narrative and Quest for "Georgianness"', in A. Assmann and L. Shortt (eds), *Memory and Political Change*, 186–200, London and New York: Palgrave Macmillan.

Batiashvili, N. 2018. *The Bivocal Nation: Memory and Identity on the Edge of Empire*, London and New York: Palgrave Macmillan.

Batiashvili, N. 2020. 'We Are Two Nations: Bivocal Nationalism in Georgia', in L. Greenfeld and Z. Wu (eds), *Research Handbook on Nationalism*, 347–60, Northampton: Edward Elgar Publishing Limited.

Blight, D. W. 2001. *Race and Reunion: The Civil War in American Memory*, Cambridge, MA and London: Harvard University Press.

Dudai, Y. 2002. *Memory from A to Z. Keywords, Concepts and Beyond*, Oxford: Oxford University Press.

Erll, A. 2011. *Memory in Culture*, trans. S. B. Young, Basingstoke: Palgrave Macmillan.

Garagazov, R. 2008. 'Characteristics of Collective Memory, Ethnic Conflicts, Historiography, and the "Politics of Memory"', *Journal of Russian and East European Psychology* 46 (2): 58–95.

Garagazov, R. 2014. 'Collective Memory and Narrative Toolkit in Turkish-Armenian Mnemonic Standoff over the Past', *Review of Armenian Studies* 30: 79–99.

Geertz, C. 1973. *The Interpretation of Cultures: Selected Essays*, New York: Basic Books.

Lotman, J. [1984] 2005. 'On the Semiosphere', trans. W. Clark, *Sign Systems Studies* 33: 205–29.

Lotman, J. [1987] 2019. 'The Symbol in the System of Culture', in J. Lotman, *Culture, Memory and History: Essays in Cultural Semiotics*, ed. M. Tamm, trans. B. J. Baer, 161–73. Cham: Palgrave Macmillan.

Lotman, Yu. M. 1990. *Universe of the Mind: A Semiotic Theory of Culture*, trans. A. Shukman, Bloomington: Indiana University Press.

Olick, J. K. 1999. 'Collective Memory: The Two Cultures', *Sociological Theory* 17 (3): 333–48.

Rose, G. 2019. 'The New Nationalism', *Foreign Affairs* 9 (March/April): 8.

Shpet, G. G. 1927. *Vnutrenniaia forma slova*, Moscow: Gosudarstvennaia akademiia khudozhestvennykh nauk.

Tamm, M. 2015. 'Semiotic Theory of Cultural Memory: In the Company of Juri Lotman', in S. Kattago (ed.), *The Ashgate Research Companion to Memory Studies*, 127–45, Farnham: Ashgate.

Wertsch, J. V. 2002. *Voices of Collective Remembering*, Cambridge: Cambridge University Press.

Wertsch, J. V. 2021. *How Nations Remember: A Narrative Approach*, New York: Oxford University Press.

Wertsch, J. V. and Batiashvili, N. 2011. 'Mnemonic Communities and Conflict: Georgia's National Narrative', in I. Markova and A. Gillespie (eds), *Trust and Conflict: Representation, Culture and Dialogue*, 42–64, London and New York: Routledge.

Winter, J. 2001. 'The Memory Boom in Contemporary Historical Studies', *Raritan* 21 (1): 52–66.

CHAPTER 29
LOTMAN AND POLITICAL THEORY
Andrey Makarychev and Alexandra Yatsyk

Introduction

An attempt to relate Lotman's scholarship to contemporary political theory can be viewed as ambiguously artificial, particularly given the fact that Lotman and his semiotic associates in Tartu and Moscow have wished to pave the way for a depoliticized school of thought, and distanced themselves from ideological engagements (Uspenskij [1993] 2016: 75). In contrast with their French semiotic contemporaries, such as Roland Barthes and Julia Kristeva, who aimed to deconstruct modern bourgeois culture and underscore the politically subversive role of language, Lotman's school emphasized the importance of the holistic nature of texts, exemplified, in particular, by Russian classical literature (Sériot 2016; see also Chapter 23).

As Maxim Waldstein pointed out, Tartu semioticians didn't fight 'against the Soviet academic order. At stake was not independence from this order but a degree of autonomy and influence *within* this order. [. . .] [T]hey in fact made use of the plasticity of official ideology by opposing some of its aspects to others for their own benefit' (Waldstein 2008: 24–5). In a sense, such a strategy of enforced depoliticization was the recipe for the school's survival under the Soviet system, which implied cultural adaptation rather than resistance (Kuzovkina 2013: 257). In Boris Uspenskij's words, the school's key term of 'secondary modelling system' was a part of the academic language game with the Soviet government: 'the ideologists of Marxism said (and they were absolutely right) that semiotics has nothing to do with Marxism. So we had to invent something enigmatic to deceive them. It sounded scientific' (Mazzali-Lurati 2014: 119).

One can agree that Lotman did not produce a coherent social theory and that the Tartu-Moscow school lacked a single methodology (Torop 1995). However, their intellectual legacy remains open to conceptual interdisciplinary development and political interpretation, particularly salient against a backdrop of the remarkable universalism of Lotman's theory, which makes it capable of transcending many conceptual and disciplinary borders (Nöth 2015).

The nexus of semiotics and political theory is instrumental for approaching power relations as a sphere of the production, communication and distribution of signs (see also Chapter 20). This sphere produces symbolic and epistemic powers of naming, qualifying and interpreting, as well as comparing, juxtaposing and connecting with each other autonomous events, policies and practices (Schönle 2002). There are a number of works extending Lotmanian ideas of translation, text, autocommunication and semiosphere into the conceptualizations of hegemony (Ventsel 2014; Madisson and Ventsel 2020; Selg 2018), totalization (Monticelli 2020; 2016; 2012) and biopolitics (Makarychev and

Yatsyk 2017). Others of Lotman's concepts, including 'boundaries', 'exclusion', 'explosion', 'imitation', 'language games' intermingle and overlap with those produced by critical political theory, namely 'foreclosure', 'suture', 'erasure' and 'politics of representation'. As products of 'translation' into the various languages of today's political philosophy, those concepts themselves become objects of political enquiry.

Since political theorizing can incorporate semiotic approaches, political theory is rich in various perspectives on the role of signs in producing, shaping and framing power relations. Therefore, 'the meaning of semiotic resources is part of a struggle over the definition of reality where the powerful in society will seek control over this process. [. . .] Signs carry traces of power relations' (Machin 2016: 331). In this vein, 'images are political', and 'the gaze is a powerful practice of power' (Schlag 2019: 110); consequently, signs ought to be approached as sources and producers of relations of hierarchy, hegemony and domination. Many schools in political philosophy are largely compatible with semiotic expertise and share a number of 'big names' who are equally renowned for their contributions to both political theory and semiotics (Julia Kristeva, Jacques Derrida, Michel Foucault, to name just a few).

This chapter explores how different schools of political theory conceptualize power as a sign-based phenomenon, and how political power manifests itself in imageries, narratives and cultural products. Lotmanian scholarship in a strict sense is not the main focus of this analysis, and neither do we use the semiotic approach as our methodological framework. However, we address some semiotic ideas to demonstrate the political implications of Lotman's reflections on meaning-making, and juxtapose them with contemporary debates on representation and signification.

Semiosis: A Lotmanian approach

For Lotman, semiosis results from dialogues between at least two meaningful totalities (texts or languages), unfolding on different levels (both vertical and horizontal). In the Lotmanian semiosphere, signs are organized in a binary and asymmetrical structure, including semantic cores and peripheries. The less equivalent are a text's signs to the semantic core, the more marginal they become, and the more innovative the semiosis itself could be (Lotman [1983] 2000: 593–4; see also Chapter 22). Lotman argued that the centre–periphery dynamics and the mechanisms of boundary construction are the most essential elements of meaning-making, and pointed out that 'texts of one specific genre can intervene in another space. Innovativeness at this juncture is seen as a realignment of one genre in accordance to the norms of another, while this "another" genre is organically inscribed in a new structure and simultaneously keeps its memory about its own coding system' (Lotman [1990/1996] 2000: 263). As Kamelia Spassova explains, the text has 'an immanent heterogeneous structure which is self-developed and subordinated. It is always coded with a dual code: one is dominant and explicit and the other is hidden and implicit, but the focus and background codes, or the dominant and local codes, could transform their positions in the process of semiosis' (Spassova 2018: 87). The heterogeneity of texts (within a text) is a driver for semiosis; even if texts could not be mutually translated, they could communicate with each other. Texts therefore work as self-referential, yet not self-sufficient, autopoetic systems, thus 'drifting down and up the sub/ meta levels outlined in the pairs of "internal/external", "core/periphery", "text/context", "unconscious/reflexive", and "hidden/visible"' (Spassova 2018: 88).

More controversial are correlations between the semiosphere as a self-generative and heterogeneous universe of signs and the non-semiotic realms. As Lotman claimed, semiosis is a process of inner hybridization, and can't exist beyond semiosphere (Lotman [1984] 1992: 13), or in the so called non-culture consisting 'of objects devoid of semiotisation, which simply are themselves and have no other meaning' (Nöth 2015: 17). This argument intends to draw a line between material objects equal to themselves, and those capable of performing a representational function, and raises a question of material reality and its semiotic representations. What lies beyond the semiosphere is unrepresented due to semantic exclusion, which involves inevitable political totalization, 'identitarian closure' (Monticelli 2012: 60), and construction of 'integrated systems of meanings that don't recognize the validity of "non-systemic elements"'. Yet since borders between 'culture' (text, semiosphere) and 'anti/non-culture' (nature) are flexible, the latter can also be signified through modelling the extra-semiotic reality (Selg and Ventsel 2008: 176). Thus, in his later works Lotman included in the concept of semiosphere 'not only people, messages, languages and texts, i.e. what is inherent in human communication and signification processes, but also signals from sputniks and animal cries' (Machtyl 2019: 447). He mentioned that what from a domestic perspective 'looks like an external, non-semiotic world, from a position of external observer can be perceived as a semiotic periphery. Therefore, where the boundary of the given culture lies, depends on observer's position' (Lotman [1984] 1992: 16). This fluidity of the boundary between the semiotically 'named' and the 'unnamed' makes Lotman's ideas close to constructivist and post-structuralist approaches, thus deploying liaisons between signified and non-signified realities into a more complex context.

A critical revisiting of Lotman's ideas on extra-semiotic realities implies that there is no 'representation of the world but the representation of a difference between signs. [. . .] All of this amounts to a fundamental and radical self-referentiality of signs: there is no escape from the world of signs' (Nöth 2011: 210). Regardless of intentions and reasoning, borders and boundaries result from 'orders of exclusion' (Monticelli 2012: 60), the rules and contours of which are defined by hegemonic discourses. In other words, 'what is absolutely excluded by self-description as a non-structural and a-semiotic instead appears, from the point of view of the bilingual belt, an otherwise structured or belonging to a different semiotic system' (Monticelli 2008: 199). This point adds one more political dimension to Lotman's analysis of literary texts, since 'perception of extra-systemic facts as allegedly non-existent created ample opportunities for making peace with the violence of the common over the private, as well as the state over the human being' (Monticelli 2012: 60). This idea could be developed even further in the case of communication established not for the sake of a dialogue but to prove its impossibility with the Other. In this context, the existence of the Other is a justification for its 'bare alterity' (Monticelli 2012: 60) and the subsequent foreclosure.

At this point, the Lotman-inspired discussion on semiosphere and its boundaries is translatable into the language of Jacques Rancière's political conceptualization of 'the distribution of the sensible' as pointing to a delimitation 'of the visible and the invisible, of speech and noise. [. . .] Politics [*la politique*] revolves around what is seen and what can be said about it, about who has the ability to see and the talent to speak' (Rancière 2004: 12). This is about those agents who 'cannot be identified with any existing or "real" part of society [and] are excess to the count' (Selmeczi 2009: 532). The distribution of the sensible determines interpretations and perceptions of reality and thus enables the formation of a semiotic sphere of shared meaning as a precondition for relations of power. In what follows we try to develop this argument and project it into the debate on representational and non-representational forms of signification.

Representation: A glance from political theory

In harmony with Lotman's thinking, a group of representation-based approaches envisage an ontological distinction between two realities – one that requires signification and the other that is constructed on the basis of 'broad systems of signification' (Tatum 2018: 346). Not only 'identity is a signifying practice' (Salin 2006: 56); what is more important is that political 'agency lies in the possibility of resignification' (Laffey 2000: 432) or attribution of different meanings to the extant concepts circulating within discursive milieus. Political subjectivity is possible only through imagination and instrumentalization of signs that create political realities. Both semiotic theory and political analysis might importantly contribute to discussions on image-centricity in the media and cultural landscapes (Stöckl 2020), as well as in the political environment.

In this context, the nexus of political semiotics and discourse analysis (Boholm 2016: 177–201) is crucial to understanding texts as chains of signs composed of such linguistic elements as words and sentences and to representing ideas of nation, ethnic community, multiculturalism, justice, dignity, equality, solidarity, modernity and many others. These concepts can't ontologically exist without or beyond representations that create hierarchies (e.g. between discursive cores and peripheries), as well as saturate political semiospheres with ideologies, myths, utopias and dystopias. By the same token, texts also have their outsides – stories and voices that are intentionally or unintentionally silenced, forgotten, forbidden or somehow removed from the semiosphere. Unwanted content can be expelled through various mechanisms of direct or indirect exclusion/non-inclusion, with the ensuing broad possibilities for manipulative, propagandistic and conspiratorial discourses (Madisson and Ventsel 2020).

For Ernesto Laclau and his multiple followers, power is generated by establishing linkages within the discursive networks of empty signifiers resembling 'spider webs:'

a bunch of peripheral signifiers are connected through discursive chains to more central signifiers, and these chains eventually all run to the heart of the network. The signifier occupying that heart, often called the nodal point, relates to many if not all the moments in this network. Every discourse has one or several such nodal points, which together define how this discourse is organized and which meanings it articulates. (Jakobs 2018: 303)

Laclau's theory explicitly discusses hegemony as a process of signification, and defines discourses as spaces for competing meaning-making: 'the outside (other potential meanings that were ruled out in the moment of fixation) is threatening because it makes the fixation of meaning unstable, and it is also constitutive because the specific understanding is only possible because the other meanings are excluded' (Stengel and Nabers 2019: 254). According to this logic, 'linking of objects without a necessary relation to each other involves power and exclusions' (Hansen 2014: 289). In the words of Laclau himself, discourse 'is a kind of link between social elements where each of the elements, considered in isolation, is not necessarily linked to the other [. . .] there is no "natural" or "necessary" relationship between elements that precedes the act of linking itself. Therefore, linking them involves some kind of intervention. This intervention is exactly what we call hegemony' (Hansen and Sonnichsen 2014: 256–7).

Significations are not stand-alone discursive events. As Thomas Diez put it, references to the existing ideational structures help 'to explain why national languages work – they do so because every word has its "proper" place in this structure of differences. Yet the fact that people often do not understand each other shows that the differences that produce meanings are not fixed but change over time, and they do so through the practices of articulation that constantly establish new meaning, not least because they add new contexts to the already existing ones' (Diez 2013: 325). Semiotics might be helpful for approaching discourses as spaces where meanings not only appear but also go through multiple transformations and deconstructions: 'Although speech is determined by convention (the repetition of these coded statements), those conventions only ever partially condition the usage of specific terms. The reason for this [. . .] is that language is subject to a universal propensity to be deployed in novel and unforeseeable ways. [. . .] Deviations in usage thus have the potential to alter meaning. All signs can be made to resignify in different ways' (Lloyd 2007: 131). For example, appeals to 'de-colonize visuality' (Steele 2017: 211), or shift focus from the dominant imageries to those that have been intentionally and artificially marginalized or sidelined, obviously constitute a political call.

Therefore, texts need some deciphering and de-coding to reveal intentions embedded in them and the ensuing discursive strategies of speaking subjects who are constructed by discursive practices. Similar to visual materials, texts might have more than one meaning and embody different logics adaptable to demands and expectations of diverse audiences. Some of these meanings are hidden, which is of particular relevance in situations involving the most sensitive or ideologically controversial issues of self-identification: extremists and radicals 'do not always show their opinions. [. . .] That is, discourse is not always ideologically transparent, and discourse analysis does not always allow us to infer what people's ideological beliefs are' (van Dijk 2006: 124).

What the school of 'new materialism' adds to this reasoning is that sign systems are not exclusively linguistic phenomena, and are in many ways related to urban landscapes, monuments, flags, posters and other material objects. 'New materialism' rejects a 'distinction between meaning-making practices on the one hand and an external material world "in need" of representation on the other' (Lundborg and Vaughan-Williams 2015: 11), along with the separation between language and materiality, as well as the human and the non-human.

Mimetic and aesthetic representations

As seen from the perspective of political theories, mimetic representations are aimed at getting as close to 'reality' as possible, and therefore at reflecting it in the most adequate way, which presumes relations of direct correspondence between signifieds and signifiers. In the twentieth century, the concept of mimesis became an ideological stumbling block between Western and Eastern schools of literary studies. The latter developed within the Marxist-Leninist framework that understood the role of the arts and literature as the 'sober mirror of reality' (Spassova 2018: 75–6). This approach was lucidly exemplified by Todor Pavlov's 'theory of reflection', which rejected the interpretative function of language and claimed that the arts are supposed to reflect reality without distortions (Pavlov 1970). Lotman, on the contrary, argued that the crucial function of the arts is their predisposition to 'an utmost possible freedom of modelling the reality. The freedom of artistic modelling is grounded in the fact that pieces of art are always breakthroughs into a new, so far non-existent sphere of artistic language. Each piece of art is a new text with its own language' (Lotman [1994] 2010: 166). He and his colleagues from the Tartu-Moscow school also used the concept of the mirror as the 'accurate' 'reduplication of the semiotic process' in the 'text within a text'. Yet they, in fact, camouflaged the idea of 'implosive' and creative mechanism of self-reflexive 'heterogeneous mimesis' of literary space with an abstract 'scientific language that was not easy to be criticized' (Spassova 2018: 82).

One of the multiple examples of mimetic representations is photography which, despite its inherent ability to reflect life 'as it is', still leaves ample space for manipulation of meaning. The very act of photographing can be placed 'in a relationship of resonance' with security issues (Simon 2012: 165): in most countries, photographing objects of critical infrastructure is prohibited, a trend that has accelerated due to terrorist threats and the increasing securitization of public life. As another piece of empirical research revealed, in European online media refugees are visualized 'as a mass of men, whose main social interaction is with police. Moreover, throughout the photographs, there are other trends that suggest refugees are invaders [. . .] they are not presented as individuals but in large groups' (Wilmott 2017: 77). Another study explains how photos of the victims of a deadly virus might become a robust source of (re)politicization:

The media coverage of the Ebola epidemic in the Global North has largely fed into a culture of fear; stigma and paranoia were on the rise, reminiscent of a colonial gaze of the 'Other' [. . .]. In response, a TV anchor and photographer, started a movement of visual resistance of her own: she produced a video that quickly spread across social media in which she declares: 'I am Liberian, not a virus' (Gessner 2020).

Documentaries can serve as another lucid illustration of mimetic representations. For example, during military campaigns many defence ministries publish online video footage of air strikes or jet flights over enemy territory, with ensuing destruction of its military objects. Usually these mimetic episodes remain almost mute and meant to serve as evidences of the power to destroy.

An additional example of mimetic representation is cartography, a field of scientific knowledge that is supposed to represent geography, yet is saturated with various signs and tropes: 'Maps communicate knowledge which can only be conveyed in a graphic format. They are deliberate constructs which possess emotional and intellectual appeal, and can potentially form a unique category of propaganda' (Foster 2013: 375). One may argue that 'historically, maps have promoted a decisive discourse underlying the configuration of a modern political authority based on strict territorial boundaries [. . .] [which] has been the basis to create hierarchies between Europeans and non-Europeans as well as among higher and lesser breeds of Europeans' (Lacy and Houtum 2015: 2).

In its turn, an aesthetic approach 'assumes that there is always a gap between a form of representation and what is represented therewith. Rather than ignoring or seeking to narrow this gap, as mimetic approaches do, aesthetic insight recognises that the inevitable difference between the represented and its representation is the very location of politics' (Bleiker 2009: 19). Aesthetics, understood in this way, envisages a certain communicative style and a certain space for authors' and producers' emotive and usually subjective interpretations of the signified events or concepts.

Emotion as an inalienable part of the representational process falls into the aesthetic niche. Arguably, 'emotions lie at the heart of how international politics is conducted. Emotions influence and in some cases underpin the normative frameworks that determine how states and other key actors should behave' (Hutchison and Bleiker 2017: 504). Therefore, the building blocks of the 'emotional construction of subjects' (Koschut 2017: 485) are representations grounded in the logic of equivalence, including a search for common grounds for collective selves.

Aesthetic significations are key for new concepts and subdisciplines to emerge. One example is popular geopolitics, a field of academic knowledge within geopolitical theorizing that studies how geographical representations contribute to a hegemonic reproduction of identity, borders, and spaces (Dittmer and Dodds 2008). Another example is the concept of borderscape, which initially appeared in the artistic milieu and then migrated to academic vocabulary to denote a specific realm of research at the intersection of border politics, aesthetics and performativity (Dell'Agnese and Szary 2015).

Aesthetic representations play a pivotal role in the symbolic usage of images for the sake of nation branding (Sengupta 2017), which requires the production of shared signifiers to aggregate multiple group identities into a relatively unified nation-centred storyline. What the semiotic gaze helps to spot behind the carnivalesque and emotionally charged commodification of national identities (Mutz and Gerke 2018) is differently expressed and manifested totalizing trends. This appears as national branding even in the most democratic countries whose governments culturally stimulate 'the renewal of social cohesion; the reaffirmation of the individuals' bonds with her or his social unit; the presentation or representation of social order; all for the purpose of social control. These characteristics comply with functionalist anthropological view of rituals as regulated symbolic expressions of sentiments and values that hold society together' (Manzenreiter 2006: 149).

Therefore, aesthetic representations are useful politico-semiotic tools for the creation of common identities, with all possible totalizing side effects. The representational and signifying functions of imageries as aesthetic constructs are particularly salient when it comes to weaponization of images, that is, their use as pivotal arguments in situations of international conflict (O'Loughlin 2011: 74–5) that trigger uniform types of discourse.

As we can see, in both aesthetic and mimetic forms representations are indispensable platforms for centralizing and unifying discourses looking for domination, even when appeared in 'mild' versions. For example, such forms of 'representational force' as soft power imply a struggle for 'prevalence of one representation over another [. . .]. [Therefore], representational force wields a blunt, nonnegotiable threat intended to radically limit the options of the subjects at whom it is directed. [. . .] [Specifically], a narrative expresses representational force when it is organized in such a way that it threatens the audience with unthinkable harm unless it submits, in word and in deed, to the term of the speaker's viewpoint' (Mattern 2005: 586). This argument is particularly worthwhile when analysing such politically divisive and inflammable issues as immigration and multiculturalism, which might be used to trigger appeals to collective (national) identity, very often with populist connotations.

Signification beyond representation

Non-representational theories are critical of the capacity of representations to generate the accurate or desired reflections of reality, and sympathetic to the idea of 'authority of the image to produce its own meanings, effects and realities [. . .] to constitute rather than to reflect' (Roberts 2012: 388). In academic literature, there are at least four different approaches to non-representational theorizing.

Firstly, one of the escapes from the logic of representation is offered by the post-structuralist concept of performativity (Larsen and Urry 2011: 1112). From this vantage point, 'every sign can be cited, and consequently it can break with every given context, and engender infinitely new contexts' (Lloyd 2007: 131). 'Discourses are performative to the extent that they co-produce what they name' (McKinlay 2010: 235) through role ascription, interpellation (Fazendeiro 2016: 498) and other linguistic means, which is of particular importance for understanding the phenomenon of populism (Thomassen 2019).

Performativity, as Cynthia Weber (1998: 90) suggested, is an explicitly deconstructive concept that 'disseminates and decenters meanings so that all meanings are ultimately undecidable. A performative understanding of state sovereignty suggests that sovereignty is undecidable because its meanings can't be fixed, for whatever the meaning of sovereignty is stabilized, one finds that the meaning of sovereignty has already moved on to something else'. Performativity therefore (re)configures social spaces, (re)draws legal, gender, race or class boundaries and (re)distributes meanings (Amicelle, Aradau and Jeandezbos 2015: 298). It 'debunks the notions of fixed identity and autonomous agency' (Nelson 1999: 340), and defies association of agency with something 'naturally existing'.

From a performative viewpoint, actors are real as soon as they are imagined, which leads to a clear anti-representational gesture: 'It is not that the theater presupposes the off-stage existence of the already formed subjects which the stage proceeds to represent' (Ringmar 2019: 906). This explains the aesthetic genealogy of the political, in other words the generation of political meaning in the sphere of cultural and artistic practice that presents or expresses 'something real that is excluded by the representational construction of reality itself' (Bencin 2019: 96).

Secondly, the logic of representation is criticized for its potential 'collectivization of emotions'. As Emma Hutchinson (2019: 296) put it, 'representations align some bodies and render certain bodies visible/invisible, "grievable"/"ungrievable"'; however, the idea of 'emotional communities presumed upon the production of shared signs of traumatic grieve or injustice might be challenged due to an inability of outsiders (those who did not experience traumatic events) to completely immerse themselves into this type of imagined community' (Auchter 2019: 283). At the core of this argument is the 'inability of representation to access, describe or give meaning to a specific experience' (Meiches 2019: 241) and, therefore, to represent the singular.

In this context, one should mention the 'new visual semiotics', a subdiscipline that is interested in covering a variety of micro-practices and micro-policies that are constitutive of communal life, such as studying and learning languages, accommodating immigrants, or media reporting. This type of semiotic analysis focuses less on 'meaning' and 'representation' and more on how individual human beings 'use the embodied and affective dimensions of visual communication to negotiate their physical experiences in the world and their relationships with others' (Jones 2020: 22).

Thirdly, semiotic linkages between signifiers and signifieds are often indirect and even arbitrary, which means that different public speakers might create dissimilar interpretations on the basis of the same reality. In critical discourse analysis, 'semiotic modalities' (visual images, or 'body languages') are often viewed as detached from language in a narrow sense (Fairclough 2013: 179–80), which turns signification into a complex process that reaches beyond representation. Semiotics has a lot to add to this reasoning: since signs are arbitrary and contingent, 'no relation between the signifier and the signified is necessary' (Selg and Ventsel 2020: 163). This reasoning seems to be in line with Jacques Rancière who argued that the breakdown of the system of representation happens when the artist suspends all messages and the relationship envisioned between the object of art and the audience [that] can freely encounter the artwork and attribute meanings to it, apart from those initially intended by the artist [. . .]. [T]he idea that such images are able to raise awareness about certain realities and drive people to take action, is completely unrealistic. (İnce 2018: 46)

Fourthly, signs can be viewed as being able to pre-empt and transform reality along the line of Slavoj Žižek's logic of looking at the 9/11 catastrophe as first experienced through mass culture and then as part of the real. It is exactly from this perspective that in 2020 multiple fiction films about pandemics could have been watched as raising issues that have either appeared or been immensely reactualized with the spread of the coronavirus. Another good example of a signifier in search of a signified is the concept of the 'global East' in the interpretation of Martin Müller. Unlike some global geographical names (South, North and West), which signify certain (geo)political and epistemological projects, the 'global East' is a signifier without a clear signified. In other words, it exists as a figure of speech, but waits for its substantiation and looks for some kind of reification (Müller 2020).

Conclusions: Do signs have political power?

To extend Lotman's theorizing into the political realm, one may conclude that signs not only have power – they are the ontological condition of political existence. The very process of semiosis is inherently political due to its dialogic nature; consequently, the generation of new meanings is possible only in dynamic interaction with the endless chain of texts and languages as semiotic units.

In conclusion, two points deserve particular attention. The first relates to the ambiguous democratic credentials of representation. On the one hand, representations 'establish how we understand different elements in reality and determine how we act according to them' (Geenens et al. 2015: 514), 'mediate access to the world' (Anderson 2019: 1121) and secure recognition (Disch 2015: 490). These functions are indispensable for political subjectivity, including the democratic subjectivity. Yet on the other hand, since each representation is incomplete, it leaves behind different singularities and minorities (individuals and groupings) that don't fit into the dominant system of representation. These exclusions explain the mechanisms of self-reproducing hierarchies: subalterns 'are bound to speak on the margins of existing discourses, rearticulating those discourses, or, alternatively, speak from positions within newly articulated discourses. Whatever the case, the subaltern can never speak for themselves because they can only ever speak as agents within a particular discourse' (Thomassen 2017: 543). In a radical version, this reasoning might imply that representations preclude 'the people from immediate participation in the political process' (Van de Sande 2020: 399).

Our second point concerns representations as ideational search engines for identifying and promoting the most essential characteristics of the signified objects. In performing this function, representations are bound to create self-referential sign systems, including simulacra, which generate fake reality that does not need objects of representation. It is exactly at this point that Lotman's semiotic theory needs cross-fertilization with the new concept of post-truth and the ensuing manipulative, misinformative and conspiratorial narratives. The global industry of nation branding demonstrates how easily the logic of representation can become simulative: a search for 'the essence of the nation' turns into a production of 'commodity-signs' detached from the represented reality (Kaneva 2018: 634). The same goes for the phenomenon of populism. Its obsession with representing the most 'essential' national traits and characteristics leads to the production of an alternative reality full of biased, oversimplified and anti-intellectual signifiers. Against this background, it is of primary importance for both semiotic and political theories to jointly identify and analyse different strategies of representation and non-representation, and the different political subjectivities produced by them.

References

Amicelle, A., Aradau, C. and Jeandesboz, J. 2015. 'Questioning Security Devices: Performativity, Resistance, Politics', *Security Dialogue* 46 (4): 293–306.

Anderson, B. 2019. 'Cultural Geography II: The Force of Representations', *Progress in Human Geography* 43 (6): 1120–32.

Auchter, J. 2019. 'Narrating Trauma: Individuals, Communities, Storytelling', *Millennium: Journal of International Studies* 47 (2): 273–83.

Bencin, R. 2019. 'Rethinking Representation in Ontology and Aesthetics via Badiou and Rancière', *Theory, Culture & Society* 36 (5): 95–112.

Bleiker, R. 2009. *Aesthetics and World Politics*, Basingstoke: Palgrave Macmillan.

Boholm, M. 2016. 'Towards a Semiotic Definition of Discourse and a Basis for a Typology of Discourses', *Semiotica* 208: 177–201.

Dell'Agnese, E. and Amilhat Szary, A.-L. 2015. 'Borderscapes: From Border Landscapes to Border Aesthetics', *Geopolitics* 20 (1): 4–13.

Diez, Th. 2013. 'Normative Power as Hegemony', *Cooperation and Conflict* 48 (2): 194–210.

Disch, L. 2015. 'The "Constructivist Turn" in Democratic Representation: A Normative Dead-End?', *Constellations* 22 (4): 487–99.

Dittmer, J. and Dodds, K. 2008. 'Popular Geopolitics Past and Future: Fandom, Identities and Audiences', *Geopolitics* 13 (3): 437–57.

Fairclough, N. 2013. 'Critical Discourse Analysis and Critical Policy Studies', *Critical Policy Studies* 7 (2): 177–97.

Fazendeiro, B. 2016. 'Rethinking Roles: Reflexive Role Ascription and Performativity in International Relations', *International Studies Review* 18 (3): 487–507.

Foster, R. 2013. 'Tabula Imperii Europae: A Cartographic Approach to the Current Debate on the European Union as Empire', *Geopolitics* 18 (2): 371–402.

Geenens, R, Decreus, T., Thewissen, F., Braeckman, A. and Resmini, M. 2015. 'The "Co-Originality" of Constituent Power and Representation', *Constellations* 22 (4): 514–22.

Gessner, I. 2020. 'Picturing Ebola: Photography as an Instrument of Biopolitical (In)Justice', Preprint, available online: https://www.researchgate.net/publication/339953286_Picturing _Ebola_Photography_as_an_Instrument_of_Biopolitical_InJustice (accessed 5 January 2021).

Hansen, A. D. 2014. 'Laclau and Mouffe and the Ontology of Radical Negativity', *Distinktion: Scandinavian Journal of Social Theory* 15 (3): 283–95.

Hansen, A. D. and Sonnichsen, A. 2014. 'Discourse, the Political and the Ontological Dimension: An Interview with Ernesto Laclau', *Distinktion: Scandinavian Journal of Social Theory* 15 (3): 255–62.

Hutchison, E. 2019. 'Emotions, Bodies, and the Un/Making of International Relations', *Millennium: Journal of International Studies* 47 (2): 284–98.

Hutchison, E. and Bleiker, R. 2017. 'Emotions, Discourse and Power in World Politics', *International Studies Review* 19 (3): 501–8.

İnce, G.. 2018. 'Biopolitics and Displaced Bodies; Gender(ed) Thoughts', *Göttingen Centre for Gender Studies, Working Paper Series* 1: 40–54.

Jacobs, T. 2018. 'The Dislocated Universe of Laclau and Mouffe: An Introduction to Post-Structuralist Discourse Theory', *Critical Review* 30 (3–4): 294–315.

Jones, R. 2020. 'Towards an Embodied Visual Semiotics: Negotiating the Right to Look', in C. Thurlow, C. Dürscheid and F. Diémoz (eds), *Visualizing Digital Discourse: Interactional, Institutional and Ideological Perspectives*, 19–42, Berlin and Boston: De Gruyter.

Kaneva, N. 2018. 'Simulation Nations: Nation Brands and Baudrillard's Theory of Media', *European Journal of Cultural Studies* 21 (5): 631–48.

Koschut, S. 2017. 'Introduction to Discourse and Emotions in International Relations', *International Studies Review* 19 (3): 482–6.

Kuzovkina, T. 2013. 'Ia poekhal v Tartu . . . K biografii Iu. M. Lotmana nachala 1950 godov', in I. Pilshchikov (ed.), *Sluchainost' i nepredskazuemost' v istorii kul'tury*, 451–74. Tallinn: Tallinn University Press.

Lacy, R. B. and van Houtum, H. 2015. 'Lies, Damned Lies & Maps: The EU's Cartopolitical Invention of Europe', *Journal of Contemporary European Studies* 23 (4): 447–99.

Laffey, M. 2000. 'Locating Identity: Performativity, Foreign Policy and State Action', *Review of International Studies* 26: 429–44.

Larsen, J. and Urry, J. 2011. 'Gazing and Performing', *Environment and Planning D: Society and Space* 29: 1110–25.

Lloyd, M. 2007. 'Radical Democratic Activism and the Politics of Resignification', *Constellations* 14 (1): 129–46.

Lotman, Ju. M. [1983] 2000. 'Asimmetriia i dialog', in Ju. M. Lotman, *Semiosfera*, 590–602, Saint Petersburg: Iskusstvo–SPB.

Lotman, Ju. M. [1984] 1992. 'O semiosfere', in Ju. M. Lotman, *Izbrannye stat'i v trekh tomakh*, vol. 1, 11–24, Tallinn: Alexandra.

Lotman, Ju. M. [1990/1996] 2000. *Vnutri mysliashchikh mirov*, in *Semiosfera*, 150–390, Saint Petersburg: Iskusstvo–SPB.

Lotman, Ju. M. [1994] 2010. *Nepredskazuemye mekhanizmy kul'tury*, Tallinn: Tallinn University Press.

Lundborg, T. and Vaughan-Williams, N. 2015. 'New Materialisms, Discourse Analysis, and International Relations: A Radical Intertextual Approach', *Review of International Studies* 41 (1): 3–25.

Machin, D. 2016. 'The Need for a Social and Affordance-driven Multimodal Critical Discourse Studies', *Discourse & Society* 27 (3): 322–34.

Machtyl, K. 2019. 'A Strawberry, an Animal Cry and a Human Subject: Where Existential Semiotics, Biosemiotics and Relational Metaphysics Seem to Meet One Another', *Sign Systems Studies* 47 (3/4): 436–52.

Madisson, M.-L. and Ventsel, A. 2020. *Strategic Conspiracy Narratives: A Semiotic Approach*, New York and London: Routledge.

Makarychev, A. and Yatsyk, A. 2017. *Lotman's Cultural Semiotics and the Political*, Lanham: Rowman & Littlefield International.

Manzenreiter, W. 2006. 'Sport Spectacles, Uniformities and the Search for Identity in Late Modern Japan', *Sociological Review* 54 (2): 144–59.

Mattern, J. B. 2005. 'Why "Soft Power" Isn't So Soft: Representational Force and the Sociolinguistic Construction of Attraction in World Politics', *Millennium: Journal of International Studies* 33 (3): 583–612.

Mazzali-Lurati, S. 2014. 'Boris Uspenskij and the Semiotics of Communication: An Essay and an Interview', *Semiotica* 199: 109–24.

McKinlay, A. 2010. 'Performativity and the Politics of Identity: Putting Butler to Work', *Critical Perspectives on Accounting* 21: 232–42.

Meiches, B. 2019. 'Traumas without Bodies: A Reply to Emma Hutchison's Affective Communities', *Millennium: Journal of International Studies* 47 (2): 237–48.

Monticelli, D. 2008. *Wholeness and its Remainders: Theoretical Procedures of Totalization and Detotalization in Semiotics, Philosophy and Politics*, Tartu: Tartu Ülikooli Kirjastus.

Monticelli, D. 2012. 'Self-Description, Dialogue and Periphery in Lotman's Later Thought', in S. K. Frank, C. Ruhe and A. Schmitz (eds), *Explosion und Periphere. Jurij Lotmans Semiotik der kulturellen Dynamic revisited*, 57–78, Bielefeld: transcript.

Monticelli, D. 2016. 'Critique of Ideology or/and Analysis of Culture? Barthes and Lotman on Secondary Semiotic Systems', *Sign Systems Studies* 44 (3): 432–51.

Monticelli, D. 2020. 'Thinking the New after the Fall of the Berlin Wall: Juri Lotman's Dialogism of History', *Rethinking History* 24 (2): 184–208.

Müller, M. 2020. 'In Search of the Global East: Thinking between North and South', *Geopolitics* 25 (3): 734–55.

Mutz, M. and Gerke, M. 2018. 'Major Sporting Events and National Identification: The Moderating Effect of Emotional Involvement and the Role of the Media', *Communication & Sport* 6 (5): 606–26.

Nelson, L. 1999. 'Bodies (and Spaces) do Matter: The Limits of Performativity, Gender, Place and Culture', *A Journal of Feminist Geography* 6 (4): 331–53.

Nöth, W. 2011. 'Self-referential Postmodernity', *Semiotica* 183 (1/4): 199–217.

Nöth, W. 2015. 'The Topography of Yuri Lotman's Semiosphere', *International Journal of Cultural Studies* 18 (1): 11–26.

O'Loughlin, B. 2011. 'Images as Weapons of War: Representation, Mediation and Interpretation', *Review of International Studies* 37: 71–91.

Pavlov, T. 1970. *Theory of Reflection. Basic Problems of the Dialectical and the Materialistic Theory of Knowledge (Fragments). The Philosophy of Todor Pavlov*, Sofia: Sofia Press.

Rancière, J. 2004. *The Politics of Aesthetics: The Distribution of the Sensible*, trans. G. Rockhill, London and New York: Continuum.

Ringmar, E. 2019. 'The Problem with Performativity: Comments on the Contributors', *Journal of International Relations and Development* 22: 899–908.

Roberts, E. 2012. 'Geography and the Visual Image: A Hauntological Approach', *Progress in Human Geography* 37 (3): 386–402.

Salin, S. 2006. 'On Judith Butler and Performativity', in K. Lovaas and M. M. Jenkins (eds), *Sexualities and Communication in Everyday Life: A Reader*, Thousand Oaks: SAGE Publications.

Schlag, G. 2019. 'Thinking and Writing Visual Global Politics – A Review of R. Bleiker's Visual Global Politics (2018, Abingdon and New York: Routledge)', *International Journal of Politics, Culture, and Society* 32: 105–14.

Schönle, A. 2002. 'Lotman and Cultural Studies: The Case for Cross-Fertilization', *Sign Systems Studies* 30 (2): 429–40.

Selg, P. 2018. 'Power and Relational Sociology', in F. Depelteau (ed.), *The Palgrave Handbook of Relational Sociology*, 539–57, Cham: Palgrave Macmillan.

Selg, P., and Ventsel, A. 2008. 'Towards a Semiotic Theory of Hegemony: Naming as Hegemonic Operation in Lotman and Laclau', *Sign Systems Studies* 36 (1): 167–83.

Selg, P. and Ventsel, A. 2020. *Introducing Relational Political Analysis: Political Semiotics as a Theory and Method*, Cham: Palgrave Macmillan.

Selmeczi, A. 2009. '"…We Are Being Left to Burn Because We Do Not Count": Biopolitics, Abandonment, and Resistance', *Global Society* 23 (4): 519–38.

Sengupta, A. 2017. *Symbols and the Image of the State in Eurasia*, Berlin: Springer.

Sériot, P. 2016. 'Barthes and Lotman: Ideology vs Culture', *Sign Systems Studies* 44 (3): 402–14.

Simon, S. 2012. 'Suspicious Encounters: Ordinary Pre-emption and the Securitization of Photography', *Security Dialogue* 43 (2): 157–73.

Spassova, K. 2018. 'Authentic and Heterogeneous Mimesis: Reflection and Self-Reflexivity in Todor Pavlov and Yuri Lotman', *Slavica Tergestina* 20 (1): 70–96.

Steele, B. 2017. 'Recognising, and Realising, the Promise of The Aesthetic Turn', *Millennium: Journal of International Studies* 45 (2): 206–13.

Stengel, F. and Nabers, D. 2019. 'Symposium: The Contribution of Laclau's Discourse Theory to International Relations and International Political Economy. Introduction', *New Political Science* 41 (2): 248–62.

Stöckl, H. 2020. 'Multimodality and Mediality in an Image-Centric Semiosphere – A Rationale', in C. Thurlow, C. Dürscheid and F. Diémoz (eds), *Visualizing Digital Discourse: Interactional, Institutional and Ideological Perspectives*, 189–202, Berlin and Boston: De Gruyter Mouton.

Tatum, D. S. 2018. 'Discourse, Genealogy and Methods of Text Selection in International Relations', *Cambridge Review of International Affairs* 31 (3–4): 344–64.

Thomassen, L. 2017. 'Poststructuralism and Representation.' *Political Studies Review* 15 (4): 539–50.

Thomassen, L. 2019. 'Representing the People: Laclau as a Theorist of Representation', *New Political Science* 41 (2): 329–44.

Torop, P. 1995. 'Tartuskaya shkola kak shkola', in E. V. Permiakov (ed.), *Lotmanovskii sbornik*, vol. 1, 223–40, Moscow: IC–Garant.

Uspenskij, B. [1993] 2016. 'O Moskovsko- Tartuskoi semioticheskoi shkole', in Ju M. Lotman and B. A. Uspenskij, *Perepiska 1964–1993*, 696–700, Tallinn: Tallinn University Press.

van Dijk, T. A. 2006. 'Ideology and Discourse Analysis', *Journal of Political Ideologies*, 11 (2): 115–40.

Ventsel, A. 2014. 'Hegemonic Signification from Perspective of Visual Rhetoric', *Semiotica* 199: 175–92.

Van de Sande, M. 2020. 'They Don't Represent Us? Synecdochal Representation and the Politics of Occupy Movements', *Constellations* 27: 397–411.

Waldstein, M. 2008. *The Soviet Empire of Signs: A History of the Tartu School of Semiotics*, Saarbrücken: VDM Verlag.

Weber, C. 1998. 'Performative States', *Millenium: Journal of International Studies* 27 (1): 77–95.

Wilmott, A. C. 2017. 'The Politics of Photography: Visual Depictions of Syrian Refugees in U.K. Online Media', *Visual Communication Quarterly* 24 (2): 67–82.

CHAPTER 30
LOTMAN AND CULTURAL STUDIES
John Hartley

In absentia

We have to broach the topic of 'Lotman and cultural studies' by means of an absence. Early cultural studies was a peculiarly English caper, like *The Italian Job* (1969). We were royally entertained by the headlong escapades of the lead cast – Stuart Hall as Charlie Croker (Michael Caine), Richard Hoggart as Professor Peach (Benny Hill), not to mention Charlotte Brunsdon as Peach's sister (Irene Handl). The *éminence grise*, Noël Coward's Mr Bridger, was unavoidably detained elsewhere, at Her Majesty's pleasure. Nevertheless, as the choreographer of 'the self-preservation society', his character motivated the plot. Lotman too was absent from 'contemporary cultural studies', but, just as our heroes couldn't have taken their urban subculture for that risky romp through Continental theory without the distant genius of a mystery mastermind, its masterplan can't be explained without him. What do we remember though? – only the *vehicle* (those iconic red, white and blue Minis), not the *tenor* (what was that all about?) (Richards 1936: 97).

This chapter concerns the 'cultural studies' that is often glossed as 'British' or 'Birmingham', not the older version that was attached to language studies, covering the cultures of particular nations or groups. Most important to the anglosphere, in that context, were Slavic Studies, which were responsible for Englishing some of Lotman's key publications. Cultural studies 'as we know it' was a child of this tradition only in the sense that its chief impetus came from English departments, insofar as these were grouped with modern languages, literature, classics and history, but of course *English* had a special – one may say imperial – status in the United Kingdom, the United States and former colonial countries. But cultural studies only gained transatlantic traction when abstracted and theorized to the point where it broke free from particular nations, empires and languages, as one manifestation of a lengthy and contested decolonization process.

Cultural studies emerged from the socially energetic interface between, on the one hand, 'power in symbolic systems' (Frow 1986: 4) and, on the other, the culture of everyday life, including the increasingly intrusive domain of popular urban culture and media (which is where I came in). This fusion of power and meaning was derived in turn from anthropological and Marxist antecedents (Williams 1977), dating from prehistorian V. Gordon Childe to philosopher Henri Lefebvre, both of whom had characterized modern human life through the concept of 'urban revolution' (Childe 1950; Lefebvre [1970] 2003).[1]

John Frow was one of the first to attempt a *synthesis* of 'system and history', combining Marxist theory, literary discourse and a 'semiotically oriented intervention in cultural politics'. Here, Frow took the further step that characterizes cultural studies: he declared himself 'not interested' in general theory or 'philosophical purification' but in 'intervention': 'the point is' to make literary, aesthetic and philosophical categories 'fit tools for critical and political uses' (Frow 1986: 4). Interestingly, Frow makes use of Lotman in this book, but never mentions cultural studies![2] Nevertheless, he put his finger on the nub of the matter, because – I argue – cultural studies emerged from a milieu in which Lotman was a familiar figure, but continued in one where he was conspicuous by his absence (see also Schönle 2006). Cultural studies itself conforms to his characterization of *art* as a 'secondary modelling system' (Lotman [1967] 2011). The crucial point here is that 'art' combines and modifies multilayered elements of both *science* (knowledge) and *play* (behaviour) in the organization of human intellect. What Lotman concludes for art applies to cultural studies:

Artistic models are a unique combination of scientific and play-type models, which simultaneously organize both the intellect and behaviour. In comparison to art, play is *without content*, while science is *without effect*. (Lotman [1967] 2011: 269)

Frow's addition of 'political intervention' to 'intellectual innovation' is the founding move of cultural studies: above all, it wanted to avoid being *without effect*.

Politically engaged cultural studies became a lingua franca across many related intellectual tendencies, philosophical movements and academic disciplines, including the following:

- Literary, cinema and media studies
- Structuralism, semiotics and deconstruction
- Marxism, feminism and postcolonialism
- Sociology, political economy and history
- Technology, education and audience studies

Under its own name, cultural studies remained preoccupied with identity and power in the social relations of discourse, ideology and inequality, leading to a continuing focus on militant, mediated and creative engagements with the cultural politics of successive subaltern groups – class, gender, race, sexuality, disability, age and so on – as ordinary populations navigated the global expansion of anglophone cultural hegemony and the dominance of American corporate/financial capitalism. It started when English and Welsh working-class 'scholarship boys' like Richard Hoggart and Raymond Williams (Lovell 1957), dubbed 'internal émigrés' by Stuart Hall, joined cosmopolitan and colonial 'exiles and migrants' at Oxbridge (Hall 2010), both to study and to critique *English*. It continues now with calls for intersectional cultural politics (Guimarães Corrêa 2020) and the critique of commodified cultural trends (Powers 2019) across the world.

Relations between academic activists (cosmopolitan but theory-driven 'praxis') and cultural practitioners (universalist but parochial 'practice') were uneasy – they spoke different languages. Even so, the connections did draw cultural studies into increasing dialogue with the creative, performing and media arts *as* interventions in cultural politics. A striking aspect was self-reflexive uncertainty about its own identity, with many publications asking 'What is cultural studies?' from the 1970s onwards (including Hartley 2003).

Already some overlap between Lotmanian (i.e. Tartu-Moscow school) cultural-semiotics and cultural studies can be observed. Both were marginal and provincial, politically and academically. Both had radical potential and implications. Both drew on multiple disciplines and on new theoretical models, especially structuralism and formalism. There were differences too. For cultural studies, Marxism was an adventurous thought experiment, something to play with (a 'caper'). For cultural semiotics, it was an everyday intellectual straightjacket, something to circumvent (a cage). Where cultural studies *must* wear its political heart on its sleeve (it was a 'unique selling point' in US academic politics), cultural semiotics *must not* (especially in buttoned-down Soviet bureaucratic politics). Where cultural studies focused on action (intervention), cultural semiotics focused on modelling (innovation). Where cultural studies leaned towards sociology (Willis 1977; Hall et al. 1978), cultural semiotics leaned towards cybernetics (Salupere 2015). In the process, cultural studies became increasingly suspicious of science, while cultural semiotics retained a commitment to it (Vernadsky, biosemiotics). The same applied to formalism: cultural semiotics continued that tradition; cultural studies nodded to it (Bennett 1979) but moved on. The newly translated work of Valentin Voloshinov ([1929] 1973) wielded some influence in early (literary) cultural studies. But his 'Russian' vision of language did not suit it. As Laura Gherlone has put it, the treatment of language marks a 'breaking point between Western and Russian cultures':

> In such a European perspective (Lacan, Freud, Piaget) the language (namely, the place of socialization and recognition of the other) is a source of anxiety, nostalgia, and eternal failure due to an otherness viewed as a *prison*. In the Russian vision (Vygotsky, Voloshinov, Bakhtin) it is instead a familiar, friendly place, because the individual is accounted as social from birth and it is such thanks to the language (Gherlone, 2016: 78)

However, Voloshinov does provide the first mention I ever saw of 'the recently developing "Tartu" or "Lotman" school', described by co-translator I. R. Titunik as 'fresh . . . vital . . . extraordinary' ([1929] 1973: 195). It was a portent of things to come, albeit *not yet*.

Cultural studies was predominantly *in* English, even as it took its politico-theoretical cues from French Theory (Saussure, Althusser, Barthes), 'Continental' philosophy (phenomenology, existentialism, structuralism, deconstruction) and Eurocommunism (Gramsci). Cultural semiotics was most active and adventurous in Russian and European 'modern languages'. Cultural studies and the Tartu-Moscow school have both been characterized as 'crossroads',[3] where scholars with 'different cultural and linguistic affiliations', 'different academic communities' came together in a 'translinguistic, transnational, transinstitutional, transdisciplinary association, or otherwise known as an "invisible college"' (Pilshchikov and Trunin 2016: 384). But the two 'schools' did not extend this productive intermingling to each other. Lotman's cultural semiotics was translated into English only after cultural studies had erected its own pantheon of founding figures, abandoning 'semiotics' to linguistics.

On reflection, the absence of Lotmanian semiotics in cultural studies can better be explained as unfinished business than as a lack. Cultural studies in its most energetic phase was not ready for Lotman; but it had – and has – a lot to learn. His work was not championed by any *grand fromage* of the field (Hoggart, Hall, Brunsdon, Williams, etc.), and anyone else's use of it did not resonate *as* cultural studies, which may have caused it to miss the crucial connection of semiosphere to biosphere (Mandelker 1994). Instead, new 'definitions' of culture continued to proliferate across intersectional borders, ignoring Lotman, in favour of what Hall himself called 'the indigenous or "native" tradition' (Gibson 2003; and see Rojek 1998).[4] Nevertheless, instead of scanning the usual suspects and exclaiming, with mock horror, 'Wot, no Lotman?', I want to focus on what cultural studies was up to when each of Lotman's most important books in English was published. I hope to indicate how much cultural studies has needed and still needs to come to terms with Lotman's own work and intellectual tradition.

The issues confronting cultural studies in its process of formation were urgent, all-encompassing and in-your-face. Iterative consolidation of the field into a 'discipline' was not a priority; indeed, it was resisted. While the Tartu-Moscow school maintained a focus on one problematic throughout, cultural studies was highly mobile, captured by successive struggles before it had resolved problems that preoccupied it only yesterday. Once cultural studies abandoned live engagement with Party Marxism, its theoretical apparatus dispersed to the point of dissipation: anything new might count; any previous work might be ignored. Subjectivity was extended from class to gender to race and other subject positions, without building an underpinning *cultural* model of class, gender, ethnicity, and so on. Instead, following critiques from Marxists, feminists, postcolonial and identity activists, it borrowed existing conceptualizations from sociology, of which Stuart Hall was a professor, and to which even Raymond Williams (Cambridge's first Professor of Drama) was posthumously recruited (Jones 2004).

The end of English

According to Simon Marginson, the opening of higher education to 'high participation' went in three steps:

- *Elite*: shaping the mind of the ruling-class (Quiller-Couch's '*noblesse oblige*');
- *Mass*: providing professional/managerial and technical skills (engineers and technicians);

- *Universal*: 'preparing the whole population in "adaptability" to social and technological change'. (Marginson 2016: 18) (knowledge economy, uncertainty)

Institutional, intellectual, artistic and musical revolution were in the air. The scions of imperial privilege, who had studied literature when *English* promoted discrimination, judgement and taste as a preparation for colonial administration (Quiller-Couch 1916) and corporate management (Leavis 1962),[5] were increasingly outnumbered by an 'influx' of white trash, Lydonesque oiks and swots (me among them), who began to crowd the groves of academe.[6] What were these socially unprivileged, low-value but high-volume cohorts to study?

Cultural studies was now an expansionary, high-participation phenomenon; you might almost say it was an entrepreneurial innovation in scaled-up educational enterprise. It was saved – if that's the right word – by what it criticized: 'neoliberal' commodifying institutionalization. Despite its own anti-disciplinary and post-disciplinary mode, cultural studies benefitted from the opening up of higher education (HE) to new cohorts and, with them, to new knowledge domains, shifting academia from 'elite' to 'mass' globally, and on to 'universal' participation (Cantwell et al. 2018), to include a significant percentage of the general population.[7] Gender disparity among students narrowed.[8] Demand for *access* quickly escalated from 'mass' to 'universal', driven by economic demand for a flexible workforce, political pressure for universities to align to industry, and by social demand for family status: 'The remarkable fact that distinguishes this period in history is that the ambition for higher education now appears unstoppable, almost everywhere, while the time span for the realization of ambition is shrinking' (Marginson 2016: 28).

This expansion of difference in the social make-up and purpose of HE changed not only who was taught but also what was taught. In the UK, the polytechnic sector offered degree courses that combined academic and vocational elements. Among such novelties were degrees in Communication Studies, at Sheffield (Hallam) Polytechnic, then in 1977 at the Polytechnic of Wales (where I worked), then Ulster Polytechnic. It took a generation, but eventually the entire HE sector followed suit (apart from Oxbridge).[9] 'Communication, cultural and media studies' were soon lumped together as a constellation which was both derivative of and a challenge to *English*.

In this context, 1977 was a decisive year, but not a mythical year zero or point of origin. If you want one of those, it's 1956 (Suez, Hungary), or 1968 (Tet, Paris, Chicago), not to mention 1989 in China, 2001 in the United States or 2011 in the Middle East (Tufekci 2017; 2018). For its part, 1977 marks a moment of 'explosion' (Lotman [1992] 2009) or 'creative destruction' (Schumpeter [1942] 1994: 82–3), where 'impact' is exorbitantly asymmetrical in relation to the unit of input energy, when irreversible change in 'the field' transforms both what is studied and why. Cultural studies was 'explosive' in the sense that it was noisy, indiscriminately expansive and irreversible. Its force transformed ideological and theoretical matter and distributed it right across the intellectual landscape. The energy of the moment explained 'the range, the diversity and the infectious excitement of the field' (Storey 1996: Preface).

1977: *Structure of the artistic text*

Would it enable *English* – hidebound but prestigious – to go mass? Would 'theory' – both cheap and abstract – loosen that discipline enough to go with the inflow? Could it gather disparate 'consumer' populations together, overriding mutual incommensurability among them, as did mass entertainment? You bet! Resist as it may, *English* had to change too, quick-smart.

Shakespearean enfant terrible Terence Hawkes had the answer. He was a doyen of *English*, but now he entered the intellectual maelstrom of *literary theory*. He launched the 'New Accents' book series, starting in 1977 with his own contribution, *Structuralism and Semiotics*. Nurtured by canny publisher Janice Price, the success of New Accents was not lost on other commercial publishers, who began to sign up all the 'critical' scholars they could find, as academic Marxism itself became a new growth industry. The forty-odd New Accents books covered all manner of previously unspeakable topics, *Englishing* the insights of continental philosophy, Russian formalism, feminist theory and, pretty soon, studies of pop culture, from *Reading Television* (Fiske and Hartley 1978) to *Subculture: The Meaning of Style* (Hebdige 1979). Unfortunately, there was no book dedicated to Lotman or Tartu-Moscow semiotics.[10]

Cultural studies itself needed a 'cultural, social energetic and systems theoretical' stance (Stokes 1995), in dialogue with appropriate intellectual traditions, including Marxism (McQuarie and Amburgey 1978). Stuart Hall sought to provide it but, even as he named it in *Marxism Today*, his efforts foundered on the rocks of Thatcherism (Callinicos 2014). The best guides to broad horizons were dynamic-systems theorists – Immanuel Wallerstein, for one (Lee 2004; 2010), and Juri Lotman ([1970] 1977; 1990; [1992] 2009), for another. But like Noël Coward's Mr Bridger, the model-builders were conspicuous by their absence from 'British' cultural studies (Turner 2003). Despite the blizzard of theorizing, there was no synthesis; there was only 'everyday life'. Cultural studies was not evolutionary, looking for origins (Sparks 1977), but insurrectionary. It wanted to break things. 'British' cultural studies wanted to break *English*. The confines of intramural English could not confine this reformist energy. The doors opened directly onto *the street*.

The year 1977 was the year that punk broke through. The Sex Pistols' 1976 'Anarchy' tour had degenerated into just that by the time they came to Wales, where I lived at the time, for a gig in Caerphilly. As England's first 'internal colony' (Hechter 1975), Wales offers a good vantage point from which to critique (the) *English* – 'Looking up England's Arsehole', as poet Harri Webb (2000) had put it. Predictably, the Pistols didn't go down well with the local powers-that-be, never mind the bemused onlookers. With populist denunciation from national media and local councillors alike ringing in their ears, 300 carol-singing opponents, a fire-and-brimstone preacher and extra police all gathered outside the venue, outnumbering the desultory crowd within by five to one. Nevertheless, a local reporter who covered the event recalled its significance:

Punk arrived as Britain was going into recession and – after teddy boys, mods and rockers and flower power – was iconoclastic: there was a feeling among some young people that the old ideas had to be challenged in a different way, that smashing things up might clear the ground to start anew. (BBC 2011)

A local fanzine interviewed various participants, including Johnny Rotten (John Lydon), asking him about the spate of cancellations the band had experienced following a notorious TV interview:

BUZZ: Does the fact that a lot of universities, who are supposedly open-minded people, pulled out of dates surprise you?

JR: Oh no, universities have proved to be the worst. They went on about us being fascist and rubbish like that. Students have proved that they're not open-minded, they've got closed minds; they're a closed shop. (*Babylon Wales* 2006)

As postcolonial, post-imperial, post-industrial Britain teetered into 1977, the Sex Pistols recruited Sid Vicious. In May they released 'God Save the Queen', providing the anti-anthem for Queen Elizabeth II's silver jubilee and propelling the band to global notoriety. The single went straight to number 1 despite being banned by the BBC, independent radio and some retail outlets. The official charts were doctored to stop it taking top slot. In a nation divided by class, race, gender and inequality, the song took sides, as John Lydon himself later commented: 'There are not many songs – written over baked beans at the breakfast table – that went onto divide a nation and force a change in popular culture.' He added: 'You don't write "God Save The Queen" because you hate the English race, you write a song like that because you love them; and you're fed up with them being mistreated.'[11] Cultural studies 101, right?

1990: *Universe of the Mind*

The year 1990 was quite a year for system collapse. The Berlin Wall fell. The Soviet Union teetered, as its constituent republics declared sovereignty or secession. Yugoslavia fragmented. Margaret Thatcher was ousted. But it was also quite a year for system creation. The two Germanys reunited. Nelson Mandela was released from Apartheid prison. Tim Berners Lee perfected the World Wide Web. The Human Genome Project commenced. The Hubble Space Telescope was launched. The Soviet Union joined the internet.[12] China was in post-Tiananmen 'damage control' (Shambaugh 1990) – 'control' being the operative word.

And *Cultural Studies* (with capital letters) went institutional. The landmark book – some Brits called it a 'tombstone' (Curran, Morley and Walkerdine 1996: 4; and see Hartley 2003: 161–6) – was by Grossberg, Nelson and Treichler (1992), a doorstopper 'reader' compiled from papers delivered at a *grand fromage*-studded conference at Illinois in 1990. This was when *Cultural Studies* shifted from activism to academic enterprise, and when publishing it shifted from London to New York, enabling scalar efficiencies in a much larger market. It was cheap to teach, it required no expensive kit or labs, anyone could do it (Courtemanche 2016), and even students could afford the textbook. *Cultural Studies* went 'global', wherever the Anglo-American publishing industry could reach.

In 1990, Lotman's *Universe of the Mind* was published in English. Its impact on cultural studies was not 'explosive'. *Universe of the Mind* came too late. I think this is a familiar story: the increasing specialization, monetization and dispersal of cultural studies meant that its centre became fixed (via ritualistic incantations of founders' names). There was no longer a core generator of new theory (aka 'Birmingham'), but rather many peripheral edges, often out of contact with each other or mutually hostile, where new work proliferated but did not reform the core tenets, which by then were 'set texts'.

Indeed, cultural studies was itself a case study of Lotman's own distinction between core and periphery, where core texts are repetitious, about identity, reducing diversity, with stories about 'us', recording principles; while peripheral texts are mobile, infringing boundaries, narratives about action, the world, difference, anomalous occurrences, with stories about 'they' identities, recording violations, crimes and events (1990: 151–3). Like any semiospheric system, its narratives about itself serve as 'myth', while stories about the outside world serve as 'news' (see Hartley 2008: 87–90). This structure is in line with the importance of what Lotman calls 'autocommunication' (self-description) in any reflexive cultural or knowledge domain, and with his insight that innovation emerges from anomaly, change, adaptation, driven by contact with *other* semiospheres and other (incommensurable, untranslatable) approximations of the world. In the 1990s, as cultural studies solidified into institutional discipline in order to be taught, the core 'myth' about itself hardened, while 'news' about 'others' proliferated.

But the dynamics of Lotman's 'two-systems' law of semiosis still hold. As cultural studies gained prominence in the university strongholds of scientific enquiry, so it gained enemies – among scientists. Most notorious was the Sokal affair of 1996 (of which the decisive account is by Wark 2016). In 1996, a physicist (Alan Sokal) claimed to have 'hoaxed' a cultural theory journal (*Social Text*) with a bogus article about quantum gravity. But the journal had published it because the item was making not truth claims about what is (physics) but ethical claims about how it ought to be interpreted (semiotics). Sokal's account (Sokal and Bricmont 1998) was gleefully reviewed in *Nature* by Richard Dawkins, fanning populist derision in the press. The whole episode was taken (by scientists) to have sounded the death knell for postmodernism, including cultural studies. Postmodernists, for their part, saw it as academic bad faith, because the journal was not about physics but discourse (Wark 2016). The contest was staged as if it concerned truth – objective versus subjective; true versus false. But actually it illustrated a new mode of textual performance, a turn from objectivity to *reflexivity* (autocommunication), where knowledge and truth are the (anomalous) problem to be tackled, not a self-evident (mythical) given.

The Sokal affair might have been more productively resolved had 'the scientists' been willing to consider discursive constraints on truth claims (Haraway 1990), and had 'the postmodernists' not rejected science altogether as a Lyotardian metanarrative, whose practical outcomes included war, imperialism, racism and environmental catastrophe.

Each knowledge domain had important concerns from which the other could have learned.

As McKenzie Wark suggests, an unforeseen consequence of the affair was that it may have done *science* more harm than good, for it contributed to a further public erosion of the authority of academic knowledge systems in general. Science itself became the target of well-funded campaigns in the populist media, giving succour to climate-change deniers, anti-vaxxers, conspiracy theorists and haters of experts (some of these in ministerial positions), who served the interests of fossil-fuel businesses and authoritarian governments. What was needed, throughout, was a Lotmanian understanding of 'at least two systems' in dialogue across incommensurable boundaries as a necessary condition for any approximation to external (extra-semiotic) reality.

2009: *Culture and Explosion*

David Beecher observes: 'The tension between change and continuity obsessed Lotman – as revealed by his idiosyncratic metaphor of the snake shedding its skin as a model for universal scholarly progress' (Beecher 2014: 379–80). Lotman himself clearly relished this metaphor, using it to close his late 'non-memoir':

> A snake sheds its skin when it grows. This is a perfect symbolic expression of scholarly process. [. . .] All that remains is to hope that the snake, having shed its skin, changed its colour, and increased in size, will preserve the very unity of itself. (Lotman [1995] 2014: 79)

With cultural studies, Tartu-Moscow cultural semiotics may need to make one last Lotmanian move – shedding its familiar skin in order to grow. As Igor Pilshchikov and Mikhail Trunin remind us:

> Historical transformations of concepts and meanings are not aggravating flaws, but inevitable conditions and even preconditions of cultural and transcultural communication. Lotman wrote of incomplete translatability, both linguistic and conceptual, as a productive mechanism of cognition and communication. (Pilshchikov and Trunin 2016: 387)

It is becoming clear that global crises affecting climate, environment, the biosphere and pandemics are 'anthropogenic'; their effect is on the world as a whole, not just the anthropos. Here, it is increasingly clear that received truths – scientific and cultural – are part of the problem. Indeed, Lotman goes so far as to claim that truth itself is not to be found in nature but in cultural history: any 'aspiration towards a single universal language (towards a single, final truth)' is itself evidence of cultural impact, not a primary origin but a later, 'secondary reality created by culture'. In response, we should not be on the lookout for a 'single perfect universal language', but for ways to *model complex dynamic systems*, where 'a multiplicity of languages is original and primary' (Lotman [1992] 2009: 2–3), and where the clash of mutually untranslatable semiosis produces new knowledge. If a 'single, final truth' is weaponized by sectional interests and fundamentalisms, how do knowledge systems across the semiosphere combine and act in corrective concert, and how can this multilayered system of systems be self-regulated, at planetary scale?

Eleanor Courtemanche (2016) thought that the 'lustre' and 'fizzy punch' of cultural studies had 'dimmed' by the early 2000s. In the aftermath of Sokal, 9/11, the Bush/Gore election and the First Gulf War, she writes:

> The movements that replaced cultural studies in the academy had a more sober, practical mood: book history, archival research, studies of realism in the novel, a tentative embrace of technology and medical history, and (at the crazy edge) interest in the dispersed and barely-perceptible agency of systems, animals, and geological fault lines. Journalists got bored and started looking for their cultural panics elsewhere. (Courtemanche 2016)

That 'crazy edge' rapidly moved centre-stage, however, because the 'barely-perceptible agency of systems' soon became all too evident in relation to planetary events: climate-change, environmental catastrophe and coronavirus pandemic. Academic cultural studies should have been reading Lotman all along:

> Lotman's later books [. . .] treat issues which are rarely associated with Tartu-Moscow School: first, the need for a common approach to natural, social, and spiritual phenomena; second, the problem of evolutionary and explosive processes in the history of culture; and, third, the question, closely linked to the previous two, of art as a workshop of indeterminism and unpredictability. These ideas have not been widely discussed; in the meantime, they can be productively developed in the context of contemporary humanities. (Pilshchikov and Trunin 2016: 389)

'Evolutionary and explosive processes' demand a 'common approach'. Culture, science and politics need coordinated action. The current academic arrangements are not ready for that challenge. But extramurally, out on the street, it is quite a different story:

> Cultural studies has turned out to be, in retrospect, a weirdly thorough success that is influencing the creation and reception of culture everywhere in the world, especially outside the academy. One might even take the omnipresence of cultural studies 2.0 as a sign that research in the humanities, though obscure at the time, ended up having transformative cultural impact. (Courtemanche 2016)

The lessons have been learned by students and young people, such as those participating in School Strike for Climate, Fridays for Future, Black Lives Matter, #MeToo and suchlike causes. Girls are already globally organized and acting together via social media to link climate justice with human and non-human rights, environmental regeneration and intersectional solidarity (e.g. Yousafzai and Lamb 2013; Thunberg 2019; Hartley 2020: Ch. 12). What's needed now from cultural studies/cultural semiotics, allied with other system sciences including the biosciences (Attenborough 2020), is a concerted effort to support everyday cultural action for system change at the core as well as the periphery. The 'explosive' moment of climate/COVID crisis activism cannot precipitate transformational change in world governance on its own. Semiospheric *models* are also needed, to clarify how reflexive knowledge and self-regulating action can be connected in sustainable practices. As Michael Stokes (1995) put it, *critique* needs to be 'cultural', 'social energetic' and 'systems theoretical' all at once, because 'a critical discourse seeks to construct openings to possible futures that are not retrogressive to a nostalgic past'.

As V. Gordon Childe wrote: 'I do not believe that there are uniformities in history of the kind from which one can make such predictions as work in natural science. I believe that the historical process as a whole is the actual creation of genuinely new values' (quoted in Gathercole 1995: 106). This is not science as commonly understood, but it's science, nonetheless. Lotman ([1967] 2011: 266), writing in 1967, makes a distinction between 'deterministic' and 'probabilistic' sciences, locating artistic texts in the quantum camp: 'a scientist creates a model based on a hypothesis, whereas an artist creates a hypothesis based on a model.' Thus:

> The work of art is not created as a strictly deterministic actualization of a given constructive principle. The constructive idea is actualized with a certain degree of independence on different levels, and if each level taken separately is constructed based on certain specific structural laws, then their combination most likely follows only probabilistic laws. ([1967] 2011: 267)

In short, from the start, cultural studies has been an 'innovation science', one that is non-linear and probabilistic, based on the interactions of multilayered complex systems, with elements of experiment (play) as well as rule (organization), its antennae tuned to '*the actual creation of genuinely new values*'. The point remains – as Frow had said at the outset – to make literary, aesthetic and philosophical categories *fit tools for critical and political uses*.

Cultural science?

In order to face the future, a synthesis of cultural studies, cultural semiotics and Earth-system sciences is urgently needed. This is the narrative trajectory that has been called 'cultural science', where a full-scale dialogue between cultural studies and Lotman has been conducted. Initially proposed as a means for theorizing the creative economy,[13] it has attracted interest from others, partly through *Cultural Science Journal* (since 2008), partly in independent studies in economics (Herrmann-Pillath [2009] 2011) and media (Ibrus 2019: 23, 216) and partly through critique. One example of the latter dismissed it as 'post-truth', lacking 'a methodologically sound and empirically rich engagement'

(De Beukelaer 2017). That is surely an incentive to rethink what counts as 'sound', truth, evidence and engagement? In the meantime, 'cultural science' is indeed a proposal rather than an achievement, provoked by the embattled state of both scientific and cultural knowledge systems in the face of global climate and humanitarian crises, hostile governments and populist media. As a thought-experiment, it seeks to develop a fully theorized methodological, conceptual and technological armamentarium while at the same time responding reflexively to the many modes of difference within and among groups, in order to understand how coordinated action may be effected at individual, institutional and planetary scale. 'Empirical richness' can only be accrued over time and across many studies: it's a collective work in progress.

The point of departure for cultural science is to treat culture functionally within evolutionary-dynamic systems. What is culture *for*? Hartley and Potts (2014) argue that:

- Culture makes groups (demes);

- Groups make knowledge;

- Cultures are competitive: their knowledge systems are both universal ('we' can explain everything) and adversarial ('they' know nothing except lies);

- Knowledge acts on the world systematically, at population scale, and probabilistically, with unforeseen consequences.

Hartley (2020) argues that polities and economies are driven as much by story as science, which is why cultural science is needed to analyse the semiotic *constitution* (not just the *administration*) of political and economic systems. We are what we mediate. In *On the Digital Semiosphere* (Hartley, Ibrus and Ojamaa 2021), we seek to integrate an explicitly Lotmanian/Earth-system model of culture, at micro-individual, meso-institutional and macro-planetary scale, and to apply it to emergent Anthropocene dynamics (see also Chapter 32 in this volume).

As previously for cultural studies, the energy of street action, globalized via social media, is well ahead of formal understanding, institutionalized via academic disciplines. In keeping with its own punk antecedents, cultural science is open to links with and learning from these sources too. The purpose is not 'philosophical purification' but practical 'intervention', in concert with those for whom science, culture, media and humanity are all part of the problem, even as they are the source of meaning, knowledge and identity. Humanity has emerged into global consciousness not as a coherent species, ready to confront planetary problems of its own making, but as contending cultures, focused on fighting each other like criminal gangs, each leader posing as a latter-day Mr Bridger, unheedingly continuing to befoul the common nest. Luckily, lurking in the background is someone who really can see the big picture. Lotman's own life's work answers the question he poses in *Culture and Explosion*, 'How can a system develop and yet remain true to itself?' ([1992] 2009: 2). It provides a model of modelling for cultural scientists, whose 'intervention' must both explain and regulate how semiosis extends beyond humans to the entire biosphere, and in turn how cultural groups may combine at scale to sustain the planetary as well as the semiotic environment.

Notes

1. Kenneth Maddock (1995: 107) used Marx to link Childe with another of the forebears of structuralist cultural studies: Claude Lévi-Strauss, commenting on the 'interesting likenesses' between them. They 'shared a largeness of view, which was connected with their old-fashioned ambitions and their common debt to Marxism'.

2. Frow has been a leading figure of literary cultural studies in Australia, from *Cultural Studies and Cultural Value* (1995) to *On Interpretive Conflict* (2019). He was Regius Professor of Rhetoric and English Literature at Edinburgh University (2000–04). He contributed the entry on 'Cultural Studies' to the *Bloomsbury Handbook of Literary and Cultural Theory* (2018). We were colleagues at Murdoch University in the 1980s.

3. Notably, for cultural studies, the 'Crossroads' conference series, organized by Pertti Alasuutari at Tampere (Finland), held biennially since 1996. With Joke Hermes and Ann Gray, Alasuutari co-founded the *European Journal of Cultural Studies*, and initiated the trans-regional Association of Cultural Studies (http://www.cultstud.org/wordpress/?page_id =83) (all links accessed on 10 November 2020).

4. The redefinition of cultural studies to suit the cultural politics of new entrants is a continuing process. The *International Journal of Cultural Studies*, which I founded and edited from the 1990s, passed into new editorial hands in 2019 (Gray et al. 2019), and began a special series on 'what is cultural studies?' with contributions from Ien Ang, Nick Couldry, Johan Fornäs, Benjamin Woo, Sarah Murray, Devon Powers (https://journals.sagepub.com/toc/icsa/23/3 and https://journals.sagepub.com/toc/icsa/23/4), and further articles by Guimarães Corrêa (2020), Johnson and Joseph (2020). None of these papers mentions Lotman.

5. The notorious 1960 'two cultures' argument between C. P. Snow (science; government) and F. R. Leavis (culture; literature) is the subject of an astute review by Julian Meyrick (2016), who concludes: 'When the bravado is stripped away, we find two visions laid out, one in which science and technology save the world, the other in which culture and language make it worth saving.'

6. 'Lydonesque' refers to John Lydon, as discussed in this chapter. Upper-class disdain for oiks and swots was given a new lease of life by UK prime minister Boris Johnson (Eton, Oxford). See: https://www.wsj.com/articles/what-is-a-swot-boris-johnson-gives-a-schoolboy-insult-a-new-political-life-11568385000; https://www.theguardian.com/uk/2009/nov/03/boris-johnson-attack-camden-london1.

7. Overall UK participation in higher education increased from 3.4 per cent in 1950, to 8.4 per cent in 1970, 19.3 per cent in 1990 (not counting polytechnics) and 33 per cent in 2000–1 (counting polytechnics). Source: https://researchbriefings.files.parliament.uk/documents/SN04252/SN04252.pdf.

8. Source: https://www.hepi.ac.uk/wp-content/uploads/2014/02/41Maleandfemaleparticipationsummary.pdf.

9. In 2020, 111 UK universities offered 502 courses including Communication Studies: https://www.whatuni.com/degree-courses/search?subject=communication-studies.

10. My own first encounter with Lotman and the Tartu-Moscow school was via the admiring footnote in Voloshinov ([1929] 1973) mentioned above. His *Marxism and the Philosophy of Language* (published in Russian in 1929) was discussed at the Cardiff Critical Theory Seminar (chaired by Terry Hawkes and attended by Catherine Belsey, Chris Norris, Chris Weedon and myself, all of whom went on to write New Accents volumes). It combined formalism and Bakhtinian literary adventurism with an early critique of Saussure.

11. Source: http://www.johnlydon.com/press/pistols.html.

12. Source: Wikipedia. For the Russian internet, see: http://www.i-love-moscow.com/russian-int ernet.html.

13. Cultural science was established as a programme of my ARC Federation Fellowship (2005– 10) in the ARC Centre of Excellence for Creative Industries and Innovation. Proceeding via a series of international workshops in Brisbane, Durham (UK) and Perth, and in *Cultural Science Journal*, the initiative has resulted in numerous publications, especially the 'trilogy' with Bloomsbury (Hartley and Potts 2014; Hartley 2020; Hartley, Ibrus and Ojamaa 2021).

References

Attenborough, D. 2020. *A Life on Our Planet: My Witness Statement and A Vision for the Future*, London: Penguin.

Babylon Wales. 2006. 'Lost Welsh Sex Pistols Interview', *Babylon Wales*, 14 December, available online: http://babylonwales.blogspot.com/2006/12/lost-welsh-sex-pistols-interview.html (accessed 15 November 2020).

BBC. 2011. 'The Sex Pistols in Caerphilly', *BBC Wales Music Archive*, available online: https://www.bbc.co.uk/wales/music/sites/history/pages/sex-pistols-caerphilly.shtml (accessed 15 November 2020).

Beecher, D. I. 2014. *Ivory Tower of Babel: Tartu University and the Languages of Two Empires, a Nation-State, and the Soviet Union*, Berkeley: University of California, PhD Dissertation, available online: https://escholarship.org/content/qt9h90g470/qt9h90g470.pdf?t=otc1m0 (accessed 15 November 2020).

Bennett, T.1979. *Formalism and Marxism*, London: Routledge.

Callinicos, A. 2014. 'Stuart Hall in Perspective', *International Socialism: A Quarterly Review of Socialist Theory*, 142, available online: http://isj.org.uk/stuart-hall-in-perspective/ (accessed 15 November 2020).

Cantwell, B., Marginson, S. and Smolentseva, A. (eds) 2018. *High Participation Systems of Higher Education*, Oxford: Oxford University Press.

Childe, V. G. 1950. 'The Urban Revolution', *The Town Planning Review* 21 (1): 3–17.

Courtemanche, E. 2016. 'The Peculiar Success of Cultural Studies 2.0', *Arcade: Literature, The Humanities, & the World*, available online: https://arcade.stanford.edu/blogs/peculiar-success-cultural-studies-20 (accessed 15 November 2020).

Curran, J., Morley, D. and Walkerdine, V (eds) 1996. *Cultural Studies and Communications*, London: Arnold.

De Beukelaer, C. 2017. 'Creative Economy and Culture', *Cultural Trends* 26 (2): 185–7.

Fiske, J. and Hartley, J. 1978. *Reading Television*, London: Routledge.

Frow, J. 1986. *Marxism and Literary History*, Cambridge, MA: Harvard University Press.

Frow, J. 1995. *Cultural Studies and Cultural Value*, Oxford: Clarendon Press.

Frow, J. 2018. 'Cultural Studies', in J. Di Leo (ed.), *The Bloomsbury Handbook of Literary and Cultural Theory*, 140–50, London: Bloomsbury.

Frow, J. 2019. *On Interpretive Conflict*, Chicago: University of Chicago Press.

Gathercole, P. 1995. 'The Relationship Between Vere Gordon Childe's Political and Academic Thought – and Practice', in P. Gathercole, T. Irving and G. Melleuish (eds), *Childe and Australia: Archaeology, Politics and Ideas*, 95–106, St Lucia: University of Queensland Press.

Gherlone, L. 2016. 'Vygotsky, Bakhtin, Lotman: Towards a Theory of Communication in the Horizon of the Other', *Semiotica* 213: 75–90.

Gibson, M. 2003. 'The Geography of Theory: Channel Crossings, Continental Invasions, and the Anglo-American "Natives"', *Symplokē* 11 (1/2): 152–66.

Gray, J., Burgess, J., Frosh, P., Fung, A., Georgiou, M. and Lopez, L. K. 2019. 'Editorial', *International Journal of Cultural Studies* 22 (1): 3–8.

Grossberg, L., Nelson, C. and Treichler, P. (eds) 1992. *Cultural Studies*. New York and London: Routledge.

Guimarães Corrêa, L. 2020. 'Intersectionality: A Challenge for Cultural Studies in the 2020s', *International Journal of Cultural Studies* 23 (6): 823–32.

Hall, S. 2010. 'Life and Times of the First New Left' *New Left Review* 61, available online: https://newleftreview.org/issues/II61/articles/stuart-hall-life-and-times-of-the-first-new-left (accessed 15 November 2020).

Hall, S., Critcher, C., Jefferson, T., Clarke, J. and Roberts, B. 1978. *Policing the Crisis: Mugging, the State, and Law and Order*, London: Hutchinson/Palgrave Macmillan.

Haraway, D. 1990. *Primate Visions: Gender, Race and Nature in the World of Modern Science*, New York: Routledge.

Hartley, J. 2003. *A Short History of Cultural Studies*, London: Sage.

Hartley, J. 2008. *Television Truths*, Malden, MA and Oxford: Wiley-Blackwell.

Hartley, J. 2020. *How We Use Stories and Why That Matters*, New York: Bloomsbury.

Hartley, J. and Potts, J. 2014. *Cultural Science: A Natural History of Stories, Demes, Knowledge and Innovation*, London: Bloomsbury.

Hartley, J., Ibrus, I. and Ojamaa, M. 2021. *On the Digital Semiosphere: Culture, Media and Science for the Anthropocene*, New York: Bloomsbury.

Hawkes, T. 1977. *Structuralism and Semiotics*, London: Methuen/Routledge.

Hebdige, D. 1979. *Subculture: The Meaning of Style*, London: Routledge.

Hechter, M. 1975. *Internal Colonialism: The Celtic Fringe in British National Development, 1536–1966*, Berkeley: University of California Press.

Herrmann-Pillath, C. [2009] 2011. *The Economics of Identity and Creativity: A Cultural Science Approach*, London: Routledge.

Ibrus, I. (ed.) 2019. *Emergence of Cross-Innovation Systems: Audiovisual Industries Co-innovating with Education, Health Care and Tourism*, Bingley: Emerald Publishing.

Johnson, M. and Joseph, R. L. 2020. 'Black Cultural Studies is Intersectionality', *International Journal of Cultural Studies* 23 (6): 833–9.

Jones, P. 2004. *Raymond Williams's Sociology of Culture: A Critical Reconstruction*, London: Palgrave Macmillan.

Leavis, F. R. 1962. *Two Cultures? The Significance of C. P. Snow*, London: Chatto & Windus.

Lee, R. E. 2004. *Life and Times of Cultural Studies: The Politics and Transformation of the Structures of Knowledge*, Durham, NC: Duke University Press.

Lee, R. E. [2010] 2017. *Knowledge Matters: The Structures of Knowledge and Crisis of the Modern World-System*, London: Routledge.

Lefebvre, H. [1970] 2003. *The Urban Revolution*. Minneapolis: University of Minnesota Press.

Lotman, J. [1967] 2011. 'The Place of Art Among Other Modelling Systems', trans. T. Pern, *Sign Systems Studies* 39 (2/4): 249–70.

Lotman, Yu. M. [1970] 1977. *Structure of the Artistic Text*, trans. R. Vroon, Ann Arbor: University of Michigan Dept of Slavic Languages and Literature.

Lotman, Yu. M. 1990. *Universe of the Mind: A Semiotic Theory of Culture*, trans. A. Shukman, Bloomington: Indiana University Press.

Lotman, J. [1992] 2009. *Culture and Explosion*, trans. W. Clark, ed. M. Grishakova, Berlin: Mouton de Gruyter.

Lotman, Y. [1995] 2014. *Non-Memoirs*, trans. C. L. Brickman, ed. E. Bershtein, Champaign, IL: Dalkey Archive Press.

Lovell, A. 1957. 'The Scholarship Boy', *Universities and Left Review* 1 (2): 33–4.

Maddock, K. 1995. 'Prehistory, Power and Pessimism', in P. Gathercole, T. Irving and G. Melleuish (eds), *Childe and Australia: Archaeology, Politics and Ideas*, 107–17, St Lucia: University of Queensland Press.

Mandelker, A. 1994. 'Semiotizing the Sphere: Organicist Theory in Lotman, Bakhtin, and Vernadsk', *PMLA* 109 (3): 385–96.

Marginson, S. 2016. 'High Participation Systems of Higher Education', *The Journal of Higher Education* 87 (2): 243–71.

McQuarie, D. and Amburgey, T. 1978. 'Marx and Modern Systems Theory', *Social Science Quarterly* 59 (1): 3–39.

Meyrick, J. 2016. 'Two Cultures (Again): Revisiting Leavis and Snow', *Sydney Review of Books*, 19 August, available online: https://sydneyreviewofbooks.com/essay/two-cultures-again-revisiting-leavis-and-snow/ (accessed 10 November 2020).

Pilshchikov, I. and Trunin, M. 2016. The Tartu-Moscow School of Semiotics: A Transnational Perspective', *Sign Systems Studies* 44 (3): 368–401.

Powers, D. 2019. *On Trend: The Business of Forecasting the Future*, Champaign: University of Illinois Press.

Quiller-Couch, A. 1916. *On the Art of Writing*, available online: https://www.bartleby.com/190/8.html (accessed 10 November 2020).

Richards, I. A. 1936. *The Philosophy of Rhetoric*, Oxford: Oxford University Press.

Rojek, C. 1998. 'Stuart Hall and the Antinomian Tradition', *International Journal of Cultural Studies* 1 (1): 45–65.

Salupere, S. 2015. 'The Cybernetic Layer of Juri Lotman's Metalanguage', *Recherches sémiotiques / Semiotic Inquiry* 35: 63–84.

Schumpeter, J. [1942] 1994. *Capitalism, Socialism and Democracy*, London: Routledge.

Schönle, A. (ed.) 2006. *Lotman and Cultural Studies: Encounters and Extensions*, Madison: University of Wisconsin Press.

Shambaugh, D. 1990. 'China in 1990: The Year of Damage Control', *Asian Survey* 31 (1): 36–49.

Sokal, A. and Bricmont, J. 1998. *Fashionable Nonsense: Postmodern Intellectuals' Abuse of Science*, New York: Picador.

Sparks, C. 1977. 'The Evolution of Cultural Studies . . .', *Screen Education* 22: 16–30, republished in Storey 1996: 14–30.

Stokes, K. 1995. *Paradigm Lost: Cultural and Systems Theoretical Critique of Political Economy*, New York: Routledge.

Storey, J. (ed.) 1996. *What is Cultural Studies: A Reader*, London: Arnold.

Thunberg, G. 2019. *No-one is Too Small to Make a Difference*, London: Penguin.

Titunik, I. R. 1973. 'The Formal Method and the Sociological Method in Russian Theory and Study of Literature', in V. N. Vološinov, *Marxism and the Philosophy of Language*, 175–200, New York: Seminar Press.

Tufekci, Z. 2017. *Twitter and Tear Gas: The Power and Fragility of Networked Protest*, New Haven, CT: Yale University Press.

Tufekci, Z. 2018. 'How Social Media Took Us from Tahrir Square to Donald Trump', *MIT Technology Review*, 14 August, available online: https://www.technologyreview.com/2018/08/14/240325/how-social-media-took-us-from-tahrir-square-to-donald-trump/ (accessed 15 November 2020).

Turner, G. 2003. *British Cultural Studies: An Introduction*, 3rd edn, London: Routledge.

Vološinov, V. N. [1929] 1973. *Marxism and the Philosophy of Language*, trans. L. Matejka and I. R. Titunik, New York: Seminar Press.

Wark, McK. 2015. *Molecular Red: Theory for the Anthropocene*, London: Verso.

Wark, McK. 2016. 'Sokal Affair', in N. Lucy (ed.), *A Dictionary of Postmodernism*, Malden, MA, and Oxford: Wiley-Blackwell.

Webb, H. 2000. *Looking up England's Arsehole – The Patriotic Poems and Boozy Ballads of Harri Webb*, ed. M. Stephens and Talybont, Ceredigion, Cymru: Y Lolfa.

Williams, R. 1977. *Marxism and Literature*, Oxford: Oxford University Press.

Willis, P. 1977. *Learning to Labour: How Working Class Kids Get Working Class Jobs*, Aldershot: Gower.

Yousafzai, M. and Lamb, C. 2013. *I Am Malala: The Girl Who Stood Up for Education and Was Shot by the Taliban*, New York: Little, Brown and Co.

CHAPTER 31
LOTMAN AND POPULAR CULTURE STUDIES
Eva Kimminich

Juri Lotman's ideas have been rather widely used in cultural studies as a complementary framework to observe the generation of meaning (Schönle 2006; see also Chapter 30). They have been applied to literature and film a number of times, for example in the essay collections *Explosion und Peripherie* (Frank, Ruhe and Schmitz 2012) and *Medien und Kommunikation* (Decker 2017a). Initial research studies can also be found in the emerging field of the semiotics of popular culture, which will be the focus of this chapter.

Youth, sub- and protest cultures as well as pop music, comics and computer games have so far received attention mainly in sociology and cultural studies, although they are well suited for analysis within semiotic research and theory-building, with their distinctive sign production, their resematizations that transcend media and codes, as well as their specific reinterpretation strategies and techniques. In Italian semiotics, popular cultural phenomena were perceived and studied by Umberto Eco and his school. Lotman's theory of semiosphere (Lotman [1984] 2005; see Chapter 22), however, has not yet been used significantly for this purpose, although it is particularly suitable for illuminating the phenomena of change in a sociocultural context and for examining the dynamics of text translation and the generation of meaning inherent in social changes (Torop 2005). In so doing, the effects of such semantic shifts on a pragmatic level can be brought into focus. Here there is a desideratum in relation to the sociocultural transformation processes of the present, which are accelerated by new media formats especially due to the extensive distribution of meaning production through internet technologies and their manipulative usage (by actors) in the political field. Initial studies of conspiracy theories and right-wing populism have already been undertaken (Kimminich and Erdmann 2018; Madisson and Ventsel 2020).

As in media semiotics (Decker 2017b), cultural semiotics works using a broad concept of text (Sedda 2015), which deliberately turns away from the literary understanding of highly cultural texts and concentrates on the creative diversity of their translations. This is based on Lotman's fundamental understanding of culture as a complex textual production mechanism and as cultural memory (see Chapter 10). It is precisely in the case of popular culture, which Lotman himself paid little attention to, that the central functions of culture as a semiosphere can be observed: specifically, the communicative function, through which texts and messages are conveyed and positioned; the creative function, which generates new texts and codes; and the mnemonic function, which keeps the diversity of texts and codes available regardless of time and place (Tamm 2019: 8–9). Observing popular cultures over recent decades therefore facilitates insightful conclusions about how meaning generates and informs identities, mentalities and opinions. The recent theoretical adaptations of Lotman's concepts, particularly translation, offer a model terminology for this (Sedda 2015: 689–93).

In this chapter, the still-undeveloped body of empirical research on popular culture semiotics will be presented in order to highlight, firstly, the benefits of applying Lotman's ideas to popular cultural phenomena and, secondly, the research in popular culture with recent theoretical refinement. The resulting observations can be useful for further empirical research and, moreover, can contribute to a version of popular culture semiotics which combines theoretical and empirical findings from its subfields into a differentiation of Lotman's cultural theory. This theory could then be updated in further research incorporating future developments in sociocultural change.

The empirical applications of Lotman's theoretical ideas (especially his semiosphere model) in this chapter come from two particular fields of research in sub- and popular culture studies. The first field of research analyses the processes of meaning formation taking place on the periphery in subcultures such as punk, glam rock, rap and pop music. The analysis will look at the diffusion of texts produced during this process and the repercussions on social realities. The second field examines right-wing populist and 'conspiracy theory' ideological reinterpretations of sociopolitical events via internet communication. Both fields of research focus on the semiosis of the subject, a process which Lotman understands as open, resulting in a multitude of possible interpretations. The analysis identifies the results of these translation processes as the critical junctions of semiospheric movements which are, in turn, indelibly linked to sociocultural change.

Semiotics of subcultures

Lotman's semiosphere model is based upon the concept of permeable buffer zones towards the outside and between internal spheres. For the semiotic analysis of subcultures, this model can provide a foundation to elucidate the continuous production of meaning generated by the mobile character of texts circulating between centre and periphery while crossing these spheres. Subcultural research considers these internal spherical processes of alteration and reinterpretation of socially acknowledged, or dominant, meaning structures, as productions of meaning by social subjects. The subjects appropriate the texts of the semiosphere within the framework of an encyclopaedic process through the lens of their subculture-specific and/or personal characteristics (Kimminich 2013: 209–26; Persello 2015; 2016). The resulting individual (multimodal) constructions of meaning consequently become the object of investigation as the smallest internal spheres of the semiosphere. The subject then establishes a balance of existing and new texts, which are again modified and then fed back into the surrounding internal spheres of the semiosphere through communication to subsequently become the basis for further appropriation processes.

This process and the interplay of translatability and untranslatability constitutes what Lotman describes 'as an accretion of meaning' (Lotman 1990: 15). Analysing the texts from the semiosphere or the internal spheres and how they have been creatively appropriated or (newly) combined opens up the possibility to re-enact the production of different interpretative patterns *in statu nascendi* and to visualize the dynamic interactions that take place between existing or already-modified interpretative patterns of collective encyclopaedias. Furthermore, empirical long-term studies of subcultural text production establish how the propagation of alternative interpretations into the semiosphere will rupture existing sociocultural patterns of self-perception and the awareness of the Other, which have been established in key cultural texts, as well as having an effect on the self-representation of social groups in everyday life, both in the present and retrospectively.

The adaptability of texts and co-texts in glam rock and punk

Mara Persello's (2016) long-term study of glam rock, which is atypical as a subculture, brings together the concepts and methods of semiotics with those of cultural studies. To do so, she uses the semiosphere model to reveal the mechanism of meaning or style generation that ultimately underlies all subcultures. This is explained through the semiosphere's inherent abolition of the fundamental distinction between text and context; accordingly, Persello understands the contexts that are linked or linkable within a network of contexts only as co-texts. This has the advantage that social realities, as perceived and represented by members of a society or community, can be seen as resulting from the interaction between discursive practices within a society. Cultural texts are consequently analysed as socio-specific practices of translation. Attention is focused on the history of a sub- or partial culture as the specific position of a text within the constellation of the semiosphere at different points in time. Evolution is then synonymous with the migration of these texts, which may (or may not) be found in different constellations in different epochs.

Persello's approach to the analysis of subcultures, derived from Lotman's concept, is to create an 'archaeology of texts', following Foucault's notion of the archaeology of knowledge. Her theoretical design thus makes it possible to go beyond a typological approach in the structuralist sense. In so doing, it allows for a meaning that emerges not from characteristics determined externally, but instead from the self-representation of the subcultural community within the texts and from the local conditions that shape it. In this way, silent forms of protest can also be more closely defined, which do not occur in the form of direct opposition, considered typical of subcultures, but in the staging of a deviant interpretation.

This emerges from Persello's textual archaeology of glam rock, traced over forty years, which observes how various products of popular culture become models for practical forms of engagement with everyday life. For example, the song lyrics of glam rock tell of artists who wanted to become rock stars but remained misunderstood by a world they perceived as dull. With the help of such explanatory patterns, social failure and frustration can be absorbed through a kind of aristocratic self-appreciation. Since the *glamsters* see themselves not as oppressed but as misunderstood heroes, they do not need to exercise protest. Their reaction to existing society and the mainstream consists, on the one hand, in indifference and disregard for the mainstream and, on the other hand, in the performance of their deviant interpretations, through which they can experience their own world view, which includes the feeling that there is 'no future'.

In her analysis of punk, Persello (2015) focuses on how connections between new and pre-existing meanings of texts are made, following Lotman's concept of translation. She states that the receiver can only understand a text if the new content is embedded in the constellation of texts from the specific, individual semiosphere. Hence, the texts must be compatible with the personal life history of each cultural actor. The process of translation is then the filter deciding if new information is included or excluded, as Persello notes: 'every new generation of punks is a demonstration of the adaptability of this text to different contexts, and of the enduring power of the no future' (Persello 2015: 98). Neither the national nor the sociopolitical contexts of the original message play the decisive role here, but rather the respective life situations. Above all else it is local circumstances that influence the individual appropriations and creative translation results, as is clear from the punk scene in rural, earthquake-ravaged Pordenone. The scene ignored the political context of the original message and instead made use of irreverence and nonsense to create meaning. This can be traced back to the founder of the scene, the art student Zigante, whose personal experience is responsible for the Dada interpretation of punk philosophy. Subsequently, the power of the receiver in the interpretation of the message is emphasized, as is the importance of the selection criteria that operate when co-texts are interlinked.

This results in a change of perspective for subculture research in general, and a move towards taking into consideration the locality and subjectivity of generation, which at the same time is based on a transnationally or transculturally formulated message. The basic idea of *cultural imperialism* must therefore be replaced by a detailed tracing of the translation processes of a subculture's central texts in order to do justice to, and acknowledge, the multiple dynamics and strands of that specific subculture.

The empirically derived conclusions of Persello's analysis can be positioned as a theoretical extension of Lotman's concept of translation, as expanded upon by Franciscu Sedda. The power of the punk or glam rock recipient within the process of translation demonstrates the differentiation made by Jacques Geninasca 'between a meaning created through the connection of the "pieces" of *commonsense systems*, which we recognize as "signs" (whatever their size or language may be), and a meaning created through the transformation of deeper nets of representations, which we generally associate with "texts"' (Sedda 2015: 691). With this distinction, as Sedda points out, continuities and ruptures in the production of meaning can be traced and explained: 'Furthermore this leads to the consideration of the possibility that the two forms of translation can be simultaneously at play and that their force can join together, move sense in a common direction, or push meaning in two different directions' (Sedda 2015: 691). This process is observed by Persello in her analysis of the divergence of the punk scene in Pordenone and in the broad individual variety of glam rock translations as distinct from other subcultures. For future research, the pioneering methodology of translation outlined in

Persello's work enables one to trace the repositioning of a central text from its original contexts into new ones. In so doing, the creative diversity and hybridization that emerge from this process can be recognized and the inner processes of transformation can be traced back to its source.

The interpretative power of rap songs

The analysis of French rap subculture and its translation processes demonstrates how reverting to texts from different internal spheres and modifying them, specifically socio-historical or political discourse fragments, is used to (re)construct the identity of a socio-ethnic group. When alternative transcriptions diffuse into the internal spheres, the newly emerging individual extends the social contingencies within the reality of everyday life (Kimminich 2013). How exactly these semiotic operations are carried out can be understood when using the framework of narratology applied in the *possible-worlds theory* (Surkamp 2002), which helps to focus more precisely on the osmotic exchange between semiospheric operations and social life. The *possible-worlds theory* conceives reality as a modal system that consists of an *actual world* and a variety of virtual alternative worlds, identities and roles: the *possible worlds*. Their possibilities are measured through the degree of accessibility in relation to the actual world, and within the frame of the narratively generated *textual actual world*, that is, in the context of a new system of perceptions and depictions, possibilities and updates. They are performed by the rapper, involving his or her recipients, the listeners, temporarily. In order to determine the validity of a story, both the authority and credibility of the rapper (the text-external narrator) and the updated text-internal narrative instances (first-person narrator and figures of their textual actual world) are crucial for listeners to receive the newly created semiotic meanings. The subjective perception of text-internal narrator instances is displayed as congruent with that of the text-external narrator by demanding that the autobiographical elements of the narrative are evaluated in the same manner. Hence, not only *narrational actual* but also *textual actual worlds* merge. The identity, credibility and authority of the rapper also guarantees an agreement of *textual actual* and *actual worlds* or *possible worlds*.

Rap's rhetorical techniques and narrative strategies enable the adoption of interpretative power and a break away from hegemonic meanings. Although this is performed in a mental space as the smallest semiospheric unit, it translates into real-life empowerment for the actants involved (the rapper and his/her recipients) at the same time. Thus, subjective perceptions can become social truths. This is particularly the case with Senegalese rap (Kimminich 2015/16). Field studies spanning over twenty years observed how an identity model disseminated via rap texts became a collective orientation for action. In three national elections, rappers mobilized the population to vote, with their credibility as rappers playing the decisive role in influencing the election. Their identity model has made them cultural actors producing a new culture that has its own values and options for action. A subculture developing on the fringes of the semiosphere can therefore also initiate sociopolitical change in the all-embracing semiosphere. Senegalese rappers reacted to the semantic categories made available to them, within the framework of their cultures, by fusing tradition and modernity. Rap builds upon the historic role of African oral culture and combines it with the core values of the still young democracies and the values of the hip-hop community, bringing them into real-life contexts. In so doing, rap enabled a change in values and categories of the then socially dominant subsphere through semiotic transfer, showing how this transfer was able to contribute to more or less concrete change according to the respective power relations and existing communication conditions.

From this research we can ascertain that, through the medium of rap, definitions and concepts at the hegemonic centre of the semiosphere are confronted with the perceptions of a subjective reality, as experienced on the margins of society. This confrontation takes place within the translation process, consisting of a producing and a receiving dimension. The rapper becomes an instance of the intersection between past, present and future, tradition and modernity, central and peripheral cultures and between history and *his(/her) story*. Telling *his story* creates a reality effect which the recipient can transfer into his or her own semiosphere allowing for unpredictable mechanisms to unfold, and generating explosive real-life actions.

In the case of France, rappers did not change society but informed the collective memory of a particular socio-ethical group through a retrospective re-evaluation of the past when the group's discrimination had been encoded. The outcome of these translations has become a recurrent subject of political debate, as exemplified quite recently in the case of Medine's song and video clip *Don't Laïk* (Kimminich 2019). This study of the trans-spherical translation of cultural texts within rap songs showed how subcultural translations and recontextualizations as semiotic operations can have an effect on social learning by confronting individual world experience with the hierarchical software of the centre of the semiosphere. In the case of Francophone rap in West Africa, the effect is still stronger because the semiotic operations mobilized the whole population to act politically (Kimminich 2015/16: 175). It even became a transcultural protest model that was reactivated in Mali, Burkina Faso and the Democratic Republic of Congo.

Pop songs as containers of meaning

The very recent practice of *Schlagersemiotik* or the semiotics of hit songs (Decker 2021) also applies Lotman's semiotic theories. Here, the focus is on movements between the canon of texts, codes and semantics that establish themselves at the centre and their subsequent transformations within *Schlagermusik*. Lotman's concept of the free structural reserve of music can also be applied to *Schlagermusik*, as the structural reserve is the prerequisite for a connotative charging of context and contextual meaning parameters with secondary meanings. The analyses of hit songs in the *Heimatfilms* of the 1950s in the Federal Republic of Germany, in the 'Sound of Austria' or in Hildegard

Knef's *Für mich soll's rote Rosen regnen* take into account the interplay of multimodal and multicodal texts in transmedial networks.

The main finding of these studies shows that hit songs (re)combine linguistic and musical empty formulas, from which an intrinsic value emerges. In so doing, a hit song is bound to the person performing it (the star) or to the performer (singing it at a specific time), who in turn can charge the hit song with new meanings of his or her own. This takes place through the empty formulas that correspond to the respective context of the person appropriating them, in his or her performance. As a result, Decker states that 'hits and hit songs [thus] become variably fillable containers of meanings, with which a permanent semiotisation and de-semiotisation is possible within the framework of a semiosphere. The hit song is, so to speak, a means of transport for the import and export of cultural meaning between different media formats, media and mentalities and cultural subsystems' (Decker 2021).

In the case of pop music, as with glam rock, punk and rap, it is the description of the re- and de-contextualization of texts in semiospheres that makes the change of identities and mentalities visible and reveals the various functions of popular cultural meaning structures.

Right-wing websites and semiospheric turbulences

Lotman's model also serves as a framework that helps to shine a light on ideological reinterpretations, especially in recent textual appropriations informed by conspiracy theories and right-wing populism on the internet (see also Chapter 33). The World Wide Web forms a media (sub-)culture that follows the same rules as the semiosphere with centres and edges, as well as permeable in-between zones, in which transformations can take place or be triggered. Due to the internet's peculiarity in allowing communication to take place in seemingly closed spaces, the formation of opinions based on translation not only is visible but can also be influenced. These otherwise invisible processes can be observed by filtering their main concepts and their symbolic values. In so doing, a new perspective can be formulated on the Lotmanian *explosions* through which change is initiated. Lotman considers the individual as a scene of the production of meaning. This brings it into focus as a user of cultural guidelines of the stabilizing centre. Here, too, semiosis is the focus of observation, this time not only with regard to the subject's (re)creative translation processes but also with regard to its influence. Thus, individual semiosis and its emerging interpretations are to be viewed as a scene onto which the social semiosis, that is the common perception and evaluation of social realities, can be shifted. This also makes semiosis attractive as a tool of manipulation, which are manifold in the digital age.

How exactly influence can be exerted on semiosis can be observed in a previous study on the PI-News website (Politically Incorrect News) (Kimminich 2016). The study analysed the website to show how the interpretation of facts and events and thus the construction of reality can be influenced. The website was classified as a right-wing, populist and Islamophobic hate blog that is considered dangerous to pluralist society. Its structure and content reveal the typical characteristics of conspiracy ideologies. Since they are aimed at shifting the perception and evaluation of social realities and events towards an alternative interpretation, a model was developed to show how such websites interpret social realities, and in the process revise or devalue existing explanatory patterns so that a different social reality is produced. The model shows how website users are given hidden instructions on how to translate and incorporate the revaluations into their personal patterns of interpretation. It clarifies how social reality is reconstructed and the strategies of the associated processes of reinterpretation that are used. It also explains the strategies that facilitate the implementation of 'PI truths' in visitors' own works of reality construction. Therefore, we have to deal with a fragmentation of reality constructs and a resemantization of reality elements with the purpose of changing the construction of their meaning.

It is thus necessary to introduce elements of 'common ground' with the website user. These are produced by disposing of some of the reality elements, such as interpretations generally discussed in media and politics, popular pictures and common citations as well as an equally important set of semantic differentiations for the re-evaluation. Once this semantic space is created, a process called *grounding* can be triggered, meaning that the website visitor can look for texts compatible with their own fears, hopes or speculations. Grounding therefore requires a 'mental meeting point' with keywords from public discussions drawing the website visitor in. In this case, the keywords are political correctness, freedom of opinion, multiculturalism and Islamization. When the reader encounters these meeting points, transmission and re-evaluation processes are initiated, as two interpretations are present and the new one has to be corroborated. This is completed through a specific offer of third-party testimony, with powerful declarations from converts and acts of self-revelation. This category of text has the function of reproducing the main ideological patterns. Grounding, re-evaluation and corroboration are the basic stages of this process to reconstruct existing constructions of reality. The internet as the technological embodiment of the semiosphere is increasingly becoming the centre of all information. It not only makes available all kinds of cultural text but also simultaneously exposes them to an endless translation and transformation process. This results in an unmanageable number of parallel meanings that put the common sense and common image of the reality of a society to the test.

In societies with advanced media landscapes, the common understanding of social realities is exposed to a multitude of levels of observation and interpretation. This, on the one hand, makes the cohesion of the construct of social reality impossible. On the other hand, in an individualized society that doubts its own interpretative agencies, the individual positioned at the intersection of social systems and semiospheric translation becomes more active in observing and in producing divergent interpretations of social realities. The individual is therefore an important resource as the reproductive agent of ideological or conspiratorial narrations. If these divergent interpretations are increasing, a fragmentation and decomposition of the common view of social realities can be set in motion. In the case of websites like PI-News or others that spread the so-called alternative information, proven knowledge and accepted semantic (moral) categories are contested, potentially resulting in their general erosion (Kimminich 2018).

A comparable observation can be found in Cassone's analysis (2018) of the political discourse around the Five Star Movement (M5S) that recontextualizes classic right-wing topics and agendas in non-ideological forms. This transformation is the outcome of a groundbreaking shift away from the traditional left versus right opposition towards a more complex overlap of establishment versus anti-establishment, as well as ideological versus non-ideological categories. As a result, several traditionally right-wing ideas have over time come to be considered as ideologically neutral and common sense driven. While Cassone demonstrated this process mainly through the example of M5S's political discourse, it seems plausible that the strategies of other political parties and events can also be described through this process. These examples could be interpreted as a confirmation of the current shift of traditional political dichotomies, in which new competing political codes emerge and fight for cultural validation. As one of the main findings, Cassone emphasizes the virality of a 'colourless right-wing' body of thought that seems to thrive and prosper in a supposedly unideological political discourse, while carrying traditional populist, neoliberal and conservative ideas and opinions (2018: 42).

This type of study helps expand Lotman's view of bifurcations in the semiosphere, which are triggered by *explosions* (see Chapter 21). The concept of bifurcation, as Grob (2012) reminds us, emerged from Lotman's discussion of Ilya Prigogine's dissipative systems, and is concerned with certain moments in which a system makes leaps in its development. These result from an unpredictable decision in favour of one of the possible paths or even simultaneously in favour of several possible paths. These decisions are irreversible and determine the direction of further development. As the analysis of PI-News and the Five Star Movement shows, the technological developments in online communication are infinitely increasing the number and scope of opportunities to influence the subject's semiotic decisions.

On social media channels, the seeker of alternative information will thus find confirmation of any statements by other existing users, particularly in filter bubbles which are steered towards a diverging narrative. Special tools of influence, such as bots, contribute to this process. The model of the presetting of semiosis (Kimminich 2018), developed by analysing PI-News as an example, makes it possible to reveal the mechanism of influence step by step and design a countermeasure. The possible decisions for the website visitor are not completely predictable but they can be made visible. The example of PI-News illustrates the importance of steering the process of individual translation in a certain direction. The direction this takes, especially when it is shared collectively, can result in momentous consequences for the social construction of reality.

Perspectives for a semiotics of popular culture

Lotman's cultural theory, especially his model of the semiosphere as a sphere of semiotic activity, provides revealing insights into the dynamics of identity formation, the shaping of mentalities as well as the forming and manipulation of opinion, as described in the examples in this chapter. Using various texts from popular culture, the analysis shows how media, modal and code-specific boundaries are crossed. Examining and further understanding individual translation processes has illustrated how existing texts are combined or modified in newer and newer constellations, thereby repositioning themselves in the semiosphere. This also results in deviations and shifts (the increase or, under certain circumstances, the weakening) of knowledge, values and power.

Coupled with the new possibilities offered by the internet for the creation and sharing of information, and new forms of communication, the individual can be considered a nerve cell or synapse in a global brain, as Marshall McLuhan (1964: 3) wrote in his rather idealistic view of the new media in the 1960s. In semiotic terms, it is clear that the receiver's individual production of meaning is a complex and powerful process.

The recent increase in protest movements worldwide, which rely on the staging and media dissemination of symbolically charged objects, gestures or monuments in order to mobilize and arouse emotions, offers an important field of research that has so far been predominantly studied in sociology, but would benefit from the application of Lotman's dynamic cultural theory as a holistic model for analysis. The theory allows us to observe which texts of cultural memory are revived, discarded or recoded during protests and in what way. In the process, information can be gained about why certain places, monuments, symbols or events become focal points of Lotmanian explosions. By analysing the translations that trigger processes of change, a direction of travel can be approximated and opportunities or even dangers can be recognized.

Lotman intended his cultural model to be expanded and updated in line with sociocultural developments; for, the semiosphere, as he wrote in *Universe of the Mind*, 'seethes like the sun, centres of activity boil up in different places, in the depths and on the surface, irradiating relatively peaceful areas with its immense energy' (Lotman 1990: 150).

References

Cassone, V. I. 2018. 'Neither Right Nor Left: The Rise of "Unpolitical" Right-wing Rhetoric', in E. Kimminich and J. Erdmann (eds), *Virality and Morphogenesis of Right Wing Internet Populism*, 29–44, Frankfurt et al.: Peter Lang.

Decker, J.-O. 2017a. 'Medienwandel', in H. Krah and M. Titzmann (eds), *Medien und Kommunikation. Eine Einführung aus semiotischer Perspektive*, 423–46, Passau: Ralf Schuster.

Decker, J.-O. 2017b. 'Strukturalistische Ansätze in der Mediensemiotik', in M. Endres and L. Herrmann (eds), *Strukturalismus heute. Brüche, Spuren, Kontinuitäten*, 79–95, Stuttgart: Metzler.

Decker, J.-O. 2021. 'Einleitung. Schlagersemiotik als Forschungsfeld der Passauer Mediensemiotik', in J.-O. Decker (ed.), *Schlagersemiotik. Beiträge der Passauer Mediensemiotik* (= *Zeitschrift für Semiotik*, 42 [1–2]), Tübingen: Stauffenburg.

Frank, S. K., Ruhe, C. and Schmitz, A. (eds) 2012. *Explosion und Peripherie. Jurij Lotmans Semiotik der kulturellen Dynamik revisited*, Bielefeld: transcript.

Grob, T. 2012. 'Der doppelte Lotman. Jurij Lotmans Konzeptionen kulturhistorischer Dynamik zwischen Gesetz und Zufall', in S. K. Frank, C. Ruhe and A. Schmitz (eds), *Explosion und Peripherie. Jurij Lotmans Semiotik der kulturellen Dynamik revisited*, 133–52, Bielefeld: transcript.

Kimminich, E. 2013. 'A Third Space for Dissent: Raps Peripherial Semiosphere, Its Making and Effects', *Lexia: Rivista di Semiotica* 13–14: 209–26.

Kimminich, E. 2015/16. 'Kollektive (R)Evolutionen: Rap als Medium der gesellschaftspolitischen Bewusstseinsbildung und der Resistenz im frankophonen Afrika', *Lied und populäre Kultur / Song and Popular Culture* 60/61: 157–75.

Kimminich, E. 2016. 'About Grounding, Courting and Truthifying: Conspiratorial Fragments and Patterns of Social Construction of Reality in Rhetoric, Media and Images', *Lexia: Rivista di Semiotica* 22–3: 33–51.

Kimminich, E. 2018. 'Instead of a Conclusion: The Shift of Meaning and Semiospheric Turbulences', in E. Kimminich and J. Erdmann (eds), *Virality and Morphogenesis of Right-Wing Internet Populism*, 179–82, Frankfurt et al.: Peter Lang.

Kimminich, E. 2019. 'RAPublicans and Jihadists or the Missed Chances of French Integration Policy: An Analysis of Rap Songs and Music Clips', available online: https://www.uni-potsd am.de/fileadmin/projects/romanistik-kimminich/docs/Kimminich_RAPublicans_and_Dj ihadists.pdf (accessed 30 December 2020).

Kimminich, E. and Erdmann, J. (eds) 2018. *Virality and Morphogenesis of Right-Wing Internet Populism*, Frankfurt et al.: Peter Lang.

Lotman, J. [1984] 2005. 'On the Semiosphere', trans. W. Clark, *Sign Systems Studies* 33 (1): 205–26.

Lotman, Yu. M. 1990. *The Universe of Mind: A Semiotic Theory of Culture*, trans. A. Shukman, London and New York: I.B. Tauris.

Madisson, M.-L. and Ventsel, A. 2020. *Strategic Conspiracy Narratives: A Semiotic Approach*, New York and London: Routledge.

McLuhan, M. 1964. *Understanding Media: The Extensions of Man*, London: Routledge & Kegan Paul.

Persello, M. 2016. 'Subcultures Creating Culture: Semiotica e studi culturali a confronto nell'interpretazione della sottocultura glam', PhD thesis, University of Potsdam and Scuola Normale Superiore, Pisa, available online: https://publishup.uni-potsdam.de/opus4-ubp/fr ontdoor/deliver/index/docId/10489/file/persello_diss.pdf (accessed 30 December 2020).

Persello, M. 2015. 'Peripheral Subcultures: The First Appropriations of Punk in Germany and Italy', *KISMIF Conference 2015, Book of Proceedings*, 93–8.

Schönle, A. (ed.) 2006. *Lotman and Cultural Studies: Encounters and Extensions*, Madison: The University of Wisconsin Press.

Sedda, F. 2015. 'Semiotics of Culture(s): Basic Questions and Concepts', in P. P. Trifonas (ed.), *International Handbook of Semiotics*, 675–96, Dordrecht et al.: Springer.

Surkamp, C. 2002. 'Narratologie und possible-worlds theory: Narrative Texte als alternative Welten', in V. Nünning and A. Nünning (eds), *Erzähltheorie transgenerisch, intermedial, interdisziplinär*, 153–83, Trier: WVT.

Tamm, M. 2019. 'Juri Lotman's Semiotic Theory of History and Cultural Memory', in J. Lotman, *Culture, Memory and History: Essays in Cultural Semiotics*, trans. B. J. Baer, ed. M. Tamm, 1–26, Cham: Palgrave Macmillan.

Torop, P. 2005. 'Semiosphere and/as the Research Object of Semiotics of Culture', *Sign Systems Studies* 33 (1): 159–73.

CHAPTER 32
LOTMAN AND MEDIA STUDIES
Indrek Ibrus and Maarja Ojamaa

Introduction

Our mission statement for this chapter is to discuss the relevance of Lotmanian cultural semiotics for media studies. This is a challenging endeavour for two reasons. Firstly, the relationships between these parties have to date been limited; and, secondly, due to broader media studies being a field constituting a moving target, as media themselves and the penumbra of approaches that study it are constantly changing. The vast domain of media and communication studies is inherently heterogeneous and only vaguely bounded.

The challenge starts with the very definition of media: Are they the material/technical channels for content delivery and access or are they the institutions of production and distribution of content? If they are institutions, then are they the producers of all content or mainly the publishers of journalistic content? Or does 'media' refer to the broader institution of content production, mediation and consumption-related practices; is it instead the 'imagined community' of media makers, audiences and users; is it the aggregate collection of all mediations in society? Different approaches within the broader domain of media studies could be seen to depart from one or the other of the aforementioned suggestions. A classic way to divide media studies into subdomains has been according to their focus on different core elements of the 'media':

- *Media industry and production studies* (including media economics and management studies, political economy of media, some sections of media innovation studies) study media content and technology production dynamics;
- *Media content studies* focus on the textual forms and representations that constitute and pervade the media;
- *Media audience studies* investigate the reach of media content and its reception and usage.

Many and generally more interesting sections of media studies research the interdependencies between these core elements. For instance, how the practices of media audiences affect the evolution of media technologies. Yet, semiotics in general, as a set of analytical frameworks, has been a natural partner and a tool for media content studies. This was especially so in the second half of the twentieth century when the broader sub-approach known as media and cultural studies was still forming. To a lesser extent, especially Umberto Eco's interpretative semiotics (and related forms thereof) have influenced audience and reception studies. Yet, since the 1990s the centrality of semiotic frameworks for media studies has been waning as those working in this subject area have become inspired by various alternatives such as (critical) discourse studies, postcolonialism, posthumanism and so on.

In contrast to general semiotics, the tools and concepts of cultural semiotics have been used very little within media studies. The few examples of more systematic and influential efforts to use Lotmanian tools to interpret media dynamics include Tom O'Regan's treatment of Australian national cinema as a system (O'Regan 1996) and John Hartley's development of the 'mediasphere' concept based on Lotman's semiosphere (Hartley 1996; 1999; 2002; 2008). Scholars from Estonia and elsewhere have also made systematic efforts to use cultural semiotics to study the emergence of mobile media or remix or transmedia storytelling practices (see Dusi 2015; Ibrus 2015; 2016; Ibrus and Ojamaa 2014; Irvine 2015; Ojamaa 2015).

Yet, despite the innovative uses of Lotman's theory by a few driving Australian scholars, in the rest of English-language media studies the take-up has been minimal. It has been argued that this is due to Lotman's post-structural works being translated into English too late, and because of his general avoidance of conceptualizing power (because he worked in the Soviet Union) and his focus on artistic texts of the eighteenth and nineteenth centuries (see Blaim 1998; Ibrus and Torop 2015). For all these reasons, his works have not appeared as immediately relevant to contemporary media studies generally interested in power dynamics represented in contemporary quotidian (non-artistic) content. Yet, we argue that extended use of cultural semiotics as a framework could present novel analytic opportunities for media studies as a field.

The central idea is that no communicative act is possible without the semiosphere being there first; the semiosphere conditions the emergence of all texts/communicative acts in culture (see also Chapter 22). But at the same time the semiosphere is inherently heterogeneous; it includes infinite numbers of subsystems and languages, and it is via their circumstantial dialogues and combinations that novel ways to signify and communicate (new) meanings could emerge. This means that change can be inflicted from anywhere: it can be conditioned by the macro-structures of the global semiosphere, but it can also emerge out of micro-level textual dynamics. Or it can be effected somewhere in between, on the (meso-) level of contemporary media industries reorganizing themselves using the ways of autocommunication. But what the semiosphere concept enables us to realize and trace is how change is systemic; it allows us to analyse the interdependencies between these different levels and across both the synchronic and the diachronic axis. Further, as it has become highly salient and visible in the Anthropocene era, communicative action in the semiosphere shapes not only the biosphere but also the geosphere and atmosphere, as well as the newcomer, the 'technosphere' (Bruni 2011, 2015; Herrmann-Pillath 2018). This means that the semiosphere model helps to analyse how culture and digital media systems are interacting and co-evolving with these other 'spheres'. All of the aforementioned suggests that the semiosphere model enables a holistic take, a system analysis of relationships not only between texts but also between meaning-making communities (be they nations, fans of a pop star or the editorial office of a small regional newspaper). In this way the concept of semiosphere allows us to trace meaning/

knowledge evolution trajectories and eventually how texts and other systems in the environment – both organic and non-organic – co-evolve.

What does this mean for media studies? And what kind of media studies? One problem with cultural semiotics, hindering its wider reception and use, is that it has not had a natural, similar enough counterpart in media studies. Perhaps closest to it, in a specific way, is the *media ecology* approach as it, too, focuses on the study of media systems holistically in terms of their internal relationships and their evolutionary dynamics. Yet, the focus of the media ecology approach is on the material aspects of media, their technological forms, while cultural semiotics departs from the ecology of meanings and meaning makers. Cultural semiotics could be understood as offering a unique and complementary perspective on media studies, something it could desperately need in the era of complex cultural systems of global reach in which different meaning systems clash, but also co-evolve and cross-fertilize via dialogues and new combinatory forms.

Yet, it needs to be emphasized that the use of cultural semiotic tools within media and communications studies is currently only a potentiality – it is used only little, mainly by specific research communities in eastern Europe, Australia and South America. Recently, however, the authors of this chapter, together with John Hartley, made a systematic effort to introduce the relevance of the Lotmanian framework to the contemporary digital and media culture research community (Hartley, Ibrus and Ojamaa 2021). In that book, but also elsewhere, we have tried to pursue dialogue between Lotmanian cultural semiotics with various subdomains within media and communications studies. We will discuss these options in the following text.

Media archaeology

A unique feature of semiosphere theory is its ability to highlight how past settings of culture, as well as existing constellations of cultural memory, condition contemporary cultural dynamics. In this area, a natural dialogue partner for cultural semiotics could be media archaeology, a close sibling to media ecology as both have grown out of the medium theory of Marshall McLuhan. Media archaeology could be related to cultural semiotics since it too is interested in how the past shapes the future. Still, the focus of media archaeology is on the materialities and technologies of the media and not on its 'semantic layer'. Media archaeology aims to understand the role of machines in the evolution of digitized culture, while cultural semiotics is known for its holistic approach and for investigating how the various processes of communication, translation and mediation (including those facilitated by digital devices) facilitate the generation of cultural novelties and shape the evolution of culture. Yet, these differences could be seen as useful complementarities.

Media archaeology has multiple roots. One of these is Michel Foucault's *The Archaeology of Knowledge* ([1969] 2002), his critique of 'old' historicism. Foucault's agenda was not to look for objectivist genealogies in historical narratives, but to seek out the dichotomies of continuities and discontinuities in these narratives and identify discursive dispersions within existing diachronic continuities. Foucault acknowledged that, as such, it is in the first place a methodology: it proposes a set of analytical–strategic questions to study 'documents' and invoke historically situated discourses ([1969] 2002: 7; Andersen 2003: 8). In relation to this, Erkki Huhtamo (1995), a media archaeologist, proposed that media archaeology has two main objectives: firstly, the study of the (cyclically recurring) discursive motifs that underlie and guide the development of media forms; secondly, the search for ways in which these discursive formations have been 'printed' on specific media machines and media systems in different historical eras.

Huhtamo (1994) argues that the first of these objectives – the media forms that disappear and reappear in the history of the media that seem to transcend specific historical contexts – are not random, produced accidentally by specific circumstances. Instead, he claims, all of these cases 'contain' certain common elements or cultural motifs that have often been found in previous cultural processes. He suggested that such motifs could be treated as *topoi*, referring to classical rhetoric. These *topoi* can be thought of as formulas that form the 'building blocks' of cultural traditions and provide 'pre-made' moulds for experience. In this context, to indicate a dialogical potential between media archaeology and cultural semiotics: the recurrence of cultural forms refers to the logics of defamiliarization and refamiliarization that Lotman borrowed from Russian Formalists: a form borrowed from culture's past/memory (which is another periphery) can sometimes accrue a potential to communicate novel meanings in new contexts. Yet, the novelty of recurring forms is depleted over time, and these may then fall back into the passively maintained reservoirs of cultural memory. In the digital culture, what has become more salient is that the older forms/motifs are often used as elements in new combinatory forms integrating elements from different contexts. And cultural dynamics is constituted by people de- and recombining elements from and to different textual constellations. Cultural semiotics insists that 'context' matters – to understand the cyclical reappearance of forms and discourses the contexts of their appearances need to be analysed to understand the reasons and outcomes of such borrowings. In other words, the dynamics of recurrence of cultural forms over time is an area of research that could benefit from the dialogue between semiosphere theory and media archaeology.

The second direction of research within media archaeology, that is, the study of how the dominant discursive formations of any age are imprinted on the media machines of that age, has been based on the works of Friedrich Kittler ([1985] 1990; [1986] 1999; [2002] 2009). Kittler studied how materiality, the technology 'underneath', limits each medium uniquely, and how it predisposes a movement towards certain cultural forms and certain discourses (Wellbery 1990: xii). Yet, despite working on media history, media archaeology is not a theory of evolution. Kittler was critical of theories of social and cultural evolution (Winthrop-Young 2000: 411). It can be suggested that in its modern form media archaeology is a rationale for an unlimited set of methodologies that can be gathered under the heading of materialistic 'discourse analysis'. It studies the forms of media technologies and what kinds of discourses and texts these technologies tend to condition in specific periods, and examines the differences between different periods. They are especially interested in the technical mediation process: 'thinking through algorithmic calculus' (Parikka 2013: 9).

The strength of cultural semiotics at the same time lies in the analysis of contingent dynamics on a synchronic axis, dialogic communication and self-communication between and within different cultural subsystems (including dialogues with their memory systems, i.e. texts preserved from previous eras), the accumulation of knowledge and the emergence of new relationships, identities and systems throughout different periods, which places, as a result, the examination of dependencies on diachronic axes (Ibrus and Ojamaa 2020a). Therefore, the archaeological gaze focuses on the materialisms of digital media, their technologies and how cultural forms are 'made by the machines'. Cultural semiotics at the same time is designed to look at the systemic processes before and after this technical calculation: how the technological forms that mediate arise as a result of the communicative mesh between the different subsystems of culture and how the mediated texts are later reused, interpreted and shaped. The complementarity of these approaches to enrich contemporary cultural analysis is evident. Furthermore, this potential is more timely and relevant, with the gradual integration of cultural semiotics with biosemiotics. It is because media archaeology has also been moving in a similar direction – towards further integration with *new materialism* – especially through the works of Jussi Parikka (2015). To work towards such further dialogues is in a way 'programmatic' for cultural semiotics, as in its view any cultural language, including analytic metalanguage, is valuable whenever it reveals new facets of cultural realities, and opens up new perspectives. In the era of the materially/technically conditioned global digital semiosphere, the interdisciplinary dialogues between cultural semiotics and media archaeology would be very much timely (see also Ibrus and Ojamaa 2020a).

Mediatization

We continue with another potentiality – mediatization studies. While this approach has been growing and has become influential in media studies, there has been very little effort to use it in combination with Lotmanian cultural semiotics. Yet, there are significant similarities, also complementarities, as well as somewhat similar ambitions. So, let us also briefly discuss this relationship. Mediatization studies have emerged both as a scholarly approach and as an argument about the changing relationship between media and society in late modernity. The idea is that the media constitutes not just a mirror to the transforming society, but is part of this change, conditioning and shaping it. Media have become part of all relationships that mediate and construct our 'social worlds' (Hepp and Krotz 2013, 2014). Societies and cultures become thoroughly mediated by media institutions and platforms with various agendas, they become 'mediatized'. Mediatization is argued to be one of the ongoing metaprocesses (Krotz 2007), part of the modernization process and parallel to processes such as urbanization, individualization, globalization, commercialization and so on.

When dissecting the media's relationship with cultural semiotics, it must be recognized that mediatization theory in the broadest sense is a sociological one. It is interested in social change, in the development of new institutions and in the shaping of 'social worlds'. It builds on traditions of sociological thought, particularly those of Elias, Bourdieu, Berger and Luckmann, and others. Its aim is to explain how mediation and communication processes are carried out by various institutions or other types of social formation and how these evolve over time (Hjarvard 2013: 4; Hepp and Hasebrink 2018: 30). That is, their purpose is to illuminate what we call the meso-level of social and cultural change.

In comparison, cultural semiotics is derived from the humanities. It interprets textual (or textualized) expressions at different levels of culture – starting from individual texts (micro-scale) and ending with the entirety of planetary culture and its inherent broad flows of textual material (macro-scale). Most importantly, cultural semiotics is explicitly interested in moving between and linking these levels, and analysing their interdependencies.

Yet, despite the differences, there are areas where cultural semiotics and mediatization theory share interests. What helps the dialogue is that mediatization researchers acknowledge that the concept is really just a 'sensitizing' one (Jensen 2013). That is, it is intended to give people a term of reference when approaching 'mediatization' phenomena. It is not intended to strictly guide or limit the analysis, but rather to enable interdisciplinary dialogue.

When it comes to more specific areas of complementarity, the first issue could be 'generativity' – how novel forms emerge in media culture. This is what cultural semiotics is all about: investigating how new forms, meanings and ideas emerge from interactions (translations, combinations) between the subsystems of the semiosphere. In contrast, most mediatization theory seems to have opted for a zero-sum game, that is, studies in this domain tend to discuss the extent to which certain social domains are mediated or not. The evolutionary dynamics of new media forms, new modalities or meanings that tend to be mediated is typically not part of the (more systematic) analysis. Thus, a dialogue between these approaches is in place to understand how 'translation' and 'mediation' interrelate and how change is conditioned in meanings and in forms of mediatization.

A concept within mediatization research that relates more immediately to semiosphere theory is that of 'communicative figurations' (see Hepp and Hasebrink 2018; 2018). This is based on the 'figuration' concept of Norbert Elias ([1970] 1978: 30), which was designed to study structural transformations in societies. Such figurations were seen to consist of individuals and other actors – organizations, institutions and so on – that are in regular contact with each other. What is important is that these were seen to evolve dynamically as resulting from communications within and between different figurations. Contemporary mediatization researchers added to this the fact that such figurations are facilitated not only by communicative *practices* but also by various modally and technologically heterogeneous constellations of *media*, more so now than in the past. Some contemporary figurations can consist entirely of some specific media and their affordances – as, for instance, the communications, communities and businesses that emerge currently on Epic's Fortnite platform or other similar 'metaverse' (Baszucki 2021) types of participatory storytelling platform. Some, however, might use multiple media, for instance, by deploying the techniques of transmedia storytelling and linking narratives on different media into one storyworld. This is, for instance, what Disney has been pursuing with its Marvel Universe; this is also what most of the contemporary news media is doing every day.

The idea of communicatively created, mediated and mediatized communities is not far from how semiosphere theory understands the ways in which culture's subsystems emerge, organize and reorganize in time. In Lotmanian terms, they autocommunicate by exchanging texts, that is, through forms of mediated communication. Such system-constituting texts/stories can be created by professional media makers or journalists (see Bell 1991), but increasingly also by all other kinds of creators: citizen journalists, activists, influencers and everybody else publishing on contemporary social media platforms (Hartley 2020). This relates to how these theoretical approaches – mediatization theory and cultural semiotics – are also similar when it comes to understanding that figurations/subsystems can be either larger or smaller, but society as a whole consists of an infinitely heterogeneous and intertwined mesh of such systems. These similarities are important as their differences could also be understood as complementarities that make furthering the dialogue between them an attractive proposition. While media archaeology focuses on the material affordances of media, mediatization theory does that too (in a different way), but includes empirical knowledge of institutions' communicative goals and practices as well as of people's usage practices and motivations. Further, mediatization research investigates how different kinds of figurations arise and how they become settled, and asks if they enable or disable participation, if they are open or closed and if they restrict or open up communicative freedoms, as well as looking at whom they empower and who gets to shape and control the communication within the figurations. This work could be seen as providing valuable explanatory evidence for cultural-semiotic investigations into the dynamics of contemporary digital culture. In return, as explained earlier, the tools of the cultural semiotic approach enable a more effective analysis of the dynamics that cause media and culture to change. These complementarities matter because both approaches have positioned themselves to make grand statements about societal and cultural change on a planetary level (see Hartley, Ibrus and Ojamaa 2021). Mediatization emphasizes therein the role of media and mediations and cultural semiotics texts and communication. These differences enable rather than hinder productive dialogue.

Studies of transmedia communication

One of the main claims about media systems of the twenty-first century is that they are characterized, even constituted, by the convergence process. If everything is digitized, if all content exists in the form of bits and bytes, their combinations become easier, enabling convergence on the level of media consumption and production practices, technologies, services and industries. Within the media studies domain, this has created a subdomain known as convergence culture studies, part of which is the study of transmedia communication.

Along with the parallel term 'crossmedia' (Davidson 2010; Erdal 2011; Ibrus and Scolari 2012), transmedia communication is most commonly understood as the set of practices and products involving transfers of meaning across media, for example communication of a story using the medium-specific modelling devices and narrative potential of multiple media (Kinder 1991; Jenkins 2003, 2006; Long 2007; Scolari 2009; Evans 2011). Scholars in media studies initially framed transmedia as 'a powerful strategy of survival' (Kinder 1991: 39) and as the 'future of entertainment' (Jenkins 2003). The core operating principles of transmedia are, however, as old as human culture, and Lotman's theory has proved useful for both analysing the structural aspects of transmedial texts and explicating the broader cultural functions of transmedial processes.

In terms of Lotman, what is perceived as a text's frame constitutes a defining dimension determining its compositional integrity, meaning and goal ([1970] 1977: 214). As transmedia stories are composed of subparts that can themselves function as separate wholes (e.g. a movie, a game, a comic strip) and often offer multiple trajectories, it is not always evident where they begin and end (compare Bolin 2010: 74); that is, there is not one frame but a crossroads of boundaries. Such compositional logic explicates most clearly the simultaneously separating and uniting function of semiotic boundaries, which operate as 'the sum of bilingual translatable "filters"' (Lotman [1984] 2005: 208). Transmedial textual space thus appears 'at the same time unequal yet unified, asymmetrical yet uniform. Composed as it is of conflicting structures, it none the less is also marked by individuation' (Lotman [1990] 2001: 131). By generalization, a similar claim can be made about media boundaries. Whereas media are heuristically describable as separate systems, in practice they appear interrelated and exchange mutual influences (compare Mitchell 2005: 257; Clüver 2007; Elleström 2010). Contemporary transmedia practices make these principles of textual and medial dynamics particularly explicit in culture.

The cultural functions of transmediality can in Lotman's framework be described as twofold, pertaining to both innovation and memory. Transmedia texts are based on intersemiotic translations, while the absence of precise semantic equivalents between media has led Lotman to describe the relationship as untranslatability. This, however, does not mean total impossibility of translation, but rather implies significant alterations of meaning, rendering the process simultaneously non-exact and non-trivial with a creative, innovative potential ([1990] 2001: 137). Understanding textual innovation processes as a kind of 'illegitimate' translation of one medium into another bears similarity to both Manovich's understanding of the language of new media (2001) and to Bolter and Grusin's concept of remediation (2000). The act of translation between media is thus culture's mechanism for supporting dynamics – a presumption that allows transmedia to generate innovation not only within global entertainment conglomerates, as referred to earlier, but also within small media markets (Ibrus and Ojamaa 2014; 2018).

While translations function as new texts on the level of communication, they can also be seen as self-reflective repetition from the viewpoint of cultural autocommunication. Thereby, the creative function of transmedia is complemented by its preservation function. Different versions of a source text are memorized as a mental whole, featuring an invariant core present in each instalment. Lotman's observation that 'being spatially limited, a work of art is a model of an infinite universe' ([1970] 1977: 210) allows for a conceptualization that balances the diversity of medium-specific parts with a perception of a whole and allows for dynamics and textual growth, while still preserving its identity (Lotman [1992] 2009: 1). According to this view, the (story)world (cf. Klastrup and Tosca 2004; Long 2007: 60; Evans 2011: 27) appears as a topological invariant of all the subtexts of the transmedia whole. Creation of such a mental whole also allocates transmedial processes to the service of cultural memory and education, especially for cultivating media and cultural literacies. For example, translating canonical texts, say Goethe's *Faust*, which have functioned as the nodal points of cultural identity in contemporary media (and reception practices) so that they can retain their position within active cultural memory is the key means for ensuring cultural continuity and sustainability. Following cultural semiotic thought, thus, we can more broadly locate the phenomenon of transmediality in the context of cultural autocommunication as a mechanism that serves both creative and mnemonic functions. By applying Lotmanian theory, the questions of transmedial textual construction can be complemented by a generalizing account of text's processual existence in culture in diverse media over time (Ojamaa and Torop 2015; Menise 2020).

Cultural analytics

Cultural analytics (Manovich 2020) is an instance of a wider search for methodology in the humanities during the digital era. This comprises attempts at exact and computational methods for traditionally qualitative fields and big data methods for traditionally close reading methods of single texts or small sets of texts. In principle, such searches are not entirely new and Lotman together with other members of the Tartu-Moscow school envisioned the discipline of 'artonics' to deal with cybernetic understanding of the mechanisms of art and creativity (Ignatiev, Nikitin and Reshetnikova 1998; Egorov 1999). However, the scale and speed of the production and consumption of networked cultural content has intensified the need for new methods to facilitate adequate analysis. Digital media platforms not only mediate information about the external world but also have in many cases been seamlessly integrated into the living environment, one of the characteristics of which is connected presence (Licoppe 2004).

Lev Manovich coined the term 'cultural analytics' in order to explore computational and visualization methods for approaching big data sets and flows of global digital culture, potentially in real time (2007). Together with Software Studies Initiative and Cultural Analytics Lab, Manovich has mainly focused on the analysis of large image and video collections, both born-digital (e.g. Instagram content) and digitized (e.g. the complete oeuvre of van Gogh or Dziga Vertov's films). The software developed allows whole collections to be visualized and ordered on the basis of metadata and/or extracted features, so it is possible to zoom in and out between recognizable single images and abstract graphs. The graphs visualize features of the texts that are both visual themselves, such as colour or shape, and non-visual attributes, such as the location of creation or gender of the author. As a result of this inclusive treatment, analysts can answer questions that are unanswerable from a close reading of individual texts. On the one hand, these concern patterns and similarities; on the other, and perhaps more importantly, it is possible to explicate variation and diversity.

In the introduction of one of his first accounts of cultural analytics, Manovich referred to Lotman's *The Structure of the Artistic Text* as a major source of inspiration, pointing out analogous analysability of artworks of different media. This analysability is based on the structural aspects of artistic texts irrespective of their medium. And, indeed, the outputs of cultural analytics case studies can also be analysed as Lotmanian texts, explicating their expression in a sign system, external boundedness and internal structuredness (Lotman [1970] 1977: 51–3). Just as Manovich's method facilitates analysis of, for example, the relationship of a single photo to all photos posted worldwide on Instagram (Manovich 2017), Lotman's isomorphic concepts of text and semiosphere allow for scale-free analysis of single text and the system that constitutes its context (see Hartley, Ibrus and Ojamaa 2021). In other words, it allows for a systematization of what resembles an unpredictable and unboundable flood in which a single photo is constantly positioned and repositioned in a myriad of configurations and series. While textual communication is habitually regarded as taking place between two separate agents, semiosphere as a holistic sphere facilitates the framing of a text as an expression of the self-description of culture, serving the autocommunicative function of organizing information.

As mentioned earlier, most big data analyses, especially in the case of visual content, rely on metadata. Pomerantz has characterized metadata schemas as 'very simple languages' (2015: 30), which we could specify in Lotmanian terms as 'modelling' systems (Lotman [1967] 2011). This is especially pertinent to content metadata systems (e.g. keywords) applied to annotation in cultural databases. This has allowed, for example, a comparative analysis of the ways that content about the same object (a historical event, a person, a location, etc.) is modelled differently in different databases and what that means for the mediation of that object in datafied cultures (see Ibrus and Ojamaa 2018). Furthermore, it is also possible to trace how metadata schemas and algorithms not only model separate objects but also create links between objects and object domains (Ibrus and Ojamaa 2020b). Such analyses allow an explanation that says that, apart from mediating and storing content/data, digital cultural databases and archives exert a strong creative influence on the operation of these databases within culture: they actively link and recombine existing texts and cultural domains, creating in effect new cultural subsystems. Cultural semiotics in combination with media archaeology could be effectively used for the analysis of such algorithmic creativity in contemporary cultures (Ibrus and Ojamaa 2020a).

Finally, the ongoing dialogues between cultural analytics and cultural semiotics (the combination being increasingly linked to the domain of cultural science (see Hartley and Potts 2014)) suggest two new potentials: firstly, to use the concepts and models of cultural semiotics and the techniques of cultural analytics to analyse the global flows of texts and discourses and the dialogues and clashes between cultural communities; and secondly to develop models to help with the forecasting of global cultural dynamics. Increasingly, the datafication of the global digital semiosphere could enable this, with the potential argued (Hartley, Ibrus and Ojamaa 2021) to be similar to weather forecasting – a once-impossible task that is now carried out routinely as a public service to inform wider publics on the dynamics in their environment. We suggest this potential to forecast the cultural climate should motivate further dialogues between cultural semiotics and cultural analytics.

Conclusion

This chapter was in the first place about potentials. The dialogues between cultural semiotics and media studies have generally been peripheral, both in the literal and in the metaphoric sense. There is more cross-fertilization in non-English-speaking countries (South America, eastern and southern Europe, China), but not so much in the English-language core of the academic semiosphere. And there are more combined uses for studying specific (related) regional cultures or topics such as cross-cultural communication or transmediality. But as Nico Carpentier commented (2015), perhaps had the Iron Curtain not hindered the dissemination of Lotman's works, the Western academic semiosphere, including media studies, could have evolved quite differently. Yet, our proposition is that the digital era with its salient complexities – multimodal textualities, remixes and transmedia communications, complex flows of culture globally, the rapid evolution of media and meaning ecosystems – make Lotman's work relevant again.

References

Andersen, P. B. 2003. 'Acting Machines', in G. Liestøl, A. Morrison and T. Rasmussen (eds), *Digital Media Revisited: Theoretical and Conceptual Innovation in Digital Domains*, 183–213, Cambridge, MA and London: MIT Press.

Baszucki, D. 2021. 'The Metaverse is Coming', *The WIRED World 2021*, 2 January, available online: https://www.wired.co.uk/article/metaverse (accessed 9 January 2021).

Bell, A. 1991. *The Language of News Media*, Malden, MA and Oxford: Wiley-Blackwell.

Blaim, A. 1998. 'Lotman in the West: An Ambiguous Complaint', in J. Andrew and R. Reid (eds), *Neo-formalist Papers: Contributions to the Silver Jubilee Conference to Mark 25 years of the Neo-Formalist Circle*, 329–37, Amsterdam: Rodopi.

Bolin, G. 2010. 'Digitization, Multiplatform Texts, and Audience Reception', *Popular Communication* 8: 72–83.

Bolter, J. D. and Richard, G. 2000. *Remediation: Understanding New Media*, Cambridge, MA, and London: MIT Press.

Bruni, L. E. 2011. 'Cognitive Sustainability in the Age of Digital Culture', *tripleC* 9 (2): 476–82.

Bruni, L. E. 2015. 'Sustainability, Cognitive Technologies and the Digital Semiosphere', *International Journal of Cultural Studies* 18 (1): 103–17.

Carpentier, N. 2015. 'Recognizing Difference in Academia: The Sqridge as a Metaphor for Agonistic Interchange', in L. Kramp, N. Carpentier, A. Hepp et al. (eds), *Journalism, Representation and the Public Sphere*, 211–26, Bremen: edition lumière.

Clüver, C. 2007. 'Intermediality and Interarts Studies', in J. Arvidson, M. Askander, J. Bruhn and H. Führer (eds), *Changing Borders: Contemporary Positions in Intermediality*, 19–37, Lund: Intermedia Studies Press.

Davidson, D. 2010. *Cross-media Communications: An Introduction to the Art of Creating Integrated Media Experiences*, Pittsburgh, PA: ETC Press.

Dusi, N. M. 2015. '*Don Quixote*, Intermediality and Remix: Translational Shifts in the Semiotics of Culture', *International Journal of Cultural Studies* 18 (1): 119–34.

Egorov, B. 1999. 'Iskusstvennyi intellekt i artonika', in B. Egorov, *Zhizn' i tvorchestvo Iu. M. Lotmana*, 205–27, Moscow: Novoe literaturnoe obozrenie.

Elias, N. [1970] 1978. *What Is Sociology?* London: Hutchinson.

Elleström, L. (ed.) 2010. *Media Borders, Multimodality and Intermediality*, London and New York: Palgrave MacMillan.

Erdal, I. J. 2011. 'Coming to Terms with Convergence Journalism: Cross-media as a Theoretical and Analytical Concept', *Convergence* 17 (2): 213–23.

Evans, E. J. 2011. *Transmedia Television: Audiences, New Media and Daily Life*, New York: Routledge.

Foucault, M. [1969] 2002. *The Archaeology of Knowledge*, trans. A. M. Sheridan Smith, London and New York: Routledge.

Hartley, J. 1996. *Popular Reality: Journalism, Modernity, Popular Culture*, London: Arnold.

Hartley, J. 1999. *Uses of Television*, London: Routledge.

Hartley, J. 2002. *Communication, Cultural and Media Studies: The Key Concepts*, London and New York: Routledge.

Hartley, J. 2008. *Television Truths: Forms of Knowledge in Popular Culture*, Malden, MA and Oxford: Wiley-Blackwell.

Hartley, J. 2020. *How We Use Stories and Why That Matters: Cultural Science in Action*, New York: Bloomsbury.

Hartley, J. and Potts, J. 2014. *Cultural Science: A Natural History of Stories, Demes, Knowledge and Innovation*, London: Bloomsbury.

Hartley, J., Ibrus, I. and Ojamaa, M. 2021. *On the Digital Semiosphere: Culture, Media and Science for the Anthropocene*, New York: Bloomsbury.

Hepp, A. and Hasebrink, U. 2018. 'Researching Transforming Communications in Times of Deep Mediatization: A Figurational Approach', in A. Hepp, A. Breiter and U. Hasebrink (eds), *Communicative Figurations: Transforming Communications in Times of Deep Mediatization*, 15–48, Cham: Palgrave Macmillan.

Hepp, A. and Krotz, F. 2014. *Mediatized Worlds: Culture and Society in a Media Age*, London: Palgrave Macmillan.

Herrmann-Pillath, C. 2018. 'The Case for a New Discipline: Technosphere Science', *Ecological Economics* 149: 212–25.

Hjarvard, S. 2013. *The Mediatization of Culture and Society*, Oxon: Routledge.

Huhtamo, E. 1994. 'From Kaleidoscomaniac to Cybernerd: Towards an Archaeology of the Media', in M. Tarkka (ed.), *ISEA '94 Catalogue*, 130–5, Helsinki: The University of Art and Design.

Huhtamo, E. 1995. 'Resurrecting the Technological Past: An Introduction to the Archaeology of Media Art', *InterCommunication* 14, available online: https://gebseng.com/media_archeolog y/reading_materials/Erkki_Huhtamo-Resurrecting_the_Technological_Past.pdf (accessed 9 January 2021).

Ibrus, I. 2015. 'Histories of Ubiquitous Web Standardization', in A. Bechmann and S. Lomborg (eds), *The Ubiquitous Internet: User and Industry Perspectives*, 97–114, London and New York: Routledge.

Ibrus, I. 2016. 'Web and Mobile Convergence: Continuities Created by Re-enactment of Selected Histories', *Convergence: The International Journal of Research into New Media Technologies* 22 (2): 147–61.

Ibrus, I. and Scolari, C. A. (eds) 2012. *Crossmedia Innovations: Texts, Markets, Institutions*, Frankfurt etc.: Peter Lang.

Ibrus, I. and Ojamaa, M. 2014. 'What Is the Cultural Function and Value of European Transmedia Independents?', *International Journal of Communication* 8: 2283–300.

Ibrus, I. and Ojamaa, M. 2018. 'Estonia: Transmedial Disruptions and Converging Conceptualizations in a Small Country', in M. Freeman and W. Proctor (eds), *Global Convergence Cultures: Transmedia Earth*, 83–97, London and New York: Routledge.

Ibrus, I. and Ojamaa, M. 2020a. 'The Creativity of Digital (Audiovisual) Archives: A Dialogue Between Media Archaeology and Cultural Semiotics', *Theory, Culture & Society* 37 (3): 49–70.

Ibrus, I. and Ojamaa, M. 2020b. 'Audiovisuaalne kultuur, metaandmed ja lingianalüüs [Audiovisual Culture, Metadata and Link Analysis]', in A. Masso, A. Siibak and K. Tiidenberg (eds), *Kuidas mõista andmestunud maailma? Metodoloogiline teejuht [How to Understand Datafied World? Methodological Guide]*, 531–68, Tallinn: Tallinna Ülikooli Kirjastus.

Ibrus, I. and Torop, P. 2015. 'Remembering and Reinventing Juri Lotman for the Digital Age', *International Journal of Cultural Studies* 18 (1): 3–9.

Ignatiev, N. B., Nikitin, A. V. and Reshetnikova, N. N. 1998. 'Komp'iuternye tekhnologii v iskusstve i sredstvakh massovoi informatsii – novoe napravlenie v obrazovanii i nauke', *EVA '98*, 1–8, Moscow: s.n, available online: https://studylib.ru/doc/4061198/komp._yuternye-teh nologii-v-iskusstve-i-sredstvah-massovoj (accessed 8 January 2021).

Irvine, M. 2015. 'Remix and the Dialogic Engine of Culture: A Model for Generative Combinatoriality', in E. Navas, O. Gallagher and X. Burrough (eds), *The Routledge Companion to Remix Studies*, 39–66, London and New York: Routledge.

Jenkins, H. 2003. 'Transmedia Storytelling', *MIT Technology Review*, 15 January, available online https://www.technologyreview.com/2003/01/15/234540/transmedia-storytelling/ (accessed 8 January 2021).

Jenkins, H. 2006. *Convergence Culture: Where Old and New Media Collide*, New York and London: New York University Press.

Jensen, K. B. 2013. 'Definitive and Sensitizing Conceptualizations of Mediatization', *Communication Theory* 23 (3): 203–22.

Kinder, M. 1991. *Playing with Power in Movies, Television and Video Games: From Muppet Babies to Teenage Mutant Ninja Turtles*, Berkeley and Los Angeles: University of California Press.

Kittler, F. A. [1985] 1990. *Discourse Networks 1800/1900*, trans. M. Metteer, with C. Cullens, Stanford, CA: Stanford University Press.

Kittler, F. A. [1986] 1999. *Gramophone, Film, Typewriter*, trans. G. Winthrop-Young and M. Wutz, Stanford, CA: Stanford University Press.

Kittler, F. A. [2002] 2009. *Optical Media*, trans. A. Enns, Cambridge: Polity Press.

Klastrup, L. and Tosca, S. 2004. *Transmedial Worlds – Rethinking Cyber-world Design*, available online: www.itu.dk/people/klastrup/klastruptosca_transworlds.pdf (accessed 8 January 2021).

Krotz, F. 2007. 'The Meta-Process of Mediatization as a Conceptual Frame', *Global Media and Communication* 3 (3): 256–60.

Krotz, F. and Hepp, A. 2013. 'A Concretization of Mediatization: How Mediatization Works and Why 'Mediatized Worlds' are a Helpful Concept for Empirical Mediatization Research', *Empedocles: European Journal for the Philosophy of Communication* 3 (2): 119–34.

Licoppe, C. 2004. '"Connected" Presence: The Emergence of a New Repertoire for Managing Social Relationships in a Changing Communication Technospace', *Environment and Planning D: Society and Space* 22 (1): 135–56.

Long, G. A. 2007. 'Transmedia Storytelling: Business, Aesthetics and Production at the Jim Henson Company', Master's dissertation, Cambridge, MA: Massachusetts Institute of Technology, available online: https://dspace.mit.edu/handle/1721.1/39152 (accessed 8 January 2021).

Lotman, J. [1967] 2011. 'The Place of Art among Other Modelling Systems', trans. T. Pern, *Sign Systems Studies* 39 (2/4): 249–70.

Lotman, J. [1970] 1977. *The Structure of the Artistic Text*, trans. R. Vroon, Ann Arbor: University of Michigan, Department of Slavic Languages and Literatures.

Lotman, Yu. [1984] 2005. 'On the Semiosphere', trans. W. Clark, *Sign Systems Studies* 33 (1): 205–29.

Lotman, Yu. M. [1990] 2001. *Universe of the Mind: A Semiotic Theory of Culture*, trans. A. Shukman, London and New York: I.B. Tauris.

Lotman, J. [1992] 2009. *Culture and Explosion*, trans. W. Clark, ed. M. Grishakova, Berlin, New York: Mouton de Gruyter.

Manovich, L. 2001. *The Language of New Media*, Cambridge, MA, and London: MIT Press.

Manovich, L. 2007. 'Cultural Analytics: Visualizing Cultural Patterns in the Era of "More Media"', available online: http://manovich.net/content/04-projects/063-cultural-analytics-visualizing-cultural-patterns/60_article_2009.pdf (accessed 8 January 2021).

Manovich, L. 2017. 'Instagram and Contemporary Image', available online http://manovich.net/index.php/projects/instagram-and-contemporary-image (accessed 8 January 2021).

Manovich, L. 2020. *Cultural Analytics*, Cambridge, MA: The MIT Press.

Menise, T. 2020. 'Fairy Tales in Transmedia Communication: Fanfiction', Doctoral dissertation, Tartu: Tartu University Press, available online: https://dspace.ut.ee/handle/10062/66923 (accessed 8 January 2021).

Mitchell, W. J. T. 2005. 'There Are No Visual Media', *Journal of Visual Culture* 4: 257–66.

Ojamaa, M. 2015. *The Transmedial Aspect of Cultural Autocommunication*, Tartu: University of Tartu Press, available online: https://dspace.ut.ee/handle/10062/45985 (accessed 8 January 2021).

Ojamaa, M. and Torop, P. 2015. 'Transmediality of Cultural Autocommunication', *International Journal of Cultural Studies* 18 (1): 61–78.

O'Regan, T. 1996. *Australian National Cinema*, London: Routledge.

Parikka, J. 2013. 'Archival Media Theory: An Introduction to Wolfgang Ernst's Media Archaeology', in W. Ernst, *Digital Memory and the Archive*, ed. J. Parikka, 1–22, Minneapolis and London: University of Minnesota Press.

Parikka, J. 2015. *A Geology of Media*, Minneapolis: University of Minnesota Press.

Pomerantz, J. 2015. *Metadata*, Cambridge, MA: The MIT Press.

Scolari, C. A. 2009. 'Transmedia Storytelling: Implicit Consumers, Narrative Worlds, and Branding in Contemporary Media Production', *International Journal of Communication* 3: 586–606.

Wellbery, D. E. 1990. 'Foreword', in F. Kittler, *Discourse Networks 1800/1900*, vii–xxxiii, Stanford, CA: Stanford University Press.

Winthrop-Young, G. 2000. 'Silicon Sociology, or, Two Kings on Hegel's Throne? Kittler, Luhmann, and Posthuman Merger of German Media Theory', *The Yale Journal of Criticism* 13 (2): 391–420.

CHAPTER 33
LOTMAN AND SOCIAL MEDIA STUDIES
Mari-Liis Madisson and Andreas Ventsel

Introduction

There are two aspects that should be emphasized when speaking of Juri Lotman's ideas in the context of social media studies. Firstly, his academically active period was a time when social media as we know it today was non-existent. The roots of social media do reach back into the 1970s, but they became an everyday phenomenon by the mid-2000s, when such popular platforms as Facebook (2004), Reddit (2005) and Twitter (2006) were launched. The real triumph of social media, however, came in the 2010s when it found mass usage with the adoption of smartphones. In 2020, the active social media population grew to 4.12 billion; Facebook, the most popular platform, has 2.7 billion active users (Statista 2020).

The other aspect is connected with the material Lotman studied. His main focus of interest was in art, literature and other forms of communication that are usually called 'high culture'. Social media, however, tends to be a hybrid information and communication environment serving as a meeting place for private users, public institutions, a wide range of service providers and mass media; the users' verbal and (audio)visual self-expression mixes with content of ephemeral authorship created in the spirit of participatory culture, official statements and commercial content. With a few exceptions (the poetics of everyday behaviour, semiotics of fear, etc.), Lotman's examples did not include phenomena of everyday culture that is of greatest interest to internet studies, including social media studies.

Applying Lotmanian semiotics to today's cultural phenomena is made rewarding by the specificity of semiotics: it focuses on constructing models and presenting abstracted communication types that can be applied to the study of many-faceted material. This chapter observes how Lotman's ideas could help interpret changes that have taken place in meaning-making processes due to the digitization of communication and the transfer to social media. We open up certain perspectives from which the cultural semiotic approach could be practised.

Defining social media

Social media are interactive computer-mediated technologies that enable the creation or communication of content via online communities and networks (Obar and Wildman 2015). According to Andreas Kaplan and Michael Haenlain's (2010: 61) famous definition, social media can be understood as Interactive Web 2.0 internet-based applications that make it possible to create and spread user-generated content (UGC). This definition emphasizes the possibilities the so-called ordinary users have in expressing their ideas and feelings on social media, sharing these with other members of the network and modifying the texts they have created as well as other communication traces.

The umbrella concept of social media covers blogs, Wikipedia-type collaborative projects and massively multiplayer online role-playing games (Kaplan and Haenlain 2010: 62). In the discourse of internet studies, Facebook, Twitter, Instagram and other such platforms typically considered as social media are classified as a subgenre called social network sites (SNSs). The SNSs enable users to (1) construct public or semi-public platform-specific profiles, (2) present a list of other users with whom they are connected (e.g. Facebook friends) and (3) view their list of connections and those made by others within the system (boyd and Ellison 2007). As SNSs uncontestedly form the most used part of social media, it is mainly these we refer to when speaking of social media in this text.

Without wishing to indulge in media determinism, we nevertheless have to admit that the mass use of smart devices and social media has left a remarkable trace both on people's private interactions as well as public communication; the cultural ley lines of the twenty-first century are clearly closely connected with this. The advancement of social media has created an unprecedented semiotic situation – in screen-mediated messages the interpreters as a rule come into contact not with things/ entities themselves, but their signs. Status updates, photos, videos, text excerpts, etc., signify things, people and various events. If in case of mass media it was customary to meet representations of events and persons perceived as socially significant that were selected by journalists and editors, in the time of social media every user of a smart device can transmit his or her thoughts and experiences both as a text and audiovisually. From the point of view of semiotics, media representations are never mere re-recordings of reality, for behind them are users' communicative choices that they may yet not need to be aware of, communication conventions, codes, genres, etc. It is also important to notice that SNSs are not neutral communication sites, but meaning-making and communication opportunities offered by platforms, and the restrictions imposed there influence the content circulating. Internet studies have adopted the notion of social media affordances to designate such platform-related possibilities and restrictions.

Social media affordances do not rigidly determine users' behaviour, but they do configure the communication environment in a way that shapes user engagement (boyd 2011: 39). Social media affordances make certain types of behaviour and usage more convenient for the users, and therefore more likely to occur than others (Tiidenberg 2017: 21). According to danah boyd (2011: 46), there are four basic affordances of SNSs: persistence, that is, automatic archiving and recording of expressions; replicability, that is, duplicability of digital content; scalability, that is, potential visibility of content for networked audience; and searchability, that is, accessibility of content through search.

The intermingling of social media (as well as, more broadly, technosphere) affordances with the sphere of our private and communal lives has introduced specific ways of representing emotions, ideas and beliefs; in addition, today's hyperaccessiblity of representations in real time has changed the geography and the cultural production of human knowledge. This leads us to the concept of digital semiosphere that facilitates the conceptualization of the communication and meaning-making tendencies that have emerged around social media affordances, as well as their broader cultural functions.

The digital semiosphere

'Semiosphere', the central concept in Lotman's later work (see Chapter 22), has found most application in analysing phenomena accompanying the digital revolution. The digital sphere, which also embraces social media, is characterized by networks, mutual influences, interactivity. In social theory of the past few decades, the non-linear network logic based on the interdependence of elements that differs from the horizontal logic of competition as well as the hierarchical logic of bureaucracy is considered a central approach in order to interpret social relations in the increasingly more globalizing world (Elias 1978; Latour 2005).

The concept of the *semiosphere* offers a new perspective on understanding the relationality and interdependence of the network-based world. Semiosphere points to a conditional space of meaning-making, embracing the coexistence of culture's sign systems, mutual connections between semiotic languages and multidimensionality. Side by side with the cultural semiosphere we need to observe the technical side of the digital semiosphere, the technosphere. Considering their interaction, it has to be noticed that 'such technological integration not only alters and introduces innovations in the interactive and representational modes of networked media, perhaps inducing changes in our cognitive functions, but also conditions the global cultural dynamics by potentially organizing, funnelling, tagging and "semantically" predigesting knowledge through the "intelligent" digital technosphere' (Bruni 2015: 103). Hartley et al. outline that 'within the digital environment several traditional cultural categories are completely reorganized owing to technological affordances. A central example is the eclipse of the boundaries between words, images and other modalities as they have been translated into bits and bytes and organised in networks, resulting in the rise of multimodal textualities and a general diversification of creative, distributive, curatorial and receptive practices' (Hartley, Ibrus, and Ojamaa 2021: 119). Thus, in summary one can claim that the cultural semiosphere and the technological design of the digital semiosphere mutually influence one another (see also Chapter 32).

At the same time, we can ask if an analogy between the semiosphere and the technosphere presented at such a level of abstraction will take us any closer to a semiotic analysis of the cultural changes accompanying the digital revolution. We should turn to other characteristics of Lotman's semiosphere that make it possible to refine such a framework for further analysis. Therefore, the focus of this chapter first and foremost lies in studying text-level meaning-making in social media communication.

The social media semiosphere

According to Peeter Torop, the semiosphere is a useful analytical tool because, from a methodological point of view, it can be studied as a separate whole, yet each semiotic whole in itself is also part of a larger whole, a more general semiosphere. A continuous dialogue occurs between the part and the whole, as cultural and textual differences develop in the course of a dialogue within and between systems (Torop 2003: 335–6).

The concept of the semiosphere has been used to interpret the media sphere by Hartley and Ibrus, who employ the concept primarily in the framework of evolutionary economic theory and in theoretical conceptualization of the innovation dynamics of new media. Thus, Hartley (1996; 2008; cf. also Hartley and McKee 2000) views mediasphere as a subpart of the semiosphere, which contains both fictional as well as actual outputs circulating on mass media.

Social media can be treated as a subsection of a general mediasphere in which a dominant public online sphere (e.g. newspaper discussion platforms) and smaller online communication spaces, with their own specific formation dynamics (e.g. closed discussion groups on Facebook), can be differentiated. In our studies of extreme-right social media communication (Madisson and Ventsel 2016a; 2016b; 2018; Madisson 2016a), we have expanded Roger Griffin's (2003) concept of the groupuscule, including the concept of the semiosphere. Groupuscular communication is characterized by such features as non-hierarchical or weblike structure, internal diversity, lack of a centre or a central axis of orientation, fluidity and temporality. The main problem here appears to be a certain reductionism: groupuscular communication is treated as analogous to the abstract textuality appearing in the hypermedia environment.

The main characteristics of semiosphere such as *boundary*, *translation*, and *core and periphery* (Lotman [1984] 2005: 208–9) offer analytical means for explaining how particular ways of interpretation and information creation are fashioned on social media. As soon as an interpreter intervenes in an ideal hypertextual system that lacks a centre and an internal hierarchy, ideas and values constituting his or her interpretation horizon start to organize the unravelling of information and set down concrete reading paths (see also Kress 2005: 4; Landow 2006: 221; Ryan 2006: 146). If we conceptualize social media first and foremost as a space for meaning-making, units communicating with one another in the internet environment can be viewed as particular semiotic wholes: a specific post, a popular discussion topic or the whole network that brings together different information nodes (Madisson and Ventsel 2018). Such a semiotic unit is a meaningful whole as well as an active generator of meaning. At the same time, on the metalevel of analysis the concept of the semiosphere will help map the temporary formation of the boundaries of semiotic units that are, for example, pointed to by automatic archiving and recording of digital traces (clicks, conversations, bits, metadata, etc.) and the emergence of communication of hierarchies.

The hierarchical nature of social media meaning-making

A concrete semiotic whole can simultaneously belong to very different units on different levels of the semiosphere, and, accordingly, it can be a part of other wholes while still retaining its unity and not being identical with itself in this connection (Lotman [1989] 1997: 12). Thus, one and the same textual excerpt that is directed into different contexts of occurrence by hyperlinks, will have different functions in the social media semiosphere. When analysing the web communication of the extreme right we have demonstrated that in mainstream media the extreme-right message mainly appears as a marginal voice that nevertheless points to democratic freedom of speech, while in an extremist right-wing semiosphere it can occur as a confirmation that 'our' (i.e. extreme right-wing) voices are represented and accepted in the mainstream media. In this case, the text's function is a positive affirmation of the adherents of the extreme right. Often such texts are accompanied by added comments that translate the texts into the language of their semiosphere and direct the interpretation paths there (Madisson and Ventsel 2016a; 2018). In the same way, Facebook selfies (Leone 2018), 'the "filters" and other conventions in use in Instagram photos or the puns in Twitter presume a wider semiotic context in order to be meaningful' (Hartley, Ibrus and Ojamaa 2021: 70).

Meaning-making (creating a meaningful whole) is based on a translation process that creates a boundary between semiotic units. During this process, external texts become modified proceeding from an internal language, and the semiotic 'self' is separated from the semiotic 'Other' (Lotman [1984] 2005: 208). Such a semiotic translation mechanism is understood as establishing a certain equivalence and correspondence rules between different semiotic systems (Lotman [1970] 2000: 451). Thus, the concept of the semiosphere and translation types helps explain why texts of a certain type will cause a stronger response in certain audiences (social media communities), while others do not (see open and closed communication in the following text).

Although at an abstract level social media communication can be characterized by the absence of a central organizing axis, in real communication it is more justified to discuss it in the light of a main characteristic of the semiosphere – the core–periphery interaction. In all semiotic wholes cores emerge that are usually more rigidly organized in comparison with more marginal semiotic units. A way for such cores to appear is the emergence of opinion leaders, whose posts are visited most and whose ideas are referenced most often. Such organizing cores of meaning-making can be the traditional opinion leaders (journalists, politicians, scientists, experts), accounts of various enterprises or institutions, discussion groups mentioned earlier, or social media influencers, for example YouTubers, Instagram celebrities, microbloggers on Twitter and so on. There seem to be several reasons for the emergence of such authorities: for instance, active and continuous posting, the existence of an 'ideological backbone' or continuity in their main opinions, the attractiveness of the posts (e.g. reliable referencing, balanced verbal and visual content, wit, consistency of style) and so on (Madisson and Ventsel 2018; 2020). Such authoritative social media mediators concentrate information connected with certain topics and often share directions as to how to interpret the information (Ventsel and Madisson 2020).

Self-model

In addition to particular opinion leaders, a system of meta-descriptions used to describe the core itself and the periphery emerges in the core of the semiosphere, whose main function is the shaping of a meaningful whole (Lotman [1984] 2005: 213). Such core structures play an important role in social media communication in which certain topics change into umbrella topics uniting several semiotic units in the course of communication, and start to determine the meaning-making by the semiotic units (e.g. the people posting on a platform) belonging to it. Such a process can be described by Lotman's concept of self-description. According to Lotman, self-description usually gives rise to dominants, on the basis of which a unified model is constructed that has to serve as the code of self-perception and -decoding of the semiotic whole (Lotman [1971] 2000: 418). It is important to note that a self-model belongs to a different level than texts that circulate in the so-called ordinary communication and which are deciphered by that self-model (Lotman and Uspensky [1971] 1978: 227). At the same time, the need for self-description that is connected to the necessity of creating a value-and-structure-based whole out of oneself at a certain stage, intensely influences culture as a phenomenon described (Lotman and Uspenskij [1977] 1984: 3). Therefore, self-description can be differentiated from culture as the object level only heuristically, for in reality the two conditions mutually affect each other.

Such communication organized by a self-model can often be met in social media discussion groups that centre on a particular topic (e.g. discussion groups linked with global warming) or content related to a general world view (e.g. the topic of feminism). At the same time, the self-model can be used to describe multimodal text creation, for instance it can be employed in analysing selfies as a mode of visual self-representation. Selfies are photos made with smartphones or webcams that people make of themselves and share on social media (Tiidenberg 2015: 2). Lotman differentiates between three types of self-models. The first type seeks maximal similarity with existing culture (Lotman [1971] 2000: 420). Under this category, we can place selfies that transmit to the subjects themselves, as well as to their social media audience, the subject's *status quo* or what they are *really* like, what they are doing *in real life*, with whom they are *really* spending their time and so on. Selfies that can be described with the help of such a self-model are not meant to be framed or saved or retain a certain place/emotion in memory, but to report on the immediate status of the moment of their maker (Fausing 2014). The selfies of many public figures (e.g. politicians and pop stars) help evoke their humanized everyday side; the audience achieves a new type of closeness with them as it is felt that characters whose images are calculated otherwise are as if offering up bits of their immediate experience (Marwick and boyd 2010: 5).

Lotman's second self-model differs from ordinary cultural practice and is designed to change those practices (Lotman [1971] 2000: 420). The function of selfies categorized under this type is first and foremost to mediate to the subject's social media audience the subject's ideal self-image; they contain the subject's more or less conscious identity options. Selfies that present people in the way they would like to be – beautiful, fashionable, active and happy – are often selected for posting on social media. Often photoshopping and several filters are used on such selfies for the purpose of visually designing one's ideal self. As selfies have an important role in creating and maintaining close relationships and communal ties (Tiideberg 2015: 4), selfies representing the self-model of the second type reflect whom we would like to show to our network of social media friends. The self-description choices one opts for, however, always have a certain reverse influence on our general self-perception and our making of behavioural choices.

Lotman's third type of self-model exists as an ideal cultural self-consciousness but is separate from culture and not oriented towards it (Lotman [1971] 2000: 420). Such a self-model is born out of a certain reaction to the premise that selfies are self-revealingly authentic, as it were. In the case of selfies, the (self-)irony, play with identities, expanding and defamiliarizing identities often emerge as an important component (Fausing 2014). Here belong, for example, the role-play selfies that 'embody' the subject as someone else via stereotypical identity markers, or give them a very context specific identity. In contrast to second type of the self-model, such selfies do not present an ideal self that is aspired to in the real world, but a possible world that is not being striven for as an end in itself.

Autocommunicative processes on social media

In addition to the aforementioned conceptions of Lotman's treatment of cultural autocommunication or self-organizing, communication with oneself has turned out to be fruitful in conceptualizing cultural phenomena relating to social media. In order to study autocommunication it is worth observing a large community as the sender/receiver of the message because individual autocommunicative processes tend to be secondary (Lotman [1973] 2000: 425–6). As particular textual traces are left on social media relating to the development of communities and the communication within them, including autocommunication, observing and analysing social media communities offers innovative possibilities for the study of collective autocommunication. This is particularly noticeable in oral or folkloric cultures (Lotman [1973] 2000: 426) and the processes of text creation therein, which are dominated by homomorphic equalizing and cyclic repetition of textual invariants or plot kernels (Lotman and Mints 1981: 39). From the perspective of studying autocommunciative processes, social media is also heuristically significant because its text creation is in many ways similar to that of oral or folkloric cultures.

A new era of orality has often been mentioned in connection with the text creation practices of participatory culture (e.g. internet memes, textual collages or creating and sharing remixed videos) that have emerged around the affordances of the technosphere and social media, particularly multimodal means of expression and copying and sharing functions (Cobley 2001: 208; Papacharissi 2015; Ventsel 2017). Digital orality is similar to folkloric culture in the constant recycling of (chunks of) texts. New text combinations are constructed on the basis of content and expression patterns with which the interpretative community is already familiar. Such a tendency is vividly expressed in meme culture, where the same images (e.g. Distracted Boyfriend, Sad Keanu and Success Kid) are constantly being given new messages. At the same time, parallels can be found between the interpersonal storytelling conditions and social media interactivity in which text creators can potentially achieve real-time contact with their audiences (Howard 2008). On the other hand, the orality emerging on social media is different in principle from that of preliterate cultures because it also contains the communication practices of mass and broadcasting culture (Papacharissi 2015: 1098–9). Social media texts can travel in an atomistic, rather unchanging shape far from the context of their creation and potentially reach a global audience (Castells 2009: 54–5). Such mass sharing of text (pieces) between users on social media, or when they go viral, is treated as a mechanism of *digital word of mouth*, which differs from traditional word-of-mouth mechanisms in its speed and often also in its low adaptivity.

Creative and mnemonic autocommunication on social media

Due to affordances that allow for interaction and shared experience of texts, social media has developed into one of the main sites of transmedia storytelling (i.e. a strategy of evoking story experience across multiple platforms and media) side by side with television and video games (see Ojamaa 2015: 16). Social media processes of transmedia storytelling offer extremely versatile material for study as these processes may embrace fictional worlds created by users or expanded by them (Menise 2019b), journalistic forwarding of messages (Borges and Gambarato 2019) or even misinformation campaigns (Madisson and Ventsel 2020: 98–9).

Using the example of thematically related sets of texts on YouTube, Torop (2013: 51) has noted that as concerns the participatory culture of social media, focusing on the abstract mental whole that arises around the texts is more important than detecting the relationships between originals and interpretations. According to a minimalist definition, transmediality refers to 'the mental aspect of the text's existence in culture' (Torop 2011: 78). According to Torop and Ojamaa (2015: 63), it is worth studying the repetition of textual invariants because it is characteristic of participatory culture and the mental whole emerging around these as the culture's autocommunication. In a Lotmanian spirit, they emphasize both the mnemonic and creative aspects of the autocommunication. On the one hand, when studying text sets that cover different media and platforms, it is important to see that in repeating an invariant in different varying sign systems the central role is adopted by the acquiring and fixing of the emerging links (Ojamaa and Torop 2015: 62). At the same time, the role of such repetition in generating new meanings should not be left unnoticed as these meanings include translations into new media and contexts, while the translations are not trivial but embrace semiotic choices and the emergence of new meaning (Ojamaa and Torop 2015: 62–3).

Tatjana Menise (2019a; 2020) has demonstrated the potential of creative autocommunication of meaning-making aspects of participatory media. She used the ficbook.net platform to observe case studies focusing on the meaning-making aspects of fan fiction centred on the motif of the Snow Queen. Her work exemplifies how the innovatory quality of fan fiction, built on the repetition of a largely similar plot core, derives from the creation of connections with novel cultural background systems and topical discourses. As regards the creative aspect of fan stories on participatory media platforms, Menise also outlines their fulfilment of an emotive function (Menise 2019b: 292), as the stories retold involve the receivers' reactions to the invariant tale.

From among theoretical frameworks offered by Lotman, the code text has also found relatively extensive application in analysing social media texts and participatory culture. According to Lotman, a code text is a textual system that originates from the collective memory of a particular culture. It is a kind of interlink that, instead of being an abstract collection of rules for constructing a text, is a textual system with a rigid syntactic order (Lotman [1981] 1988: 35–6). Several authors have been discussing invariant text patterns repeated on social media as code texts, for instance the invariant elements repeated in restaged videos on YouTube or TikTok (Hartley, Ibrus and Ojamaa 2021: 169) or the appearance of the Disney Princess motif in user-generated content, for example memes (Menise 2019b) have been described as code texts. In addition, invariant connection frameworks of conspiracy theories repeated in social media communities have been treated as code texts (Kimminich 2016; Madisson 2016b). We have demonstrated the central role of the New World Order (NWO) conspiracy theory code texts in the social media communication of the extreme right and explained the logic of self-descriptions based on this (Madisson and Ventsel 2016a).

The enclosing autocommunication of social media echo chambers

Several authors have pointed out the enclosing communication communities, or echo chambers, emerging on social media as a problematic issue. These bring together conversation partners and information sources with very similar views; long-term participation in such a homogeneous sphere of communication is often connected with shared standpoints and the polarization of views (see Benkler et al. 2018; Singer and Brooking 2018; Warner and Neville-Shepard 2014). Proceeding from the framework of Lotman's cultural semiotics and observations on extreme-right social media (primarily blogs), we have detected three main meaning-making dominants that, when in co-existence, cause autocommunicative meaning-making to lose its innovative potential and start to produce polarized connections tangled in stereotypes (Madisson 2016a; Madisson and Ventsel 2016b).

Although the notion of echo chambers is still widely used in works focusing on radicalized social media communities, the extent and relevance of the problem of social media echo chambers have been questioned in the academic debates of recent years. Social media platforms have taken steps, for example changing their recommendation algorithms in a way that leads users to more diverse information. In addition, it has been pointed out that using the metaphor of the echo chamber overshadows the potential of social media to serve as a diverse communication channel and misrepresents 'the connective and communicative patterns they describe as symptomatic of users' entire experience of social media platforms, rather than as only one aspect of a much more diverse range of encounters' (Bruns 2019: 7). The arguments surrounding the echo chamber have also been criticized from the point of view of media determinism, that is, seeing causal relationships between polarization and social media affordances despite this being one-sided and misleading, as the amplification of certain oppositional stances is primarily a social and cultural issue (see Bruns 2019; Dutton et al. 2017). However, as semiotics is engaged with the latter aspect, the criticism will not be extended to the approach discussed in the following text. We have focused on explicating the meaning-making mechanisms that prevail in social media communities and tend towards closing and polarization.

We have used antithetical modelling, which will not allow acknowledgement of the relativity of values and plurality of interpretation paths as a cornerstone of the autocommunication in echo chambers (Madisson and Ventsel 2016b: 333–6). Antithetical logic divides the world into two opposing camps: moral and immoral, true and false, friends and enemies and so on (Lotman and Uspensky [1971] 1978: 219). The antithetical modelling type will need the existence of a villain to be sustainable, which is why increasingly more representations are being created of the adversary's dangerousness (Lotman [1992] 2002: 45). It is typical of enclosing social media communities that they repeat examples, of one and the same type, that confirm the dangerousness of ideological opponents, and the use of mirror projection is also relatively widespread. In such echo chambers the adversary's dangerousness is significant not as an isolated case but primarily because it corroborates the community stereotype of 'their' immorality and, accordingly, 'our' morality. This dominant of enclosing autocommunication has also been foregrounded in a study of Croatian right-wing public Facebook pages (Damcevic and Rodik 2018).

As a second dominant of enclosing autocommunication, we have outlined the hermetic creation of connections based on seemingly arbitrary analogies (Madisson and Ventsel 2016b: 336–7). In communicative echo chambers, a type of connection reigns that Lotman ([1978] 2019) has called homomorphic resemblance, that is, a tendency to recognize signs of one and the same phenomenon in different real-world phenomena, and a unified object instead of different objects of the same class. Such a meaning-making dominant is manifested in enclosing social media communities, for example in sketching one-to-one parallels between the situation at the moment and code texts (e.g. the pattern of the NWO conspiracy theory) stored in communal memory (Madisson and Ventsel 2018).

As a third dominant of enclosing autocommunication, we have seen the considerable number of messages with a phatic orientation (Madisson and Ventsel 2016b: 343–5). A large proportion of echo chamber communication consists in providing mutual recognition and showing familiarity with one another's messages. Several social media affordances, for example liking, linking, sharing, copying authoritative sources and so on, create particularly convenient opportunities to fulfil phatic communication aims. At the same time, phatic communication becomes manifest in the thriving of a lexicon that marks belonging to the so-called inner circle. Lotman has noted that an important device for creating trusting contact lies in activating connections in communal memory, while the value of messages can in this case be heightened by the degree of their opaqueness in the eyes of others (i.e. third parties) (Lotman [1977] 1982). The function of creating such trusting contact in echo chambers is often served by acronyms or number combinations that are understandable only to a community's inner circle. In extreme right-wing social media communities, number combinations and acronyms (e.g. *88*[1], *RAHOWA*[2] and *PWA*[3]) are used to strengthen group feeling and mark belonging (see Madisson and Ventsel 2016b: 346); various memes (Loonde 2018: 83) and GIFs are also shared, performing the same function.

Although these examples mainly concentrate on the discourse of the extreme right, we can meet similar mechanisms of enclosing meaning-making in the social media communication of different ideologies. Cultural semiotics first and foremost focuses on modelling sign processes, that is, the level of form.

Future directions

This chapter demonstrated several ways in which Lotman's theoretical frameworks have helped explain modes of communication characteristic of social media and meaning-making practices connected with particular affordances. The referenced research has made the first important steps towards showing the potential of Lotman's theory when used to interpret and analyse today's media-saturated culture and enrich the metalanguage of social media studies.

As a central path of future development, we can certainly see clear relations being forged between the theoretical trajectories presented in the examples analysed here and the rich textual material offered by social media. Semiotic works have occasionally been criticized for insufficient empirical grounding and providing just single examples that fit a theory. For our part, however, we see the methods of digital ethnography, creative research, multimodal discourse analysis and link analysis (Ibrus and Ojamaa 2019) as particularly promising.

The popularity of reactions referred to as social media affordances, for example copying and sharing functions, has been connected with making public discussion space emotion based and less reliant on argumentation. Brief social media texts are often based on associative connections, a typical example of which is hash tagging in Twitter and Facebook (tagging allows for the easy linking of semiotic modalities and signifiers that derive from different discourses (Gyorl 2013: 487)). The potential receiver of the texts has to work out the more specific connections between the elements during the interpretation process, as these connections are often marked merely by the act of naming only.

We see the potential of cultural semiotics in conceptualizing the association- and emotion-based culture of expression that could be called the affective social media semiosphere. Affective meaning-making in many ways marks the collective realization that some aspects are relevant in interpreting certain viral texts, although they are not arranged into clearly distinguishable logical-discrete structures but rather seem intuitively relevant and meaningful. The affective meaning-making described earlier is to a great degree reduced to naming, which can be called approximate or surface (Lotman [1989] 1997) semiotization, or making connections that proceed from a non-discrete logic of signification and is based on equating, creating analogies and finding homeo- and isomorphisms (Lotman [1978] 2019). Lotman's conception of iconic-continuous and verbal-discrete modes of encoding makes it possible to expand on the existing discussions of affective social media communication and foreground its meaning-making aspects more clearly and systematically.[4]

Notes

1. 88 means '*Heil Hitler*', due to the fact that H is the eighth letter in the alphabet.
2. RAHOWA is the abbreviation of the expression *Racial Holy War*.
3. PWA is the abbreviation of the expression *Preserve White Aryans*, also the name of an Estonian skinhead punk band.
4. This work was supported by Estonian Research Council grants PRG314 and PUTJD804.

References

Benkler, Y., Faris, R. and Roberts, H. 2018. *Network Propaganda: Manipulation, Disinformation, and Radicalization in American Politics*, New York: Oxford University Press.

Borges, P. M. and Gambarato, R. R. 2019. 'The Role of Beliefs and Behavior on Facebook: A Semiotic Approach to Algorithms, Fake News, and Transmedia Journalism', *International Journal of Communication* 13: 603–18.

boyd, d. 2011. 'Social Network Sites as Networked Publics: Affordances, Dynamics, and Implications', in Z. Papacharissi (ed.), *A Networked Self: Identity, Community, and Culture on Social Network Sites*, 39–58, New York and London: Routledge.

boyd, d. and Ellison, N. B. 2007. 'Social Network Sites: Definition, History, and Scholarship', *Journal of Computer-Mediated Communication* 13 (1): 210–30.

Bruni, L. E. 2015. 'Sustainability, Cognitive Technologies and the Digital Semiosphere', *International Journal of Cultural Studies* 18 (1): 103–17.

Bruns, A. 2019. *Are Filter Bubbles Real?* Cambridge: Polity Press.

Castells, M. 2009. *Communication Power*, Oxford: Oxford University Press.

Cobley, P. 2001. *Narrative*, London: Routledge.

Damčević, K. and Rodik, F. 2018. 'Ready for the Homeland: Hate Speech on Croatian Right-Wing Public Facebook Pages', *Romanian Journal of Communication and Public Relations* 20 (3): 31–52.

Dutton, W., B. Reisdorf, E. Dubois and Blank, G. 2017. 'Social Shaping of the Politics of Internet Search and Networking: Moving Beyond Filter Bubbles, Echo Chambers, and Fake News', *Quello Center Working Papers, No. 2944191*, Lansing: Michigan State University.

Elias, N. 1978. *What Is Sociology?* New York: Columbia University Press.

Griffin, R. 2003. 'From Slime Mould to Rhizome: An Introduction to the Groupuscular Right', *Patterns of Prejudice* 37 (1): 27–50.

Gyorl, B. 2013. 'Naming Neda: Digital Discourse and the Rhetorics of Association', *Journal of Broadcasting& Electronic Media* 57 (4): 482–503.

Fausing, B. 2014. 'Selfies Shape the World: Selfies, Healthies, Usies, Felfies . . .'. Available online: http://www.scribd.com/doc/213679678/Selfies-shape-the-World-Selfies-Healthies-Usies-F elfies (accessed 5 January 2021).

Hartley, J. 1996. *Popular Reality: Journalism, Modernity, Popular Culture*, London: Bloomsbury.

Hartley, J. 2008. *Television Truths: Forms of Knowledge in Popular Culture*, Malden, MA and Oxford: Wiley-Blackwell.

Hartley, J. and McKee, A. 2000. *The Indigenous Public Sphere: The Reporting and Reception of Aboriginal Issues in the Australian Media*, Oxford: Oxford University Press.

Hartley, J., Ibrus, I. and Ojamaa, M. 2021. *On the Digital Semiosphere: Culture, Media and Science for the Anthropocene*, London: Bloomsbury.

Ibrus, I. and Ojamaa, M. 2019. 'The Creativity of Digital (Audiovisual) Archives: A Dialogue Between Media Archaeology and Cultural Semiotics', *Theory, Culture & Society* 37 (3): 49–70.

Ibrus, I. and Ojamaa, M. 2020. 'Audiovisuaalne kultuur, metaandmed ja lingianalüüs [Audiovisual Culture, Metadata and Link Analysis]', in A. Masso, A. Siibak and K. Tiidenberg (eds), *Kuidas mõista andmestunud maailma? Metodoloogiline teejuht [How to Understand Datafied World? Methodological Guide]*, 531–68, Tallinn: Tallinna Ülikooli Kirjastus.

Kimminich, E. 2016. 'About Grounding, Courting and Truthifying Conspiratorial Fragments and Patterns of Social Construction of Reality in Rhetoric, Media and Images', *Lexia* 23/24: 35–53.

Kress, G. 2005. *Literacy in the New Media Age*, London and New York: Routledge.

Landow, G. P. 2006. *Hypertext 3.0: Critical Theory and New Media in an Era of Globalization*, Baltimore, MD, and London: The Johns Hopkins University Press.

Latour, B. 2005. *Reassembling the Social: An Introduction to Actor-Network-Theory*, Oxford and New York: Oxford University Press.

Leone, M. 2018. 'Semiotics of the Selfie: The Glorification of the Present', *Punctum* 4 (2): 33–48.

Loonde, E. 2018. 'Internetimeemid EKRE poliitilises kommunikatsioonis [Internet Memes in the Political Communication of Estonian Conservative People's Party]', *Acta Semiotica Estica* 15: 64–88.

Lotman, Ju. M. [1970] 2000. 'O tipologicheskom izutchenii kul'tury', in Ju. M. Lotman, *Semiosfera*, 447–59. Saint Petersburg: Iskusstvo–SPB.

Lotman, Ju. M. [1971] 2000. 'Problema "obucheniia kul'ture" kak ee tipologicheskaia kharakteristika', in Ju. M. Lotman, *Semiosfera*, 417–25, Saint Petersburg: Iskusstvo–SPB.

Lotman, Ju. M. [1973] 2000. 'O dvukh tipakh orientirovannosti kul'tury', in Ju. M. Lotman, *Semiosfera*, 425–7, Saint Petersburg: Iskusstvo–SPB.

Lotman, Yu. M. [1977] 1982. 'The Text and the Structure of Its Audience', *New Literary History* 14 (1): 81–7.

Lotman, J. [1978] 2019. 'The Phenomenon of Culture', in J. Lotman, *Culture, Memory and History: Essays in Cultural Semiotics*, trans. B. J. Baer, ed. M. Tamm, 33–49, Cham: Palgrave Macmillan.

Lotman, Yu. M. [1981] 1988. 'Text Within a Text', *Soviet Psychology* 26 (3): 32–51.

Lotman, Yu. [1984] 2005. 'On Semiosphere', trans. W. Clark, *Sign Systems Studies* 33 (1): 205–29.

Lotman, J. [1989] 1997. 'Culture as a Subject and an Object in Itself', *Trames* 1 (51/46): 7–16.

Lotman, Ju. M. [1992] 2002. 'Mekhanizm smuty', in Ju. M. Lotman, *Istoriia i tipologiia russkoi kul'tury*, 33–46, Saint Petersburg: Iskusstvo–SPB.

Lotman, Ju. and Mints, Z. 1981. 'Literatura i mifologiia', *Trudy po znakovym sistemam* 13: 35–55.

Lotman, Yu. M. and Uspensky, B. A. [1971] 1978. 'On the Semiotic Mechanism of Culture', trans. G. Mihaychuk, *New Literary History* 9 (2): 211–32.

Lotman, Yu. M. and Uspensky, B. A. [1977] 1984. 'The Role of Dual Models in the Dynamics of Russian Culture (Up to the End of the Eighteenth Century)', trans. F. C. Owen, in Yu. M. Lotman and B. A. Uspenskij, *The Semiotics of Russian Culture*, ed. A. Shukman, 3–35, Ann Arbor, MI: Department of Slavic Languages and Literatures, University of Michigan.

Madisson, M.-L. 2016a. *The Semiotic Construction of Identities in Hypermedia Environments: The Analysis of Online Communication of the Estonian Extreme Right*, Tartu: Tartu Ülikooli Kirjastus.

Madisson, M.-L. 2016b. 'NWO Conspiracy Theory: A Key Frame in Online Communication of Estonian Extreme Right', *Lexia* 23/24: 189–208.

Madisson, M.-L. and Ventsel, A. 2016a. '"Freedom of Speech" in the Self-Descriptions of the Estonian Extreme Right Groupuscules', *National Identities* 18 (2): 89–104.

Madisson, M.-L. and Ventsel, A. 2016b. 'Autocommunicative Meaning-making in Online-Communication of Estonian Extreme Right', *Sign Systems Studies* 44 (3): 326–54.

Madisson, M.-L. and Ventsel, A. 2018. 'Groupuscular Identity-Creation in Online-Communication of Estonian Extreme Right', *Semiotica* 222: 25–46.

Madisson, M.-L. and Ventsel, A. 2020. *Strategic Conspiracy Narratives: A Semiotic Approach*, London and New York: Routledge.

Marwick, A. E., boyd, d. 2010. 'I Tweet Honestly, I Tweet Passionately: Twitter Users, Context Collapse, and the Imagined Audience', *New Media and Society* 20 (10): 1–20.

Menise, T. 2019a. 'Fairy Tales Between Transformation and Repetition: How Audiences Rethink the Big Romantic Myth Through Disney Princess Stories', *Sign Systems Studies* 47 (3/4): 526–51.

Menise, T. 2019b. '"The Snow Queen" in Russian Fan Fiction: Voices of Readers and Viewers', *Marvels & Tales* 33 (2): 283–301.

Menise, Tatjana 2020. *Fairy Tales in Transmedia Communication: Fanfiction*, Tartu: University of Tartu Press.

Obar, J. A. and Wildman, S. 2015. 'Social Media Definition and the Governance Challenge: An Introduction to the Special Issue', *Telecommunications Policy* 39 (9): 745–50.

Ojamaa, M. 2015. *The Transmedial Aspect of Cultural Autocommunication*, Tartu: University of Tartu Press, available online: https://dspace.ut.ee/handle/10062/45985 (accessed 8 January 2021).

Ojamaa, M. and Torop, P. 2015. 'Transmediality of Cultural Autocommunication', *International Journal of Cultural Studies* 18 (1): 61–78.

Papacharissi, Z. 2015. 'The Unbearable Lightness of Information and the Impossible Gravitas of Knowledge: Big Data and the Makings of a Digital Orality', *Media, Culture & Society* 37 (7): 1095–100.

Ryan, M.-L. 2006. *Avatars of Story*, Minneapolis: University of Minnesota Press.

Singer, P. W. and Brooking, E. T. 2018. *LikeWar: The Weaponization of Social Media*, Boston and New York: Eamon Dolan/Houghton Mifflin Harcourt.

Statista 2020. Available online: https://www.statista.com/statistics/272014/global-social-net works-ranked-by-number-of-users/ (accessed 5 January 2021).

Tiidenberg, K. 2015. 'Self-Making and Significant Relationships: Understanding Selfie-Practices', Doctoral thesis, Tallinn: Tallinn University.

Tiidenberg, K. 2017. *Ihu ja hingega internetis: kuidas mõista sotsiaalmeediat? [Body and Soul on the Internet: Making Sense of Social Media]*, Tallinn: Tallinna Ülikooli Kirjastus.

Torop, P. 2003. 'Semiospherical Understanding: Textuality', *Sign Systems Studies* 31 (2): 323–37.

Torop, P. 2011. *Tõlge ja kultuur [Translation and Culture]*, Tallinn and Tartu: Tartu Ülikooli Kirjastus.

Torop, P. 2013. 'Vanad raamatud ja uus meedia' [Old Books and New Media], *Vikerkaar* 28 (12): 50–62.

Ventsel, A. 2017. 'Viral Communication and the Formation of Counter-publics', *Lexia* 25–6: 365–80.

Ventsel, A. and Madisson, M.-L. 2017. 'Tõejärgne diskursus ja semiootika' [Post-truth Discourse and Semiotics], *Acta Semiotica Estica* 14: 93–116.

Ventsel, A. and Madisson, M.-L. 2020. 'Socio-political Discussion in the Digital Public Space', in H. Sooväli-Sepping (ed.), *Spatial Choices for an Urbanised Society. Estonian Human Development Report 2019/2020*, Tallinn: SA Estonian Cooperation Assembly, available online: https://www.inimareng.ee/en/socio-political-discussion-in-the-digital-public-space.html (accessed 5 January 2021).

Warner, B. R. and Neville-Shepard, R. 2014. 'Echoes of a Conspiracy: Birthers, Truthers, and the Cultivation of Extremism', *Communication Quarterly* 62 (1): 1–17.

CHAPTER 34
JURI LOTMAN AND LIFE SCIENCES
Kalevi Kull and Timo Maran

What is similar in animals and humans is very interesting, and in general I think that zoosemiotics should become a part of linguistics or linguistics a part of zoosemiotics – we will not argue about ranks, but it seems to me that a zoologist should be linguist, or maybe a linguist must be zoologist.

> – Juri Lotman (1990b: 19)

Apart from an impact on and belongness to the local intellectual sphere – in Juri Lotman's case both to Estonian (Tamm and Kull 2016) and to Russian (Torop 2019) cultures – the work of a scholar can contribute to scientific understanding in general. Lotman's major and deep theoretical interest was (in addition to the poetics of text and the theory of culture) in semiotics, the area in which he became a classic author. His relationships with life sciences exist mainly via his fundamental effect on general semiotics, the potentials of which are far from entirely explored.

Lotman's life-long project was to understand the mechanisms of artistic text.

For the Tartu-Moscow School the shift from gradual processes to explosive moments was determined when the centre of scholarly attention was relocated from the field of linguistics to the semiotics of art. Art is a child of explosion. The work of art is born in a moment of explosion and cannot be understood without taking into account the very nature of that birth. (Lotman [1994/2010] 2013: 87)

Moreover: 'The actual artistic text reproduces that interlacing of the predictable and the unpredictable that brings it near to life itself, not just to a model of life' (Lotman [1994/2010] 2013: 220). Because 'it is not so that the artistic texts are extreme expressions of some normal non-artistic texts, but I think that non-artistic texts are a special case of artistic texts' (Lotman 1981: 7). Going the long way of studies through the various aspects of such modelling, Lotman's theory of semiotics was built.

The semiotics of the 1960s and 1970s was mainly limited to human sciences and logic (and to some extent cybernetics). The application of semiotics to biology and the development of biosemiotics has grown to a noticeable extent only since the 1980s, and more extensively since the 1990s. Therefore, it is rather obvious that semiotics for Lotman mainly speaks in human sciences. However, as much as his work on general semiotic models describes the deep mechanisms of meaning-making and communication – the mechanisms that are general throughout the entire area of semiotics – his work unwittingly contributes to biosemiotics and to a theory of life. This connection through general semiotics is the aspect of Lotman's relation to biosemiotics – and via this to life sciences in general – that we focus on in the following paragraphs.

Sources

While the main topic of Lotman's works in the 1960s and 1970s was structural poetics and semiotic theory of culture (Żyłko 2016), in the 1980s he turned towards the problems of general semiotics, and accordingly there are more connections to life sciences in the works from that last period of his life. International reception of Lotman's work in general semiotics grew after the publication of *Universe of the Mind* in 1990; his work appears in the international anthologies of semiotics only since 2000 (see Kull 2011).

In addition to Lotman's published works, there is also a link to life sciences via his talks to and conversations with biologists, and these too have not been without influence. We can thus list four types of source that deserve attention when reviewing the Lotman–biosciences bridge:

(A) Lotman's writings in which he formulates principles of general semiotics. These are particularly his works from the last decade of his life (Lotman [1984] 2005; 1990a; [1992] 2009; [1994/2010] 2013), however, a scattering of these principles can also be found in several works from the 1960s and 1970s.

(B) Various examples and expressions in works on different subjects in which the features of non-human life were briefly characterized or discussed or mentioned in the context of comparison with the phenomena of human culture (e.g. Lotman 1967).

(C) A few writings in which biological problems were directly addressed. These include a couple of short articles (Lotman 1984; 1988), two interviews (Lotman 1990b; Kull and Lotman [1992] 2015) and some lectures he gave by invitation of a theoretical biology group in Tartu.

(D) Talks (e.g. Lotman 1981), correspondence (Raudla and Pern 2011) and conversations in which biological questions were explicitly or implicitly addressed.

Since the Tartu-Moscow school of the 1960s and 1970s did not include biologists, both their works and the main literature about the school has said almost nothing (with very few exceptions, like Andrews 2003) on the topic of Lotman and life sciences.

In addition, (C) and (D) belong mainly to the period when active collaboration within the Tartu-Moscow school was over (cf. Avtonomova 2014: 219–27). The relevant texts for (C) were both not published in Russian, and appeared in editions outside the interests of the Slavists.

The previous works in which Lotman's relationships to life sciences (or the topic of Lotman and biology) have been analysed include, in particular, Alexandrov (2000), Andrews (2003), Favareau (2010), Kotov (2002), Kotov and Kull (2011), Kull (1999; 2005; 2015a), Kull and Lotman (2012), Kull and Velmezova (2018), M. Lotman (2002),

Machtyl (2019), Mandelker (1994), Maran (2020), Marinakis (2012), Markoš (2014), Nöth (2006), Patoine and Hope (2015), Sebeok (1988; 1998), Semenenko (2016) and so on. Remarkably, almost all these belong to the twenty-first century.

Lotman's general semiotics and its relevance for biology

Lotman was interested in general principles of meaning-making from his works of the early 1960s. For instance, in 1964 he says that art has features that enable it to specifically describe life. In saying this, Lotman attempts to describe how the non-verbal aspects of life can be best modelled by non-verbal aspects of poetic description. 'Art learns life recreating it. [. . .] Art is a modelling system' (Lotman 1964: 18, 27). Without having in mind non-human examples, what Lotman was to discover was a deep and general mechanism that includes the working of forms of non-human life. In the conclusion to the same work, Lotman provides an explicit comparison between the study of art, and biology:

> The parallelism between the phenomena of life and the phenomena of art has, for all its conventionality, one additional aspect. Just as in the science of a living organism we understand that the phenomenon of life, being a qualitative specificity of biological processes, cannot be represented for a single moment outside the material structure of cells; just as the materialist biologist understands that by linking life with a certain system of relations and organization of material substance, he does not humiliate life, but only fences himself off from vitalism, – the art theorist must clearly understand that the idea of art, constituting its basis, cannot exist outside the material structure of the work. Talking about a useful idea and poor performance is the same as studying the 'life force' that exists outside of living cells. (Lotman 1964: 189)

Or, for instance, another simple example of Lotman's generalization, which states that 'in examining the nature of semiotic structures, we observe that the complexity of a structure is directly proportional to the complexity of the information transmitted. As the nature of the information grows more complicated, the semiotic system used to transmit that information grows more complicated' (Lotman [1970] 1977: 10). This rule is probably applicable on all levels of semiotic systems – from a cell, from vegetative and animal semiosis to culture and its structures.

Throughout his many writings, Lotman formulated a series of characteristics that describe various universal aspects of a general semiotic process – of semiosis (cf. Lepik 2008). Through these characteristics or principles, he built a model of semiosis that – as we assume – would describe semiosis from its emergence in the first meaning-making living systems.

The model of semiosis, as based on Juri Lotman's approach, can be described as consisting of a series of logically connected basic principles (cf. Kull 2015a):

(1) The principle of *code plurality* – one code is insufficient for semiosis, and at least two codes are necessary; 'semiotic dualism is the minimal form of organisation of a working semiotic system' (Lotman 1990a: 124);

(2) The principle of *incompatibility* or *nontranslatability* or confusion or conflict – meaning-making requires an incompatibility of codes; incompatibility is the source of indeterminacy, non-predictability and freedom; 'transmitter and receiver use different codes [. . .] which overlap but are not identical. [. . .] The asymmetrical relationship, the constant need for choice, make translation in this case an act of generating new information' (Lotman 1990a: 14–5). 'Particularly indicative is the situation where it is not simply difference which exists between codes, but mutual untranslatability (for instance, in the translation of a verbal text into an iconic one)' (Lotman 1990a: 15); 'across any synchronic section of the semiosphere different languages at different stage of development are in conflict, and some texts are immersed in languages not their own, while the codes to decipher them with may be entirely absent' (Lotman 1990a: 126);

(3) The principle of *asymmetry* – semiotic structures are inherently asymmetrical or in imbalance; this principle is present in different topics and discussions for Lotman as, for instance, relations between left and right hemisphere of the brain, between centre and periphery of culture, between inside and outside of semiotic space and so on; the principle of asymmetry leads to the dynamic and developmental view of semiotic systems and processes;

(4) The principle of *autocommunication* or *translation* or negotiation – autocommunication is the most general form of communication; it must be present for sign interpretation; autocommunication underlies the ability to qualitatively restructure and translate; 'culture is a vast example of autocommunication' (Lotman 1990a: 33);

(5) The principle of *semiotic inheritance* – every sign comes from another sign, every text from another text; 'semiotic experience precedes the semiotic act' (Lotman 1990a: 123); 'the semiotic situation precedes the instruments of semiosis' (Lotman 1990a: 144);

(6) The principle of the *semiosphere* – the principle of the relationality of semiotic systems: semiotic space must be regarded as a unified mechanism; semiosis cannot exist outside of the semiosphere, of 'that synchronic semiotic space [. . .] without which separate semiotic systems cannot function or come into being' (Lotman 1990a: 3);

(7) The principle of *non-gradual (punctuated) evolution* – in the development of a semiotic system, explosive or disrupted and continuous or orthogenetic processes alternate and co-occur; 'Neither a system made up of explosions alone nor a system devoid of explosions can exist as a healthy organism. [. . .] Gradual evolution and shifts to unpredictability must form a complex whole. [. . .] Unpredictability experienced in the realm of art can be carried over into

reality in a form free of catastrophes, similar to the way an injection provides an organism with immunity' (Lotman [1994/2010] 2013: 131);

(8) The principle of *modelling* – semiotic systems are themselves modelling systems; 'A modelling system is a structure of elements and rules of their combination, existing in a state of fixed analogy to the whole sphere of the object of perception, cognition, or organization' (Lotman [1967] 2011: 250);

(9) The principle of *boundaries* – boundaries are the source of diversity and creativity of semiotic systems; 'One of the fundamental concepts of semiotic delimitation lies in the notion of boundary' (Lotman [1984] 2005: 208). 'The border of semiotic space is the most important functional and structural position, giving substance to its semiotic mechanism. The border is a bilingual mechanism, translating external communications into the internal language of the semiosphere and vice versa' (Lotman [1984] 2005: 210);

(10) The principle of *unpredictability* and *choice* – semiosis presupposes the situation of unpredictability that forces a choice; 'Every time when we talk about unpredictability, we mean a certain set of equipossible choices, of which only one becomes realized' (Lotman 1992: 190); 'The unpredictable element becomes an act, is unavoidably subjected to interpretation, and is attributed with additional motivation after the fact' (Lotman [1994/2010] 2013: 67); 'The translator is forced to *make a choice*' (Lotman 1990a: 14).

These interconnected principles can be seen as the universal characteristics of a meaning-making mechanism, the semiosis, wherever and whenever it may occur. And as much as semiosis is widely existent in living organisms, these principles should unavoidably be applicable to non-human forms of semiosis – that is to say, in the realm of life sciences.

Links via shared methodology

In addition to semiosis as a shared object between anthroposemiotics and biosemiotics, Lotmanian approach also shares something with biological (biosemiotic) methodology.

Firstly, this is an emphasis on a *scientific* approach, often repeated by Lotman. Semiotics is viewed as science, according to Lotman. This emphasis does not characterize all schools of semiotics, but in the case of the Tartu school it is certainly important (see also Salupere 2011). Its roots are, of course, in structuralism and attempts to apply mathematical models to literary studies, which was the main context during the formation of Tartu-Moscow School of Semiotics in the 1960s. However, in Lotman's case the view of semiotics as a science persisted, even into the 1990s.

Secondly, and this is related to the foregoing, the emphasis on *mechanisms*. For Lotman, it is natural to speak about the mechanisms of meaning-making, mechanism of semiosis, mechanisms of cultural dynamics and structure. This, of course, has nothing to do with mechanicism. The roots of his view were rather, first, in the semiotics of Russian formalism (where the term 'mechanism' was widely used, cf. Steiner [1984] 2014), and second, in general systems theory, which largely stemmed from biology, from the works of Ludwig von Bertalanffy.

Thirdly, again related to the latter, is the emphasis on *modelling*. On the one hand, modelling is seen as the general means of cognition, and on the other hand the means of knowledge transfer from one field to another (supported by the popularity of general systems theory in the 1960s and 1970s – *Sistemnye issledovaniia*, in Russian – which emphasize modelling as the basis of interdisciplinarity). Theoretical biology and semiotics became neighbouring disciplines in this context.

And fourth, holism, *organicism*. Organicism does not characterize all approaches in life sciences, although it is certainly an essence of biology. Lotman's semiotics was, no doubt, holistic. He writes: 'we are proposing a "semiotic physiology", a study of the functional connection between the different languages in the single functioning whole. By posing the question: "In what way is this particular language essential for the general functioning of culture and what is its special function in the single cultural organism?" we will be able to elucidate what is specific in each language' (Lotman and Uspenskij 1984: ix).

One of the fundamental features of semiotic systems, according to Lotman, is the incompatibility or partial untranslatability of the languages or codes that are included in the semiotic system (see aforementioned principle 2). Using the ways in which different fields deal with (logical) incompatibilities or conflicts, a rather clear distinction is observable (see also Kull 2015a: 263):

The arts – use incompatibilities (often implicit) to make meanings;

The sciences – make the incompatibilities explicit:

- either removing them (*physical sciences*) so that objects do not include incompatibilities
- or describing them (*semiotic sciences*) so that objects can include incompatibilities.

Indeed, life (the research object for biology) as well as art (the research object for Lotman) both essentially include incompatibilities: conflict is what drives them, what makes them alive.

Semiotics of animals in Lotman's works

Lotman uses a very broad concept of language (see also Chapter 8) that enables the creation of a connection between human cultural semiosis and semiosis of other organisms:

Every system whose end is to establish communication between two or more individuals may be defined as language ([. . .] the case of auto-communication implies that one individual functions as two). The common allegation that language implies communication *in human society* is not, strictly speaking, binding, for, on the one hand, linguistic communication between man and machine, and today between machines themselves, is no longer a theoretical problem but a technological reality. On the other hand, the existence of certain forms of linguistic communication between animals has also ceased to be questioned. In contrast, systems of communication inside an individual (for example, the mechanisms of biochemical regulation or of signals transmitted through an organism's nervous system) are not languages. [. . .] Every language makes use of signs which constitute its 'vocabulary'. (Lotman [1970] 1977: 7)

He admits that 'it would be possible to identify cases of sharp, individual markings, especially in pairs of animals during the mating period. But still there remains one indisputable fact: the language of animals does not "know" proper names' (Lotman [1992] 2009: 30).

In his article 'Natural Environment and Information' (Lotman 1988), Lotman analysed animal communication that is based on movement. He states that animals with elaborate repertoires of movement can play, in which case 'the movement system can be viewed as language' (Lotman 1988: 46).

The problem of difference between human beings and animals is discussed, for instance, in some chapters of the books *Unpredictable Workings of Culture* (Lotman [1994/2010] 2013, 'A Dialogue in Different Languages', 'Fashion and Dress', 'A Workshop of Unpredictability', 'In Place of a Conclusion') and *Culture and Explosion* (Lotman [1992] 2009, 'Thinking Reed', 'The World of Proper Names', 'The Fool and the Madman', 'The Moment of Unpredictability'). In many of these contexts, animals have been used as a counterexample to highlight human cultural and semiotic abilities. For instance, in *Culture and Explosion* Lotman stresses the rituality and regularity of animal communication (in courtship behaviour, in conflicts to regulate social hierarchies, in territorial disputes), contrasting this to creativity and inventiveness in human communication. Accordingly, 'From man's point of view, animals are stupid; from the animal's point of view, man is dishonest (he doesn't play by the rules). Man constructs his view of the animal as a foolish person. The animal constructs his view of man as a dishonourable animal' (Lotman [1992] 2009: 29).

In Lotman's earlier writings, we can see some occasional comparisons between literature and biological (non-human) life, pointing to analogies of cultural and textual phenomena in prelinguistic life. For instance, he has compared the functional structure of literary text and living organism:

Relationship between the artistic idea and the construction of a literary work reminds one of the relationship *between life and the biological structure of a cell*. In biology, there is no vitalist any more who would investigate life outside the real organization of matter, its carrier. In the science of literature they still exist. Also, a listing of the *material 'inventory' of a living tissue cannot unlock the secrets of life*: the *cell is given as a complex functioning self-accommodating system. Realization of its functions turns out to be life. A literary work is also a complex self-accommodating system* (indeed, of an other type). The idea represents the life of a literary work, and this is similarly impossible in a body dissected by an anatomist or outside this body. Mechanicism of the former and idealism of the latter should be replaced by the dialectics of functional analysis. (Lotman 1967: 97, our emphases)

It is interesting that in some contexts Lotman denies the existence of sign processes inside the organism ('systems of communication inside an individual [. . .] are not languages'), and in another context speaks about the similarity between the dynamic structure of the brain and of culture. Such contradictions can be at least partly explained by the datings of the works, as Lotman's views change gradually from structuralism towards more open post-structural and organicist semiotics.

In the article 'Culture and the Organism' (Lotman 1984), Lotman lists some general features, which are common to the organism and to culture, at a certain level of abstraction – memory, the symmetric mechanism of homeostasis and asymmetric mechanisms generating new information, the explosive growth of information content in certain stages of development and so on. He adds: 'Similarly to the living organism, whose normal contact to the insentient nature means the prevenient "translation" of information into the structural language of biosphere, also the contact of every intellectual being with outward information requires its translation into the sign system' (Lotman 1984: 216).

In some definitions of semiosphere, Lotman has explicitly included all living beings:

The semiosphere, if pictured in the momentary film-still of a synchronic cross-section, should include in itself all the totality of semiotic acts, from the signals of animals to the verses of poets and the call-signs of artificial satellites. (Lotman and Uspenskij 1984: x)

and

By analogy with the biosphere, our planet is surrounded by a real semiosphere, synchronously including all the variety of signals from bird singing to radio signals from artificial satellites, and diachronously including the entire cultural memory of mankind, from 'recordings' of neurons in the brain and genetic memory to libraries, film collections and museums. Each semiotic system functions, being in certain relations with other systems and levels of the semiosphere. (Lotman 1991: 4)

While accepting semiotic activity in other living species, Lotman pointed out a strong difference between humans and animals. We may not agree with the source of that difference as described by Lotman, but at the same time his descriptions of semiotic mechanisms are widely applicable.

Ecosemiotic aspects

By ecosemiotics we mean the study of semiotic aspects of human relationships with nature, and in connection with this, with semiosic relations in ecosystems and the biosphere. Juri Lotman has made some remarkable observations in this area.

In his work of 1970 (Lotman [1970] 2002: 151), he writes: 'Mastering of the world via turning it into the text, its "culturization", includes two opposite approaches.' In the first case, the world is considered as text (either made by God or by the natural laws of nature, or by the absolute idea, etc.). Then its mastering means the deciphering of this text and translation of the nature's text to the language of human culture. This is largely the way characteristic to the medieval, baroque and romanticist relation to nature. The book of nature is rather stable, and accordingly this approach rather sustainable. In the second case, the world is not a text. In this case, a deep divide between nature and culture appears:

the culturization means giving to the world the structure of culture. [. . .] This is analogical to the concept of mastering the 'barbarian' world by introducing into it the structures of civilization [. . .]. In this case it is not a translation of a text, but turning a non-text into a text. Turning a forest into a ploughland, drainage of swamps or irrigation of deserts – i.e. any transformation of non-cultural landscape into a cultural one – can also be seen as turning a non-text into a text. (Lotman [1970] 2002: 152)

As noted in Maran (2020), Lotman's cultural semiotics includes several concepts with ecological potential, for example semiosphere, cultural boundary and semiotics of space, but what is most relevant among these is probably the idea of semiotic modelling (see also Chapter 12). Lotman describes cultural boundaries as semi-permeable translation mechanisms that allow culture–nature relations to be redefined based on modelling and semiosis. In this vein, Kati Lindström (2010) has applied Lotman's concept of autocommunication to analyse landscape as a source of secondary code for culture; and Maran (2014) has used Lotman's concept of text to study literary representations of nature.

Lotman's broad understanding of text as an internally organized semiotic structure makes it possible to analyse parts of nature as semiotic in relation to human culture. Lotman and Piatigorsky ([1968] 1977: 129) consider the concept of text to cover also 'inscriptions left by a population that has already disappeared from a region, ruins of buildings of unknown purpose'. Alfred Siewers has elaborated on Lotman's perception of the volatile boundaries of culture in the concept of *ecosemiosphere* as 'an ecological bubble of meaning' (Siewers 2014: 4) that 'extends earlier definitions of specific symbolic cultures as semiospheres, or meaningful environments, into physical environments' (Siewers 2011: 41; cf. the concept of *semiobiosphere* in Ponzio and Petrilli 2001).

Conversations with biologists

Reviewing the link between Lotman and biology, it is obvious to ask what were Lotman's (personal) relationships to life sciences.

Lotman had an interest in biology during his school years before the war (Lotman 1994: 468). Later, however, he did not read much on biological research; instead, his biological knowledge was mainly kept up-to-date via conversations with biologists. His son Aleksei Lotman, who expressed early interest in zoology and studied biology at the University of Tartu, played an important role among those with whom he held conversations on biology. Among Juri Lotman's students and colleagues, there were no biologists. However, he may have had some conversations with Aleksei Turovski, who often appeared in the circles of Lotman's students (Velmezova and Kull 2016); and perhaps with Oleg Mutt, a philologist, who helped in the translation of abstracts for Lotman's journal *Trudy po znakovym sistemam* (Sign Systems Studies) and had an interest in zoosemiotics (Vaiksoo 2018); and on some occasions with Kalevi Kull, and with the biologists in theoretical biology seminars which Lotman attended (among these 'Biology and Linguistics' in 1978 in Tartu, and 'Theory of Behaviour' in 1982 in Puhtu – see Kull 1999; 2006).

A group of biologists with whom Lotman shared an interest and had many conversations were neurophysiologists, who studied the phenomena of hemispheric asymmetry in the brain – Lev J. Balonov, Vadim L. Deglin and Tatjana V. Chernigovskaja from Saint Petersburg. On 13–15 March 1981, Lotman and his colleagues organized a seminar titled 'Functional parallelism between the asymmetry of functions of the cerebral hemispheres and the semiotic asymmetry of culture as a mechanism of collective consciousness' in Tartu (Egorov et al. 2018: 516). The meeting was attended by, among others, Suren Zolyan (with a talk), Mihhail Kotik and Aleksei Lotman.

Biological ideas for a theory of culture?

Did Lotman give ideas to life science or rather did he receive inspiration from biology? Amy Mandelker's analysis tends to favour the latter:

> The spatialised and biologised concept of the semiosphere enhances the earlier Moscow-Tartu school notion of inner and outer cultural perspectives. [. . .] The sphere also invites the borrowing of some suggestive topics from biophysics and cell biology: enclosure and disclosure, resistance and responsiveness to penetration, and the assimilation of intruding and extruding elements. [. . .] Lotman's sphere of silence embraces, encloses, and embodies the utterance just as the biosphere [. . .] embraces all life and lies passively open to men's husbandry. (Mandelker 1994: 390, 392)

In addition, the reconstructions of the formation of the concept of semiosphere via Lotman's reading on the history of the concept of biosphere in Vladimir Vernadsky tells us that Lotman received ideas from life science. It may also be that Lotman had more personal contacts with biologists after the end of 1970s. Be that as it may, it is important to see that the ideas taken from biology were not of the kind often meant by biologization, that is, the struggle for existence and natural selection. Not at all. The ideas that attracted Lotman were those of living memory – *omne vivum e vivo* – of a boundary that translates, of asymmetry, of the organic whole.

Lotman's influence on biosemiotics

Lotman's influence on biosemiotics is obvious. Without Lotman's semiotics in Tartu, the Tartu biosemiotics group would either not exist or have a rather different form. And later via biosemiotics, Lotman may have had an indirect effect on theoretical biology and ecology.

Some fundamental ideas on general meaning-making mechanisms – code incompatibility and the related code plurality and untranslatability – are used in works on the mechanism of semiosis (Kull 2015b). When comparing the description of communication with that provided by Thomas Sebeok, Lotman adds an important aspect to the understanding of the mechanism of meaningful communication, that of incompatibility, the necessary difference.

The concept of semiosphere, which is widely used in contemporary biosemiotics, has a separate source from the works of Jesper Hoffmeyer (1996; 1997; 1998), who introduced the concept initially without having read Lotman; however, later he reconstructed the link to Lotman (see Kull and Velmezova 2019: 374). Kaie Kotov (2002) has clarified the relationship between these concepts. That Donald Favareau (2010) included a chapter on Lotman in the major anthology of biosemiotics is both a reflection of Lotman's existing role, and its further propagation.

Since Lotman's definition of culture, which uses as a criterial feature the non-hereditary information ('we understand culture as the *nonhereditary memory of the community*, a memory expressing itself in a system of constraints and prescriptions' – Lotman and Uspensky [1971] 1978: 213), is applicable – due to common epigenetic and social inheritance – in many species other than humans, an additional path opened to use Lotman's general model of cultural semiosis in the pre-human realm. Anton Markoš (2014) speaks along these lines about lineages as cultures and concludes that semiosphere is coextensive with biosphere.

Lotman's theoretical models have been used in various analyses of non-human life, for instance in studying urban trees (Magnus and Remm 2018), hedge mazes and landscape gardens (Kaczmarczyk and Salvoni 2016), and human interpretation of river landscapes (Kruis 2017).

In addition to the results gained in post-Lotmanian-era Tartu semiotics, one of the strong trends has been the synthesis of Lotman's and Uexküll's theories, including the relationships between umwelt and semiosphere (Kull and Lotman 2012; Kull 1998a; Kotov 2002). Uexküll-Lotman conceptual proximity has been noted by several scholars

(Andrews 2003; Andrews and Maksimova 2008; M. Lotman 2002). Indeed, reading, for instance, the following, it is hard not to recognize a similarity to Jakob von Uexküll's description of umwelt:

Any act of semiotic recognition must involve the separation of significant elements from insignificant ones in surrounding reality. Elements which, from the point of view of that modelling system, are not bearers of meaning, as it were do not exist. The fact of their actual existence recedes to the background in face of their irrelevance in the given modelling system. (Lotman 1990a: 58)

Integration of umwelt and modelling system approaches was clearly one of the main points of Sebeok and Danesi's project (Sebeok and Danesi 2000; with an earlier attempt in Sebeok 1988). As John Deely believes, 'Jakob von Uexküll and Juri Lotman [. . .] the heritage of these two figures have proved to be the foundation-stones, in some ways more important even than the, so far, more widely recognized figures of Ferdinand de Saussure and Charles Peirce – for the future of semiotics within university life and intellectual life generally' (Deely 2012: 214).[1]

Note

1. Acknowledgements: we thank Silvi Salupere, Tatiana Kuzovkina and the Juri Lotman Semiotics Repository for their help in supplying material for this research, Marek Tamm for helpful comments, and the Estonian Research Council (project PRG314) for their support.

References

Alexandrov, V. E. 2000. 'Biology, Semiosis, and Cultural Difference in Lotman's Semiosphere', *Comparative Literature* 52 (4): 339–62.

Andrews, E. 2003. *Conversations with Lotman: Cultural Semiotics in Language, Literature, and Cognition*, Toronto: University of Toronto Press.

Andrews, E. and Maksimova, E. 2008. 'Semiospheric Transitions: A Key to Modelling Translation', *Sign Systems Studies* 36 (2): 259–69.

Avtonomova, N. S. 2014. *Otkrytaia struktura: Iakobson – Bakhtin – Lotman – Gasparov*. Moscow: ROSSPEN.

Deely, J. 2012. 'The Tartu Synthesis in Semiotics Today Viewed From America', *Chinese Semiotics Studies* 8: 214–26.

Egorov, B. F., Dmitriev, A. P., Kuzovkina, T. D. and Poselyagin, N. V. (eds) 2018. *Ju. M. Lotman, Z. G. Mintz – B. F. Egorov: Perepiska 1954–1993*, Saint Petersburg: OOO 'Poligaf'.

Favareau, D. 2010. 'Introduction and Commentary: Juri Mikhajlovič Lotman', in D. Favareau (ed.), *Essential Readings in Biosemiotics: Anthology and Commentary*, 191–6, Berlin: Springer.

Hoffmeyer, J. 1996. *Signs of Meaning in the Universe*, trans. B. J. Haveland, Bloomington: Indiana University Press.

Hoffmeyer, J. 1997. 'The Global Semiosphere', in I. Rauch and G. F. Carr (eds), *Semiotics Around the World: Synthesis in Diversity. Proceedings of the Fifth Congress of the International Association for Semiotic Studies. Berkeley 1994*, 933–6, Berlin: Mouton de Gruyter.

Hoffmeyer, J. 1998. 'The Unfolding Semiosphere', in G. van de Vijver, S. Salthe and M. Delpos (eds), *Evolutionary Systems: Biological and Epistemological Perspectives on Selection and Self-Organization*, 281–93, Dordrecht: Kluwer.

Kaczmarczyk, K. and Salvoni, M. 2016. 'Hedge Mazes and Landscape Gardens as Cultural Boundary Objects', *Sign Systems Studies* 44 (1/2): 53–68.

Kotov, K. 2002. 'Semiosphere: A Chemistry of Being', *Sign Systems Studies* 30 (1): 41–55.

Kotov, K. and Kull, K. 2011. 'Semiosphere is the Relational Biosphere', in C. Emmeche and K. Kull (eds), *Towards a Semiotic Biology: Life Is the Action of Signs*, 179–94, London: Imperial College Press.

Kruis, J. L. 2017. 'Shoshone as a Text: A Structural-Semiotic Analysis of Reading the River as a Whitewater Raft Guide', in A. Kannike, M. Tasa and E.-H. Västrik (eds), *Body, Personhood and Privacy: Perspectives on the Cultural Other and Human Experience*, 245–65, Tartu: University of Tartu Press.

Kull, K. 1998a. 'On Semiosis, Umwelt, and Semiosphere', *Semiotica* 120 (3/4): 299–310.

Kull, K. 1998b. 'Semiotic Ecology: Different Natures in the Semiosphere', *Sign Systems Studies* 26: 344–71.

Kull, K. 1999. 'Towards Biosemiotics with Juri Lotman', *Semiotica* 127 (1/4): 115–31.

Kull, K. 2005. 'Semiosphere and a Dual Ecology: Paradoxes of Communication', *Sign Systems Studies* 33(1): 175–89.

Kull, K. 2006. 'Semiosfäär, 1982: kommentaariks' ['Semiosphere' in 1982: A Comment]', *Acta Semiotica Estica* 3: 222–24.

Kull, K. 2011. 'Juri Lotman in English: Bibliography', *Sign Systems Studies* 39 (2/4): 343–56.

Kull, K. 2015a. 'A Semiotic Theory of Life: Lotman's Principles of the Universe of the Mind', *Green Letters: Studies in Ecocriticism* 19 (3): 255–66.

Kull, K. 2015b. 'Semiosis Stems from Logical Incompatibility in Organic Nature: Why Biophysics Does Not See Meaning, While Biosemiotics Does', *Progress in Biophysics and Molecular Biology* 119 (3): 616–21.

Kull, K. and Lotman, Y. [1992] 2015. 'Au sujet de la sémiotique de la vie et de l'évolution. (Entretien de Kalevi Kull avec Youri Lotman. Tartu, juin 1992)', in E. Velmezova (ed.), *L'École sémiotique de Moscou-Tartu / Tartu-Moscou. Histoire. Épistémologie. Actualité*, 165–82 (Slavica Occitania 40), Toulouse: Université de Toulouse.

Kull, K. and Lotman, M. 2012. 'Semiotica Tartuensis: Jakob von Uexküll and Juri Lotman', *Chinese Semiotic Studies* 6: 312–23.

Kull, K. and Velmezova, E. 2018. 'O paradokse "semiotiki zhizni": raboty poslednikh let Iuriia Lotmana', *Slovo.ru: Baltiiskii aktsent* 9 (4): 6–14.

Kull, K. and Velmezova, E. 2019. 'Jesper Hoffmeyer: Biosemiotics is a Discovery', *Biosemiotics* 12 (3): 373–9.

Lepik, P. 2008. *Universals in the Context of Juri Lotman's Semiotics*, Tartu: Tartu University Press.

Lindström, K. 2010. 'Autocommunication and Perceptual Markers in Landscape: Japanese Examples', *Biosemiotics* 3 (3): 359–73.

Lotman, Ju. M. 1964. *Lektsii po struktural'noi poetike. Vyp. 1. Vvedenie, teoriia stikha*, Tartu: Izdatel'stvo Tartuskogo universiteta (Trudy po znakovym sistemam, 1).

Lotman, Ju. M. 1967. 'Literaturovedenie dolzhno byt' naukoi', *Voprosy literatury* 1: 90–100.

Lotman, J. [1967] 2011. 'The Place of Art Among Other Modelling Systems', trans. T. Pern, *Sign Systems Studies* 39 (2/4): 249–70.

Lotman, J. [1970] 1977. *The Structure of the Artistic Text*, trans. R. Vroon, Ann Arbor: University of Michigan, Department of Slavic Languages and Literatures.

Lotman, Ju. M. [1970] 2002. 'Kultura i informatsia', in Ju. M. Lotman, *Stati po semiotike kultury i iskusstva*, ed. R. G. Grigorev, 143–53, Saint Petersburg: Gumanitarnoe agentstvo 'Akademicheskii proekt'.

Lotman, Ju. M. 1981. 'Doklad 13 marta 1981 goda' [Typewritten from tape]. Manuscript in Juri Lotman Semiotics Repository, Tallinn University, 19 pages.

Lotman, J. 1984. 'Kultuur ja organism' [Culture and Organism], in T. Tiivel, K. Kull, T. Neuman and U. Sutrop (eds), *Teooria ja mudelid eluteaduses [Theory and Models in Life Sciences]*, 215–20, Tartu: TA.

Lotman, J. [1984] 2005. 'On the Semiosphere', trans. W. Clark, *Sign Systems Studies* 33 (1): 215–39.

Lotman, J. 1988. 'Natural Environment and Information', in K. Kull and T. Tiivel (eds), *Lectures in Theoretical Biology*, 45–7, Tallinn: Valgus.

Lotman, Yu. M. 1990a. *Universe of the Mind: A Semiotic Theory of Culture*, trans. A. Shukman, London: I.B. Tauris.

Lotman, J. 1990b. "'Vita aeterna' intervjuu' [Interview to 'Vita aeterna'], T. Tammaru (ed.), *Vita aeterna* 5: 12–20.

Lotman, J. 1991. 'Eessõna eestikeelsele väljaandele' [Introduction to the Estonian Edition], trans. R. Veidemann, in J. Lotman, *Kultuurisemiootika: Tekst – kirjandus – kultuur [Semiotics of Culture: Text – Literature – Culture]*, 3–6, Tallinn: Olion.

Lotman, Ju. M. 1992. *Kultura i vzryv*, Moscow: Gnozis.

Lotman, J. [1992] 2009. *Culture and Explosion*, trans. W. Clark, ed. M. Grishakova, Berlin and New York: Mouton de Gruyter.

Lotman, Ju. M. 1994. "'Prosmatrivaia zhizn s ee nachala": Vospominaniia', in A. D. Koshelev (ed.), *Iu. M. Lotman i tartusko-moskovskaya semioticheskaya shkola*, 465–74, Moscow: Gnozis.

Lotman, J. M. [1994/2010] 2013. *The Unpredictable Workings of Culture*, trans. B. J. Baer, ed. I. Pilshchikov and S. Salupere, Tallinn: TLU Press.

Lotman, Yu. and Pjatigorskij A. [1968] 1977. 'Text and Function', in D. P. Lucid (ed. and trans.), *Soviet Semiotics: An Anthology*, 125–35, Baltimore, MD: The Johns Hopkins University Press.

Lotman, Yu. M. and Uspenskij, B. A. [1971] 1978. 'On the Semiotic Mechanism of Culture', trans. G. Mihaychuk, *New Literary History* 9 (2): 211–32.

Lotman, Ju. M. and Uspenskij, B. A. 1984. "Authors' Introduction', in Ju. M. Lotman and B. A. Uspenskij, *The Semiotics of Russian Culture*, ed. A. Shukman, ix–xiv, Ann Arbor: Department of Slavic Languages and Literatures, University of Michigan.

Lotman, M. 2002. 'Umwelt and Semiosphere', *Sign Systems Studies* 30 (1): 33–40.

Machtyl, K. 2019. 'A Strawberry, an Animal Cry and a Human Subject: Where Existential Semiotics, Biosemiotics and Relational Metaphysics Seem to Meet One Another', *Sign Systems Studies* 47 (3/4): 436–52.

Magnus, R. and Remm, T. 2018. 'Urban Ecosemiotics of Trees: Why the Ecological Alien Species Paradigm Has Not Gained Ground in Cities?', *Sign Systems Studies* 46 (2/3): 319–42.

Mandelker, A. 1994. 'Semiotizing the Sphere: Organicist Theory in Lotman, Bakhtin, and Vernadsky', *Publications of the Modern Language Association* 109 (3): 385–96.

Maran, T. 2014. 'Biosemiotic Criticism: Modelling the Environment in Literature', *Green Letters: Studies in Ecocriticism* 18 (3): 297–311.

Maran, T. 2020. *Ecosemiotics: The Study of Signs in Changing Ecologies*, Cambridge: Cambridge University Press.

Marinakis, Y. 2012. 'On the Semiosphere, Revisited', *Signs* 6: 70–126.

Markoš, A. 2014. 'Biosphere as Semiosphere: Variations on Lotman', *Sign Systems Studies* 42 (4): 487–98.

Nöth, W. 2006. 'Yuri Lotman on Metaphors and Culture as Self-referential Semiospheres', *Semiotica* 161 (1/4): 249–63.

Patoine, P.-L. and Hope, J. 2015. 'The Semiosphere, Between Informational Modernity and Ecological Postmodernity', *Recherches sémiotiques / Semiotic Inquiry* 35 (1): 11–26.

Ponzio, A. and Petrilli, S. 2001. 'Bioethics, Semiotics of Life, and Global Communication', *Sign Systems Studies* 29 (1): 263–76.

Raudla, T. and Pern, T. 2011. The Tartu Connection: Thomas Sebeok's Correspondence with Juri Lotman', in P. Cobley, J. Deely, K. Kull and S. Petrilli (eds), *Semiotics Continues to Astonish: Thomas A. Sebeok and the Doctrine of Signs*, 475–84, Berlin: De Gruyter Mouton.

Salupere, S. 2011. 'Semiotics as Science', *Sign Systems Studies* 39 (2/4): 271–89.

Sebeok, T. A. 1988. 'In What Sense is Language a 'Primary Modeling System?', in H. Broms and R. Kaufmann (eds), *Semiotics of Culture: Proceedings of the 25th Symposium of the Tartu-Moscow School of Semiotics, Imatra, Finland, 27th–29th July, 1987*, 67–80, Helsinki: Arator.

Sebeok, T. A. 1998. 'The Estonian Connection', *Sign Systems Studies* 26: 20–41.

Sebeok, T. A. and Danesi, M. 2000. *The Forms of Meaning: Modeling Systems Theory and Semiotic Analysis*, Berlin: Mouton de Gruyter.

Semenenko, A. 2016. '*Homo polyglottus*: Semiosphere as a Model of Human Cognition', *Sign Systems Studies* 44 (4): 494–510.

Siewers, A. K. 2011. 'Pre-modern Ecosemiotics: The Green World as Literary Ecology', in T. Peil (ed.), *The Space of Culture – The Place of Nature in Estonia and Beyond*, 39–68, Tartu: University of Tartu Press.

Siewers, A. K. 2014. 'Introduction: Song, Tree, and Spring: Environmental Meaning and Environmental Humanities', in A. K. Siewers (ed.), *Re-imagining Nature: Environmental Humanities and Ecosemiotics*, 1–41, Bucknell: Bucknell University Press.

Steiner, P. [1984] 2014. *Russian Formalism: A Metapoetics*, Geneva: sdvig press.

Tamm, M. and Kull, K. 2016. 'Toward a Reterritorialization of Cultural Theory: Estonian Theory from Baer via Uexküll to Lotman', *History of Human Sciences* 29 (1): 75–98.

Torop, P. 2019. 'Russian Theory and Semiotics of Culture: History and Perspectives', *Bakhtiniana: Revista de Estudos do Discurso* 14 (4): 19–39.

Vaiksoo, R. M. 2018. 'Oleg Mutt tõi zoosemiootika eestikeelsesse kirjandusse' [Oleg Mutt Introduced Zoosemiotics in Estonian Language], *Acta Semiotica Estica* 15: 225–7.

Velmezova, E. and Kull, K. 2016. 'Tõlkimine kui zoosemiootika põhiküsimus: Aleksei Turovski ja Tartu–Moskva koolkond' [Translation as a Key Issue in Zoosemiotics: Aleksei Turovski and Tartu-Moscow School], *Acta Semiotica Estica* 13: 197–210.

Żyłko, B. 2016. 'Jurij Łotman: od poetyki strukturalnej do semiotycznej teorii kultury', *Konteksty* 314 (3/4): 143–46.

CHAPTER 35
LOTMAN AND COGNITIVE NEUROSCIENCE
Edna Andrews

Более того, чем труднее и неадекватнее перевод одной непересекающейся части пространства на язык другой, тем более ценным в информационном и социальном отношениях становится факт этого парадоксального общения. Можно сказать, что перевод непереводимого оказывается носителем информации высокой ценности.

Moreover, the more difficult the translation of a non-intersecting space into another language, the more valued this paradoxical interaction becomes in terms of informativeness and social relationships. One might say that the translation of the untranslatable turns out to be the carrier of highly valuable information.

– Juri Lotman (1992: 15)

The breadth of Juri Lotman's impact on contemporary semiotic theory has been profound, and the current volume attests to the importance of his major contributions. This final chapter will focus on the future of Lotmanian semiotic theory and how it impacts and will continue to inform developments in cognitive neuroscience. Previous chapters have examined Lotman in the context of intellectual figures who have contributed to his theories, his role in the Tartu-Moscow school, fundamental contributions and modelling, and how his work engages across disciplines and periods of time.

In the context of cognitive neuroscience, I have selected contributions by Lotman that speak to the shift from cognitive science to cognitive neuroscience. The following analysis includes the newer trends and best practices for analysing the interaction of brain and language, and more precisely brains and languages, including research focusing on embodied cognition, as well as neuroimaging studies that illuminate how human brains process languages. As the opening quote demonstrates, the *plural* is imperative in Lotman's work, and it is equally imperative in scientific research on brain and language given the fact that most of the world's speakers are bi- or multilingual (de Bot 2009: 425).

We begin our journey with Lotman's notions of communication acts, his relationship to Jakobson and Peirce, and his modelling of the semiosphere, followed by the critical role of collective memory and culture texts and the relevance of key Lotmanian concepts in contemporary cognitive neuroscience. Our analysis will conclude with a recontextualization of Lotman's cultural semiotics and other semiotics, including biosemiotics and zoosemiotics.

Background: Lotman, Sebeok and moving toward the cognitive sciences

As early as the 1970s, Thomas Sebeok introduces a terminological distinction ('perception' instead of 'cognition') that underscores his positioning of semiotics and its potential relationship to the original *cognitive sciences* (computer science, philosophy, psychology and linguistics) (Andrews 2003: 53). By the 1980s, semiotics became known not only in the context of human anthropological and linguistic systems (anthroposemiotics) but also in reclaiming earlier semiotic models found in Jakob von Uexküll's theory of biology (*Umwelt*) (1928; [1940] 1982). And it is at this point that Lotman articulates his theory of the *semiosphere*, a term derived from Vladimir Vernadsky's *biosphere* (1926).

In his introduction to *Universe of the Mind* (1990: ix–x), Umberto Eco summarizes Lotman's key theoretical positions in four statements: (1) the call for the elimination of the opposition between exact science and humanities, (2) to present semiotic systems as *modelling systems* that both *construct* and *explain* the world in which humans live (systems that are a-historical and embedded in complex systems of 'non-hereditary collective memory' (Lotman and Uspenskij 1971)), (3) to require that all cultural spaces are based on multiple linguo-cultural codes and (4) to position semiotics to be a *cognitive science.*

Modelling meaning generation: Jakobson and Lotman

At the very beginning of his chapter on autocommunication and speech acts, Lotman immediately states that he is using Roman Jakobson's modelling of communication as the basis for his work (Lotman 1990: 20ff; Andrews 2003; 2012). In order to fully appreciate Lotman's innovation to this model, a few words are appropriate to contextualize Jakobson's speech act model (also referred to as the speech event model). According to Jakobson, any speech act requires a minimum of six factors and functions as the 'constitutive factors in any speech event, in any act of verbal communication' and 'each of these six factors determines a different function of language' (Jakobson [1960] 1987: 66). Jakobson takes these six factors and maps them onto six functions to yield the diagram reproduced in Figure 35.1 (adapted from Jakobson [1960] 1987: 66–71).

This important heuristic is not a description of speech acts, but rather *explains* the mechanism for the generation of meaning(s) in any linguistic act – a mechanism based on the constant dynamic of shifting hierarchies and emergent, negotiated meanings. Jakobson's *minimalist model* is defined to accommodate all languages of the world and schematize how meanings emerge in linguistic interaction (oral/aural, visual, gestural, etc.). Figurative and literal meanings are treated as different points on a continuum, not as different *types* of meanings. JSAM is valid for describing ecologically valid speech acts within speech communities (with healthy subjects and in pathology), and anticipates the relevance of both intended and non-intended participants. *All six factors and functions are obligatorily present in any speech event, but they exist in a relatively determined hierarchy that is renegotiated anew in each instantiation and retrospectively.* Furthermore, one and the same speech act may be apprehended and comprehended by speakers and

Factors		
	Context	
	Contact	
Addresser		Addressee
	Code	
	Message	

Functions		
	Referential	
	Phatic	
Emotive		Conative
	Metalingual	
	Poetic	

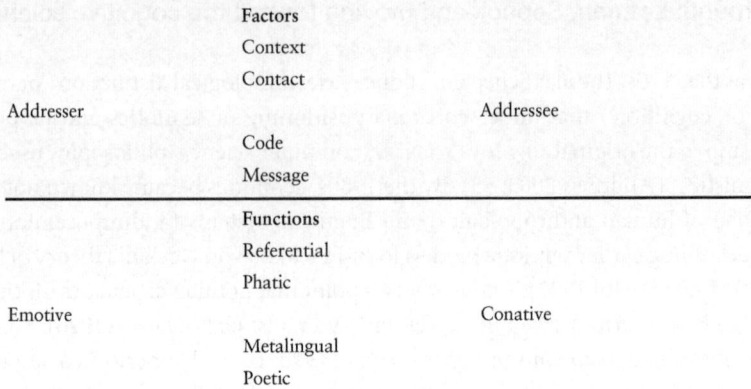

Figure 35.1 Jakobson's speech act model of six factors mapped onto six functions.

hearers in varying ways with different hierarchical realizations and unique mappings to any of the factors and their functional interrelations. The dominant factor/function of any given speech act may be singular or multiple, and the emergent meanings remain dynamic and may be renegotiated over time. There are multiple significant outcomes of the application of this model: (1) The Jakobsonian model requires the recognition that *referential* meaning is *a* type of meaning, but not the only type (or even the most important type) that emerges in language; (2) the language users/participants are defined internally within the factors and functions of the speech act itself, not 'add-ons' to a disembodied code and message. There is no question that the cognitive linguistic approach to meaning as 'constructed' and the importance of speakers and hearers as 'active participants in constructing meaning on-line in specific contexts' (Kövecses 2006: 249) is compatible with Jakobson's speech act model.

Lotman contributes his own extension to this robust modelling system through his important doubling of the factors and functions of Jakobson's model with a focus on addresser, message, code and channel. This doubling is required to accommodate the important baseline requirement for two or more languages and the notion of *autocommunication*. The primary role of autocommunication is to create new information, it is not defined by redundancy and is not self-contained (Lotman 1990: 20–2, Andrews 2003: 28ff). As I have noted earlier, Lotman's description of communication systems and the generation of new information shares interesting parallels with Gerald Edelman's (1987) and Rosenfield's (1989) modelling of dynamic human memory systems (Andrews 2003: 166). Lotman's revision of Jakobson's model is a central component of *culture texts* and text generation in the *semiosphere* (see the following section).

Culture texts

Culture texts, as defined by the Tartu-Moscow School, is defined as a set of functional principles and is the central structure through which a cultural space acquires information about itself and the surrounding context. All culture texts are (1) dynamic semiotic unities, (2) serve as carriers of any and all integrated messages (including verbal, visual, art forms, rituals, etc.) and (3) not all usages of language are automatically defined as texts (Lotman et al. [1973] 2013: 57–8). Culture texts include not only artistic (aesthetic) forms of literary and visual arts texts, but also simple speech acts as described earlier and other meaning-generating symbolic systems. All text generation requires 'semiotic transformations' and obligatory acts of translation across semiospheric boundaries (cf. opening epigraph of this analysis), where emergent meanings may be unpredictable (Lotman 1990: 77).[1]

Structuralist and non-structuralist semiotics: Lotman and Peirce

> There are two scientific traditions that given the foundation of semiotics. One comes from Peirce and Morris, and begins with the concept of the sign as the primary element of any semiotic system. The second is based on Saussure and the Prague School, where the basis is the antinomy of language and speech (text) . . . in the first case we have the isolated sign, [. . .] the second point of view is specifically expressed in the desire to examine the discrete communication act.
>
> *– Juri Lotman ([1984] 1992: 11)*

Given the absence of translations of Peirce's work in Russian and because of Lotman's focus on binarism, it is clear that Lotman's introduction to and understanding of Peircean signs came through Jakobson's work. In fact, in the single reference to Peirce in Lotman's 1990 book, the reference is to Jakobson 'reflecting' on Peirce, not to Peirce directly. Thus, we see Jakobson as a bridge connecting Lotman to Peircean sign theory (Peirce 1957; 1931–58). Jakobson's semiotics blends both structuralist and non-structuralist trends by bringing together European and Soviet structural semiotics with Peircean non-structuralist semiotics. Peircean semiotics, with its deep connection to the philosophy of science and clear departure from the structuralist tradition, provides a framework for categorizing irreducible triadic sign types into a theory of signs, modes of inquiry and types of inference (e.g. abduction, induction, deduction). For Peirce, the triadic sign includes three relationships: sign–sign, sign–dynamic object and sign–final interpretant. The icon/index/symbol triad is part of the sign–dynamic object relationship (Peirce 2.246; Savan 1976; Andrews 1990: 46–64).

Following Jakobson's introduction of the Peircean sign-object triad into the vocabulary of modern linguistics in the 1940s, these sign types became a prominent feature of linguistic theory. Jakobson linked Peircean categories to metaphor and metonymy, to verbal grammatical categories called *shifters* in his landmark study originally published in 1957 ('Shifters, Verbal Categories and the Russian Verb'), and deixis in this first wave of iconicity and indexicality. These influences are present in Lotman's characterizations of iconicity and the symbolic level. However, Lotman only makes limited reference to indexicality. Lotman articulates the view that it is the Saussurean, not Peircean, tradition, that places communication acts as starting points for semiotic analysis, while Peircean sign theory only focuses on the individual sign (Lotman [1984] 1992: 11). And it is signification and communication acts that build the fundamental semiotic mechanism of Lotman's semiosphere.

Semiosphere

> Semiotic space stands before us as a multilayered intersection of differentiated texts brought together into a specific level, including complex internal correspondences reflecting different degrees of translatability and spaces of untranslatability.
>
> – *Juri Lotman (1992: 42)*

Lotman defines the *semiosphere* as 'the semiotic space necessary for the existence and functioning of languages, not the sum total of different languages; in a sense the semiosphere has a prior existence and is in constant interaction with languages [. . .] a generation of information' (1990: 123, 127). This space is both a *precursor to* and *a result of* cultural development (1990: 125). One of the most important structural and functional semiotic mechanisms of the semiosphere is the notion of *boundary* (Russian *granitsa*).

All semiospheres are by definition heterogeneous, dynamic and asymmetrical semiotic spaces that guarantee future changes within the functioning system. Note that the importance of heterogeneity is a principle of all *speech communities* (following Dell Hymes,) and this principle plays a central role in all of modern sociolinguistic theory. Lotman also includes binarism as a defining characteristic of the semiosphere, but in a very specific way: 'Binarism, however, must be understood as a principle which is realized *in plurality* since every newly formed language is in turn subdivided on a binary principle' (Lotman 1990: 124).

Lotman's application of this definition of binaries occurs in two instances: (1) centre versus periphery and (2) the fundamental types of dynamic change – continuous and discontinuous. How Lotman's notion of binarism is implemented has a direct impact on determining compatibility between Lotman's theory and Peircean sign theory.

The ideological fundamentals of *Culture and Explosion* (1992) imply Lotman's concept of the *semiosphere*, originally introduced in 1984. In addition to the four defining characteristics given earlier, Lotman includes a fifth point – the 'development of a metalanguage' as the final act of the system's structural organization (1990: 124–40). Of these five points, only one is discussed in *Culture and Explosion*. In fact, the term *semiosphere* only appears in *Culture and Explosion* on two occasions. Specifically, in the chapter entitled 'The Logic of Explosion', Lotman focuses on the notion of heterogeneity as a characteristic of not only spatial differentiation, but also different rates of change between and within individual subspaces of the semiosphere:

> Semiological space is filled with the freely moving fragments of a variety of structures which, however, store stably within themselves a memory of the whole

which, falling into a strange environment, can suddenly and vigorously restore themselves [. . .].

Completely stable invariant semiotic structures apparently do not exist at all. (Lotman 1992: 177)

Lotman's reiteration of the importance of a complex *dynamic* within and around the semiosphere speaks to its critical role in capturing the essence of its explanatory power as a modelling system. The fundamental tenet of Lotman's approach to semiotics is the importance of semiotics as a dynamic process of *semiosis,* which is a system-level phenomenon engaging multiple sign complexes that are given simultaneously across spatiotemporal boundaries. As Lotman's work is contextualized into the broader fields of structuralist and non-structuralist-semiotic paradigms (e.g. comparisons with the works of Saussure, Hjelmslev, Peirce, Jakobson and others) and more recently the cognitive sciences, it is crucial to understand Lotman's decision to target his theoretical models at the system level, and not at the individual sign level. This fact may explain, for example, why Lotman does not devote more works to explications of Peircean sign types (iconicity, indexicality and symbolic distinctions).

Lotman's work has often been read through the prism of other semiotic contributors of the twentieth century, resulting in what often appears to be an attempt to position Lotman as more of a borrower of ideas than an innovator of ideas. While it is certainly true that Lotman was deeply influenced by his own professors and some of the most outstanding intellectuals of his day, Lotman's work is unique in its achievement of a broadly based *metalanguage* for the *modelling* of cultures, *a system of systems.* Lotman's interest in modelling systems involves two major trajectories: (1) the creation of metasemiotics, which focuses more on modelling the text than the text itself, and (2) the specific semiotic functioning of actual texts ([1981] 1992: 129). It is the second trajectory that gives rise to a developed discipline of cultural semiotics. Lotman's formulation and explication of semiospheric space is the single most powerful contributing factor to his success in presenting a usable metalanguage for cultural analysis. Vyacheslav Ivanov, Lotman's colleague and co-founder of the Tartu-Moscow school, is very emphatic in his refocusing of the semiotic agenda to contextualize itself within the defining principles and mechanisms of the semiosphere itself (Ivanov 1998: 792).

Lotman's requirement of multiple languages as 'the minimal meaning-generating unit' (1992: 16) may be interpreted in a variety of ways and on a variety of levels. For instance, these different languages could be the languages of the internal spaces of the semiosphere and the surrounding spaces in which the semiosphere is situated or could include Lotman's fundamental distinction between I–I (also called *autocommunication*) and I–s/he models of communication as presented in *Universe of the Mind* (1990: 21–33). As autocommunication creates *new information* at both the cultural and individual levels, specific characteristics are manifested, including (1) its qualitative reconstruction, (2) not being self-contained or redundant and (3) the doubling and redefinition of both the *message* and the *code* (1990: 21–2).

An interesting corollary of Lotman's requirement of a minimum of two languages is that all phenomena must be translated in order to be perceived in semiospheric space. Such a formulation brings Lotman closer to Peircean *interpretants*. Furthermore, all translations necessarily change meaning, and the act of non-comprehension is as salient as the act of comprehension.

The relationship between translatability and nontranslatability in Lotmanian theory is an important source of *tension*, which is a basic structural principle of all semiotic space and plays an integral part in the realization of discontinuities in the dynamic form of *explosions*. In the introductory chapter of *Culture and Explosion*, Lotman describes the interrelationship of the multiple languages that lie at the heart of semiotic space and their mutual untranslatability (or limited translatability) as the 'source of adjustment of the extra-lingual object to its reflection in the world of languages' (1992: 10). Lotman expands this description in his definition of semiotic space:

> Semiotic space appears before us as the multi-layered intersection of various texts, which are woven together in a specific layer characterized by complex internal relationships and variable degrees of translatability and spaces of untranslatability. (1992: 42)

Collective memory, semiosphere and the *distributive cognitive-cultural network*

Lotman's focus on the importance of collective memory and collective intellect plays an essential role in defining the structure of the semiosphere and, in fact, all linguistic signification and communication.

> ... culture is both collective intellect and collective memory, i.e. a supra-individual mechanism of preservation and the conveyance of specific messages (texts) and the generation of new ones [...].
> Cultural memory is not only unified, but also has internal heterogeneity. This means that its unity exists only at a specific level, and presupposes the existence of discrete 'dialects of memory' that correspond to the internal organization of collectives that constitute the world of a particular culture. (Lotman [1985]1992: 200)

Collective memory is a mechanism for self-preservation and cultural propagation. Lotman's perspective on the importance of oral and written culture texts as the basis for collective memory is central to explaining the role of language in this process. In shifting the burden of memory from the individual to an externalized symbolic system collectively maintained through the process of writing, we are able to see more clearly how oral texts place a greater load on the individual's memory system (1990: 246–7). Thus, language becomes the symbolic condenser of the different levels of semiosis and different temporal segments (1990: 110). Lotman combines the forces of collective memory and collective intellect to construct a model of culture in which knowledge is maintained and transferred through time, and the actualization of codified and innovative information are guaranteed (Lotman [1985] 1992: 200; Andrews 2003: 157). Lotman's semiosphere is critical for understanding the construction and maintenance of *non-hereditary collective memory*, and it is precisely non-hereditary collective memory that is central to the identity of cultural spaces and their languages. There are interesting parallels to be found in cognitive neuroscience research of memory systems. Steven Rose consistently points out the importance of the interaction of collective and individual memory systems: 'Individual our memories may be, but they are structured, their very brain mechanisms affected by the collective, social nature of the way we as humans live' (Rose 1992: 60).

There is one other important connection that should be noted between Lotman's definition of the semiosphere and collective memory – Merlin Donald's *distributed cognitive-cultural network* (2004: 34–58). Lotman and Donald share the view of human nature based on flexibility of cognition and 'novel ways' of conducting cognitive activity. First and foremost, all conducting of cognitive activity is given in the interaction of cognition with the cultural context. Lotman's construction of the semiosphere and its role in cognition and cultural meaning is in keeping with the central notions in Donald's *distributed cognitive-cultural network*:

> The human mind has evolved a symbiosis that links brain development to cognitive networks who properties can change radically. Critical mental capabilities, such as language and symbol-based thinking (as in mathematics) are made possible only by evolving distributed systems. Culture itself has network properties now found in individual brains. The individual mind is thus a hybrid project, partly organismic in origin, and partly ecological, shaped by a distributed network whose properties are changing. (2004: 35)

I would also like to suggest that there are important synergies between Lotman's semiosphere and the mechanisms for meaning generation and the twenty-first-century neuroscience perspective of the importance of bilateral processing of languages and music, default mode networks, multimodal interactions and innovative approaches to memory systems, including updates to the components framework and *process-specific alliances* (PSA) (Cabeza and Moscovitch 2013). For an extensive examination of these questions, see Andrews et al. 2013 and Andrews 2014.

We also see important discussions and analyses focusing on *embodied cognition* and neural processing of language (Gallese and Lakoff 2005). Vittorio Gallese and George Lakoff make a compelling argument in favour of a view of the sensory-motor system of the brain as a multimodal system, where conceptual knowledge, including human language, is embodied in the multimodality of the sensor-motor system which links 'sight, hearing, touch, motor actions, and son on' (Gallese and Lakoff 2005: 456). Their work provides evidence for a rejection of older and more controversial modular views of language(s) and brain. One of the components of embodied cognition research is given by a 'unified explanatory framework' that provides a path for reconciling neuroscience and neural computational research with cognitive linguistics. The conclusions of their research are focused on strong statements about how language(s) are mapped in the brain, and include a reaffirmation that language piggybacks on the same neurological systems critical for perception and action and rejection of any type of 'language module' (Gallese and Lakoff 2005: 474). An examination of how Lotmanian semiotics might inform, contextualize and deepen approaches grounded in embodied cognition is worth pursuing. Future research is needed to develop and elucidate detailed interactions between Lotman's cultural semiotic theory, Donald's distributed cognitive-cultural network and neuroimaging studies of languages and other complex sensory-motor processes.

Connecting cultural semiotics and biosemiotics: Lotman and the University of Tartu

By way of conclusion, I would like to return to Lotman's life in Tartu beginning in 1950 at the Tartu Teachers Institute, and where he stayed until his death in 1993. In 1952, Lotman declined a position offered to him at the University of Tartu, but he did accept a position there in 1954. Lotman chaired the Department of Russian Literature at the university from 1960 to 1977, and subsequently moved to the Department of Literary Theory while continuing to teach in the Russian literature department. Kalevi Kull's 1999 paper, 'Towards Biosemiotics with Yuri Lotman', does an outstanding job of revealing Lotman's deep interest in biological sciences and biosemiotics and his 'sense of biological holism' as an important aspect of Lotman's oeuvre (Kull 1999: 127). A common ground between von Uexküll's theory of *Umwelt* and Lotman's modelling of the semiosphere is the requirement for autocommunication in order for sign interpretation to occur (Lotman 1990: 21–35) and the importance of the metatextual level (for Lotman – metatexts and for Uexküll – metainterpretations) (Andrews 2003: 66–8).

Lotman's focus on more general principles of complexity and information transmission and his important connections with von Uexküll are explored by Kalevi Kull and Timo Maran in Chapter 34 of this volume. Lotman directly draws analogies between his notion of *semiosphere* and Vernadsky's *biosphere* and reminds the reader that all living organisms, including humans, are a 'function of the biosphere' (Lotman 1990: 125; [1984] 1992: 12). Lotman reiterates the significance of 'energy production' and entropy, and information flow in his writings, and brings them into his explanation of the impact of 'self-description' within the semiosphere, which more closely connects him to Sebeok's work in bio- and zoosemiotics:

> The highest form and final act of a semiotic system's structural organization is when it describes itself. This is the stage when grammars are written, customs and laws codified. When this happens, however, the *system gains the advantage of*

greater structural organization, but loses its inner reserves of indeterminacy which provide it with flexibility, heightened capacity for information and the potential for dynamic development.

The stage of self-description is a necessary response to the threat of too much diversity within the semiosphere: the system might lose its unity and definition, and disintegrate. Whether we have in mind language, politics or culture, the mechanism is the same: one part of the semiosphere (as a rule one which is part of its nuclear structure) in the process of self-description creates its own grammar; this self-description may be real or ideal[ized] depending on whether its inner orientation is towards the present or the future. (Lotman 1990: 128 [my emphasis in italics])

The works of Juri Lotman and his profound contribution to a theory of semiotics will continue to generate new research and new connections across not only the empirical, biological cognitive, social and neurosciences, but also the humanities, including research on Russian culture and Russian culture texts for many years to come.

Note

1. All translations except for Lotman 1990 are the author's. The Russian original for each quote from Lotman in English will appear in this note section in the order that it appears in the text.

    Общеизвестно, что у истоков семиотики лежат две научные традиции. Одна из них восходит к Пирсу Моррису и отправляется от понятия знака как первоэлемента всякой семиотической системы. Вторая основывается на тезисах Соссюра и Пражской школы и кладет в основу антиномию языка и речи (текста) [...] в первом случае в основу анализа кладется изолированный знак [...]. Вторая точка зрения, в частности, выразилась в стремлении рассматривать отдельный коммуникативный акт. (Lotman [1984] 1992: 11)

    Семиотическое пространство предстает перед нами как многослойное пересечение различных текстов, вместе складывающихся в определенный пласт, со сложными внутренними соотношениями, разной степенью переводимости и пространствами непереводимости. (Lotman 1992: 42)

    Семиологическое пространство заполнено свободно передвигающимися обломками различных структур, которые, однако, устойчиво хранят в себе память о целом и, попадая в чужие пространства, могут вдруг бурно реставрироваться [...]. Полностью стабильных, не изменяющихся семиотических структур, видимо, не существует вообще. (Lotman 1992: 177)

    Семиотическое пространство предстает перед нами как многослойное пересечение различных текстов, вместе складывающихся в определенный пласт, со сложными внутренними соотношениями, разной степенью переводимости и пространствами непереводимости. (Lotman 1992: 42)

    ... культура представляет собой коллективный интеллект и коллективную память, т.е. надындивидуальный механизм хранения и передачи некоторых сообщений (текстов) и выработки новых [...]. Память культуры не только едина, но и внутренне разнообразна. Это означает, что ее единство существует лишь на некотором уровне и подразумевает наличие частных «диалектов памяти», соответствующих внутренней организации коллективов, составляющих мир данной культуры. (Lotman [1985] 1992: 200)

References

Andrews, E. 1990. *Markedness Theory: The Union of Asymmetry and Semiosis in Language*, Durham, NC: Duke Univeristy Press.

Andrews, E. 2003. *Conversations with Lotman: Cultural Semiotics in Language, Literature, and Cognition*, Toronto: Toronto University Press.

Andrews, E. 2012. 'Lotman and the Cognitive Sciences: The Role of Autocommunication in the Language of Memory', in S. Frank, C. Ruhe and A. Schmitz (eds), *Explosion und Peripherie. Jurij Lotmans Semiotik der kulturellen Dynamik revisited*, 175–92, Bielefeld: transkript.

Andrews, E. 2014. *Neuroscience and Multilingualism*, Cambridge: Cambridge University Press.

Andrews, E., Frigau, L., Voyvodic-Casabo, C., Voyvodic, J. and Wright, J. 2013. 'Multilingualism and fMRI: Longitudinal Study of Second Language Acquisition', *Brain Sciences* 3 (2): 849–76.

Cabeza, R. and Moscovitch, M. 2013. 'Memory Systems, Processing Modes, and Components: Functional Neuroimaging Evidence', *Perspectives on Psychological Science* 8 (1): 49–55.

de Bot, K. 2009. 'Multilingualism and Aging', in T. K. Bhatia and W. C. Ritchie (eds), *The New Handbook of Second Language Acquisition*, 425–42, Bingley: Emerald Group Publishing.

Donald, M. 2004. 'The Definition of Human Nature', in D. Rees and S. Rose (eds), *The New Brain Sciences. Perils and Prospects*, Cambridge: Cambridge University Press.

Eco, U. 1990. 'Introduction', in Yu. M. Lotman, *Universe of the Mind: A Semiotic Theory of Culture*, trans. A. Shukman, vii–xiii, Bloomington: Indiana University Press.

Edelman, G. M. 1987. *Neural Darwinism: The Theory of Neuronal Group Selection*, New York: Basic Books.

Gallese, V. and Lakoff, G. 2005. 'The Brain's Concepts: The Role of the Sensory-Motor System in Conceptual Knowledge', *Cognitive Neuropsychology* 22: 455–79.

Ivanov, V. V. 1998. *Izbrannye trudy po semiotike i istorii kul'tury*, vol. 1, Moscow: Iazyki russkoi kul'tury.

Jakobson, R. [1960] 1987. 'Linguistics and Poetics', in R. Jakobson, *Language in Literature*, eds. K. Pomorska and S. Rudy, 62–94, Cambridge, MA: Belknap Press of Harvard University Press.

Kövecses, Z. 2006. *Language, Mind and Culture: A Practical Introduction*, Oxford: Oxford University Press.

Kull, K. 1999. 'Towards Biosemiotics with Yuri Lotman', *Semiotica* 127 (1/4): 115–31.

Lotman, Ju. M. [1981] 1992. 'Semiotika kul'tury i poniatie teksta', in Ju. M. Lotman, *Izbrannye stat'i v trekh tomakh*, vol. 1, 129–32, Tallinn: Aleksandra.

Lotman, Ju. M. [1984] 1992. 'Semiosfera', in Ju. M. Lotman, *Izbrannye stat'i v trekh tomakh*, vol. 1, 11–24, Tallinn: Aleksandra.

Lotman, Ju. M. [1985] 1992. "Pamiat' v kul'turologitcheskom osveshchenii', in Ju. M. Lotman, *Izbrannye stat'i v trekh tomakh*, vol. 1, 200–2, Tallinn: Aleksandra.

Lotman, Yu. M. 1990. *Universe of the Mind: A Semiotic Theory of Culture*, trans. A. Shukman, Bloomington: Indiana University Press.

Lotman, Ju. M. 1992. *Kul'tura i vzryv*, Moscow: Gnozis.

Lotman, Ju. M. and Uspenskij, B. A. 1971. 'O semioticheskom mekhanizme kul'tury', *Trudy po znakovym sistemam* 5: 144–66.

Lotman, J. M., Ivanov, V. V., Pjatigorskij, A. M., Toporov, V. N. and Uspenskij, B. A. [1973] 2013. 'Theses on the Semiotic Study of Cultures (as Applied to Slavic Texts)', in S. Salupere, P. Torop and K. Kull (eds), *Beginnings of the Semiotics of Culture*, 53–77, Tartu: University of Tartu Press.

Peirce, C. S. 1957. *Essays in the Philosophy of Science*, New York: Liberal Arts Press.

Peirce, C. S. 1931–58. *Collected Papers of Charles Sanders Peirce*, Cambridge, MA: Harvard University Press.

Rose, S. 1992. *The Making of Memory: From Molecules to Mind*, New York and London: Anchor Books.

Rosenfield, I. 1989. *The Invention of Memory*, New York: Basic Books.

Savan, D. 1976. *An Introduction to Peirce's Semiotic*, Toronto: Victoria University.

Uexküll, J. von. 1928. *Theoretische Biologie*, Berlin: Springer.

Uexküll, J. von. [1940] 1982. 'The Theory of Meaning', *Semiotica* 42 (1): 25–82.

Vernadsky, V. I. 1926. *Biosfera*, Leningrad: Nauchno-techn. Izd.

JURI LOTMAN IN ENGLISH
A BIBLIOGRAPHY
Remo Gramigna

Introduction

While in the past cataloguing and listing was a common modality of representation (Eco 2009), compiling bibliographies is something out of fashion today. The present work is the result of several years of research carried out while teaching at the Department of Semiotics of the University of Tartu, in Estonia.[1] The purpose of this study is to offer to all those, students and experts in the field, who are interested in the scholarship of Juri Lotman a bird's eye view of his work. Undoubtedly, this is a very ambitious project, and it is by no means exhaustive. However, it is my hope that this endeavour will be useful to all the students and researchers who are interested in the subject.

This bibliography lists the writings of Lotman translated or published in English that have appeared between 1973 and 2020. This list includes a wide range of items: articles, books, anthologies, book chapters, special issues, bibliographies and doctoral dissertations that have appeared in English since the inception of the Tartu-Moscow school, of which Lotman was the founder and the *spiritus movens*. Publications were selected on the basis of their relevance to the subject and were consulted *de visu*.

The bibliography has a limited scope and follows a practical criterion, for it covers publications only in the English language by and about Lotman. The works of Lotman have been reaching the West since the late 1960s and have been translated into many languages (Prevignano 1979; Winner 2002). The reader may find relevant information by consulting bibliographies of Lotman's works in different languages (Cáceres Sánchez 1995; Elkouch 2016; Fleishman 1976; Fleisher and Grzybek 1995; Gherlone 2015; Makura 1994; Sedda 2006; Volkova 2019).

Needless to say, a bibliography always faces the difficult issue of the criteria used for the selection of the writings catalogued. This point is worth pondering. Would a bibliography on the works of and by Lotman include exclusively publications that have his name explicitly next to the title? Or should those articles that – even starting from different premises and without mention of Lotman's name in the title – provide the reader with important data useful to the student of Lotman's thought also be listed? This is not a trivial question. Secondary literature devoted to the subjects of the Tartu-Moscow school, so-called 'Soviet semiotics', as well as the 'semiotics of culture' generally also provide useful insights on Lotman, and for this reason are listed in this bibliography, although these entries are not exclusively about Lotman. Although this may be a quite arbitrary choice, it is my contention that it is also the most appropriate one. Thus, in selecting the secondary literature I kept in mind that in the articles and books that deal with the Tartu-Moscow school, 'Soviet semiotics' and the 'semiotics of culture' – which are larger areas than Lotman's thought – valuable and relevant ideas can often be found that are sometimes tangentially, and at other times more directly, related to Lotman. Moreover, the list includes short encyclopaedic articles on Lotman because, even in their concise form, they offer valuable information to the reader.

Similar attempts at providing an overview of literature about Lotman's writings in English are not entirely a novelty. Ann Shukman (1978), Karl Eimermacher and Serge Shishkoff (1976; 1977) included in their own bibliographies on the Tartu-Moscow school a specific section devoted to the 'writings on Soviet semiotics' (Shukman 1978: 594–6) or 'selected writings on Soviet semiotics and structuralism' (Eimermacher and Shishkoff 1977: 131–40). More recently, Kalevi Kull (2011) compiled the first bibliography of the works of Lotman published in English, which has since been updated (Kull and Gramigna 2014). The first publication included 109 entries published from 1973 to 2011 and the second bibliography updated the list to 2014, reaching 122 entries. I am very much indebted to these two previous works; the present endeavour may be considered as a continuation of the same effort. Yet, about ten years have passed and since then we have witnessed an increase in publication on this subject. Indeed, Lotman's scholarship has seen a re-emergence in the international panorama of the humanities as is apparent from the proliferation of publications devoted to Lotman's thought.

Thus, the present bibliography seeks to continue the work already done in cataloguing Juri Lotman's scholarly achievement by presenting an updated version of the English bibliography on Lotman published earlier and by mapping the most relevant literature on the topic. This list includes 404 entries in total, of which 148 are the writings of Lotman published from 1973 to 2020 in English. As compared to previous bibliographies of Lotman in English published in recent years, the present work is not limited to primary sources. Indeed, it includes a separate section devoted exclusively to the secondary literature on Lotman published in English.

Thus, the enumerative bibliography consists of two parts. While Part I lists English translations of Lotman's writings (from 1973 to 2020), Part II lists writings published in English about Lotman. Part I is listed in chronological order and follows, updates and provides some correction to the work carried out previously in the same field. Part II follows alphabetical and chronological order. I divided Part II into four subsections: (II.1) bibliographies, (II.2) special issues, (II.3) anthologies and (II.4) writings on Lotman, with the hope of facilitating the use of the bibliography.

Note

1. I would like to thank Kalevi Kull, Silvi Salupere, Peter Grzybek, Marek Tamm, Peeter Torop and Pietro Restaneo for reading the several earlier drafts of this bibliography and for providing me with valuable feedback.

References

Cáceres Sánchez, M. (1995), 'Iuri M. Lotman y la escuela semiótica de Tartu-Moscú: Bibliografía en español, francés, inglés, italiano, portugués y alemán', *Signa: Revista de la Asociación Española de Semiótica*, 4: 45–76.

Eco, U. (2009), *Vertigine della lista*, Milan: Bompiani.

Eimermacher, K. and Shishkoff, S. (1976), 'Selected bibliography of soviet semiotics', *Dispositio*, 1 (3): 364–70.

Eimermacher, K. and Shishkoff, S. (1977), *Subject Bibliography of Soviet Semiotics: The Moscow-Tartu School*, Ann Arbor: Michigan Slavic Publications.

Elkouch, H. (2016), 'Juri Lotman in Arabic: A bibliography', *Sign Systems Studies*, 44 (3): 452–5.

Fleishman, L. (1976), 'A bibliography of the works of Yury Lotman', in Y. Lotman, *Analysis of the Poetic Text*, ed. and trans. D. B. Johnson, 299–309, Ann Arbor: Ardis.

Fleisher, M. and Grzybek, P. (1995), 'Bibliographie der wissenschaftlichen Arbeiten von Ju. M. Lotman (1949–1992)', *Znakolog: An International Yearbook of Slavic Semiotics*, 5: 209–25.

Gherlone, L. (2015), 'Bibliografia essenziale', in M. Bertelé, A. Bianco and A. Cavallaro (eds.), *Le Muse fanno il girotondo Jurij Lotman e le arti. Studi in onore di Giuseppe Barbieri. Atti del convegno internazionale Università Ca' Foscari Venezia 26–28 novembre 2013*, 186–91, Crocetta del Montello: Terra Ferma.

Kull, K. (2011), 'Juri Lotman in English', *Sign Systems Studies*, 39 (2/4): 343–56.

Kull, K. and Gramigna, R. (2014), 'Juri Lotman in English: Updates to bibliography', *Sign Systems Studies*, 42 (4): 549–52.

Makura, V. (1994), 'A bibliography of Lotman, Yurii: Works published in Czech and Slovak', *Ceska Literatura*, 42 (1): 107–8.

Prevignano, C., ed. (1979), *La semiotica nei paesi slavi. Programmi, problemi, analisi*, Milan: Feltrinelli.

Sedda, F. (2006), 'Bibliografia dei testi di Jurij M. Lotman pubblicati in italiano', in J. M. Lotman, *Tesi per una semiotica delle culture*, ed. F. Sedda, 303–11, Rome: Meltemi.

Shukman, A. (1978), 'The Moscow-Tartu semiotic school: A bibliography of works and comments in English', *PTL: A Journal for Descriptive Poetics and Theory of Literature*, 3: 593–601.

Volkova, E. A. (2019), 'The language of the Tartu–Moscow semiotic school and the translations of Yuri Lotman's works in Brazil', *Bakhtiniana: Revista de Estudos do Discurso*, 14 (4): 40–60.

Winner, T. (2002), 'How did the ideas of Yuri Lotman reach the west?' *Sign Systems Studies*, 30 (2): 419–27.

I. Juri Lotman's works in English translation

1. Uspenskij, B. A., Ivanov, V. V., Toporov, V. N., Pjatigorskij, A. M. and Lotman, Ju. M. (1973), 'Theses on the semiotic study of cultures (as applied to Slavic texts)', in Jan van der Eng and Mojmír Grygar (eds.), *Structure of Texts and Semiotics of Culture*, 1–28, The Hague, Paris: Mouton.

2. Lotman, Juri (1973), 'Different cultures, different codes', *Times Literary Supplement*, 3736 (12 October): 1213–15.

3. Lotman, Ju. M. (1974), 'The sign mechanism of culture' (Ann Shukman, trans.), *Semiotica*, 12 (4): 301–5.

4. Lotman, Ju. M. (1974), 'On some principal difficulties in the structural description of a text', *Linguistics*, 12 (121): 57–63.

5. Lotman, Iu. M. (1974), 'Analysis of a poetic text: The structure of poetry', [Excerpt], *Soviet Studies in Literature: A Journal of Translations*, 10 (2): 3–41.
6. Lotman, Iu. M. (1974), 'Observations on the structure of the narrative text', *Soviet Studies in Literature: A Journal of Translations*, 10 (4): 75–81.
7. Lotman, Iu. M. (1974), 'On the mythological code of plotted texts', *Soviet Studies in Literature: A Journal of Translations*, 10 (4): 82–7.
8. Mints, Z. G. and Lotman, Iu. M. (1974), 'The individual creative career and the typology of culture codes', *Soviet Studies in Literature: A Journal of Translations*, 10 (4): 88–90.
9. Lotman, Iu. M. and Uspenskii, B. A. (1975), 'Myth – name – culture', *Soviet Studies in Literature: A Journal of Translations*, 11 (2/3): 17–46.
10. Lotman, Iu. M. (1975), 'Theater and theatricality in the order of early nineteenth century culture', *Soviet Studies in Literature: A Journal of Translations*, 11 (2/3): 155–85.
11. Lotman, Ju. M. (1975), 'On the metalanguage of a typological description of culture', *Semiotica*, 14 (2): 97–123.
12. Lotman, Juri M. (1975), 'Notes on the structure of a literary text', *Semiotica*, 15 (3): 199–205.
13. Lotman, J. M. (1975), 'The discrete text and the iconic text: Remarks on the structure of narrative' (Frances Pfotenhauer, trans.), *New Literary History*, 6 (2): 333–8.
14. Lotman, J. M. (1975), 'Point of view in a text' (L. M. O'Toole, trans.), *New Literary History*, 6 (2): 339–52.
15. Lotman, Jurij M., Uspenskij, B. A., Ivanov, V. V., Toporov, V. N. and Pjatigorskij, A. M. (1975), 'Theses on the semiotic study of cultures (as applied to Slavic texts)', in Thomas A. Sebeok (ed.), *The Tell-Tale Sign: A Survey of Semiotics*, 57–84, Lisse, Netherlands: The Peter de Ridder Press.
16. Lotman, Ju. M., Uspenskij, B. A., Ivanov, V. V., Toporov, V. N. and Pjatigorskij, A. M. (1975), *Theses on the Semiotic Study of Cultures (As Applied to Slavic Texts)*, Lisse, Netherlands: The Peter de Ridder Press, 29 p. [Reprint from 15].
17. Lotman, Iu. M. (1975), 'Observations on the structure of the narrative text', *The Soviet Review*, 14 (2): 59–65.
18. Lotman, Iu. M. (1975), 'Theater and theatricality in the order of early nineteenth century culture', *The Soviet Review*, 16 (4): 53–83.
19. Lotman, Yury (1976), *Analysis of the Poetic Text* (D. Barton Johnson, trans. With a bibliography of Lotman's works compiled by Lazar Fleishman), Ann Arbor, MI: Ardis, 309 p.
20. Lotman, Jurij (1976), *Semiotics of Cinema* (Mark E. Suino, foreword and trans.) (Michigan Slavic Contributions 5), Ann Arbor: The University of Michigan, ix+106 p.
21. Lotman, Jurij (1976), 'Culture and information' (Stephen White, trans.), *Dispositio: Revista Hispánica de Semiótica Literaria*, 1 (3): 213–15.
22. Lotman, Iu. M. (1976), 'O. M. Freidenberg as a student of culture', *Soviet Studies in Literature: A Journal of Translations*, 12 (2): 3–11.

23. Lotman, Iu. M. (1976), "Gogol' and the correlation of "the culture of humor" with the comic and serious in the Russian national tradition", *Soviet Studies in Literature: A Journal of Translations*, 12 (2): 40–3.

24. Lotman, Iu. M. (1976), 'On the reduction and unfolding of sign systems (The problem of "Freudianism and semiotic culturology")', *Soviet Studies in Literature: A Journal of Translations*, 12 (2): 44–52.

[A] Baran, Henryk, ed. (1976), *Semiotics and Structuralism: Readings from the Soviet Union*, White Plains, NY: International Arts and Sciences Press. (Translated by William Mandel, Henryk Baran, and A. J. Hollander.) xxvi+369. [This anthology includes the following articles 25–29:]

25. Lotman, Iu. M. and Uspenskii, B. A. (1976), 'Myth – name – culture', in: ibidem [A], 3–32.

26. Lotman, Iu. M. (1976), 'Theater and theatricality in the order of early nineteenth century culture', in: ibidem [A], 33–63.

27. Lotman, Iu. M. (1976), 'O. M. Freidenberg as a student of culture', in: ibidem [A], 257–68.

28. Lotman, Iu. M. (1976), '"Gogol" and the correlation of "the culture of humor" with the comic and serious in the Russian national tradition', in: ibidem [A], 297–300.

29. Lotman, Iu. M. (1976), 'On the reduction and unfolding of sign systems (The problem of "Freudianism and semiotic culturology")', in: ibidem [A], 301–9.

30. Lotman, Jurij (1976), 'The content and structure of the concept of "literature"' (Christopher R. Pike, trans.), *PTL: A Journal for Descriptive Poetics and Theory of Literature*, 1 (2): 339–56.

31. Lotman, Yu. M. (1976), 'The structure of ideas in Pushkin's poem 'Andzhelo" (Ann Shukman, trans.), in: L. M. O'Toole and A. Shukman (eds.), *Poetry and Prose (Russian Poetics in Translation 2)*, 66–84, Colchester: University of Essex.

32. Lotman, Yu. M. (1976), 'The modelling significance of the concepts "end" and "beginning" in artistic texts' (Wendy Rosslyn, trans.), in: Lawrence Michael O'Toole and Ann Shukman (eds.), *General Semiotics. (Russian Poetics in Translation 3)*, 7–11, Colchester: University of Essex.

33. Lotman, Juri (1976), 'Program proposal of the fourth summer workshop on secondary modeling systems' (Martha Defoe, trans.), *Dispositio: Rivista Hispánica de Semiótica Literaria*, 1 (3): 216–18.

34. Lotman, Jurij (1977), *The Structure of the Artistic Text* (Gail Lenhoff and Ronald Vroon, trans.) (Michigan Slavic Contributions 7), Ann Arbor: University of Michigan, Department of Slavic Languages and Literatures. 300 p.

[B1] Lucid, Daniel P., ed. and trans. (1977), *Soviet Semiotics: An Anthology*, Baltimore: The Johns Hopkins University Press. [This book includes the following articles 35–42:]

35. Lotman, Ju. M. (1977), 'Primary and secondary communication-modeling systems', in: ibidem [B1], 95–8.

36. Lotman, Ju. M. (1977), 'Two models of communication', in: ibidem [B1], 99–101.

37. Lotman, Ju. M. (1977), 'Problems in the typology of texts', in: ibidem [B1], 119–24.
38. Lotman, Ju. M. and Pjatigorskij, A. M. (1977), 'Text and function', in: ibidem [B1], 125–35.
39. Lotman, Ju. M. (1977), 'The structure of the narrative text', in: ibidem [B1], 193–7.
40. Lotman, Ju. M. (1977), 'Problems in the typology of culture', in: ibidem [B1], 213–21.
41. Lotman, Ju. M. (1977), 'Numerical semantics and cultural types', in: ibidem [B1], 227–31.
42. Lotman, Ju. M. and Uspenskij, B. A. (1977), 'Myth – name – culture', in: ibidem [B1], 233–52.
43. Lotman, Ju. M. (1977), 'The dynamic model of a semiotic system' (Ann Shukman, trans.), *Semiotica*, 21 (3/4): 193–210.
44. Lotman, Ju. M. and Uspenskij, B. A. (1978), 'Myth – name – culture', *Semiotica*, 22 (3/4): 211–33.
45. Lotman, Yu. M. and Uspenskij, B. A. (1978), 'On the semiotic mechanism of culture' (George Mihaychuk, trans.), *New Literary History*, 9 (2): 211–32.
46. Lotman, Yu. M. and Pjatigorskij, A. M. (1978), 'Text and function' (Ann Shukman, trans.), *New Literary History*, 9 (2): 233–44.
47. Lotman, Jurij (1978), 'Theme and plot: The theme of cards and the card game in Russian literature of the Nineteenth century' (Christopher R. Pike, trans.), *PTL: A Journal for Descriptive Poetics and Theory of Literature*, 3 (3): 455–92.
48. Lotman, Yury (1978), 'Language and reality in the early Pasternak', in: Victor Erlich (ed.), *Pasternak: A Collection of Critical Essays*, 21–38, Englewood Cliffs, NJ: Prentice-Hall.
49. Lotman, Yu. M. (1979), 'Culture as collective intellect and the problems of artificial intelligence' (Ann Shukman, trans.), in: Lawrence Michael O'Toole and Ann Shukman (eds.), *Dramatic Structure: Poetic and Cognitive Semantics* (Russian Poetics in Translation 6), 84–96, Colchester: University of Essex.
50. Lotman, Jurij M. (1979), 'The future for structural poetics', *Poetics*, 8 (6): 501–7.
51. Lotman, Jurij M. (1979), 'The origin of plot in the light of typology' (Julian Graffy, trans.), *Poetics Today*, 1 (1/2): 161–84.
52. Lotman, Yu. M. (1980), 'The natural language/metre interrelationship in the mechanism of verse' (Gerry S. Smith, introduction and trans.), in: Lawrence Michael O'Toole and Ann Shukman (eds.), *Metre, Rhythm, Stanza, Rhyme (Russian Poetics in Translation 7)*, 86–9, Colchester: University of Essex.
53. Lotman, Yu. (1981), 'On the language of animated cartoons' (Ruth Sobel, trans.), in: Lawrence Michael O'Toole and Ann Shukman (eds.), *Film Theory and General Semiotics (Russian Poetics in Translation 8)*, 36–9, Colchester: University of Essex.
54. Lotman, Jurij (1981), *Semiotics of Cinema* (Mark E. Suino, foreword and trans.) (Michigan Slavic Contributions 5.), Ann Arbor: University of Michigan, xi+106 p. [New edition of 20].
55. Lotman, Yury M. (1982), 'The text and the structure of its audience' (Ann Shukman, trans.), *New Literary History*, 14 (1): 81–7.

[C] Lotman, Ju. M. and Uspenskij, B. A. (1984), *The Semiotics of Russian Culture*. Edited by Ann Shukman. (Michigan Slavic Contributions 11), Ann Arbor: Department of Slavic Languages and Literatures, University of Michigan, xiv+341. [This anthology includes the following articles 56–66:]

56. Lotman, Jurij M. and Uspenskij, Boris A. (1984), 'Authors' introduction', in: ibidem [C], ix–xiv.

57. Lotman, Ju. M. and Uspenskij, B. A. (1984), 'The role of dual models in the dynamics of Russian culture (up to the end of the eighteenth century)' (N. F. C. Owen, trans.), in: ibidem [C], 3–35.

58. Lotman, Ju. M. and Uspenskij, B. A. (1984), 'New aspects in the study of early Russian culture', in: ibidem [C], 36–52.

59. Lotman, Ju. M. and Uspenskij, B. A. (1984), 'Echoes of the notion "Moscow as the third Rome" in Peter the Great's ideology' (N. F. C. Owen, trans.), in: ibidem [C], 53–67.

60. Lotman, Ju. M. (1984), 'The Decembrist in everyday life: Everyday behavior as a historical-psychological category' (C. R. Pike, trans.), in: ibidem [C], 71–123.

61. Lotman, Ju. M. (1984), '"Agreement" and "self-giving" as archetypal models of culture' (N. F. C. Owen, trans.), in: ibidem [C], 125–40.

62. Lotman, Jurij M. (1984), 'The theater and theatricality as components of early nineteenth-century culture' (G. S. Smith, trans.), in: ibidem [C], 141–64.

63. Lotman, Ju. M. (1984), 'The stage and painting as code mechanisms for cultural behavior in the early nineteenth century' (Judith Armstrong, trans.) in: ibidem [C], 165–76.

64. Lotman, Ju. M. (1984), 'Gogol's Chlestakov: The pragmatics of a literary character' (Ruth Sobel, trans.), in: ibidem [C], 177–212.

65. Lotman, Ju. M. (1984), 'Gogol's "Tale of captain Kopejkin": Reconstruction of the plan and ideo-compositional function' (Julian Graffy, trans.), in: ibidem [C], 213–30.

66. Lotman, Ju. M. (1984), 'The poetics of everyday behavior in Russian eighteenth century culture' (N. F. C. Owen, trans.), in: ibidem [C], 231–56.

[D] Nakhimovsky, Alexander D. and Nakhimovsky, Alice Stone, eds. (1985), *The Semiotics of Russian Cultural History: Essays by Iurii M. Lotman, Lidiia Ia. Ginsburg, Boris A. Uspenskii*, Ithaca, NY, and London: Cornell University Press. [This book includes the following articles 67–70:]

67. Lotman, Iurii M. and Uspenskii, Boris A. (1985), 'Binary models in the dynamics of Russian culture (to the end of the eighteenth century)' (Robert Sorenson, trans.), in: ibidem [D], 30–66.

68. Lotman, Iurii M. (1985), 'The poetics of everyday behavior in eighteenth-century Russian culture' (Andrea Beesing, trans.), in: ibidem [D], 67–94.

69. Lotman, Iurii M. (1985), 'The Decembrist in daily life (everyday behavior as a historical-psychological category)' (Andrea Beesing, trans.), in: ibidem [D], 95–149.

70. Lotman, Iurii M. (1985), 'Concerning Khlestakov' (Louisa Vinton, trans.), in: ibidem [D], 150–87.

71. Lotman, Yuri M. (1985), 'The problem of artistic space in Gogol's prose', in: George Gibian (ed.), *Gogol, Nikolai, Dead Souls: The Reavey Translation, Backgrounds and Sources, Essays in Criticism*, 577–83, New York: W.W. Norton.

72. Lotman, Jurij M. (1987), 'Semiotics and culture in the second half of the twentieth century' (Jostein Børtnes, trans.), *Livstegn: Tidsskrift for Norsk forening for semiotikk [Proceedings of the first symposium] "Semiotics in Theory and Practice"*, 2–3 Oct. *1986, Bergen (Norway), Norwegian Association for Semiotic Studies*, 3 (1): 9–11.

73. Lotman, Jurij M. (1987), 'On the contemporary concept of the text' (Jostein Børtnes, trans.), *Livstegn: Tidsskrift for Norsk forening for semiotikk / Journal of the Norwegian Association for Semiotic Studies [Proceedings of the first symposium "Semiotics in Theory and Practice"*, 2–3 Oct. 1986, Bergen (Norway)*], 3: 159–63.

74. Lotman, Yuri (1987), 'Architecture in the context of culture', *Architecture and Society* (Архитектура и общество) [Sofia], 6: 8–15. [Parallel text in Russian.]

75. Lotman, Yuri M. (1987), 'The text and the structure of its audience', in: F. Shirley Staton (ed.), *Literary Theory in Praxis*, 380–85, Philadelphia, The University of Pennsylvania Press. [Reprint of 55]

76. Lotman, Juri (1988), 'Natural environment and information', in: Kalevi Kull and Toomas Tiivel (eds.), *Lectures in Theoretical Biology*, 45–7, Tallinn: Valgus.

77. Lotman, Yury (1988), 'The structure of Eugene Onegin', in: Sona Stephan Hoisington and Walter Arndt (eds.), *Russian Views of Pushkin's Eugene Onegin.* (Verse passages translated by Walter Arndt, foreword by Caryl Emerson), 91–114, Bloomington: Indiana University Press.

78. Lotman, Yury (1988), 'The transformation of the tradition generated by Onegin in the subsequent history of the Russian novel', in: Sona Stephan Hoisington and Walter Arndt (eds.), *Russian Views of Pushkin's Eugene Onegin.* (Verse passages translated by Walter Arndt, foreword by Caryl Emerson), 169–77, Bloomington: Indiana University Press.

79. Lotman, Yu M. (1988), 'Text within a text', *Soviet Psychology*, 26 (3): 32–51.

80. Lotman, Yu. M. (1988), 'The semiotics of culture and the concept of a text', *Soviet Psychology*, 26 (3): 52–8.

81. Lotman, Yuri and Henri Broms (1988), 'Greetings to the symposium. An interview with Yuri Lotman in Helsinki, June 1987' (The interviewer Henri Broms; Holman, Eugene, trans.), in: Henri Broms and Rebecca Kaufmann (eds.), *Semiotics of Culture: Proceedings of the 25th Symposium of the Tartu–Moscow School of Semiotics, Imatra, Finland, 27th–29th July, 1987*, 115–23, Helsinki: Arator.

[B2] Lucid, Daniel P., ed. (1988), *Soviet Semiotics: An Anthology.* (New foreword by T. A. Sebeok.) Baltimore, London: Johns Hopkins University Press. [The new edition of Lucid 1977 [B1]. This book includes the following articles 81–9:]

82. Lotman, Ju. M. (1988), 'Primary and secondary communication-modeling systems', in: ibidem [B2], 95–8.

83. Lotman, Ju. M. (1988), 'Two models of communication', in: ibidem [B2], 99–101.

84. Lotman, Ju. M. (1988), 'Problems in the typology of texts', in: ibidem [B2], 119–24.

85. Lotman, Ju. M. and Pjatigorskij, A. M. (1988), 'Text and function', in: ibidem [B2], 125–35.

86. Lotman, Ju. M. (1988), 'The structure of the narrative text', in: ibidem [B2], 193–7.

87. Lotman, Ju. M. (1988), 'Problems in the typology of culture', in: ibidem [B2], 213–21.

88. Lotman, Ju. M. (1988), 'Numerical semantics and cultural types', in: ibidem [B2], 227–31.

89. Lotman, Ju. M. and Uspenskij, B. A. (1988), 'Myth – name – culture', in: ibidem [B2], 233–52.

90. Lotman, Yu. M. (1989), 'The semiosphere', *Soviet Psychology*, 27 (1): 40–61.

91. Lotman, Yuri M. (1990), *Universe of the Mind: A Semiotic Theory of Culture* (Ann Shukman, trans; Eco, Umberto, introduction), London and New York: I. B. Tauris & Co Ltd. xiii+288 p.

92. Lotman, Yury (1990), 'Artistic space in Gogol's prose', *Russian Literature Triquarterly*, 23: 199–241.

93. Lotman, Iurii (1991), 'Semiotics and the historical sciences', in: Bo Göranzon and Magnus Florin (eds.), *Dialogue and Technology: Art and Knowledge*. (The Springer Series of Artificial Intelligence and Society.), 165–80, London: Springer.

94. Lotman, Jurij M. (1991), 'Technological progress as a problem in the study of culture' (Ilana Gomel, trans.), *Poetics Today*, 12 (4): 781–800.

95. Lotman, Yu. M. (1991), 'Technical progress as a cultural problem', *Soviet Psychology*, 29 (1): 6–28.

96. Lotman, Yury M. (1994), 'The text within the text' (Jerry Leo and Amy Mandelker, trans.), *Publications of the Modern Language Association (PMLA)*, 109 (3): 377–84.

97. Lotman, Yury (1994), 'Theses towards a semiotics of Russian culture', *Elementa*, 1 (3): 219–27.

98. Lotman, Yuri (1994), 'Painting and the language of theater: Notes on the problem of iconic rhetoric', in: Alla Efimova and Lev Manovich (eds. and trans.), *Tekstura: Russian Essays on Visual Culture*, 45–55, Chicago and London: The University of Chicago Press.

99. Lotman, Juri (1997), 'Culture as a subject and an object in itself', *Trames*, 1 (1): 7–16.

100. Lotman, Iurii M. (1997), 'Conversations on Russian culture. Russian noble traditions and lifestyle in the eighteen and early nineteenth centuries', *Russian Studies in History*, 35 (4): 6–34.

101. Uspenskij, B. A., Ivanov, V. V., Toporov, V. N., Pjatigorskij, A. M. and Lotman, Ju. M. (1998), *Theses on the semiotic study of cultures (as applied to the Slavic texts)* (Tartu Semiotics Library 1), 33–60. [Facsimile of 1973 publication 1].

102. Lotman, Jurij (1999), 'The truth as lie in Gogol's poetics', in: Sven Spieker (ed.), *Gogol: Exploring Absence: Negativity in 19th Century Russian Literature*, 35–54, Bloomington: Slavica Publishers.

103. Lotman, Yuri M. (2000), *Universe of the Mind: A Semiotic Theory of Culture* (Ann Shukman, trans; Eco, Umberto, introduction), Bloomington and Indianapolis: Indiana University Press, xiii+288. [The new edition of 91]

104. Lotman, Yuri M. (2001), *Universe of the Mind: A Semiotic Theory of Culture* (Ann Shukman, trans; Eco, Umberto, introduction.) London and New York: Tauris transformations, xiii+288. [The new edition of 91]

105. Lotman, Juri (2002), 'Semiotics of the individual and society', *Sign Systems Studies*, 30 (2): 573–6.

106. Uspenskij, B. A., Ivanov, V. V., Toporov, V. N., Pjatigorskij, A. M. and Lotman, Ju. M. (2003), 'Theses on the semiotic study of cultures (as applied to Slavic texts)', in: Mark Gottdiener, Karin Boklund-Lagopoulou and Alexandros Ph. Lagopoulos (eds.), *Semiotics*, vol. 1, 293–316, London: SAGE Publications. [Republication of 1].

107. Lotman, Juri M. (2003), 'On the metalanguage of a typological description of culture', in: Mark Gottdiener, Karin Boklund-Lagopoulou and Alexandros Ph. Lagopoulos (eds.), *Semiotics*, vol. 3, 101–25, London: SAGE Publications, 101–25. [Republication of 11]

108. Lotman, Juri (2005), 'On the semiosphere' (Wilma Clark, trans.), *Sign Systems Studies*, 33 (1): 215–39.

109. Lotman, Yuri M. (2006), 'The text and the structure of its audience' (Ann Shukman, trans.) in: Paul Cobley (ed.), *Communication Theories: Critical Concepts in Media and Cultural Studies*, vol. 3, 64–70, London: Routledge.

110. Lotman, Juri (2008), 'Semiotics of personality and society', in: Peet Lepik (ed.), *Universals in the Context of Juri Lotman's Semiotics* (Tartu Semiotics Library 7), 225–44, Tartu: Tartu University Press. [Three lectures of Juri Lotman from 1967 published from the notes of Marju Lauristin, edited by Peet Lepik, translated by Tiia Raudma].

111. Lotman, Juri (2009), *Culture and Explosion* (Wilma Clark, trans; Marina Grishakova, ed.), Berlin: Mouton de Gruyter, xxxix+195.

112. Lotman, Juri Mikhajlovič (2010), 'Excerpts from 'Universe of the mind: A semiotic theory of culture (1990)', in: Donald Favareau (ed.), *Essential Readings in Biosemiotics: Anthology and Commentary*, 197–214, Berlin: Springer.

113. Lotman, Yuri (2011), 'Art as language', in: Frederik Stjernfelt and Peer F. Bundgaard (eds.), *Semiotics: Critical Concepts in Language Studies. Vol. 3: Text and Image*, 88–112, London: Routledge. [Excerpt from 34, pp. 7–31]

114. Lotman, Yuri (2011), 'Semiotic space', in: Frederik Stjernfelt and Peer F. Bundgaard (eds.), *Semiotics: Critical Concepts in Language Studies. Vol. 4: Logic, Biology, Psychology, Culture and Anthropology*, 489–96, London: Routledge. [Excerpt from 91, pp. 123–30.]

115. Lotman, Yuri (2011), 'The notion of boundary', in: Frederik Stjernfelt and Peer F. Bund-gaard (eds.), *Semiotics: Critical Concepts in Language Studies. Vol. 4: Logic, Biology, Psychology, Culture and Anthropology*, 497–509, London: Routledge. [Excerpt from 91, pp. 131–42.]

116. Lotman, Juri (2011), 'The place of art among other modelling systems' (Tanel Pern, trans.), *Sign Systems Studies*, 39 (2/4): 249–70.

117. Lotman, Juri (2012), 'Text and cultural polyglotism' (Tanel Pern, trans.), in: International Congress Cultural Polyglotism (to the Anniversary of Juri Lotman's 90th Birthday. Tartu, February 28–March 2, 2012). Abstracts. Tartu, 9–14.

118. Lotman, Juri (2013), 'On the dynamics of culture' (Tyler Adkins, trans.), *Sign Systems Studies*, 41 (2/3): 355–70.

119. Lotman, Juri (2013), 'Canonical art as informational paradox' (Montana Salvoni and Oleg Sobchuk, trans.), *Sign Systems Studies*, 41 (2/3): 371–77.

120. Lotman, Juri M. (2013), *The Unpredictable Workings of Culture* (Brian James Baer, trans.; Igor Pilshchikov; Silvi Salupere, eds.), Tallinn: TLU Press.

121. Lotman, Juri (2013), 'Proposals for the programme of the 4th Summer school on secondary modelling systems' (Tanel Pern, trans.), in: Silvi Salupere, Peeter Torop and Kalevi Kull (eds.), *Beginnings of the Semiotics of Culture* (Tartu Semiotics Library 13), 41–3, Tartu: University of Tartu Press. [See also 33].

122. Lotman, Juri M., Ivanov, Vjacheslav V., Pjatigorskij, Aleksandr M., Toporov, Vladimir N. and Uspenskij, Boris A. (2013), 'Theses on the semiotic study of cultures (as applied to Slavic texts)', in: Silvi Salupere, Peeter Torop and Kalevi Kull (eds.), *Beginnings of the Semiotics of Culture* (Tartu Semiotics Library 13), 53–77, Tartu: University of Tartu Press. [The earlier English versions – [1, 15, 16, 101, 106]. This is the most updated translation with some corrections]

123. Lotman, Juri M. and Uspenskij, Boris A. (2013), 'Heterogeneity and homogeneity of cultures: Postscriptum to the collective theses' (Remo Gramigna, trans. from Italian), in: Silvi Salupere, Peeter Torop and Kalevi Kull (eds.), *Beginnings of the Semiotics of Culture* (Tartu Semiotics Library 13), 129–32, Tartu: University of Tartu Press.

124. Lotman, Yuri M. and Pogosjan, Jelena A. (2014), *High Society Dinners: Dining in Tsarist Russia.* (Marian Schwartz, trans.; Darra Goldstein, ed. and introduction). Totnes: Prospect Books. 444 pp.

125. Lotman, Yuri (2014), *Non-Memoirs* (Brickman, Caroline Lemak, trans. and annot.; Bershtein, Evgenii, ed.; Brickman, Caroline Lemak; Bershtein, Evgenii, afterword.) Champaign: Dalkey Archive Press. 108 pp.

[E] Tamm, Marek, ed. (2019), Juri Lotman. *Culture, Memory and History: Essays in Cultural Semiotics* (translated by Brian James Baer), Cham: Palgrave Macmillan. [This anthology includes the following articles 126–39:]

126. Lotman, Juri (2019), 'The phenomenon of culture' (Brian James Baer, trans.), in: ibidem [E], 33–48.

127. Lotman, Juri (2019), 'The "contract" and "self-surrender" as archetypal models of culture' (Brian James Baer, trans.), in: ibidem [E], 49–65.

128. Lotman, Juri (2019), 'Toward a theory of cultural interaction: The semiotic aspect' (Brian James Baer, trans.), in: ibidem [E], 67–81.

129. Lotman, Juri (2019), 'Culture as a subject and its own object' (Brian James Baer, trans.), in: ibidem [E], 83–93.

130. Lotman, Juri (2019), 'On the dynamics of culture' (Brian James Baer, trans.), in: ibidem [E], 95–113,

131. Lotman, Juri (2019), 'The role of art in the dynamics of culture' (Brian James Baer, trans.), in: ibidem [E], 115–30.

132. Lotman, Juri (2019), 'Memory in a culturological perspective' (Brian James Baer, trans.), in: ibidem [E], 133–37.

133. Lotman, Juri (2019), 'Cultural memory' (Brian James Baer, trans.), in: ibidem [E], 139–48.

134. Lotman, Juri (2019), 'Some thoughts on typologies of culture' (Brian James Baer, trans.), in: ibidem [E], 149–59.

135. Lotman, Juri (2019), 'The symbol in the system of culture' (Brian James Baer, trans.), in: ibidem [E], 161–73.

136. Lotman, Juri (2019), 'Clio at the crossroads' (Brian James Baer, trans.), in: ibidem [E], 177–87.

137. Lotman, Juri (2019), 'A divine pronouncement or a game of chance? The law-governed and the accidental in the historical process' (Brian James Baer, trans.), in: ibidem [E], 189–99.

138. Lotman, Juri (2019), 'Technological Progress as a Culturological Problem' (Brian James Baer, trans.), in: ibidem [E], 201–23.

139. Lotman, Juri (2019), 'The time of troubles as a cultural mechanism: Toward a typology of Russian cultural history' (Brian James Baer, trans.), in: ibidem [E], 225–43.

[F] Schönle, Andreas, ed. (2020), Yuri Lotman. *Culture and Communication. Signs in Flux. An Anthology of Major and Lesser-known works* (translated by Benjamin Paloff), Boston: Academic Series Press (Cultural Syllabus Series), 254 p. [This anthology includes the following articles 140–48:]

140. Lotman Yuri (2020), 'From "Universe of the mind"' (Benjamin Paloff, trans.), in: ibidem [F], 3–47.

141. Lotman Yuri (2020), '"Noise" and artistic information' (Benjamin Paloff, trans.), in: ibidem [F], 48–60. [Excerpt from *The Structure of the Artistic Text*]

142. Lotman Yuri (2020), 'The interrupted and the uninterrupted' (Benjamin Paloff, trans.), in: ibidem [F], 61–78. [Excerpt from *Culture and Explosion*]

143. Lotman Yuri (2020), 'Memory in a culturological light' (Benjamin Paloff, trans.), in: ibidem [F], 79–83.

144. Lotman Yuri (2020), 'The language of theater' (Benjamin Paloff, trans.), in: ibidem [F], 84–90.

145. Lotman Yuri (2020), 'The role of dual models in the dynamics of Russian culture (until the end of the Eighteenth century' (Benjamin Paloff, trans.), in: ibidem [F], 93–123.

146. Lotman Yuri (2020), 'The symbolism of Petersburg and the problems of the semiotics of the city' (Paloff, Benjamin, trans.), ibidem [F], 124–39.

147. Lotman Yuri (2020), 'The duel' (Benjamin Paloff, trans.), in: ibidem [F], 140–57. [Excerpt from *Conversation on Russian Culture*]

148. Lotman Yuri (2020), 'A woman's world' (Benjamin Paloff, trans.), in: ibidem [F], 158–96. [Excerpt from *Conversation on Russian Culture*].

II. Selected writings on Juri Lotman in English

II.1 Juri Lotman Bibliographies

149. Cáceres Sánchez, M. (1995), 'Iuri M. Lotman y la escuela semiótica de Tartu-Moscú: Bibliografía en español, francés, inglés, italiano, portugués y alemán', *Signa: Revista de la Asociación Española de Semiótica*, 4: 45–76.
150. Eimermacher, Karl and Sege Shishkoff (1976), 'Selected bibliography of Soviet Semiotics', *Dispositio*, 1 (3), Special Issue: *Soviet Semiotics of Culture*: 364–70.
151. Eimermacher, Karl and Serge Shishkoff (1977), *Subject Bibliography of Soviet Semiotics: The Moscow-Tartu School*, Ann Arbor: Michigan Slavic Publications.
152. Kull, Kalevi (2011), 'Juri Lotman in English', *Sign Systems Studies*, 39 (2/4): 343–56.
153. Kull, Kalevi and Gramigna, Remo (2014), 'Juri Lotman in English: Updates to bibliography', *Sign Systems Studies*, 42 (4): 549–52.
154. Shukman, Ann (1978), 'The Moscow-Tartu Semiotics School: A bibliography of works and comments in English', *PTL: A Journal for Descriptive Poetics and Theory of Literature*, 3: 593–601.

II.2 Special Issues in journals devoted to Juri Lotman and 'Soviet semiotics'

153. Andrew, Joe, Polukhina, Valentina and Reid, Robert, eds. (1994), Special Issue. Ju. M. Lotman I. *Russian Literature* XXXVI (III), Amsterdam: North-Holland, 243–369.
154. Andrew, Joe, Polukhina, Valentina and Reid, Robert, eds. (1994), Special Issue. Ju. M. Lotman II. *Russian Literature* XXXVI (IV), Amsterdam: North-Holland, 243–369.
155. Andrews, Edna, ed. (2015), Special issue. Juri M. Lotman. *Recherches sémiotiques / Semiotic Inquiry*, 35 (1): 1–162.
156. Baran, Henryk, ed. (1975), *Structuralism. Soviet Studies in Literature*, 11 (2/3): 3–243.
157. Cohen, Ralph, ed. (1978), *Soviet Semiotics and Literary Criticism. New Literary History*, 9 (2), Baltimore, Maryland: The Johns Hopkins University Press, 189–413.
158. Ibrus, Indrek and Torop, Peeter, eds. (2015), Special Issue: The uses of Juri Lotman. *International Journal of Cultural Studies*, 18 (1): 1–151.
159. Koten, Bernard L. and Hollander, Joseph A. (1976), 'Semiotics', *Soviet Studies in Literature*, 12 (2): 3–91.
160. Machado, Irene and Barei, Silvia, eds. (2019), 'Between Turbulences and Unpredictability of Historical Time: The Semiotics of Yuri Lotman', *Bakhtiniana: Revista de Estudos do Discurso*, 14 (4). [Available online: https://revistas.pucsp.br/index.php/bakhtiniana/issue/view/2280/showToc]
161. Mignolo, Walter, ed. (1976), 'Soviet semiotics of culture', Special Issue. *Dispositio. Rivista Hispánica de Semiótica Literaria*, 1 (3): 207–370.
162. Shukman, Ann, ed. (1978), Special Issue: Soviet Semiotics. *PTL: A Journal for Descriptive Poetics and Theory of Literature*, 3 (3), North-Holland Publishing Company, Amsterdam.

163. Valentina, Polukhina, Joe Andrew and Robert Reid, eds. (1993), *Literary Tradition and Practice in Russian Culture. Papers from an International Conference on the Occasion of the Seventieth Birthday of Yury Mikhailovich Lotman*. Russian Culture: Structure & Tradition. 2–6 July 1992, Keele University, United Kingdom.

164. Van der Eng, Jan and Nilsson, Nils Åke, eds. (1977), Special Issue. Jurij M. Lotman. *Russian Literature*, 5 (1), Amsterdam: North-Holland Publishing Company, 1–116.

II.3 Anthologies

165. Baran, Henryk, ed. (1976), *Semiotics and Structuralism: Readings from the Soviet Union*, White Plains, NY: International Arts and Sciences Press. (Translated by William Mandel, Henryk Baran and A. J. Hollander) xxvi+369.

166. Halle, Morris, Ladislav, Matejka, Krystyna, Pomorska and Boris, Uspenskij, eds. (1984), *Semiosis. Semiotics and the History of Culture: In Honorem Georgii Lotman* (Michigan Slavic Contributions 10), Ann Arbor: Department of Slavic Languages and Literatures, The University of Michigan.

167. Lotman, Ju. M. and Uspenskij, B. A. (1984), *The Semiotics of Russian Culture*, Ed. Ann Shukman. (Michigan Slavic Contributions 11), Ann Arbor: Department of Slavic Languages and Literatures, University of Michigan, xiv+341.

168. Lucid, Daniel P., ed. and trans. (1977), *Soviet Semiotics: An Anthology*, Baltimore: The Johns Hopkins University Press.

169. Nakhimovsky, Alexander D. and Nakhimovsky, Alice Stone, eds. (1985), *The Semiotics of Russian Cultural History: Essays by Iurii M. Lotman, Lidiia Ia. Ginsburg, Boris A. Uspenskii*, Ithaca, NY, and London: Cornell University Press.

170. Schönle, Andreas, ed. (2006), *Lotman and Cultural Studies: Encounters and Extensions*, Madison, WI: The University of Wisconsin Press.

171. Schönle, Andreas, ed. (2020), Yuri Lotman. *Culture and Communication. Signs in Flux. An Anthology of Major and Lesser-known works*, trans. Benjamin Paloff, Boston: Academic Series Press.

172. Tamm, Marek, ed. (2019), Juri Lotman, *Culture, Memory and History. Essays in Cultural Semiotics* (translated by Brian James Baer), Cham: Palgrave Macmillan.

II.4 Writings on Juri Lotman

173. Alexandrov, Vladimir E. (1998), 'Lotman's "semiosphere" and varieties of the self', *Working Papers and Pre-Publications, Centro Internazionale di Semiotica e di Linguistica*, Serie C 270, Università di Urbino, Italia.

174. Alexandrov, Vladimir E. (2000), 'Biology, semiosis, and cultural difference in Lotman's semiosphere', *Comparative Literature*, 52 (4): 339–62.

175. Andrews, Edna (1999), 'Lotman's communication act and semiosis', *Semiotica*, 126 (1/4): 1–16.

176. Andrews, Edna (2001), 'Text and culture: Continuous discontinuity in Lotman and Zamjatin', *Russian Literature*, 49 (4): 347–69.

177. Andrews, Edna (2003), *Conversations with Lotman: Cultural Semiotics in Language, Literature and Cognition*, Toronto, Buffalo and London: University of Toronto Press.

178. Andrews, Edna (2009), 'Introduction', in: Juri Lotman, *Culture and Explosion*, trans. Wilma Clark, ed. Marina Grishakova, XIX–XXVI, Berlin and New York: Mouton de Gruyter.

179. Andrews, Edna (2012), 'Lotman and the cognitive sciences. The role of autocommunication in the language of memory', in: Susi K. Frank, Cornelia Ruhe and Alexander Schmitz (eds.), *Explosion und Peripherie: Jurij Lotmans Semiotik der kulturellen Dynamik revisited*, 175–90, Bielefeld: transkript.

180. Andrews, Edna (2015a), 'Presentation: Juri M. Lotman', *Recherches sémiotiques / Semiotic Inquiry*, 35 (1): 7–10.

181. Andrews, Edna (2015b), 'The importance of Lotmanian semiotics to sign theory and to cognitive neurosciences', *Sign Systems Studies*, 43 (2/3): 347–64.

182. Avtonomova, Natalia S. (2009), 'History, structure, explosion', *Russian Studies in Philosophy*, 48 (2): 28–46.

183. Bailey, James (1972), 'Some recent developments in the study of Russian versification', *Language and Style*, 3: 155–91.

184. Bailey, Richard W. (1976), 'Maxwell's demon and the muse', *Dispositio. Rivista Hispánica de Semiótica Literaria*, 1 (3): 293–301.

185. Baer, Brian James (2013), 'Translator's preface', in: Juri M. Lotman, *The Unpredictable Workings of Culture*, trans. Brian James Baer, eds. Igor Pilshchikov and Silvi Salupere, 17–26, Tallinn: TLU Press.

186. Baer, Brian James (2019), 'Translator's preface', in: Juri Lotman, *Culture, Memory and History. Essays in Cultural Semiotics*, ed. Marek Tamm, 27–30, Cham: Palgrave Macmillan.

187. Baran, Henryk (1975), 'A review of structural-semiotic research in the Soviet-Union', *Soviet Studies in Literature*, 11 (2/3): 3–16.

188. Baran, Hendryk (1976), 'Introduction', in: Hendryk Baran (ed.), *Semiotics and Structuralism: Readings from the Soviet Union*, VII–XXVI, White Plains, NY: International Arts and Sciences Press.

189. Bethea, David M. (1997), 'Bakhtinian prosaics versus Lotmanian "poetic thinking". The code and its relation to literary biography', *The Slavic and East European Journal*, 41 (1): 1–15.

190. Bethea, David M. (1998), *Realizing Metaphors: Alexander Pushkin and the Life of the Poet*, Madison, WI: The University of Wisconsin Press ['Lotman: The Code and Its Relation to Literary Biography', pp. 118–33].

191. Birnbaum, Henrik (1990), 'Semiotic modeling systems, primary and secondary', *Language Sciences*, 12 (1): 53–63.

192. Blaim, Artur (1992), 'Constructivist aspects of cultural semiotics', in: Joe Andrew (ed.), *Poetics of the Text. Essays to Celebrate Twenty Years of the Neo-Formalist Circle*, 17–27, Amsterdam: Rodopi.

193. Blaim, Artur (1994), 'Cultural semiotics – The use of a theory', *Russian Literature*, 36 (3): 243–54.

194. Blaim, Artur (1998), 'Lotman in the West: An ambiguous complaint', in Joe Andrew and Robert Reid (eds.), Neo-Formalist Papers. *Contributions to the Silver Jubilee Conference to Mark 25 Years of the Neo-Formalist Circle*, 329–33, Amsterdam, Atlanta: Rodopi.

195. Bonafin, Massimo (1997), 'Typology of culture and carnival: Notes on the models of Bachtin and Lotman', *Russian Literature*, 41 (3). Special Issue. *Italian Contributions to the International Bachtin Dialogue: 1981–1986*: 255–68.

196. Brickman, Caroline Lemak and Bershtein, E. (2014), 'Afterword: Yuri Lotman's semiotic memoirs'Lotman', in: Yuri Lotman, *Non-Memoirs*, trans. Caroline Lemak Brickman, ed. Evgenii Bershtein, 95–107. Champaign: Dalkey Archive Press.

197. Broms, Henri and Yuri Lotman (1988), 'Greetings to the symposium. An interview with Yuri Lotman in Helsinki, June 1987', in: Henri Broms and Rebecca Kaufmann (eds.), *Semiotics of Culture: Proceedings of the 25th Symposium of the Tartu-Moscow School of Semiotics, Imatra, Finland, 27th–29th July, 1987*, 115–23, Helsinki: Arator Inc.

198. Boyko, Taras (2014), 'Tartu-Moscow School of semiotics and history', *Historein*, 14 (2): 51–70.

199. Boyko, Taras (2015), 'Describing the past: Tartu-Moscow school ideas history, historiography, and the historian's craft', *Sign Systems Studies*, 43 (2/3): 269–80.

200. Champagne, Roland A. (1978), 'A grammar of the languages of culture: Literary theory and Yury M. Lotman's semiotics', *New Literary History*, 9 (2): 205–10.

201. Chang, Han-liang (2003), 'Is language a primary modeling system? On Juri Lotman's concept of semiosphere', *Sign Systems Studies*, 31 (2): 1–15.

202. Clark, Wilma Anne (2010), *Lotman's Semiosphere: A Systems Thinking Approach to Students' Meaning-making Practices with Digital Texts*, Ph.D. Diss. University of London [unpublished manuscript].

203. Chernov, Igor (1988), 'Historical survey of Tartu-Moscow Semiotic School', in: Henri Broms and Rebecca Kaufmann (eds.), *Semiotics of Culture. Proceedings of the 25th Symposium of the Tartu-Moscow School of Semiotics, Imatra, Finland, 27th-29th July 1987*, 7–16, Helsinki: Arator.

204. Cornwell, Neil (1992), 'Lotman's semiosphere', *Irish Slavonic Studies*, 13: 163–67.

205. Danesi, Marcel (2000) 'A note on Vico and Lotman: Semiotics as the "science of the imagination"', *Sign Systems Studies*, 28: 99–115.

206. Danow, David K. (1986), 'Dialogic perspectives: The East European view (Bachtin, Mukařovský, Lotman)', *Russian Literature*, 20 (2). Special Issue. *Developments of the Theory of Literature 7*: 119–41.

207. Danow, David K. (1988), 'Bakhtin and Lotman: Novel and culture', in Henri Broms and Rebecca Kaufmann (eds.), *Semiotics of Culture: Proceedings of the 25th*

Symposium of the Tartu-Moscow School of Semiotics, Imatra, Finland, 27th–29th July, 1987, 233–44, Helsinki: Arator.

208. Deltcheva, Roumiana and Eduard Vlasov (1996), 'Lotman's culture and explosion: A shift in the paradigm of the semiotics of culture', *Slavic and East European Journal*, 40 (1): 148–52.

209. Eagle, Herbert J. (1976), 'The semiotics of the cinema: Lotman and Metz', *Dispositio: Rivista Hispánica de Semiótica Literaria*, 1 (3): 303–14.

210. Eco, Umberto (1990), 'Introduction', in: Yuri M. Lotman, *Universe of the Mind: A Semiotic Theory of Culture*, trans. Ann Shukman, vii–xiii, London and New York: I. B. Tauris & Co Ltd.

211. Eimermacher, Karl (1977), 'Some aspects of semiotic studies of the Moscow and Tartu schools', in: Karl Eimermacher and Serge Shishkoff (eds.), *Subject Bibliography of Soviet Semiotics: The Moscow-Tartu School*, vii–x, Ann Arbor: Michigan Slavic Publications.

212. Eimermacher, Karl (1987), 'Cultural semiotics in the Soviet Union', in: Achim Eschbach and Walter A. Koch (eds.), *A Plea for Cultural Semiotics*, 23–35, Bochum: Brockmeyer.

213. Emerson, Carol (2003), 'Jurij Lotman's last book and filiations with Baxtin', *Die Welt der Slaven*, 48 (2): 201–16.

214. Eng, Jan van der (1977), 'The poetic text: A complicated and accessible semantic structure', *Russian Literature*, 5 (1): 103–13.

215. Fokkema, D. W. (1976), 'Continuity and change in Russian Formalism, Czech Structuralism, and Soviet Semiotics', *PTL: A Journal for Descriptive Poetics and Theory of Literature*, 1: 153–96.

216. Gasparov, Boris (1994), 'In memoriam: Iurii Mikhailovich Lotman (1922–1993)', *The Slavic and East European Journal*, 38 (4): 731–39.

217. Gherlone, Laura (2013a), 'Lotman's epistemology: Analogy, culture, world', *Sign Systems Studies*, 41 (2–3): 312–38.

218. Gherlone, Laura (2013b), 'Semiotics and interdisciplinarity: Lotman's legacy', *Sign Systems Studies*, 41 (4): 391–403.

219. Gherlone, Laura (2016), 'Vygotsky, Bakhtin, Lotman. Towards a theory of communication in the horizon of the other', *Semiotica*, 213: 75–90.

220. Gherlone, Laura (2017), 'Waiting for history: At the eve of explosion', in: Kristian Bankov (ed.), *New Semiotics Between Tradition and Innovation. Proceedings of the 12th World Congress of the International Association for Semiotic Studies (IASS/ AIS), Sofia, 16–20 September 2014*, 97–103, Sofia: NBU Publishing House & IASS Publications.

221. Gherlone, Laura (2019) 'Lotman continues to astonish. Revolutions and collective emotions', *Bakhtiniana: Revista de Estudos do Discurso*, 14 (4): 163–83.

222. Goldstein, Darra (2014), 'Introduction to the English edition', in: Yuri M. Lotman and Jelena A. Pogosjan, *High Society Dinners: Dining in Tsarist Russia*, trans. Marian Schwartz, ed. and introduction Darra Goldstein, 11–31, Totnes: Prospect Books.

223. Gómez Ponce, Ariel (2013), 'Lotman's tradition: Semiotics of culture from a Latin American perspective', *Sign Systems Studies*, 41 (4): 528–32.

224. Gramigna, Remo (2013), 'The place of language among sign systems: Juri Lotman and Émile Benveniste', *Sign Systems Studies*, 41 (2/3): 339–54.

225. Gramigna, Remo (2018), 'A report on the symposium "Juri Lotman and sociosemiotics" (Elva, Estonia, 19–20 May 2017), *Sign Systems Studies*, 46 (1): 178–80.

226. Gramigna, Remo and Silvi Salupere (2017), 'Umberto Eco and Juri Lotman on communication and cognition', in: Torkild Thellefsen and Bent Sørensen (eds.), *Umberto Eco in His Own Words*, 248–57, Berlin, Munich, Boston: Mouton de Gruyter.

227. Grigorjeva, Jelena (2003), 'Lotman on mimesis', *Sign Systems Studies*, 31 (1): 228–37.

228. Grishakova, Marina (2009), 'Afterword: Around "Culture and Explosion:" J. Lotman and Tartu-Moscow School in the 1980s–90s', in: Juri Lotman, *Culture and Explosion*, trans. Wilma Clark, ed. Marina Grishakova (Semiotics, Communication and Cognition 1), 175–87, Berlin and New York: Mouton de Gruyter.

229. Grishakova, Marina (2018), 'Semiotics and structuralism', in: David H. Richter (ed.), *The Blackwell Companion to Literary Theory*, 48–59, Malden-Oxford: Wiley-Blackwell.

230. Grishakova, Marina and Silvi Salupere (2015), 'A school in the woods: Tartu-Moscow semiotics', in: Marina Grishakova and Silvi Salupere (eds.), *Theoretical Schools and Circles in the Twentieth-Century Humanities: Literary Theory, History, Philosophy*, 173–95, London and New York: Routledge.

231. Grygar, Moimír (1977), 'On the specificness of the literary work', *Russian Literature*, 5 (1): 91–101.

232. Grzybek, Peter (1994), 'The concept of "model" in Soviet Semiotics', *Russian Literature*, 36 (3): 285–300.

233. Grzybek, Peter (1998a), 'Lotman, Jurij M.', in: Paul Bouissac (ed.), *Encyclopedia of Semiotics*, 375–7, New York and Oxford: Oxford University Press.

234. Grzybek, Peter (1998b), 'Moscow-Tartu School', in: Paul Bouissac (ed.), *Encyclopedia of Semiotics*, 422–5, New York and Oxford: Oxford University Press.

235. Haidar, Julieta (2019), 'Iuri Lotman: The analysis of culture from complexity and transdisciplinarity', *Bakhtiniana: Revista de Estudos do Discurso*, 14 (4): 99–116.

236. Hammarberg, Gitta (1984), 'A reinterpretation of Tynjanov and Jakobson on prose (with some thoughts on the Baxtin and Lotman connection)', in: Benjamin A. Stolz, I. R. Titunik and Lubomor Dolezel (eds.), *Language and Literary Theory: In Honor of Ladislav Matejka*, 379–401 (Papers in Slavic Philology 5), Ann Arbor: University of Michigan.

237. Hartley, John, Indrek Ibrus and Maarja Ojamaa (2020), *On the Digital Semiosphere: Culture, Media and Science for the Anthropocene*, New York: Bloomsbury Academic.

238. Hong, Guo (2009), 'A brief introduction to and semiotic analysis of Lotman's cultural semiotics', *Chinese Semiotic Studies*, 1 (1): 158–70.

239. Hu, Yuanyan (2014), 'Intertextuality in writing under Lotman's late text view', *Chinese Semiotic Studies*, 10 (4): 565–78.

240. Hymes, David (1978), 'Comments on Soviet Semiotic and criticism', *New Literary History*, 9 (2): 399–411.

241. Ibrus, Indrek and Torop, Peter (2015), 'Introduction: Remembering and reinventing Juri Lotman for the digital age', *International Journal of Cultural Studies*, 18 (1): 3–9.

242. Ioffe, Dennis (2012), 'The cultural "text of behaviour": The Moscow-Tartu school and the religious philosophy of language', *Cultura: International Journal of Philosophy of Culture and Axiology*, 9 (2): 175–94.

243. Ivanov, Vyacheslav (2013), 'Preface to the Russian edition', in: Juri M. Lotman, *The Unpredictable Workings of Culture*, trans. Brian James Baer, eds. Igor Pilshchikov and Silvi Salupere, 7–16, Tallinn: TLU Press.

244. Johnson, Barton (1976), 'The structural poetics of Yuri Lotman', in: Yury Lotman, *Analysis of the Poetic Text*, ix–xxix, Ann Arbor, MI: Ardis.

245. Kim, Soo Hwan (2014), 'Lotmanian explosion: From peripheral space to dislocated time', *Sign Systems Studies*, 42 (1): 7–30.

246. Kim, Soo Hwan (2015), 'Photogénie as "the other" of the semiotics of cinema: On Yuri Lotman's concept of "the mythological"', *Semiotica*, 207: 395–409.

247. Kiseleva, Lyubov (1992), 'The archaistic model of behaviour as a semiotic object', in: Joe Andrew (ed.), *Poetics of the Text: Essays to Celebrate Twenty Years of the Neo-Formalist Circle*, 28–34, Amsterdam: Rodopi.

248. Kliger, Ilya (2010), 'World literature beyond hegemony in Yuri M. Lotman's cultural semiotics', *Comparative Critical Studies*, 7 (2/3): 257–74.

249. Konstantinov, Mihael (2017), 'Model of communication act in art: Ju. M. Lotman', *European Philosophical and Historical Discourse*, 3 (1): 98–104.

250. Kotov, Kaie (2002), 'Semiosphere: A chemistry of being', *Sign Systems Studies*, 30 (1): 41–55.

251. Kotov, Kaie and Kalevi Kull (2011), 'Semiosphere is the relational biosphere', in: Claus Emmeche and Kalevi Kull (eds.), *Towards a Semiotic Biology: Life is the Action of Signs*, 179–94, London: Imperial College Press.

252. Kourdis, Evangelos (2017), 'The semiotic school of Tartu-Moscow: The cultural 'circuit' of translation', in: Larisa Schippel and Cornelia Zwischenberger (eds.), *Going East: Discovering New and Alternative Traditions in Translation Studies*, 149–68, Berlin: Frank & Timme.

253. Kristeva, Julia (1994) 'On Yury Lotman', *Publications of the Modern Language Association (PMLA)*, 109 (3): 375–6.

254. Kull, Kalevi (1999), 'Towards biosemiotics with Yuri Lotman', *Semiotica*, 127: 115–31.

255. Kull, Kalevi (2005), 'Semiosphere and dual ecology: Paradoxes of communication', *Sign Systems Studies*, 33 (1): 175–89.

256. Kull, Kalevi (2014), 'The manifesto of Tartu-Moscow semiotics since 1973', *Chinese Semiotic Studies*, 10 (1): 101–7.

257. Kull, Kalevi (2015), 'A semiotic theory of life: Lotman's principles of the universe of the mind', *Green Letters: Studies in Ecocriticism*, 19 (3): 255–66.

258. Kull, Kalevi and Lotman, Mihhail (2012), 'Semiotica Tartuensis: Jakob von Uexküll and Juri Lotman', *Chinese Semiotic Studies*, 6 (2): 312–23.

259. Lachmann, Renate (1987), 'Value aspects in Jurij Lotman's "semiotics of culture/ semiotics of text"', *Dispositio: Rivista Hispánica de Semiótica Literaria*, 12 (30/32): 13–33.

260. Laferrière, Daniel (1977), 'On semioticians and slavists', *Semiotic Scene*, 1 (4): 28–33.

261. Laferrière, Daniel (1978), 'Semiotica sub specie sovietica. Anti-Freudianism, pro-Marrism, and other disturbing matters', *PTL: A Journal for Descriptive Poetics and Theory of Literature*, 3: 437–54.

262. Le Grande, Eva (1993), 'Lotman, Iurii Mikhailovich', in: Irena Makaryk (ed.), *Encyclopedia of Contemporary Literary Theory. Approaches, Scholars, Terms*, 407–10, Toronto, Buffalo, and London: University of Toronto Press.

263. Lepik, Peet (2002), 'On universalism in connection with the interpretation of magic in the semiotics of Juri Lotman', *Sign Systems Studies*, 30 (2): 555–76.

264. Lepik, Peet (2008), *Universals in the Context of Juri Lotman's Semiotics* (Tartu Semiotics Library 7), Tartu: Tartu University Press.

265. Lorusso, Anna Maria (2019), 'Between times and spaces. Polyglotism and polychronism in Yuri Lotman', *Bakhtiniana: Revista de Estudos do Discurso*, 14 (4): 83–98.

266. Lorusso, Anna Maria (2019), 'Jurij Lotman', in: *Oxford Bibliographies*, Oxford: Oxford University Press, 1–13. [electronic publication] https://www.oxfordbibliog raphies.com/view/document/obo-9780190221911/obo-9780190221911-0074.xml (accessed 15 January 2021).

267. Lotman, Mihhail (2000), 'A few notes on the philosophical background of the Tartu School of Semiotics', *S: European Journal for Semiotic Studies*, 12 (1): 23–46.

268. Lotman, Mihhail (2001), 'The paradoxes of semiosphere', *Sun Yat-sen Journal of Humanities*, 12: 97–106.

269. Lotman, Mihhail (2002), 'Umwelt and semiosphere', *Sign Systems Studies*, 30 (1): 33–40.

270. Lotman, Mihhail (2013), 'Afterword: Semiotics and unpredictability', in: Juri Lotman, *The Unpredictable Workings of Culture*, 239–78, Tallinn: Tallinn University Press.

271. Lotman, Mihhail (2019), 'Afterword: (re)constructing the drafts of past', in: Juri Lotman, *Culture, Memory and History: Essays in Cultural Semiotics*, ed. Marek Tamm, 245–65, Cham: Palgrave Macmillan.

272. Lucid, Daniel Peri (1977), 'Introduction', in: Daniel Peri Lucid (ed.), *Soviet Semiotics: An Anthology*, 1–23, Baltimore, London: The John Hopkins University Press.

273. Lutfurahman, Jonaid-Sharif (1984), *Text-Sign-Structure: The Poetics of Jurij Lotman*, Ph.D. Diss. University of Southwestern Louisiana [unpublished manuscript].

274. Machado, Irene (2011), 'Lotman's scientific investigatory boldness: The semiosphere as a critical theory of communication in culture', *Sign Systems Studies*, 39 (1): 81–104.

275. Machado, Irene and Silvia Barei (2019), 'Between turbulences and unpredictability of historical time: The semiotics of Yuri Lotman', *Bakhtiniana: Revista de Estudos do Discurso*, 14 (4): 7–18.

276. Makarychev, Andrey and Yatsyk, Alexandra (2017), *Lotman's Cultural Semiotics and the Political*, London and New York: Rowman and Littlefield.

277. Makarychev, Andrey and Alexandra Yatsyk (2018), 'Unpacking the Post-Soviet: Political legacy of the Tartu Semiotic School', *All Azimuth*, 7 (2): 31–45.

278. Mandelker, Amy (1994), 'Semiotizing the sphere: Organicist theory in Lotman, Bakhtin, and Vernadsky', *Publications of the Modern Language Association (PMLA)*, 109 (3): 385–96.

279. Mandelker, Amy (1995), 'Logosphere and semiosphere: Bakhtin, Russian organicism, and the semiotics of culture', in: Amy Mandelker (ed.), *Bakhtin in Contexts Across the Disciplines*, 177–90, Evanston: Northwestern University Press.

280. Mandelker, Amy (2006), 'Lotman's Other: Estrangement and ethics in culture and explosion', in: Andreas Schönle (ed.), *Lotman and Cultural Semiotics: Encounters and Extensions*, 59–83, Madison, WI: University of Wisconsin Press.

281. Margolin, Uri (1975), 'Juri Lotman and the creation of meaning in literature', *Canadian Review of Comparative Literature/Revue Canadienne de Littérature Comparée*, 2 (3): 262–82.

282. Markoš, Anton (2014), 'Biosphere as semiosphere: Variations on Lotman', *Sign Systems Studies*, 42 (4): 487–98.

283. Matejka, Ladislav (1976), 'Languages of art in soviet semiotics', *Dispositio. Rivista Hispánica de Semiótica Literaria*, 1 (3): 207–12.

284. Mayenowa, Maria R. (1977), 'Lotman as a historian of literature', *Russian Literature*, 5 (1): 81–90.

285. Meijer, Jan M. (1973), 'Literature as information. Some notes on Lotman's book: Struktura xudožestvennogo teksta', in: Jan van der Eng and Monéir Grygar (eds.), *Structure of Texts and Semiotics of Culture*, 209–23, The Hague and Paris: Mouton.

286. Meijer, Jan M. (1977), 'A reply to Ju. Lotman', *Russian Literature*, 5 (1): 55–60.

287. Meijer, Jan M. (1979), 'Semiotics in Russia', *Canadian Slavonic Papers/ Revue Canadienne des Slavistes*, 21 (1): 92–7.

288. Meletinsky, E. M. and Dimitri Segal (1971), 'Structuralism and semiotics in USSR', *Diogenes*, 73: 88–125.

289. Merrell, Floyd (2008), 'Lotman's semiosphere, Peirce's signs, and cultural processes', *Russian Journal of Communication*, 1 (4): 372–400.

290. Mihkelsaar, Janar (2018), 'Lotman's semiotic theory of culture *or* Laclau's political ontology?' *Semiotica*, 224: 135–63.

291. Monticelli, Daniele (2012a), 'Self-description, dialogue and periphery in Lotman's later thought', in: Susi K. Frank, Cornelia Ruhe and Alexander Schmitz (eds.), *Explosion und Peripherie: Jurij Lotmans Semiotik der kulturellen Dynamik revisited*, 57–78, Bielefeld: transkript.

292. Monticelli, Daniele (2012b), 'Challenging identity: Lotman's "translation of the untranslatable" and Derrida's différance', *Sign Systems Studies*, 40 (3/4): 319–39.

293. Monticelli, Daniele (2019), 'Borders and translation: Revisiting Juri Lotman's semiosphere', *Semiotica*, 230: 389–406.

294. Monticelli, Daniele (2020), 'Thinking the new after the fall of the Berlin Wall: Juri Lotman's dialogism of history', *Rethinking History*, 24 (2): 184–208.

295. Myasnikov, Georgy (1973), 'Jury Mikhailovich Lotman: An essay-tribute on the fiftieth anniversary of his birth', *Russian Literature Triquarterly*, 6: 575–78.

296. Nascimento, Rodrigo Alves do (2019), 'Yuri Lotman and the semiotics of theatre', *Bakhtiniana*, 14 (3): 208–29.

297. Norimatsu, Kyohei (2018), 'Within or beyond policing norms: Yuri Lotman's theory of theatricality', in: Călin-Andrei Mihăilescu and Takayuki Yokota-Murakami (eds.), *Policing Literary Theory*, 111–34 (Textxet: Studies in Comparative Literature, 86), Leiden: Brill.

298. Nöth, Winfried (2006), 'Yuri Lotman on metaphors and culture as self-referential semiospheres', *Semiotica*, 161 (1/4): 249–63.

299. Nöth, Winfried (2015), 'The topography of Yuri Lotman's semiosphere', *International Journal of Cultural Studies*, 18 (1): 11–26.

300. Novikova, Anna A. and Varvara P. Chumakova (2015), 'Yuri Lotman's cultural semiotics as a contribution to media ecology', *Explorations in Media Ecology*, 14 (1–2): 73–85.

301. Ojamaa, Maarja and Peeter Torop (2015), 'Transmediality of cultural autocommunication', *International Journal of Cultural Studies*, 18 (1): 61–78.

302. Paterson, Janet M. (1993), 'Tartu school', in: Irena Makaryk (ed.), *Encyclopedia of Contemporary Literary Theory. Approaches, Scholars, Terms*, 208–11, Toronto, Buffalo, and London: University of Toronto Press.

303. Patoine, Pierre-Louis and Jonathan Hope (2015), 'The semiosphere: Between informational modernity and ecological postmodernity', *Recherches sémiotiques / Semiotic Inquiry*, 35 (1): 11–26.

304. Perlinska, Agnieszka (1992), 'A semiotic analysis of eighteenth-century Russian culture: Discovering the past and modeling the present', *Historical Reflections / Réflexions Historiques*, 18 (3), The Eighteenth Century and Uses of the Past: 45–57.

305. Pilshchikov, Igor and Mikhail Trunin (2016), 'The Tartu-Moscow School of Semiotics in transnational perspective', *Sign Systems Studies*, 44 (3): 368–401.

306. Priimägi, Linnar (2005), 'The problem of the autocatalytic origin of culture in Juri Lotman's cultural philosophy', *Sign Systems Studies*, 33 (1): 191–203.

307. Randviir, Anti(2007), 'On spatiality in Tartu-Moscow cultural semiotics: The semiotic subject', *Sign Systems Studies*, 35 (1/2): 137–59.

308. Randviir, Anti (2005), 'Cultural semiotics and social meanings', in: Kristian Bankov (ed.), *EFSS'2004 Culture and Text*, 114–28, Sofia: New Bulgaria University Press.

309. Raudla, Tuuli (2008), 'Vico and Lotman: Poetic meaning creation and primary modelling', *Sign Systems Studies*, 36 (1): 137–65.

310. Raudla, Tuuli and Pern, Tanel (2011), 'The Tartu connection: Thomas Sebeok's correspondence with Juri Lotman', in: Paul Cobley, John Deely, Kalev Kull and Susan Petrilli (eds.), *Semiotics Continues to Astonish: Thomas A. Sebeok and the Doctrine of Signs*, (Semiotics, Communication and Cognition 7), 473–84, Berlin: de Gruyter Mouton.

311. Reid, Allan (1990a), 'Who is Lotman and why is Bakhtin saying those nasty things about him', *Discours social/Social Discourse*, 3 (1/2): 325–38.

312. Reid, Allan (1990b), *Literature as Communication and Cognition in Bakhtin and Lotman*, New York: Garland.

313. Restaneo, Pietro (2018), 'Lotman, Leibniz, and the semiospheric monad: Lost pages from the archive', *Semiotica*, 224: 313–36.

314. Restivo, Giuseppina (1999), 'The Enlightenment code in Yuri Lotman's theory of culture', *Slavica tergestina*, 7: 5–31.

315. Revzina, Olga G. (1972), 'The fourth summer school of on secondary modelling systems', *Semiotica*, 6: 222–43.

316. Rewar, Walter (1972), *Semiotics and Literature*, Ph.D. diss, Language and Literature, University of California, San Diego [unpublished manuscript].

317. Rewar, Walter (1976a), 'Notes for a typology of culture', *Semiotica*, 18: 361–78.

318. Rewar, Walter (1976b), 'Semiotics and communication in Soviet criticism', *Language and Style*, 11: 55–69.

319. Rewar, Walter (1976c), 'Tartu semiotics', *Bulletin of Literary Semiotics*, 3: 1–16.

320. Rosner, Katarzyna (1984), 'On some difficulties involved in Lotman's concept of the semiotics of culture', in: Jerzy Pelc, Thomas A. Sebeok, Edward Stankiewicz and Thomas G. Winner (eds.), Sign, System, and Function. Papers of the First and Second Polish-American Semiotics Colloquia (Approaches to Semiotics 67), 355–9, Berlin: de Gruyter Mouton.

321. Rudy, Stephen (1986), 'Semiotics in the URSSR', in: Thomas A. Sebeok and Donna Jean Umiker-Sebeok (eds.), *The Semiotic Sphere*, 555–82, New York: Plenum Press.

322. Salupere, Silvi (2012), 'Tartu summer schools of semiotics at the time of Juri Lotman', *Chinese Semiotic Studies*, 6: 303–11.

323. Salupere, Silvi and Torop, Peeter (2013), 'On the beginnings of the semiotics of culture in the light of the Theses of the Tartu-Moscow School', in: Silvi Salupere, Peeter Torop and Kalevi Kull (eds.), *Beginnings of the Semiotics of Culture* (Tartu Semiotics Library 13), 15–37, Tartu: Tartu University Press.

324. Salupere, Silvi (2015), 'The cybernetic layer of Juri Lotman's metalanguage', *Recherches sémiotiques / Semiotic Inquiry*, 35 (1): 63–84.

325. Sánchez, Manuel Cáceres 'Scientific thought and work of Yuri Lotman', *Sign Systems Studies*, 27: 46–59.

326. Schönle, Andreas (2001a), 'Lotman in an interdisciplinary context: A symposium held at the University of Michigan', *Sign Systems Studies*, 29 (2): 745–8.

327. Schönle, Andreas (2001b), 'Social power and individual agency: The self in Greenblatt and Lotman', *The Slavic and East European Journal*, 45 (1): 61–79.

328. Schönle, Andreas (2002), 'Lotman and cultural studies. The case for cross-fertilization', *Sign Systems Studies*, 30 (2): 429–0.

329. Schönle, Andreas (2006), 'The self, its bubbles, and its illusions: Cultivating autonomy in Greenblatt and Lotman', in: Andreas Schönle (ed.), *Lotman and Cultural Studies: Encounters and Extensions*, 183–207, Madison, WI: The University of Wisconsin Press.

330. Schönle, Andreas (2020), 'Introducion', in: Yuri Lotman, *Culture and Communication. Signs in Flux. An Anthology of Major and Lesser-known works*, trans. Benjamin Paloff, ed. Andreas Schönle, xiii–xxiv, Boston: Academic Series Press.

331. Schönle, Andreas and Shine, Jeremy (2006), 'Introduction', in Andreas Schönle (ed.), *Lotman and Cultural Studies: Encounters and Extensions*, 3–35, Madison, WI: The University of Wisconsin Press.

332. Sebeok, Thomas A. (1998a), 'The Estonian connection', *Sign Systems Studies*, 26: 20–41.

333. Sebeok, Thomas A. (1988b), 'In what sense is language a "primary modeling system?"', in: Henri Broms and Rebecca Kaufmann (eds.), *Semiotics of Culture*: *Proceedings of the 25th Symposium of the Tartu-Moscow School of Semiotics, Imatra, Finland, 27th-29th July, 1987*, 67–80, Helsinki: Arator Inc.

334. Segal, Dmitri (1974), *Aspects of Structuralism in Soviet Philology*. Papers on Poetics and Semiotics 2, Tel-Aviv: Tel-Aviv University, Department of Poetics and Comparative Literature.

335. Segre, Cesare (1978), 'Culture and modeling systems', *Critical Enquiry*, 4 (3): 525–37.

336. Semenenko, Aleksei (2012), *The Texture of Culture: An Introduction to Yuri Lotman's Semiotic Theory*, New York: Palgrave Macmillan.

337. Semenenko, Aleksei (2016), 'Homo polyglottus: Semiosphere as a model of human cognition', *Sign Systems Studies*, 44 (4): 494–510.

338. Semenenko, Aleksei (2019), 'Semiotics of nonsense and non-sense: A lotmanian perspective', *Bakhtiniana: Revista de Estudos do Discurso*, 14 (4): 152–62.

339. Sériot, Patrick (2016), 'Barthes and Lotman: Ideology vs culture', *Sign Systems Studies*, 44 (3): 402–14.

340. Seyffert, Peter (1985), *Soviet Literary Structuralism: Background, Debate, Issues*, Columbus, OH: Slavica Publishers.

341. Shore, Bradd (1998), 'Semiotics of culture', in: P. Bouissac (ed.), *Encyclopedia of Semiotics*, 165–8, New York and Oxford: Oxford University Press.

342. Shukman, Ann (1974), *Structuralist literary criticism in the Soviet Union, 1962-1970, with special reference to the work of Yu. M.Lotman*, Ph.D. Diss. University of Oxford [unpublished manuscript].

343. Shukman, Ann (1976), 'The canonization of the real: Jurij Lotman's theory of literature and analysis of poetry', *PTL: A Journal for Descriptive Poetics and Theory of Literature*, 1 (2): 317–38.

344. Shukman, Ann (1977a), *Literature and Semiotics: A Study of the Writings of Yu. M. Lotman* (Meaning and Art 1), Amsterdam, New York and London: North Holland Publishing.

345. Shukman, Ann (1977b), 'Jurij Lotman and the semiotics of culture', *Russian Literature*, 5 (1): 41–53.

346. Shukman, Ann (1978a), 'Lotman: The dialectic of a semiotician', in: R. W. Bailey, Ladislav Matejka and Peter Steiner (eds.), *The Sign: Semiotics Around the World* (Michigan Slavic Contributions 9), 194–206, Ann Arbor: The University of Michigan.

347. Shukman, Ann (1978b), 'Soviet semiotics and literary criticism', *New Literary History*, 9 (2), *Soviet Semiotics and Criticism: An Anthology*: 189–97.

348. Shukman, Ann (1981), 'The dialectics of change: Culture, codes and the individual', in: Pierre V. Zima (ed.), *Semiotics and Dialectics: Ideology and the Text*, 311–29, Amsterdam: John Benjamins.

349. Shukman, Ann (1988), 'Semiotic aspects of the work of Jurij Michajlovic Lotman', in: Thomas A. Sebeok and Jean Umiker-Sebeok (eds.), *The Semiotic Web 1987*, 65–78, Berlin and New York: De Gruyter.

350. Shukman, Ann (1989), 'Semiotics of culture and the influence of M. M. Bakhtin', in: Karl Eimermacher, Peter Grzybek and Georg Witte (eds.), *Issues in Slavic Literary and Cultural Theory*, 193–207, Bochum: Universitätsverlag Dr. Norbert Brockmeyer.

351. Sörensen, Dolf (1987), *Theory Formation and the Study of Literature*, Amsterdam: Rodopi. [See chapter 10, 'Lotman's semiotics of art and literature'].

352. Spassova, Kamelia (2018), 'Authentic and heterogeneous mimesis: Reflection and self-reflexivity in Todor Pavlov and Yuri Lotman', *Slavica Tergestina*, 20 (1): 70–96.

353. Spassova, Kamelia (2019), 'Dual codes: Text within a text in Lotman and Kristeva', *Prace Filologiczne. Literaturoznawstwo*, 8 (11), part 2: 13–28.

354. Steiner, Lina (2003), 'Toward an ideal universal community: Lotman's revisiting of the Enlightenment and Romanticism', *Comparative Literature Studies*, 40 (1): 37–53.

355. Steiner, Lina (2011), *For Humanity's Sake: The Bildungsroman in Russian Culture*, Toronto: University of Toronto Press. [See Part 1, Chapter 3, 'Yurii Lotman's idea of the 'semiosphere']

356. Steiner, Peter (1976), 'On semantic poetics', *Dispositio*, 1 (3): 339–48.

357. Sturrock, John (1991), 'Inside the semiosphere', *Times Literary Supplement*, 3 May: 9–10.

358. Suino, Mark E. (1976), 'Translator's foreword', in: Juri Lotman, *Semiotics of Cinema* (Michigan Slavic Contributions N.5), trans.Mark E. Suino, VII–VIX, Ann Arbor: University of Michigan.

359. Sutrop, Urmas (2011), 'Towards a semiotic theory of basic colour terms and the semiotics of Juri Lotman', in: Carole P. Biggam, Carole Hough, Christian J. Kay and

David R. Simmons (eds.), *New Directions in Colour Studies*, 39–48, Amsterdam: Benjamins.

360. Tamm, Marek (2015), 'Semiotic theory of cultural memory: In the company of Juri Lotman', in: Siobhan Kattago (ed.), *Ashgate Research Companion to Memory Studies*, 127–41, Farnham: Ashgate.

361. Tamm, Marek. (2017), 'Introduction: Semiotics and history revisited', *Sign Systems Studies*, 45 (3/4): 211–29.

362. Tamm, Marek (2019), 'Introduction: Juri Lotman's semiotic theory of history and cultural memory', in: Juri Lotman, *Culture, Memory and History: Essays in Cultural Semiotics*, ed. Marek Tamm, 1–26, Cham: Palgrave Macmillan.

363. Thibault, Mattia (2016), 'Lotman and play: For a theory of playfulness based on semiotics of culture', *Sign Systems Studies*, 44 (3): 295–325.

364. Thompson, Ewa M. (1977), 'Jurij Lotman's literary theory and its context', *The Slavic and East European Journal*, 21 (2): 225–38.

365. Titunik, Irwin R. (1976), 'M. M. Baxtin (The Baxtin School) and Soviet Semiotics', *Dispositio. Rivista Hispánica de Semiótica Literaria*, 1 (3): 327–38.

366. Todd, William Mills (1998), 'Moscow-Tartu school', in: Edward Craig (ed.), *Routledge Encyclopedia of Philosophy*, vol. 6, 583–8, London: Routledge.

367. Torop, Peeter (1998), 'Semiotics in Tartu', *Sign Systems Studies*, 26: 9–19.

368. Torop, Peeter (1999), 'Cultural semiotics and culture', *Sign Systems Studies*, 27: 9–23.

369. Torop, Peeter (2000), 'New Tartu semiotics', *S: European Journal for Semiotic Studies*, 12 (1): 5–22.

370. Torop, Peeter (2001), 'Lotman, Jurij', in: Paul Cobley (ed.), *The Routledge Companion to Semiotics and Linguistics*, 218–19, London: Routledge.

371. Torop, Peeter (2002), 'Introduction: Rereading of cultural semiotics', *Sign Systems Studies*, 30 (2): 395–404.

372. Torop, Peeter (2004), 'Semiospherical understanding: Textuality', *Sign Systems Studies*, 31 (2): 323–39.

373. Torop, Peeter (2005), 'Semiosphere and/ as the research object of semiotics of culture', *Sign Systems Studies*, 33 (1): 159–73.

374. Torop, Peeter (2008), 'Lotman, Iurii Mikhailovich', in: David G. Hundert (ed.), *The YIVO Encyclopedia of Jews in Eastern Europe*, vol. 1, 1088, New Haven: Yale University Press.

375. Torop, Peeter (2011), 'Identity, creolisation and cultural semiotics', *Chinese Semiotic Studies*, 5 (1): 233–45.

376. Torop, Peeter (2014a), 'Foreword. Lotmanian explosion' in: Juri Lotman, *Culture and Explosion*, ed. Marina Grishakova, trans. Wilma Clark, xxvii–xxxix, Berlin: Mouton de Gruyter.

377. Torop, Peeter (2014b), 'Semiotics and the possibilities of cultural analysis: Experience of the Tartu-Moscow School', *Chinese Semiotic Studies*, 10 (1): 109–17.

378. Torop, Peeter (2015), 'Cultural semiotics', in: Farzad Farzad (ed.), *The Routledge Handbook of Language and Culture*, 170–80, London and New York: Routledge.

379. Torop, Peeter (2017) 'Semiotics of cultural history', *Sign Systems Studies*, 45 (3/4): 317–34.

380. Torop, Peeter (2019), 'Russian theory and semiotics of culture: History and perspectives', *Bakhtiniana: Revista de Estudos do Discurso*, 14 (4): 19–39.

381. Trunin, Mikhail (2017), 'Semiosphere and history: Toward the origins of the semiotic approach to history', *Sign Systems Studies*, 45 (3/4): 335–60.

382. Umiker-Sebeok, Jean (1977), 'Semiotics of culture: Great Britain and North America', *Annual Review of Anthropology*, 6: 121–35.

383. Ventsel, Andreas and Peeter Selg (2008), 'Towards a semiotic theory of hegemony: Naming as hegemonic operation in Lotman and Laclau', *Sign System Studies*, 36 (1): 167–83.

384. Vetik, Raivo (1994), 'The Platonism of J. Lotman', *Semiotica*, 99 (1–2): 67–80.

385. Voigt, Vilmos (1995), 'In memoriam of "Lotmanosphere"', *Semiotica*, 105: 191–206.

386. Volkova, A. A. (2020), 'From dialogical ontology to the theory of semiosphere: The idea of the dialogue of cultures in the philosophical concepts of M. Buber and Yu. M. Lotman', *RUDN Journal of Philosophy*, 24 (2): 276–85.

387. Vroon, Ronald (1977), 'Preface', in: Jurij Lotman, *The Structure of the Artistic Text*, trans. Gail Lenhoff and Ronald Vroon (Michigan Slavic Contributions 7), vii–xiii, Ann Arbor: University of Michigan, Department of Slavic Languages and Literatures.

388. Zorin, Andrey (2001), 'Ideology, semiotics and Clifford Geertz', *History and Theory*, 40: 57–73.

389. Żyłko, Bogusław (2001), 'Culture and semiotics: Notes on Lotman's conception of culture', *New Literary History*, 32 (2): 391–408.

390. Żyłko, Bogusław (2015), 'Notes on Yuri Lotman's structuralism', *International Journal of Cultural Studies*, 18 (1): 27–42.

391. Waldstein, Maxim (2007), 'Russifying Estonia? Iurii Lotman and the politics of language and culture in Soviet Estonia', *Kritika: Explorations in Russian and Eurasian History*, 8 (3): 561–96.

392. Waldstein, Maxim (2008a), *The Soviet Empire of Signs: A History of the Tartu School of Semiotics*. Saarbrücken: VDM Verlag.

393. Waldstein, Maxim (2008b), 'The mangle of practice and the practice of mangle: Toward a dialogue between science studies and soviet semiotics', in: Andrew Pickering and Keith Guzik (eds.), *The Mangle in Practice: Science, Society, and Becoming*, 221–42, Durham and London: Duke University Press.

394. Weidlé, Wladmir (1974), 'Critical observations: On the interpretation of poetry, primarily concerning the works of R. O. Jakobson, Iu. M. Lotman, and K. F. Taranovski', *Soviet Studies in Literature*, 10 (4): 3–33.

395. Winner, Irene Portis (1978), 'Cultural semiotics and anthropology', in: R. W. Bailey, Ladislav Matejka and Peter Steiner (eds.), *The Sign: Semiotics Around the World* (Michigan Slavic Contributions, 9), 335–63, Ann Arbor, Michigan Svavic Publications.

396. Winner, Irene Portis (1982), *Semiotics of Culture: The State of the Art* (Toronto Semiotic Circle. Monographs, Working Papers and Prepublications), Toronto: Victoria University.

397. Winner, Irene Portis (1984), 'Some comments upon Lotman's concepts of semiotics of culture: Implications for the study of ethnic culture texts', in: Morris Halle, Ladislav Matejka, Krystyna Pomorska and Boris Uspenskij (eds.), *Semiosis. Semiotics and the History of Culture: In Honorem Georgii Lotman* (Michigan Slavic Contributions 10), 28–36, Ann Arbor, Department of Slavic Languages and Literatures, The University of Michigan.

398. Winner, Irene Portis (1987), 'Cultural semiotics vs. other cultural sciences', in: Achim Eschbach and Walter A. Koch (eds.), *A Plea for Cultural Semiotics*, 4–22, Bochum: Brockmeyer.

399. Winner, Irene Portis (1994), *Semiotics of Culture: "The Strange Intruder"*, Bochum: Universitätsverlag Dr. Norbert Brockmeyer.

400. Winner, Irene Portis (1998), 'Lotman's semiosphere: Some comments', in: Jacek J. Jadacki and Witold Strawiński (eds.), *In the World of Signs: Essays in Honour of Professor Jerzy Pelc*, 235–44, Amsterdam, Atlanta, GA: Rodopi.

401. Winner, Irene Portis (1999), 'The dynamics of semiotics of culture: Its pertinence to anthropology', *Sign Systems Studies*, 27: 24–45.

402. Winner, Irene Portis and Thomas G. Winner (1976), 'The semiotics of cultural texts', *Semiotica*, 18 (2): 101–56.

403. Winner, Thomas (2002), 'How did the ideas of Yuri Lotman reach the west?' *Sign Systems Studies*, 30 (2): 419–27.

404. Weidlé, Wladimir (1974), 'Critical observations: On the interpretation of poetry, primarily concerning the works of R. O. Jakobson, Iu. M. Lotman, and K. F. Taranovski', *Soviet Studies in Literature*, 10 (4): 3–33.

405. Zenkin, Sergey (2012), 'Continuous models after Lotman', in: Susi K. Frank, Cornelia Ruhe and Alexander Schmitz (eds.), *Explosion und Peripherie: Jurij Lotmans Semiotik der kulturellen Dynamik revisited*, 119–32, Bielefeld: transkript.

INDEX

Index

Index

Index

Index

semiosphere 8–9, 19, 24, 41–3, 58, 81, 82, 84, 110,
    124, 136, 142, 144, 150, 152, 161–2, 165–6,
    168–9, 177, 201–2, 205–9, 214–15, 219, 277,
    285, 315, 325–7, 330, 353, 361–2, 370–2,
    379–83, 392, 411, 414, 421–3, 426–30,
    433–8, 441–2, 450–1, 457, 464, 468, 470–1,
    476–8, 480–2, 484–5
  anatomy of 296–9
  concept of *post factum* 299–301
  culture and 304–5
  dialogic 301–2
  digital 448–9
  social media 449
  text and 302–4
semiotic model of power 270, 272–7
  description 276–7
  dominant 274–6
  self-description 273–4
semiotic(s) 33–4, 36, 38, 40, 43, 48, 56, 58,
    62, 66–7, 71, 78, 81, 86, 91, 93, 101, 108,
    111–14, 124, 131, 136, 148–9, 155, 168, 177,
    184, 212–14, 216, 221 n.3, 241, 245–6, 248,
    254, 300, 304, 322, 324, 330, 335, 390, 394,
    398, 423, 432, 481
  activity 274–8, 282
  analysis 202, 398
  of animals 466–8
  approach 105, 108, 185 n.2, 286, 391
  of behaviour 261
  of cultural emotions 340–1
  individuality 277–8, 374
  literary comparatistic sand 360–2
  models 158, 243, 334–6, 339, 344, 345 n.1,
    461, 477
  of popular culture 421–2, 429
  processes 205, 207–8, 313–14
  reality 202, 205–9
  spaces 41, 58, 140, 153, 165–6, 201–2, 205,
    230, 276, 297, 326–7, 482
  structuralist and non-structuralist 479–80
  structures 6, 24, 149, 152–3, 158, 168, 171,
    181, 206, 236, 314, 388, 463–4, 469, 481
  of subcultures 422–3
  systems 6, 21, 41–2, 64, 68, 95, 123, 136,
    149–51, 162, 168, 175, 180, 201, 203, 228,
    231, 234–6, 299–300, 318, 326, 355, 392,
    450, 463, 466, 468, 479
  theory 79, 100, 128, 164, 184, 213, 216, 270,
    323, 393, 400, 426, 476
Semiotics of Cinema and Problems of Film Aesthetics
    (*Semiotika kino i problemy kinoestetiki*,
    Lotman) 1, 21, 36, 228, 230
semiotization and desemiotization 141, 155, 169,
    209, 235–6, 297–9, 457
Sex Pistols 409–10

Shahadat, Schamma 368
Shakespeare, William 85, 194, 367
Shannon, Claude Elwood 162–3
Shcheglov, Yuri 48, 358
Shishkoff, Serge 490
Shklovsky, Viktor 47–53, 106, 189
Shpet, Gustav 99, 386
Shtoff, Victor 176
Shukman, Ann 2, 490
Siewers, Alfred 469
signification 68, 214–5, 217, 218, 300, 314, 370,
    391–4, 397–9, 480, 482
signified and signifier 39–40, 128, 213–14, 216,
    324, 356–7, 395, 398–400
sign(s) 3, 6, 8, 35, 129–30, 156–8, 191, 203, 217,
    220, 231, 235, 314, 391–4
  culture as 149–52
  exchange 42
  and symbol 211–13
  systems 19, 40, 56, 62, 124–5, 140, 142, 155,
    175, 178–81, 225, 234, 236, 241–2, 303, 314,
    324, 395, 399–400, 441, 448, 453
  vs. text 136–7
Simonides Melicus 240
simulacra 316, 400
Sinyavsky, Andrei 22
Slovo o Polku Igoreve (The Tale of Igor's
    Campaign) 64–5, 354
Smirnov, I. 357
social media 396, 413, 415, 429, 438
social media studies 446
  autocommunicative processes 452–3
  creative and mnemonic
    autocommunication 453–4
  definition 446–8
  digital semiosphere 448–9
  echo chambers 454–6
  meaning-making 450
  self-model 451–2
  semiosphere 449
Solovyov, Vladimir 216
Soviet semiotics 5, 92, 108, 112, 257, 489–90
Soviet Union. *See* USSR
space 200–1, 215
  and border 188–9
  end of 205–7
  functionality of text and 203–5
  modelling aspects 202–3
  primary modelling system 201–2
  and spatiality 184–5
  spatialization and 'real' 207–9
Spassova, Kamelia 391
spatial organization 201, 204
spatial semantics 188, 193
spatial semiotics 86, 195

Index